Clio in the Italian Garden

Twenty-First-Century Studies in Historical Methods and Theoretical Perspectives

Dumbarton Oaks Colloquium on the History of Landscape Architecture XXXII

Clio in the Italian Garden

Twenty-First-Century Studies in Historical Methods and Theoretical Perspectives

Mirka Beneš *and* Michael G. Lee
Editors

Dumbarton Oaks Research Library and Collection, Washington, D.C.

Printed in the United States of America

Library of Congress Cataloging-in-Publication Data

Clio in the Italian garden : twenty-first-century studies in historical methods and theoretical perspectives / edited by Mirka Beneš and Michael G. Lee.
p. cm. — (Dumbarton Oaks colloquium on the history of landscape architecture ; XXXII)
Includes bibliographical references and index.
ISBN 978-0-88402-367-8 (pbk. : alk. paper)
1. Gardens, Italian—Congresses. 2. Gardens—Italy—History—Congresses.
I. Beneš, Mirka. II. Lee, Michael G.
SB457.85 C59 2011
712.0945—dc22
2010035588

Art Director: Kathleen Sparkes
Design and Composition: Melissa Tandysh
Managing Editor: Sara Taylor

Volume based on papers presented at the symposium “Recent Issues in Italian Garden Studies” organized by the Garden and Landscape Studies program at Dumbarton Oaks. The symposium was held on 19–20 October 2007.

www.doaks.org/publications

Contents

Foreword

THIS VOLUME PRESENTS THE PROCEEDINGS OF the thirty-second Dumbarton Oaks symposium in the history of landscape architecture, held in October 2007 and entitled "Recent Issues in Italian Garden Studies." The symposium represented both the continuation of a tradition for which Dumbarton Oaks is deservedly celebrated—the sponsorship of advanced scholarship in the history of gardens and designed landscapes—and the capacity for innovation that is essential to the survival and growth of any institution. Organized by Michel Conan during his final year as director of the Garden and Landscape Studies program at Dumbarton Oaks, the symposium presented new directions in research on Italian gardens by an international group of scholars. The presentations have been edited for this publication by Mirka Beneš, an associate professor in the School of Architecture at the University of Texas at Austin and one of the participants in the symposium, and Michael G. Lee, a landscape historian who is currently a postdoctoral associate in Garden and Landscape Studies at Dumbarton Oaks.

The commitment of Dumbarton Oaks to the study of Italian gardens has been particularly pronounced. In April 1971, the institution convened its first symposium in the history of landscape architecture. Broadly titled "The Italian Garden," it focused on sixteenth- and seventeenth-century creations, particularly in Rome, Florence, and the Veneto, and resulted in a 1972 publication of the same name edited by David R. Coffin. Six years later, Dumbarton Oaks reprised the subject, this time with attention to Renaissance garden fountains; the publication, edited by Elisabeth Blair MacDougall and titled *Fons Sapientiae: Renaissance Garden Fountains*, appeared in 1978. In the years since, Dumbarton Oaks symposia have addressed a remarkable range of topics, from theme parks to environmentalism, but Italian garden topics have continued to be featured on a regular basis. The proceedings of the twenty-first symposium, for instance, published in 1999 as *Perspectives on Garden Histories*, featured two texts on the historiography of Italian gardens, by David R. Coffin and Mirka Beneš. Essays on Italian subjects also appeared in the Dumbarton Oaks publications *Bourgeois and Aristocratic Cultural Encounters in Garden Art, 1550–1850* (2002); *Baroque Garden Cultures: Emulation, Sublimation, Subversion* (2005); *Botanical Progress, Horticultural Innovation, and Cultural Change* (2007); *Gardens, City Life, and Culture: A World Tour* (2008); and *Gardens and Imagination: Cultural History and Agency* (2008). Moreover, Italian garden scholars have been frequent fellows at the institution. This is all as it should be: Italianate traditions cast a long shadow over the gardens at Dumbarton Oaks. Their chief designer, Beatrix Farrand, was the niece of Edith Wharton, author of *Italian Villas and Their Gardens*. Farrand was partially educated on trips abroad, sometimes in the company of her aunt. A grand tour to Italy, Germany, England, and France in 1895 left particularly strong impressions on her; she visited some twenty Italian gardens, including the Villa Aldobrandini at Frascati, the Villa Lante at Bagnaia, and the Boboli Gardens in Florence, on that trip.

In their excellent introduction to this volume, Mirka Beneš and Michael G. Lee make plain that while Dumbarton Oaks has been steadfast in its attention to Italian gardens, the field has changed dramatically over the past generation. Studies in garden history and landscape architecture have become increasingly interdisciplinary, drawing on methods from the social sciences, literature, and philosophy, among other fields; at the same time, scholars are giving greater attention to gardens in their larger political, geographical, and productive contexts. Challenging the notion of uniform national or cultural traditions, historians are also sorting out regional and chronological variations and examining the changing intellectual conceptions of gardens and nature over time. These transformations are as evident in the study of Italian gardens at Dumbarton Oaks as they are in the field at large; a review of the essays on Italian subjects published by Dumbarton Oaks over the years reveals a steady widening of geographical, chronological, and social focus, as well as a proliferation of methodological approaches. Mapping these changes motivated Michel Conan to organize a symposium dedicated once again to Italian gardens in 2007.

For this volume, we have followed the structure that Michel Conan created for the symposium; we are grateful to him both for selecting the topic and for assembling a distinguished international group of scholars to examine it. The editors wish to extend their personal thanks to him, to Shannon Leahy, former assistant to the director of Garden and Landscape Studies, and to all the other members of the staff of Dumbarton Oaks who worked tirelessly to bring the 2007 symposium to fruition. Jane Padelford, current assistant to the director of Garden and Landscape Studies, coordinated many of the practical matters required to assemble this volume. We are also grateful for the insights of the two anonymous reviewers of the manuscript; their careful attention to the task improved the volume immeasurably. Special thanks and gratitude are due to the publications staff at Dumbarton Oaks, especially Kathy Sparkes, publications manager, and Sara Taylor, art and archaeology editor. Finally, but most emphatically, we wish to thank the director of Dumbarton Oaks, Jan Ziolkowski, for his steadfast support of research in the humanities and the intellectual life of the institution, of which these symposium publications are among the most enduring parts.

John Beardsley
Director of Garden and Landscape Studies
Dumbarton Oaks Research Library
and Collection

Introduction

The Study of Italian Gardens: A Newly Expanding Field

Mirka Beneš and Michael G. Lee

I

THIS VOLUME CONTAINS THE PAPERS PRESENTED in the symposium, "Recent Issues in Italian Garden Studies," held at Dumbarton Oaks in October 2007. The symposium was organized by Michel Conan, who from 1998 to 2008 was director of Garden and Landscape Studies at Dumbarton Oaks; we are very thankful to him for focusing on historical methodologies and theoretical perspectives and for advocating a current assessment of a time-honored field of study. As editors of the resultant volume, we inherited the structure he gave to the symposium, and are pleased to situate that structure intellectually in two broad fields: first, in the wide-ranging concerns he brought to a decade of symposia at Dumbarton Oaks, and second, in the larger perspectives of the field of studies on Italian gardens.[1]

The 2007 meeting has a prehistory. In June 2005, Conan sent out a call for papers for a symposium, "Recent Issues in Italian Garden Studies: Sources, Methods, and Theoretical Perspectives," to be jointly sponsored by Dumbarton Oaks and the Accademia delle Arti del Disegno and held in June 2006 in Florence, Italy.[2] Conan noted that, since the first Dumbarton Oaks symposium devoted to the Italian garden in 1971, "a large body of research on Italian gardens has been developed by scholars working on both sides of the Atlantic. Many new directions of research have been put to the test, accepted versions of garden history have been revised, and many archives have been brought to life." Working in conjunction with the noted Italian garden historians Lucia Tongiorgi Tomasi and Luigi Zangheri, Conan sought to bring Italian, American, and French scholars together to discuss the key issues, advances, and methodological debates found in the research on Italian gardens during the previous ten years.[3] At the same time, Tongiorgi Tomasi and Zangheri planned to prepare a new comprehensive bibliography of research on Italian gardens since 1980; the bibliography was published in 2008 on a CD-ROM, and was accompanied by a book of historiographical essays by Italian scholars.[4] This bibliography and book constitute an extraordinary contribution and research tool for the field.

The Florence meeting did not occur as originally planned, but Conan organized a symposium with a smaller number of participants, namely the

Map of Italy.

Reprinted from Philipp Clüver, *Introductio in universam geographiam* (Guelferbyti, 1667). Rare Book Collection, Dumbarton Oaks Research Library and Collection, Washington, D.C.

authors represented in this volume, in October 2007 at Dumbarton Oaks. The symposium was an international event, and the resultant publication—which is published by an American institution—showcases mostly European scholars (including seven Italians, one Frenchman, and one American), thus providing a window onto the new geography of scholarship on Italian gardens. Margherita Azzi Visentini was part of the original 2007 symposium. Regrettably, her excellent contribution could not be included here in time for the publishing deadline. The title of her presentation was "The Gardens of the Veneto and Friuli, Thirty Years of Studies: State of the Question, New Critical Perspectives, and New Methodological Approaches"; she plans to publish it in English in an Anglo-American venue so as to continue the kind of international bridging currently of interest for scholarship on Italian gardens, art, and architecture.

Italian gardens have been the subject of two prior symposia at Dumbarton Oaks: "The Italian Garden" (1971) and "*Fons Sapientiae*: Renaissance Garden Fountains" (1977).[5] The speakers of the first symposium included the Briton Georgina Masson, the Italians Lionello Puppi and Eugenio Battisti, and the American Elisabeth Blair MacDougall, as well as the organizer, David R. Coffin, who at that time was one of the few specialists on Italian Renaissance gardens.[6] Their methodologies were quite diverse, ranging from the iconographical approach of Erwin Panofsky to Marxism. Following the symposium, MacDougall was appointed the first director of the Studies in Landscape Architecture program. She later organized a second symposium on Italian gardens that focused on fountains—a topic that had received little previous attention. "*Fons Sapientiae*: Renaissance Garden Fountains" featured five speakers (four Americans and one German) who used research methods drawn from several fields, including archaeology, literary criticism, and art history. MacDougall's collected essays on Italian gardens, fountains, and plants were published in *Fountains, Statues, and Flowers: Studies in Italian Gardens of the Sixteenth and Seventeenth Centuries* (1994). The other symposia held during her tenure (1972–88) covered mostly other historical periods and geographical areas.

MacDougall's successors, among them John Dixon Hunt (1988–91) and Joachim Wolschke-Bulmahn (1991–96), organized many symposia—but not on Italian gardens. They promoted interdisciplinary approaches to the study of gardens, and went beyond the study of garden typologies to consider topics debated in the social sciences and of contemporary social relevance, such as the vernacular, ideology, political engagement, memory, and identity.[7] Hunt, a garden historian with a background in literature and criticism, advanced the study of Italian gardens through his own research and produced a number of key publications on the subject.[8] Wolschke-Bulmahn, a German landscape architect and currently professor of garden history at Leibniz Universität Hannover, did not focus on Italian gardens in his personal research. However, his interest in methodological issues and the social dimensions of garden design led him to pursue projects that included this topic. In March 1996, he organized "Evolution and Perspectives of the Study of Garden History," the first colloquium at Dumbarton Oaks to consider the historiography of gardens and designed landscapes.[9] This colloquium, which included a discussion of Italian gardens, was followed by the 1997 symposium "Perspectives on Garden Histories," which featured two historiographical assessments of Italian garden studies.[10] In these years, as well, the directors welcomed noted scholars from Italy—for example, the historian of Veneto gardens Margherita Azzi Visentini of the Politecnico di Milano and the historian of botanical gardens and illustration Lucia Tongiorgi Tomasi of the Università di Pisa—to conduct research at Dumbarton Oaks.

The subsequent director of Garden and Landscape Studies, Michel Conan, brought new perspectives that left a firm imprint on the expanding field of Italian garden studies. As a French sociologist and a professor of sociology and urban and landscape studies in France before coming to Dumbarton Oaks, he had long focused his scholarship on the history of gardens, on their social and literary contexts, and, above all, on the theoretical approaches to their study. He had also been interested in the world of contemporary landscape architecture, and had published several studies on the French landscape architect Bernard Lassus, with whom he had also collaborated on research.[11] Based on this experience, and during his time as director, he was able to bring together at Dumbarton Oaks several worlds that had previously existed mostly separate from each other in garden studies. See, for example, the symposia acts he edited and published, including *Perspectives on Garden Histories* (1999), *Baroque Garden Cultures: Emulation, Sublimation, Subversion* (2005), and *Gardens and Imagination: Cultural History and Agency* (2008). He connected, quite concretely, the worlds of universities and architecture schools in France with those in Italy, Turkey, England, Germany, and the United States. He also amplified the methodological and historiographical direction in garden studies already started by Hunt and Wolschke-Bulmahn, and he really made that direction flourish. All of this came to bear on his selection of the topics and participants for the 2007 symposium on Italian gardens.

Conan's methodological models came from new interdisciplinary research that united the study of gardens with literary theory and the social sciences. His milieu consisted of scholars and practitioners (e.g., landscape architects), especially in France and Italy, where the study of gardens and landscapes was reconfigured as a new field in the late 1980s and early 1990s.[12] Geographers, philosophers, sociologists, art historians, architects, and literary critics began to join forces in considering the garden as both an object of historical study and a medium through which questions of contemporary societal interest could be discussed.[13] During his tenure as director of Garden and Landscape Studies at Dumbarton Oaks, Conan collaborated (as he still does) on publications—many of them involving Italian gardens—with other scholars in Europe and the United States and with professional landscape architects and preservationists.[14]

Conan brought these interests to bear on the symposia he organized, and worked closely with symposia participants to develop and elaborate the common themes linking their papers. For example, his concept of "the social reception of gardens," which was based on ideas about reception theory in literature and art,[15] was woven into the themes of many of his symposia, including *Baroque Garden Cultures: Emulation, Sublimation, Subversion* (2005) and *Gardens and Imagination: Cultural History and Agency* (2008). A number of the concepts underlying his symposia derive from his own immersion in French philosophy and critical theory, whether phenomenology, literary theory—for example, Louis Marin's use of Jacques Lacan's notion of three "orders" (i.e., the real, the symbolic, and the imaginary) in *Le portrait du roi* (1981)—or the notion of agency in Lacan and others. These concepts provided stimuli and vehicles for the dialogue that Conan had with prospective symposia participants, attracting at times "like minds," and this is evident in the acts of the symposia he organized, including this volume. It is seen, for example, in his selection of Antonella Pietrogrande and Denis Ribouillault as participants. Both of their essays, especially Ribouillault's, are situated within this intellectual tradition of French theoretical approaches, leading us to title the section of this volume containing their essays "Ways of Seeing the Landscape: Reconstructing Horizons of Perception and the Imaginary." Moreover, the contributions of many symposia participants (such as Lionella Scazzosi) reflect in specific ways the panorama of the new European theoretical approaches to landscape and gardens.

During Conan's tenure at Dumbarton Oaks, from 1998 to 2008, single studies of Italian gardens were incorporated into broadly defined symposia and symposia volumes that considered gardens from many different countries and periods. For example, Lauro Magnani discussed the social background of Genoese villa gardens from the sixteenth through nineteenth centuries in *Bourgeois and Aristocratic Cultural Encounters in Garden Art, 1550–1850* (2002). In *Baroque Garden Cultures: Emulation, Sublimation, Subversion* (2005), Margherita Azzi Visentini looked at the design and travelers' perceptions of the Borromean island gardens on Lake Maggiore, while Tracy L. Ehrlich considered the social competition among papal and aristocratic families in Baroque Rome as expressed through villa garden design, as well as issues of social emulation, perception, and misunderstanding by later visitors to these gardens. Mauro Ambrosoli studied the conservation and diffusion of species diversity in Renaissance peasant gardens of northern Italy, a topic that stems from his research as a historian of Italian agrarian life and practices, in *Botanical Progress, Horticultural Innovation, and Cultural Change* (2007). And in *Gardens and Imagination: Cultural History and Agency* (2008), Kathleen Christian considered poetical inscriptions and gatherings in early Renaissance sculpture gardens in Rome as repeated reenactments of an imagined connection to the world of ancient Rome and its culture by using the Renaissance's own "concept of the imagination as a cultural construct."[16] Christian's essay on Renaissance Rome was placed alongside studies of gardens in medieval and early modern Persia, Turkey, Japan, China, Russia, and Spain.

II

The essays in this volume are presented in four thematic groupings: Historiography of Italian Gardens and Landscapes, The Notion of Territorial Systems in Italian Villa Gardens, Agents of Landscape Transformation: From Microstoria to Policies of Stewardship, and Ways of Seeing the Landscape: Reconstructing Horizons of Perception and the Imaginary. Our organization largely reflects the one established by Conan for the symposium in 2007.

Historiography of Italian Gardens and Landscapes

The first two essays—"Methodological Changes in the Study of Italian Gardens from the 1970s to the 1990s: A Personal Itinerary" by Mirka Beneš and "'Grafting the Edelweiss on Cactus Plants': The 1931 Italian Garden Exhibition and Its Legacy" by Raffaella Fabiani Giannetto—sketch out some of the major issues that have emerged during the past decades in the historiography of Italian gardens. Working from complementary perspectives, they each propose that developments at the macrolevel of historical study, such as the establishment of widely used analytic categories and periodizations, are best explained in relation to exemplary case studies.

Beneš approaches this task by focusing on an important strand of Italian garden scholarship since the 1970s: the convergence of traditional art historical methods with those derived from the social sciences. At the same time, she traces the emergence of the Italian garden as a distinct field of study from its origins as a branch of architectural history. Beneš shows that the past and present contours of the field have assumed their various shapes according to global and individual forces—from the profound, culture-wide shifts associated with the year 1968 to the particular intellectual trends that are more directly the result of pedagogical lineages, scholarly networks, and even individual biographies. The latter is underscored by Beneš's account of her own intellectual formation, which, when seen against this broader backdrop, shows how seemingly disparate factors can converge in the solution of specific problems, such as the development of a framework to explain the creation of Roman villa parks during the seventeenth century. The synthetic picture of the field that emerges from her analysis, then, is that of a layered accumulation of contributions whose research agendas are not always closely aligned.

In contrast, Fabiani Giannetto looks to one historical moment to draw lessons about the field as a whole. Taking as her point of departure the first Italian garden exhibition, held in Florence in 1931, she demonstrates how political-ideological imperatives that have impinged on the scholarly endeavors of one period—or even one event—can have lasting, distorting effects on subsequent scholarship. Her object of inquiry is no less than the category of the Italian garden, which for much of the twentieth century denoted primarily the Roman and Florentine villa gardens of the fifteenth through eighteenth centuries. Such gardens were narrowly construed as quintessentially architectonic designs composed of terraces, axially arranged paths, evergreen vegetation, fountains, and sculptures. Fabiani Giannetto argues that this stereotype was constructed through the fascist appropriation of late nineteenth- and early twentieth-century scholarship, which was produced primarily by Anglo-American and German expatriate historians whose celebration of the Italian Renaissance stemmed from their own cultural agendas. After tracing this history, she casts a critical eye on the characterization of Italian gardens since World War II, and calls for a more comprehensive history that embraces broader temporal and geographic frames and formal types.

The Notion of Territorial Systems in Italian Villa Gardens

The next two essays explore the interpretive possibilities that are afforded by villa gardens that occur in clusters, and propose that we analyze these gardens as components of landscape "systems" rather than as isolated objects or units. Drawing upon methods that have been in development since the early 1970s, Marcello Fagiolo and Vincenzo Cazzato look comparatively at a series of representative situations, many of which occur in geographical areas of Italy that are underrepresented in the mainstream literature.

In "Systems of Gardens in Italy: Princely Residences and Villas in Rome and Latium, Savoy Piedmont, Royal Bourbon Naples, and Bagheria, Sicily," Fagiolo explains his conceptualization of villa systems through "ideograms," which map the physical, symbolic, and visual relations between villa properties and other points of interest. Radiating or crossing axes, usually drawn in plan view, trace the linkages between villas and historical and mythological sites, routes of movement (such as royal roads and hunting allées), and sight lines that frame views to built structures and topographical features. The resulting diagrams, although perhaps at first glance appearing to denote merely formal relationships, in fact show what Fagiolo refers to as "lines of force"—the vectors of social practices and territorial economies that shape the landscape but otherwise remain imperceptible. Fagiolo further demonstrates that regional variations in the territorial organization of villa systems in early modern Italy typically arose from a complex intersection of the symbolic requirements of court life and the economic realities of landscape management. This was particularly true of courts that favored hunting rituals, as their large-scale territorial configurations tended to reflect the exacting requirements of the chase rather than agricultural or pastoral patterns of land use. Such regional specificity assumes added significance when Fagiolo situates Italy's villa systems within a pan-European context, where he notes concurrent territorial formations in France and Austria.

Vincenzo Cazzato takes a similar approach in "Residences of the Emergent Classes in Two Areas of Southern Italy," where he analyzes two major villa systems, one in the Salento region of Puglia and another along the "Golden Mile" between Naples and Torre del Greco. Whereas the latter—which was centered on a strong court culture—closely resembled the villa systems examined by Fagiolo, the villa system in the Salento region was formed in the absence of a centralizing political force. Cazzato traces how the Salento villa gardens drew upon local agricultural traditions and typologies, such as the *masseria* (farm compound), for their basic elements and formal vocabulary. He also shows how these ties to agriculture embedded the villa gardens within broader territorial systems. This dual link with agriculture, both typological and territorial, contributed significantly to the popular image of the Italian countryside as a "gardened" landscape—a major historiographical theme that is elaborated on by several contributors to this volume.

Agents of Landscape Transformation: From Microstoria to Policies of Stewardship

Through the sheer force of multiplication, the notion of villa systems expands our traditional understanding of agency in the landscape and invites a reappraisal of design as a privileged category for understanding human alterations of landscape. Mauro Ambrosoli and Lionella Scazzosi push the field of inquiry even further with essays that deal with highly diffuse and jointly shared forms of agency: for Ambrosoli, a mode of landscape transformation distributed across multiple social strata and marked by both cooperation and conflict; and for Scazzosi, an accumulation of traces left behind by actors whose work spans centuries and must be evaluated anew by each succeeding generation. The issues raised by the authors have forced each of them to refine, and sometimes to reframe, their object of study and, by implication, the object of study for the field as a whole.

For Ambrosoli, this frame of reference is the agricultural landscape of Italy, which was collectively designed and managed by both villa owners and peasant farmers. It was this cultural landscape, far more than formal gardens per se, that was admired and copied by European, and especially English, travelers during the early modern period. In "From the Italian Countryside to the Italianate Landscape: Peasants as Gardeners and Foreign Observers in Italy, 1500–1850," Ambrosoli reconstructs the evolution of the Italian countryside through a combination of methods, including a close reading of travel literature, an analysis of the representations of peasant labor in landscape painting, and an extensive use of archivally based microhistories of Italian agriculture. A significant result is that the essay not only expands the frame of analysis to admit a composite "gardened" landscape, viewed as a synthesis of aristocratic and peasant activities, but also subtly shifts the depiction of agency in the landscape by foregrounding largely anonymous, repetitive acts occurring over long periods of time rather than singular interventions of individual, well-known designers. This result could be seen as one example of the convergence of the formal and the social traced by Beneš.

Writing from a perspective deeply informed by the practical concerns of stewardship, Scazzosi recounts how conceptual developments in Italian garden historiography have become increasingly intertwined with the technical problems and policy decisions faced by administrators of historical sites. In "Gardens and Landscapes as 'Open-Ended Works' between Continuity and Transformation: Notes on the Role of Historical Studies," she revisits two concepts—"vegetal architectures" and "open-ended artifacts"—from her previous work to contextualize these notions in relation to the broader field of historic preservation and to ask whether they remain relevant for the management of historical gardens and landscapes today. Her analysis, which shows how conservation has gradually come to encompass an array of landscape situations (not just gardens) and to value the contributions of actors across broad stretches of time, underscores the degree to which these concepts parallel recent developments in other disciplinary branches of garden history. Most of Scazzosi's critical discussion is reserved for the complexities of open-ended artifacts, and she acknowledges that the term has sometimes been abused to justify changes in historical landscapes that should be considered inappropriate. Following Alois Riegl, Scazzosi argues that the open-endedness of her approach does not mean openness to innovations of any kind but only those that preserve the existing character of a site and enhance its function as a vehicle of collective identity. She maintains that historical scholarship is one of the most effective tools for guiding decisions that will preserve this identity, as it both informs operational choices made by officials and technicians and shapes public opinion. The commitment to openness acknowledges that landscapes are dynamic and change over time, sometimes rapidly, and echoes Ambrosoli's emphasis on the *longue durée* of landscape transformation.

Ways of Seeing the Landscape: Reconstructing Horizons of Perception and the Imaginary

Antonella Pietrogrande and Denis Ribouillault address a central issue raised in both Ambrosoli's and Scazzosi's work by exploring how scholarship itself functions as an agent in the landscape. What roles did antiquarian scholarship play in the creation of Renaissance gardens and in the decisions regarding their conservation in the twenty-first century? How has this knowledge informed the perceptions of sophisticated audiences and conditioned how they see these gardens? This final section can also stand for the entire symposium and publication, as it effectively refocuses the broadened perspectives of current scholarship onto a few well-known Renaissance gardens, coming full circle, as it were, in dialogue with the state of the field as it stood in 1971.

In "The Imaginary of Generative Nature in Italian Mannerist Gardens," Pietrogrande seeks to uncover the motivations that led many creators of Renaissance and Mannerist villa gardens to include representations of pre-Olympian female deities in their decorative programs. Drawing upon studies in anthropology and the history of religion, she interprets this proliferation of images not only as a manifestation of the intellectual curiosity of antiquarian scholars but also as a more emotional desire to sacralize nature, to reawaken "the spirit of the place," and to experience imaginatively the generative capacity of nature. Focusing primarily on images of the Great Mother in the Villa d'Este at Tivoli, Pietrogrande expands the scope of the major iconographical studies of this garden, such as those of David R. Coffin, by invoking Lacan's sense of the imaginary as a "horizon of perception," that is, as the unconscious emotional, intellectual, and behavioral structures shared by particular social cohorts that condition their expectations prior to any actual phenomenal experience (such as strolling in a garden). By reconstructing the sixteenth-century emotional and intellectual nexus associated with the Great Mother, Pietrogrande asks her audience to step inside the perceptual world that the garden's creators intended to conjure through the deity's image.

Like Pietrogrande, Ribouillault works within an intellectual framework that includes the notion of horizons of perception, but he more specifically links physical artifacts with habituated forms of visual perception—a strategy that he terms an "archaeology of the gaze." Analyzing the representational strategies and uses of painted garden views within the architectural structures of Renaissance villas, particularly those of the Medici villas surrounding Florence, the Villa d'Este at Tivoli, and the Palazzo Farnese at Caprarola, he proposes that these views be understood as ideal ways of seeing the gardens rather than as artifacts documenting their actual state. In "Toward an Archaeology of the Gaze: The Perception and Function of Garden Views in Italian Renaissance Villas," Ribouillault demonstrates that, in most cases, the images, with regard to both their content and their location, are in complex dialogue with the gardens and their surrounding territories. Whether their visual strategies juxtapose painted views of garden scenery against actual views through windows, distill the mental geography of a landscape into a three-dimensional self-referential environment, or visually supplant a garden's present reality with its projected state, such virtuosic displays reveal a cultural imagination fascinated by the liminal qualities of representation. Ribouillault grounds this perceptual analysis within the broader Renaissance culture of image-making, and shows that garden views functioned historically as didactic and mnemonic devices, closely connected with Renaissance understandings of memory and place. His synthetic approach proposes a model for future studies that seeks to expand traditional iconographic methods with more recent cultural analyses of imagination, and in doing so highlights the unique possibilities that are offered to such endeavors by the field of garden studies.

III

The essays in this volume should be seen against the changing picture of scholarship today on Italian gardens. In terms of broad developments, we have seen over the last decade a growing diversity in the professional training of those writing on Italian gardens, an increasing collaboration among scholars (especially in Europe), a shift in interest from gardens to larger landscape systems, an expansion of methodologies, a change in the canon of exemplary Italian gardens, and a new interest in taking stock of it all through historiographical writing.

Behind these changes, we can see the impact of two driving forces, institutional and intellectual. At the institutional level in Europe, research on gardens and landscapes is increasingly done by large teams in targeted documentary campaigns and in research institutions, such as the Centre National de la Recherche Scientifique (CNRS) in France or the Consiglio Nazionale delle Ricerche (CNR) in Italy. Their work is usually supported by grants from governmental institutions at the municipal, national, or European Union level, and is manifest in exhibitions, conferences, and other activities engaging the public, such as garden tours, agro-tourism, and preservation campaigns. Recent decades have seen a huge expansion of this kind of research. But while European scholars emphasize teamwork, their American colleagues tend to work as individuals. At the intellectual level on both sides of the Atlantic, an equally strong driving force has been the growing interest in interdisciplinarity.[17] In Europe, the institutional model undoubtedly reinforces this interest, which is also rooted in deeper methodological shifts within intellectual life.

Italian and French researchers on Italian gardens became much more professionally diversified in the 1980s.[18] Besides art historians, they include important philosophers (such as Rosario Assunto and Massimo Venturi Ferriolo), landscape architects, ecologists, and policymakers directly involved in the preservation, restoration, and redesign of Italian gardens. This trend—which resulted in an expansion in the number of Italian publications on garden design—would continue in the 1990s and 2000s.[19]

The growth of collaboration across Europe can be seen in the recent volumes edited by Laura Sabrina Pelissetti and Lionella Scazzosi, Sabine Frommel, Monique Chatenet, and Francesco Ceccarelli and Gianni Venturi.[20] For example, Frommel is a German art and architectural historian who teaches at the École Pratique des Hautes Études en Sciences Sociales (Paris) and conducts research in both Italy and France. Her recent edited books, *Villa Lante a Bagnaia* (2005) and *Bomarzo: Il sacro bosco* (2009), include essays by Italian, German, French, and English scholars. The other collaborative volumes just mentioned include the same range.

Both in the history of Italian gardens and in the public service of land stewardship and historic preservation, attention has shifted from the microunit of the individual garden to the macroscale of larger, often regional, landscape systems, as is discussed in this volume by Mirka Beneš, Marcello Fagiolo, Vincenzo Cazzato, Mauro Ambrosoli, and Lionella Scazzosi. From a garden historian's perspective, this shift may be motivated by a desire to interpret the meanings of the large parklands that appeared in early seventeenth-century Rome or the large-scale territorial organizations that were required for royal hunting rituals in Baroque Piedmont or Bourbon Naples. From the viewpoint of a historian of the Italian landscape, the "gardened" agrarian landscape of Italy forms a larger system of practices based on the maintenance of myriad properties. From the perspective of a historic preservationist, this shift is driven by the need to deal with the changing landscape around historical gardens during conditions of rapid urban expansion.

New scholarship on Italian gardens emerged in France in the late 1990s. Although it was partially influenced by the wealth of Italian research, it had its own theoretical frameworks deriving from André Chastel and his disciples, and from the major French contribution to philosophy and theory that began in the 1960s.[21] Philosophers, geographers, and sociologists—including Alain Roger, Augustin Berque, Jean-Marc Besse, and Michel Conan—are interested in theoretical topics involving landscape and vision, reception theory, philosophical concepts of the garden, and representation and the garden, specifically in landscape painting of the Italian Renaissance.[22] At the same time, Italian scholars of gardens, such as Antonella Pietrogrande, turn in multidisciplinary ways to French and Italian anthropologists in order to forge new understandings of Renaissance gardens, such as the Villa d'Este at Tivoli.[23]

Working more independently, the American art historians concerned with Italian gardens have introduced distinctive intellectual frameworks to the field.[24] For example, they have been interested in appropriating theoretical perspectives from literary theory, history, and geography to the study of gardens. The themes of geographical structures, representation, and landscape and vision have been repeatedly addressed in their writings.[25] Their work has been particularly strong in its extensive use of a new body of historical literature, namely the social, economic, and cultural history of the Italian medieval and early modern states, as well as regional studies.[26]

The possibilities for study in the field of Italian gardens are much richer and larger today than they were several decades ago, not only in the thematic realm, but also in the geographical and chronological ones. The Dumbarton Oaks symposium of 1971 reflected a consensus that there existed, since the Renaissance, a unified stylistic and cultural concept—"the Italian garden," tied to a single ideal construct, likely represented by a Florentine or a Roman garden. Thirty-five years later, scholars on both sides of the Atlantic have come to view the material reality of gardens in Italy as a highly varied group of historical typologies grounded in the entire Italian peninsula. Nearly ten years ago, in "Italy is a Garden: The Idea of Italy and the Italian Garden" (2001), Claudia Lazzaro had already begun to question the construct of the Italian garden, arguing that Italy did not politically and physically exist as a unified country until 1861, before which it comprised several republics and states, each with its own agricultural landscapes, economies, and political structures. The issue of how the Italian garden came to be constructed in the late nineteenth and twentieth centuries is taken up in several of the essays in this volume.

From the 1980s on, and especially in the 1990s, a broader geographical coverage developed in the study of Italian gardens. Here, again, both institutional and intellectual forces were responsible. Institutionally, Italian scholars and garden preservationists needed to deal with gardens and designed landscapes in every corner of their country.[27] Intellectually, following their colleagues in history and art history, garden historians expanded their focus from Florence and Rome to all of the Italian states.[28] This volume considers many of these regions, from the Po Valley in the north to the southern realms of Naples and Sicily.

This broader geographical inclusiveness is linked to a new historical periodization for Italian gardens that reaches far beyond the Renaissance. In contrast to even two decades ago, studies today investigate Italian gardens in diachronic ways, over the longue durée, leading to a revision of previous chronological delimitations of research. The study of Italian gardens is no longer limited to Renaissance and Baroque examples, but includes medieval and modern ones as well. Recent historical research on the Mediterranean world, its port cities, trade routes, political embassies, and migrations provides evidence of the impact of international exchanges on the conceptualization, design, and plant materials of gardens in a wide range of Mediterranean and adjacent regions—from Spain and Italy to Ottoman Turkey and Safavid Persia.[29] As a result, Italian gardens are now seen in a continuum of developments from late antiquity onward—for example, the gardens at the Villa Rufolo and other villas at Ravello south of Naples are reconstructed in their intermingled Byzantine, Islamic, and Italian contexts.[30]

Partly because of this new literature, recent studies also upend the view that Italian Renaissance gardens were historically and formally derived solely from the great monuments of Roman antiquity, such as Hadrian's Villa at Tivoli, or from surviving texts, such as Pliny the Younger's description of his two villas in central Italy. New research reveals that Italian ambassadors and travelers, such as Andrea Navagero at the Alhambra in Granada, Spain, in 1526, brought plant specimens, hydraulic knowledge, and concepts of palace gardens back to Italy. These elements became defining features of Italian gardens such as the Villa Madama in Rome and the Villa d'Este at Tivoli, which were previously thought to be purely the result of the study of Roman antiquity on Italian soil.[31] Additionally, scholars now consider the influence of Persian garden design on the conceptualization of the Villa d'Este at Tivoli and other Renaissance gardens in and near Rome.[32] Thus, we see that the field of Italian garden history is undergoing striking transformations, both quantitative and methodological. This volume is a reflexive and historiographical meditation on some of those transformations, and is part of the current desire of both historians and practitioners of landscape architecture to situate their work in today's rapidly changing fields of intellectual life and professional design practice.

Notes

1 Historiographical background to this introduction can be found in Mirka Beneš, "Recent Developments and Perspectives in the Historiography of Italian Gardens," in *Perspectives on Garden Histories*, ed. Michel Conan, 37–76 (Washington, D.C.: Dumbarton Oaks Research Library and Collection, 1999); David R. Coffin, "The Study of the History of the Italian Garden until the First Dumbarton Oaks Colloquium," in *Perspectives on Garden Histories*, ed. Michel Conan, 27–36 (Washington, D.C.: Dumbarton Oaks Research Library and Collection, 1999); Mirka Beneš, "Italian and French Gardens: A Century of Historical Study (1900–2000)," in *Villas and Gardens in Early Modern Italy and France*, eds. Mirka Beneš and Dianne Harris, 1–16 (Cambridge: Cambridge University Press, 2001); Margherita Azzi Visentini, "Storia dei giardini: Osservazioni in margine al recente sviluppo di questa disciplina in Italia," in *Storia e storie di giardini: Fortune e storia del giardino italiano e verbanese nel mondo; Atti del Convegno, Verbania, sabato 31 agosto 2002*, eds. Leonardo Parachini and Carlo Alessandro Pisoni, 45–86 (Verbania: Alberti Libraio, Comune di Verbania, Magazzeno Storico Verbanese, 2003); Mirka Beneš, "A Tribute to Two Historians of Landscape Architecture: David R. Coffin and Elisabeth B. MacDougall," *Journal of the Society of Architectural Historians* 63, no. 2 (June 2004): 248–54; Margherita Zalum, "La storia del giardino italiano: Lineamenti ed evoluzione di una giovane disciplina," in *Bibliografia del giardino e del paesaggio italiano, 1980–2005*, eds. Lucia Tongiorgi Tomasi and Luigi Zangheri, 1–14 (Florence: L. S. Olschki, 2008); Luigi Zangheri, "Il restauro dei giardini storici in Italia dal 1980," in *Bibliografia del giardino e del paesaggio italiano, 1980–2005*, eds. Lucia Tongiorgi Tomasi and Luigi Zangheri, 135–59 (Florence: L. S. Olschki, 2008); and Margherita Azzi Visentini, "Riflessioni intorno alla fortuna critica del giardino storico italiano negli Stati Uniti negli ultimi trentacinque anni," in *Giardini storici: A 25 anni dalle Carte di Firenze; Esperienze e prospettive*, eds. Laura Sabrina Pelissetti and Lionella Scazzosi, 1:31–46 (Florence: L. S. Olschki, 2009). For bibliographies of the literature, see Lucia Tongiorgi Tomasi and Luigi Zangheri, eds., *Bibliografia del giardino e del paesaggio italiano, 1980–2005* (Florence: L. S. Olschki, 2008); and Uwe Schneider and Gert Gröning, eds., *Stolo: Bibliographische Findmittel zur Gartenkultur*, vol. 1, *Italien* (Worms: Wernersche Verlagsgesellschaft, 2009).

2 The central concern—an assessment of recent developments in the field—was similar to that of the symposium on Mughal gardens. See James L. Wescoat Jr. and Joachim Wolschke-Bulmahn, "Sources, Places, Representations, and Prospects: A Perspective of Mughal Gardens," in *Mughal Gardens: Sources, Places, Representations, and Prospects*, eds. James L. Wescoat Jr. and Joachim Wolschke-Bulmahn, 5–29 (Washington, D.C.: Dumbarton Oaks Research Library and Collection, 1996).

3 Michel Conan, call for papers for the "Recent Issues in Italian Garden Studies: Sources, Methods, and Theoretical Perspectives" symposium, 14 June 2005, Dumbarton Oaks Research Library and Collection. He specified that proposals for papers "should present new results brought by recent investigations, and place these results in a critical perspective." He called for each paper to include a discussion of new sources or methods, especially theoretical perspectives. The call for papers went out to a range of scholars, including the philosopher Massimo Venturi Ferriolo; the preservation scholar and theoretician Lionella Scazzosi; the historian of botany Alessandro Tosi; the historians of Genoese, Veneto, and Medici Tuscan gardens, Lauro Magnani, Margherita Azzi Visentini, and Raffaela Fabiani Giannetto, respectively;

the handful of American art historians who focus on Italian gardens, Claudia Lazzaro, Dianne Harris, Tracy L. Ehrlich, Mirka Beneš, and Kathleen W. Christian; and a new generation of French art historians who have very recently emerged with substantial studies on Italian gardens, namely Hervé Brunon and Denis Ribouillault.

4 Tongiorgi Tomasi and Zangheri, *Bibliografia del giardino e del paesaggio italiano, 1980–2005*.

5 David R. Coffin, ed., *The Italian Garden* (Washington, D.C.: Dumbarton Oaks Research Library and Collection, 1972); and Elisabeth Blair MacDougall, ed., *Fons Sapientiae: Renaissance Garden Fountains* (Washington, D.C.: Dumbarton Oaks Research Library and Collection, 1978).

6 For what follows on studies of Italian gardens at Dumbarton Oaks since the 1971 symposium and for the centers and figures in American scholarship, see the excellent new article by Azzi Visentini, "Riflessioni intorno alla fortuna critica del giardino storico italiano," 33–42. Azzi Visentini notes that the 1971 symposium had an impact on scholarship in Italy—for example, through Lionello Puppi's teaching at Padua—and that Dumbarton Oaks became a training ground for American scholars of Italian gardens. Ibid., 38–40.

7 For a general overview of garden and landscape studies at Dumbarton Oaks from 1971 to 1996, see Joachim Wolschke-Bulmahn, *Twenty-Five Years of Studies in Landscape Architecture at Dumbarton Oaks: From Italian Gardens to Theme Parks* (Washington, D.C.: Dumbarton Oaks Research Library and Collection, 1996). Hunt's first symposium, "Garden History: Issues, Approaches, Methods" (1989), opened the way to broad reflection on the field. John Dixon Hunt, ed., *Garden History: Issues, Approaches, Methods* (Washington, D.C.: Dumbarton Oaks Research Library and Collection, 1992); and John Dixon Hunt and Joachim Wolschke-Bulmahn, eds., *The Vernacular Garden* (Washington, D.C.: Dumbarton Oaks Research Library and Collection, 1993).

8 In a major collection of essays, Hunt brought together an international array of scholars to write on a wide range of topics, from literature to hydraulics, from social life to nineteenth-century Italian gardens. John Dixon Hunt, *The Italian Garden: Art, Design, and Culture* (Cambridge: Cambridge University Press, 1996). In effect, his publication both joined the widening of the canon for the Anglo-American scholarship of Italian gardens and reflected a growing reality, the emergence of a new body of impressive scholarship in Italy during the 1980s and 1990s. See Azzi Visentini, "Storia dei giardini," on Italian scholarship in the 1980s and 1990s; and Azzi Visentini, "Riflessioni intorno alla fortuna critica del giardino storico italiano," 38–39, on Hunt's bridging of the Anglo-American and Italian worlds of scholarship.

9 Mirka Beneš, "Society, Culture, and Geography in European Garden History, 1950–1995: From Art History to Heritages of Marxism, the *Annales*, and Foucault" (paper presented at the "Evolution and Perspectives of the Study of Garden History" colloquium, Dumbarton Oaks, 23 March 1996).

10 Coffin, "The Study of the History of the Italian Garden until the First Dumbarton Oaks Colloquium"; and Beneš, "Recent Developments and Perspectives in the Historiography of Italian Gardens."

11 See Thierry Paquot, "Invité(s): Michel Conan," in *Urbanisme: Villes-Sociétés-Cultures* 333 (November-December 2003), http://www.urbanisme.fr/issue/contents.php?code=333.

12 For the French renewal of landscape studies and the practice and theory of landscape architecture since the 1980s, which was centered on the École Nationale Supérieure du Paysage de Versailles (ENSP), see Pierre Donadieu, "Eléments pour une histoire de la recherche à l'École Nationale Supérieure du Paysage de Versailles (ENSP)," 26 June 2006, http://www.projetsdepaysage.fr. Conan's role in the renewal at the ENSP is discussed here.

13 See, for example, Alessandro Tagliolini and Massimo Venturi Ferriolo, eds., *Il giardino: Idea natura realità* (Milan: Guerini, 1987); Massimo Venturi Ferriolo, *Nel grembo della vita: Le origini dell'idea di giardino* (Milan: Guerini, 1989); Rosario Assunto, *Retour au jardin: Essais pour une philosophie de la nature, 1976–1987* (Besançon: Les Éditions de l'Imprimeur, 2003); Domenico Luciani, "Ritrovare e reinventare i 'giardini italiani': L'aporìa del restauro," in *Storia e storie di giardini: Fortune e storia del giardino italiano e verbanese nel mondo; Atti del Convegno, Verbania, sabato 31 agosto 2002*, eds. Leonardo Parachini and Carlo Alessandro Pisoni, 35–43 (Verbania: Alberti Libraio, Comune di Verbania, Magazzeno Storico Verbanese, 2003); and the bibliographies in Azzi Visentini, "Storia dei giardini"; and Hervé Brunon, "L'essor artistique et la fabrique culturelle du paysage à la Renaissance," *Studiolo: Revue d'histoire de l'art de l'Académie de France à Rome* 4 (2006): 261–90. For the parallel phenomenon in garden studies in France, see Brunon, "L'essor artistique et la fabrique culturelle du paysage à la Renaissance"; and Brunon, "Questions et méthodes de l'histoire des jardins en France," in *Giardini storici: A 25 anni dalle Carte di Firenze; Esperienze e prospettive*, eds. Laura Sabrina Pelissetti and Lionella Scazzosi, 1:11–21 (Florence: L. S. Olschki, 2009).

14 For example, Michel Conan, José Tito Rojo, and Luigi Zangheri, eds., *Histories of Garden Conservation: Case-Studies and Critical Debates* (Florence: L. S. Olschki, 2005).

15 Reception theory can be traced to a range of philosophers, literary theorists, and art historians from the 1960s on, for example, Hans Robert Jauss, Richard Wollheim, Michael Baxandall, and Wolfgang Kemp. See Hans Robert Jauss, *Literaturgeschichte als Provokation* (Frankfurt: Suhrkamp, 1970); Wolfgang Kemp, *Der Anteil des Betrachters: Rezeptionsästhetische Studien zur Malerei des 19. Jahrhunderts* (Munich: Mäander, 1983); and Richard Wollheim, *Painting as an Art* (Princeton, N.J.: Princeton University Press, 1987). Conan frequently cites Jauss and

Maurice Merleau-Ponty in his introductions to symposium volumes from Dumbarton Oaks. See Maurice Merleau-Ponty, *Phénoménologie de la perception* (Paris: Gallimard, 1945). Other garden historians are also interested in the reception and perception, not necessarily social, of gardens by their viewers and users; see John Dixon Hunt, *The Afterlife of Gardens* (Philadelphia: University of Pennsylvania Press, 2004), for an analysis of literary theory and reception of gardens since the eighteenth century in England.

16 Kathleen W. Christian, "Landscapes of Ruin and the Imagination in the Antiquarian Gardens of Renaissance Rome," in *Gardens and Imagination: Cultural History and Agency*, ed. Michel Conan (Washington, D.C.: Dumbarton Oaks Research Library and Collection, 2008), 122.

17 An assessment of the growing interdisciplinarity in studies of landscape architecture is given in Dianne Harris, "Landscape in Context," in *Villas and Gardens in Early Modern Italy and France*, eds. Mirka Beneš and Dianne Harris (Cambridge: Cambridge University Press, 2001), 16–19.

18 For the diverse professional backgrounds of scholars and the rich range of their writings, see Azzi Visentini, "Storia dei giardini"; Brunon, "L'essor artistique et la fabrique culturelle du paysage à la Renaissance"; Zalum, "La storia del giardino italiano"; Zangheri, "Il restauro dei giardini storici in Italia dal 1980"; and Laura Sabrina Pelissetti and Lionella Scazzosi, eds., *Giardini storici: A 25 anni dalle Carte di Firenze; Esperienze e prospettive*, 2 vols. (Florence: L. S. Olschki, 2009).

19 This new Italian literature on Italian gardens is exemplified by the *Giardini e paesaggio* series published by L. S. Olschki in Florence. The first volume (*Fitocronologia d'Italia*) was published by Federico Maniero in 2000. The series now counts twenty-five volumes with the publication of *Giardini storici* by Pelissetti and Scazzosi in 2009.

20 See, as examples, the excellent new collaborative works: Sabine Frommel, ed., *Villa Lante a Bagnaia* (Milan: Electa, 2005); Brunon, "L'essor artistique et la fabrique culturelle du paysage à la Renaissance"; Gianni Venturi and Francesco Ceccarelli, eds., *Delizie in villa: Il giardino rinascimentale e i suoi committenti* (Florence: L. S. Olschki, 2008); and Pelissetti and Scazzosi, *Giardini storici*. See also the edited volumes that contextualize gardens through analyses of a single theme, such as country life or hunting. Monique Chatenet, ed., *Maisons des champs dans l'Europe de la Renaissance: Actes des premières rencontres d'architecture européenne, Château de Maisons 10–13 juin 2003* (Paris: Picard, 2006); and Claude d'Anthenaise and Monique Chatenet, eds., *Chasses princières dans l'Europe de la Renaissance: Actes du colloque de Chambord, 1er et 2 octobre 2004* (Arles: Actes Sud, 2007). A model for such dialogues were the architectural history "colloques" that Jean Guillaume organized for many years at the Centre d'Études Supérieures de la Renaissance at Tours, France, and that included studies of villas and gardens. Jean Guillaume, ed., *Architecture, jardin, paysage: L'environnement du château et de la villa aux XVe et XVIe siècles* (Paris: Picard, 1999).

21 For the emergence of the vibrant new field of French studies of gardens, see Beneš, "Italian and French Gardens"; Brunon, "L'essor artistique et la fabrique culturelle du paysage à la Renaissance"; and Brunon, "Questions et méthodes de l'histoire des jardins en France." See the numerous publications of Monique Mosser, who was a leader of French scholarship on gardens for three decades. For background on the historical studies and theoretical works that have had a large impact on the new garden studies, see François Bédarida, ed., *L'histoire et le métier d'historien en France 1945–1995* (Paris: Éditions de la Maison des Sciences de l'Homme, 1995); and François Cusset, *French theory: Foucault, Derrida, Deleuze & Cie et les mutations de la vie intellectuelle aux États-Unis* (Paris: Découverte, 2003). See also Beneš, "Recent Developments and Perspectives in the Historiography of Italian Gardens," 66–69; and Beneš, "Italian and French Gardens," 12–15.

22 Brunon, "L'essor artistique et la fabrique culturelle du paysage à la Renaissance," 265–69; and Denis Ribouillault, "Toward an Archaeology of the Gaze: The Perception and Function of Garden Views in Italian Renaissance Villas," this volume.

23 Antonella Pietrogrande, "The Imaginary of Generative Nature in Italian Mannerist Gardens," this volume.

24 On these frameworks, see Beneš, "Methodological Changes in the Study of Italian Gardens from the 1970s to the 1990s: A Personal Itinerary," this volume. Besides those mentioned above, a few American art historians of the Italian Renaissance are now focusing on gardens: Katherine Bentz and Yvonne Elet on Renaissance Rome, and Christopher Pastore on the Renaissance Veneto.

25 See, for example, the effect of the work of Denis Cosgrove on Tracy L. Ehrlich, *Landscape and Identity in Early Modern Rome: Villa Culture at Frascati in the Borghese Era* (Cambridge: Cambridge University Press, 2002); and Dianne Harris, *The Nature of Authority: Villa Culture, Landscape, and Representation in Eighteenth-Century Lombardy* (University Park: Pennsylvania State University Press, 2003). For recent theoretical works on the key topics just discussed, see Dianne Harris, "The Post-Modernization of Landscape: A Critical Historiography," *Journal of the Society of Architectural Historians* 58, no. 3 (September 1999): 434–43; Mirka Beneš, "Pastoralism in the Roman Baroque Villa and in Claude Lorrain: Myths and Realities of the Roman Campagna," in *Villas and Gardens in Early Modern Italy and France*, eds. Mirka Beneš and Dianne Harris, 88–113 (Cambridge: Cambridge University Press, 2001); and Dianne Harris and D. Fairchild Ruggles, eds., *Sites Unseen: Landscape and Vision* (Pittsburgh, Pa.: University of Pittsburgh Press, 2007).

26 This new historical work began in the 1970s and today is a flourishing field. For these developments, see Beneš, "Recent Developments and Perspectives in the Historiography of Italian Gardens," 54, 59, and 65–66; and

Beneš, "Methodological Changes in the Study of Italian Gardens from the 1970s to the 1990s," this volume. For examples of essays on villas and villa culture by social historians, see Irene Fosi, "Fra Siena e Roma: Famiglie, mercanti, pontefici fra Cinquecento e Seicento," in *I giardini Chigi tra Siena e Roma: Dal Cinquecento agli inizi dell'Ottocento*, ed. Carla Benocci, 13–38 (Siena: Protagon, Fondazione Monte dei Paschi di Siena, 2005); and Michael Lingohr, "The Palace and Villa as Spaces of Patrician Self-Definition," in *Renaissance Florence: A Social History*, eds. Roger J. Crum and John T. Paoletti, 240–72 (New York: Cambridge University Press, 2006).

27 The need to restore and administer their country's historical gardens has led scholars and preservationists to inventory, document, and analyze an astounding number and range of gardens, larger designed landscapes, garden ornaments such as fountains and grottoes, and designers. See Vincenzo Cazzato, ed., *Atlante del giardino italiano, 1750–1940: Dizionario biografico di architetti, giardinieri, botanici, committenti, letterati e altri protagonisti*, 2 vols. (Rome: Istituto Poligrafico e Zecca dello Stato, Libreria dello Stato, 2009).

28 Among the many top-notch Italian publications that cover the peninsula, see Vincenzo Cazzato, Marcello Fagiolo, and Maria Adriana Giusti, eds., *Atlante delle grotte e dei ninfei in Italia*, vol. 1, *Toscana, Lazio, Italia meridionale e isole* (Milan: Electa, 2001) and vol. 2, *Italia settentrionale, Umbria e Marche* (Milan: Electa, 2002); and Cazzato, *Atlante del giardino italiano*. For examples of regional studies in English, see Margherita Azzi Visentini, "Islands of Delight: Shifting Perceptions of the Borromean Islands," in *Baroque Garden Cultures: Emulation, Sublimation, Subversion*, ed. Michel Conan, 245–89 (Washington, D.C.: Dumbarton Oaks Research Library and Collection, 2005); and Harris, *The Nature of Authority*. On the origins of the broadening in geographical scope, see Beneš, "Recent Developments and Perspectives in the Historiography of Italian Gardens," 51–53; and Azzi Visentini, "Storia dei giardini." Gardens are notably prominent in the magisterial series, *Atlante tematico del Barocco in Italia*, started in 2003 and directed at the national level in Italy by Marcello Fagiolo. See Mario Bevilacqua and Maria Luisa Madonna, eds., *Stato pontificio e granducato di Toscana*, vol. 2 of *Il sistema delle residenze nobiliari*, ed. Marcello Fagiolo (Rome: De Luca, 2003).

29 David Abulafia, ed., *The Mediterranean in History* (Los Angeles: J. Paul Getty Museum, 2003).

30 Forty years ago, art historian Eugenio Battisti was an exception: at the Dumbarton Oaks symposium of 1971, he discussed fifteenth-century gardens in many Italian regions and probed the exchange of ideas on gardens between the Italian peninsula and the larger Mediterranean world, including Islamic cultures. See Eugenio Battisti, "*Natura Artificiosa* to *Natura Artificialis*," in *The Italian Garden*, ed. David R. Coffin (Washington, D.C.: Dumbarton Oaks Research Library and Collection, 1972), 3–6, 10–13; and Eugenio Battisti, *Iconologia ed ecologia del giardino e del paesaggio*, ed. Giuseppa Saccaro Del Buffa (Florence: L. S. Olschki, 2004). In the symposium of 1977, George Hersey went outside the established canon by discussing early Renaissance Naples; see "Water-Works and Water-Play in Renaissance Naples," in *Fons Sapientiae: Renaissance Garden Fountains*, ed. Elisabeth Blair MacDougall, 59–84 (Washington, D.C.: Dumbarton Oaks Research Library and Collection, 1978).

31 Cammy Brothers, "The Renaissance Reception of the Alhambra: The Letters of Andrea Navagero and the Palace of Charles V," *Muqarnas* 11 (1994): 79–102.

32 Many new publications and conferences are exploring the intercultural connections of the Mediterranean in terms of garden design. See Brothers, "The Renaissance Reception of the Alhambra"; Gülru Necipoglu, "The Suburban Landscape of Sixteenth-Century Istanbul as a Mirror of Classical Ottoman Garden Culture," in *Gardens in the Time of the Great Muslim Empires: Theory and Design*, ed. Attilio Petruccioli, 32–71 (Leiden and New York: Brill, 1997); Luciani, "Ritrovare e reinventare i 'giardini italiani'," 38–40; Jill Caskey, *Art and Patronage in the Medieval Mediterranean: Merchant Culture in the Region of Amalfi* (Cambridge: Cambridge University Press, 2004); Luigi Zangheri, Brunella Lorenzi, and Nausikaa M. Rahmati, *Il giardino islamico* (Florence: L. S. Olschki, 2006); Howard Burns and Paul Davies, "Mediterranean Dialogues: Palladio and Sinan," in *Palladio*, eds. Guido Beltramini and Howard Burns, 236–43 (London: Royal Academy of Arts, 2008); and Lisa Golombek, "From Timur to Tivoli: Reflections on *Il Giardino All'Italiana*," in *Frontiers of Islamic Art and Architecture: Essays in Celebration of Oleg Grabar's Eightieth Birthday*, eds. Gülru Necipoglu and Julia Bailey, special issue, *Muqarnas* 25 (2008): 243–54. An example of this new interest was "East, West, North, South: A Broader Geography for the Culture of Gardens, 800–1700 AD," a session chaired by Mirka Beneš and Cammy Brothers at the annual meeting of the Society of Architectural Historians in April 2008.

PART I

Historiography of Italian Gardens and Landscapes

CHAPTER 1

Methodological Changes in the Study of Italian Gardens from the 1970s to the 1990s: A Personal Itinerary

MIRKA BENEŠ

SINCE THE 1980S, THE HISTORICAL STUDY OF Italian villas and gardens of the Renaissance and Baroque periods has been undergoing large shifts. First, there has been an explosion in the amount of published work by Italian (and, more recently, French) researchers, while the share produced by German and American scholars has decreased.[1] Second, there has been a shift in the emphasis and the methodology of the research, from formal gardens to parks and surrounding landscapes and territories, and from methods derived from traditional art history to methods influenced by the social sciences, history, linguistics, and preservation policies (figs. 1.1–1.3).[2]

It is this second aspect, the shift in emphasis and methodology, that I want to address here. Given the complexity and multilayering of the work produced today, I will focus on one recent methodological strand alone, that of my own research. Encouraged by Michel Conan, who, as the organizer of the Dumbarton Oaks symposium in October 2007, suggested this approach, I take a somewhat autobiographical viewpoint and revisit my own intellectual itinerary in writing on Roman villa gardens, trying to understand the conditions that enabled and spurred my thinking in the direction that it took. One by-product of retracing my own itinerary is that, in the background, I sketch several strands of the history of Italian gardens as a discipline.[3] The primary aim of this paper, however, is to consider, through a quite personal case study, the broader question of how methodological changes happen in a given field. Thus, of the two issues that Conan asked us to address—where our particular methodology comes from, and how it has evolved in the last ten years—it is the first one that I will emphasize.

I was first trained as an art historian in the 1970s and early 1980s in the United States. Like many others in my generation, I searched for a way to bring together the study of the aesthetic qualities of gardens and the study of their social dimensions—political, economic, and cultural. There was no established model for this approach within the field of Roman Renaissance and Baroque garden studies, or even garden studies at large, where a strictly art historical approach was used, especially in the United States.

But a broader intellectual picture was evolving, and I fed on a convergence taking shape between the

FIGURE 1.1.
Villa Barbaro, Maser, built ca. 1550–59.
Photograph by the author.

FIGURE 1.2.
Villa Barbaro, Maser, built ca. 1550–59.
Photograph by the author.

FIGURE 1.3.
Villa Barbaro, Maser, built ca. 1550–59.
Photograph by the author.

FIGURE 1.4.
Villa Medici, Rome, built ca. 1564–74.
Photograph by the author.

FIGURE 1.5.
View of the Water Theater and the Columns of Hercules at the Villa Aldobrandini, Frascati, built ca. 1592–1620.
Photograph by the author.

FIGURE 1.6.
View of the park from the top-floor loggia of the palace at the Villa Aldobrandini, Frascati, built ca. 1592–1620.
Photograph by the author.

two domains of art history and the social sciences, which were beginning to be connected by Marxist concepts of "mediating structures."[4] The art historical study of gardens and the social sciences were worlds apart before the 1960s, but have greatly overlapped since the 1980s. During the two intervening decades, developments internal to each of these domains pushed each in the direction of the other. On the one hand, Italian garden studies expanded their focus from formal Renaissance gardens to Baroque gardens with large park areas; the older categories developed to analyze Renaissance gardens did not provide explanation for the Baroque ones or the parks, thus pushing historians like myself to look for new categories (figs. 1.4–1.6). On the other hand, the social sciences increasingly moved toward the study of concrete situations, artifacts, and specific mediating structures (rather than abstract systems), thus providing a link with the focus on the art object, in formal and iconographical terms, that was traditional in art history.

This broad process of convergence and mediation—observed from the angle of my own personal evolution—is what I will try to outline in this essay. But, first, I will sketch out what was for me the point of departure of this process: the art historical approach to Italian gardens of the Renaissance and Baroque periods prior to 1970. My examples will be chosen primarily from studies on Roman villa gardens, although the larger development of the field of Italian garden studies cannot be entirely excluded. A few words are needed here about the terms "villa" and "garden." From at least the fifteenth to the eighteenth centuries, Rome's gardens were usually part of villas, or complexes that included houses or palaces and their surrounding gardens. Therefore, the term "villa garden" is used here.[5]

This essay is structured in two parts with an epilogue. Part one, Worlds Apart: The 1940s to 1970s, looks at the methodologies used in art historical studies on Italian gardens from the 1940s to the 1970s, and at their separateness from the methodologies of the social sciences, using scholarship on Roman villa gardens as a case in point. Part two, Worlds Converging: The 1970s to 1980s, considers the start of a convergence of interests between social sciences and art history, especially in the 1970s, and examines its implications for Italian and Roman garden studies. The epilogue, Worlds Together: The 1980s to 1990s, concludes by briefly tracing the use I made of those convergences during the 1980s and 1990s, when I developed my own methodology on Roman seventeenth-century villa gardens.

Worlds Apart: The 1940s to 1970s

I begin with the scholarly generation that was born about 1920 and educated during and just after World War II.[6] These scholars can be roughly divided between those who worked in the mainstream of academic art history and those who pursued other professions.

The Mainstream of Art History

The American scholars included David R. Coffin (1918–2003), James S. Ackerman (b. 1919), and Elisabeth Blair MacDougall (1925–2003).[7] They attended elite American universities and were taught by German émigré art historians.[8] Ackerman, though not a specialist on gardens, was deeply interested in the concept, culture, and forms of Renaissance villas.[9] By contrast, Coffin and MacDougall focused specifically on gardens, especially Roman ones. Coffin remained at Princeton University throughout his career, teaching Italian garden studies, including Roman subjects, to several American students of the next generation.[10] MacDougall became the director of the newly founded Studies in Landscape Architecture program at Dumbarton Oaks, an institute of Harvard University in Washington, D.C., in 1972; she remained in this position until her retirement in 1988.[11]

Throughout their careers, and during their field study in Rome, these garden historians kept company mainly with other American art historians in a milieu centered on the American Academy in Rome and the Bibliotheca Hertziana, the German art history institute.[12] For example, MacDougall's teachers included Richard Krautheimer and Wolfgang Lotz, as well as Ackerman. After the mid-1960s, Ackerman also engaged in dialogue with his milieux of contemporary art, social historical studies, and European art historians, some of them of neo-Marxist bent, such as Michelangelo Muraro, the author of studies on Veneto villas.[13]

The American scholars, like their German teachers, relied considerably on an approach that came from the art historical study of paintings, namely the catalogue raisonné, in which written and visual archival sources were gathered, ordered chronologically, compared, indexed, and "reasoned" in order to document objectively the works of art.[14] German and Italian scholars followed suit. This approach, which is still very important and highly successful, is evident in some of the finest writings on Roman Renaissance and Baroque architecture and has greatly influenced the field of garden studies.[15] Overall, the work of these art historians had its origins in German aesthetics and art history, as will be discussed later in this essay.[16]

The Italian scholars included the art historians Paola della Pergola (ca. 1900–93) and Isa Belli Barsali (1920–86), who trained at elite universities (e.g., the Università di Pisa and the Università di Firenze) under renowned art historians and critics, such as Adolfo Venturi (1856–1941) and his son Lionello Venturi (1885–1961).[17] Belli Barsali's catalogue raisonnées of the villa gardens of Rome and Latium from 1500 to modern times were exceptional and farsighted; they are goldmines that have still not been fully plumbed.[18] She was the first to recover relevant historical and economic contexts for the villas of the Roman countryside (the Roman Campagna) by discussing the tradition of the Roman *casale* (farmhouse, fortified farm) (fig. 1.7). Della Pergola became director of the Galleria Borghese from the 1950s to the 1970s, and was highly prolific in publishing on museology and artworks from

Veronese to Bernini. In 1962, she published *Villa Borghese*, one of the first modern, documentary monographs on a Roman Baroque villa and its gardens (built 1606–33 on the Pincian Hill) that covered the entire complex (i.e., artworks, architecture, and gardens).[19] Her book became the benchmark for modern studies on the Villa Borghese, and was conceived from the perspective of an art historian and museum curator (fig. 1.8).

The German scholars who researched Roman villa gardens from the 1940s to the 1970s were embedded in the German academic world of art historical scholarship. They included the art historians Carl Lamb (1905–68), Klaus Schwager (b. 1925), and Christoph Heilmann (act. after ca. 1967), and the architect Carlludwig Franck (act. 1930s–60s).[20] All of these scholars, apart from Lamb on the Villa d'Este at Tivoli, pioneered by steering German art history, with its documentary and archivally based approach, into new territory: the early seventeenth-century Roman villa garden. Their approaches paralleled those of Ackerman, Coffin, and Belli Barsali, and stemmed from the German art historical methodologies outlined here. Franck emphasized qualities of landscape that were ultimately derived from Heinrich Wölfflin's theories in *Die Barockvillen in Frascati, ihre Gestaltung aus den landschaftlichen Gegebenheiten* (prepared in 1932 and published in 1956), which was translated in 1966 as *The Villas of Frascati, 1550–1750*. The English title did not contain the connotations of the original "Gestaltung" or structure that arose from the physical circumstances of the Frascati landscapes.[21]

Schwager contributed a documentary, book-length article on the Villa Aldobrandini (built ca. 1592–1620) at Frascati outside of Rome, published in the *Jahrbuch* of the Bibliotheca Hertziana.[22] Heilmann, like Lamb and Schwager, was based at the Bibliotheca Hertziana, and published a very substantial documentary article on the Villa Borghese.[23] Rich archival work and chronological documentation in the archives of the Aldobrandini, Borghese, Ludovisi, and other Roman papal families provided a strong basis for their examinations of form and style, their typologies of architectural and garden forms, and their iconographic analyses of villa complexes and their parts. This new archival research was very much the result of the fuller opening of the Vatican Secret Archives and Roman family archives after World War II. Their archival and documentary

FIGURE 1.7. Villa La Magliana, near Rome, built ca. 1460–1520.

Photograph by the author.

approach contrasted with the solely aesthetic and architectural approach used earlier by Franck.

In the late 1950s and 1960s, an important bridge between the German work and the American field of studies on Roman villa gardens was provided by the art and architectural historian Howard Hibbard (1928–84), who taught at Columbia University from 1959 until his early death. From the late 1950s on, Hibbard frequently engaged the topic of Roman villas and gardens and published important archival discoveries. His teachers, among them Rudolf Wittkower, had considered mainly the recognized "heroes" of the Roman Baroque who worked from the 1630s to the 1670s—Bernini, Borromini, Cortona, and Carlo Rainaldi. Focusing instead on the architect Carlo Maderno and the years from Michelangelo's death in 1564 to the 1630s, Hibbard undertook vast archival campaigns on a period in Rome that, coincidentally, had seen one of the greatest flourishings of villa architecture and gardens.[24] He was unique among the contemporary art historians who worked on Renaissance and Baroque Rome in that he framed his book *Carlo Maderno and Roman Architecture, 1580–1630* with an historical first chapter ("Rome and the Popes in the Later Cinquecento") that was based on Jean Delumeau's monumental social and economic study of Rome in the period 1550–1600, as well as on the accounts of contemporaries in Rome, such as Botero and Montaigne.[25] Hibbard's particular sensitivity to the social, cultural, and economic dimensions of later sixteenth-century Rome—i.e., to the world of the papal court and to the realities of urban and country life—can perhaps be partly explained by the fact that he was the son of a renowned American historian of the agrarian economy.[26]

We will now consider the art historical mainstream's intellectual and theoretical underpinnings. Art history in the 1950s, 1960s, and 1970s at most American and European universities was a field thoroughly focused on the arts as a scientific or intellectual inquiry; this approach had German origins, as did art history in Italy. For example, around 1970 at Princeton University, where Erwin Panofsky (1892–1968) had influenced the study of gardens through his graduate student, David R. Coffin, key topics in art history were Iconography and the Study of Meaning in Art, Psychology and Perception, and the "structural" analysis of works of art.[27] The Social History of Art, was confined mainly to the study of Arnold Hauser, the author of *The Social History of Art* (4 vols., 1951), a Marxist-Leninist interpretation of artworks as capital, of the forces of production as the base in society, and of art as the raw superstructure, unmediated. Hauser's work was mentioned, but was thoroughly discredited, by contemporary scholars. Italian or European political and social history entered art history courses only through one or two works, principally the *Civilization of the Renaissance in Italy* by Jacob Burckhardt (1818–97), which had been published first in 1860, but still framed the criteria by which one regarded works of Italian art in the 1970s.[28]

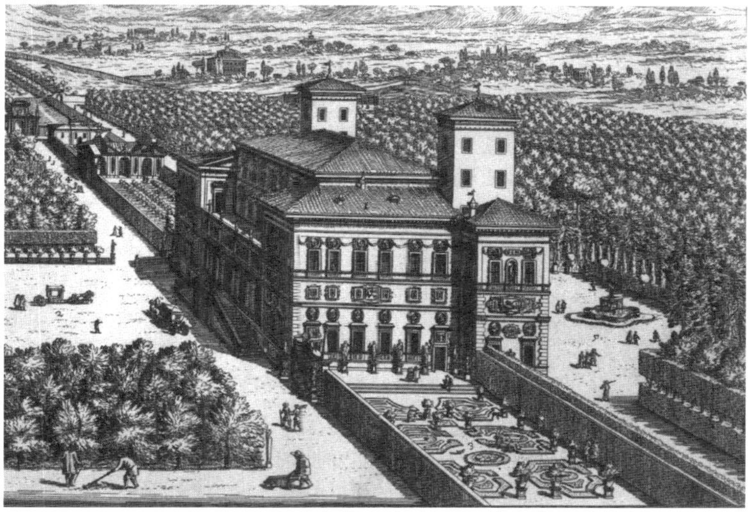

FIGURE 1.8.
Detail of an engraved view of the palace and park at the Villa Borghese, Rome.
Reprinted from Giovanni Battista Falda, *Li giardini di Roma* (Rome, ca. 1675).

Although it might seem a digression to go back in time from the 1970s, it is nonetheless crucial to understand that the methodological approaches to the art historical study of Roman gardens even then continued to be grounded in the principles formulated by Burckhardt's student Heinrich Wölfflin (1864–1945) around 1900. Wölfflin was concerned with "structures," namely the visual and perceptual qualities of works of art.[29] He and his contemporaries, including Alois Riegl, applied these aesthetic categories to architecture—and to gardens, especially Roman ones, emphasizing *Raum* (space), axes, tectonic qualities, movement of the spectator in space, and empathy with architectural qualities as if they were projections of human feelings.[30] Italian gardens—especially Roman villa gardens with their terraces, staircases, fountains, and often parklike settings articulated by strong contrasts of sunlight, shadows, open spaces, and groves of trees—provided Wölfflin and Riegl with the perfect medium for their investigations of visual and perceptual structures. Such strong formal contrasts can be seen in the gardens of the Villas Aldobrandini and Borghese, especially between the dark green foliage and light-colored stonework and between areas of shade and sunlight (figs. 1.5 and 1.9). Later, the concepts of iconography and iconology—the study of symbolic meanings in art and their cultural resonances—developed by Edgar Wind, Fritz Saxl, and Panofsky were, interestingly, paired with *Raumforschung* in the study of architecture and gardens.[31] This pairing was the primary methodology adopted by art historians of all nationalities who focused on Roman Renaissance and Baroque architecture and ventured into garden studies.[32]

Let us read the words of several early art historians on Roman villa gardens to see how they adopted the criteria discussed above, which were then absorbed by Lotz, Ackerman, Coffin, Schwager, MacDougall, and others. Wölfflin dedicated a third of his short book, *Renaissance und Barock: Eine Untersuchung über Wesen und Entstehung des Barockstils in Italien* (1888), to the chapter, "The Villa and the Garden." In it, he focused on the rise of new formal qualities in "the baroque garden,"[33] the start of which he identified in the Villa d'Este at Tivoli (ca. 1550–72):

> It must seem strange that landscape, the most painterly of all subjects, should be most rigorously subordinated to architectural rules in the period of the "painterly" style. But the paradox is only superficial: the baroque stylised nature in order to give it greater poise and dignity, and this was in answer to the demands of the age. But the natural park did not entirely disappear under this schematic treatment; the formless and unconfined were drawn into the composition—a fact which accounts for the development of the landscape painting of Poussin and Gaspar Dughet . . . The garden architecture of the baroque worked with more space and larger motifs than the Renaissance.[34]

Albert E. Brinckmann, a student of Wölfflin, followed him with a rhapsody about "the full triumph of the rhythmically-developed spatial axis" ("den vollen Sieg der rhythmisch entwickelten Raumachse") in the parkland planted uphill from the main palace at the Villa Aldobrandini at Frascati.[35]

The voice of Wölfflin can be heard in the major Italian study on Italian gardens of the early twentieth century. This is *Il giardino italiano* (1924), published immediately in English as *The Italian Garden* (1925), by the art historian Luigi Dami (1882–1926); the book has a significant section on Rome and Latium.[36] It is fascinating to watch Dami reach back to the seventeenth-century art theory of "il pittoresco," expounded by Marco Boschini (1613–78) in *La carta del navegar pittoresco* (Venice, 1660), and to combine it with Wölfflin's approach (perhaps based on the same) in order to account for the changes that took place around 1600 in the conception of the Roman villa gardens (fig. 1.10).[37]

The anchoring of analyses of the gardens in the perceptual qualities of architectural space as voiced by Wölfflin, Riegl, and Brinckmann was robustly continued by German and American art historians. The discourse on Raum and composition can be found in Ackerman's synthetic analysis of Bramante's Cortile del Belvedere.[38] Iconographic analyses are also applied to architecture in Ackerman's description of a fresco by Perino del Vaga that depicted the Cortile: "It was, in fact, so composed as to force us to recognize the 'iconography' of the architecture. Throughout the first half of the sixteenth century, Bramante's Cortile was seen as he meant it to be seen: a re-embodiment of the [ancient] Roman villa or palace garden."[39]

These discourses are subsequently found in one of MacDougall's most important articles on the underpinnings of Roman garden iconography in Renaissance literary theory. In discussing stylistic changes in the later sixteenth century, she overlaid spatial concepts in architecture with genres in literature: "For the Renaissance these various literary genres provided specific themes associated both with gardens and with natural landscape."[40] The architectural and the natural were examined together in spatial terms.[41] MacDougall, who was one of the first art historians to address the change

FIGURE 1.9.
Villa Borghese, Rome, built 1606–33.

Photograph by the author.

FIGURE 1.10.
Giovanni Francesco Venturini, view of a pedestal fountain at the Villa Borghese, Rome, ca. 1680, engraving.

Reprinted from Luigi Dami, *Il giardino italiano* (Milan: Bestetti and Tumminelli, 1924).

in Roman garden design from the sixteenth to the seventeenth centuries, interpreted it as a change "in the traditional Roman garden style" that was manifest in revisions made in 1590–1623 to the Villa Montalto-Peretti of Pope Sixtus V (r. 1585–90) and also to the Villa Borghese (1606–33). "Garden style" was equated with both spatial experience and iconographical associations. On the one hand, her language and interpretative frameworks continued those of Wölfflin, Riegl, and Brinckmann[42] as bequeathed through her teachers, Krautheimer, Lotz, and Ackerman. This is evident, for example, in her analysis of the experiential features of the early seventeenth-century gardens at the Villas Montalto-Peretti and Borghese: "There are still the familiar grids of *compartimenti*, the enclosing and delimiting walls, the cross axes. High hedges, however, transformed the spectator's experience of the garden. It was now impossible to experience the garden without moving through it, and movement once again became strictly controlled as it had been early in the sixteenth century." The changes from the sixteenth century, where enclosed planting beds (compartimenti) were bordered by low hedges (thus allowing for open views across the beds), to the seventeenth century, where high evergreen hedges created the experience of walking through tunnels, can be seen in two different areas of the Villa Medici. Compare the open view over low hedges in figure 1.4 with the high hedges of box and laurel in figure 1.11. The high hedges of the Villa Borghese can be seen in figures 1.8 and 1.10.[43] On the other hand, she made a paradigmatic step in discussing style by reading garden forms, such as the *boschetto*, through the lens of contemporary literary culture.[44]

These examples, taken from the German and American art history of gardens, can stand for the larger picture. In general, before the 1970s, history as a field—with its social, political, and economic approaches—was absent from Roman garden studies (as it was for all Italian regions, except for the Veneto, where agrarian history had entered discussion of the Palladian estates).[45] The art historians working on Rome, such as Wittkower, Lotz, Frommel, Coffin, Ackerman, and MacDougall, considered the arts, including Roman gardens, to be "autonomous" and used history to illuminate

FIGURE 1.11. Villa Medici, Rome, built ca. 1564–74.

Photograph by the author.

the intentions of the artist.[46] But Ackerman was beginning to reconsider his intellectual perspective on the social sciences and their relation to art history. With a very prescient viewpoint, he called already in 1960 for a broader, contextual history of style, noting that "autonomous" should not mean "isolated" and that the artist's intentions should be investigated through the study of "contexts."[47] How those historical contexts could be studied was something that Ackerman and the next generation of art historians would tackle in the 1970s and 1980s.[48]

Outside the Mainstream of Art History

At this point, it is important to discuss some key "outsiders" to the mainstream academy. As outsiders, they had greater freedom than scholars operating within a large, structured discipline, such as art history, and they established countless new connections among unrelated fields. But at the same time, precisely because they were outsiders, their contributions remained isolated until broader developments provided a context in which they could be used. They include Georgina Masson (1912–80), Renato Lefevre (1910–2004), Cesare d'Onofrio (1921–94), Beata di Gaddo (1921–2007), Eugenio Battisti (1924–89), Luigi Devoti (b. 1931), and Alessandro Tagliolini (1931–2000). Although they came from very different worlds, they all delved into the study of political, social, and local cultural history far more than their peers.[49] All, except Battisti, focused their research on Roman medieval and modern history and on villa gardens in Rome and the Roman Campagna. (Battisti was broadly concerned with the methodologies of Renaissance art history.) All, except Battisti, an art historian, had experience outside the academy in various professions, such as law, architecture, journalism, and medicine.

Marion (Babs) Johnson, who published under the pen name of Georgina Masson, came to the study of Roman gardens from a quite different perspective than those of the academics.[50] A journalist, she wrote historical biographies on Renaissance courtesans, the Borgia popes, and Queen Christina of Sweden (who settled in Rome in 1656). These works are truly social histories, and were researched extensively in the Vatican and Roman family archives. Her book *Italian Gardens* (1961) was the result of her vast fieldwork, photography, historical reading, and archival research. It has been and is still highly valued by academics, from Coffin's friendship with and esteem for Masson to Margherita Azzi Visentini's forthcoming critical edition. Masson aptly characterized the seventeenth-century Roman villa gardens as "park villas," an idea that influenced Coffin and the generation that followed.[51] As an Italian correspondent for *The Architectural Review* (published in London), she looked at these novel park designs through the lens of their societal origins and their owners. A broad context for Masson's writing can be found in the social and economic histories published in England after World War II—for example, in the works of E. P. Thompson (1924–93) and her contemporary, William George Hoskins (1908–92), the author of *The Making of the English Landscape* (1955).

The architect Beata di Gaddo made a major contribution to the study of seventeenth-century Roman villas with her monograph *Villa Borghese: Il giardino e le architetture* (1985).[52] Architectural and garden histories written by architects had been common in Italy since the early twentieth century—one need only think of Marcello Piacentini and Gustavo Giovannoni.[53] In her book, di Gaddo focused on the gardens and park between the 1600s and 1950s, and brought into discussion key aspects of villa design, such as geology, soil, and materials; scale, proportion, and geometry; water systems; and the integration of architecture and topography in each part of the gardens. These issues were not normally treated by the art historians who dominated the field.

Renato Lefevre and his younger peer Luigi Devoti are representatives of an important strand of the local, antiquarian history of Rome, the Roman Campagna, and the Castelli Romani (the fief towns in the hills at the outer edge of the Roman Campagna) that was rooted in the topographical and socio-cultural studies dating to the unification of Italy in 1861. That tradition resulted in numerous publications, ranging in content from archaeology to feudalism to folklore, by archaeological researchers such as Rodolfo Lanciani and Giuseppe Tomassetti, whose specialization was the Roman Campagna. The tradition still flourishes today in the journal *Archivio della Società Romana di Storia Patria* (1878–)

(henceforth, *ASRSP*), which by 1970 was opening its doors to historians influenced by the *Annales* approach, founded in France in the 1930s, that paired history with geography—to be discussed in part two of this essay. Heirs to this tradition, Lefevre, a journalist, high government functionary, and university professor, and Devoti, a medical doctor, devoted particular attention to archival research and to Roman villa gardens. Devoti continues to publish extensively on the villas at Frascati. From the 1950s until his death in 2004, Lefevre was a prominent member or director of many local Roman cultural institutions (such as the Gruppo Culturale di Roma e del Lazio) and was featured prominently in their publications, such as the series *Lunario romano* and the journals *Strenna dei Romanisti*, *Castelli Romani*, and *Lazio ieri e oggi*. He was well regarded by the academic art historical community for his books on the Villa Madama and the Palazzo Chigi and its park at Ariccia, as well as for his countless essays on the villa gardens at Frascati and in the Castelli Romani. Because he studied economics and politics and chose to write on economic, family, and property histories, his work formed a bridge between scholars of local Roman history and topography and scholars concerned with broader issues in the historical disciplines; this bridge would be directly fruitful for Roman villa gardens as a developing field of study.[54]

D'Onofrio, who appears to have studied art history, devoted his life to the study of Rome and its arts, publishing scores of books filled with archival discoveries and documentation. Baroque Rome was his special field, and his books, *Le fontane di Roma* (1957), *La Villa Aldobrandini a Frascati* (1963), *Roma nel Seicento* (1969), and *Il Tevere e Roma* (1970), laid some of the foundations for the study of seventeenth-century Roman gardens. His book on the Tiber River is a remarkable synthesis of local history, representations in art, and topographical study. These books also opened the door to a potential social history of Roman art, architecture, and gardens, because d'Onofrio plumbed seventeenth-century personal documents—such as diaries, memoirs, and correspondence—and public printed ones—from papal edicts to opera libretti—to recreate a lively panorama of Roman lives, rich and poor.

Tagliolini, a sculptor, practiced landscape architecture and restoration, and studied Italian, and especially Roman, gardens from the 1970s on, contextualizing them with studies of local culture and folklore and shepherding the production of an array of significant conferences and publications on Italian gardens.[55]

Eugenio Battisti, an art historian, was born (in Turin in 1924) into a lively and rich intellectual setting that reflected the imprint of many important historians and intellectuals, including the Italian Marxist theoretician and politician Antonio Gramsci (1891–1937), who had made Turin his base in the 1910s. A prodigious writer from an early age, Battisti published art, theater, and music criticism in a number of newspapers. He studied aesthetics and the philosophy of art at the Università di Torino, and trained in the art historical methodologies (especially iconography and iconology) of Lionello Venturi, Roberto Longhi, Panofsky, and the scholars of the Warburg Institute in London. Early on in the 1950s, he engaged in the debates on the formal definitions of Renaissance and Baroque art—on which he published *Rinascimento e Barocco* (1960), a revision of the Wölfflinian view—and also in the study of art as symbol. At the same time, he focused on what could be called the "dark side" of the Italian Renaissance, as manifest in astrology, folklore, peasant rituals, the occult and witchcraft, the hermetic, and the "anti-classical." The history of Italian gardens, fountains, grottoes, and garden automata—in mostly Tuscan and north Italian gardens, but also Roman ones—was woven throughout his work.[56] His approach to Italian gardens was thus unlike anything produced to that date by other garden scholars. He published the results in a massive, two-volume study, *L'antirinascimento* (1962), in which he thanked his father for giving him "the courage to venture into unfamiliar areas of research" ("il coraggio di avventurarmi in campi di ricerca non miei") and cited the studies by René Hocke, Jurgis Baltrušaitis, and Hiram Haydn that had inspired him.[57]

Indeed, the convergence of Battisti's interests in history, anthropology, philosophy, and semiotics, with those of historians, anthropologists, and writers (his friends included Umberto Eco) in those years is notable, even if one can literally say that Battisti's intellectual interests were "all over the map."[58] Turin-born historian Carlo Ginzburg (b. 1939) was likely influenced by Battisti; he was from the same milieu and completed his earliest studies on French historians of the Annales group as well as on witchcraft and agrarian culture in Counter-Reformation Italy.[59] In *L'antirinascimento*, Battisti made ample reference to Ginzburg, to Annales historians (such as Marc Bloch, Georges Duby, and Jacques Le Goff), and to Italian *Annalistes* (such as Emilio Sereni) who researched Italian rural settlements and landscapes. Battisti would later found a center for the study of modern industrial technologies, a field he studied in a dialectical relation to the preindustrial worlds of medieval Islam and Renaissance Italy that so interested him.

When the first Dumbarton Oaks symposium on Italian gardens was convened in 1971, the four speakers were Battisti, MacDougall, Lionello Puppi, and Masson. The participant list offers a sense of the field of Italian garden studies at that date and hints at its internationalism, which then somewhat disappeared and has only very recently resurfaced in Italian garden studies. Battisti was the most internationally minded of the four speakers—between 1964 to 1984, he taught at the Pennsylvania State University during half of the year and at a succession of universities—the Università di Reggio Calabria, di Milano, di Firenze, and di Roma-Tor Vergata—during the other half. His intellectual world was broadly based.[60] His symposium paper was remarkable: he played a tape of an original composition, with sung madrigals, sounds of water, and bird songs, to convey aurally "the sensual impact of a fifteenth-century garden," and he provided both synchronic and diachronic frameworks for understanding the gardens of Rome and other Italian urban centers by probing the breadth of their cultures and their not-so-distant medieval Mediterranean and Islamic connections.[61] Its implications still have not been fully plumbed, but the garden historian Luigi Zangheri (b. 1954) has explored the connections with the broader Mediterranean and Islamic worlds.[62] Battisti may be the only art historian of his generation working on Italian gardens who made meaningful use of the writings of Emilio Sereni, the great historian of the Italian agricultural landscape. Sereni's *Storia del paesaggio agrario italiano* was first published in 1961, but was mostly ignored by art-historically trained garden historians until the 1990s because of the methodological distance between the disciplines and because Sereni had a Marxist-Leninist formation and was politically engaged in his writing throughout his distinguished career.[63] Although Battisti produced encyclopedic (rather than coherently structural) writings and did not explicitly embrace a synthetic kind of Marxist thinking and history writing, it is clear that he knew the Marxist concept of the interrelatedness of all dimensions in a given society and that he saw the Italian and Roman gardens as tied to the larger, agrarian landscape and to the complex, multidimensional cultures in which they were embedded. Certainly, Fernand Braudel's statement in 1946 that his own book *La Méditerranée et le monde méditerranéen à l'epoque de Philippe II* (1949) "will perhaps prove that history can do more than study walled gardens" applied to Battisti.[64]

Worlds Converging: The 1970s to 1980s

As mentioned in the introduction, I, like many graduate students in art history during the 1970s and 1980s, was searching for a way to bring together the approaches of art history and social history. In this second part of this essay, I will track the convergence of interests between the social sciences and art history that was then taking place and on which I was able to feed. Part of this convergence was enabled by new forms of "mediation," in which a new order of complexity was acknowledged in both Marxist and non-Marxist thinking about the domain of "the social." We shall look at some of the steps that led to the more social approaches to the art history of Italian gardens and to the more mediated approaches that we find in Italian garden studies today. My choice of steps to consider reflects my own academic itinerary, including my own path of research on Roman Baroque gardens, even though this kind of experience was common to quite a few garden scholars in my generation on both sides of the Atlantic, whether art historians or geographers.[65]

These concerns about the social dimensions of art were at the heart of many of our art historical readings, whether by T. J. Clark, Michael Baxandall, Svetlana Alpers, or Enrico Castelnuovo.[66] At this time, American art historical study was being pressured by social historians at graduate schools such as Yale University, where I studied, and our professors, among them Robert L. Herbert and Vincent J. Scully, were considering how to treat the social dimension of art. In the political and cultural aftermath of 1968, I spent as much time reading the works of Karl Marx, Max Weber, Antonio Gramsci, György Lukács, and Raymond Williams, whose *The Country and the City* (1973) had just been published, as I did reading art history. I also spent a year in Venice, where I took the courses of the Italian architectural historian Manfredo Tafuri at the Istituto Universitario di Architettura di Venezia.[67] Earlier, in college, I had absorbed Clifford Geertz's writings on anthropology, especially *The Interpretation of Cultures* (1973), and after 1979, I collected and read Pierre Bourdieu's journal, *Actes de la recherche en sciences sociales*, which contained many articles that worked out approaches to a social, if not sociological, study of art, and which published essays by an international array of critics and scholars, including Williams and Baxandall. My PhD advisor at Yale University, Scully, was then studying the gardens of André Le Nôtre, and I had the benefit of his large interpretative view, which was influenced by existentialist philosophy and by the French art historians who had taught him at Yale University, and likely also by French Annales history writing. Scully pioneered in studying French classical garden design in terms of national infrastructural systems and territorial organization. He called his broad study of Le Nôtre's garden forms "The Shape of France."[68] Yet, as I delved deeper into my topic, I realized that seventeenth-century papal Rome and its surrounding Campagna looked nothing like the France of Louis XIV with its dynastic monarchy. In Rome, there was hardly any state infrastructure; the papal states were governed by papal monarchs, who ruled by means of nepotistic kinship ties and who rotated in and out of power with the death of each pope. What, I wondered, would "The Shape of Rome and Its Territory" look like?

One answer appeared to lie in applying Annales historical approaches to the art historical study of the landscapes of Roman villas. In my research, I

FIGURE 1.12. Villa Pamphilj, Rome, built 1644–70. Photograph by the author.

focused on the Villa Pamphilj (1644–70), the largest and latest villa built among the group of papal villa gardens that manifested the change in concept from garden to park in papal Rome in the late sixteenth to the mid-seventeenth century (figs. 1.12 and 1.13). I was looking for theoretical approaches that would bring together, synthetically, the formal and symbolic, and the social and geographical aspects of designed landscapes. And I would eventually find them in a new generation of Annales studies on the city of Rome and its countryside, and in the new concern with structures of meaning that was developing in the social sciences and soon would spread into art and architectural history.

The Annales in Italy: Landscape and Rome

A major enabling development in the transformation of the field of Italian history was the large impact in Italy and worldwide of the interdisciplinary work of the Annales group of historians in France, whose best-known figures were Marc Bloch (1886–1944), Lucien Febvre (1878–1956), and Fernand Braudel (1902–85).[69] Bloch and Febvre, followed by their disciple Braudel, shared a sense of the limitations in the kind of political and diplomatic history written by the generations preceding them.[70] The Annales, the short name of the journal founded in 1929 by the group, rejuvenated the study of history through the perspective of geographical and anthropological frameworks and through an emphasis on the larger landscape as a set of living systems. Such larger landscape features and systems were the setting of the Villa Pamphilj, for example, and they were reflected in its design. The geographical slant of the Annaliste enterprise would make its approaches particularly apt for the study of landscape, topography, and agriculture by geographers, historians, and, ultimately, as I hope to show in this essay, garden historians.[71] Spurred by Braudel's *La Méditerranée et le monde méditerranéen à l'epoque de Philippe II* (1949), which used a framework exploring "the connections between history and geographical space,"[72] French Annales historians in France and their contacts in Italy went to work on the structures of Italian geographical and social systems. Their studies proliferated immediately after World War II, and emphasized collaborative work and international exchanges, allowing for massive archival campaigns on social, political, and financial institutions and on *longue durée* agrarian and trading cycles.[73] Anthropology and ethnography also entered into their approaches. In 1953, Braudel's book was translated into Italian; it was followed by Italian translations of Marc Bloch's works during the 1950s and 1960s. In dialogue with the Annales, Sereni had published for several decades on all aspects of ancient, medieval, and modern Italian agrarian history and the etymology of agrarian terms; as noted, his *Storia del paesaggio agrario italiano* appeared in 1961, was soon translated into French (1965), and went through many Italian editions.[74] Several of his chapters dealt directly with the organizational units of agrarian properties and their plantings in central Italy, including the Roman Campagna.[75]

FIGURE 1.13. Villa Pamphilj, Rome, built 1644–70.
Photograph by the author.

The historical study of the Italian landscape and the art historical study of Italian gardens have crossed paths since the 1970s. One example is the new *Storia d'Italia* series, begun in 1971, strongly influenced by Annales approaches, and still ongoing.[76] Its fifth volume, *Il paesaggio* (published in 1982 in the sub-series *Annali*), was edited by the art and architectural historian Cesare de Seta, and featured contributors ranging from the Annales historian Jacques Le Goff to literary historians concerned with Italian garden culture, such as Gianni Venturi.[77] Its several lengthy essays were dedicated to the history of the Italian landscape—seen as a cultural construct (by foreign visitors), as painted and drawn representations, as an economic and agricultural phenomenon in dialectical relationship to the Italian city, and as an enduring literary theme. It was an interdisciplinary beginning that would have ramifications for scholars for several decades thereafter.

One of the new areas of Annales research soon after World War II was papal Rome and its countryside. Prior to this time, research on Rome had focused on political and diplomatic papal histories, for example Ludwig von Pastor's multivolume *The History of the Popes from the Close of the Middle Ages* (English trans., 1891–1940). But from their base at the École Française de Rome, and inspired by Braudel, Annales historians focused on Rome in the pivotal period of the Counter-Reformation, when the Catholic papacy expanded the curial bureaucracy, sponsored the reforms of the Council of Trent, and anchored its wealth in the building industry and in the image of the city of Rome as the world capital of Christianity. For example, Jean Delumeau (b. 1923) founded his career with his monumental two-volume study, *Vie économique et sociale de Rome dans la seconde moitié du XVIe siècle* (1957–59), which included studies of the road and postal systems, the revenues and expenditures of popes and churchmen, and "le problème du grain" in the Roman Campagna.[78] His 1948–50 sojourn at the École in Rome was followed by that of Pierre Toubert (b. 1932) in 1958–61, who produced a two-volume work, *Les structures du Latium médiéval: Le Latium méridional et la Sabine du IXe siècle à la fin du XIIe siècle* (1973). Many of those "structures" were landscape structures.

Structures of Meaning

A second broad intellectual development important for me was the rise of a wide-ranging interest in the mechanisms by which social meanings are communicated; this rise was apparent in several fields, including anthropology, sociology, philosophy, and cultural criticism, from the 1950s and 1960s on. The interest in social meanings was driven by several overlapping trends that can only be mentioned here. On the one hand, there was a general effort by intellectuals to deal with the social in response to the political and social maelstrom of the 1960s. On the other hand, there was a serious rethinking of Marxist theory, driven by intellectuals who, while committed to a Marxist view, were disillusioned by the rigidity of communist parties and by the Soviet crushing of the Hungarian uprising in 1956 and the Prague Spring in 1968. This rethinking resulted in new interest for strands of Marxism that had preceded or bypassed the Leninist-Stalinist phase, in particular for philosophers connected with the Frankfurt School, such as Walter Benjamin and Theodor Adorno. Finally, linguistics and theories of language, with a long history from the work of Ferdinand de Saussure and Claude Lévi-Strauss, were reinterpreted in many fields, especially in anthropology, but also in the new Marxist thinking and in history.

Common to all of these trends was a synthetic interest in the social dimensions of life, in language, culture, symbols, artifacts, and the communication of social meanings. This interest can be observed in the work of scholars as diverse as Raymond Williams (1921–88) on literature and cultural theory in England; Roland Barthes (1915–80), Henri Lefebvre (1901–91), Michel Foucault (1926–84), and Pierre Bourdieu (1930–2004) on semiology, philosophy, sociology, and cultural history in France; and Clifford Geertz (1926–2006) and Robert Darnton (b. 1939) on anthropology and history in the United States.[79] Of these scholars, I will discuss Williams, Bourdieu, and Geertz in detail, as they were particularly relevant to my intellectual development.[80] I will not address Foucault—his work influenced the current generation of French art historians who now work on Italian and Roman gardens (such as Denis Ribouillault and Hervé Brunon), but did not play a big role in my own development.[81]

In a politically engaged way, from the 1950s to the 1970s, Raymond Williams published Marxist critiques of English literature, arts, and rural realities of the eighteenth, nineteenth, and twentieth centuries.[82] His book *The Country and the City* (1973) became very important for landscape historians and cultural geographers after the 1980s, particularly in Anglo-American scholarship. By conceptualizing the literary culture of landscape as an artistic mediating structure in the dialectical relationships between city and country and agrarian labor and urban cultural retreats, Williams showed how landscape forms in eighteenth-century English gardens and paintings could be understood as formal naturalizations of conflicted social spaces.[83]

Since the late 1960s, Pierre Bourdieu had researched the actors and fields ("champs") in the culture of museums, art scenes, and artistic reception.[84] Early on, he became interested in the work of Erwin Panofsky on iconography and symbols, including Panofsky's early essay, "Perspective als symbolische Form" (1924–25).[85] In the journal *Actes de la recherche en sciences sociales*, which he founded in 1975, Bourdieu brought together not only the young neo-Marxist sociologists and literary critics studying with him, but also art historians and literary critics from the English strand of Marxist or related cultural criticism, among them Williams, Baxandall, Francis D. Klingender, and Francis Haskell.[86] Many of the historians in contact with Bourdieu had been trained in Annales history, and Bourdieu himself contributed articles to the group's journal, *Annales: Économies, sociétés, civilisations*, including one in 1977 entitled "Sur le pouvoir symbolique."[87] Bourdieu's importance for me was as a linchpin: it was now at least possible to bring together Bourdieu's concept of symbolic power, Williams's notion of mediation in landscape culture, and the Annales' synthesis of history, geography, and anthropology in the study of Italy's landscapes and villa culture.

For Clifford Geertz, who had taken his BA in philosophy (1950) and then his PhD in anthropology (1956), the development of what he called an "interpretative anthropology," also called symbolic anthropology, was a spur to go back to two German sources: the philosopher Ludwig Wittgenstein's studies on language as a social activity or a "form of life," and the sociologist Max Weber's studies of culture and shared beliefs as a means to study modernization.[88] Geertz put it this way in *The Interpretation of Cultures* (1973): "The concept of culture I espouse, and whose utility the essays below attempt to demonstrate, is essentially a semiotic one. Believing, with Max Weber, that man is an animal suspended in webs of significance he himself has spun, I take culture to be those webs, and the analysis of it to be therefore not an experimental science in search of law but an interpretative one in search of meaning."[89] In order to articulate the key concept of his ethnographic "intellectual effort," Geertz borrowed the notion of "thick description" of cultural activities and artifacts from the philosopher Gilbert Ryle, and defined his own anthropological approach to the analytical study of cultures as "sorting out the structures of signification," in other words of meanings.[90]

In concluding this section, it is worth noting that both Williams and Bourdieu directly spanned the two worlds of social sciences and art history—Bourdieu through his connection with Panofsky and his publication of the work of so many art historians in *Actes de la recherche en sciences sociales*, and Williams through his writings on landscapes in literature and art. This is one among many reasons why these figures could act as bridges and mediate between the two worlds.

Social Art and Architectural Histories of Gardens

It was in the above context of searches to understand how cultures communicate social meanings that attempts to write a social history of Italian villa forms and culture arose as part of a new "social history of art" that started to develop in the 1960s and 1970s.[91] While not directly translatable to my study on Roman Baroque villa parks, these social histories of villas provided examples of how the methods of the social sciences and art history could be brought together.

In studies of Italian Renaissance art and architecture, German art historians with connections to the sociology of the Frankfurt School, Adorno, and Jürgen Habermas led the way. The Italian Renaissance villa—particularly in northern Italy and the Veneto, where villas consisted of a main house, gardens, and an agrarian estate rationally managed for profit— provided a case study for the dialectical relationship of a utopian withdrawal from the city to the countryside by a landed elite of urban origin, to the economic agrarian base of peasant labor on the land, which supported this villa culture. At the Villa Barbaro at Maser (Treviso), for example, the views of the owner or his visitors across the fields of the estate—either toward or away from the front facade of the villa palace—to the agrarian landscapes in the distance, which were possessed by the owner or his neighbors, encompass this dialectical expression of urban elite culture in the countryside (figs. 1.1–1.3). Most well known was the study of Reinhard Bentmann and Michael Müller on Veneto villas, their estates, and their painted decorations, *Die Villa als Herrschafts-architektur: Versuch einer kunst- und sozialgeschichtlichen Analyse* (1970); the book was translated into French as *La villa, architecture de domination* in 1975, but was only relayed to the Anglo-American world with an English translation in 1992.[92]

To one audience, their study was the logical outcome of social studies of the Frankfurt School; to another, namely in the American and European mainstreams of art history, it appeared as a radical, if not threatening, neo-Marxist narrative that prompted its own failure by articulating too literal and simplistic a connection between the ideological claims of the villa owners and the structural organization of the Veneto villas' layouts. However, following in the steps of the Venetian art historian Michelangelo Muraro (1913–91), whose neo-Marxist ideas influenced Muraro's friend James S. Ackerman, Bentmann and Müller successfully took the interpretation of Renaissance villas in a new social direction, ultimately enriching the standard iconographical interpretation of Roman and Florentine villa gardens seen in the writings of MacDougall, Coffin, and Ackerman.[93] Bentmann and Müller provided a basic political and social framework in which to understand the organization and the components of the Veneto villa:

> Standing at the center of the *podere*, the villa ordered the landscape, compartmentalized it. As a whole organism, however, it not only framed its overall natural environment autocratically but also expressed hierarchical structures through its internal articulation, thus signifying the claim to hegemony. The full range of functions necessitated by agricultural estate management converged in the *casa di villa*, . . . the heart . . . for the *latifundium*'s various arteries: the country roads, the canal system, and the irrigation ditches of the agriculturally utilized *possessioni* (country estate), that in turn articulated the artistic prospects, avenues, gardens, fruit orchards, and plantations.[94]

This was no highly documented history or interpretation of the social and physical infrastructure of Veneto villas, but it was the start of a new paradigm, as it introduced the notion of social space and the spatialization of the owner's power in a hierarchical organization of architectural and landscape forms.[95] Bentmann and Müller's book would also provide a basic theoretical structure for the geographer Denis Cosgrove's *The Palladian Landscape: Geographical Change and its Cultural Representations in Sixteenth-Century Italy* (1993) and for the German art historian Martin Warnke's *Politische Landschaft: zur Kunstgeschichte der Natur* (1992), which took a more mediated approach.[96]

Bentmann and Müller wrote about villas, not gardens, in the Veneto, and they did not address the very different case of the Roman Renaissance villa gardens, which generally were not part of agrarian estates, as were their counterparts in the Veneto and Tuscany. For members of my generation studying Roman art history in the 1970s and 1980s, their approach needed further translation into the social and economic frameworks of a specifically Roman historical setting. Important and influential benchmarks for such cross-regional translation were Vittorio Franchetti Pardo's studies of the fifteenth- and sixteenth-century Medici villas in Tuscany, which was closer to the Venetian model because its villas were part and parcel of a productive agricultural estate.[97] Franchetti Pardo stressed the political ideology and strategy of Medici land investments, and his approach and sources ranged from art history (Ackerman, André Chastel, and Howard Saalman) to history (Richard Goldthwaite, Alberto Tenenti, Gene Brucker, Anthony Molho, and Giorgio Spini) and to history and economics of the Italian agricultural landscape (Emilio Sereni and Giovanni Cherubini). In 1986, English art and architectural historian Amanda Lillie would greatly expand on Franchetti Pardo's core studies, using Tuscan social and economic history in her study of early Renaissance Florentine villas.[98]

It was in this context that Ackerman published a comprehensive book, *The Villa: Form and Ideology of Country Houses* (1990), in which he openly acknowledged his indebtedness "for the articulation of villa ideology" to Bentmann and Müller, and carried the social art historical approach over a broad spectrum of villa cultures.[99] In this book, Ackerman built upon, and introduced to the Anglo-American literature on villas, Italian and other historians who had written on the ancient and Renaissance agricultural economics of villa estates. The book was translated into Italian in 1992 and Spanish in 1997. Although his focus was the villa complex in its entirety, and not specifically the gardens, Ackerman's engagement with the topic of social and political ideology in villas had a very significant, positive, and stimulating effect on the study of Roman villa gardens. It provided a framework for thinking about villa culture; this framework was followed, for example, in Tracy Ehrlich's important, recent work on the seventeenth-century Borghese villas in and around Rome.[100]

In an intellectual world separate from that of Bentmann and Müller, the reading of Italian Renaissance architecture, art, and gardens in terms of political history and patronage merged with the traditional study of "iconography" in several exceptional studies in the 1970s, many of them in German. See, for example, the studies by Christoph L. Frommel, Kurt W. Forster, Martin Warnke, and Stanislaus von Moos.[101] This approach soon became mainstream for plantings, fountains, statues, and theatrical festivals in gardens.[102] In Von Moos's book on the iconography of military architecture, *Turm und Bollwerk: Beiträge zu einer politischen Ikonographie der italienischen Renaissancearchitektur*, which included villas, it was the "Symbolisierung politischer Macht," the visual expression of political power, that interested him, not the social and geographical structures and networks of this power, as might have been studied by an Annales historian or by a Clifford Geertz.[103] This focus on the political was more thematic and associational than structural and social, and it characterized the later work of MacDougall and Coffin on Roman Renaissance gardens, including the magisterial work that Coffin brought together during the 1960s and 1970s, *The Villa in the Life of Renaissance Rome* (1979).[104]

However many its theoretical shortcomings, Coffin's documentary contribution in *The Villa in the Life of Renaissance Rome* laid the basis for evolving a key theme or strand in the weave between art history and social history that would be attempted for Roman villa gardens during the later 1980s and the 1990s. This key theme comprised the unique structure of the papal court in Rome—represented by its celibate male monarch and his courtiers (i.e., the cardinals)—and the role it played not only in the choices of design and decoration, but also in the uses and functions of the villas and their gardens.[105] In 1980, ten years before he published his own book on the villa, Ackerman wrote a concise review of Coffin's book; the review was a farsighted and rich summation of the peculiarities of the Roman Renaissance social setting for villa life.[106] For the high-ranking churchmen who could afford to commission villas, "activities were few: eating and drinking headed the list, followed by walking in the garden, conversation (. . . undoubtedly devoted chiefly to politics and gossip), meditation and prayer, and, for those raised in great families, hunting." By the seventeenth century, social activities (such as hunting and strolling in villas) were so important that they were incorporated into specific design features in Roman villa gardens. For example, each of the Roman papal villas built in the five decades following the creation of the Villa Montalto-Peretti for Pope Sixtus V, including the Villa Pamphilj, had extraordinarily long avenues for strolling and carriage riding, and several had designed hunting parks (figs. 1.13 and 1.14)[107]

Critical of Coffin's lack of a historical framework for presenting his vast documentation, Ackerman provided in his short review likely the very first synthetic account of "the implications of the unique conditions depicted in his [Coffin's villa] documents relating to curial and papal patronage," namely just what it meant to build villas in the Counter-Reformation in Rome.[108] Ackerman pointed to the key issues that Coffin's documents evoked: namely,

FIGURE 1.14. Dominique Barrière, view of the entrance to the Villa Pamphilj, Rome, detail of an etching.

Reprinted from Dominique Barrière, *Villa Pamphilia eiusque palatium* (Rome, ca. 1670).

gender, "no mention is made of a woman"; visualizing "the way the different rooms were used, how the staff was organized"; the inheritance of villas belonging to childless churchmen; and the apparent contradictions between the Counter-Reformation's efforts at curbing financial abuses and the requirement that churchmen spend lavishly on architecture, gardens, and entertainment and "display the magnificence appropriate to a great family; and should he be of more obscure origins, . . . the obligation to ennoble, to enrich, and to advertise an emergent family."[109] Overall, concluded Ackerman, "the majority of Roman villas, then, were designed less as elegant living accommodations than as political and dynastic instruments."[110]

Although not directly engaged with the social issues discussed here, Claudia Lazzaro's work should be discussed at this point because of her evolving interest in the cultural and intellectual frameworks through which meanings were articulated in central Italian Renaissance gardens. After an early influential article on the Villa Lante at Bagnaia, her major book of 1990 provided a new paradigm for reading the garden narratives of many Renaissance gardens through the Italian intellectual and cultural frameworks of the time.[111] Her contribution is methodologically important because of its emphasis on the frameworks, treated as interpretive structures, by which she advanced the field significantly beyond the customary identification of isolated iconographical motifs and the simple one-to-one relationship between motifs and political expression seen in the aforementioned studies on the political iconography of villas and gardens.

The limitations of some of these early attempts at engaging the social and political dimensions of Renaissance art, architecture, and gardens were contested not only by Ackerman, but also, and especially, by the Italian architectural historian Manfredo Tafuri (1935–94), who developed some of the most significant "mediating structures" available to scholars in my generation who wrote on Renaissance and Baroque Rome. Well known to theorists and historians of modern architecture for his neo-Marxist critical theories, Tafuri also published key works on Renaissance and Baroque Rome that were supported by exemplary philological and archival research. In "Via Giulia: Storia di una struttura urbana," his first major study of Roman Renaissance architecture and urbanism, he analyzed the new straight street cut for Pope Julius II through the curvilinear network of medieval urban fabric in the heart of Rome not only in political and ideological terms—as a reified political act ("un atto concreto politico")—but also in social and geographical ones, thus making a synthetic interpretation and providing a model for how to write about "the social" and "the formal" dimensions of architecture.[112] The complex and contested relationships between all protagonists—including the pope, the old baronial aristocracy, the municipal urban nobility (the *Senatus Populusque Romanus*, or

SPQR), the city folk, and the architects—are considered. Tafuri did not remain at the generic conceptual level of Bentmann and Müller, and did not argue only that architecture and its forms can express political power; rather, he situated their designs and their formal and symbolic means as the actions, to cite Geertz, of man "suspended in webs of significance he himself has spun."[113]

To do this, Tafuri synthesized several levels of interpretation available to him in the late 1960s—the critiques of the Marxist philosophy of Adorno and Benjamin; the semiology of Barthes (as seen in *Mythologies* [1957]) and Eco; the anthropological structuralism of Lévi-Strauss and its critics (such as Bourdieu); and the study of history, in particular the works of Annales historians, from Bloch to François Furet.[114] He read in documentary, historical terms the semantic social structures identified by thinkers like Bourdieu and Geertz; his interpretation of the Via Giulia takes place at something like the level of Bourdieu's "champs social." It is an approach that he continued to elaborate in later studies on Rome.[115]

From 1969, when he began the Via Giulia study, Tafuri was in contact not only with Frommel, Wittkower, and other mainstream architectural historians, but also with an emerging generation of new historians who worked on Roman medieval and Renaissance society and economy—i.e., family ties, papal bureaucracy, investments, and landholdings—such as Massimo Miglio and Clara Gennaro.[116] Years later, in 1992, Tafuri noted that the readings he did while writing *Teorie e storia dell'architettura* (1968) covered "the great masters of history writing—for me, principally [Marc] Bloch and [Lucien] Febvre, but also Delio Cantimori. They had really been a shock for me in terms of the history of mentalities . . ."[117] He and his close colleagues envisioned an interdisciplinary kind of history: "our goal was always to construct history as interconnections, wherein the discipline of art history was taken apart and reassembled in a configuration that embraced all the other histories—social, political, legal, etc."[118] We see that in Tafuri's case, by his strong bridging between his own work in art and architectural history, on the one hand, and others' work in the historical disciplines and social sciences, on the other, the distinct worlds of these formerly separate disciplines began firmly to converge, in an approach rooted in his particular education and milieux.[119]

After the 1970s and 1980s, several other art and architectural historians of Renaissance and Baroque Italy went beyond mainstream art historical iconographical analysis and political iconography. For example, the writings of Michael Baxandall and Joseph Connors have been of great interest to my Anglo-American generation of Roman garden historians, as both likened the structures of social networks and daily life to language—just as they had been in the Renaissance and Baroque periods.[120] The notion of symbol (iconography) is still operative, but, in Tafuri's case, the symbol is shown to be embedded in the political and ideological structures of early modern Italian society, through a marriage of Annaliste history and Marxist perspective; in Baxandall's case, it is embedded in social and linguistic "webs of meanings" derived from anthropologists of Geertz's generation;[121] and in Connors's case, it is embedded in the complex intertwining of vernacular practices with elite architectural ones and in the structuralist importance of language in so many disciplines by that time.[122]

The few American scholars who conduct research on Roman and Italian Baroque villa gardens—for example, Tracy Ehrlich, Dianne Harris, and myself—have also been deeply influenced by Connors's work and by his reading of architectural and artistic forms of the Roman Baroque through the lenses of the political networks, social life, scientific research, and reading practices of seventeenth-century Romans and their visitors.[123]

Worlds Together: The 1980s to 1990s

I would now like to look, in the last pages of this article, at how some of my own work has intersected with the historiography I have just described. I will do so by focusing on one particular concept that I introduced in my doctoral dissertation, "The Villa Pamphilj (1630–70): Family, Land, and Gardens in Seventeenth-Century Rome" and subsequent essays, including "Landowning and the Villa in the Social Geography of the Roman Territory: The Location and Landscapes of the Villa Pamphilj, 1645–70," "The Social Significance of Transforming the Landscape of the Villa Borghese, 1606–1630: Territory, Trees, and Agriculture in the Design of the First Roman Baroque Park," and "Pastoralism in the Roman Baroque Villa and in Claude Lorrain: Myths and Realities of the Roman Campagna." I singled out a specific way that Romans read their landscapes in terms of social and geographical categories, and I identified this way of reading the landscape as a mediating structure, thus allowing me to interpret a key aspect of the specific character of the large park landscapes that began to appear in Rome with the seventeenth-century villas. These park landscapes were formally defined by their juxtapositions of open meadowlands with dense, forestlike groves of different tree species, and it was hard for contemporaries in the seventeenth century to define them as traditional *giardini*. Even in their somewhat altered forms of today, they are more like parks and landscapes than gardens (see figs. 1.5, 1.8, 1.12, and 1.13). I will refer to this mediating structure by the shorthand words "three rings" for reasons that will soon become clear. After introducing the concept of three rings below, I will discuss how my identification of its potential was made possible by the broad stream of convergences and methodological shifts that I sketched out in part two of this essay. Finally, I will discuss some of the implications of the concept of three rings.

In a nutshell, the concept of three rings can be described as follows. Since at least medieval times, Romans conceived of the territory around their city in terms of three concentric belts of properties encircling the city center. Each belt corresponded to a specific type of property—for example, the inner ring immediately surrounding the city contained small properties or *vigne* (vineyards or rustic plots) used for growing vegetables, fruit trees, and grape vines; the next ring (extending for nearly thirty miles on relatively flat land) featured very large *casali* (farming estates) of hundreds of acres; and the outer ring contained fief towns with their surrounding agrarian lands and forests. For the Romans, each of these three types of property had not only physical and topographical connotations (near or far, small or large, flat or hilly, wooded or open), but also economic and social ones connected to their use and ownership. The land around Rome, then, could be read by the Romans as a social geography of properties and as a system of meanings. Specific statements could be communicated through this system by transposing landscape features across locations (for example, by making a villa park in the first ring look like open pastureland from the second ring).

The concept of three rings arose as a way of explaining the Villa Pamphilj, and before proceeding, it is useful to describe the villa itself. Built in 1644–70, it was the largest and latest of the papal villa gardens created between the late sixteenth and the mid-seventeenth centuries. It was constructed on the Janiculum Hill, just south of the Vatican, for the papal family of Innocent X Pamphilj (r. 1644–55), whose family palace was in the Piazza Navona. The concept of three rings can also explain the Villa Montalto-Peretti (1576–90, park revised 1618–23), the Villa Borghese (1606–33), and the Villa Ludovisi (1621–23).[124] These grand Roman villas were characterized by their layout as estates; they were organized around a small core of formal gardens extending in architectural terraces from a casino or small palace. Each architectural core was set within vast tracts of stately trees like the umbrella pine (*Pinus pinea*), and was surrounded by elements of rural landscape scenery from the Roman Campagna, such as farm buildings, meadows, Mediterranean maquis (*macchia mediterranea*), hills, dales, streams, and even lakes. Each villa was hundreds of acres in size—they were ten to fifteen times the size of earlier giardini (such as the Villa Medici), and their landscaped parklands, usually containing hunting grounds, were called *parchi* or *barchi* (parks or hunting enclosures). Their position in the midst of small vigne close to the walls of Rome emphasized their deliberately large size, their unusual character as vast estates, and their landscape elements (such as their lakes), and positioned them conceptually as the heirs of the emperor Nero's Golden House (64–68 AD), built at the center of ancient Rome, with its artificial forests and large lake.[125]

The key feature that I was trying to explain in this group of villas was the obvious re-creation, within their parks, of several discrete landscapes from specific geographical zones around Rome, such as the open meadows and macchia mediterranea of the Campagna or the lake landscapes in the Campagna and the hill towns.[126] I framed the concept of three rings to interpret this feature. Crucial enabling factors were the recent bodies of historical research on the social and economic history of Rome and the social-topographical history of the Roman Campagna.

The first factor was a new kind of historical writing on early modern Rome by a range of historians who followed the lead of Jean Delumeau on the Counter-Reformation economy and society.[127] Several of these historians—including Wolfgang Reinhard, Renata Ago, and Laurie Nussdorfer—were trained with a mediated perspective, and often melded history and anthropology.[128] Both Reinhard and Nussdorfer provided groundbreaking syntheses on the structures of Roman papal society in the seventeenth century; they defined the tiers of the nobility and explained the roles of papal nepotism in anchoring the wealth and status of papal families like the Borghese and Pamphilj. Their studies were particularly appropriate for the Roman villa gardens because they looked at the social dimensions of the early modern absolutist state and its administrative bureaucracy, whose top members commissioned the villas. Reinhard and Nussdorfer were especially able to trace early modern Roman "systems of meaning" and "styles of thought" (to quote Geertz) in social networks and kinship ties because of their association with anthropologists, including Geertz himself.[129] Nussdorfer noted the mediated quality of the new perspective: "Social history and anthropology have suggested by implication that the history of power and politics is more complicated than the old authoritarian model of Baroque monarchy assumed. Social history . . . has demonstrated the vivid political effects of social networks of kinship and patronage."[130]

The second enabling factor was the new scholarship on the land properties of the Roman Campagna in the medieval period. These publications were characterized by synthetic, Annales-influenced social and geographical histories of Roman families, property ownership, categories of property (such as the vigne and casali), and definitions of territorial jurisdictions of Rome over its countryside. Key historians in this specialized field were Pierre Toubert, Jean Coste, and Jean-Claude Maire-Vigueur. I received training both in primary documentation and in the field from Coste, an eminent medievalist and historian of the Roman Campagna, whose decades of study of medieval and early modern Roman land deeds resulted in seminal publications, including "I casali della Campagna di Roma all'inizio del Seicento" (1969); "La topographie médiévale de la campagne romaine et l'histoire socio-économique" (1976); and "Description et délimitation de l'espace rural dans la campagne romaine" (1984).

It soon became clear that these historians of the Roman Campagna were writing the history of the very land units on which the great Baroque villa gardens stood (e.g., of the many small vigne that had been aggregated to create the large estates of the Villas Borghese and Pamphilj).[131] They were also analyzing the land units to which the villa gardens referred, namely the grazing meadows that were recreated within the assembled estates.[132] The meaning of the Villas Borghese, Ludovisi, and Pamphilj, as designed parklands, lay partly in the histories of vernacular lands and distinct units of landscape, which were made over by powerful new aristocratic owners into noble landscape preserves.

Studies by Coste and his colleagues (such as Maire-Vigueur) had revealed that in medieval times Romans conceived of the territory around their city in terms of property belts that were arranged in three concentric rings encircling the city center. Each ring corresponded to a specific category or type of property—namely, the suburbs of vigne, the Roman Campagna of farms, and the fief-towns surrounded by forests and agrarian holdings.[133] Coste and his colleagues were medievalists, and they did not apply this geographical understanding of the organization of the medieval Roman territory to other periods of Roman history or other Roman systems of land use or organization. But their work allowed me to test the enduring vitality of the concept of the three rings of land around Rome, and to transpose it to an analysis of the seventeenth-century villas with parks. In studying seventeenth-century documents (such as maps, descriptions of properties, legal documents, and travel journals), I found confirmation that Romans and their foreign visitors read the territory around their city in terms of the same social geography of properties. Each of the three rings of land, in other words, was associated with specific social groups in early modern Rome.

In their studies on the seventeenth-century Roman nobility and the social rise of families (especially papal families) in Roman society, Reinhard and Nussdorfer had reconstructed many of the specific relations between noble groups and their land properties. Specifically, they noted the ideological value of landowning for these groups: titled rank was hereditary and took its ideological meaning from land.[134] Landowning on a large scale was not only an economic investment, but had symbolic associations with the old feudal aristocracy. A major transfer of lands was then taking place in Rome—moving with the lands were rank and titles from the old baronial nobility to the emerging papal aristocracy. The former was burdened by debts, while the latter was recently enriched from church offices and, for the papal families, from new financial uses of the traditional institution of nepotism.[135]

Seen against the work of Reinhard and Nussdorfer, the three rings of properties identified by Coste and his colleagues acquired an expanded meaning. For seventeenth-century Romans, who were aware of these major and symbolically laden land transfers, the three rings of land around Rome constituted "a mental map" not only of geography, but also of property and history. When the Pamphilj or other Roman papal families built their villas, they could read in them the changing structure of Roman society during the later sixteenth and seventeenth centuries—a period of great social mobility in the upper tiers of the patriciate.[136]

By bringing together the work of historians, both of Roman society and of Roman territory, with the analysis of the physical forms and designs of the seventeenth-century Roman villa gardens, I was able to identify a mediating structure in the ways Romans looked at their landscapes. Identifying the symbolic social dimensions of the Roman mental map of landscapes could not have been accomplished without the perspectives of Annales studies on the social and geographical "spaces" and relations that operated in medieval and early modern Italian societies, starting with what Braudel had called "the connections between history and geographical space."[137] And behind the concepts of the spatialization of power and social relations—evident in the diverse writings of Tafuri and Nussdorfer[138]—lay the varied writings of French theorists, from Foucault to Bourdieu, who, as we recall, had published "Sur le pouvoir symbolique" (1977) in *Annales: Économies, sociétés, civilisations*. Geertz was also important in my reconstructions of Roman social-geographical mental frameworks: the Roman mental construct about physical realities—namely, the three rings of land around Rome—constituted "systems of meaning" and "styles of thought" that Romans in the seventeenth century had about the landscapes in which they were raised. The Roman landscape, too, was a living set of systems and structures "suspended in webs of significance he himself [man] has spun."[139]

The construct of the three rings can have a much broader application than to the seventeenth-century Roman villa gardens. As a social geography of properties, as a mental map, and as a mediating structure for viewing landscape, it can provide a useful model for the study of other cities and their countrysides in the medieval and early modern periods. Of course, the construct must be translated to the realities of other early modern cities and their subject territories, such as London, Paris, Madrid, or Istanbul. These cities may not have three rings; they may have two or seven rings, or radiating spokes, or completely different social-geographical structures.

The mental map is also applicable as an interpretative structure in other disciplines and in other artistic media within the same culture. For example, landscape paintings and pastoral literature also functioned as key mediating structures in the patrician experience of the complex relationships between the Roman countryside and their anchor in urban life in Baroque Rome. I have shown this to be the case with the work of Claude Lorrain (ca. 1604–82), the French landscape painter in Rome.[140] Such different art forms as parks and paintings articulated those relationships through a common expressive structure, such as the pastoral, which was devised in ancient times and strongly reasserted in the Renaissance as a means of articulating the dialectical relationships between urban and rural spheres. But the structure of the pastoral in Baroque Rome was predicated on the existence of the mental map of the three land rings through which Romans interpreted the landscape around their city and its territory. The heightened contrasts and dialectics of the pastoral mode functioned specifically on the basis of such a mental geography. Transposition and displacement of landscape elements were key visual and formal techniques in the contemporary Roman discourses about the land, the actual pastoralist economy (i.e., livestock raising), and the artistic pastoral mode. This kind of methodology has a broad similarity with other approaches of the 1980s and 1990s, which were even more directly influenced by Raymond Williams. See, for example, the study of eighteenth-century English landscape gardens and their pictorial representations by the geographer Stephen Daniels.[141]

The geographical range of the three rings, which reaches from the urban center of Rome to the outer edges of its territory, also connects with some trends in current studies of gardens. Seventeenth-century Romans were aware of both the larger landscape systems and the microsystems of small vernacular gardens such as the Roman vigne. Indeed, their ability to "read" the great villa parks, with their transposed landscapes, rested on an awareness of the full range from center to periphery. On the one hand, this has resonance today, when current attention in many areas of the historical study of gardens has shifted from enclosed gardens to larger landscape systems and notions of territory, particularly with respect to the stewardship and preservation of historical gardens in Italy and elsewhere.[142] On the other hand, the work of social historians of Rome, such Daniela Esposito, investigates microsystems in the form of vernacular gardens in Rome, opening the door to a much needed new avenue of research: the gardens of ordinary citizens in medieval and early modern times.[143] This research promises to bring us closer to a history of vernacular Roman gardens, and, inspired by the writings of Emilio Sereni, it will do for Rome what the historian Mauro Ambrosoli has done for northern Italy.[144]

My earlier iterations of the approach that I have just described have had their shortcomings.[145] By focusing on the social strategies of Roman families (such as the Pamphilj) and on the representation of these strategies in villa garden design, the larger social-geographical structures of the Roman countryside became the protagonists of my research, and, often because of a lack of documentation, I gave short shrift to the signs of individual human intention (fig. 1.14).[146] But this is not a problem inherent in the concept of three rings. For example, in my recent work, besides showing that the web of meanings constituted a language that went beyond the specifics of architecture or garden design, I have tried to recapture individual voices from the past. These voices are those of members of the papal Pamphilj family, Claude Lorrain, Romans from all walks of life, and their visitors.[147] And in the current work of Ehrlich on the Villa Mondragone—the Borghese palace (built 1613–20) with designed rural landscapes and a hunting park near Frascati—the implications of the work of Reinhard, Nussdorfer, and Coste, as well as that of Williams and the concept of the three rings, are integrated in a very rich synthesis on the formal and the ideological dimensions. She has expanded the social-geographical approach to Roman villa gardens by taking it to the third ring of properties around Rome, by emphasizing the centrality of the papal court in the conception of villa culture, by showing how the ideology of Borghese landowning and contemporary pastoral poetry conditioned the experience of visitors to their lands, and by giving a rich and complex picture of the Borghese protagonists and seventeenth-century Roman villa culture in general.[148] In Ehrlich's writings, as well as in the recent work of Claudia Lazzaro (such as her article "Italy is a Garden: The Idea of Italy and the Italian Garden Tradition" [2001]), the voices and opinions of Italians and their many visitors come alive in the written descriptions and visual constructs that manifest broad cultural frameworks for understanding the roles that gardens played in Italian cultural traditions. Today, some of the most interesting research on Italian and Roman gardens is concerned with reading and interpreting these earlier voices and constructs as seen in the many prints that were made of the Italian gardens from the sixteenth century on (see figs. 1.8 and 1.14).[149]

To conclude an essay devoted to methodological issues, I would like to reconnect with the larger picture of studies on Roman seventeenth-century gardens. The concept of three rings arose from the search for a synthetic nexus, one that would bring out the complex layering of Roman villas and life, and pull it together at the same time. But equally important to a complex understanding of the subject is the multisided picture of seventeenth-century

Roman villa gardens that is emerging from a different effort, namely the major research campaigns carried out in the last thirty years by those responsible for the administration and conservation of the gardens, above all the art historians Alberta Campitelli and Carla Benocci in Rome. By building their studies on the notion of comprehensive documentation and contextualization, they have done more than anyone to recover the realities of what seventeenth-century Roman villa gardens were about.[150]

Acknowledgments

I warmly thank Michel Conan for convening the symposium for which this essay was written and for encouraging dialogue among the international participants. I am also grateful to the two anonymous reviewers who generously gave of their time in reviewing the draft and suggesting revisions. In this historiographical essay, the illustrations are few and are intended as evocations of the larger themes treated.

Notes

Unless otherwise noted, all translations are my own.

1 For a historiographical mapping of the field of Italian garden studies and for background to this article, see Mirka Beneš, "Recent Developments and Perspectives in the Historiography of Italian Gardens," in *Perspectives on Garden Histories*, ed. Michel Conan, 37–76 (Washington, D.C.: Dumbarton Oaks Research Library and Collection, 1999); David R. Coffin, "The Study of the History of the Italian Garden until the First Dumbarton Oaks Colloquium," in *Perspectives on Garden Histories*, ed. Michel Conan, 27–36 (Washington, D.C.: Dumbarton Oaks Research Library and Collection, 1999); Mirka Beneš, "Italian and French Gardens: A Century of Historical Study (1900–2000)," in *Villas and Gardens in Early Modern Italy and France*, eds. Mirka Beneš and Dianne Harris, 1–16 (Cambridge: Cambridge University Press, 2001); Margherita Azzi Visentini, "Storia dei giardini: Osservazioni in margine al recente sviluppo di questa disciplina in Italia," in *Storia e storie di giardini: Fortune e storia del giardino italiano e verbanese nel mondo; Atti del Convegno, Verbania, sabato 31 agosto 2002*, eds. Leonardo Parachini and Carlo Alessandro Pisoni, 45–86 (Verbania: Alberti Libraio, Comune di Verbania, Magazzeno Storico Verbanese, 2003); Mirka Beneš, "A Tribute to Two Historians of Landscape Architecture: David R. Coffin and Elisabeth B. MacDougall," *Journal of the Society of Architectural Historians* 63, no. 2 (June 2004): 248–54; Hervé Brunon, "L'essor artistique et la fabrique culturelle du paysage à la Renaissance," *Studiolo: Revue d'histoire de l'art de l'Académie de France à Rome* 4 (2006): 261–90; Margherita Zalum, "La storia del giardino italiano: Lineamenti ed evoluzione di una giovane disciplina," in *Bibliografia del giardino e del paesaggio italiano, 1980–2005*, eds. Lucia Tongiorgi Tomasi and Luigi Zangheri, 1–14 (Florence: L. S. Olschki, 2008); Luigi Zangheri, "Il restauro dei giardini storici in Italia dal 1980," in *Bibliografia del giardino e del paesaggio italiano, 1980–2005*, eds. Lucia Tongiorgi Tomasi and Luigi Zangheri, 135–59 (Florence: L. S. Olschki, 2008); and Margherita Azzi Visentini, "Riflessioni intorno alla fortuna critica del giardino storico italiano negli Stati Uniti negli ultimi trentacinque anni," in *Giardini storici: A 25 anni dalle Carte di Firenze; Esperienze e prospettive*, eds. Laura Sabrina Pelissetti and Lionella Scazzosi, 1:31–46 (Florence: L. S. Olschki, 2009). For the first comprehensive bibliographies on the field, see Lucia Tongiorgi Tomasi and Luigi Zangheri, eds., *Bibliografia del giardino e del paesaggio italiano, 1980–2005* (Florence: L. S. Olschki, 2008) (including the CD); and Uwe Schneider and Gert Gröning, eds., *Stolo: Bibliographische Findmittel zur Gartenkultur*, vol. 1, *Italien* (Worms: Wernersche Verlagsgesellschaft, 2009). For French scholars, see in particular Brunon, "L'essor artistique et la fabrique culturelle du paysage à la Renaissance."

2 See, for example, the range in Laura Sabrina Pelissetti and Lionella Scazzosi, eds., *Giardini storici: A 25 anni dalle Carte di Firenze; Esperienze e prospettive*, 2 vols. (Florence: L. S. Olschki, 2009).

3 This, naturally, has an Anglo-American cast, as Italian colleagues have correctly noted in response to my historiographical essays of 1999 and 2001, which indeed could not cover the Italian literature in the way Italian scholars can. See Azzi Visentini, "Storia dei giardini"; Zalum, "La storia del giardino italiano: Lineamenti ed evoluzione di

una giovane disciplina," 2 ("quest'ultimo testo condizionato da un'angolatura fortemente anglocentrica") and 11; and Azzi Visentini, "Riflessioni intorno alla fortuna critica del giardino storico italiano negli Stati Uniti negli ultimi trentacinque anni," 42n20 ("vista da una prospettiva americana") and 45.

4 For "mediation," also in the Marxist sense, see Raymond Williams, *Keywords: A Vocabulary of Culture and Society*, rev. ed. (1976; reprint, New York: Oxford University Press, 1983), 204–7. Williams also refers the reader to the related sense of "dialectic" (106–8). Since the later nineteenth century, the word "mediation" has been construed as "describing the interaction of two opposed concepts or forces within the totality to which they are assumed to belong, or do really belong; . . . describing such interaction as in itself substantial, with forms of its own, so that it is not the neutral process of the interaction of separate forms, but an active process in which the form of the mediation alters the things mediated, or by its nature indicates their nature" (205). Williams draws on the work of Theodor Adorno and the Frankfurt School from the 1930s to the 1970s, adding: "all 'objects,' and in this context notably works of art, are mediated by specific social relations but cannot be reduced to an abstraction of that relationship; . . ." (206).

5 The term "villa," as used here and historically in Rome from 1400 to 1800, refers to the entire landholding of the villa (gardens included) and not to the main building alone. The literature has focused on gardens owned by the elite social classes (i.e., popes, cardinals, and the nobility) for at least two reasons: they were the best preserved, and their contents (e.g., sculptures, fountains, and balustrades) were high-style arts. There has been recent interest in Roman villa gardens owned by people from different social classes—from the *vigna* (vineyard, or small rustic plot) of merchants or notaries to the highly decorated villas of cardinals or popes. For the vigne, see Daniela Esposito, "Vigneti e orti entro le mura: Utilizzo del suolo e strutture insediative," in *Roma: Le trasformazioni urbane nel Quattrocento*, ed. Giorgio Simoncini, 2:205–28 (Florence: L. S. Olschki, 2004).

6 For background to what follows, see the works listed in note 1. For biographical information on the scholars discussed here, see s.v. in Udo Kulterman, *Storia della storia dell'arte* (Vicenza: Neri Pozza, 1997); Marcello Barbanera, *L'archeologia degli italiani: Storia, metodi e orientamenti dell'archeologia classica in Italia* (Rome: Editori Riuniti, 1998); and www.dictionaryofarthistorians.org.

7 These art historians have already been discussed in the recent literature; see Beneš, "Recent Developments and Perspectives in the Historiography of Italian Gardens"; Beneš, "A Tribute to Two Historians of Landscape Architecture"; Tracy L. Ehrlich, *Landscape and Identity in Early Modern Rome: Villa Culture at Frascati in the Borghese Era* (Cambridge: Cambridge University Press, 2002); and Azzi Visentini, "Riflessioni intorno alla fortuna critica del giardino storico italiano negli Stati Uniti negli ultimi trentacinque anni."

8 Ackerman did his PhD dissertation at New York University (1952) with Richard Krautheimer (1897–1994) on Bramante's Cortile del Belvedere in the Vatican; his book appeared in 1954. Coffin did his PhD at Princeton University (1954) with Erwin Panofsky (1892–1968) on the Villa d'Este at Tivoli; his book appeared in 1960. MacDougall studied for her PhD at Harvard University in the late 1950s and received her degree in 1970; she studied late sixteenth- and early seventeenth-century Roman villa gardens with John Coolidge, who had published a seminal study on the Villa Giulia in Rome (1943), and with Ackerman, who had come to Harvard University in 1960 to teach in the Department of Fine Arts.

9 James S. Ackerman, *The Villa: Form and Ideology of Country Houses* (Princeton, N.J.: Princeton University Press, 1990).

10 Coffin's doctoral students included Claudia Lazzaro, who completed her dissertation on the Villa Lante at Bagnaia in 1974.

11 On Dumbarton Oaks's contributions to Italian garden studies, see Azzi Visentini, "Riflessioni intorno alla fortuna critica del giardino storico italiano negli Stati Uniti negli ultimi trentacinque anni."

12 They did field trips in Rome with the German art historians Rudolf Wittkower, professor of art and architectural history at Columbia University, and Wolfgang Lotz, later director of the Bibliotheca Hertziana. For their professional circles, see Henry A. Millon, *A Life of Learning: Charles Homer Haskins Lecture for 2002* (New York: American Council of Learned Societies, 2002); and Beneš, "A Tribute to Two Historians of Landscape Architecture."

13 See James S. Ackerman, "Art History and the Problems of Criticism," in *The Visual Arts Today*, ed. Gyorgy Kepes (Middletown, Conn.: Wesleyan University Press, 1960), 262–65. See also Beneš, "Recent Developments and Perspectives in the Historiography of Italian Gardens," 47–50 and 58–59; and Beneš, "Italian and French Gardens," 5.

14 The written and visual archival documentation of the Roman Renaissance villa gardens included land acquisition records, payment records for construction, planting, and decoration, surveys of terrain (few existed), printed maps of Rome, printed views of the gardens, records of the antique sculptures in the gardens, and drawings and paintings that recorded the villas and their gardens from the sixteenth century on.

15 Among them, James S. Ackerman, *The Cortile del Belvedere* (Vatican City: Biblioteca Apostolica Vaticana, 1954); Christoph Luitpold Frommel, *Die Farnesina und Peruzzis Architektonisches Frühwerk* (Berlin: De Gruyter, 1961); Arnaldo Bruschi, *Bramante architetto* (Bari: Laterza, 1969); Howard Hibbard, *Carlo Maderno and Roman Architecture,*

1580–1630 (London: Zwemmer, 1971); Christoph Luitpold Frommel, *Der römische Palastbau der Hochrenaissance*, 3 vols. (Tübingen: E. Wasmuth, 1973); and Joseph Connors, *Borromini and the Roman Oratory: Style and Society* (New York: Architectural History Foundation, 1980).

16 Ackerman noted: "I felt that my German mentors . . . had all the benefit of a German philosophical background . . . For example, Panofsky was very consciously founding his work in a philosophical base of [Ernst] Cassirer and Kant." James S. Ackerman, *Interviews with Art Historians, 1991–2002* (Malibu, Calif.: Getty Research Institute, 1994), 32.

17 Evelina Borea, "La scomparsa di Paola della Pergola: La signora della Galleria Borghese," *Il giornale dell'arte* 11, no. 108 (1993): 3.

18 Isa Belli Barsali, *Ville di Roma* (1970; reprint, Milan: Rusconi, 1983); and Isa Belli Barsali and Maria Grazia Branchetti, *Ville della campagna romana* (Milan: SISAR, 1975). For Belli Barsali, see "Nota biografica su Isa Belli Barsali" and her "Scritti" at www.pacinifazzi.it/scheda_perlacitta.htm. She studied with Mario Salmi and Roberto Longhi, and, in addition to Roman villas, focused on the arts and villas of Tuscany, especially Lucca.

19 Paola della Pergola, *Villa Borghese* (Rome: Istituto Poligrafico dello Stato, Libreria dello Stato, 1962).

20 For Lamb, see www.carl-lamb.de and Carl Lamb, *Die Villa d'Este in Tivoli* (Munich: Prestel, 1966), 7. He began his research on the Villa d'Este in 1938 in Rome; it was interrupted by World War II. A professional filmmaker, photographer, and art historian, Lamb frequented the Bibliotheca Hertziana and became acquainted with architect-historians, such as Furio Fasolo. He followed the German methodology and paired it with original surveys of the architecture, gardens, and water systems of the Villa d'Este in his 1966 book. In going outside the art historical box, his book adds much to David R. Coffin's key study, *The Villa d'Este at Tivoli* (Princeton, N.J.: Princeton University Press, 1960).

21 Franck approached the villa gardens at Frascati as architectural gardens, following the methodologies of German scholars Jacob Burckhardt, Heinrich Wölfflin, Albert E. Brinckmann, Cornelius Gurlitt, and Marie Luise Gothein, among others. Carlludwig Franck, *Die Barockvillen in Frascati, ihre Gestaltung aus den landschaftlichen Gegebenheiten* (Munich: Deutscher Kunstverlag, 1956). In Rome, he frequented the American Academy and the Bibliotheca Hertziana.

22 Klaus Schwager, "Kardinal Pietro Aldobrandinis Villa di Belvedere in Frascati," *Römisches Jahrbuch für Kunstgeschichte* 9–10 (1961–62): 291–382. Schwager trained with Georg Weise (1888–1978) at the Kunsthistorisches Institut at the Universität Tübingen, where he served as ordinarius professor from 1971 to 1990. Heilmann became a museum curator and researched German artists in Rome and modern art.

23 Christoph H. Heilmann, "Die Entstehungsgeschichte der Villa Borghese in Rom," *Münchner Jahrbuch für Kunstgeschichte* 15 (1973): 97–158.

24 In a review of his *Carlo Maderno and Roman Architecture, 1580–1630* (London: Zwemmer, 1971), published in the *Times Literary Supplement*, 6 April 1973, Hibbard was called Maderno's "brilliant new apologist," but his subject matter, Rome in 1580–1630, was denigrated as "a low period of Roman architecture, perhaps of Italian architecture generally" (374). For Hibbard on Roman villas and gardens, see his important review of Franck, *Die Barockvillen in Frascati* in *The Art Bulletin* 40, no. 4 (December 1958): 354–59, and his publications: "Palazzo Borghese Studies, 1. The Garden and its Fountains," *The Burlington Magazine* 100, no. 663 (June 1958): 204–12, 215; "Scipione Borghese's Garden Palace on the Quirinal," *Journal of the Society of Architectural Historians* 23, no. 4 (December 1964): 163–92; and *Carlo Maderno and Roman Architecture*. Hibbard's nucleus of work on the Frascati villas was brought to an entirely new level of art historical and historical study by Tracy Ehrlich (PhD, art history, Columbia University, 1995); see her magisterial study, *Landscape and Identity in Early Modern Rome*, and especially p. 6 for a historiography of the Frascati villas.

25 Hibbard, *Carlo Maderno and Roman Architecture*, 7–21; Jean Delumeau, *Vie économique et sociale de Rome dans la seconde moitié du XVIe siècle*, 2 vols. (Paris: E. de Boccard, 1957–59); Giovanni Botero, *The Reason of State*, and *The Greatness of Cities* (New Haven: Yale University Press, 1956); and Michel de Montaigne, *The Complete Works: Essays, Travel Journal, Letters*, trans. Donald M. Frame (Stanford: Stanford University Press, 1958).

26 Hibbard's special feeling for Roman Baroque society and country life may have been affected by his father's research. The numerous works of Benjamin H. Hibbard (1870–1955) were devoted to Midwestern land policies, agricultural economics, and cheese prices.

27 My account here is based on my BA studies in art history at Princeton University in the 1970s, where the Methods of Art History seminars included such syllabus topics as "Art History as a Humanistic Discipline" (from Panofsky's work; he died in 1968 after a long career at Princeton); "Ekphrasis: Description of an Individual Object, Real or Imaginary"; "Style: The Language of Art," in which we studied "theory of period styles, theory of the 'spirit of the times' (*Kunstwollen* or *Zeitgeist*), theory of individual styles"; "Iconography: The Content of Art"; and "The Quality of Art" on aesthetic state, judgment, and connoisseurship.

28 Burckhardt himself framed the criteria for viewing Italian gardens early on in his substantial chapter on Roman villas and gardens in *Der Cicerone: Eine Anleitung zum Genuss Der Kunstwerke Italiens* (Basel: Schweighauser'sche Verlagsbuchhandlung, 1855). Burckhardt, in *Der Cicerone*, and his student Heinrich Wölfflin, in *Renaissance und Barock: Eine Untersuchung über Wesen und Entstehung des*

Barockstils in Italien (Munich: T. Ackermann, 1888), were among the first to characterize the formal and stylistic changes—the expansion from gardens to parks—in Roman villa gardens in the century between 1580 and 1680, and they did so in aesthetic-spatial terms, as in Burckhardt's "the [Baroque] garden however becomes dedicated, more harmoniously than before, to grand lines and perspectives, to the simplest contrasts possible." ("der Garten aber wird harmonischer als früher den grossen Linien und Perspektiven, den möglichst einfachen Kontrasten gewidmet.") Burckhardt, *Der Cicerone*, 379–80.

29 Wölfflin and Alois Riegl, who used the Roman villa gardens of 1550–1650 to exemplify stylistic change, viewed the notion of artistic style as an entity or will-to-form that transcended the single work of art and manifested itself in a determined way in it—a concept inspired by Kantian and Hegelian philosophy. This approach was also called *Strukturforschung*.

30 See the texts in *Empathy, Form, and Space: Problems in German Aesthetics, 1873–1893* (Santa Monica, Calif.: The Getty Center for the History of Art and the humanities, 1994).

31 Iconography and the study of symbols, too, had origins in German philosophy of the later eighteenth century. For iconography and iconology, two terms on which Panofsky based much of his work, see Erwin Panofsky, "Three Decades of Art History in the United States: Impressions of a Transplanted European," in *Meaning in the Visual Arts*, 321–46 (Garden City, N.Y.: Doubleday, 1955); Karen Michels, *Transplantierte Kunstwissenschaft: Deutschsprachige Kunstgeschichte in amerikanischen Exil* (Berlin: Akademie, 1999); and Allen J. Grieco, Michael Rocke, and Fiorella Gioffredi Superbi, eds., *The Italian Renaissance in the Twentieth Century: Acts of an International Conference, Florence, Villa I Tatti, June 9–11, 1999* (Florence: L. S. Olschki, 2002).

32 The Germans who focused on Raum-forschung included Riegl and Albert E. Brinckmann, while those who brought iconography and Raum-forschung to bear in their studies included Wolfgang Lotz (1912–81), Ludwig Heydenreich (1903–78), and, somewhat younger, Klaus Schwager (b. 1925) and Christoph L. Frommel (b. 1933). Richard Krautheimer (1897–1994), mentor of many of these figures and a seminal art historian, did not work on Roman gardens per se, but his transposition of the Panofskian concept of "iconography" or "iconology" from art works to architecture, made about 1940, affected the developing field of Roman garden studies. See Richard Krautheimer, "Introduction to an 'Iconography of Medieval Architecture,'" *Journal of the Courtauld and Warburg Institutes* 5 (1942): 1–33; James S. Ackerman, "Richard Krautheimer, 6 July 1897–1 November 1994," *Proceedings of the American Philosophical Society* 148, no. 2 (June 2004): 229–34; and Beneš, "A Tribute to Two Historians of Landscape Architecture."

33 Following his teacher Burckhardt's approach, Wölfflin qualified the change thus: "The baroque garden did not follow the terrain; it subordinated it to a unified scheme. The whole design was dominated by one all-embracing view . . ." Heinrich Wölfflin, *Renaissance and Baroque*, trans. Kathrin Simon (Ithaca, N.Y.: Cornell University Press, 1966), 150.

34 Ibid., 150–52.

35 Albert E. Brinckmann, *Baukunst des 17. und 18. Jahrhunderts in den romanischen Ländern* (Berlin-Neubabelsberg: Athenaion, 1919), 178. Discussions of Raum pervade Brinckmann's many influential writings on the architecture, gardens, and urban spaces of Renaissance and Baroque Rome. See Albert E. Brinckmann, *Platz und Monument als künstlerisches Formproblem* (Berlin: E. Wasmuth, 1923). Raum (space) and the development of *Raumgefühl* (feeling for space) in design are central in his thought, and he continued Wölfflin's and Riegl's concepts of art's will-to-form (*Kunstwollen*). See *Baukunst des 17. und 18. Jahrhunderts in den romanischen Ländern*, where Raum and its qualities are used to discuss Italian gardens.

36 Dami's wide-ranging bibliography included—unusually—historical sources and studies on Florentine, Roman, Venetian, and other Italian societies. Luigi Dami, *Il giardino italiano* (Milan: Bestetti and Tumminelli, 1924), 50–53. For Rome, Dami referred the reader to historians who also doubled as art historians, such as Eugène Müntz, Ludwig von Pastor, Federico Hermanin, and J. A. F. Orbaan.

37 "Nel seicento anche per il giardino si tratta del preponderare o almeno dell' accentuarsi a poco a poco di alcuni elementi 'pittoreschi.' . . . Villa Borghese ha tre recinti, e il terzo è quasi campagna schietta. Villa Doria [Pamphilj] ha il suo pineto 'irregolare.' . . . Sebbene la regola architettonica domini immutata e nessuno pensi neanche da lontano a mutarla, si sente che siamo ai giorni in cui si va creando la pittura di paese di Annibale Carracci e poi di Claudio e di Poussin." Dami, *Il giardino italiano*, 25–26. On Boschini and the "pittoresco," see Francis Haskell, *Patrons and Painters: A Study in the Relations between Italian Art and Society in the Age of the Baroque* (London: Chatto and Windus, 1963); and Philip L. Sohm, *Pittoresco: Marco Boschini, His Critics, and Their Critique of Painterly Brushwork in Seventeenth- and Eighteenth-Century Italy* (Cambridge: Cambridge University Press, 1991). Dami's book was very influential; his conception of the Roman parks as "pittoreschi," painterly, was used by Italian architects who wrote histories of Italian gardens. See, for example, Francesco Fariello, *Architettura dei giardini* (Rome: Edizioni dell'Ateneo, 1967).

38 "But the profound effect of the Cortile on later generations was due not so much to mere novelties as to radical changes in the concept of space and composition. For the first time in Renaissance architecture the out-of-doors became an element in architectural thought . . . It is evident then that Bramante . . . brought to the design

concepts which were to be fully grasped only in Baroque architecture: movement and climax." Ackerman, *Cortile del Belvedere*, 121–22 and 125.

39 Ackerman, *Cortile del Belvedere*, 137–38.

40 Elisabeth Blair MacDougall, "*Ars Hortulorum*: Sixteenth-Century Garden Iconography and Literary Theory in Italy," in *The Italian Garden*, ed. David R. Coffin (Washington, D.C.: Dumbarton Oaks Research Library and Collection, 1972), 47.

41 "At the same time that the *boschetto* was growing in importance a change took place in the relationship between the spectator and the garden. The early Renaissance garden was primarily static and could be viewed in its entirety from a fixed point of view. To borrow from literary terminology, it had a unity of space and time. The gardens after the 1520s consisted of a series of successive spaces, isolated from each other physically and visually. They could only be experienced through movement, and the relationship between spectator and garden became active rather than passive." MacDougall, "*Ars Hortulorum*," 46.

42 See Henny Weber, *Achsialität und Symmetrie im Grundriss des italienischen Profanbaus von der Frührenaissance bis zum Frühbarock* (Berlin, 1937), quoted in Elisabeth Blair MacDougall, "The Villa Mattei and the Development of the Roman Garden Style" (PhD diss., Harvard University, 1970).

43 MacDougall, "Villa Mattei and the Development of the Roman Garden Style," 74–75.

44 MacDougall acknowledged gardens as part of a broader cultural history of social spaces: "Finally, I have invented a name, *giardino a soggetto*, to describe a garden with a unified iconographical theme. This is an adaptation of the term *torneo a soggetto*, which refers to the sixteenth-century tourneys organized around a literary theme, really a ballet on horseback rather than a mock combat. The subject matter and the clientele were the same for both gardens and tourneys." The term *torneo a soggetto* derived from treatises of the time. Ibid., xi. Since the 1950s, her teachers, Richard Krautheimer and Wolfgang Lotz, wrestled with the question of "style," and attempted to move beyond a Wölfflinian to a Panofskian notion of art as part of culture—"iconology." See their essays in Richard Krautheimer, ed., *Redefinitions of Style*, special issue, *College Art Journal* 17, no. 2 (Winter 1958).

45 The only historical studies on the Roman Renaissance and Baroque that were regularly consulted were works by Burckhardt, Leopold von Ranke, and Ludwig von Pastor (1854–1928) in Von Pastor's multivolume *The History of the Popes from the Close of the Middle Ages* (1891–1940); these works were used essentially for data and general background. Von Pastor's monumental history was first published in German in sixteen volumes in 1886–1933. Both Coffin and MacDougall were interested in a broader European historical context for Roman gardens, comparing them with gardens of other cultures. See, for example, MacDougall's reference to studies of French and English gardens; Franklin Hamilton Hazlehurst, *Jacques Boyceau and the French Formal Garden* (1966); and Edward Greenway Malins, *English Landscaping and Literature, 1660–1840* (1966). MacDougall, "Villa Mattei and the Development of the Roman Garden Style."

46 Ackerman, "Art History and the Problems of Criticism," 265.

47 "Starting with the premise of the autonomy of the individual work, we would seek out the intention and the experiences of the artist as he produced it . . . he cannot work in a historical vacuum . . . Every tool of history must be at hand to understand all this, and some new ones, too, such as those of psychology and other social sciences. In short, we would formulate the history of art primarily in terms of contexts rather than developments . . . History in terms of contexts should foster a broader definition of style by its awareness of the *intentions* of the artist." Ibid. (emphasis in the original).

48 One key result for the Anglo-American study of Italian and Roman gardens would be Ackerman's important book on *The Villa: Form and Ideology of Country Houses* (1990).

49 An anonymous reviewer of this article's draft noted, aptly, that England and Italy both have traditions of scholarship conducted by people from all walks of life and often from outside the academy.

50 Masson was born in British colonial India at Rawalpindi near the Kyber Pass (now Pakistan), never went beyond secondary school, perhaps worked in intelligence in Paris during World War II, came to Rome about 1945, settled there definitively, and took up journalism and writing to make ends meet. Alessandra Capodiferro and Cornelia Lauf, eds., *Georgina Masson (1912–1980): Selections from the Photographic Archive* (Milan: Charta, 2003).

51 "Villa Borghese was the earliest of the great Roman park villas of modern times, in which the gardens and park dominated and the house and other buildings were mere incidents in the vast layout . . . Although the villa was laid out as park it should not be imagined that it was a park in the English landscape sense." Georgina Masson, *Italian Gardens* (New York: Harry N. Abrams, 1961), 194–95. Masson's historical work was comparable to that of Marchesa Iris Origo in *The Merchant of Prato* (1957).

52 For di Gaddo, see the website of Giorgio Muratore, http://www.archiwatch.it/2007/05/28/beata.html. Born in Rome, di Gaddo studied at the Facoltà di Architettura, Università di Roma, and graduated in 1946. She taught in Rome and Palermo, also practicing architecture. From 1977 to 1991, she taught Disegno e Rilievo, namely, architectural drawing and survey; her students' surveys of the Villa Borghese are key to the *Villa Borghese: Il giardino e le architetture* (Rome: Officina Edizioni, 1985).

53 Giorgio Simoncini, "Gustavo Giovannoni, Vincenzo Fasolo e la concezione integrale della storia dell'architettura," in *Principi e metodi della storia dell'architettura e l'eredità della "Scuola Romana,"* eds. Flavia Colonna and Stefania Costantini, 63–72 (Rome: Centro Stampa Ateneo, 1994); and Maria Piera Sette, ed., *Gustavo Giovannoni: Riflessioni agli albori del XXI secolo* (Rome: Bonsignori, 2005).

54 Historians in the ambit of the *ASRSP* influenced by the Annales include Jean Coste, who studied topography, property, and landowning in the Roman Campagna. See "I casali della Campagna di Roma all'inizio del Seicento," *Archivio della Società Romana di Storia Patria* 92 (1969): 41–115; "La topographie médiévale de la campagne romaine et l'histoire socio-économique: Pistes de recherche," *Mélanges de École Française de Rome: Moyen âge, temps modernes* 88, no. 2 (1976): 621–75; and "Description et délimitation de l'espace rural dans la campagne romaine," in *Sources of Social History: Private Acts of the Late Middle Ages*, eds. Paolo Brezzi and Egmont Lee, 185–200 (Toronto: Pontifical Institute of Mediaeval Studies, 1984). For Lefevre's approach on the Villa Madama, see Renato Lefevre, "Il patrimonio cinquecentesco dei Medici nel Lazio e in Abruzzo," *Archivio della Società Romana di Storia Patria* 98 (1975): 95–133. On Lefevre, see Maria Teresa Bonadonna Russo, "Renato Lefevre," *Archivio della Società Romana di Storia Patria* 127 (2004): 293–99. On the impact of the *ASRSP* on medieval Roman studies, see Letizia Ermini Pani, "Il contributo della Società Romana di Storia Patria allo studio della topografia di Roma e del Lazio nel medioevo," *Archivio della Società Romana di Storia Patria* 130 (2007 [2008]): 123–37.

55 See Azzi Visentini, "Storia dei giardini"; Ines Romitti, *Alessandro Tagliolini paesaggista, scultore e storico del giardino* (Florence: Alinea Editrice, 2001); and http://www.fondazionetagliolini.it. In the 1980s and 1990s, Tagliolini began convening both international and interdisciplinary scholars on Italian and Roman gardens in conferences held at his Centro Studi Giardini Storici e Contemporanei at Pietrasanta in Tuscany. He also sought to connect Roman gardens with larger cultural and anthropological concerns of society in *I giardini di Roma: Folclore, poesia e storia della città attraverso l'evoluzione delle 'isole verdi,' la riscoperta di una rinascimentale bellezza in un'ideale sintesi tra natura e arte* (Rome: Newton Compton, 1980).

56 See Eugenio Battisti, *Iconologia ed ecologia del giardino e del paesaggio*, ed. Giuseppa Saccaro Del Buffa (Florence: L. S. Olschki, 2004) for the posthumous publication of these garden studies. For a very recent assessment of Battisti's studies on gardens, see Marcello Fagiolo, "Battisti, il giardino delle idee," in *Eugenio Battisti: Storia, critica, progetto nella continuità della ricerca*, eds. Antonio Piva and Pierfranco Galliani, 33–39 (Rome: Gangemi, 2009).

57 Eugenio Battisti, *L'antirinascimento* (1962; reprint, Milan: Garzanti, 1989), 1:5–10.

58 Eugenio Battisti, "The Role of Semiology in the Visual Arts," in *A Semiotic Landscape: Proceedings of the First Congress of the International Association for Semiotic Studies*, eds. Seymour Chatman, Umberto Eco, and Jean-Marie Klinkenberg, 744–48 (The Hague: Mouton, 1979).

59 Carlo Ginzburg, "A proposito della raccolta dei saggi storici di Marc Bloch," *Studi medievali*, 3rd ser., 6, no. 1 (1965): 335–53; and Carlo Ginzburg, *I benandanti: Ricerche sulla stregoneria e sui culti agrari tra Cinquecento e Seicento* (Turin: G. Einaudi, 1966).

60 Battisti, *L'antirinascimento*, 2:7–17.

61 Eugenio Battisti, "*Natura Artificiosa* to *Natura Artificialis*," in *The Italian Garden*, ed. David R. Coffin (Washington, D.C.: Dumbarton Oaks Research Library and Collection, 1972), 3–6 and 10.

62 Zangheri has focused on Florentine gardens since his magisterial monograph, *Pratolino, il giardino delle meraviglie* (Florence: Gonnelli, 1979). However, like Battisti, he has great range; see Luigi Zangheri, Brunella Lorenzi, and Nausikaa M. Rahmati, *Il giardino islamico* (Florence: L. S. Olschki, 2006).

63 On Sereni's importance for the study of Italian gardens, see Beneš, "Recent Developments and Perspectives in the Historiography of Italian Gardens," 48–50. Key Italian art historians who study gardens respected Battisti; see, for example, Marcello Fagiolo, "Ricordo di Eugenio Battisti: il cavaliere dell' Antirinascimento," *Quaderni di storia dell'architettura e restauro* 3 (1990): 101–2; and Fagiolo, "Battisti, il giardino delle idee."

64 Fernand Braudel, *The Mediterranean and the Mediterranean World in the Age of Philip II*, trans. Siân Reynolds, 2 vols. (New York: Harper and Row, 1972), 22.

65 A few examples with respect to landscape and garden studies of the earlier periods are Mirka Beneš, "Villa Pamphilj (1630–1670): Family, Land, and Gardens in Papal Rome" (PhD diss., Yale University, 1989); Stephen Daniels, "Marxism, Culture, and the Duplicity of Landscape," in *New Models in Geography*, eds. Richard Peet and Nigel Thrift, 196–220 (London and Boston: Unwin-Hyman, 1989); Tom Williamson, *Polite Landscapes: Gardens and Society in Eighteenth-Century England* (Baltimore: Johns Hopkins University Press, 1995); Mirka Beneš, "Landowning and the Villa in the Social Geography of the Roman Territory: The Location and Landscapes of the Villa Pamphilj, 1645–70," in *Form, Modernism, and History: Essays in Honor of Eduard F. Sekler*, ed. Alexander von Hoffmann, 187–209 (Cambridge, Mass.: Harvard University Graduate School of Design, 1996); Chandra Mukerji, *Territorial Ambitions and the Gardens of Versailles* (Cambridge: Cambridge University Press, 1997); Stephen Daniels, *Humphry Repton: Landscape Gardening and the Geography of Georgian England* (New Haven: Yale University Press, 1999); Dianne Harris, "The Post-Modernization of Landscape: A Critical Historiography," *Journal of the Society of Architectural Historians* 58, no. 3 (September 1999): 434–43; D. Fairchild Ruggles, *Gardens, Landscape, and Vision in the Palaces of*

Islamic Spain (University Park: Pennsylvania State University Press, 2000); Mirka Beneš, "Pastoralism in the Roman Baroque Villa and in Claude Lorrain: Myths and Realities of the Roman Campagna," in *Villas and Gardens in Early Modern Italy and France*, eds. Mirka Beneš and Dianne Harris, 88–113 (Cambridge: Cambridge University Press, 2001); and Dianne Harris, *The Nature of Authority: Villa Culture, Landscape, and Representation in Eighteenth-Century Lombardy* (University Park: Pennsylvania State University Press, 2003). For the "generation," in terms of scholarly generation, that followed, see, for example, Hervé Brunon, "Pratolino: Art des jardins et imaginaire de la nature dans l'Italie de la seconde moitié du XVIe siècle" (Doctoral thesis, Université Paris 1 Panthéon-Sorbonne, 2001); Ehrlich, *Landscape and Identity in Early Modern Rome*; Brunon, "L'essor artistique et la fabrique culturelle du paysage à la Renaissance"; and Georges Farhat, ed., *André Le Nôtre, fragments d'un paysage culturel: Institutions, arts, sciences & techniques* (Sceaux: Musée de l'Ile-de-France, Domaine de Sceaux, 2006).

66 See, for example, Michael Baxandall, *Giotto and the Orators: Humanist Observers of Painting in Italy and the Discovery of Pictorial Composition, 1350–1450* (Oxford: Clarendon Press, 1971); Michael Baxandall, *Painting and Experience in Fifteenth-Century Italy: A Primer in the Social History of Pictorial Style* (Oxford: Oxford University Press, 1972); Hanna Deinhard, "Reflections on Art History and Sociology of Art," *Art Journal* 35, no. 1 (Fall 1975): 29–32; Enrico Castelnuovo, "Per una storia sociale dell'arte," *Paragone* 27, no. 313 (March 1976): 3–30 and 27, no. 314 (January 1977): 3–34; Svetlana Alpers, "Is Art History?" *Daedalus* 106, no. 3 (Summer 1977): 1–13; and Svetlana Alpers, ed., "Art or Society: Must We Choose?" special issue, *Representations* 12 (Fall 1985). Similar convergences, in an explicit neo-Marxist vein, were occurring in the thinking of cultural geographers; see Daniels, "Marxism, Culture, and the Duplicity of Landscape," for an excellent synthesis on the English filiation, from Raymond Williams and John Berger to "a new cultural geography [that in 1990] is emerging" (196).

67 In 1977–78, at the Istituto Universitario di Architettura di Venezia, I took Tafuri's and Massimo Cacciari's courses on early twentieth-century Vienna, including "La 'Grande Vienna': Dalla formazione del mito asburgico alla crisi dell'Austromarxismo," in which Tafuri defined the central theme as "la crisi semantica come problema di 'nuovi linguaggi' e di nuove 'tecniche.'"

68 That infrastructure included the roads and canals set up from 1600 by Henri IV following the French religious wars and the fortifications built by Sébastien LePrestre de Vauban for Louis XIV. See Vincent J. Scully, *Architecture: The Natural and the Manmade* (New York: St. Martin's Press, 1991), 221–73 and 284–92. For Scully's formation, see Neil Levine, "Introduction" and "Vincent Scully: A Biographical Sketch," in *Modern Architecture and Other Essays*, ed. Vincent Scully, 8–11 and 12–33 (Princeton, N.J.: Princeton University Press, 2003), and pp. 12–13 for Focillon and Aubert. For a recent study of Le Nôtre's gardens in this vein, see Thierry Mariage, *L'univers de Le Nostre* (Brussels: P. Mardaga, 1990). For Scully on the symbolic relationships of ancient buildings and landscapes, see *The Earth, the Temple and the Gods: Greek Sacred Architecture* (New Haven: Yale University Press, 1962), written 1957–58. Levine, "Vincent Scully: A Biographical Sketch," 18. Scully's unique perspective at the time was noted by Eugenio Battisti: "Although many visitors, and even specialists, such as Dami, are convinced of the importance of the surrounding landscape to the Italian garden, we are actually in the situation of critical indifference similar to that regretted by Scully for Greek temples." Battisti, "*Natura Artificiosa* to *Natura Artificialis*," 24.

69 The Annales group of historians derives its name from the journal, *Annales d'histoire économique et sociale*, founded in 1929 by Marc Bloch. The journal had various titles, and from 1946 on was known as *Annales: Économies, sociétés, civilisations*. Although historians who espoused Annales approaches have been referred to as a school, it was not one in the official sense. For the Annales, see Peter Burke, *The French Historical Revolution: The Annales School, 1929–89* (Stanford: Stanford University Press, 1990); Stuart Clark, ed., *The Annales School*, 4 vols. (London and New York: Routledge, 1999); and André Burguière, *L'école des Annales: Une histoire intellectuelle* (Paris: O. Jacob, 2006).

70 François Bédarida, ed., *L'histoire et le métier d'historien en France 1945–1995* (Paris: Éditions de la Maison des Sciences de l'Homme, 1995).

71 A brief introduction to this concept is in Beneš, "Recent Developments and Perspectives in the Historiography of Italian Gardens," 65–66.

72 Braudel, *Mediterranean and the Mediterranean World in the Age of Philip II*, 22.

73 Burke, *French Historical Revolution*; Bédarida, *L'histoire et le métier d'historien en France 1945–1995*; Clark, *Annales School*; and Burguière, *L'école des Annales*.

74 See R. Burr Litchfield in Emilio Sereni, *History of the Italian Agricultural Landscape*, trans. R. Burr Litchfield (Princeton, N.J.: Princeton University Press, 1997), xxviii–xliv; and Sereni's many articles in *Quaderni storici* and *Critica marxista*.

75 In Sereni, *History of the Italian Agricultural Landscape*, see esp. chap. 57, "Agricultural Systems of Temporary Clearings, and the New Extension of Pastoral Landscapes between the Fifteenth and Eighteenth Centuries," 188–93, and chap. 59, "Classic and Romantic Landscape in Italian Reality and Art of the Seventeenth Century," 199–201.

76 In fact, Sereni had contributed the article "Agricoltura e mondo rurale" to the first volume (*I caratteri originali*) of the series *Storia d'Italia*.

77 See Lionello Puppi, "L'ambiente, il paesaggio e il territorio," in *Materiali e problemi: Ricerche spaziali e tecnologiche*, pt. 1, vol. 4 of *Storia dell'arte italiana*, ed. Giovanni

Previtali, 44–99 (Turin: G. Einaudi, 1980); Cesare de Seta, ed., *Il paesaggio*, vol. 5 of *Storia d'Italia: Annali* (Turin: G. Einaudi, 1982); Maurice Aymard, "Les *Annales* et l'Italie," *Mélanges de l'École Française de Rome: Moyen âge* 93, no. 1 (1981): 401–17; Gianni Venturi, "Picta poësis: Ricerche sulla poesia e il giardino dalle origini al Seicento," in *Storia d'Italia: Annali*, eds. Ruggiero Romeno and Corrado Vivanti, vol. 5, *Il Paesaggio*, ed. Cesare de Seta, 665–749 (Turin: G. Einaudi, 1982); and Gianni Venturi and Francesco Ceccarelli, eds., *Delizie in villa: Il giardino rinascimentale e i suoi committenti* (Florence: L. S. Olschki, 2008).

78 This was the era of an international Annales. See, for example, the *X° Congresso Internazionale di Scienze Storiche* that took place in Rome in 1955; its participants included historians who would become immensely influential in their fields: Braudel, Hubert Jedin (a historian of the Counter-Reformation papacy), Jean Meuvret (a historian of French and European agriculture), W. G. Hoskins (whose *The Making of the English Landscape* had just appeared), and Delio Cantimori (the noted historian of the Italian Renaissance). For expansion of Annales historical methods to Italy, see Aymard, "Les *Annales* et l'Italie"; and Jacques Le Goff, "Les *Annales* et l'histoire de l'Italie médiévale," *Mélanges de l'École Française de Rome: Moyen âge* 93, no. 1 (1981): 349–60.

79 For example, the historian of Enlightenment France and reading culture, Robert Darnton recalled recently: "The most exciting kind of history in 1965 was known as 'history from below.' It was an attempt to recapture the experience of ordinary people, especially those in the bottom ranks of society, and to see the past from their perspective. They had never made it into history books . . ." Robert Darnton, "'What Is the History of Books?' Revisited." *Modern Intellectual History* 4, no. 3 (November 2007): 501. Darnton suggests that the impact of Annales history on Anglo-American historians like him came about 1970. See also Robert Darnton, "Two Paths through the Social History of Ideas," in *The Darnton Debate: Books and Revolution in the Eighteenth Century*, ed. Haydn T. Mason, 251–96 (Oxford: Voltaire Foundation, 1998).

80 As an undergraduate in art history at Princeton University in the 1970s, I tried to find common ground between the lectures of Clifford Geertz on the meanings of modernization and of, say, the cockfight in contemporary Bali and those of my professors of art history, who espoused Kantian aesthetics and the iconographical tools of Panofsky's *Meaning in the Visual Arts* (1955) as the means of interpretation for art.

81 For the impact of French theoretical work in America, see François Cusset, *French theory: Foucault, Derrida, Deleuze & Cie et les mutations de la vie intellectuelle aux États-Unis* (Paris: Découverte, 2003).

82 By bringing together English landscape, literature, and painting, Williams influenced an entire generation of English art historians who came of age in the late 1950s and the 1960s and who articulated social histories of art. These included Francis Haskell on early modern European arts, Michael Baxandall on Italian Renaissance arts, Timothy J. Clark on Courbet and French painting, and John Barrell on eighteenth-century English literature, painting, and landscape. See John Barrell, *The Dark Side of the Landscape: The Rural Poor in English Painting, 1730–1840* (Cambridge: Cambridge University Press, 1980). Williams's legacy was transmitted to subsequent generations of scholars interested in the culture of landscapes, including cultural geographers Denis Cosgrove and Stephen Daniels and art historians Ann Bermingham, David Solkin, and Adrian Rifkin. See Denis Cosgrove and Stephen Daniels, eds., *The Iconography of Landscape: Essays on the Symbolic Representation, Design, and Use of Past Environments* (Cambridge: Cambridge University Press, 1988); and Daniels, "Marxism, Culture, and the Duplicity of Landscape."

83 For mediation, base, and superstructure in Raymond Williams, see his publications: "Base and Superstructure in Marxist Cultural Theory," *New Left Review* (November–December 1973): 3–16, and *The Country and the City* (London: Chatto and Windus, 1973). See also Raymond Williams, *Marxism and Literature* (Oxford: Oxford University Press, 1977); and the essays in Terry Eagleton, ed., *Raymond Williams: Critical Perspectives* (Boston: Northeastern University Press, 1989), esp. "Base and Superstructure in Raymond Williams," 165–75.

84 See the following publications by Pierre Bourdieu: "Champs intellectuel et projet créateur" (1966; reprinted in *Anthologie des sociologues français contemporains*, ed. Jean Duvignaud, Paris: Presses Universitaires de France, 1970); "Champs du pouvoir, champs intellectuel et habitus de classe," *Scolies* 1 (1971): 7–26; and "The Genesis of the Concepts of *Habitus* and of *Field*," *Sociocriticism* 2 (December 1985): 11–25.

85 Aron Vinegar and Helene Lipstadt are among the scholars currently working on the relationship between Panofsky and Bourdieu, including Bourdieu's derivation of his notion of "habitus" from Panofsky's study of medieval scholasticism.

86 In 1963, Haskell published *Patrons and Painters: A Study in the Relations between Italian Art and Society in the Age of the Baroque*, which was one of the first attempts to structure the topic of artistic patronage as a social one, although it contained very little on Italian history and society.

87 In a 1977 issue of *Actes de la recherche en sciences sociales*, Bourdieu published Raymond Williams in translation, "Plaisantes perspectives: Invention du paysage et abolition du paysan," alongside his own editorial critique on attitudes to peasantry, "Une classe objet." Raymond Williams, "Plaisantes perspectives: Invention du paysage et abolition du paysan," *Actes de la recherche en sciences sociales* 17–18 (November 1977): 29–36. The June 1979 issue of *Actes de la recherche en sciences sociales* was dedicated to *Les fonctions*

de l'art, and articles by art historians were flanked by those by historians on art, for example, Maurice Agulhon in dialogue with Eric Hobsbawn. The November 1981 issue was dedicated to *Sociologie de l'oeil*, and included Baxandall on "L'oeil du Quattrocento" and Enrico Castelnuovo and Carlo Ginzburg, who together contributed "Domination symbolique et géographie artistique dans l'histoire de l'art italien."

88 Clifford Geertz, *A Life of Learning: Charles Homer Haskins Lecture for 1999* (New York: American Council of Learned Societies, 1999).

89 Clifford Geertz, *The Interpretation of Cultures* (New York: Basic Books, 1973), 5.

90 Ibid., 6 and 9. Some while later, the historian Peter Burke saw the merit of such anthropological and sociological concerns with "the place of symbolism in everyday life," and made them the centerpiece of his *The Historical Anthropology of Early Modern Italy: Essays on Perception and Communication* (Cambridge: Cambridge University Press, 1987), 3–4.

91 See, for example, the response to Bourdieu's writings in Deinhard, "Reflections on Art History and Sociology of Art." See also Baxandall, *Giotto and the Orators*; Baxandall, *Painting and Experience in Fifteenth-Century Italy*; and Castelnuovo, "Per una storia sociale dell'arte."

92 They were preceded in the idea of the villa as a "negative utopia" by Bernhard Rupprecht in his publications: "Villa: Zur Geschichte eines Ideals," in *Wandlungen des Paradiesischen und Utopischen: Studien zum Bild eines Ideals*, ed. Hermann Bauer, 210–50 (Berlin: De Gruyter, 1966); and "L'iconologia nella villa veneta," *Bollettino del Centro Internazionale di Studi di Architettura 'Andrea Palladio'* 10 (1968): 299–340. See also the publications by Reinhard Bentmann and Michael Müller: *Die Villa als Herrschafts-architektur: Versuch einer kunst- und sozialgeschichtlichen Analyse* (Frankfurt: Suhrkamp, 1970); and *The Villa as Hegemonic Architecture*, trans. Tim Spence and David Craven (Atlantic Highlands, N.J.: Humanities Press, 1992).

93 It is important to note that Bentmann and Müller and their followers were indebted to a neo-Marxist strand of art history in Venice itself, in particular that of Michelangelo Muraro (1913–91) on Venetian villas, architecture, and paintings. See his publications: "Civiltà delle ville venete," in *Arte in Europa: Scritti di storia dell'arte in onore di Edoardo Arslan* (Milan: Tipografia Artipo, 1966), 533–43; and "Feudo e ville venete," *Bollettino del Centro Internazionale di Studi di Architettura 'Andrea Palladio'* 10 (1978): 203–23. Muraro first presented his renowned lecture, "Civiltà delle ville venete" at the Bibliotheca Hertziana, Rome, on 23 October 1964.

94 Bentmann and Müller, *Villa as Hegemonic Architecture*, 33–34.

95 Concomitantly with Bentmann's and Müller's book, the Venetian art historian Lionello Puppi contributed a paper on "The Villa Garden of the Veneto from the Fifteenth to the Eighteenth Century" to the Dumbarton Oaks symposium of 1971. David R. Coffin, *The Italian Garden* (Washington, D.C.: Dumbarton Oaks Research Library and Collection, 1972). It too had a neo-Marxist approach, and hewed to the same type of model for base, superstructure, and ideology as theirs. Although Puppi could not demonstrate, in a mediated way, the weave that drew ideological intentions through the design of the Veneto gardens, his was a groundbreaking study.

96 See also Denis Cosgrove, "Venice, the Veneto and Sixteenth-Century Landscape," in *Social Formation and Symbolic Landscape* (London: Croom Helm, 1984), 102–41; and Denis Cosgrove, *The Palladian Landscape: Geographical Change and Its Cultural Representations in Sixteenth-Century Italy* (Leicester: Leicester University Press, 1993).

97 Vittorio Franchetti Pardo, "Le ville medicee nel contado fiorentino (sec. XV–XVI): Ideologia di un investimento patrimoniale," *Storia della città* 6 (1978): 42–57; and Vittorio Franchetti Pardo and Giovanna Casali, *I Medici nel contado fiorentino: Ville e possedimenti agricoli tra Quattrocento e Cinquecento* (Florence: Cooperativa Editrice Universitaria, 1978).

98 See Amanda Lillie, "Florentine Villas in the Fifteenth Century: A Study of the Strozzi and Assetti Country Properties" (PhD diss., Courtauld Institute of Art, 1986), which was recently published as a book, *Florentine Villas in the Fifteenth Century: An Architectural and Social History* (Cambridge: Cambridge University Press, 2005). The very recent Italian literature on the design and use of Veneto villas is particularly rich from the social and economic standpoints.

99 Ackerman, *Villa*, 287n2. Ackerman describes ideology roughly in the sense that Bentmann and Müller used it, but sees himself separate from Marxist interpretation. In an interview of 19 March 1991, situating his own evolution, he said: "For me the big thing in my career has been to get beyond what comes naturally to an American, which is the detective, the positivist, unfolding of what happened when . . . For two-thirds of my career, people weren't even trying to overcome that limitation. Alternatives only began to emerge, all heavily impacted by Europe, in the seventies as a result of the upheavals of the sixties." Ackerman, *Interviews with Art Historians*, 32.

100 Ehrlich, *Landscape and Identity in Early Modern Rome*, 8.

101 As examples, see Frommel, *Der römische Palastbau der Hochrenaissance*, 11–24; Martin Warnke, *Bau und Überbau: Soziologie der mittelalterlichen Architektur nach den Schriftquellen* (Frankfurt: Syndikat, 1976); Martin Warnke, *Politische Architektur in Europa vom Mittelalter bis heute: Repräsentation und Gemeinschaft* (Cologne: DuMont, 1984); Frommel, "Papal Policy: The Planning of Rome during the Renaissance," *Journal of Interdisciplinary History* 17, no. 1 (1986): 39–65; and Martin Warnke, *Politische Landschaft: Zur Kunstgeschichte der Natur* (Munich: C. Hamer,

1992). Chapter two ("Palastbau und Urbanistik im Rom der Hochrenaissance") of Frommel's monumental, three-volume study interprets the political nature of urbanistic interventions by Roman families in the siting and decoration of their palaces.

102 See, for example, MacDougall's essays, republished in *Fountains, Statues, and Flowers: Studies in Italian Gardens of the Sixteenth and Seventeenth Centuries* (Washington, D.C.: Dumbarton Oaks Research Library and Collection, 1994); and Roy C. Strong's very original study of courtly festivals in Europe, *Splendour at Court: Renaissance Spectacle and the Theatre of Power* (London: Weidenfield and Nicolson, 1973), expanded with a new title, *Art and Power: Renaissance Festivals 1450–1650* (Woodbridge, Suffolk: Boydell, 1984). For the context, see Beneš, "Recent Developments and Perspectives in the Historiography of Italian Gardens," 47–58.

103 Stanislaus von Moos, *Turm und Bollwerk: Beiträge zu einer politischen Ikonographie der italienischen Renaissancearchitektur* (Zurich: Atlantis, 1974), 9. Von Moos worked on his book, a revision of his dissertation, in 1964–71, at the Bibliotheca Hertziana in Rome. Like Frommel at this time, he was attempting to break out of the box of the iconographical study of architecture. Other early examples of the approach include Kurt W. Forster's articles: "Metaphors of Rule: Political Ideology and History in the Portraits of Cosimo I de' Medici," *Mitteilungen des Kunsthistorischen Institutes in Florenz* 15, no. 1 (1971): 65–104; and "Back to the Farm: Vernacular Architecture and the Development of the Renaissance Villa," *Architectura* 1 (1974): 1–12.

104 On Coffin's methodologies, see James S. Ackerman, review of *The Villa in the Life of Renaissance Rome*, by David R. Coffin, *Journal of the Society of Architectural Historians* 39 (1980): 242–43; and Beneš, "Recent Developments and Perspectives in the Historiography of Italian Gardens," 58–59. MacDougall's article, "A Circus, a Wild Man and a Dragon: Family History and the Villa Mattei" (1983), reprinted in *Fountains, Statues, and Flowers*, did not treat the Mattei family's history as social history but as relevant background. Coffin's approach was similar in his other publications: *The Villa in the Life of Renaissance Rome* (Princeton, N.J.: Princeton University Press, 1979); and *Gardens and Gardening in Papal Rome* (Princeton, N.J.: Princeton University Press, 1991).

105 Ehrlich, *Landscape and Identity in Early Modern Rome*, 8 and passim.

106 Ackerman, review of *Villa in the Life of Renaissance Rome*, 242–43.

107 Ibid., 242.

108 Ibid., 243. Ackerman's criticism centered on Coffin's lack of conclusions and synthesis: "it leaves the book without an interpretation of the rich data it offers, and without a thesis."

109 Ibid., 242–43.

110 Ackerman continued: "In their instrumental role, they had utilitarian functions, relating less to the comfort of the owner than to his ambitions." However, Ackerman is more hesitant on the potential of studying the historical, spatial, and formal embedding of social structures in architecture and gardens: "Although there is no way to validate securely observations on the impact of such particular social situations on design, speculation on the subject is warranted . . ." Ibid., 243.

111 Claudia Lazzaro, "The Villa Lante at Bagnaia: An Allegory of Art and Nature," *The Art Bulletin* 40, no. 4 (December 1977): 553–60; and Claudia Lazzaro, *The Italian Renaissance Garden: From the Conventions of Planting, Design, and Ornament to the Grand Gardens of Sixteenth-Century Central Italy* (New Haven: Yale University Press, 1990).

112 Manfredo Tafuri, "Via Giulia: Storia di una struttura urbana," in *Via Giulia: Una utopia urbanistica del 500*, eds. Luigi Salerno, Luigi Spezzaferro, and Manfredo Tafuri (Rome: A. Staderini, 1973), 72.

113 Geertz, *Interpretation of Cultures*, 5.

114 Manfredo Tafuri, *Teorie e storia dell'architettura* (Bari: Laterza, 1968), 8–10; and Manfredo Tafuri, "History as Project: An Interview with Manfredo Tafuri," by Luisa Passerini, *Architecture New York (ANY)* 25–26 (2000): 36, 43, 46–47, 60, and 67.

115 See the following publications by Manfredo Tafuri: *Materiali per il corso di storia dell' architettura II.a A. 1978/79 (Francesco Borromini)* (Venice: CLUVA Libreria Editrice and Istituto Universitario di Architettura di Venezia, Dipartimento di Analisi Critica e Storica, 1979); "'Roma instaurata': Strategie urbane e politiche pontificie nella Roma del primo '500," in *Raffaello Architetto*, eds. Christoph Luitpold Frommel, Stefano Ray, and Manfredo Tafuri, 59–106 (Milan: Electa, 1984); and *Ricerca del Rinascimento: Principi, città, architetti* (Turin: G. Einaudi, 1992).

116 See Tafuri, "History as Project," 36 and 44. By comparison, Frommel addressed the same key issues about palaces and streets in Renaissance Rome, but considered them as an iconography of architectural history, using the frameworks of Richard Krautheimer. Frommel, *Der römische Palastbau der Hochrenaissance*, 11–24.

117 Tafuri, "History as Project," 43. The question was "how to invent forms of aggregation . . . in such a way that the art historian, instead of always looking at paintings and drawings of architecture, would come into direct confrontation with those who study social history, the history of women in the Veneto, and so on . . . To us, it seemed logical to say that there is the history of art, the history of religion, the history of Turkish literature, because only in this way could we create a context in which the disciplines would be forced to rethink themselves in a mutual context, that is, the context of history." Ibid., 46–47.

118 Ibid., 59–60.

119 The study of Annales historians was key for Tafuri: "I believe that the theme of history as a grand construct of many histories was a turning point for me around 1979 or 1980 . . . It shouldn't be the case that philology is done by one scholar and history by another . . . Then I did seminars on historiographic methods that touched on the subject of art history only slightly, if at all, and entered very deeply into the work of historians of the *Annales* school." Ibid., 59–60, 62, 63, and 67.

120 See the two books by Baxandall (*Giotto and the Orators* and *Painting and Experience in Fifteenth-Century Italy*) and the publications of Joseph Connors: "The Casa dei Filippini in Rome" (PhD diss., Harvard University, 1978); *Borromini and the Roman Oratory*; "Alliance and Enmity in Roman Baroque Urbanism," *Römisches Jahrbuch für Kunstgeschichte* 25 (1989): 207–94; and "Virtuoso Architecture in Cassiano's Rome," in *Cassiano Dal Pozzo's Paper Museum*, eds. Ian Jenkins et al., 2:23–40 (Milan: Olivetti, 1992).

121 While preparing this article for publication, I read Allan Langdale's excellent essay, "Aspects of the Critical Reception and Intellectual History of Baxandall's Concept of the Period Eye," in *About Michael Baxandall*, ed. Adrian Rifkin, 17–35 (Oxford and Malden, Mass.: Blackwell, 1999), in which he dissects the intellectual heritage of Baxandall's early books, and identifies the Marxist critique of them. He also, as I do here, connects him with Geertz and Bourdieu.

122 "On one level architectural history is simply the record of a building's construction . . . It tells the story of an outer shell. But on another level it is the history of the intangible elements that surround a building, such as the financial institutions that allowed or encouraged the shell to be built, the ephemeral life that formerly unfolded within it, and the language of corporate symbolism that the structure once spoke." Connors, *Borromini and the Roman Oratory*, 59.

123 See the following publications by Connors: *Borromini and the Roman Oratory*; "Alliance and Enmity in Roman Baroque Urbanism"; and "Virtuoso Architecture in Cassiano's Rome." Connors's article, "Ars Tornandi: Baroque Architecture and the Lathe," *Journal of the Warburg and Courtauld Institutes* 53 (1990): 217–36, has a particular resonance with Baxandall's approach. Using the example of Borromini's spiral lantern atop Sant'Ivo alla Sapienza in Rome, Connors has recently pointed out how an educated reading public, from the Baroque until today, discerns meanings and loads an architectural form with meanings inspired by their readings, "broder des couches de figures rhétoriques autour d'un noyau symbolique." This reading public, then and now, and not the creator-architects nor the users, become "les faiseurs de sens." Joseph Connors, "Comment interpréter un édifice? Le cas de Saint-Yves-de-la-Sapience," in *Méthodes en histoire de l'architecture*, ed. Sabine Frommel (Paris: Monum, 2002), 108.

124 Elisabeth Blair MacDougall, "Villa Mattei and the Development of the Roman Garden Style," 68–72, identified a major turning point in the development of what she called "the Roman garden style" in the creation of the Villa Montalto-Peretti, which was begun around 1576 on the Viminal Hill for Cardinal Felice Peretti, later Pope Sixtus V (r. 1585–90). Coffin concurred: "the significant history of the seventeenth-century Roman villa is more a history of garden and landscape design than of architectural design." Coffin, *Villa in the Life of Renaissance Rome*, 366–69. For the shift in the design of Roman gardens, from villa gardens to villas as estates, see Beneš, "Villa Pamphilj (1630–1670)," 139–58; Beneš, "Landowning and the Villa in the Social Geography of the Roman Territory," 9–11, 13–16, and 187–88; and Ehrlich, *Landscape and Identity in Early Modern Rome*, 7 and passim. Earlier literature on the Roman villa parks includes Armando Schiavo, *Villa Doria Pamphilj* (Milan: Alfieri and Lacroix, 1942); Schwager, "Kardinal Pietro Aldobrandinis Villa di Belvedere in Frascati"; Heilmann, "Die Entstehungsgeschichte der Villa Borghese in Rom"; Armando Schiavo, *Villa Ludovisi e Palazzo Margherita* (Rome: Editrice Roma Amor, on behalf of the Banca Nazionale del Lavoro, 1981); di Gaddo, *Villa Borghese*; Beneš, "Villa Pamphilj (1630–1670)"; Coffin, *Gardens and Gardening in Papal Rome*, 139–158; and Matthias Quast, *Die Villa Montalto in Rom: Entstehung und Gestalt im Cinquecento* (Munich: Tuduv, 1991). More recently, see for example, Carla Benocci, *Villa Doria Pamphilj* (Rome: Editalia, 1996); Beneš, "The Social Significance of Transforming the Landscape of the Villa Borghese, 1606–1630"; Alberta Campitelli, *Villa Borghese: Da giardino del principe a parco dei romani* (Rome: Istituto Poligrafico e Zecca dello Stato, Libreria dello Stato, 2003); Carla Benocci, ed., *I giardini Chigi tra Siena e Roma: Dal Cinquecento agli inizi dell'Ottocento* (Siena: Protagon, Fondazione Monte dei Paschi di Siena, 2005); Hervé Brunon, "Dalle 'fiere non rapaci' ai 'fruttiferi e pomati arbori': Villa Lante a Bagnaia e l'evoluzione del barco nel Rinascimento," in *Villa Lante a Bagnaia*, ed. Sabine Frommel, 31–43 (Milan: Electa, 2005); Tracy L. Ehrlich, "Pastoral Landscape and Social Politics in Baroque Rome," in *Baroque Garden Cultures: Emulation, Sublimation, Subversion*, ed. Michel Conan, 131–81 (Washington, D.C.: Dumbarton Oaks Research Library and Collection, 2005); and Marcella Culatti, *Villa Montalto Negroni: Fortuna iconografica di un luogo perduto di Roma* (Venice: Istituto Veneto di Scienze, Lettere ed Arti, 2009).

125 During this period, the villa grounds in the Roman Campagna and castle fieflands in the hilltowns were also transformed into parks, as at the Villa Mondragone at Frascati, and older castle parks were modernized, as at the Palazzo Chigi at Ariccia (1656–70). Ehrlich, *Landscape and Identity in Early Modern Rome*; Benocci, *I giardini Chigi tra Siena e Roma*; and, for an earlier model of villa parklands, such as the Villa Lante at Bagnaia, Brunon, "Dalle 'fiere non rapaci' ai 'fruttiferi e pomati arbori'."

126 A convincing explanation of another feature of the Montalto-Peretti, Borghese, Ludovisi, and Pamphilj villas, namely the duality of formal gardens and parkland,

had already been proposed by Claudia Lazzaro for the Villa Lante at Bagnaia (ca. 1568–78), which also comprises formal gardens and a park. Lazzaro interpreted the contrast as a metaphor of that between art and nature, readable through the symbolic representations of that duality in the sculptures and fountains that are laid out in both parts of the villa. Lazzaro, "Villa Lante at Bagnaia."

127 Delumeau, *Vie économique et sociale de Rome dans la seconde moitié du XVIe siècle.*

128 See, for example, Wolfgang Reinhard, "Papa Pius: Prolegomena zu einer Sozialgeschichte des Papsttums," in *Von Konstanz nach Trient: Beiträge zur Geschichte der Kirche von den Reformkonzilien bis zum Tridentinum; Festgabe für August Franzen*, ed. Remigius Bäumer, 261–99 (Munich: F. Schöningh, 1972); Wolfgang Reinhard, "Ämterlaufbahn und Familienstatus: Der Aufstieg des Hauses Borghese 1537–1621," *Quellen und Forschungen aus Italienischen Archiven und Bibliotheken* 53 (1974): 328–427; Wolfgang Reinhard, *Papstfinanz und Nepotismus unter Paul V (1605–1621): Studien und Quellen zur Struktur und zu quantitativen Aspekten des päpstlichen Herrschaftsystems*, 2 vols. (Stuttgart: A. Hiersemann, 1974); Wolfgang Reinhard, "Nepotismus: Der Funktionswandel einer papstgeschichtlichen Konstanten," *Zeitschrift für Kirchengeschichte* 86 (1975): 145–85; Wolfgang Reinhard, "Herkunft und Karriere der Päpste, 1417–1963: Beiträge zu einer historischen Soziologie der römischen Kurie," *Mededelingen van het Nederlands Instituut te Rome* 38 (1976): 87–108; Renata Ago, "Gli storici italiani e le fortune dell'antropologia: Il dibattito sulla storia sociale in Italia," in *Orientamenti marxisti e studi antropologici italiani: Problemi e dibattiti*, eds. Renata Ago et al., 223–29 (Milan: F. Angeli, 1980); Laurie Nussdorfer, "City Politics in Baroque Rome, 1623–1644" (PhD diss., Princeton University, 1985); Renata Ago, *Carriere e clientele nella Roma barocca* (Rome: Laterza, 1990); Laurie Nussdorfer, *Civic Politics in the Rome of Urban VIII* (Princeton, N.J.: Princeton University Press, 1992); Laurie Nussdorfer, "The Politics of Space in Early Modern Rome," *The Memoirs of the American Academy in Rome* 42 (1997): 161–86; and Maria Antonietta Visceglia and Gianvittorio Signorotto, eds., *La corte di Roma tra Cinque e Seicento: Teatro della politica europea* (Rome: Bulzoni, 1998).

129 "Styles of thought" is a phrase from Geertz. For his focus on "systems of meaning, beliefs, values, world views, forms of feeling, styles of thought, in terms of which particular peoples construct their existence," see www.ias.edu/newsroom/announcements/view/geertz-1926-2006.html, an obituary of Clifford Geertz, who from 1970 to his death in 2006 was on the faculty of the School of Social Sciences at the Institute of Advanced Study, Princeton University. For anthropology and history, see Ago, "Gli storici italiani e le fortune dell'antropologia." Reinhard came to these studies from German, French, and American anthropology and sociology, as indicated in his study of patronage and clientele systems at the papal court, *Freunde und Kreaturen: 'Verflechtung' als Konzept zur Erforschung historischer Führungsgruppen; Römische Oligarchie um 1600* (Munich: Ernst Vögel, 1979). See Nussdorfer, *Civic Politics in the Rome of Urban VIII*, 3–16 (which was based on her PhD dissertation at Princeton University); and Mark Silk, "The Hot History Department: Princeton's Influential Faculty," *New York Times Magazine*, 19 April 1987. On "historical anthropology," see Burke, *Historical Anthropology of Early Modern Italy*, 3–24. Clifford Geertz and several historians merged forces at Princeton University, among them Natalie Davis, Lawrence Stone, Robert Darnton, and Peter Brown.

130 Nussdorfer, *Civic Politics in the Rome of Urban VIII*, 4–5.

131 On the land properties for the Villa Pamphilj and their contexts, see Beneš, "Villa Pamphilj (1630–1670)," 539–69 and 599–853; and Beneš, "Landowning and the Villa in the Social Geography of the Roman Territory."

132 Coste, "I casali della Campagna di Roma all'inizio del Seicento"; Jean-Claude Maire-Vigueur, "Les grands domaines de la Campagne Romaine dans la seconde moitié du XIVe siècle" (Thèse d'état, Université Paris I Sorbonne, 1974); and Volker Reinhardt, *Kardinal Scipione Borghese (1605–1633): Vermögen, Finanzen und sozialer Aufstieg eines Papstnepoten* (Tübingen: M. Niemeyer, 1984).

133 Maire-Vigueur, "Les grands domaines de la Campagne Romaine dans la seconde moitié du XIVe siècle," 40–42; and Coste, "La topographie médiévale de la campagne romaine et l'histoire socio-économique," 621.

134 Reinhard, *Papstfinanz und Nepotismus unter Paul V (1605–1621)*; and Nussdorfer, "City Politics in Baroque Rome, 1623–1644."

135 Since the later sixteenth century, the Roman barons had become increasingly indebted and had to sell their lands, because on the one hand they attempted to remain competitive in the increasingly luxurious way of life of the new aristocracy, and because on the other, they did not have access to the system of papal nepotism that was enriching their rivals. See Delumeau, *Vie économique et sociale de Rome dans la seconde moitié du XVIe siècle*, 1:457–58 and 1:469–85 (for the barons' debts), and 1:471–81 (for the sale of the lands).

136 Beneš, "Villa Pamphilj (1630–1670)"; and Beneš, "Landowning and the Villa in the Social Geography of the Roman Territory."

137 Braudel, *Mediterranean and the Mediterranean World in the Age of Philip II*, 22.

138 Tafuri, "Via Giulia: Storia di una struttura urbana"; Tafuri, "'Roma instaurata': Strategie urbane e politiche pontificie nella Roma del primo '500"; and Nussdorfer, "The Politics of Space in Early Modern Rome."

139 Geertz, *Interpretation of Cultures*, 5.

140 Beneš, "Pastoralism in the Roman Baroque Villa and in Claude Lorrain"; and Mirka Beneš, "Claude Lorrain's Pendant Landscapes of 1646–50 for Camillo Pamphilj, Nephew of Pope Innocent X: Classicism, Architecture, and

Gardens as Contexts for the Artist's Roman Patronage," *Storia dell'arte* 112 (2005): 37–90.

141 See Daniels, "Marxism, Culture, and the Duplicity of Landscape"; and Daniels, *Humphry Repton*.

142 Lionella Scazzosi, "Giardini e paesaggi 'opera aperta': I limiti delle trasformazioni," in *Giardini storici: A 25 anni dalle Carte di Firenze; Esperienze e prospettive*, eds. Laura Sabrina Pelissetti and Lionella Scazzosi, 2:131–57 (Florence: L. S. Olschki, 2009); and Lionella Scazzosi, "Gardens and Landscapes as 'Open-Ended Works' between Continuity and Transformation: Notes on the Role of Historical Studies," this volume.

143 Esposito, "Vigneti e orti entro le mura."

144 Mauro Ambrosoli, *Scienzati, contadini e proprietari: Botanica e agricoltura nell'Europa occidentale, 1350–1850* (Turin: G. Einaudi, 1992); and Mauro Ambrosoli, "From the Italian Countryside to the Italianate Landscape: Peasants as Gardeners and Foreign Observers in Italy, 1500–1850," this volume.

145 For concerns that the influence of Annales and interdisciplinary studies might lead to scholarly neglect of the material and formal qualities of Italian gardens, for example in my own work, see Azzi Visentini, "Storia dei giardini: Osservazioni in margine al recente sviluppo di questa disciplina in Italia"; Zalum, "La storia del giardino italiano," 2 and 11; and Azzi Visentini, "Riflessioni intorno alla fortuna critica del giardino storico italiano negli Stati Uniti negli ultimi trentacinque anni," 42n20 and 45.

146 This is, as well, a general critique that has been made of Annales writing. A later phase of Annales studies focused on mental habits or conceptions in societies (*histoire des mentalités*), and these provide a bridge to understanding the vast range of cultural signs, including the literary associations that iconography could decode, in the study of landscapes. For history of mentalités, see Burke, *French Historical Revolution*, 17–18, 67–74, and 115; and Bédarida, *L'histoire et le métier d'historien en France 1945–1995*.

147 Beneš, "Pastoralism in the Roman Baroque Villa and in Claude Lorrain"; and Beneš, "Claude Lorrain's Pendant Landscapes of 1646–50 for Camillo Pamphilj, Nephew of Pope Innocent X."

148 Ehrlich, *Landscape and Identity in Early Modern Rome*; and Ehrlich, "Pastoral Landscape and Social Politics in Baroque Rome." How specifically the intentions of the owner-patrons can be documented in the conception and design of the pastoral landscape at Frascati, and similar designed landscapes, is questioned in Hervé Brunon, "Articuler pratiques et représentations paysagères en histoire de l'art: Recherches récentes sur l'Italie à la Renaissance," in *Paysage et environnement: De la reconstitution du passé aux modèles prospectifs*, ed. Didier Galop, 461–69 (Besançon: Presses Universitaires de Franche-Comté, 2008).

149 Examples are Dianne Harris, "Landscape and Representation: The Printed View and Marc'Antonio dal Re's *Ville di Delizie*," in *Villas and Gardens in Early Modern Italy and France*, eds. Mirka Beneš and Dianne Harris, 178–206 (Cambridge: Cambridge University Press, 2001); Harris, *Nature of Authority*; and Claudia Lazzaro, "Representing the Social and Cultural Experience of Italian Gardens in Prints," in *The Changing Garden: Four Centuries of European and American Art*, ed. Betsy G. Fryberger, 29–39 (Berkeley, Calif.: Iris and B. Gerald Cantor Center for Visual Arts at Stanford University, 2003).

150 See, most recently, the publications written by Benocci (*Villa Doria Pamphilj*; *Villa Il Vascello* [Rome, Erasmo, 2003]; and *I giardini Chigi tra Siena e Roma*) and written and edited by Campitelli (*Villa Borghese: Da giardino del principe a parco dei romani*; *Villa Borghese: I principi, le arti, la città dal Settecento all'Ottocento*; *Verdi delizie: Le ville, i giardini, i parchi storici del Comune di Roma* [Rome: De Luca, 2005]; and *Villa Borghese: Storia e gestione* [Milan: Skira Editore, 2005]). Both Benocci and Campitelli work in the Roman municipal administration, in dual roles as historians and curators. Campitelli is a trained architect and art historian, and has been the curator of Villa Borghese for two decades. She has published many books on Roman villa gardens and their sculpture and horticulture collections from the seventeenth through the nineteenth centuries, and on the principles of garden restoration. Today she is Dirigente dell'Ufficio Ville e Parchi Storici della Sovrintendenza ai Beni Culturali del Comune di Roma, and she is in charge of some forty gardens and parks in Rome. Carla Benocci, who also trained as an art historian, has dual responsibilities like Campitelli; she is in charge of the Villa Pamphilj and many other villa gardens in the area of the Via Aurelia on the Janiculum Hill. Both have devoted their careers and studies to Roman villa gardens with a particular approach: they have worked for decades in the Vatican archives (for the Borghese papers) and the private Pamphilj family archive (for the Pamphilj papers), and have sought a very wide range of materials in order to document and fully reconstruct every historical structure and designed planting in the Villas Borghese and Pamphilj, respectively. Both of them collaborate interdisciplinarily in their publications with a range of scholars, from historians (see Benocci, *I giardini Chigi tra Siena e Roma*) to garden preservationists (see Campitelli, *Villa Borghese: Storia e gestione*).

CHAPTER 2

"Grafting the Edelweiss on Cactus Plants": The 1931 Italian Garden Exhibition and Its Legacy

RAFFAELLA FABIANI GIANNETTO

AN ITALIAN GARDEN IS OFTEN PERCEIVED AS a work of art designed according to the same principles of symmetry and proportion that guided Renaissance architects in the composition of buildings (fig. 2.1). This type of garden is praised for its enchanting timelessness, which can be attributed to its use of stonework, evergreen trees, and clipped hedges that appear as if they never grow. This very quality has informed, and still informs, our perception of the Italian garden tradition, which is often understood as something that has always existed—just like the idea of Italy, even though Italy became a unified political entity only in 1861. But while notions of Italy informed Italian culture long before the Risorgimento, the identification of the Italian garden with the geometric type—which is said to have taken shape between the sixteenth and eighteenth centuries—is an entirely modern construct.

This paper will address some of the cultural, political, and methodological explanations for the genesis of the Italian garden concept in the first half of the twentieth century, when Italian scholars promoted the idea of a national garden as part of their effort to document a continuous cultural tradition under the auspices of local fascist authorities. The historical narratives produced during the years of the fascist regime, as we shall see, had an impact on the following sixty years of Italian garden studies, as is particularly evident in the scholarship on Medici gardens.

In the early twentieth century, an effort was made to unify the diversity and richness of the Italian regions, each with its different artistic traditions, under a common cultural and political umbrella. Italian scholars constructed a generalized ideal of the national garden coincident with the architectonic type, which they documented at the first Mostra del Giardino Italiano held in Florence at the Palazzo Vecchio in 1931 (fig. 2.2).[1] The exhibition signaled the awakening of Italian scholarly interest in a subject that had previously attracted the attention of foreign intellectuals almost exclusively.[2] But the motivations behind the Italians' identification of the architectonic garden with their own nation were altogether different from those of their English and American predecessors. The Italian garden was described by the exhibition catalogue as the "garden of the intellect," thereby reflecting the chauvinistic ideals brought about by the fascist ideology of the second quarter of the century.[3] The aim of the

FIGURE 2.1. Giusto Utens, *Castello*, 1599. Museo Firenze Com'era, Florence.

Photograph courtesy of the Ministero per i Beni e le Attività Culturali.

exhibition was to "revive" the *giardino all'italiana*, which had been pronounced dead by Luigi Dami in 1924. He associated the decline of the national garden style with the eighteenth-century moment when painting replaced architecture as the most important source of inspiration for garden design. It seems that Dami, together with architectural critic Ugo Ojetti, considered the possibility of an exhibition focused on the architectonic garden style as early as 1912. However, according to Nello Tarchiani, the secretary general of the 1931 exhibition, the time was not right for a public display of national gardens.[4]

There are a number of reasons why the 1930s were considered the most propitious time for the Mostra del Giardino Italiano. In the exhibition catalogue, Ojetti wrote that the Italian garden had recently come back to life—"torna di moda"—outside of Italy, and especially in North America, where one could see an "ostentatious return of reason in architecture."[5] Some scholars have taken this statement to suggest that the revival of the Italian garden had been brought about by the so-called Rationalism that was guiding the development of contemporary architecture.[6] On the contrary, a review of the exhibition published in the architectural journal of the Italian rationalists, *Casabella*, said precisely the opposite—that is, that the revival of the Italian tradition of garden art was yet to take place, and that the efforts of the exhibition organizers to present their agenda as something that had already happened were vain and unrealistic.[7]

The 1930s saw intense debates between rationalists and traditionalists: the rationalists accused the traditionalists (also called the *culturalisti*) of promoting a sterile revival of Neoclassical and Baroque architecture in order to shape the monumental scale that was increasingly demanded of state architecture, with the sole result of transforming Italy into a museum of itself; the traditionalists accused the members of the Movimento Italiano per l'Architettura Razionalista (MIAR) of being iconoclasts, betraying their home country, and consorting with foreign ideas while producing an architecture without content or spirit.[8] Notwithstanding these criticisms, the traditionalists and rationalists had something in common—they both competed for the approval of Il Duce, without which their initiatives—so they thought—were either destined to remain unborn or bound to a very short life.

On 14 February 1931, the Milanese newspaper *L'ambrosiano* published "Petizione a Mussolini per l'architettura" by Pietro Maria Bardi. The petition was a public defense of rational architecture. This, the author maintained, had Italian, even Roman, roots; one of its exemplary structures, the Coliseum, was cited as a model of rational building. Bardi argued that it was not unreasonable for architects to draw inspiration from foreign examples while they "took a vacation" from Italian traditions. The petition was also an attempt to gain governmental support for an ideal that was widely shared among fascism's proponents: the moral renewal of Italy. The author suggested that the legislation governing urban planning and building, and in particular the committees who made use of such legislation, were impediments to the restoration of architecture's artistic freedom.[9] The traditionalist committees that Bardi asked Il Duce to abolish, however, had been created with the intent of defining a shared Italian culture and promoting it by means of public events, which became venues for political propaganda. Thus, the rationalists and the traditionalists competed to determine whose philosophy adhered more closely to the fascist ideal. Although both groups maintained that their perspectives were rooted exclusively in the purest Italian tradition, the local fascist authorities would come to favor the traditionalists in their definition of the national garden, as their arguments could appeal to the masses more than the (perhaps too sophisticated) arguments offered by the rationalists.[10]

Therefore, the political and intellectual climate—which involved not only aesthetic concerns but also cultural matters, issues of national identity, and civilization—explains the timing of the first exhibition of the Italian garden. In the early 1920s, the concept of a national garden would probably not have made much sense to the average working-class Italian—whom the government now considered the most important audience for the exhibition—because it was mostly foreign scholars who visited, wrote about, and owned the most beautiful of the "Italian" villas, at least in Florence. Ten years later, however, the high profile of foreigners helped fuel the regime's strategy for a new political and cultural propaganda within the Tuscan region. Fascist leaders sought to protect Florence from the interests of the "foreign expatriates who had for decades served as its unofficial guardians."[11] By founding such institutions as the Accademia Reale d'Italia[12] and, in particular, the Florentine Exhibition Committee, the regime encouraged Italian scholars to regain possession of their cultural patrimony and to make it available to all Italians by means of public events in which all were encouraged to participate as a patriotic duty.

FIGURE 2.2.
Lithograph printed for the Mostra del Giardino Italiano, 1931.
Photograph courtesy of the Archivio Storico Comune di Firenze.

In Florence, the most important event was the *Primavera Fiorentina*, which occurred every year from the spring to the autumn equinox. The program, which was organized by the fascist secretary of the city, Alessandro Pavolini, included a number of cultural, historical, religious, commercial, folkloristic, and sporting events that engaged and entertained a heterogeneous group of people.[13] Among the most celebrated and popular events was the *calcio fiorentino*, a soccer game in which players wore Renaissance costumes to commemorate a sport played in sixteenth-century Florence. The event, which occurred in 1930 and 1931, was promoted by foreign newspapers in conjunction with ads for guided tours of the Tuscan villas.[14]

However, as D. Medina Lasansky has pointed out, the cultural heritage offered to the people of Italy was reinterpreted—and sometimes rewritten, with a de-emphasis on historical accuracy—in order to achieve public consensus.[15] For instance, certain festivals that were said to date to a very specific historical time—such as the Renaissance—were reintroduced by the regime without regard to the changes that inevitably occurred during the intervening centuries. Lasansky noted: "It was not until the Fascist era that each of these festivals assumed [particularly in Tuscany] an identifiably medieval/Renaissance form, a fixed location within the city, and a fixed date on the national ritual calendar."[16] The staging of these festivals was a political strategy, and a very effective one, as it allowed the regime not only to bring a number of Italian intellectuals, those who were entrusted with the organization of specific cultural events, into the fold of fascism, but also to manipulate, through them, the unaware masses.

The Mostra del Giardino Italiano was probably the most important and ambitious event of the Primavera Fiorentina. Presented to Il Duce, the program had been approved for the year 1931. In addition to the exhibition at the Palazzo Vecchio, the original proposal called for the organization of tours at the most famous Tuscan villas, the re-creation of historical gardens at the Parco delle Cascine, and the design of four modern giardini all'italiana by public competition. Although more than one million programs for the Primavera Fiorentina had been printed and distributed in Italy and abroad by fall 1930, the organizers themselves raised doubts as to whether the promised program could be carried out. The reconstruction of the historical gardens, in particular, proved to be a difficult enterprise, especially with regard to the economic and time constraints. Some committee members suggested that they limit the construction of new gardens to modern ones: "We should highlight as much as possible the art of the modern garden by inviting noted architects to work together with horticulturists and compete to create some modern gardens. We will spend much less money this way and can be sure to have the gardens completed by next spring."[17]

But emphasizing modern gardens was not a simple task. Committee member Carlo Mercatelli argued that "the modern Italian garden does not exist;"[18] others maintained that, in order to create a modern garden, architects would have to spend a long time studying and drawing inspiration from the historical gardens of Italy. But, the question was, which ones in particular? The answer here was an easy one. As in the case of the calcio fiorentino, the preference was given to the Renaissance gardens, with no consideration whatsoever for examples from other historical periods. Thus, Romantic gardens—"that are, in the end, only a derivation of the old Italian gardens"[19]—were purposefully ignored in order to highlight only one type of garden to represent the nation.[20] In order to make the intentions of the exhibition clear to everybody, it was necessary, as Ojetti remarked, "to give precise instructions to these [regional] committees from here . . . We must hire architects . . . to draw plans and rough sketches of the [types of] gardens that we want to create."[21]

For the exhibition at the Palazzo Vecchio, the regional committees could not interpret freely their idea of the national garden. They were given specific instructions on the types of materials needed to illustrate the characteristics of the Italian garden and to testify to its presence throughout the country. Committee members were supposed to make an inventory of regional Italian-style gardens: those that still existed, those that had been modified, and those that were no longer extant but had been reproduced in paintings, prints, and drawings. Particularly difficult was the task of documenting fourteenth- and fifteenth-century gardens. With regard to these, the regional committees were told to look for paintings and tapestries. Thus, for example, the lunettes painted by Giusto Utens in 1599 for Ferdinando de'Medici were exhibited to illustrate the appearance of the early Medici villas of Il Trebbio and Cafaggiolo.

But not everyone agreed with the instructions. Francesco Fichera, a member of the Sicilian committee in charge of looking for those insular gardens that could be considered exemplary of the architectonic style, asked: "How will Sicily participate in the garden exhibition, which will open soon in Florence, and where the norm will be architectonic Italian gardens? *Architectonic gardens*: were this not the definition, three-quarters of Sicily could be represented . . . [If] *Architectonic gardens* [are the norm] . . . our contribution will be very modest" (emphasis in original).[22]

In their correspondence, the members of the organizing committee in Florence said that the exhibition needed to present gardens from nearly one hundred of the most famous villas—that is, those with which the hypothetical visitor (or *mediamente intelligente*) would be familiar.[23] Moreover, in the documents related to the construction of model gardens exhibited in the Salone dei Cinquecento, they argued that their intention was to have each model represent a particular garden type "because in the minds of the public, not used to abstractions or synthesis, it will be easier to understand what a sixteenth-century Florentine garden . . . was like through an ideal model that does not represent the numerous variations of specific gardens that exist or once existed" (fig. 2.3).[24] These instructions were not motivated by historical accuracy, but rather driven by a hastily put together historicism. Their goal was to achieve a garden archetype to convince middle-class Italians of the existence of a common and national cultural patrimony. In short, the aim of the model gardens was to offer a static image of a shared artistic past where garden art had always been homogeneous and stylistically consistent.

According to Fichera, the appeal to the spirit of the common people was the only positive aspect of the Mostra del Giardino Italiano. He sarcastically wrote that the Italians visiting the exhibition would not familiarize themselves with useless contemporary debates between traditionalists and rationalists;

FIGURE 2.3. Enrico Lusini, model of the Quattrocento Florentine garden exhibited in the Mostra del Giardino Italiano.

Photograph courtesy of Alinari Archives, Florence.

rather, they would learn how to distinguish Italian flowers from foreign ones: "It is precious knowledge at a moment like today when—in the name of youth, modernity, and fascism—some attempt to graft the edelweiss on cactus plants."[25] But Italians already knew how to distinguish native plants from imported ones. What they did not recognize, as Fichera's ironic metaphor suggests, was that by grafting northern edelweiss flowers onto southern cacti, the Florentine Exhibition Committee was attempting to impose the idea of a unique national garden—an idea that they imported from Germany—on a Mediterranean country that was characterized by multiple regional differences.[26] These differences, which included variations in garden architecture, were ignored by the organizers of the exhibition in the name of a nationalistic rhetoric aimed at establishing an officially sanctioned version of Italian art. Part of the regime's political strategy was to actively encourage middle-class citizens to visit the cultural events, such as the Mostra del Giardino Italiano. For example, they printed thirty thousand lithographs to advertise the *riduzioni ferroviarie* (reduced train fares) and extended opening hours for the exhibition. These efforts attracted a large number of visitors, who left the premises with a clear sense of their own country's cultural identity.[27]

Within this climate, Ojetti's remarks in the exhibition catalogue are self-evident: "the goal of this exhibition is to reclaim a place of honor for our singular art, which, after having conquered the world, has been obfuscated by other fashions and hidden under foreign names."[28] The exhibition sought to reclaim the national garden from the Italian scholars who had associated it with the natural or modern garden in the Risorgimento and from the foreign scholars who had carefully created the image of the architectonic Italian garden at the turn of the twentieth century. Before that time, the garden tradition of Italy was not associated with the principles of formal design. In 1792, for example, the poet Ippolito Pindemonte tried to establish the Italian claim to the picturesque garden, whose morphology is not at all architectural. Moved by patriotic emotions, he wrote that John Milton derived his descriptions of untamed nature—from which the English picturesque garden was said to have originated—from the poet Torquato Tasso, who described, in *La Gerusalemme liberata* (1580), a garden that, despite its "natural" appearance, was created by the art of man.[29] Hence, Pindemonte argued that the picturesque garden had originated in Tasso's Italy rather than in Milton's England. It was not until the end of the nineteenth century that the Italianness of geometric layouts, symmetry, and clipped hedges would be spelled out by the American and British citizens—including men and women of letters, art historians and critics, collectors of Quattrocento Italian art, and connoisseurs—who traveled to Italy in an effort to shorten the cultural distance between the Old and the New Worlds.[30] These foreign intellectuals produced the first narratives of the history of what they thought was the Italian garden. In order to narrate the origin of its design, a few of them systematically toured and surveyed the most important villas in Italy. Their objective was not only to write a history of Italian gardens, but also to identify and explain the architectonic garden's principles of design, so that their readers could easily employ them at their villas in Tuscany or in their home countries. Although most of these studies constituted an invaluable source of information for subsequent scholars, they also contributed to the construction of the Italian garden myth.

Vernon Lee—the pseudonym of the English novelist Violet Paget—lived at the Villa del Palmerino (Maiano, San Gervasio) and wrote an early history of Italian gardens that was included in *Limbo, and Other Essays* (1897). In the chapter entitled "Old Italian Gardens," Lee gave a general definition of gardens before explaining why the typical Italian pleasance is identified with the Renaissance gardens of Rome. She wrote: "Gardens have nothing to do with Nature, or not much. Save the garden of Eden, which was perhaps no more a garden than certain London streets so called, gardens are always primarily the work of man."[31] She then traced the origin of the Italian garden to the descriptions and illustrations of the *Hypnerotomachia Poliphili* (1499) and argued that the best gardens are to be found "in the Roman villas of the late sixteenth and seventeenth centuries," which present "naturally an element of architectural ground-plan and decoration which is easily followed: the terraces of quincunxes, the symmetrical groves, the long flights of steps, the triumphal arches, the big ponds, come, as it were, of themselves, obeying the order of what is below."[32] As a result of such analyses by Vernon Lee and other scholars, toward the end of the nineteenth century, the architectonic garden began to be considered as typically Italian—however, it is significant that this assessment was made by foreign writers who were perhaps moved by the desire to distinguish the gardens of Italy from the noticeably different ones of their home countries.

The influence of Vernon Lee's insights on Italian gardens is felt in the pages of Edith Wharton's *Italian Villas and Their Gardens* (1904).[33] Like Lee, Wharton associated the Italian garden par excellence with the geometric gardens of Renaissance Rome—but she noted that a few examples could be found in Florence. By describing their ethos in terms of magic, she contributed to the myth of the Italian garden. Although she noted that the magic of the Italian garden was ineffable, she was able to identify the principles of design from which its charm stemmed. One of the most important qualities of the geometric garden was the timelessness of its stonework and evergreen foliage, arranged in such a way as to mirror the architecture of the house. Wharton's study allowed the garden lover "to extract" from these Italian gardens "principles which may be applied at home."[34] Similar attempts to encourage the design of architectonic gardens outside of Italy were made by Charles A. Platt and George Sitwell in *Italian Gardens* (1894) and *On the Making of Gardens* (1909), respectively.

The principles of design described by Wharton, Platt, and Sitwell proved very useful, as indicated by the frequent restoration or re-creation of gardens according to the fabricated Italian tradition that their fellow citizens commissioned, both in Italy and abroad, in the years following the publication of their books.[35] It is clear that the critical fortunes of the Italian Renaissance, in terms of its artistic, architectural, and literary achievements, had a bearing on the identification of the formal garden with the Italian nation. A consequence of the new enthusiasm toward the Renaissance was the rejection of anything that recalled earlier centuries of Italian history or any imported trend.

For example, Wharton complained that "the English who have colonized in such numbers the slopes above the Arno have contributed not a little to the destruction of the old gardens by introducing into their horticultural plans two features entirely alien to the Tuscan climate and soil, namely, lawns and deciduous shade-trees. Many, indeed, are the parterres and terraces which have disappeared before the Britannic craving for a lawn." She suggested that "there is much to be learned from the old Italian gardens, and the first lesson is that . . . they must be copied."[36] Similarly, Sitwell judged the whole theory of the English natural garden, which "spread like a plague all over Europe," to be "absolutely unsound." He claimed that the new generation of designers would be responsible for reviving the gardens of the Italian Renaissance, which "for more than two centuries" had lain "under a cloud, exciting . . . little but contempt and disgust in all who viewed them."[37]

Sitwell's call for a revival of Italian Renaissance design principles was answered by Cecil Pinsent and Geoffrey Scott, two English architects who shared a taste for geometric topiary and classical layouts, and who reacted against the English Romantic garden, which was still in vogue in Italy at that time. Pinsent and Scott were also steeped in the debates on the primacy of the Renaissance, and had the cultural background and intellect necessary to satisfy the demands of their patrons, some of whom, like Bernard Berenson were notable Renaissance scholars, art critics, and dealers. In 1914, Scott published his most important theoretical work, *The Architecture of Humanism*, in which he claimed that by replacing the aesthetic interest of form with nature's variety and irregularity, the adherents of Romanticism had caused the disappearance of the formal garden of the Renaissance. He defined this Renaissance garden as "an extension of the main design of the house, which mediates between architecture and Nature insofar as it combines formality of design with naturalness of material."[38]

It is not surprising that most of the wealthy foreigners who owned properties on the outskirts of Florence commissioned their new "old Italian gardens" and villas—which sought to respond to the schemata described by Wharton, Sitwell, and others—from Pinsent and Scott.[39] Among their most notable projects are the Villa I Tatti, which

FIGURE 2.4.
Villa I Tatti, Settignano.
Photograph by John Dixon Hunt.

FIGURE 2.5.
Villa Le Balze, Fiesole.
Photograph by John Dixon Hunt.

was purchased by Bernard and Mary Berenson in 1905 (fig. 2.4); the Villa Le Balze, which was constructed anew together with its architectonic garden for Charles Augustus Strong in 1911 (fig. 2.5); and the Villa Medici at Fiesole, which was restored for Lady Sybil Cutting in 1915 (fig. 2.6).

Foreign writers defined the principles of the architectonic garden and determined that the formal style was most representative of Italy, but they maintained that the typical Italian garden was not to be found everywhere in the country. For example, when describing the gardens of central Italy—such as those of Lorenzo de'Medici in Florence, Caterina Cornaro near Asolo, and the Gonzaga family near Mantua—Vernon Lee pointed out that "they had waterworks already, and aviaries full of costly birds . . . they were the gardens of the castle, of the farm, magnified and made magnificent, spread over a large extent of ground. But they were *not* . . . the typical Italian gardens of later days," as they lacked those elements of "perspective, architecture, decoration" that characterized the Roman gardens created for the popes, cardinals, and their nephews during the Renaissance (emphasis added).[40]

FIGURE 2.6.
Villa Medici, Fiesole.

Photograph by the author.

The historical narratives produced at the beginning of the twentieth century by foreign intellectuals were useful to the fascist scholars in charge of constructing the notion of a unified Italian garden tradition. But the fascist leaders did more than simply appropriate a concept that had largely been defined by foreign scholars. Whereas these scholars stressed the link between Renaissance villas and Rome, the regime went to great lengths to grant the primacy to Florence in an effort to maximize its Renaissance resources. The Florentine Exhibition Committee initiated the reading of the early Medici villas in Florence as the prototypes of the giardino all'italiana.[41] In the exhibition catalogue, the organizers argued that Roman gardens descended from Florentine examples.[42] The Medici family, in particular, was credited with making "the greatest contribution to the art of the garden,"[43] and Lorenzo de'Medici's villa at Poggio a Caiano was described as "the first real grand villa of the Renaissance."[44] In an article about the tour of Tuscan villas organized during the exhibition, Gherardo Bosio described the Medici gardens as the "source out of which flowed the grand river of the Italian garden, which wound its way from the fifteenth century . . . to the 1700s."[45]

Therefore, although the regime's objective was to strengthen a recently formed national identity by insisting on the country's shared culture, the fascist leaders selectively emphasized specific local resources and traditions. Thus, if the celebration of *romanità* and the rhetoric of antiquity took place in Rome,[46] and served to authorize the regime's empire-building agenda, Florence was identified with the Renaissance image of the city, to the shaping of which scholars and foreign intellectuals had already contributed in the nineteenth and early twentieth centuries. The fascist leaders' selective view of history may explain why the celebration of the Italian garden tradition, which was traced back to the Renaissance and the Medici villas, took place in Florence, while the two Esposizioni di Architettura Razionale Italiana (1928 and 1931)—which, as Bardi and other rationalists claimed, drew inspiration from Roman imperial architecture—were held in Rome, the city that had been, and was now again, celebrated as the *caput mundi*. And it is probably for this reason that Rome was not considered an appropriate venue for the first exhibition of Roman Renaissance and Baroque gardens, which was instead held in Turin in 1928.

Whereas foreign scholars regarded the study of Renaissance Florence as an elite preoccupation, the regime transformed it into an experience for the masses. Moreover, whereas English and American scholars acknowledged regional differences and indicated Rome as the birthplace of the formal garden, their Italian successors extended the architectonic garden tradition to the rest of Italy, and made it appear timeless.

The Italian garden discourse that fascist scholars inherited from their foreign predecessors and reshaped during the 1930s had a long-lasting legacy. For many years after the Florentine exhibition, scholars produced formal analyses of gardens that were inspired either by the teleological quest for a prototype of the national garden style or by the urge to represent an improbable continuity within the Italian garden tradition. Moreover, the fact that nineteenth- and twentieth-century gardens (which were typically not designed in the formal style) have only recently begun to receive scholarly attention attests to the profound impact of the 1930s debates on Italian garden studies—in particular their insistence on the formal garden as the only type worthy of attention.[47]

In his two-volume study, *Le ville di Firenze* (1954), Giulio Cesare Lensi Orlandi Cardini identified Florentine gardens as early examples of the formal garden, and described the Medici gardens—whose original layouts are illustrated in the lunettes by Giusto Utens—as the most typical of Florentine gardens.[48] Cardini praised Il Trebbio, which he described as a masterwork that challenged the passing of time with its "impeccable garden,"[49] but he lamented the loss of the garden at Careggi, which Francis Sloane replaced with a Romantic park that "forever disfigured the villa."[50] He considered the transformation of Italian gardens into English-style parks a disgrace. On the contrary, he praised Cecil Pinsent for assimilating and re-creating the spirit of Renaissance architecture in his buildings and small gardens (such as those at the Villa Le Balze).[51]

In his *Arte dei giardini* (1956), Francesco Fariello adopted a more objective approach to the study of garden art. The book—which was intended as a textbook for landscape architecture courses in the Facoltà di Architettura at the Università di Roma—includes a brief description of Pratolino, whose layout, according to the author, presents "a freer general design intent if compared to more geometric Renaissance schemes."[52] Because of its freer layout and its inclusion of landscape forms that would be developed in subsequent centuries, Pratolino occupies an important place in the history of garden art. The same chapter contains a brief description of northern Italian gardens, which are described in the measure in which they depart from the Roman and Florentine models. Fariello characterized the latter as "all order, clarity, and a wealth of plastic form."[53] The author emphasized the semirustic and agricultural character of these northern gardens; he also remarked that they possessed only a few elements reminiscent of Roman and Florentine gardens—namely, their overall axial layout and their use of tree-lined avenues. Although Fariello did not disparage these exceptional gardens for diverging from the Renaissance ideal, his preference for the Italian garden definition spelled out during the regime is evident in the chapter's conclusion, which summarized the main characteristics of Italian Renaissance gardens and excluded all the exceptions to the rule of geometry and number. Moreover, some of the typical elements described by Fariello are more likely to be found in the so-called Italian gardens restored during the 1930s than in the gardens of the Renaissance period: "The end result of the Renaissance conception is a tight and completely predetermined composition, where every space is defined, and nothing is left to chance. A garden conceived in this way will accept only those plants that may contribute to the overall architectonic effect . . . Therefore, evergreens, such as cypresses, pines, holm oaks that are aligned along the alleys and in bosquets, are the preferred plants . . . There is no room for flowers, and small plants in this type of garden. They would not offer a valuable contribution to the overall chromatic effect, essentially based on the shades of plants and tree masses, from the dark green of holm oaks to the lighter green of citrus plants . . . the strong light of the Italian sky and the geometric rhythms of an essentially architectonic garden would not adapt well to the presence of lively colors, that will create confusion and disturbance."[54]

In the 1960s, the geometric or formal garden continued to be considered representative of Italy in Camillo Fiorani's *Giardini d'Italia: Arte, carattere e storia del giardino italiano* (1960) and in Georgina Masson's *Italian Gardens* (1961). Not only do these books offer historical accounts that focus exclusively on the genesis and development of the architectonic garden in Italy, but, like Cardini a decade earlier, they formulate negative judgments on alternative forms of garden design. For example, when describing the geometric garden, Fiorani wrote: "The vitality of a concept that draws its origin from the very character of our race will influence, for quite some time, the European builders who will look for inspiration to the original and insuperable examples of Rome and Florence, considered, because of their unmistakable peculiarity, the model of the 'Italian garden.'"[55] In a chapter dedicated to the landscape garden of the Romantic period, Fiorani explained the cultural change taking place in the 1800s:

> Naturally, even the gardens were affected by the new climate. Of all the arts, that of the garden was the most affected. A real crusade. The classic idea based on measure and order had lasted unchanged until the end of the eighteenth century. The changes that had occurred till then were due to logical evolutions based on the times, taste, and fashion. If a tendency to move away from Renaissance canons was manifested in France, with the development of the garden on level ground, it was only, in the end, a new application of the founding Italian principle.[56]

Fiorani claimed that it was only after the work of André Le Nôtre was imitated extensively that garden design became a sterile academic exercise, which led to an inevitable return to nature. Thus, toward the end of the nineteenth century, the landscape garden had become the most fashionable style both in Italy and in Europe. But, according to the author:

> That which was made, when it was not the work of foreigners, was without dignity. The gardens are usually assigned to gardeners, who are more concerned with the fate of the plants' welfare than with perspective, and who only roughly copy from the few examples they have in front of them . . . A green lawn or a lush blooming of exotic trees, even if beautiful to look at, do not have anything in common with art, which is made of proportions and harmony beyond that mysterious quality that animates every soul but which only a few are allowed to express. In the last century it was believed that architects were not qualified to work on gardens because of their scant botanical knowledge. As if a painter were not able to make a beautiful painting only because he did not know how to make the colors he needed.[57]

The influence of the 1930s debates is evident. Fiorani was familiar with the critical literature, and mentioned publications such as Ojetti's *I palazzi e le ville che non sono più del re* (1921)[58] in his bibliography. Moreover, the catalogue of the Mostra del Giardino Italiano is among the recommended readings in Masson's *Italian Gardens*. Even the layout of her book resembles that of the exhibition catalogue, where the gardens are grouped geographically and chronologically. Like Fiorani, Masson regarded the English landscape garden as a disruptive craze in Italy: "In attempting the impossible by trying to create an English landscape even in the confined limits of the gardens of many small Tuscan villas, the formal parterres, which were an integral part of the original design, were destroyed and their place was taken by meandering paths and ugly irregular beds that bear no relation to the scale, character or site."[59]

Masson's descriptions of extant examples of architectonic gardens show that the Italian garden tradition established during the fascist regime was consolidated by the 1960s. However, like others, she overlooked the misreading of primary sources by the Florentine exhibition committee in their effort to validate the idea of a national garden. For example, the exhibition committee initiated the anachronistic association of early fifteenth-century gardens, such as Il Trebbio and Cafaggiolo, with late sixteenth-century paintings of these gardens, such as the lunettes by Utens; thus, they fostered a rather narrow interpretation of the early Medici villas. This anachronistic association has been accepted by many subsequent scholars, who consider the lunettes to be accurate depictions of fifteenth-century Florentine gardens. It has lead these scholars to emphasize the

FIGURE 2.7.
Giusto Utens,
Il Trebbio, 1599.
Museo Firenze
Com'era, Florence.
Photograph courtesy of the Ministero per i Beni e le Attività Culturali.

improbable timelessness of the gardens. For example, Masson wrote: "An interesting picture of what a Medici villa of this period [fifteenth century] looked like is to be seen in one of the fascinating lunettes of the Medici properties . . . Although this painting representing the villa of Cafaggiolo dates from the end of the sixteenth century, from the very simplicity of the layout it is probable that it had not been changed in the hundred and fifty years since it was first laid out."[60] Similarly, she described Il Trebbio as a "rare treasure," a fifteenth-century garden that "has retained its simple charm almost untouched through centuries . . . A lunette . . . painted possibly by Utens or an unknown artist of the early seventeenth century, shows the layout of the house, chapel, farm, and walled garden, just as it probably looked in Cosimo's time and almost exactly as it is today."[61] When describing the garden at Castello, one of the later Medici villas, she wrote: "Although Utens's picture does not correspond exactly with earlier descriptions of the garden, this is only in small details, and broadly speaking its basic lines are the same as those that we see today, so that it may be taken as a fairly reliable guide."[62] She went on to recommend the use of this picture as a guide for the re-creation of the garden; this would become a common approach to the restoration of the Medici gardens in subsequent years.[63]

Studies of the early Medici villas dating from the 1980s and 1990s tend to reiterate the information made available fifty years earlier. Most authors do not consult the fifteenth-century sources; instead, they rely on Utens's images of Il Trebbio and Cafaggiolo (figs. 2.7 and 2.8) as the primary visual record of these gardens. For example, Alessandro Tagliolini described Il Trebbio as "a charming small garden, surrounded by walls with flowerbeds and pergolas."[64] When describing Cafaggiolo, he pointed to "the simplicity of the lawn, bordered with a fence in the front, [which] is contrasted with the refinement of the vegetal pavilion and even more with the elegant fountain that rises over the grass, having as its backdrop the severe image of the fortified villa."[65] In "Il giardino del Trebbio" (1996), Mariachiara Pozzana wrote:

> We are dealing with an almost unique example of a fifteenth-century garden whose main structures have been preserved . . . The large *orto* located on the right hand side of Trebbio was created on two terraces, the first was completely occupied by a large pergola and the

FIGURE 2.8.
Giusto Utens, *Cafaggiolo*, 1599. Museo Firenze Com’era, Florence.

Photograph courtesy of the Ministero per i Beni e le Attività Culturali.

> second by the actual *orto* and a second pergola, now lost . . . In front of the house and on the left appeared a particularly unique vegetal architecture: a sort of *berceau,* that in the past has been interpreted as an aviary. Actually, it is a pavilion formed with evergreens (perhaps ilex) whose foliage is pruned into a dome-shape that shields the bench underneath with its shade.[66]

It is obvious that both Tagliolini and Pozzana do not describe the actual fifteenth-century gardens, but rather use Utens's paintings as the basis of their descriptions, as the authors themselves make clear. Tagliolini wrote: “The rustic aspect of the gardens was documented at the end of the sixteenth century in one of the lunettes that decorated the villa of Artimino, painted by the Flemish artist Giusto Utens, who gave an idealized version of the gardens, but one that was perhaps not dissimilar from the fifteenth-century reality.”[67] And Pozzana acknowledged: “The analysis of the lunette by Utens, a well-known source . . . informs us of the characteristics of the fifteenth-century garden [at Cafaggiolo].”[68]

The fact that the lunettes were painted more than a hundred years after the gardens were created does not hinder these scholars. But even if we accepted that the appearance of the gardens, which are made of ephemeral materials, remained unchanged for more than a century, the question of why the lunettes are treated as photographs remains to be answered. Although it is true that Flemish painters were known for the accuracy of their representations, a comparison of later gardens and their corresponding lunettes shows that Utens chose, in some cases, to not be very faithful to the subjects he was to paint. The lunette representing Castello, for instance, shows a garden whose central axis corresponds to that of the building, but this alignment was not present in the actual garden. (Niccolò Tribolo probably intended to expand the building so that the two axes coincided, but his intention was never realized.) The lunette also regularized the perimeter of the upper terrace at Castello. The documentary value of the lunettes is limited, particularly vis-à-vis the layout of Medici gardens in the fifteenth century. Nevertheless, because these lunettes are the earliest visual rendering of the gardens at Il Trebbio and Cafaggiolo, and because other kinds of documentary sources (such as drawings and detailed written descriptions) are scarce, the anachronistic reading of the past on the basis of later historical evidence has been legitimized. An immediate consequence is that the gardens of the fifteenth and sixteenth centuries are described as fixed and immutable works of art that have always existed.

In addition to the timelessness of the gardens, their formality is another important feature that is usually drawn from the lunettes; it is this quality that made scholars point to the Medici villas as early examples of the Italian garden style, which, they maintained, flowered more vigorously later in the Renaissance. In an essay on the transformation of the Tuscan landscape and society in the fifteenth and sixteenth centuries, Adriano Gradi wrote: "The high bourgeoisie merchants become landowners: the giardino all'italiana spreads to all of their villas in imitation of those at the Medici residences."[69] A few years later, Cristina Acidini Luchinat associated principles of formal design with the very definition of a garden and referred to the scholarly literature produced during the fascist regime to support her point: "Beginning in the thirteenth and fourteenth centuries, order, the quintessential expression of rationality, is the first and foremost requisite such that a defined portion of space could be called a 'garden.' And that is not only the case in Tuscany, but in all the states of the peninsula. In fact, the scholarly literature has for a long time consolidated this interpretation, starting from the early twentieth-century superimposition of the term 'Italian garden' onto the 'garden of reason' *tout court* until today."[70]

When we compare the research on Il Trebbio and Cafaggiolo published before and after the 1930s, we see how the exhibition changed the course of Italian garden historiography, especially in regard to the early Medici gardens. In *Il giardino italiano* (1924), Luigi Dami wrote: "Cafaggiolo, in spite of Vasari's assertion, probably never had gardens in the strict sense of the word. Even less Trebbio and the others."[71] A few years later, Rose Standish Nichols, drawing on Dami, Vernon Lee, and the garden designer and historian Inigo Triggs, wrote in *Italian Pleasure Gardens* (1931): "After Cosimo's purchase of Careggi, in his rebuilding of the old house and in the additions to the gardens, Renaissance influence becomes clearly apparent as it had *not* been in his castles—Trebbio and Cafaggiuolo [*sic*]—surrounded only by ilex woods and farmlands in the more remote valley in the Mugello" (emphasis added).[72] In contrast, few scholars since the 1930s have doubted that beautiful gardens, such as those represented by Utens, adorned the early Medici villas.

One last trace of the influence of the 1930s on Italian garden historiography emerges in very recent scholarship that associates the Italian garden tradition with the centuries in which the geometric garden developed. Claudia Lazzaro's "Politicizing a National Garden Tradition: The Italianness of the Italian Garden" (2005) exemplifies this scholarship, as it claims that "the Italian garden tradition comprises gardens of three centuries, the sixteenth through the eighteenth, created in diverse climates and topographies, and influenced by different regional artistic traditions. Nevertheless, this variety has come to be understood as a distinct Italian tradition, which has roots in ancient Roman gardens, and which provides evidence of an Italian 'nation' long before the existence of such a political entity."[73] By emphasizing only three centuries of garden history, the author has clearly singled out the geometric garden; in doing so she has also echoed the early twentieth-century argument that this garden type was conceptualized as early as the Renaissance. Although Lazzaro analyzed the political ideology that tainted the studies produced during the 1930s, she does not question the basic premises of fascist scholars, who took pride in preserving a continuous, but fictitious, national cultural heritage, which, they claimed, included the purely Italian tradition of the architectonic garden.[74] In addition, Lazzaro maintained that all Italian gardens produced during the sixteenth, seventeenth, and eighteenth centuries represented an idea of Italy. Just as Italy has always been compared to a garden, "so too gardens from the Renaissance to the eighteenth century embodied the current notions of Italy. Some Renaissance gardens reproduced the local region in microcosm, while many others alluded more generally to the surrounding landscape. Gardens implicitly represented the idea of Italy with imagery that celebrated Italy's natural gifts and cultural riches."[75] This claim generalizes the complex and diverse history of garden art in Italy. The reason is self-evident: although some gardens were constructed with the specific purpose of representing the country (or portions of it, as in the representation of Tuscany at Castello), it is unlikely that all gardens planted in Italy between the sixteenth and eighteenth centuries embodied, either implicitly or explicitly, an idea of the "nation." In fact, there were other, perhaps more worthy, themes (such as ideas of paradise or notions of class distinction) that were more likely to be associated with gardens.

Lazzaro acknowledged that the scholarship produced during the years of the fascist regime "had a profound influence on the received notion of the Italian garden in the second half of the twentieth century."[76] She rightly observed that gardens restored between the 1920s and 1940s "were planted with boxwood in massive geometric and architectonic forms in hedges and borders, patterns in the parterres, and labyrinths, in contrast to the great variety of plant materials in Renaissance gardens, the low and narrow hedges, and the blossoming herbs and flowers in the parterres."[77] But if it is true that "the restored gardens represented an idea of the Italian garden outside of time,"[78] as Lazzaro claimed, then it is no less true that timelessness was attributed also to an invented Italian tradition of the formal garden. On the one hand, Lazzaro seemed to denounce the conception of the Italian garden produced during the 1930s—she claimed that it was "not a false conception, only an exaggerated and partial one taken for the whole,"[79]—but, on the other hand, she was too quick to accept the idea, promoted by fascist scholars, of a unique Italian garden that corresponded exclusively with the formal garden style. Thus, her general conclusions on the recurring idea of nationhood embodied by Italian gardens resonated with the 1930s discourses on the national garden: "In their origins, as in the twentieth century, gardens are highly charged with issues of national identity, since they represent how a culture shapes the very land of the nation."[80]

The Mostra del Giardino Italiano, and especially the archival documents that reveal its objectives, sheds light on a moment in Italian cultural history in which scholarship was influenced by political propaganda. It is surprising, however, that even after the fall of the regime, the course of historiography maintained the same premises set up by fascist scholars. The motivations of Italian intellectuals writing in the 1930s may have been clear, but one wonders what justified the perpetuation of their views on the Italian garden (and particularly early Medici gardens) in the following years. Perhaps the endorsement of modern aesthetics, which may explain the continued use of formal analyses of gardens, substituted for the political motivations of the early twentieth century. The theoretical leanings of some scholars, in fact, bear a very close resemblance to the modernist discourses that informed the theory and practice of architecture in the first half of the century.[81] In the same way that modernists created an architecture of pure volumes and condensed its essence into a few structural components that were independent of time and specific regions, garden historians reduced early Medici gardens to art objects that seem to exist only within an autonomous space. Moreover, just as modernists recontextualized the architectural object as a "'visual representation' [of an ideal] to be judged on specifically aesthetic and formalist terms,"[82] garden historians have recontextualized the fifteenth-century Medici gardens within the single ideal of the national garden type, whose formal characteristics are represented by Utens's lunettes. Described in these terms, the early Medici gardens appear as intentional works of pure and rational geometry, as practical materializations of lofty concepts, and as products of the application of design theory. This insistence on formal analysis, which is motivated by a desire to reconstruct the appearance of the garden object, has, therefore, isolated the gardens from their social, political, cultural, and physical contexts.

There are a few exceptions to this method of historical inquiry, however. An example is Emilio Sereni's *Storia del paesaggio agrario italiano*, which was written in the mid-1950s and published in 1961. Like other historians, Sereni used the Utens lunette to describe the Medici villa at Cafaggiolo. But he did not use it to describe the garden as the prototype of the giardino all'italiana; his observations focused instead on the surrounding landscape: "One sees in the illustration the important part still assumed by woods, farms, and rustic works of construction in the landscape of the villa at Cafaggiolo, in comparison with the relatively modest importance of the seigneurial villa and its gardens."[83] Sereni placed Cafaggiolo in the larger context of the Tuscan landscape, whose "pattern of symmetrical simplicity"[84] was the result of agricultural and practical economies more than aesthetic concerns. By placing gardening in relation to farming, Sereni's work suggested that gardens, however modest, played a role in the cultural and social history of the Italian landscape. His different approach may be explained by his training in agriculture and his concern for the long history of the human transformation of the natural environment.[85] But although Sereni was not interested in depicting an Italian garden tradition that fit a formal ideal, he—like his contemporaries, a generation of scholars who conceived their work in the aftermath of fascism—was interested in describing a sense of Italian national identity. Sereni spoke of this identity in terms of the obstacles to the progress of the nation imposed not only by local resources and conditions but by people, both landowners and industrialists.

Following in the footsteps of Sereni, Vittorio Franchetti Pardo and Giovanna Casali published *I Medici nel contado fiorentino* (1978), the earliest comprehensive study of the Medici properties in the Florentine countryside. Unlike writings that examine these villas from a stylistic point of view and trace a gradual and continuous development of landscape forms, this account points to a discontinuity of formal arrangements, which depended on the contingent situations in which different Medici patrons operated. By consulting the archival documents related to the transfer of ownership, bequest, and acquisition of Medici properties in the fifteenth and sixteenth centuries, the authors were able to identify the criteria that guided and motivated their land investments. The typical pattern of Medici land investment was disrupted by Lorenzo de'Medici's commission of Poggio a Caiano from Giuliano da Sangallo.[86] When Lorenzo purchased this land in the 1470s, the economic as well as the political power of the Medici in Florence had already been established. The villa at Poggio a Caiano was not just the center of a large farm—it was also regarded as a pleasurable place that was less charged with economic tensions and emotional values. On the contrary, the Medici land investments in the fifteenth century were motivated by a desire to confirm and expand the possessions around the Mugello area near Florence, where the family ancestors lived. Moreover, the Medici typically invested in land whose productivity, especially with regard to its vine crops, was well established. Land cultivation was mainly motivated by private consumption, and was considered a secure investment, which would have helped the family during dire financial crises. The buildings of Il Trebbio and Cafaggiolo—which were more fortresses than villas—were of secondary importance to the agricultural products of the properties. Their fortified appearance—created by towers and crenellated walls—stressed their isolation from the agricultural life of their respective estates. The concept of the *villa di delizie* (a place dedicated to literary *otia*) cannot be applied to these early properties. In fact, the length of the Medici family's sojourns on these properties was linked to the rhythms of agricultural production, thereby confirming that these villas were essentially farms. In this context, it is obvious why Franchetti Pardo and Casali do not address the gardens attached to Il Trebbio and Cafaggiolo. The archival documents indicate that these gardens were more often referred to as *orti* (kitchen gardens), which were likely set aside for the production of vegetables and herbs for family use. And the role of Michelozzo di Bartolomeo, whom Cosimo de'Medici commissioned to restore the buildings and to whom Vasari attributed the design of the gardens, was more that of a technician than an artist in charge of giving form to a clear aesthetic ideal. This view is shared by Hervé Brunon, who described the *ragnaie* (or structures for fowling) at Cafaggiolo, which were planted by Michelozzo and survived until the seventeenth century.

In "La chasse et l'organisation du paysage dans la Toscane des Médicis" (2007), Brunon placed the Medici gardens within a larger cultural context, which included social and political aspects and involved the regional landscapes in which the villas were located. Instead of using Utens's lunettes for formal analyses of gardens, Brunon pointed to the Flemish painter's integration of hunting scenes into his painted views of the Medici villas. He argued that the lunettes accurately reflect the landscapes depicted in Anton Francesco Doni's treatise on *villeggiatura*—*Le ville* (Bologna, 1566)—which hardly dissociated Renaissance villa life from the princely hunts practiced by itinerant courts. The Medici villas carried out an essential agricultural function, but, nonetheless, hunting was important not only in dictating the seasonal itinerary of the Medici entourage, but also in determining the morphological structure of the Tuscan landscape. This landscape was subdivided into a number of reserves, or *bandite*, dedicated to hunting, fowling, and fishing; the reserves had boundaries that encompassed and extended beyond those of agricultural terrains, and they often included territories that belonged to the crown, private individuals, and the community. Brunon explained the creation of such protected areas in the general context of a slow appropriation of the hunting rights by the seigneurial elite, which appear to have been concentrated to their advantage by the beginning of the modern period. The main bandite surrounded the Medici villas and were located in areas that were richer in game, such as the Mugello.

Like the bandite, the ragnaie (which were used to capture thrushes, blackbirds, and warblers) had an impact, both physical and visual, on the structure of the landscape. As Brunon wrote, one can only imagine the monumental effect that the narrow and tall ragnaie must have produced in the configuration of the rural landscape, especially in a territory that mostly included vineyards and olive trees and was scarcely equipped with woods. Perfectly integrated into the framework of plots, these structures contributed to a strong geometrization of the land. This formal regularity—seen, for example, in the cultivated fields, which were subdivided into regular plots for ease of cultivation following sharecropping practices—was due to the exigencies of fowling, rather than to an attempt to conform to a specific aesthetic type.

With the exception of the work published by Franchetti Pardo and Casali, and to a certain extent the work published by Brunon, the *longue durée* approach that forms the basis of Sereni's history and that has been described as a monument of synthesis[87] has remained isolated; this isolation can be partially explained by the fact that this method of historical analysis, which has its roots in the French *Annales* paradigm, was later supplanted by other theories. Historians of subsequent generations became preoccupied by multiple voices that were previously marginalized and ignored; their work is characterized by an increasing fragmentation. For example, in an essay on Pratolino that was published in a volume edited by Mirka Beneš and Dianne Harris in 2001, Suzanne Butters addressed the unusual topic of the wretched conditions endured by conscripted countrymen in the construction of the park of the Medici villa at Pratolino, thus going beyond the typical reading of Pratolino as a microcosmic representation of the Tuscan state by adding multiple layers of cultural and social meanings to garden iconography. Butters's approach is comparable to that of other historians, in particular the proponents of *microstoria*, who focus on the documented actions and beliefs of individuals in order to understand the social and cultural systems in which they act.

In a sense, the methods of Sereni and the microhistorians stand at two opposite ends, or scales, of historical investigation. Nevertheless, both offer very useful tools for historians of the Italian garden. The bottom-up approach of the microhistorians demonstrates that certain developments may be contingent and uneven. Moreover, their attention to ordinary people enables garden historians to consider that gardens are not only luxuries commissioned by wealthy clients and created by well-known architects but can also involve anonymous makers whose work is motivated more by the needs of everyday living than of display. Design may be understood as a process that is as important as its material product. Understanding its evolution can offer glimpses of changing cultural structures and values contingent on specific times and milieux. At the same time, the microhistorians suggest an alternative to the urge to construct general typologies (i.e. the Italian garden) by focusing instead on the concrete details of individual cases. This does not mean that individual gardens should not be studied as part of larger systems, but rather that these systems may not necessarily be typified or represented by them.

The attention to long-term and large-scale processes that stems from Sereni's scholarship, on the other hand, compensates for the limitations of a narrow and detailed approach that cannot take into account recurrent phenomena (i.e. economic, social, and cultural cycles). Moreover, his emphasis on processes and human agencies suggests that the creation of a garden may be dependent on unwritten and empirical traditions that did not drip down from garden theorists to the common people but were, instead, handed down from one generation to another and transformed in time as a result of practice and technological progress. These are the lessons that have guided my own research on the Medici gardens, published in *Medici Gardens: From Making to Design* (2008). By resisting the usual temptation to reconstruct the layout of gardens such as Il Trebbio and Cafaggiolo, for which we lack contemporary documentary evidence, I tried to distance my research from the scholarship of my predecessors, most of whom, as I think I have shown, have adopted the same methods and, to a certain extent, conclusions of the studies carried out during the years of the fascist regime.

In conclusion, the idea of the Medici gardens as prototypes of the Italian garden, and the very notion of a national style, is a modern phenomenon that rests on historical, political, cultural, and methodological reasons. The effort of the fascist regime to form and corroborate a national garden tradition that disallowed regional differences, the fascination of many foreign intellectuals with an idea of Italy resting solely on its Renaissance past, and the essentialist approach and methodology of certain Medici garden scholarship—all contribute to define the Italian garden as a work of art as fixed as a painting and as unaffected by the passage of time. On the contrary, the renunciation of mythical reconstructions of the past governed by certain needs and meant to sustain certain expectations can not only do justice to the Medici villas but also encourage the study of less-explored gardens in Florence or elsewhere in Italy. Micro- and macrohistorical methods of analysis suggest new paths for the development of Italian garden history. For example, the role of women in making and writing about gardens, the relationship between garden making and material culture, and the economic and political aspects of gardens vis-à-vis social hierarchy and class structure are all avenues of investigation that have recently started to receive scholarly attention and that should be encouraged in order to broaden the horizons of historiography.

Acknowledgments

I wish to express my deep gratitude to Michel Conan for inviting me to present a first version of this essay at the 2007 Dumbarton Oaks symposium on Italian gardens. I would also like to thank him for encouraging me to pursue my research on Italian garden historiography. I am very grateful to Richard Etlin for his thoughtful comments on my study of fascist Italy, and to John Dixon Hunt for reading the last drafts of this essay and for offering critical advice. This study owes much to two anonymous readers, whose specific suggestions for improvement guided my revisions.

Notes

Unless otherwise noted, all translations are my own.

1 Archival documents related to the organization of the exhibition are at the Archivio Storico Comunale di Firenze (henceforth ASCF), "Mostra del Giardino Italiano, 1931," buste 5087–93 and C.F. 9260; and the Biblioteca della Facoltà di Architettura di Firenze (henceforth BFAF), Fondo Roberto Papini, filza 117, "Mostra del Giardino Italiano." Secondary sources on the 1931 exhibition include Vincenzo Cazzato, "I giardini del desiderio: La Mostra del Giardino Italiano (Firenze 1931)," in *Il giardino romantico*, ed. Alessandro Vezzosi, 80–88 (Florence: Alinea, 1986); Vincenzo Cazzato, "Firenze 1931: La consacrazione del 'primato italiano' nell'arte dei giardini," in *Il giardino: Idea natura realtà*, eds. Alessandro Tagliolini and Massimo Venturi Ferriolo, 77–108 (Milan: Guerini, 1987); Vincenzo Cazzato, *Ville e giardini italiani: I disegni di architetti e paesaggisti dell'American Academy in Rome* (Rome: Istituto Poligrafico e Zecca dello Stato, Libreria dello Stato, 2004); and Claudia

Lazzaro, "Politicizing a National Garden Tradition: The Italianness of the Italian Garden," in *Donatello among the Blackshirts: History and Modernity in the Visual Culture of Fascist Italy*, eds. Claudia Lazzaro and Roger J. Crum, 157–69 (Ithaca, N.Y.: Cornell University Press, 2005).

2 During the Risorgimento, a few Italian scholars, including Ippolito Pindemonte and Pier Luigi Mabil, expressed their ideas on nationhood and national gardens. Their discussions of the regular garden were limited to short descriptions in narratives focused on the natural or modern garden, which seemed "to represent a distinctive Italianness." John Dixon Hunt, *The Picturesque Garden in Europe* (London: Thames and Hudson, 2002), 187. It was not until the early twentieth century, with the writings of Maria Pasolini Ponti and Luigi Dami and the organization of the 1931 exhibition, that the interest of Italian intellectuals shifted toward the geometric or regular garden, which was considered more Italian than any other type of garden. For the writings of Pindemonte, Mabil, and the contemporary garden theorist Ercole Silva, see Margherita Azzi Visentini, ed., *L'arte dei giardini: Scritti teorici e pratici dal XIV al XIX secolo* (Milan: Il Polifilo, 1999), 2:155–273.

3 *Mostra del Giardino Italiano: Catalogo*, 2nd ed. (Florence: Comune di Firenze, 1931), 24.

4 Nello Tarchiani, "La Mostra del Giardino Italiano in Palazzo Vecchio a Firenze," *Domus* 38 (1931): 15.

5 "Ostentato ritorno della ragione nell'architettura," *Mostra del Giardino Italiano*, 24.

6 Lazzaro, "Politicizing a National Garden Tradition," 166; Cristina Acidini Luchinat, "Il modello del giardino fiorentino del Quattrocento nella mostra del 1931," in *Giardini medicei: Giardini di palazzo e di villa nella Firenze del Quattrocento*, ed. Cristina Acidini Luchinat (Milan: F. Motta, 1996), 140.

7 "Da codesto carattere documentario . . . all'ambizioso proposito, assai trasparente anche se non confessato, di volere attraverso l'odierna Mostra determinare un risveglio e un ritorno alla tradizione italiana nell'arte del Giardino, il passo ci sembra lungo." Mario Tinti, "La Mostra del Giardino Italiano," *La casa bella* 41 (May 1931): 39. Only Cazzato has found the rationalists' negative reaction puzzling, especially if compared to Ojetti's words in "La mostra fiorentina del giardino italiano," an article published in the journal *Il giardino fiorito*: "Questo tipo di giardino [all'italiana] . . . dai nuovi architetti detti razionali è amorosamente studiato appunto per la sua nitida e riposante razionalità." Cazzato, *Ville e giardini italiani*, 105–6.

8 Giuseppe Pagano, "I 'materiali' nella nuova architettura," *La casa bella* 41 (May 1931): 14. See also Movimento Italiano per l'Architettura Razionale (MIAR), "L'architettura razionale italiana, 1931," *La casa bella* 40 (April 1931): 71.

9 "Bisogna . . . unificare, coordinare, combattere le idee parassitarie e favorire i tentativi, levar di mezzo l'ufficio intralciatore delle Commissioni e quello dei Consigli inferiori e superiori, in modo da agevolare la gara, e dunque il beneficio di progredire. E' da un'attenta considerazione della formula proposta, 'Architettura, arte di Stato,' che potranno scaturire nuovi germi di vita e di prosperità per l'arte principe." The petition was also published in MIAR, "L'architettura razionale italiana, 1931," 79.

10 Only a few traditionalists believed that drawing inspiration from foreign models would not compromise the *italianità* of the country's art and architecture. See the polemic between Ugo Ojetti and Roberto Papini in BFAF, Fondo Roberto Papini, filza 33c, "Influenze straniere sull'arte italiana—polemica con Ojetti 1932."

11 For example, Frederick Stibbert and John Temple Leader contributed funds for the completion of the facade at Santa Maria del Fiore, whereas Francis Sloane donated funds for the construction of the neo-Gothic facade of Santa Croce. D. Medina Lasansky, *The Renaissance Perfected: Architecture, Spectacle, and Tourism in Fascist Italy* (University Park: Pennsylvania State University Press, 2004), 57.

12 The Accademia, which was founded in 1925, promoted the study of the arts and sciences as a means of protecting the "purity of national character according to the genius and traditions of the people." Ibid., 78.

13 "La seconda 'Primavera Fiorentina,'" *Il Popolo d'Italia*, 20 January 1931. See also ASCF, fascicolo "Ritagli di giornali," busta 5090.

14 "Spring To Bring Many To Lovely Tuscan Gardens. Motor Bus Service To Link Up Points of Interest," *Chicago Tribune*, 25 January 1931, European edition. See also ASCF, fascicolo "Ritagli di giornali," busta 5090.

15 This, however, was not an exclusive characteristic of fascism, nor was it a prerogative of Italian scholars. The rewriting of tradition occurred earlier and in other countries. Eric Hobsbawm and Terence Ranger, eds. *The Invention of Tradition* (Cambridge: Cambridge University Press, 1983), 1–14. See also John Dixon Hunt, "The Garden as Cultural Object," in *Denatured Visions: Landscape and Culture in the Twentieth Century*, eds. Stuart Wrede and William Howard Adams, 19–32 (New York: Museum of Modern Art, 1991).

16 Lasansky, *Renaissance Perfected*, 66.

17 "Occorre valorizzare quanto più è possibile l'arte moderna del giardino invitando qualche architetto di nome a mettersi d'accordo con degli orticultori che concorrano per fare dei giardini moderni. Si spenderà così molto meno e si avrà la sicurezza di esser pronti per la prossima primavera." Remarks of Antonio Maraini in a Florentine Exhibition Committee meeting, 19 November 1930, ASCF, "Fascicolo Commissione Museo del Giardino a Castello e Mostra del Giardino Italiano a Palazzo Vecchio," busta C.F. 9260.

18 "Il giardino italiano moderno non esiste." Remarks of Carlo Mercatelli in a Florentine Exhibition Committee meeting, 19 November 1930, ASCF, "Fascicolo Commissione Museo del Giardino a Castello e Mostra del Giardino Italiano a Palazzo Vecchio," busta C.F. 9260.

19 "Che del resto sono una derivazione degli antichi giardini italiani." Remarks of Ugo Ojetti in a Florentine Exhibition Committee meeting, 19 November 1930, ASCF, "Fascicolo Commissione Museo del Giardino a Castello e Mostra del Giardino Italiano a Palazzo Vecchio," busta C.F. 9260.

20 Committee members rejected a proposal to construct a romantic garden as a negative model to be compared with the traditional Italian garden.

21 "Non basta fidarsi dell'opera delle Commissioni Regionali. Bisogna che anche di qui possiamo dare delle indicazioni precise a queste commissioni . . . Si dovrà incaricare degli architetti di studiare, secondo le indicazioni che verranno date dal comitato, piante e bozzetti di massima dei giardini che vogliamo costruire." Remarks of Ugo Ojetti in a Florentine Exhibition Committee meeting, 19 November 1930, ASCF, "Fascicolo Commissione Museo del Giardino a Castello e Mostra del Giardino Italiano a Palazzo Vecchio," busta C.F. 9260. In the end, the reconstruction of historical gardens did not take place, although a public competition for the design of two gardens (one public, one private) was launched. The competition was opened only to those architects belonging to the fascist *sindacati architetti* and to fourth-year architecture students.

22 "Come figurerà la Sicilia alla mostra del giardino che sarà aperta prossimamente a Firenze, e dove è norma mandare esempi di giardini architettonici italiani? *Giardino architettonico,* se così non fosse i tre quarti della Sicilia avrebbero potuto figuravi . . . *Giardino architettonico,* e perciò sarà modesto il nostro contributo." Francesco Fichera, "La Sicilia orientale e i suoi giardini alla prossima mostra di Firenze," *Giornale d'Italia,* 25 March 1931, ASCF, fascicolo "Ritagli di giornali," busta 5090.

23 Tarchiani wrote to Roberto Papini, the secretary of the Roman committee, on 12 January 1931: "Ci siamo messi a fare la parte del pubblico . . . mediamente intelligente. Ed abbiamo fatto una lista di ville che crediamo essere rappresentate al più completamente possibile." BFAF, Fondo Roberto Papini, filza 117, "Mostra del Giardino Italiano."

24 "Perché nella mente del pubblico, non facile alle astrazioni e alle sintesi, sarà più facile comprendere che cosa fosse il giardino cinquecentesco fiorentino ecc. da una scenografia ideale, che non da numerose raffigurazioni di singoli giardini realmente esistenti o esistiti." ASCF, "Mostra del Giardino Italiano, 1931," busta 5088.

25 "Ci abitueremo ancor meglio a distinguere i nostri fiori, sbocciati al sole, da quelli d'importazione, curati e cresciuti in serra. Conoscenza assai preziosa oggi che—in nome della giovinezza, della modernità, del fascismo—si tenta da alcuni di innestare gli edelweiss nelle piante di cactus." Francesco Fichera, "La Sicilia orientale e i suoi giardini alla prossima mostra di Firenze," 25 March 1931, ASCF, fascicolo "Ritagli di giornali," busta 5090.

26 During a discussion about the nonexistence of—and need for—a national garden at an exhibition committee meeting, Antonio Maraini said that a similar attempt had been carried out in Germany: "Si è tentato qualche cosa in Germania, ma poco." ASCF, "Fascicolo Commissione Museo del Giardino a Castello e Mostra del Giardino Italiano a Palazzo Vecchio," busta C.F. 9260.

27 The special train tickets (called *della Primavera Fiorentina*) are mentioned in ASCF, "Mostra del Giardino Italiano, 1931," busta 5087. Florentines also benefited from a generous reduction in ticket prices from five liras (the cost of the regular ticket) to one lira. ASCF, "Mostra del Giardino Italiano, 1931," busta 5089.

28 "Anche questa Mostra intende rimettere in onore un'arte singolarmente nostra che dopo avere conquistato il mondo sembrò offuscata da altre mode o nascosta sotto nomi stranieri." *Mostra del Giardino Italiano,* 23.

29 "Apriche collinette, ombrose valli, / Selve, e spelonche in una vista offerse; / E quel, che il bello e il caro accresce all'opre, / L'arte, che tutto fa, nulla si scopre." Ippolito Pindemonte, *Su i giardini inglesi e sul merito in cio dell'Italia* (Verona: Dalla Tipografia Mainardi, 1817), 51.

30 The art and literature of medieval Florence attracted a few scholars who attended the universities of New England, such as Henry W. Longfellow, James R. Lowell, and Charles E. Norton. Their translation of Dante's *Commedia* into English in 1867, and later the foundation of the Dante Society of America, surely contributed to the promotion of Italian culture. Margherita Ciacci, "Non tutti i giardini di delizie sono uguali," in *I giardini delle regine: Il mito di Firenze nell'ambiente preraffaellita e nella cultura americana fra Ottocento e Novecento,* eds. Margherita Ciacci and Grazia Gobbi Sica, 12–39 (Florence: Sillabe, 2004).

31 Vernon Lee, "Old Italian Gardens," in *Limbo, and Other Essays* (London: G. Richards, 1897), 110–11.

32 Ibid., 115 and 121.

33 Edith Wharton, *Italian Villas and Their Gardens* (1904; reprint, with introductory notes by Arthur Ross, Henry Hope Reed, and Thomas S. Hayes, New York: Da Capo Press, 1988), 25.

34 Ibid., 11.

35 See the residences commissioned by John Pierpont Morgan, Andrew Carnegie, and Egisto Fabbri in the United States. Ciacci, "Non tutti i giardini di delizie sono uguali," 23.

36 Wharton, *Italian Villas and Their Gardens,* 12.

37 George Sitwell, *On the Making of Gardens* (1909; reprint, with a foreword by John Dixon Hunt, Boston: David R. Godine, 2003), 7, 8, and 14.

38 Geoffrey Scott, *The Architecture of Humanism: A Study in the History of Taste* (1914; reprint, New York: W. W. Norton, 1999), 60–61.

39 Pinsent listed his works in an article by John Fleming that was never published. His list was partly

published in Erika Neubauer, "The Garden Architecture of Cecil Pinsent, 1884–1964," *Journal of Garden History* 3, no. 1 (1983): 35–48.

40 Lee, "Old Italian Gardens," 44.

41 In an editorial announcing the exhibition, the committee wrote: "Particolarmente Firenze, coi suoi colli festanti e le opere d'arte che ripetono per virtù degli uomini il miracolo d'Iddio, fu la terra destinata alla gaiezza e ai fiori . . . A Luigi Dami, geniale cultore della storia dell'arte, spetta il merito di aver rivendicato a Firenze il primato nella costruzione del giardino italiano." Venturino Lucchesi, "La 'Primavera Fiorentina'—Giardini l'Italia," *Corriere Padano* (Ferrara), 9 April 1931, ASCF, fascicolo "Ritagli di giornali," busta 5090.

42 "E come da Firenze l'impero dell'architettura era passato a Roma, così dal giardino fiorentino, tutto disegnato in piano e rinchiuso e limitato, s'era passati al giardino romano, tutto plastico sulle masse accidentate del terreno e digradante per terrazzo e aperto sugli orizzonti." *Mostra del Giardino Italiano*, 71.

43 "Il maggiore incremento all'arte del giardino." Ibid., 45.

44 "La prima vera grande villa del Rinascimento." Ibid.

45 "Sorgente di ciò che fu il grandioso fiume del 'Giardino all'italiana" snodantesi dal '400, attraverso i secoli, sino al '700 . . . Soluzioni abbozzate più che realizzazioni d'arte, ma che già segnano sulle colline fiorentine . . . la rinascita dell'arte del giardino, la sottomissione del terreno e della vegetazione alla volontà dell'artista in un disegno ordinato e definito." Gherardo Bosio, "Invito alla visita delle Ville Medicee a proposito della mostra fiorentina del giardino," *Domus* 39 (March 1931): 56.

46 A Mostra Augustea della Romanità was organized in Rome in 1937 in order to celebrate the two thousandth anniversary of Augustus's birth. Given the emphasis on empire, the study of Republican Rome was somewhat neglected during the fascist years.

47 See Hunt, *Picturesque Garden in Europe*, 187–93; Vezzosi, *Il giardino romantico*; Alessandro Tagliolini, ed., *Il giardino italiano dell'Ottocento nelle immagini, nella letteratura, nelle memorie* (Milan: Guerini, 1990); Milena Matteini, *Pietro Porcinai, architetto del giardino e del paesaggio* (Milan: Electa, 1991); Pier Fausto Bagatti Valsecchi and Andreas Kipar, eds., *Il giardino paesaggistico tra Settecento e Ottocento in Italia e in Germania: Villa Vigoni e l'opera di Giuseppe Balzaretto* (Milan: Guerini, 1996); Massimo Venturi Ferriolo, *Giardino e paesaggio dei romantici* (Milan: Guerini, 1998); Mariachiara Pozzana, ed., *I giardini del XX secolo: L'opera di Pietro Porcinai* (Florence: Alinea, 1998); and Vincenzo Cazzato, *La memoria, il tempo, la storia nel giardino italiano fra '800 e '900* (Rome: Istituto Poligrafico e Zecca dello Stato, 1999). See also Giovanna Ragionieri, ed., *Il giardino storico italiano: Problemi di indagine, fonti letterarie e storiche* (Florence: L. S. Olschki, 1981); this book is a collection of essays delivered at the first conference on gardens organized in October 1978 at San Quirico d'Orcia by the Giunta Regionale Toscana. As the adjective *storico* suggests, the essays included in the book do not give a categorical definition of the Italian garden. On the contrary, they call for an expansion of horizons, and cover gardens from the late Renaissance, Mannerist, and Baroque periods to gardens from the eighteenth and nineteenth centuries. Each essay studies gardens from a morphological, historical, and cultural point of view, and pays considerable attention to archival sources.

48 Giulio Cesare Lensi Orlandi Cardini, *Le ville di Firenze*, 2 vols. (Florence: Vallecchi, 1954).

49 Ibid., 58.

50 Ibid., 38.

51 Ibid., 92–93.

52 Francesco Fariello, *Arte dei giardini* (Rome: Edizioni dell'Ateneo, 1956), 102.

53 "tutto ordine, chiarezza e ricchezza plastica." Ibid., 105.

54 Ibid., 111–12.

55 "La vitalità di una concezione che trae le sue origini nei caratteri stessi della nostra razza influenzerà per molto tempo i costruttori europei che guarderanno, per le loro ispirazioni, ai modelli originali ed insuperabili di Roma e di Firenze considerati, proprio per le loro peculiarità inconfondibili, i modelli del 'giardino italiano.'" Camillo Fiorani, *Giardini d'Italia: Arte, carattere e storia del giardino italiano* (Rome: Edizioni Mediterranee, 1960), 44.

56 "Naturalmente anche i giardini risentirono del nuovo clima. Di tutte le arti, quella dei giardini fu la più colpita. Una vera crociata. La concezione classica fatta di misura e di ordine era giunta sino alla fine del secolo diciottesimo quasi immutata. I cambiamenti non erano stati fino allora che logiche evoluzioni dovute ai tempi, ai gusti, alle mode. Se qualche tendenza a svincolarsi dai canoni rinascimentali si era manifestata in Francia, con la creazione del giardino di pianura, quella non era stata, in fondo, che una nuova applicazione del principio generatore italiano." Ibid., 93.

57 "Quello che si fece, quando non fu opera di stranieri, è senza dignità. I giardini vengono affidati di solito ai giardinieri i quali, preoccupati più della sorte delle piante che della prospettiva, copiano con approssimazione i pochi modelli che hanno davanti agli occhi . . . Un prato verde o una rigogliosa fioritura di alberi esotici, anche se belli a vedersi, non hanno nulla in comune con l'arte che è fatta di proporzioni, di armonia oltre a quel 'quid' misterioso che si agita in ogni anima ma che a pochi soltanto è concesso di esprimere. Si riteneva nel secolo scorso che gli architetti non fossero idonei a occuparsi di giardini per le loro scarse conoscenze botaniche. Come se un pittore non fosse in grado di fare un bel quadro soltanto perchè non sa fabbricare da sè i colori che gli occorrono . . ." Ibid., 202.

58 Ugo Ojetti, ed., *I palazzi e le ville che non sono più del re* (Milan: Fratelli Treves, 1921).

59 Georgina Masson, *Italian Gardens* (New York: Harry N. Abrams, 1961), 71.

60 Ibid., 63.

61 Ibid., 72.

62 Ibid., 79.

63 Ibid., 83.

64 "Un grazioso giardinetto, cinto da mura con aiole e pergolati, lo troviamo anche nella residenza chiamata il Trebbio, un'antica costruzione medievale situata su una collina nei pressi di Cafaggiolo, trasformata da Michelozzo in un'accogliente villa di campagna, che si collocava al centro di una vasta tenuta comprendente ventotto poderi." Alessandro Tagliolini, *Storia del giardino italiano: Gli artisti, l'invenzione, le forme, dall'antichità al XIX secolo* (1988; reprint, Rome: Ponte alle Grazie, 1994), 66.

65 "La semplicità del prato, recinto sul fronte da uno steccato, contrasta con la ricercatezza del padiglione di verdura ed ancor più con l'elegante fontana che si innalza sull'erba, avendo come sfondo la severa immagine della villa fortificata." Ibid.

66 "Si tratta di un esempio quasi unico di giardino quattrocentesco conservatosi nelle sue strutture principali . . . Il grande orto posto sul lato destro del Trebbio è realizzato in due terrazze, la prima occupata completamente dal grande pergolato e la seconda dall'orto vero e proprio e dal secondo pergolato oggi perduto . . . Davanti alla casa sulla sinistra compare una architettura vegetale piuttosto singolare: una sorta di *berceau*, che nel passato è stato interpretato come un'uccelliera. Si tratta in realtà di un padiglione, realizzato con sempreverdi (forse lecci) la cui chioma è potata a cupola, che ripara con la sua ombra un sedile sottostante." Mariachiara Pozzana, "Il giardino del Trebbio," in *Giardini medicei: Giardini di palazzo e di villa nella Firenze del Quattrocento*, ed. Cristina Acidini Luchinat (Milan: F. Motta, 1996), 148 and 150–51.

67 "L'aspetto rustico dei giardini è documentato, sul finire del Cinquecento, in una delle lunette che ornavano la villa di Artimino, dipinta dal pittore fiammingo Giusto Utens, che ne dette una versione idealizzata ma forse non troppo dissimile dalla realtà quattrocentesca." Tagliolini, *Storia del giardino italiano*, 65–66.

68 "L'analisi della lunetta dell'Utens, testo molto noto, ma forse non ancora a fondo indagato per quanto riguarda l'intorno, ci informa sui caratteri del giardino quattrocentesco." Pozzana, "Il giardino del Trebbio," 155.

69 "L'alta borghesia mercantile divenne terriera: in tutte le ville si diffuse il giardino all'italiana ad imitazione di quelli delle residenze medicee." Adriano Gradi, "Il paesaggio agrario-forestale toscano nel XV secolo e sue trasformazioni," in *L'arte al potere: Universi simbolici e reali nelle terre di Firenze al tempo di Lorenzo il Magnifico*, eds. Domenico A. Conci, Vittorio Dini, and Francesco Magnelli (Bologna: Editrice Compositori, 1992), 51.

70 "L'ordine appunto, nella sua quintessenza di espressione della razionalità, si presenta infatti fin dal Due e Trecento come primo e fondamentale requisito affinché una porzione definita di spazio possa dirsi un "giardino," e ciò non solo in Toscana, ma in tutti gli stati della penisola; un'interpretazione questa che, del resto, si è consolidata da tempo nella letteratura critica, partendo dalla sovrapposizione tipica del primo Novecento del "giardino italiano" al "giardino della ragione" *tout court*, per giungere ai giorni nostri." Cristina Acidini Luchinat, "I giardini dei Medici: Origini, sviluppi, trasformazioni; L'architettura, il verde, le statue, le fontane," in *Giardini medicei: Giardini di palazzo e di villa nella Firenze del Quattrocento*, ed. Cristina Acidini Luchinat (Milan: F. Motta, 1996), 48.

71 "Cafaggiolo, nonostante l'affermazione del Vasari, probabilmente non ebbe giardini nel senso stretto della parola. Meno ancora Trebbio e le altre." Luigi Dami, *Il giardino italiano* (Milan: Bestetti and Tumminelli, 1924), 31n4. Earlier books on Italian gardens relied solely on Vasari's testimony. See Mrs. Julia Mary Cartwright Ady, *Italian Gardens of the Renaissance* (London: Smith, Elder, 1914), 13: "Cafaggiolo was another villa which Michelozzo built for Cosimo. Vasari describes this as a castle with moat and drawbridge, built for defense, but surrounded with ilex-woods, gardens, fountains, aviaries, and all that makes a villa fair and pleasant."

72 Rose Standish Nichols, *Italian Pleasure Gardens* (New York: Dodd, Mead, 1931), 100–101.

73 Lazzaro, "Politicizing a National Garden Tradition," 157.

74 Lazzaro distinguished her study of the Italian garden "from modern notions . . . which were largely recast in the first four decades of this century" in "Italy is a Garden: The Idea of Italy and the Italian Garden Tradition," in *Villas and Gardens in Early Modern Italy and France*, eds. Mirka Beneš and Dianne Harris, 29–60 (Cambridge: Cambridge University Press, 2001). But while she questioned the "homogeneity of the Italian garden tradition" that was emphasized during the regime, and contrasted it with the diverse topography, flora, and culture of Italy, she also insisted on "the idea of a unified garden tradition," for which, she claimed, there was considerable evidence. Rather than proving the unity of the Italian garden tradition, however, her study successfully pointed to the diversity within what has been called "Italian" from the eighteenth century onward. Yet it failed to acknowledge that the English landscape garden was also considered "Italian" during the years of the Risorgimento, when issues of national identity urged Italian intellectuals to focus their attention on notions of heritage and tradition, which they construed and constructed as they saw fit.

75 Lazzaro, "Politicizing a National Garden Tradition," 157.

76 Ibid., 169.

77 Ibid., 159.

78 Ibid.

79 Ibid., 169.

80 Ibid.

81 It is probably not a coincidence that most Italian scholars who write about gardens are, in fact, architects. What is surprising, however, is that their writings on gardens do not reflect the more recent postmodern approaches that have otherwise informed the architectural discourse.

82 Ritu Bhatt, "The Significance of the Aesthetic in Postmodern Architectural Theory," *Journal of Architectural Education* 53 (May 2000): 230.

83 Emilio Sereni, *History of the Italian Agricultural Landscape*, trans. R. Burr Litchfield (Princeton, N.J.: Princeton University Press, 1997), 148

84 Ibid.

85 Charles S. Maier, foreword to *History of the Italian Agricultural Landscape*, xxi.

86 The Medici villa at Fiesole, however, can be considered an earlier exception.

87 Maier, foreword to *History of the Italian Agricultural Landscape*, xxv.

PART II

The Notion of Territorial Systems in Italian Villa Gardens

CHAPTER 3

Systems of Gardens in Italy: Princely Residences and Villas in Rome and Latium, Savoy Piedmont, Royal Bourbon Naples, and Bagheria, Sicily

MARCELLO FAGIOLO

THE MAIN OBJECTIVE OF THIS PAPER—WHICH is complementary to that of Vincenzo Cazzato—is to study certain systems of extraurban gardens. In recent decades, scholars have focused their attention on many of these systems, but a comparative critical analysis that demonstrates congruities and correlations of formal and social-political character among extraurban garden systems is still lacking. From these characters, or essences, either similar or complementary, are bequeathed formal design choices that we will examine in parallel, if even with differences linked to the diversity of patronage and to the range of historical periods.

I will, therefore, examine synthetically four systems of princely residences in Italy. These systems have very homogeneous and strongly coherent features from historical and cultural points of view. They also share geographic and historical characteristics (i.e., they are restricted to certain geographic areas and, in some cases, to very limited historical periods), similarities of function (e.g., hunting), and common visual and structural elements (e.g., the use of scenographic layouts and "theatricality," the interrelationship between the villa and the capital city, and the privileged positions of viewing "belvederes" onto the surrounding territories).[1]

The concept of a "system of gardens" has also been a central tenet of the cultural strategy of the Italian Committee for the Study and Conservation of Gardens and Historical Parks (Comitato per lo studio e la conservazione dei giardini e dei parchi storici) of the Ministero per i Beni Culturali e Ambientali (where I acted as vice-chairman from 1983 to 2004 and chairman after 2004). This cultural strategy is directed toward conserving and enhancing the status of gardens and their territorial contexts, which should be preserved and defended against the aggressions of building speculation and of the policies tied to large transportation infrastructure.

The decision to focus on systems instead of single residences allows me to include residences that are devoid of formal gardens but connected to woods or hunting parks—both of which are fundamental elements in the systems selected for study. I will not be considering other notable or important systems of villas that—because they do not adhere to the criteria of selection discussed here—show different formal and functional parameters and are characterized by other dominant motivating circumstances. For example, I will not examine the Baroque villas around Milan, which were mostly connected with urban palaces and which functioned not only as sites of *villeggiatura* (sojourns and life in the villa) and emblems of status, but also as centers of control over agricultural work; the Genoese villas, which were largely created for aristocratic villeggiatura or as residences representative of status; or the Veneto villas of the Renaissance and Baroque periods, which were embedded in programs of rationalization of productive yields or the agricultural transformation of the region.[2] Similarly, certain systems of the Renaissance are excluded, such as the *delizie* (delights) of the Este family in Ferrara[3] and the Medici villas around Florence.[4] In both types of villas, the function of hunting was dominant but did not affect significantly the formal structure of the villas (something that happens, on the contrary, in the Baroque villa systems that are studied). Although it is restricted to the four selected villa systems, this comparative analysis has been made possible through the use of the multidisciplinary studies carried out in recent decades; these studies offer a consolidated

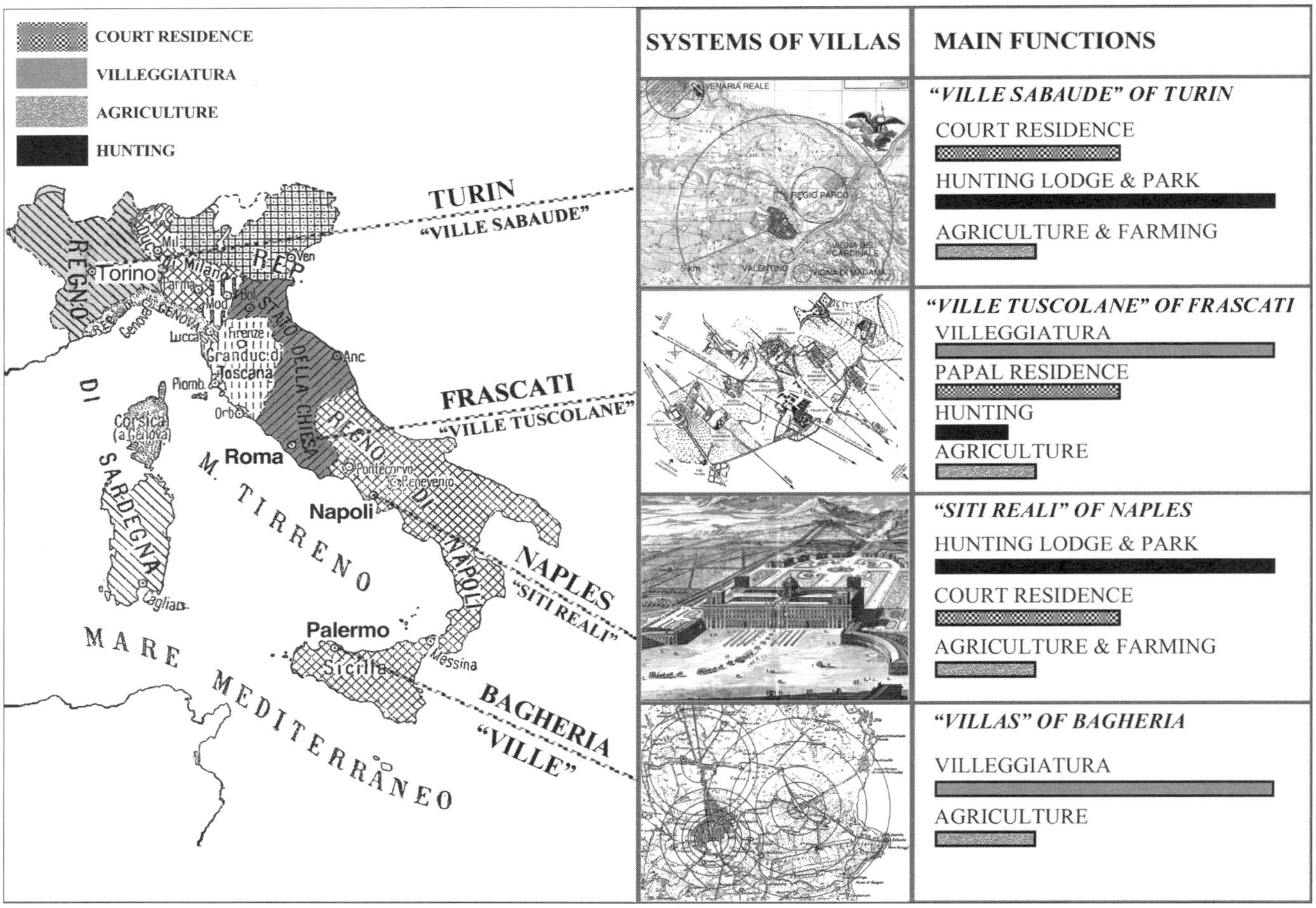

FIGURE 3.1.
Ideogrammatic scheme showing the four key systems of villas in Italy: the Savoy villas around Turin (the capital of the Duchy of Savoy), the papal and cardinalate villas at Frascati near Rome (the capital of the papal states), the "royal sites" of the Bourbon dynasty around Naples, and the villas of the nobility at Bagheria near Palermo.

Illustration by Marcello Fagiolo.

point of departure regarding the complementary or similar typologies, the compositional layouts, the choices of design language, and the different political, economic, and social functions.

Figure 3.1 provides a comprehensive ideogrammatic scheme, or visual ideation, of the four geographical systems of villas that I have laid out. This early modern map of Italy indicates the geographical and political regions of each system: the Savoy villas around Turin (the capital of the Duchy of Savoy), the papal and cardinalate villas at Frascati near Rome (the capital of the papal states), the "royal sites" of the Bourbon dynasty around Naples, and the villas of the nobility at Bagheria near Palermo. For each system, I have highlighted the quantitative significance of the four main functions—court residence, villeggiatura, hunting, and agriculture and forestal exploitation—that I have discerned as a basis for comparative analysis:

- *court residence,* with fluctuations between the extremes of the long-term residence (such as the Royal Palace in Caserta, the new eighteenth-century Bourbon capital that was conceptualized on the model of Versailles) and the temporary residence connected to the rituals of hunting (such as the residences of the House of Savoy and the "royal sites" of Naples) or to the summer villeggiatura (such as the Tusculan villas near Frascati)
- *villeggiatura,* with the setting up of representational spaces or those of "splendid isolation," and with the creation of gardens and parks
- *hunting,* with all the pertinent territorial organization and practices
- the control and transformation of the larger territory through *agricultural and forestal exploitation,* animal breeding, and the livestock industry

Always at the level of the ideogrammatic, we will begin by discussing some models in the region of Latium, namely villas conceived in relation to the territory and to the capital, Rome, or to the nearest town. We will immediately recall the importance of the genius loci, which is expressed in each of the relationships between the villas, hills, lakes, and ancient shrines. In an ideogrammatic drawing (fig. 3.2) based on an intuitive concept by Christian

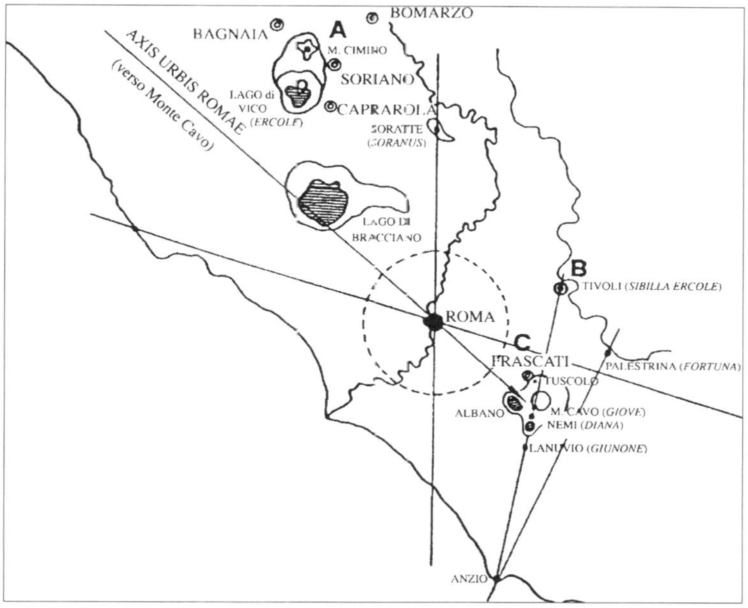

FIGURE 3.2.
Ideogrammatic map of the relationships between villas, mountains, lakes, and ancient sanctuaries in Latium. The map shows the historical and mythical rooting of the three main groups of villas in Latium (with their different genii loci); these villas are gathered around the *axis urbis Romae* and are directed toward the Alban Hills and the Sanctuary of Jupiter/Latium.

Illustration by Marcello Fagiolo; adapted from a scheme in Christian Norberg-Schulz, *Genius loci: Paesaggio, ambiente, architettura* (Milan: Electa, 1979).

Norberg-Schulz,[5] I have illustrated the profound historical-mythical rooting of the three main nuclei of the Latium villas around the *axis urbis Romae* pointing in the direction of the Alban Hills and the Sanctuary of Jupiter/Latium. The letter A refers to the Renaissance villas and nymphaea of the Tuscia region near Viterbo, including the Villa Orsini at Bomarzo (also called the Sacro Bosco); the Villa Lante at Bagnaia; the Palazzo Madruzzo and the Forte Madruzzo at Soriano nel Cimino; and the Villa Farnese at Caprarola. These villas are arrayed around the sacred centers of the territory: Lago di Vico (tied to the myth of Hercules), Mount Cimino, and Mount Soratte (tied to the cult of Soranus). The letter B indicates the Villa d'Este at Tivoli, which was consecrated to the local cults of Hercules Saxanus and the Sibyl Albunea (Tiburtine Sibyl). The letter C refers to the villas of Frascati, which are centered around ancient

Tusculum (now Tuscolo, the dwelling of Castor and Pollux) and the Albanus Mons in the Alban Hills (the site of the Sanctuary of Jupiter/Latium, the barycenter of an extensive system of sanctuaries).

The Villa as a Territorial Barycenter: Tivoli, Bagnaia, and Genzano

Villa d'Este at Tivoli

The Villa d'Este at Tivoli lies at the crossing of two ideal Cartesian territorial axes (fig. 3.3). The relationship between the Villa d'Este, the town of Tivoli, and the ruins interpreted by Pirro Ligorio as ancient villas can be visualized through a grid of lines that accompany these two crossing axes. The villa has been placed in an orthogonal grid that shows some important analogies of orientation with Tiburtine antiquities. Particularly interesting is the *cardo maximus* in the garden, placed along the axis A–B that leads from the Fortress (Rocca Pia) of Pope Pius II and the amphitheater of Tivoli to the villa of Quintilius Varus (at B) and the landscape highlights of the Monti Corniculani and Mount Soratte. The most important *decumani* are those of the Avenue of

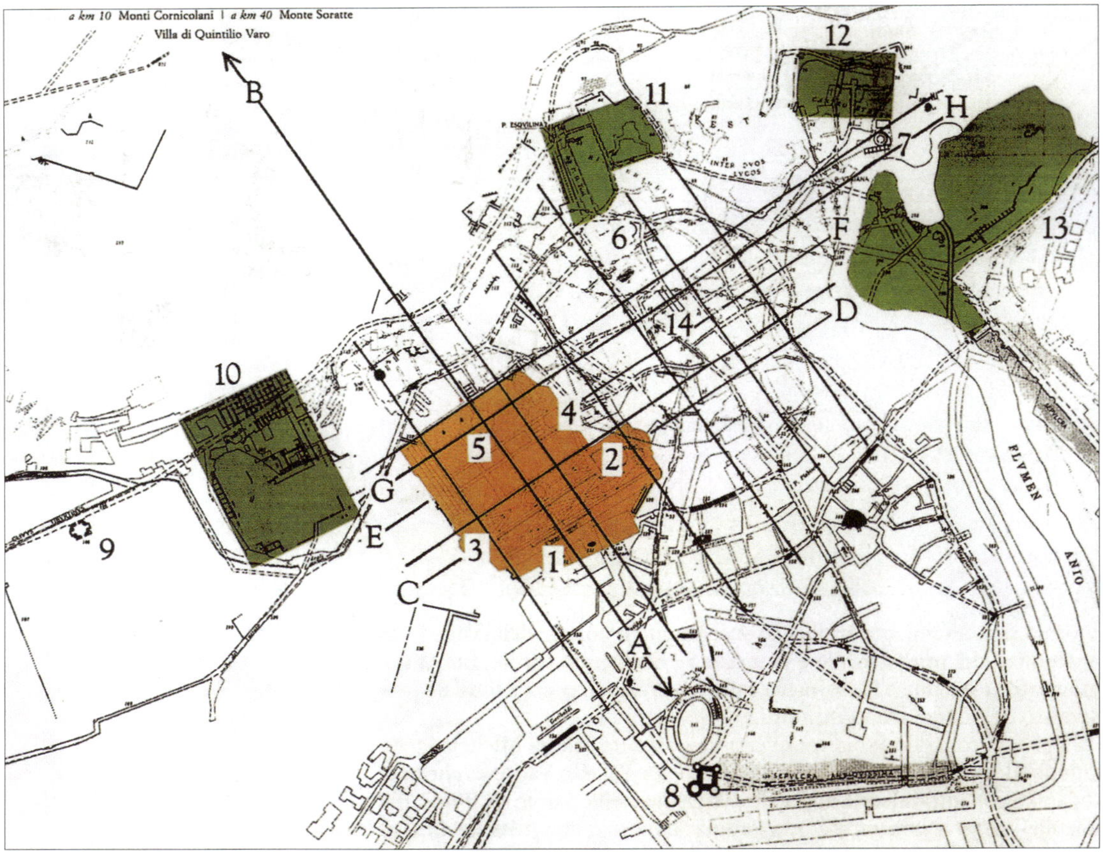

FIGURE 3.3.
The relationship between the Villa d'Este, the town of Tivoli, and the ruins interpreted by Pirro Ligorio as ancient villas. The following sites are indicated in the drawing: Palace at the Ville d'Este (1), Fountain of Tivoli (2), Fountain of Rome (3), Fountain of the Organ (4), Cypress Rotunda (5), Temple of Hercules (Cathedral) (6), Acropolis and Temple of the Sibyl (7), Fortress (Rocca Pia) of Pope Pius II (8), Temple "della Tosse" (9), villa of Augustus (Temple of Hercules Victor) (10), villa of Horace (11), Villa Gelliana (12), and villa of Manlius Vopiscus (13).

Illustration by Marcello Fagiolo; adapted from the Archaeological Map of Tivoli by Cairoli Fulvio Giuliani in Isabella Barisi, Marcello Fagiolo, and Maria Luisa Madonna, *Villa d'Este* (Rome: De Luca, 2003).

the Hundred Fountains (axis C–D) and the avenue of the fishpools (axis E–F), while from a territorial point of view the axis of the Cypress Rotunda (axis G–H) contained between the villa of Augustus and the Temple of the Sibyl is of particular relevance. The southwest-northeast axis links the Tiburtine acropolis with the city of Rome, while the northwest-southeast axis (which coincides with the central avenue of the garden) runs from the Rocca Pia of Pius II, to the palace of the villa, to the ancient villa of Quintilius Varus, and to the landscape features of the Monti Cornicolani (approximately ten kilometers away), beyond which the distant peak of Mount Soratte rises almost seven hundred meters at a distance of forty kilometers. It was the mythical site of "Soranus," identified in antiquity with Pluto or Apollo.[6] The view—at once mountainous, georgic, and paradisiacal—was described by Antonio del Re in 1611:

> You see the mount of Viterbo and that of Santo Oreste in ancient times called Soracte with all the mountains and sites interposed—between you and them; and from the right side there are beautiful mounts, and hills nearby; and beneath the mount of Viterbo we discover the green vegetation of very tall olive trees, gardens of pomegranates and other fruits, with a plain of meadows and fields to be sown, and the river Aniene which, meandering in the midst of all this like a serpent, descends toward the Tiber.[7]

The Villa d'Este was unique in its efforts to emulate Hadrian's Villa. Its designer, Pirro Ligorio, also intended that it should be integrated at the very center of a basin of land, like an amphitheater, of ancient villas (real or presumed), including the villa of Augustus, the villa of Horace, the Villa Gelliana, and the villa of Manlius Vopiscus.

Before the creation of the *vie d'acqua* (waterways) of the gardens at Bagnaia and Caprarola, the Villa d'Este had the first astonishing example of an *asse acquatico* (water axis): the Avenue of the Hundred Fountains. Stretched between the Fountain of the Sybil and the Fountain of Rome, it lies along the axis C–D that effectively joins the two opposing poles (nature and culture) of the Temple of the Tiburtine Sibyl and of the city of Rome, far off on the horizon.

Villa Lante at Bagnaia

At the Villa Lante (ex-Gambara) at Bagnaia, a design was conceived to order the two organic systems—the feudal village dominated by the castle, and the park around the preexisting hunting casino of the Riario family—that were previously governed by what seemed like chaos (fig. 3.4).[8] In the analytic plan of the villa, I have highlighted the north-south axis of equilibrium between the geometric garden (A) and the park (B); along this axis we find the secondary portal of the villa (D) and the tower of the castle inside the medieval town (E) toward which the four streets of the town converge. The geometric genesis of the villa, built on three modules almost squared, has also been identified. The main portal (C) is placed equidistantly from the northern end of the garden (Fountain of the Great Flood) and the tower (E). For this plan, one can imagine a discussion between the patron, Vignola, and Tommaso Ghinucci, who—as the overseer of all architectural and urban planning work at Bagnaia—was commissioned by the Comune di Bagnaia in February 1567 to carry out the urbanistic systematization of the area between the market square and the park.[9] It is probable, however, that it was Vignola who devised the trident of avenues, which, after the construction of the new town quarter, introduced into this previously chaotic area a sense of order that was both natural and urban.[10]

The first design intervention consisted, in my view, of creating a divide or *spartiacque* (literally, a watershed) between the wild nature of the park and the artificial nature of the garden. A north-south line was drawn from the castle keep to separate these two systems. Along this axis opens the lower portal of the villa; the entrance drive then runs upward to the side entrance to the garden (which is still used as the start of the visitors' circuit). Precisely in order to privilege this *asse di bilanciamento* (axis restoring the balance), it was decided not to make the garden axis coincide with the one that connects its portal with the castle. The dimensions of the garden were then set out according to a rational logic. The main entrance gate was established in a position exactly barycentral with respect to the castle keep's tower, which functioned as a kind of generator of historical

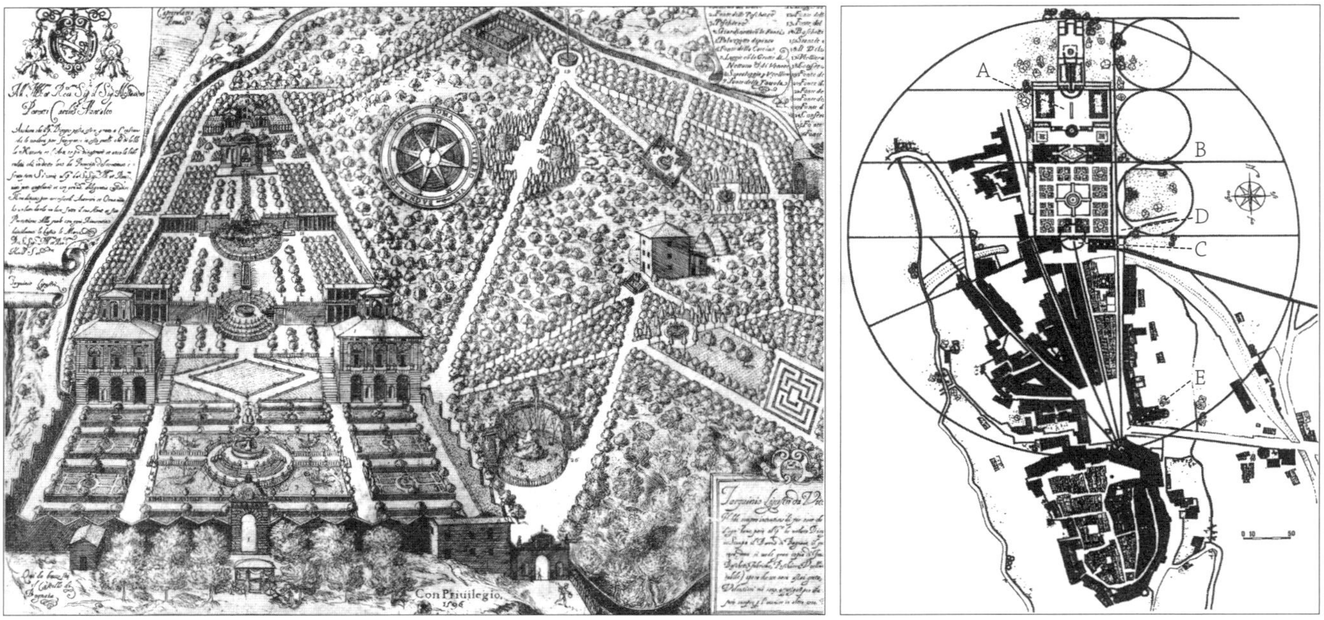

a b

FIGURE 3.4. Plan of the Villa Lante and the town of Bagnaia. (a) Engraving by Tarquinio Ligustri, 1596. (b) Illustration by Marcello Fagiolo; adapted from a survey in Margherita Asso, Marisa Cuppini, and Adriana Montori, "Bagnaia," *Quaderni dell'Istituto di Storia dell'Architettura* 17 (1956).

and urbanistic meaning, and the end of the garden, where the water of the Fontana del Diluvio (Fountain of the Great Flood), the natural generator of the axial waterway, poured forth. Lastly, the geometrical grid of the garden was determined and three identical ideal squares were laid out. The first square contained a garden organized in parterres, a second square included the two pavilions and the two upper terraces, and a third square formed the vanishing point of the entire composition.

The Villa Lante at Bagnaia echoed the balancing act between the axial order of Bramante's Belvedere Court at the Vatican and the relative disorder of the Vatican *bosco* (woodland). Furthermore, one should note that this bosco, with its system of avenues around the Casino of Pius IV and its *orto dei semplici* (garden of simples) laid out as a spray of radiating avenues in front of the loggia-fishpond, had come to be a model for a park, such as the complex of the Villa Lante, in the 1560s.

Later examples of tridents in the architecture of villas include the trident designed by Domenico Fontana around 1580 in front of the *palazzina* (pavilion) at the Villa Montalto-Peretti (Rome), the three avenues designed by Giacomo della Porta in front of the main building at the Villa Aldobrandini (Frascati), and the large piazza with sixteen avenues built after 1640 at the Villa Mattei Celimontana (Rome).

Genzano

Far more complex is the case of Genzano, a park that over the centuries became the spine of a new town.[11] The *borgo* (town) of Genzano originated in 1636–43 between the poles of the old cathedral and the Palazzo Baronale, and had a system of roads designed according to the triangulation method (fig. 3.5). Of particular interest is the trivium of avenues of elm trees, which was laid out in front of the palace in 1643 at the behest of Giuliano Cesarini. A fourth avenue of elms formed a transversal axis starting from the "Palatine" Church of the Capuchins. The trivium of elm avenues is replicated in the urbanized trivium at the foot of the old town, which constitutes an ideal half of a Renaissance model of a radial-centric town with eight radii. The difficulties of the topographic relief perhaps advised against executing the three radii missing toward the valley. The most exalted and highest status road, the Via Livia, presents the same template as that of the elm avenues. With its width of twenty meters, it can be hypothesized

a

b

FIGURE 3.5.
Two views of the level of the elm avenues and groves in relation to the Palazzo Sforza Cesarini in Genzano. (a) Engraving showing the visit of Pope Alexander VII by Gregorio Tomasini; (b) Domenico Jacovacci, view of Genzano and its streets, 1638, watercolor.

Photograph 3.5b courtesy of the Palazzo Chigi di Ariccia.

that this road was also to have been lined with elm trees. Cesarini's master plan designated Genzano as the *umbilicus Latii*—the barycenter of the complex territorial relationships between Rome, the Tyrrhenian Sea, and the Prenestine Mountains (fig. 3.6). The center of the trivium in front of the palace is singled out along the axis that joins the palace with Rome, and in particular to the rising mass of Saint Peter's. (This axis also joins the sanctuary of Galloro, the park in Ariccia, and the church of San Paolo at Albano with the axis's trivium of streets.) The second avenue of elms links the Capuchin church with an ideal axis that ends on the sea at Ostia Antica and Porto. The third avenue symbolically connects Marino with Lanuvio. The fourth (transversal) avenue is singled out along the axis that joins a number of highly significant points of ancient Latium: Mount Cavo, Tusculum, and Hadrian's Villa at Tivoli (in the northwest) to Anzio (in the southeast). Furthermore, the central road of the trivium appears to be correlated with a sacred territorial axis in the direction of the Temple of Diana Nemorense (Nemi) and Palestrina. The Palazzo Cesarini complex was thus inserted into the arcane system of sacred hills and great sanctuaries of eastern Latium.

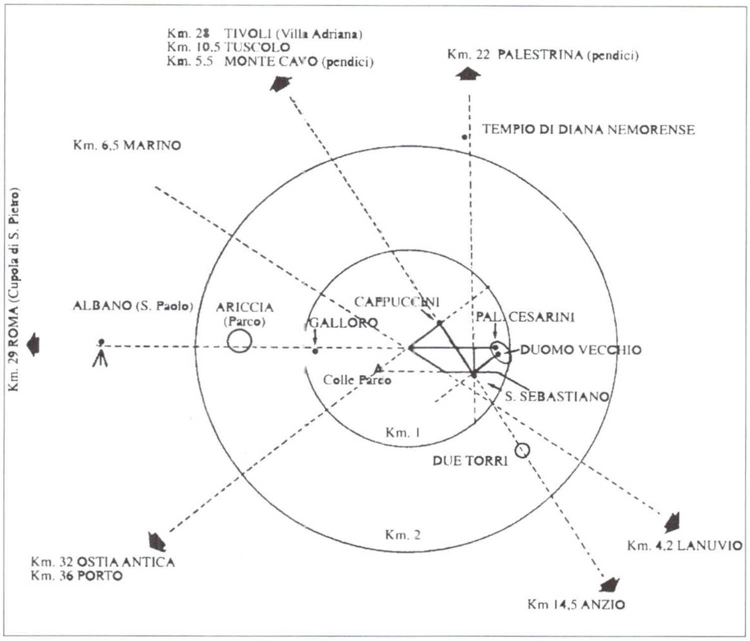

FIGURE 3.6.
Ideogrammatic scheme of the seventeenth-century urban plan of Genzano. The trident of elm avenues west of the Palazzo Sforza Cesarini and the new axes to the south point toward the main historical and geographical highlights of Latium.

Illustration by Marcello Fagiolo.

The Tusculan Villas

Within the span of fifty years—between the pontificates of Gregory XIII (1572–85) and Gregory XV (1621–23)—a glowing constellation of twelve villas was created at Frascati to revive the memory of Tusculum, an ancient site that had been annexed to the system of *villae tusculanae* and that had belonged to Cato, Lucullus, Sallust, Pompey, Cicero, and Tiberius.[12] TUSCOLO RESTITUTA is inscribed on a medal of Pope Paul III (1534–49), who regained the borough of Frascati for the church in 1537, transformed it into a town, and established the custom of papal and cardinalate villeggiatura in the Tusculan area. The town was extended southward in the direction of the future cathedral and the Villa Rufina (later the Villa Falconieri), which was built by Bishop Alessandro Rufini in 1546 as a summer residence for himself and for refreshing the troubled mind of the pope (who was popularly rumored to be his father). This villa-fortress, together with the Caravilla (the small villa of Annibale Caro), was to be the seed of the rebirth of the ancient *otia tusculana,* which gained strength with Pius IV (1559–65) and Gregory XIII.

Writing to his friend Torquato Conti in 1564, Caro looked forward to establishing a "borough of villas from Poli to Rome."[13] (Poli is a village north of Palestrina and southeast of Tivoli.) While the dream of a club of gentlemen with political careers tied to the idea of a chain of villas remained an intellectual metaphor, it is true that a "city of villas" was established around Frascati that was comparable in extent and quality not only to the system of villae tusculanae, but to the suburban villas of powerful men and emperors in ancient Rome. Some of the new villas were literally grafted onto the remains of ancient buildings,[14] and it can also be said that they began to dialogue with the two centers of aggregation of the territory. These two centers were: to the southeast, Mount Tusculum (with the ancient remains at the summit of the hill); and to the northwest on the valleyside, the city of Rome,

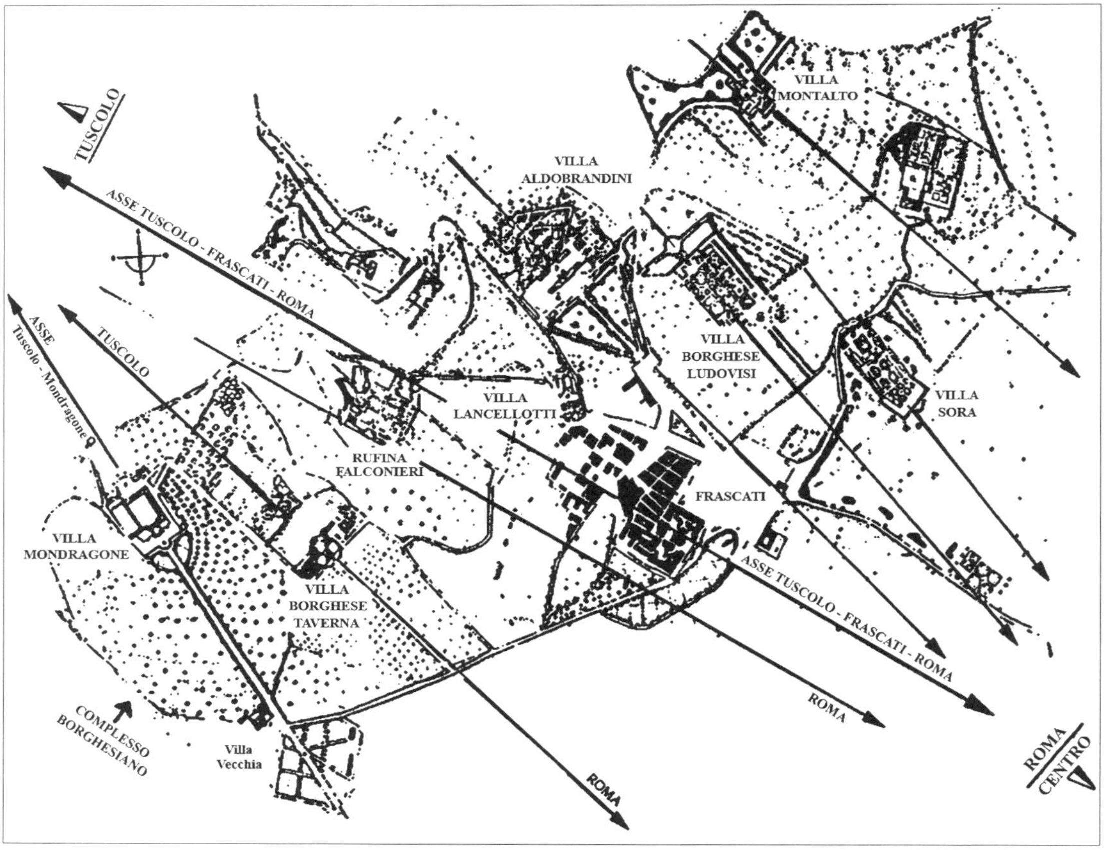

FIGURE 3.7. The villas of the popes, cardinals, and nobility at Frascati. The prevalent orientation of the villas follows the axis connecting the ancient town of Tusculum (at upper left) with Rome (off the map, at lower right).

Illustration by Marcello Fagiolo; adapted from a map by Isa Belli Barsali in *Per le ville di Roma e del Lazio* (Rome: Ist. Grafico Tiberino, 1968).

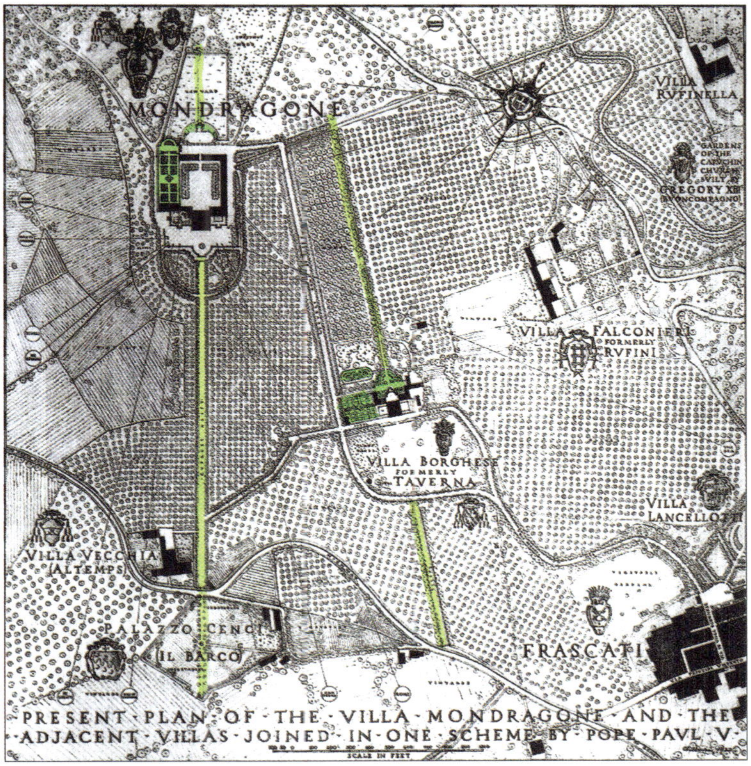

FIGURE 3.8.
Plan of the Villa Mondragone and two villas—Villa Vecchia and Villa Borghese (formerly Taverna)—acquired by Cardinal Scipione Borghese.

Drawing by J. H. Chillman, 1922. Photographic Archive, American Academy in Rome.

barely seventeen or eighteen kilometers away, toward which the front facades of the villas were turned, almost heliotropically (fig. 3.7). The whole sloping area of the Tusculan hills is understood as a theater or "amphitheater" (to borrow a Plinian topos used in the description of the upper Tiber valley) formed by the sum of individual villas-as-theaters that are strategically arranged to exploit their differences in level, their connections with preexisting elements, and, above all, their extraordinary views of Rome.

It can be observed that the town of Frascati is placed on the axis that joins Tusculum with Rome, and that the longitudinal bodies of two of the oldest Frascati villas (the Villas Rufina and Rufinella) lie along an analogous axis. A somewhat different orientation—almost radiating from the theater of Tusculum—is commanded by the three villas in the eastern sector which, in the early seventeenth century, formed a Borghese family fief: Villa Mondragone, Villa Vecchia, and Villa Borghese (formerly Taverna) (fig. 3.8). (All three villas were acquired by Cardinal Scipione Borghese, who, in turn, sold the Caravilla after refashioning it with its spectacular multiplicity of cascades.)[15] Similar to the axis just described is the axis of orientation—perhaps regarded as ideal from the heliothermal standpoint—of the four villas in the western sector: Villa Aldobrandini, Villa Ludovisi (formerly Borghese), Villa Sora, and Villa Montalto-Peretti. We are thus witnessing an intense conversation between villa and metropolis and between natural and artificial landscapes.

In 1601, Cardinal Pietro Aldobrandini, the nephew of Clement VIII (1592–1605), commissioned Giacomo della Porta to convert the casino of the Villa di Belvedere (later Villa Aldobrandini). After della Porta's death in 1602, Carlo Maderno and Giovanni Fontana took over and started to lay out the garden and to convey water to the site. Work began on the nymphaeum (also called the Water Theater) in 1604, and on the fountains higher on the slope after 1610 (fig. 3.9). The spectacular via d'acqua thus

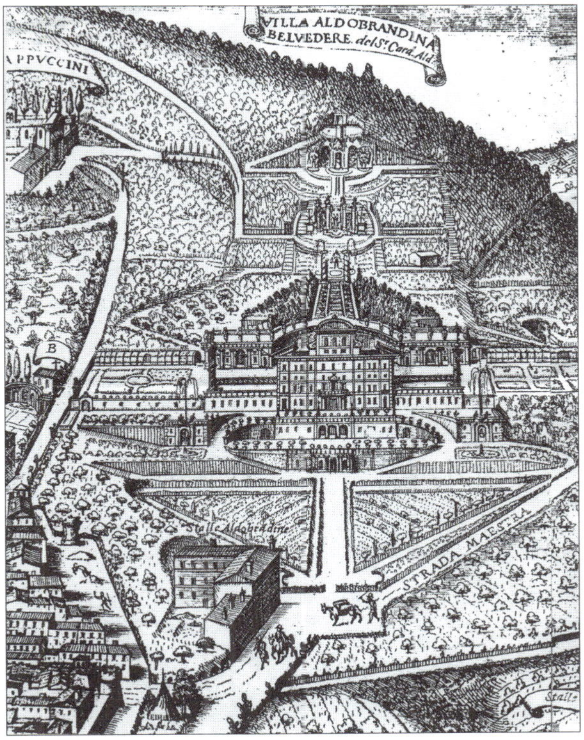

FIGURE 3.9.
Villa Aldobrandini at Frascati, detail of a 1620 engraving by Matteo Greuter.

Centro Documentazione del Centro di Studi sulla Cultura e l'Immagine di Roma, Rome.

a

b

c

FIGURE 3.10. Water theaters of the (a) Villa Aldobrandini; (b) Villa Borghese Ludovisi; and (c) Villa Mondragone at Frascati.

Reprinted from Giovanni Battista Falda, *Le fontane di Roma* (Rome, ca. 1683).

took shape; it was based less on the *scale d'acqua* (water stairs) of ancient nymphaea than on the Villa Lante (Bagnaia) and Villa Farnese (Caprarola), and it eventually became the model for other Roman and Tusculan inventions (fig. 3.10a). The water, which gushes forth high up on the hill, passes the Columns of Hercules with a nearly vertical rush and then flows back down, twisting along the ridges of the mosaic-clad column trunks and hurtling down the steps of a long iridescent ladder. It then bathes the rocky sides of the waterway, plunges into a basin, and disappears—only to reappear immediately afterward in the Aldobrandini Star (a heraldic figure) and in a cosmic epiphany, where it splashes with the incandescence of a thousand stars from the heavenly globe held up by Atlas (an allusion to Pope Clement VIII), who was originally assisted by Hercules (an allusion to Cardinal Aldobrandini). The exedra of the nymphaeum advances and recedes with the rhythm of a *scaenae frons*; indeed the single scene shatters into various minor scenes, which are presented in the series of aedicules and tabernacles dedicated to mythical personages and gladdened by the music of the waters that gave life to the panpipe of the statue Polyphemus and to the horn of the statue Centaur, while the jet of water exhaled by the giant Enceladus thundered.

A second *teatro d'acqua* (water theater) is in the Caravilla, which was bought and held briefly by Scipione Borghese; this theater was designed by Maderno and Fontana (fig. 3.10b). (The Caravilla was formerly owned by Annibale Caro, and later owned by the Ludovisi and Torlonia.) The water, which originated in a large mask, hurtled noisily down in six successive leaps into a series of big oval basins; the form of these basins was visually amplified and echoed in the wavy, curving flights of steps that descended from the upper fish pond to the lower basin between the two tall cypresses that framed the waterway in the guise of two green pillars of Hercules. To crown the waterway, after he had bought it from Cardinal Borghese, Cardinal Ludovico Ludovisi commissioned Maderno to make the nymphaeum (completed in 1621–23). At the foot of the cascade just described, the nymphaeum appears as a pacifying intervention, as a sort of dam raised to arrest the advance of the waters. This monumental scaenae frons, which has been recently restored, aligned its two openings and twenty niches with fountains; for example, in its two wings, tritons and water-spurting vases follow one another in an alternating rhythm, while in its center, the rhythm became more pressing with "sweating" rockeries (like the *Meta Sudans* of ancient Rome) and colossal figures of standing river gods who poured water from amphorae.[16]

Cardinal Borghese was also the patron of the nymphaeum in the Villa Mondragone, created by

Giovanni Vasanzio between 1616 and 1620, which had a theatrical exedra raised on a podium in the guise of a stage to allow for a better view of the garden. The scaenae frons, which is curved like a cavea, reminds one of the concept of a "theater in a theater" that was to triumph above all in the theatrical performances of Gianlorenzo Bernini (fig. 3.10c). Since almost all of the decorative elements of the nymphaeum have been lost, the recital of the waters can be reconstructed only through graphic documentation and written descriptions. For example, Deseine writes that in the seven (now empty) niches "are beautiful statues . . . jets of water gush in all directions and in the middle is a spraying waterwheel (*girandola*) that fills the ears with a deafening roar imitating thunder, rain and hail."[17]

Another theatrical element is the perspectival splay of coffers in each niche, which illusionistically augments the depth of the niches and evokes the passages that open in the scenes of Palladio's Teatro Olimpico (which the nymphaeum also resembles with its crowning element of a balustrade and statues). Thus, the central niche with water brings to mind the *via regia* (royal street, reserved here for the Regina Aqua) of the ancient theater. In these same years, the banker of the Borghese family, Roberto Primo, constructed in his villa (now the Villa Lancellotti) a nymphaeum that was very similar to and disposed in visual dialogue with the Villa Aldobrandini. His nymphaeum consisted of seven niches, originally without statues and the crowning balustrade.

The "Crown of Delights" of the House of Savoy

Shifting our attention to the eighteenth century, we will now concentrate on the two most important Italian states (besides that of the papal states): the Duchy of Savoy (later the Kingdom of Sicily and the Kingdom of Sardinia) and the Realm of Naples (which became independent with the accession of Carlo di Borbone in 1734). It is only in these two states that royal constructions were made on a European scale—in particular, Turin asserted itself, thanks also to the work of the architect Filippo Juvarra, as one of the most beautiful and modern cities in Europe.

The Savoy residences around Turin, the new capital of the Duchy, constitute a *corona di delitie* (crown of delights).[18] Built starting in the years 1563–65 with a unified strategy, albeit in successive phases, they comprised thirteen residences, including four fluvial homes (Regio Parco, Lucento, Mirafiori, and Valentino); two hillside *vigne*, or villas with vineyards (Madama Reale and that of Cardinal Maurizio); two castles in the mountains (Rivoli and Moncalieri); two hunting estates in the plain (Venaria Reale and Stupinigi); and three royal residences for villeggiatura around Turin (Agliè, Racconigi, and Pollenzo) (fig. 3.11). We will dwell on the residences that gravitate most strongly toward the capital; they are the Regio Parco, the Vigna del Cardinale, the Venaria Reale, the castles of Mirafiori, Valentino, and Rivoli, and the hunting estate at Stupinigi.

In parallel with his project of fortifying the capital with the Citadel (designed by Francesco Paciotto), Duke Emanuele Filiberto (r. 1553–80) pursued "an intense and targeted policy of land purchases, destined to establish around Turin, beyond the limits of the city walls, a vast zone of ducal property, which came to form a sort of personal domain of the sovereign"[19] (fig. 3.12). He immediately acquired the Castello di Valentino, with its gardens on the Po River, and the Viboccone, the estate that was incorporated into the Regio Parco. These constituted the first nuclei of the state property close to the urban fortifications, to which were then added other possessions further away from the city. The plan for the system of residences took on more concrete form with Duke Carlo Emanuele I (r. 1580–1630), who at the same time created the urban focus of the Palazzo Ducale and then expanded Turin with the Città Nuova, where incentives were offered to noblemen if they resided there. The duke used as his architect Ascanio Vitozzi, and the work was later continued by Carlo di Castellamonte.

The Viboccone (later the Regio Parco), which was created by Ascanio Vitozzi for Carlo Emanuele I at the beginning of the seventeenth century, is a veritable *speculum sapientiae*, in which the ideals of the Christian prince join with the moralizing demands of the Counter-Reformation. The park is known through a written description by the artist Federico Zuccaro. If, as Zuccaro wrote, other gardens contain iconographic elements and themes

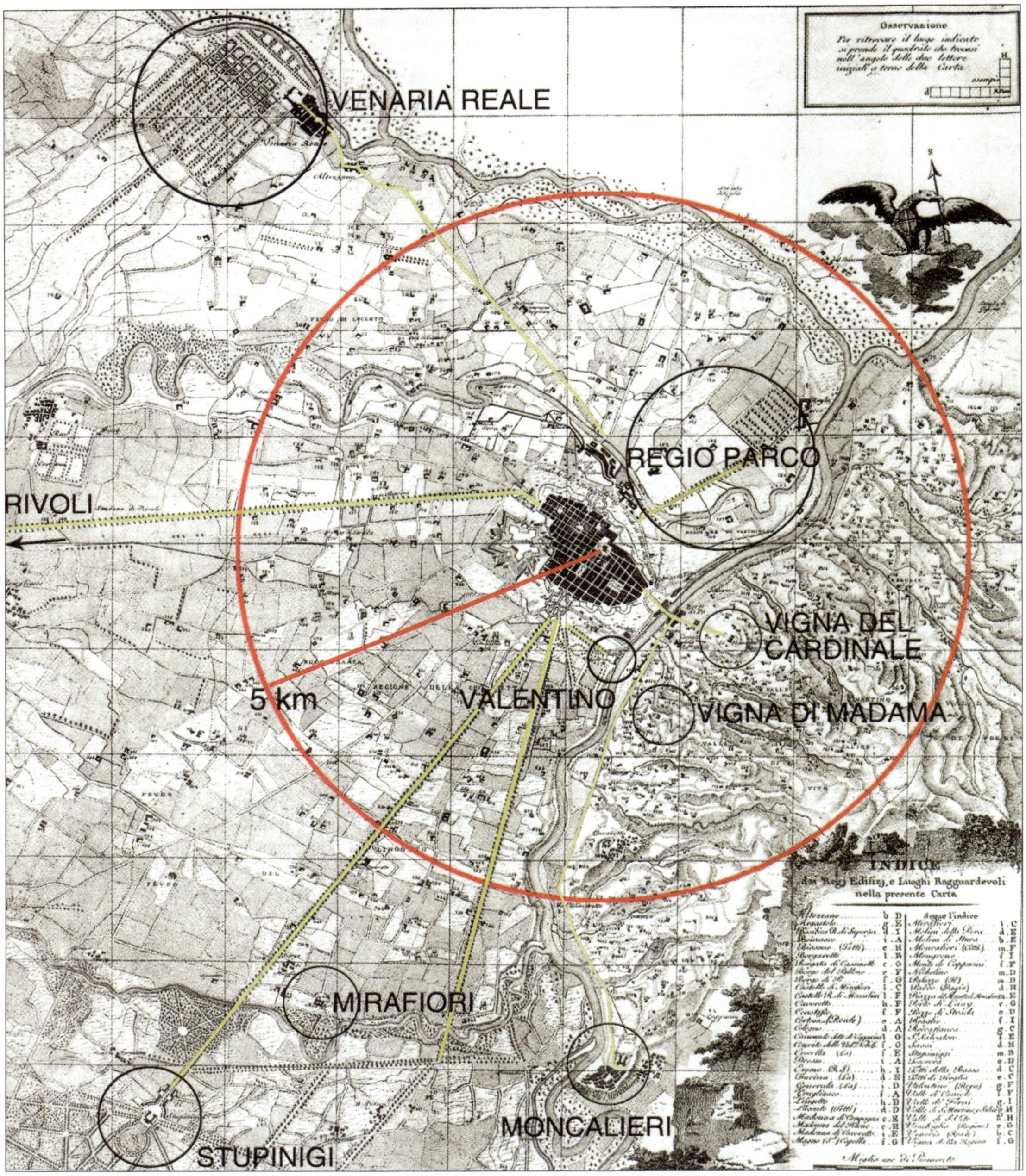

FIGURE 3.11. The system of the Savoy residences. Sites within a five-kilometer radius of the town center are enclosed within the circle.

Map engraved by Antonio Maria Stagnon after a drawing by Carlos Randoni, and published ca. 1800. Reproduced by permission from Costanza Roggero Bardelli, Maria Grazia Vinardi, and Vittorio Defabiani, *Ville Sabaude* (Milan: Rusconi, 1990).

of pure delight, the Turin park is much more than those. It was:

> arranged to show active and contemplative life forming a mirror of human life; walking through it you will discover the road that not only princes but everybody should keep to, to live well and to work virtuously, to become powerful, munificent and glorious, and, without any fear or terror, to see always to the end any praiseworthy and virtuous enterprise. It is a place, in sum, that reveals all the Ethics of Aristotle which is the true way to rule and to govern oneself and others too: thoughts that transcend human minds, corporal delight being joined with the pleasure of the spirit.[20]

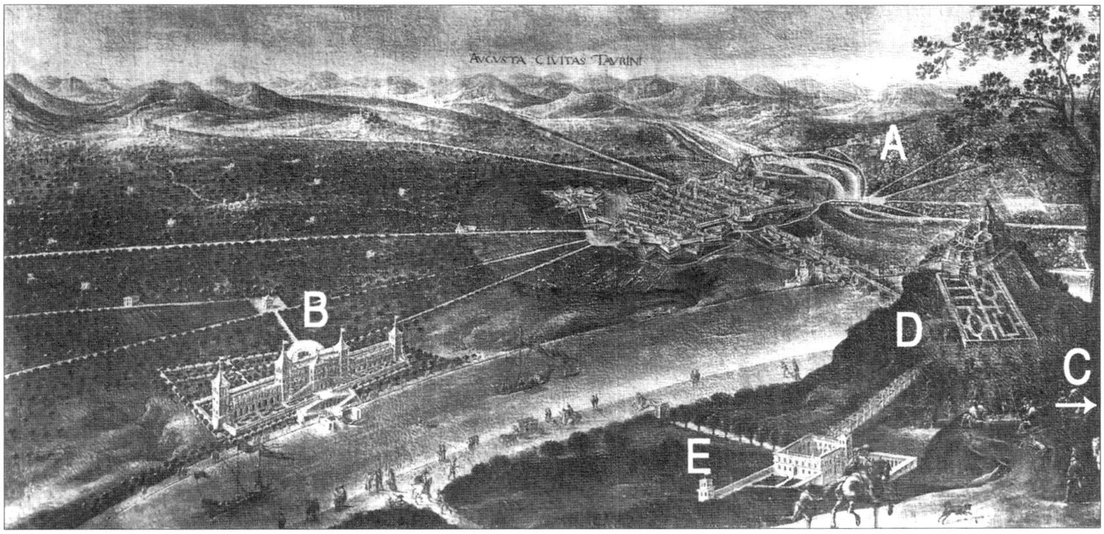

FIGURE 3.12. *Augusta Civitas Taurini (The August Town of Turin)*, ca. 1640, oil on canvas. The following Savoy residences near Turin have been marked: Regio Parco (A), Castello di Valentino (B), *vigna* of Cardinal Maurizio (C), and Madama Reale (D).

Reproduced by permission from Costanza Roggero Bardelli, Maria Grazia Vinardi, and Vittorio Defabiani, *Ville Sabaude* (Milan: Rusconi, 1990).

The park was conceived as a garden or *montagna della virtù* (mountain of virtue) following the archetypal myths of Hercules at the crossroads or the *Tabula Cebetis*, in which the allegorical path to knowing oneself posits itself as a road to knowledge of this and higher worlds. More precisely, the fanning out of five roads perhaps refers to the use of the hand and of its fingers in the "art of memory." Beyond the bridge on the Dora Riparia River (F), the park designed by Vitozzi was articulated by five roads converging in a semicircular piazza: Road of the Senses (1), Road of the Liberal Arts (2), Great Road of Sacred Theology (3), Road of Higher Studies (4), and Road of the Mathematical Sciences (5) (fig. 3.13).

The park is a peninsula surrounded by the Stura, Po, and Dora Riparia rivers. Beyond a bridge over the latter river "start five large roads . . . each of these roads arranged prettily to show various sensations and actions of ours and of virtue and vice."[21] The choice between virtue and vice is introduced by the first road, which—through the attraction of a beautiful garden at its terminus (in the manner of a backdrop, like the backdrops of two of the five roads that seem to refer to theatrical or scenographic experiences)—expresses the temptations and the perils of the senses. The second road is dedicated to the first victory of virtue over vice by means of human intellect or genius.[22]

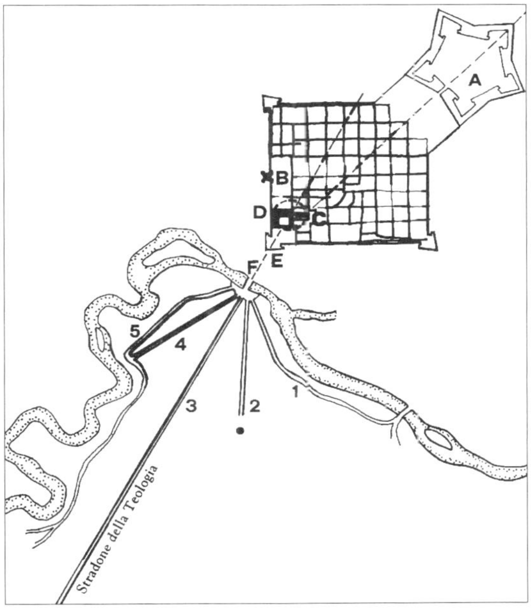

FIGURE 3.13. Reconstruction of the plan of the Regio Parco in relation to the city of Turin.

Illustration by Marcello Fagiolo.

Zuccaro then described the third and fourth roads, to the right:

> This long one [no. 4 in fig 3.13] is straight and dedicated to higher studies and here all men of letters may find every enjoyment, as there are various rest spots with niches, mottoes and figures of lawmakers and poets. The fourth one [no. 5], close behind, skirts the right side

> of the wood at greater length than the others, and it has various branches and pleasant paths, along which one goes in gentle recreation and in philosophizing; and this road is dedicated to the speculative mathematical sciences, according to the variety of which there are various roads . . . which properly invite one to philosophize and to contemplate the sky, the stars, the planets and all the sovereign spheres.[23]

The fifth and main road (now the Corso Regio Parco) is the only one whose trace is preserved. Zuccaro wrote that "the fifth large road [no. 3] in the middle claims the role of contemplating the heavens and the divine mysteries revealed by Sacred Theology, and for this reason on the one side and on the other there are shrines and chapels in rest spots, with priestly statues, rooms of small buildings dedicated to prudence, to counsel, with most graceful mottoes and writings, in Greek and Latin, which lift the mind to divine contemplation."[24]

The park's extraordinary master plan has led me to carry out research on its possible connection with the city, which was expanded after the mid-sixteenth century with the addition of the pentagonal Citadel (fig. 3.13). This first plan is of great interest as a rereading of the original square layout of *Augusta Taurinorum* (the Roman city on which Turin was built). The central road was to have pointed toward the Green Bulwark (at the end of the axis town–citadel A–E), near the pivot between the Palazzo Ducale (D) and the Cathedral (C). By extending diagonally the axis of the Citadel one obtains an ideal axis[25] that traverses the entire city as far as the Cathedral and the bastion, where Vitozzi built the Casino del Baloardo Verde (Casino of the Green Bastion) in 1586–87. The Casino del Baloardo Verde was described anthropomorphically by Zuccaro: "this most noble tower is constructed in the shape of the helmet of a man at arms who stands at sentinel watch over all Italy, as well as over his own city, and under this great helmet, whose visor seems to be raised, there is a graceful little loggia where all the winds are figured. The plume, or pennant, is the little cupola and the weathervane that while turning shows which winds are blowing."[26] The belvedere is here identified with the sentinel, or rather with his helmeted head, an obvious reference to the caput of the Citadel at the far end of the city. The typology of Tower of the Winds calls to mind the two towers built by Gregory XIII in the Vatican and on the Quirinal Hill in Rome that dominated in like manner the gardens, the city, and the surrounding territory. Zuccaro himself took note of the straight axis on which the loggia was sited: "Over here is a most charming view . . . This loggia is *in a straight line with the bridge over the Dora, the park, and that large middle road* and the view of both sides of the woods, the countryside open to the left, and the very high mountains, and to the right the plain and the delightful hills already mentioned, with a wide sweep of the said Dora River ahead . . . "[27] (emphasis added).

From the anthropomorphic loggia-belvedere one, therefore, enjoys a view of the Great Road of Sacred Theology in the park—vice versa, from the park, which was conceived in close connection with the ducal garden,[28] one was proffered the visual terminus of the "Green Bastion" or *Garittone dei fiori* ("Sentinel Box with Flowers"), the outpost of a garden designed by Vitozzi, beyond which is the urban hinge between the new Palazzo Ducale and the Cathedral, more or less in the place where, in 1611–12, again on Vitozzi's design, construction started on the Chapel of the Holy Shroud. Hence we like to think that Vitozzi programmatically oriented his Great Road of Sacred Theology toward the most prestigious relic of Christianity and the pride of the House of Savoy, which had transferred it to Turin in 1578 from Chambéry.

It is, thus, evident that there is a close connection between the Regio Parco and the urban planning of Turin. An analogous situation can be seen at the Vigna del Cardinale ("The Cardinal's Vineyard"), which was begun in 1615 by Cardinal Maurizio di Savoia on the hill south of Turin across the Po River and was connected to the city by a straight street leading to the only bridge over the river; this line would be continued immediately afterward with the axis of the Via Po, on which the expansion of the capital in the direction of the river was based (fig. 3.14). From an architectural standpoint, the spatial composition of the Vigna del Cardinale must be linked above all with the Villa

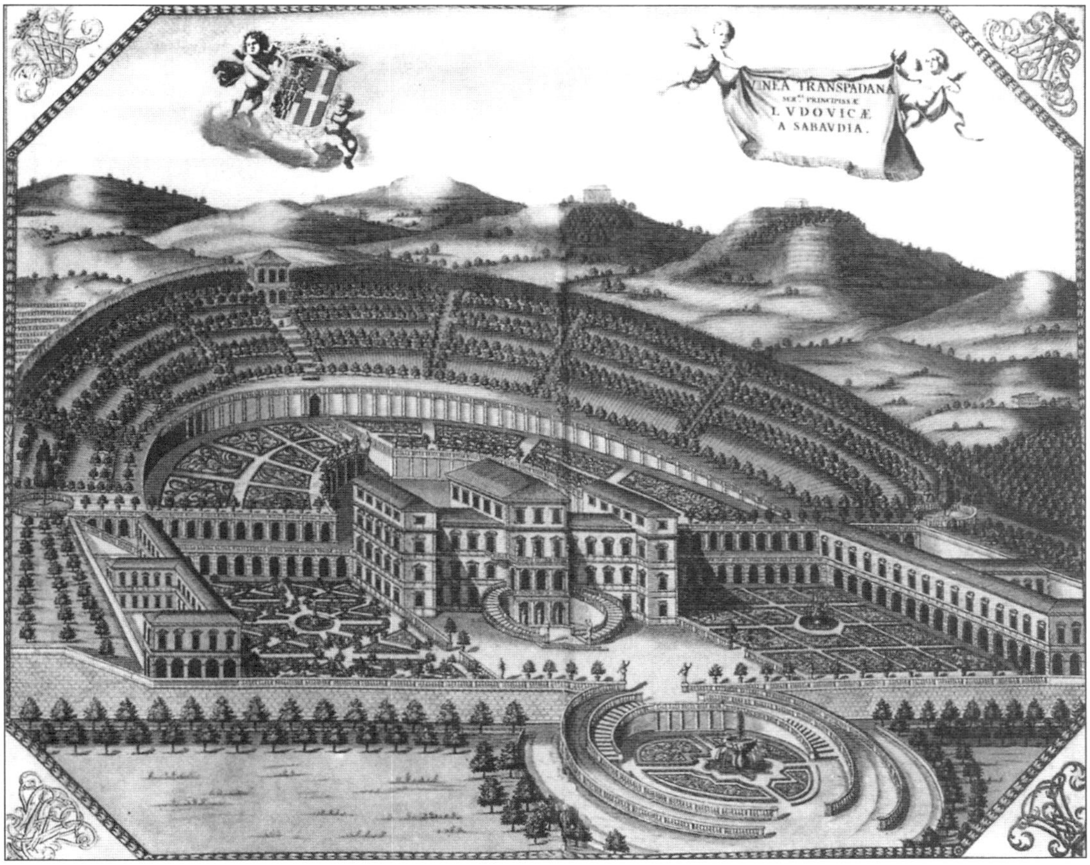

FIGURE 3.14.
Vigna del Cardinale, Turin.

Engraving by G. T. Borgonio; reprinted from *Theatrum statuum regia celsitudinis sabaudia ducis* (Amsterdam: Apud Haeredes Ioannis Blaev, 1682).

Aldobrandini (Frascati), which was the inspiration for the large retaining wall theater on the hillside and the amphitheatrical system of ramps that lead to the palace. (These ramps can also be related to the models of the villas at Caprarola and Tivoli.) It should be emphasized that the celebrated description of the Villa Aldobrandini was conceived by its author, Giovanni Battista Agucchi, in the form of a 1611 letter to the Duke of Savoy.

The third node directly connected with the city is the Castello di Valentino, which was rebuilt by Maria Cristina of France (the "Madama Reale" and wife of the crown prince Vittorio Amedeo) in 1620. On the one hand, the palace was connected with a straight avenue to the Porta Nuova of Turin, while, on the other hand, it was connected across the river to the Vigna di Madama Reale, which was also conceived in the 1620s as a project for terraces in the form of a theater behind the palace, analogous to that of the

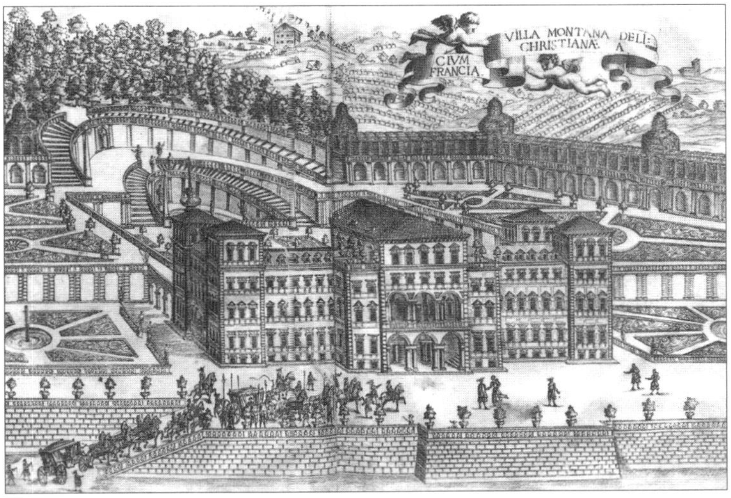

FIGURE 3.15.
Vigna di Madama Reale, Turin.

Engraving by G. T. Borgonio; reprinted from *Theatrum statuum regia celsitudinis sabaudia ducis* (Amsterdam: Apud Haeredes Ioannis Blaev, 1682).

Vigna del Cardinale. Work stopped on the Vigna di Madama Reale after her death in 1663 (fig. 3.15).

By the 1660s, the project of a corona di delitie bordering the capital was extended to include more distant properties that were favored as hunting residences. The greater distance of these residences from Turin can be seen in figure 3.11. A true *città della caccia* (city for the hunt)—the Venaria Reale (or Royal Venery, from the Latin *venatio*)—was built northwest of Turin in the 1660s. Its very name was inspired by the name used for the hunts of the French monarchy (e.g., the treatise *La vénerie royale* was published in 1655).[29] In a book containing an idealized dialogue with Gianlorenzo Bernini, who visited the Duchy in 1665, the architect Count Amedeo di Castellamonte explained the playful and ceremonial liturgy of the "itinerary of delights" followed by the sovereign and his court: "One who leaves from the Castle of Rivoli, and makes a tour of these Palaces, little more than three miles distant from one another, and equally spaced apart, when arriving at the Venaria Reale will have accomplished a fair day's travel amid the delights of Woods, Magnificent Buildings, the amenities of fountains, of allées, and of gardens; something truly rare, and perhaps not observed by you, my Lord (*Vostra Signoria*), in other parts of Italy."[30] Obviously this tourist's itinerary of a quick twenty-four hours contrasted with the much longer journey actually traveled by the itinerant court as it moved from one hunting residence to another.[31]

Castellamonte's description of the theatrical exedra at the termination of the first part of the garden beyond the palace at the Venaria Reale is noteworthy: ". . . that loggia in the form of a Theater rises so high, that one's gaze remains imprisoned in its heart"[32] (fig. 3.16). The exedra backdrop, which was planned or executed in various other Savoy residences, is seen as a *prospettiva* (perspective), to use a term that became fashionable with the architects and scenographers of the Emilia Romagna. Castellamonte went on to add some interesting information on the proportions of the garden: "in length one did not wish to exceed double the width, to give it better proportions and not to lose it in the vastness of the Air, which there reaches as far as the mountains . . ."[33] The alternative was to create a perspective open toward the distant natural backdrop of the Alps; this option was complementary to the roadway perspectives prolonged to infinity in the *rotte di caccia* (hunting routes) that, by then, characterized the whole of the Turinese territory. One formal solution, which found its highest expression in Juvarra's conception of the hunting lodge of Stupinigi, was to create an apparently infinite perspective for whoever departs Turin by coach or on horseback. Once in sight of Stupinigi, this traveler would discover the distant backdrop of the hunting lodge, and meanwhile would view the lodge like an object seen through telescopic focusing in a progressive visual frame. This kind of perspective refers to a form of dynamic perception, what can be called the "aesthetics of hunting." A synthetic study of the Savoy residences has characterized the hunting landscape of Stupinigi in these terms: "The complex play of the routes, integrated with the marking of the meeting places in the *étoiles*, reinvents a form of hunting based on movement tied to the magnificent ritual of the Court."[34]

Developed in the seventeenth and eighteenth centuries with new buildings and wide roads creating axial connections to Turin, the corona di delitie was enlarged to become a more ample circuit of residences, a sort of semicircular theater with a radius of eight to twelve kilometers (beyond which the amphitheater of the Alps stretched into the distance). In addition to the Venaria Reale, the circuit comprised the residences of Rivoli, Mirafiori, Stupinigi, and Moncalieri, and, much further to the south, the castle of Racconigi (which was redesigned by Guarino Guarini, with a large exedra, and whose formal garden was designed by André Le Nôtre).[35] The project of the corona di delitie was already made clear in Maria Cristina's decree of 1638, which delimited the ducal hunting reserve by enacting a "prohibition to hunt any type of game for only ten miles around the city of Turin, thus on this side of the Po River, including the whole said river, in which circuit we declare comprised the lands and places listed at the bottom of the following order." (See figure 3.11 for a basic scheme of this territorial extension, although it shows a radius of only five kilometers.[36] In 1675, the circuit was reduced to eight miles.) The control of the territory destined for the hunt foresaw the construction and maintenance of roads and bridges and the conservation and even expansion of the forestal domain.

The process of connecting the residences to the capital had already been started in 1587 with the

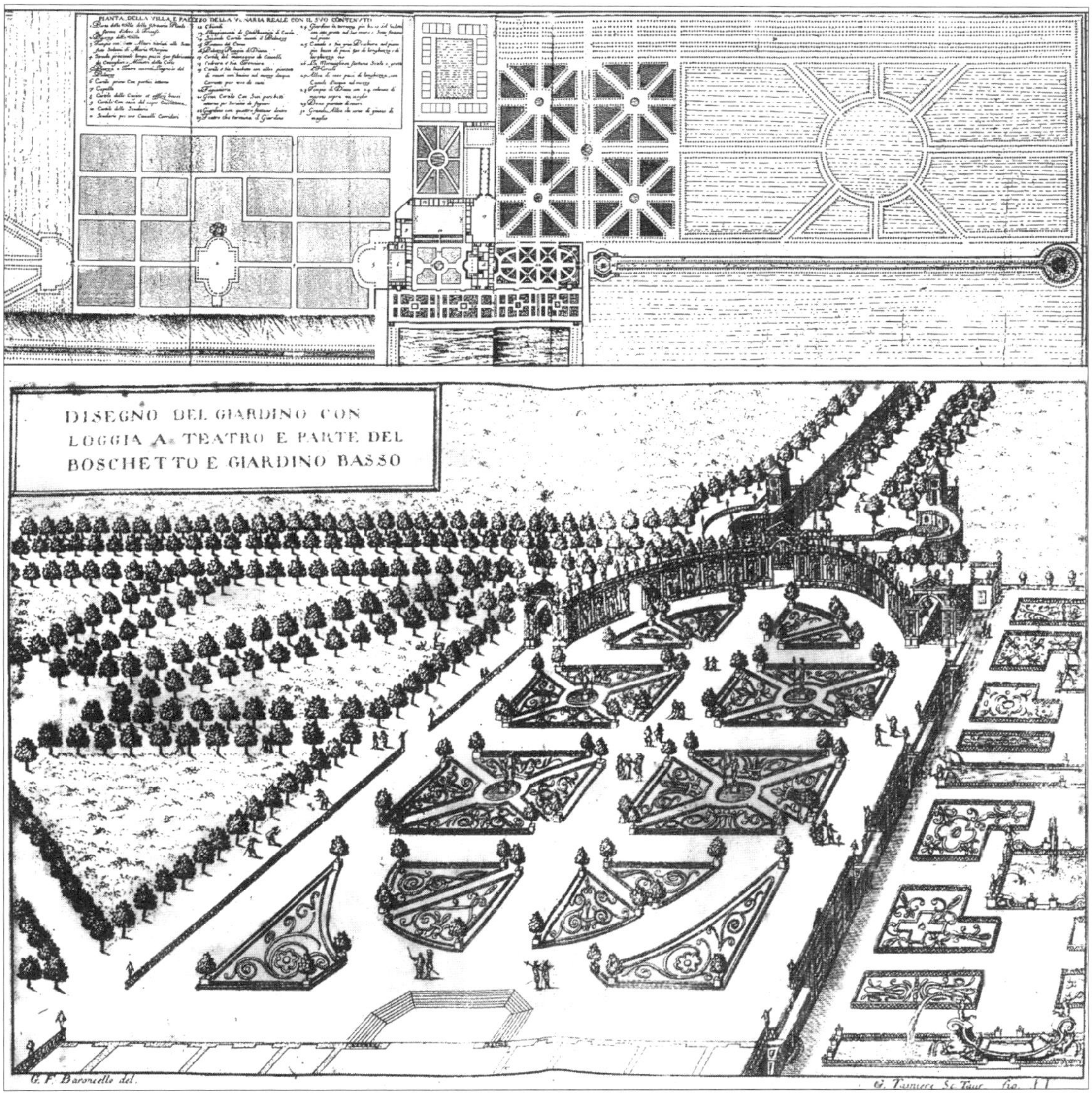

FIGURE 3.16.
Palace and gardens of the Venaria Reale.

Engravings by Georges Tasnière; reprinted from Amedeo di Castellamonte, *Venaria reale, palazzo di piacere, et di caccia: Ideato dall'Altezza reale di Carlo Emanvel II, duca di Sauoia, Re di Cipro* (Turin: B. Zapatta, 1674).

creation of the straight road between the Castello di Mirafiori (and further on, the forest of Stupinigi) and the Porta Nuova, which was opened in the Turin city wall on that occasion. In the design made in the early seventeenth century, the castle was preceded by a wood with a trident of roads leading into a semicircular piazza. Beyond the castle, one descended two long flights of stairs (which were inspired by the Belvedere Court and by French models) to a formal garden laid out on a square island, followed by another hunting wood, both contained within a trident of roads leading to the Sangone River. In 1661, Bernini was asked for his advice on the enlargement of the castle, and his subsequent design, sent from Rome in November, was perhaps represented in the book *Theatrum sabaudiae* (1682). Instead of the earlier semicircular piazza, he imagined almost a lay version of the colonnade at Saint Peter's in Rome. We know that the design was considered "so beautiful, that neither with regard to the site, nor for the building, will Rome have anything that can bear comparison with Mirafiore," and, in any case, the spatial containment is fairly analogous to Bernini's project, drawn up in 1665, for a great amphitheater between the Louvre and the Palace of the Tuileries in Paris, in which two spiral-scroll columns marked the ends. Mirafiori's design is intertwined with the unexecuted project for a large courtyard amphitheater in front of the Castello di Rivoli (as it appears in the etching of the *Theatrum sabaudiae*)[37] and with Castellamonte's design for the piazza of the Venaria Reale, where two spiral columns were deployed instead of the two fountains of Mirafiori. Like the Venaria Reale, the Castello di Rivoli, Vittorio Amedeo II's extraurban royal palace, had a history of construction, destruction, and reconstruction at the hands of the same architects and ultimately remained unfinished.

The construction that perhaps best synthesizes the complexity of the system is the 1729–31 *palazzina di caccia* (hunting lodge) at Stupinigi, with its composition and interpenetration of massing that dissolves into a ceaseless pulsation of undulating vibrations, an infinite production of kinetic energy, and an unheard-of tentacular emanation (fig. 3.17). All of this spatial dynamic is anchored by the oval salon at the very center of the palazzina.

One should note that the compositional geometry of Stupinigi must be interpreted within the preexisting road system—that is, the highway to Turin and the system of straight hunting routes that intersect in the surrounding territory (fig. 3.18). From this system arises the idea of a fulcrum in the guise of a Saint Andrew's cross (which, moreover, is found in the designs of Sebastiano Serlio, Johann Bernhard Fischer von Erlach, and Germain Boffrand) and of the great hexagonal piazza, the axes of which irradiated out to the paths of the hunting expeditions. From this system also arises the theme of the étoile (frequent in the intersections of hunting routes) in the vast circular and radially structured rear garden.

The oval salon is defined as the center "of a branching system that organizes the territory, becoming the centrifugal element of spatial appro-

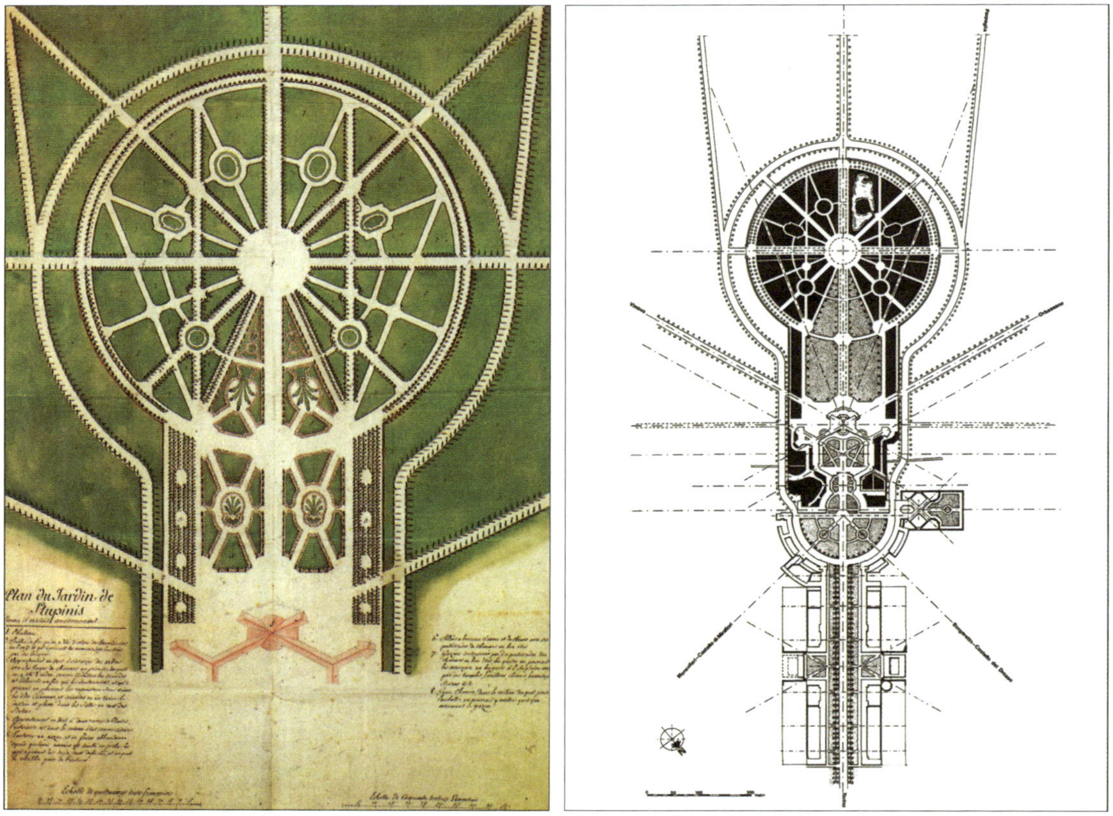

a

b

FIGURE 3.17. Plans of the garden at Stupinigi in (a) ca. 1802 and (b) as it exists today.

Reproduced by permission from Gianfranco Gritella, *Stupinigi: Dal progetto di Juvarra alle premesse neoclassiche* (Modena: Panini, 1987).

FIGURE 3.18.
Distribution of *rondeaux* along the hunting roads at Stupinigi.

Reproduced by permission from Gianfranco Gritella, *Stupinigi: Dal progetto di Juvarra alle premesse neoclassiche* (Modena: Panini, 1987).

priation, in an explicit invitation to the hunt and to flight."[38] More generally, it appears ever clearer that "the adaptation to the model and to the hunting rite of French custom and that of the other European courts, required a territory adequate for the choreography (of the rite) and suitable for an extensive and varied design project for the hunting routes."[39] The central salon itself is viewed as a ducal pavilion crowning the whole, symbolically surmounted by the image of the stag.

A few decades later, we witness with great interest the geometry of the new garden created around the Vigna di Madama Reale (fig. 3.19), with experiments

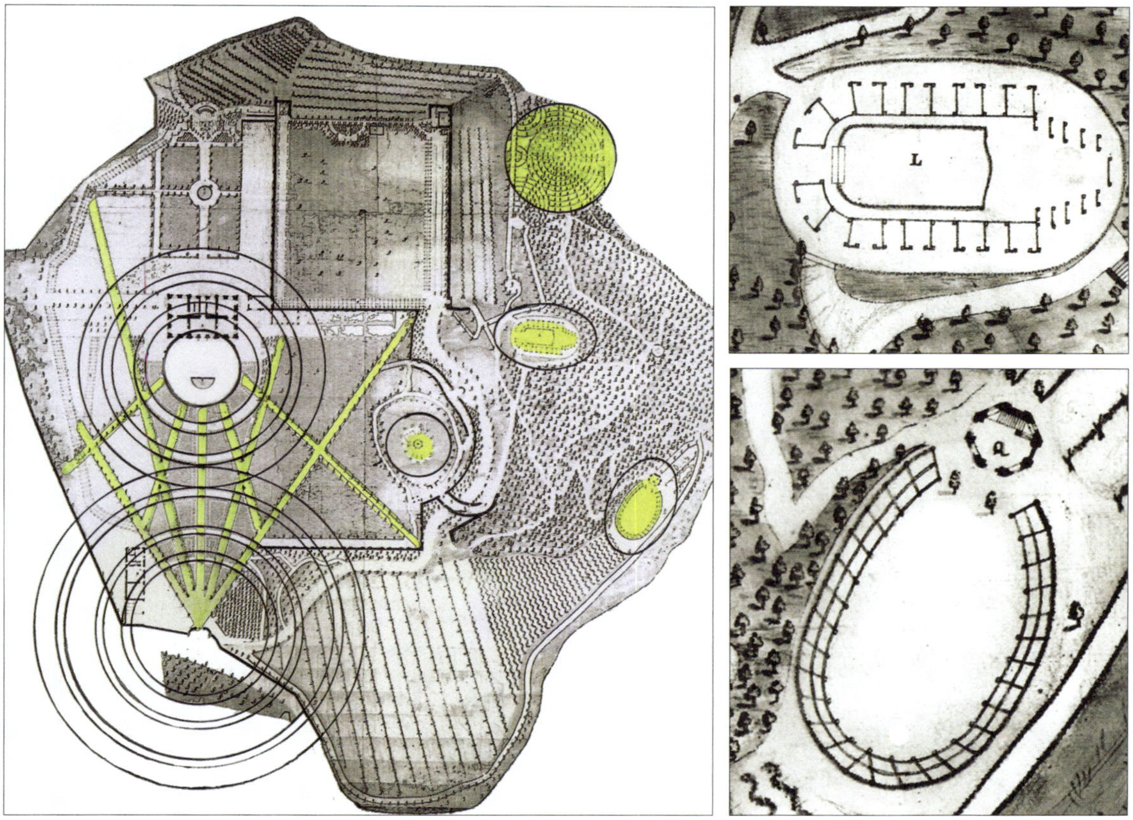

FIGURE 3.19.
Vigna di Madama Reale, Turin. Radial-centric junctions and theatrical spaces have been highlighted. Details of the theater and of the amphitheater of verdure are seen on the right.

Illustration by Marcello Fagiolo; adapted from a late-eighteenth-century drawing, private collection, Turin.

made of interpenetrating radial and concentric systems, according to scientific models of visualizing fields of force and of vortices (e.g., Cartesian ideograms) (fig. 3.29). Here we can emphasize, at the level of visuality, not only the theme of the perspectival avenue pointing toward the obelisk (in the manner of the straight streets in the urban planning of Rome by Sixtus V), but also the proliferation of theatrical structures made of green vegetation (namely the U-shaped theater, with its stage, traditional theater wings, and oval amphitheater topped by an octagonal belvedere functioning as backdrop).[40]

The System of Bourbon Royal Residences in Naples

The first architectural commissions of Carlo di Borbone, the king of the Two Sicilies from 1734 to 1759, were determined by his passion for hunting and fishing; this passion also led to the

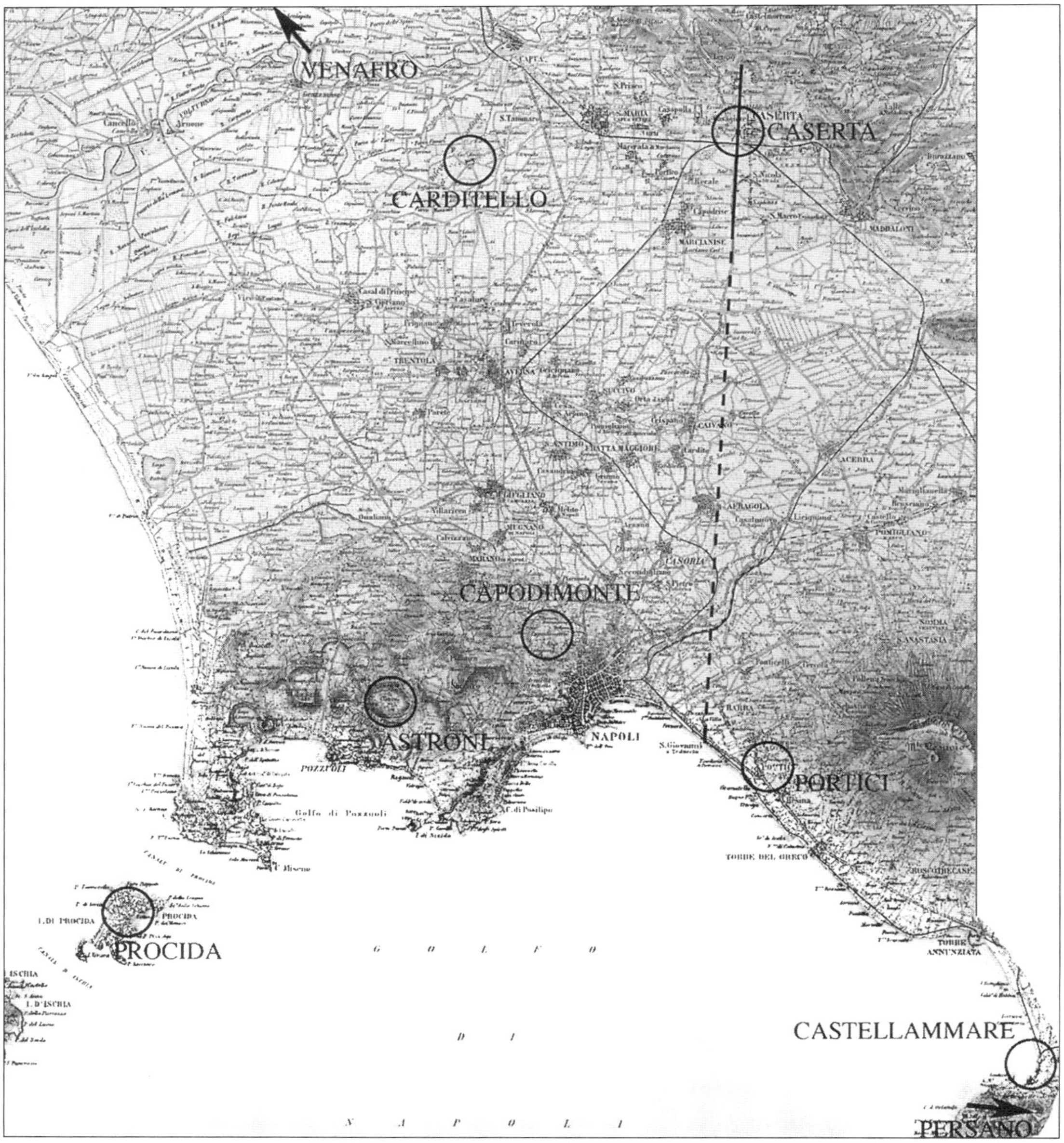

FIGURE 3.20. Plan of the Bourbon "royal sites" in Naples. The barycentric axis of the main road Caserta–Naples points toward the Gulf of Naples and further (beyond the map) to the island of Capri. (Original scale 1:100.000). Illustration by Marcello Fagiolo.

creation of a system of one dozen principal "royal sites," including the three new palaces at Caserta, Capodimonte, and Portici, which were either constructed *ex novo* or restructured (fig. 3.20).[41] One historian has noted the importance of hunting for all of these royal residences:

> The great ordinary business of the court, the most assiduous task, the most enduring toil, consisted of the king's hunts. He remained very little in the capital, and this little was interspersed with hunting parties in the immediate vicinity; then there were the not-so-near and the distant places, and hence the continuous motion of travel. Residence at Caserta, which occupied the first months of the year, was interrupted by the hunt at Torre di Guevara and Bovino for some twenty days, and then by that at Venafro. In mid-September came the "campaign" against the pheasants on the island of Procida; at Portici, the "campaign" against the partridges at Ottaiano. Immediately after this came the commemoration of the dead at Persano.[42]

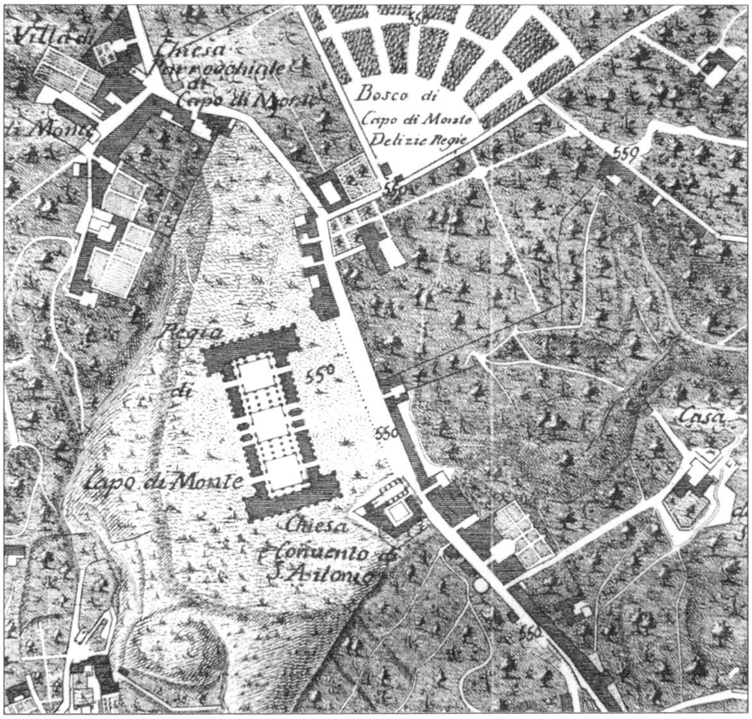

FIGURE 3.21. Giovanni Carafa, Duke of Noja, royal palace and bosco of Capodimonte, Naples, detail of the *Mappa topografica della città di Napoli e de' suoi contorni* (Naples, 1775).

In 1735, the king had the forest of Caserta supplied with *caccia di pelo* (large game); this forest included a park with a wealth of fountains and waterworks (which were later incorporated in the park of the royal palace at Caserta). In 1738, he carried on simultaneously with building the royal palaces at Capodimonte and Portici. Originally a small casino with two different woods for game and fowl hunting was to have been erected at Capodimonte, but then the king decided to create—on the designs of the architects Giovanni Antonio Medrano and Antonio Canevari—a palace-museum to display the Farnese collections and the artworks coming from the excavations at Herculaneum. A century later, the palace was completed as a royal residence and no longer as a museum. The bosco of Capodimonte is of considerable interest; it was designed by Ferdinando Sanfelice, and has five extremely long avenues fanning out from the initial rondeau (fig. 3.21). The palace at Portici, which was carried out by Antonio Canevari with subsequent improvements by Ferdinando Fuga and Luigi Vanvitelli, soon proved to be unsatisfactory to the king, despite its most fortunate natural situation as a site for hunting and fishing, apart from being a delightful bathing resort.

Meanwhile, through an impressive series of public works, Naples became one of the greatest capitals of Europe, with all the advantages and disadvantages of a metropolis. In 1750, Carlo di Borbone decided to move permanently outside of Naples because the royal palace had become insufficient for his very numerous and heterogeneous court, which was composed of Tuscans, Parmesans, Spaniards, as well as Neapolitan barons and notables. Attention was then concentrated on Caserta, which provided double advantages as a delightful natural site and as a militarily secure site, and which replaced Naples as the capital—in clear emulation of Versailles—and accommodated ministers, magistrates, and public offices (fig. 3.22). The construction of the royal palace at Caserta, the most imposing royal residence in Italy, thus commenced; its longitudinal axis measuring three kilometers was directed toward the Bay of Naples, halfway between the capital and Mount Vesuvius, which loomed over

FIGURE 3.22.
View of the royal palace and gardens of Caserta.

Reprinted from Luigi Vanvitelli, *Dichiarazione dei disegni del reale palazzo di Caserta* (Naples: Regia Stamperia, 1756).

FIGURE 3.23.
Axis of the royal palace and the wide road of Caserta, which points toward the Gulf of Naples and the island of Capri.

Photograph by Giulio Bulfoni.

the complex system of Vesuvian villas dominated by the royal palace of Portici (fig. 3.23). Leaving aside here the analysis of the park of Caserta and of its clear connections—which Carlo di Borbone surely wished for—with Versailles (for the general design of the garden) and with La Granja (for the cascades and for the iconography linked especially to Diana and hunting as well as to the winds, rivers, and elements), I would like to focus on the meaningful epilogue of this story, namely Persano and Carditello.

Apart from Portici and the Quisisana palace at Castellammare, Persano emerges in the south-eastern sector of the "royal sites," with its bosco reale situated between the Sele and Calore rivers.[43] The palace at Persano (under construction in 1752 and completed in 1754) is a square structure resembling a monastery or fortress. Possibly designed by the Spanish military engineer Juan Domingo Piana, it features a chapel in the guise of a caput (in a similar position to the chapel at the Escorial). One should note, in particular, the four corner turrets, partly used as stairwells, in the large colonnaded courtyard.[44] In an 1808 plan, this "royal site" appears to be intersected by a polycentric system of hunting routes modeled after the Franco-Savoy ones.

The "royal site" of Carditello developed under Ferdinando IV as a productive farm and hunting residence.[45] The royal casino—which was begun in 1787 to the design of Francesco Collecini, formerly Vanvitelli's principal assistant at Caserta—is preceded by an impressive open piazza (resembling a circus or hippodrome) with a "spine" formed by two fountains with obelisks (in a clear imitation of the arrangement at the Piazza Navona) and by a small, centrally placed temple that perhaps was originally intended as a royal viewing box. The parallels with the royal palace of Caserta include the trident of avenues converging at the royal balcony of the palace, almost an imperial "loggia of appearances" by the king.

The System of Villas in Bagheria

The last case study, the villas at Bagheria outside of Palermo, does not seem to be a system of princely villas, because the viceregal regime did not permit any widespread property ownership by the viceroys, who, as a rule, were not Sicilians and were only elected for limited terms. This homogeneous system of villas, which was created by the powerful neo-feudal aristocracy, appears to have been governed by a learned, albeit not very visible, geometry, which is today in large part concealed or obliterated.

While Palermo was the "urban theater" of the Sicilian nobility, the Piana dei Colli and especially the Bagheria area to its southeast, were presented as the "natural theater" of leisure pursuits. It was to be precisely the need for this dialogue with nature, which we find in the great French, Austrian, and German princely and palatial residences built between the seventeenth and the eighteenth centuries, that

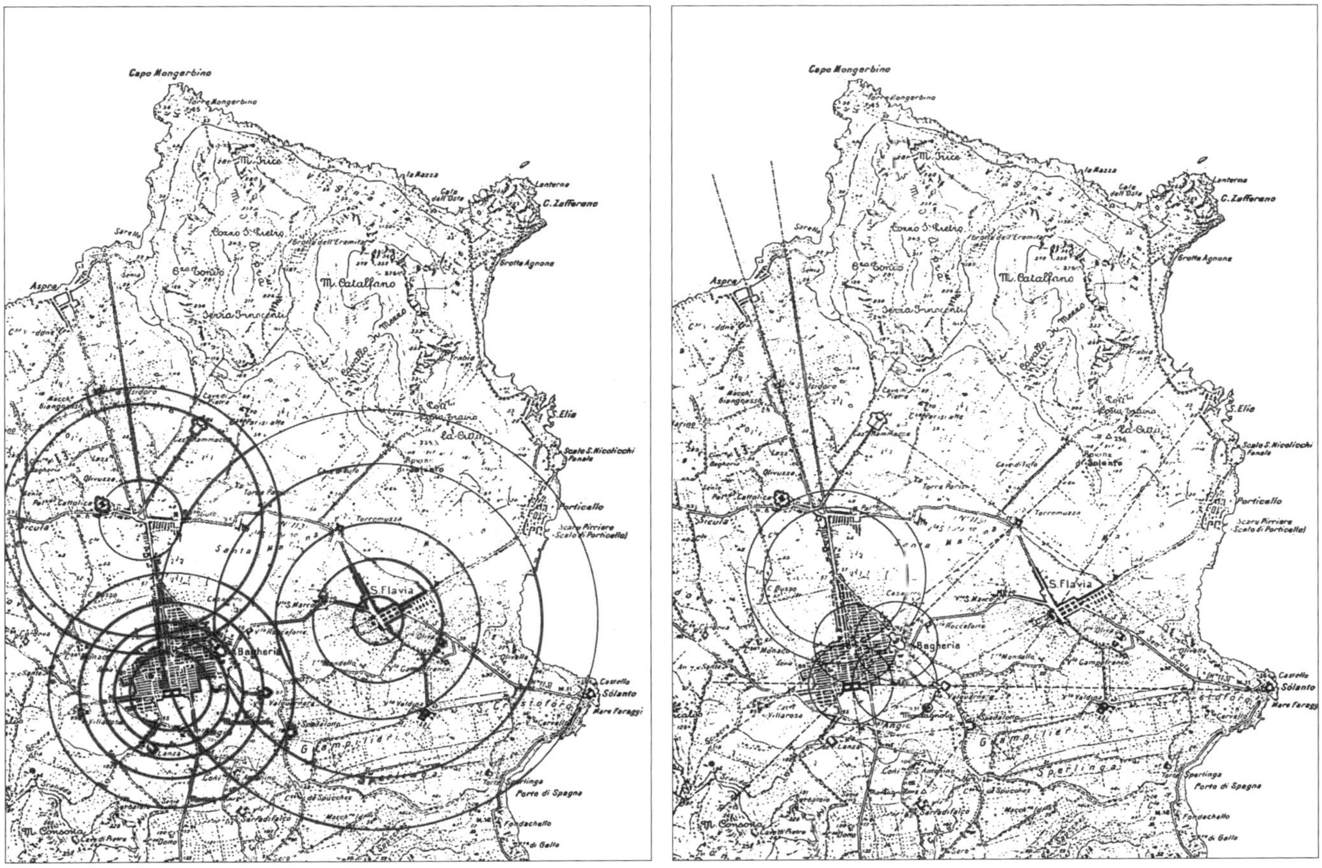

FIGURE 3.24. The system of villas in Bagheria. Grid of axes and interrelations between villas and territorial highlights.

Illustration by Marcello Fagiolo; reprinted from Marcello Fagiolo and Maria Luisa Madonna, "Sicilia: La ristrutturazione del territorio; Una realpolitik feudale," in *San Leucio: Archeologia, storia, progetto* (Milan: Il Formichiere, 1977).

imposed a new architectural vision for royal residence. This new vision linked building design with urban planning and territorial survey.

As Maria Luisa Madonna and I clarified in 1977, some of the villas at Palermo were devised according to a very great spatial range and with precisely corresponding elements at all levels.[46] The villas are inserted into the territory according to an elaborate system of road and/or visual axes that place them in reciprocal relationships; the whole territory is triangulated, and is studied in terms of its areas or nuclei of influence, taking into account both the natural elements (the sea and the hillocks) and the historical elements (villas, castles, villages, and archaeological centers) (fig. 3.24).

In contrast to the orthogonal system prevalent in most master plans of Sicilian cities in the Baroque period, in the plan for Bagheria the axes of the villas intersect at various angles, thereby introducing a whole series of bivia and trivia (complex virtual crossings of visual axes), which can be compared with the triangular layout of the casino of the Villa Palagonia and with the triradial layout of the Villa Larderia. In the diagrams that we have elaborated, the axial visual connections can clearly be seen between the villas and the town nuclei of Bagheria, Santa Flavia, and Solanto. Alongside a number of radial joints (such as the one in the vicinity of the Cattolica and Ramacca villas), the towns of Bagheria and Santa Flavia are revealed to be at the center of fields of radial forces that support the spatial intention of certain architectural layouts of villas. The play of the equal distances and the reciprocal relationships between the five villas (Butera, Trabia, Valguarnera, Palagonia, and Larderia) gravitating on the town of Bagheria can be figured by a geometric ideogram that coincides with the quadrilobite geometric layout of the Villa Palagonia and the Villa Cattolica (fig. 3.25).[47]

But even without analyzing these spatial relations, it is clear that the villas designed by Tommaso Maria Napoli or inspired by his teaching (i.e., the Villas Palagonia, Cattolica, and Larderia in Bagheria, as well as the Villa Partanna in the Piana dei Colli) define the whole countryside around Palermo as an inexhaustible laboratory of architectural research, comparable to the crown of the Savoy villas or to the villas on the outskirts of Vienna.

The central role of the Villa Palagonia is a case in point.[48] Built for Prince Ferdinando Francesco Gravina after 1715, its layout reflects the experience of Tommaso Maria Napoli as a mathematician, a theologian, a writer of architectural treatises, a builder of fortresses in Hungary and Greece, and, from 1711, a military engineer for the Senate of Palermo. The pavilion is laid out in the guise of a bastion: it

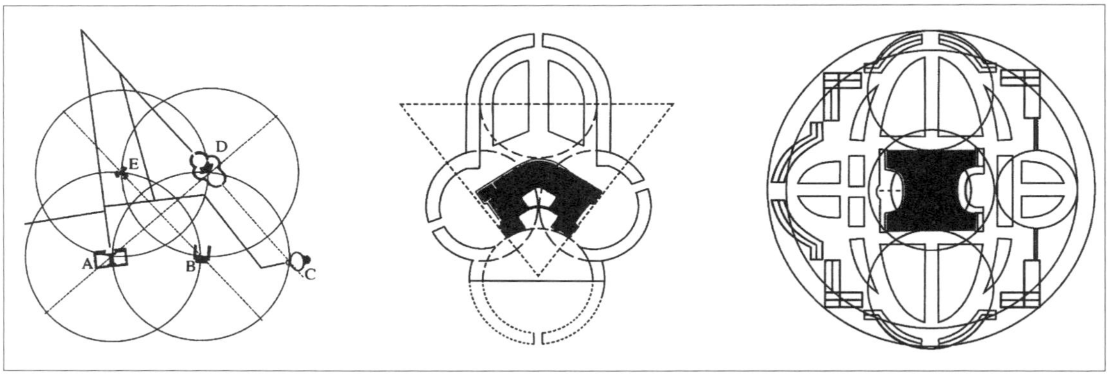

FIGURE 3.25.
Geometries of the town of Bagheria (left), the Villa Palagonia (center), and the Villa Cattolica (right). The following villas are indicated on the diagram of Bagheria: Villa Butera (A), Villa Trabia (B), Villa Valguarnera (C), Villa Palagonia (D), and Villa Larderia (E).

Illustration by Marcello Fagiolo; reprinted from Marcello Fagiolo and Maria Luisa Madonna, "Sicilia: La ristrutturazione del territorio; Una realpolitik feudale," in *San Leucio: Archeologia, storia, progetto* (Milan: Il Formichiere, 1977).

has corner turrets with escarped bases and a main facade that encases a concave wall between two turrets. Between these turrets runs the open-air, scenographic main flight of stairs, analogous to that of the Villa Valguarnera. The flight of stairs in the facade can be contextualized within the similar experimentations of late Baroque architecture in Central Europe.[49] Napoli had followed Prince Eugenio of Savoy to the court of Vienna, where he met Fischer von Erlach. Subsequently, Sicilian ties with Austria would become reinforced when Emperor Charles VI became King of Sicily in 1718. The circular open space in front of the palazzina presents a crenellated edge that crowns the exterior wall, while inside, as at the Villa Valguarnera, it forms a rustic version of the colonnade of Saint Peter's. (The fountain, designed in 1753 together with a twin fountain, has been dismantled.)

The Villa Palagonia stands at the end of a long axis that, starting from a now lost triumphal arch, encounters the Portal of the Giants and a series of linked open spaces of differentiated forms. The general composition exalts the complementary principles of the articulated circuit, of permeability (the entire axis can be perceived, in view of the presence of an open corridor at the center of the pavilion), of military-type defense, of the hierarchy of volumetric masses, and of the virtual interpenetration of linked circles, making it a masterpiece of spatial geometry, the heir of the geometric inventions of Francesco Borromini, Guarino Guarini, and Fischer von Erlach, the parallel to the inventions of Filippo Juvarra, and the precursor to other masters of the Sicilian Baroque, such as Giovanni Biagio Amico, Rosario Gagliardi, and Giovan Battista Vaccarini.

The Portal of the Giants (which is rounded externally, and is followed by a circular open space) recalls, in addition to the Giants of the Porta Nuova in Palermo, a 1699 triumphal arch erected by Fischer von Erlach in Vienna as well as his studies for portals of villas having a round plan, which are mostly based—due to their perspectival arrangement with their central opening onto the avenues—on the concept of the permeable axis of the Villa Palagonia, which permits the visual and physical crossing of the building.

Added to Fischer von Erlach's military experience and to his re-evocations of the "Imperial style" was his study of antiquity, which was tied to a sojourn in Rome and to his possible frequenting of Carlo Fontana's studio. The curvilinear rear facade, with its loggias later filled-in, can lead back to the theaters and amphitheaters of Roman tradition. The palace, in fact, building on the quadrilobite plan of the Villa Cattolica at Bagheria, is surrounded by four lower building elements with different curvilinear profiles, reminding us of the polylobate layouts of ancient Roman baths—such as those of Caracalla and Diocletian—and the two exedras of the Forum of Augustus in Rome. The interlinking of these spatial and cultural motifs demonstrates, in sum, the complexity of an architectural reasoning that goes far beyond the limits of the individual villas, thereby inducing us to accumulate a whole series of data in support of our hypotheses about an integrated design at territorial scale.

Conclusion: The Spatiality of the Networks of Villas

The main function of a retreat or hunting residence in the proposed systems of villas does not exclude ceremonial rituals and characteristics of leadership when the sovereigns temporarily established themselves in the villas, with their courts or large numbers of courtiers. Think in this regard of the macroscopic examples of Versailles or Schönbrunn, which were the inspiration for many residences in the late Baroque period.

Although in various sixteenth-century villas the garden was conceived as an image enclosed in itself and as a metaphor of a physical territory (or even of an ideal territory), with the advent of the systems of villas, the opposite trend took place. The system of villas transformed the territory into a garden or park of outspread type, thereby developing Dante's metaphor of Italy as a "garden of the Empire" (i.e., a garden that would be abandoned or "deserted" as a result of war and decline).[50] Dante hoped that an emperor would return and restore the garden as a token of peace and universal order; in the seventeenth and eighteenth centuries, there were princes and aristocrats who partially realized this idea, while simultaneously oppressing their subordinates and privatizing their territory.[51]

The Tusculan villas constitute an extraordinary system, in which the character of the balcony-belvedere—which overlooks the panorama of Rome and northern Latium—resides with the agricultural fertility of the volcanic soil (vineyards and olive groves) and with the presence of woods suitable for hunting. In the major villas, the frequent sojourns of the popes (who often chose the Alban Hills as their summer residences because of their healthy air and temperate climate) also made it necessary to combine *otium* with the *negotia* in rituals that, at times, endeavored to emulate, *all'antica*, the life of sites consecrated to the memories of Lucullus and Cicero.

From the comparison of the two truly princely systems dealt with here—those around Turin and Naples—we see that, after the late sixteenth century, royal patrons almost completely neglected the two preceding models of the villa as a retreat (with the accent on otium) and of the villa as an agricultural enterprise (not a secondary matter, in terms of agriculture), and created villas almost exclusively for hunting activities, to the obvious detriment of the agricultural economy. On the one hand, the French royal model in Piedmont led to the creation of a very extensive Savoy hunting domain, to the redesign of the territory's existing forms by triangulating the hunting routes, and to the abandonment of an economy based on agriculture and animal husbandry (with the exception of horse or poultry farms). On the other hand, the Spanish model of the "royal sites" imposed in Campania the formation of a constellation of residences with highly differentiated settlement characteristics and more dislocated distributions over the territory. Such residences gravitated, as stated above, around the axis of the royal palace of Caserta. In effect, it becomes clear that Italian patrons rejected earlier villa models in favor of French and Spanish models of extraurban centers for hunting activities.

In the Baroque hunting ceremonies, we find the intersection of techniques of warfare and of exhibitions of court ritual, in which power and hierarchy are represented with an explicit ideal of knowledgeable acquisition of territory. For the Baroque aristocracy, hunting functioned as the pedagogical model for training for the dynamic of war. As Castellamonte wrote:

> With the hunt of the Stag, Princes and Noblemen (*Cavalieri*) become accustomed to enduring the fatigue and discomforts that are encountered in war; with this, they learn to know the roads, the villas (or towns), the places to ford rivers in their own countryside, to make use thereof on the occasions of war, such that a Nobleman who dares to confront the most ferocious animals in

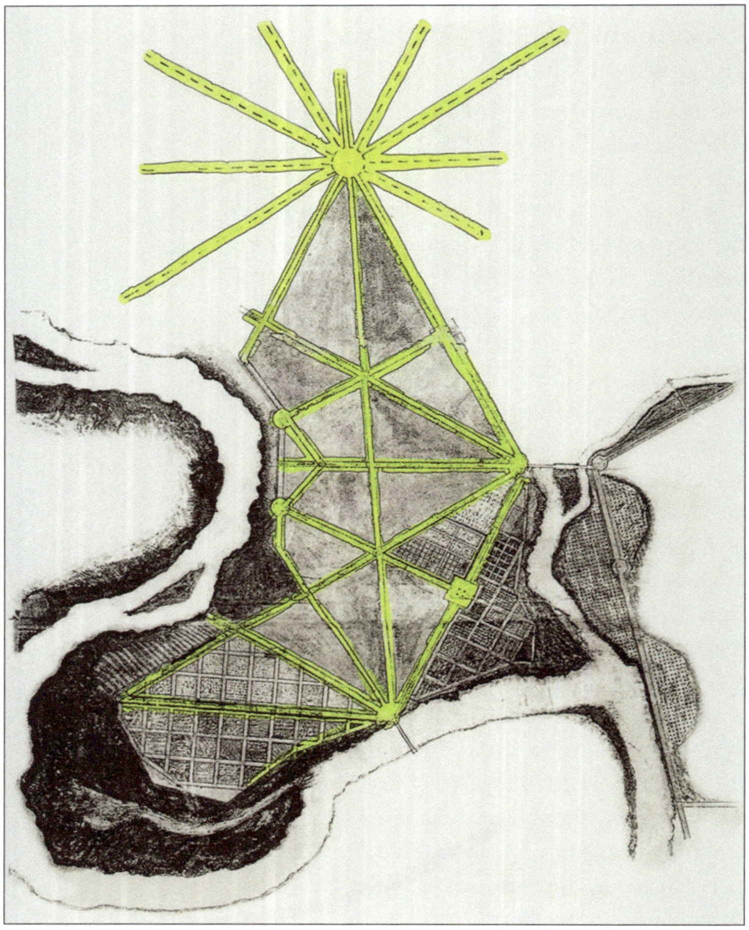

FIGURE 3.26.
Juan de Herrera, project for the Huertas de Picotajo in the park of Aranjuez, Spain.

Illustration by Marcello Fagiolo; adapted from a ca. 1580 drawing at the Library of The Royal Palace, Madrid.

FIGURE 3.27. Reconstruction of the plan of the gardens at Aranjuez in the time of Philip II.

Reproduced by permission from Carmen Añon, José Luis Sancho, and José Martínez Millán, eds., *Jardín y naturaleza en el reinado de Felipe II* (Madrid: Sociedad Estatal Conme. Centenarios Felipe II–Carlos V, 1998).

> the forests, will not fear on the fields of battle meeting the fiercest enemies, so that we may conclude that warfare is truly the art of Princes, and that Hunting is their teacher.[52]

A knowledge of the territory, thus, defines itself as an act of consciousness regarding the dominion of monarchial power. In this regard, the hypothesis that the expansion of the hunting grounds was paralleled, on the one hand, by the publication of the *Theatrum sabaudiae* (with its engraved views of all Savoy seats and lands) and, on the other, by the creation of detailed cartographic surveys that accompanied the formation of the innovative Savoy general land cadaster appears ever more illuminating.[53]

This discussion about the polycentric design of the garden and landscape should put the aforementioned Italian realities side by side with the realities of the Parisian region, where a true network of parks and gardens was largely created by Louis XIV.[54] The model of Versailles and other gardens (such as Meudon) by Le Nôtre was widely diffused in European gardens.

Perhaps the most intriguing starting point for such comparisons is the park of Aranjuez in Spain, and in particular the Huertas de Picotajo, designed as early as 1580 by Juan de Herrera, with the geometric intersection of the axes culminating on a hill with a star with twelve rays, which, in my opinion, is related to the symbolism of the Sun (figs. 3.26 and 3.27).[55] The main avenue, or Avenue of the Mulberry

FIGURE 3.28.
Battista Agnese, nautical chart of Italy, ca. 1550.

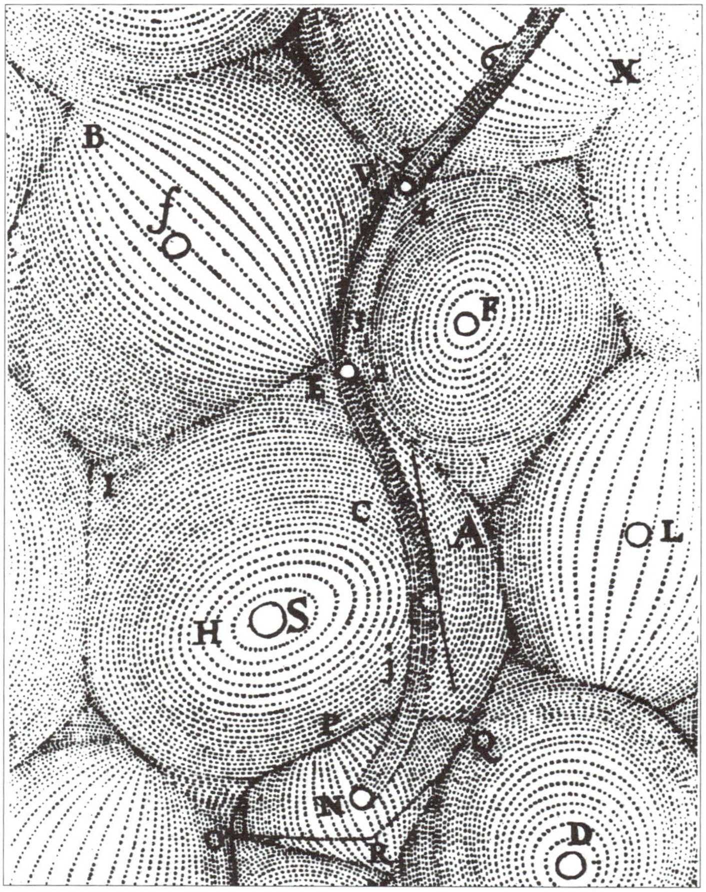

FIGURE 3.29.
René Descartes, ideogram of the vortex theory, 1637.

Reprinted from René Descartes, *Principia philosophiae* (Amsterdam, 1644).

Trees (*Calle de las Moreras*), leads from the bridge over the Jarama River to the twelve roads (*doce calles*) and continues as a long ring-road, which is punctuated at intervals by square or circular open spaces (*piazzali*), until it reaches the royal palace. We should note that engineers and technicians of various nations worked in this park, because their multinational expertise was required for the complex hydraulic works of land reclamation, and that thus it was a case of a true European laboratory of farsighted design, which anticipated not only polycentric urbanistic concepts (that were built upon the experiments of treatise writers on the subject of "ideal cities"), but also the French and Savoy *geometria della caccia* (geometry of the hunt).

The polycentric geometry of these systems of avenues should also be related, in my view, to the

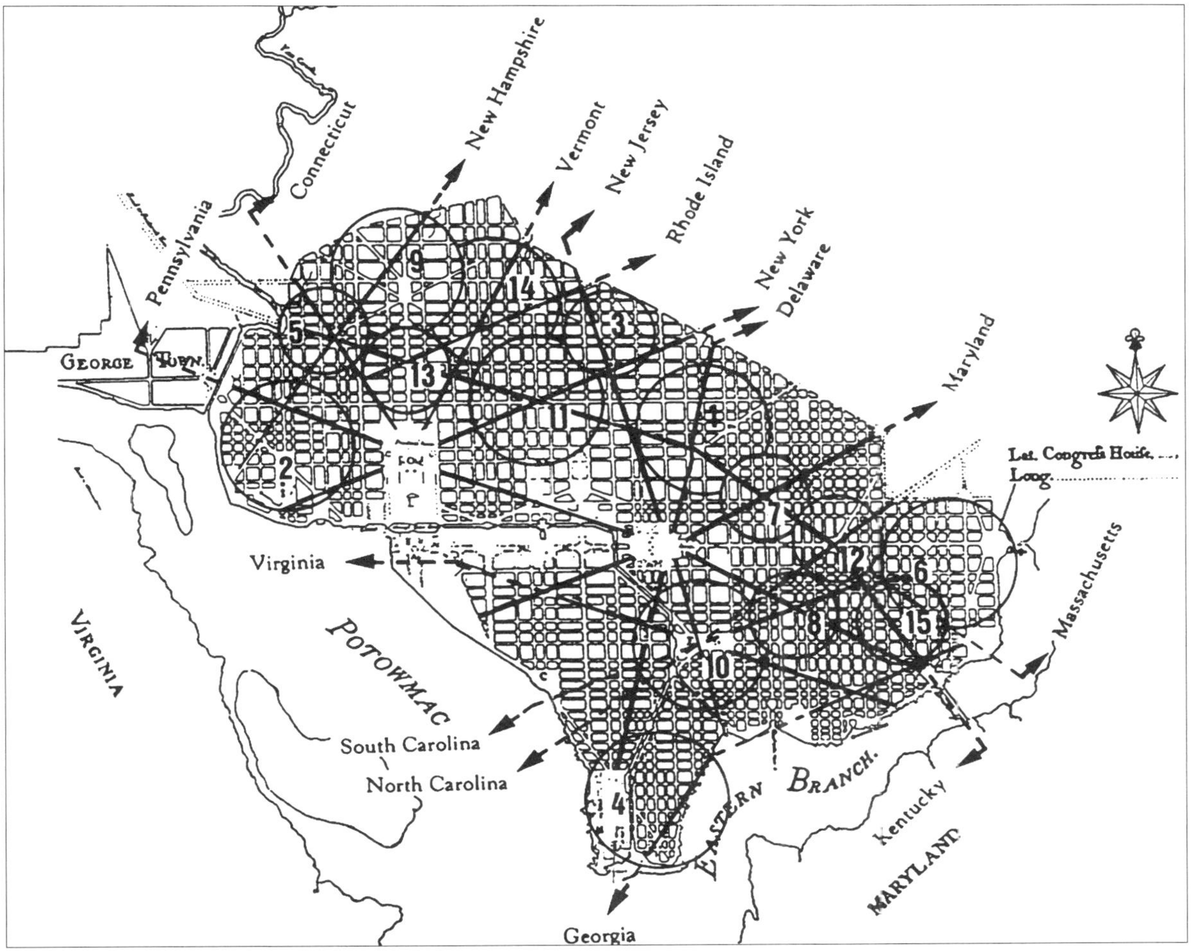

FIGURE 3.30. Washington, D.C. Ideogram of the polycentrism of the squares as a synthetic image of the United States.

Illustration by Marcello Fagiolo; reprinted from Marcello Fagiolo and Vincenzo Cazzato, eds., *Architettura e massoneria: L'esoterismo della costruzione* (Rome: Gangemi, 2007).

cartographic methods of trigonometric triangulation of territory (carried out for the first time after 1562 by Pedro de Esquivel for King Philip II of Spain) or to the system of multiple wind roses in nautical charts (used for the first time in terrestrial surveys in Mexico in the age of Philip II) (fig. 3.28).[56] The technology of topographic surveying and of nautical mapmaking was well known by Herrera, who was a scientist, architect, and inventor of new instruments for nautical surveying. Thus, his designs for the park of Aranjuez deserve a clear place in the discussion on the relationship between the design of the garden and the science of representation (figs. 3.26–3.28).

I have dealt with these topics in previous studies on the history of town planning, in those particular cases where urban design may be compared to or assimilated with the design of the garden or forest. An example is the case of the polycentric urban design by Sixtus V for Rome, for which I have suggested various connections with the methods for land surveying (triangulation) and maritime surveying (nautical charts).[57] Another scientific source may be found in the ideograms of the vortex theory elaborated by René Descartes (fig. 3.29); these ideograms visually display a diagrammatic system of fields of power that can be connected to the compositional methods of Baroque architecture.[58] But I will not dwell, in concluding, on the polycentric design of Washington, D.C., which I have many times connected with the polycentrism of the various states of the United States (fig. 3.30) and with the aesthetics of the connubium town-garden-forest.[59]

Notes

Translation revised by Mirka Beneš.

1 For the overall framework of this question—as well as its experimental application to the systems of gardens at the villas of Tuscany and Latium—see the following studies by Marcello Fagiolo: "Villa Aldobrandina Tusculana," *Quaderni dell'Istituto di Storia dell'Architettura* 62–66 (1964): 61–92; *Natura e artificio: L'ordine rustico, le fontane, gli automi nella cultura del Manierismo europeo* (Rome: Officina, 1981); "Le due anime nelle ville della Tuscia," in *Il giardino d'Europa: Pratolino come modello nella cultura europea*, ed. Alessandro Vezzosi, 68–81 (Milan: Mazzotta, 1986); Introduction to *Lazio delle delizie: Le dimore della nobiltà, teatro del lusso e dell'illusione*, eds. Marco Fabio Apolloni et al., 15–22 (Milan: Franco Maria Ricci, 1988); "Gli assi segreti delle ville nel sistema sacrale del *Latium vetus*," in *Atti del Convegno "Il giardino storico nel Lazio": Indirizzi per la conservazione e il restauro*, 16–26 (Rome: Associazione Dimore Storiche Italiane, 1990); *Roma delle delizie: I teatri dell'acqua, grotte, ninfei, fontane* (Milan: Franco Maria Ricci, 1990); "Da Villa Madama a Villa Giulia e al Gianicolo: Gli assi della memoria storica," in *Roma: Il verde e la città; Giardini e spazi verdi nella costruzione della forma urbana*, eds. Roberto Cassetti and Marcello Fagiolo, 2:31–47 (Rome: Gangemi, 2002); "Sistemi di ville in Italia: Roma e il Lazio, il Piemonte Sabaudo, i Siti Reali borbonici, le ville di Bagheria," in *Paesaggi e sistemi di ville nel Salento*, ed. Vincenzo Cazzato, 14–33 (Galatina: Mario Congedo, 2006); and *Vignola: L'architettura dei principi* (Rome: Gangemi, 2007), 185–256. On the theme of stage design and theatricality, which I have newly articulated for the field of study of historical gardens, see in particular Marcello Fagiolo, *La città effimera e l'universo artificiale del giardino* (Rome: Officina, 1980); Fagiolo, *Roma delle delizie*; Vincenzo Cazzato, Marcello Fagiolo, and Maria Adriana Giusti, *Teatri di verzura: La scena del giardino dal barocco al Novecento* (Florence: Edifir, 1993); and Marcello Fagiolo and Maria Adriana Giusti, eds., *Lo specchio del paradiso: L'immagine del giardino dall'antico al Novecento* (Cinisello Balsamo [Milan]: Silvana, 1996).

2 For a general view of the systems of villas and gardens in northern Italy, see Marcello Fagiolo, ed., *Il sistema delle residenze nobiliari*, vol. 1, *Italia settentrionale* (Rome: De Luca, 2009). For the villas near Milan, see Dianne Harris, *The Nature of Authority: Villa Culture, Landscape, and Representation in Eighteenth-Century Lombardy* (University Park: Pennsylvania State University Press, 2003).

3 For the *delizie estensi* (Este delights), see Marco Folin, "Borso a Schifanoia: Il Salone dei Mesi come *speculum principis*," in *Il Palazzo Schifanoia a Ferrara*, eds. Salvatore Settis and Walter Cupperi, 9–38 (Modena: F. C. Panini, 2007); and Francesco Ceccarelli and Marco Folin, eds., *Delizie estensi: Architetture di ville nel Rinascimento italiano ed europeo* (Florence: L. S. Olschki, 2009). Of particular interest is the policy of Borso d'Este, who, according to Giuliano Antigini's chronicle, "began to build several villas for himself and his favorites, in which 'he held a great and magnificent court with falcons, sparrow-hawks and dogs.' . . . In the Palazzo Schifanoia's Hall of the Months hunting is celebrated as the aristocratic—if not royal—recreation par excellence, *ludus honestus* and more than anything else worthy of a ruler, as had already been claimed for centuries by the authors of the *Specula principum* and of hunting treatises." ("tegneva grandissima e pompoxa corte cum falchuni, sparivieri e chani.") Folin, "Borso a Schifanoia," 11 and 17.

4 On hunting in the Medici villas, see Fauzia Farneti, "La legislazione medicea sulle bandite, la caccia e la pesca," in *La legislazione medicea sull'ambiente*, eds. Giovanni Cascio Pratilli and Luigi Zangheri, 95–117 (Florence: L. S. Olschki, 1988); Susanna Pietrosanti, *Le cacce dei Medici* (Florence: Vallecchi, 1992); and Hervé Brunon, "La chasse et l'organisation du paysage dans la Toscane des Médicis," in *Chasses princières dans l'Europe de la Renaissance: Actes du colloque de Chambord, 1er et 2 octobre 2004*, eds. Claude d'Anthenaise and Monique Chatenet, 219–46 (Arles: Actes Sud, 2007). The latter volume, *Chasses princières*, presents a bibliographically up-to-date overview on hunting during the Renaissance, with contributions by Margherita Azzi Visentini on the Duchy of Milan and Sabine Frommel on hunting residences in Italy.

5 Christian Norberg-Schulz, *Genius loci: Paesaggio, ambiente, architettura* (Milan: Electa, 1979), 142–47.

6 See Isabella Barisi, Marcello Fagiolo, and Maria Luisa Madonna, *Villa d'Este* (Rome: De Luca, 2003).

7 "Si vede la montagna di Viterbo, con quella di Santo Oreste anticamente detto Soratte con tutte montagne, et luoghi fraposti; et dal lato destro ha vaghi monti, et colli vicini; et sotto a lei si scorgono verdure d'altissime olive, giardini di mele granate, et altri frutti, con una pianura di prati e terreni da seminare, et il fiume Aniene, che fra mezzo serpendo a guisa di biscia fra loro se ne descende verso il Tevere." Antonio del Re, *Dell'antichità tiburtine: Capitolo V* (Rome: Appresso Giacomo Mascardi, 1611), book V.

8 For centuries, the design of the Villa Lante at Bagnaia was attributed deductively to Jacopo Barozzi da Vignola; in some cases, his authorship was soundly rejected. Moreover, one can note the presence of Tommaso Ghinucci, a Sienese *familiare* and trusted house architect of Cardinals Nicolò Ridolfi and Giovan Francesco Gambara, in Bagnaia between 1538 and 1587. Marcello Fagiolo, "Struttura e significato di Villa Lante a Bagnaia," in *Ville e parchi storici: Storia, conservazione e tutela*, ed. Alberta Campitelli, 219–30 (Rome: Argos, 1994); and Fagiolo, "Sistemi di ville in Italia."

9 This information—which was provided by the eighteenth-century historian of Bagnaia, Arcangelo Carones—is reported in Claudia Lazzaro, *The Italian Renaissance Garden: From the Conventions of Planting, Design, and Orna-*

ment to the Grand Gardens of Sixteenth-Century Central Italy (New Haven: Yale University Press, 1990), 247; and Fabiano Tiziano Fagliari Zeni Buchicchio, "Tommaso Ghinucci," in *Dizionario biografico degli Italiani* (Roma: Istituto della Enciclopedia Italiana, 1999), 53:781–83. Only during the seventeenth century would a new quarter be built between the town and the villa.

10 It seems plausible that, at Bagnaia, Vignola tried to rationalize the relationship that existed in Rome between the Castel Sant'Angelo and the nearby urban trident. The two portals and the left flank of the villa (from whence began the route to Caprarola) were connected to the town by three avenues directed toward the tower keep. If this hypothesis is correct, then the transformation by Vignola would later have been *pietrificata*, realized in stone, in the quarter that arose between the seventeenth and eighteenth centuries on the lines of the three avenues. At the end of the sixteenth century, the area between the villa and the borough was in any case uninhabited—in front of the central portal was an enclosure with a little grove, a *boschetto*, a sort of woodland *ouverture* to the formal garden.

11 Marcello Fagiolo, introduction to *Tracce di memoria: Arte e cultura a Genzano di Roma*, by Mariano Apa, 11–16 (Genzano di Roma: Comune di Genzano, 1982).

12 In addition to the publications mentioned in note 1, see the following bibliography on Tusculan villas: Carlludwig Franck, *Die Barockvillen in Frascati, ihre Gestaltung aus den landschaftlichen Gegebenheiten* (Munich: Deutscher Kunstverlag, 1956); Almamaria Tantillo Mignosi, ed., *Villa e paese: Dimore nobili del Tuscolo e di Marino* (Rome: De Luca, 1980); and Tracy L. Ehrlich, *Landscape and Identity in Early Modern Rome: Villa Culture at Frascati in the Borghese Era* (Cambridge: Cambridge University Press, 2002). See also the publications by Maria Barbara Guerrieri Borsoi: *Villa Belpoggio a Frascati: Storia della villa dei Vestri, Cesi, Borromeo, Visconti, Pallavicini, Sciarra dal XVI al XX secolo* (Rome: Gangemi, 1997); *Villa Sora a Frascati* (Rome: Gangemi, 2000); "I Contugi e Francesco da Volterra: Il palazzo romano all'Aracoeli e la villa tuscolana," *Palladio* 40 (2007): 103–16; and *Villa Rufina Falconieri: La rinascita di Frascati e la più antica dimora tuscolana* (Rome: Gangemi, 2008).

13 Annibale Caro, *Lettere familiari*, ed. Aulo Greco, 3 vols. (Florence: Le Monnier, 1957–61).

14 The medieval borough of Frascati itself was likely built on the remains of a Roman villa.

15 The Caravilla, together with the Villa Acquaviva, constituted a first villa system of the Borghese family.

16 Perhaps here came alive again not only the memory of the villa of Lucullus but also of some other ancient building types: from the spine of the Circus (a long canal, crossed by little bridges corresponding to the openings, evokes precisely the *euripus* of the circus) to the linear nymphaea such as the "Naumachia" of Taormina or the Neronian nymphaeum embedded in the substructures of the ancient "Claudianum" in Rome.

17 "Si trovano belle statue . . . getti d'acqua zampillano da tutte le parti e in mezzo è una girandola che riempie le orecchie di un rumore spaventoso imitando il tuono, la pioggia, la grandine." François-Jacques Deseine, *Rome moderne, premiére ville de l'Europe, avec toutes ses magnificences et ses delices* (Leiden: P. Vander Aa, 1713).

18 On the Savoy residences, see Vera Comoli Mandracci, *Torino* (Rome: Laterza, 1983); Costanza Roggero Bardelli, Maria Grazia Vinardi, and Vittorio Defabiani, *Ville Sabaude* (Milan: Rusconi, 1990); and Gianfranco Gritella, *Juvarra: L'architettura* (Modena: Panini, 1992).

19 Roggero Bardelli, Vinardi, and Defabiani, *Ville Sabaude*, 13.

20 "Disposto a vista di vita attiva e contemplativa per formare uno specchio alla vita umana, per il quale caminando scuopre la strada che non solo i Prencipi, ma ciascuno deve tenere per ben vivere e virtuosamente operare, per riuscire forte, magnanimo et glorioso e, senza timore o spavento alcuno, seguire sempre ogni lodevole e virtuosa impresa. È un luogo, in somma, che scuopre tutta l'Etica d'Aristotele che è la vera strada di reggere e governare se stesso et altri ancora: pensieri che trascendano gli umani intelletti essendo congionto il gusto corporale co'l piacere dello spirito." The description by Zuccaro (1608) was republished in Detlef Heikamp, "I viaggi di Federico Zuccaro," pt. 1, *Paragone* 9, no. 105 (1958): 48–49; and studied in Nino Carboneri, *Ascanio Vitozzi: Un architetto tra Manierismo e Barocco* (Rome: Officina Edizioni, 1966); Aurora Scotti, *Ascanio Vitozzi: Ingegnere ducale a Torino* (Florence: La Nuova Italia, 1969); and Roggero Bardelli, Vinardi, and Defabiani, *Ville Sabaude*.

21 "hanno principio cinque stradoni . . ciascuna di queste strade disposte gratiosamente a vari effetti et operationi nostre e di virtù e di vitio." Heikamp, "I viaggi di Federico Zuccaro," 49.

22 "La strada a questa vicina ha per fine di vista un bellissimo tempio rotondo dedicato alle arti liberali: nel suo principio dimostra orridezza d'alberi e sterpi, e quanto più avanti si va, tanto più bella et gratiosa riesce per le spalliere di rose e fiori che gli fanno ornamento, et a luogo a luogo vi sono riposi di nicchie e statue di uomini di singolar virtù e fama in professioni nobili, con taluni motti a quelle aspettanti." Ibid., 49.

23 "Questa lunga e diritta è dedicata alli studii maggiori e ponno qui godere a voglia loro tutti i letterati, poiché vi sono varii riposi con nicchie, motti e figure di legisti e poeti. La quarta appresso a questa gira la parte destra del bosco più lungamente dell'altre et ha varii bracci e piacevoli vie, per le quali si va soavemente diportando e filosofando; e questa è dedicata alle mattematiche scientie speculative,

secondo la varietà delle quali vi sono diverse strade . . . che invitano propriamente a filosofare e contemplare il cielo, le stelle, i pianeti e tutte le sfere sovrane." Ibid., 50.

24 "Et in questa strada delle virtù attive e contemplative si scorgano la teorica e la prattica, e con ragione è posta in mezzo a gli altri per avere figurato d'esser il più degno luogo nell'intelletto dell'uomo: è larga, lunga, spatiosa et aperta, come quella che più apertamente conosce i più alti e nobili misteri che imaginar si possa mente umana; è chiara, risplendente e luminosa, perché non ci è il velo della oscurità delle cose terrene che gli possa fare ombra o macchia alcuna." Ibid., 50–51.

25 For a comparison, see the urban design of Caprarola, where the axial road terminates at the front facade of the Palazzo Farnese.

26 "Questo nobilissimo torrione è fabricato in forma di un elmo d'uomo d'arme che stia alla veduta per guardia di tutta l'Italia, non che della propria città, et sotto questo grand'elmo, che sembra d'avere alzato la visiera, è una gratiosa loggietta ove sono figurati tutti i venti. Il pennacchio, o pennone è la cupoletta e banderola che mostra girando i venti che tirano." Heikamp, "I viaggi di Federico Zuccaro," 55.

27 "È una gratiosissima vista . . . Questa loggia ha per linea diritta il ponte della Dora, il parco e quel gran stradone di mezzo e la vista dell'una e l'altra parte del bosco, la campagna aperta a sinistra, e l'altissime montagne, et a destra il piano e le colline delitiose già dette, con un gran giro di detta Dora avanti . . . " Ibid., 55–56.

28 "The park—in its structural extension of the water ways and road systems—was intended as a natural expansion beyond the walls of the internal garden of the city palace. The direct connection was constituted by 'the exit, if not secret then private, of Sua Altezza (His Highness, the Duke) for his tour of the Park,' a passageway that linked the 'private garden of His Highness and of The Most Serene Infantas (the Crown Princesses)' with the hunting estate across the Dora River." ("Il parco—nella sua estensione strutturale delle vie d'acque e dei percorsi—fu inteso come naturale protendimento oltre le mura del giardino interno del palazzo urbano. Il tramite diretto era costituito da quella 'se non segreta almeno particolare uscita di S. A. per la gita del Parco', un passaggio che univa il 'giardino particolare di S. A. e delle Serenissime Infante' con la tenuta venatoria oltre la Dora.") Heikamp, "I viaggi di Federico Zuccaro," quoted in Roggero Bardelli, Vinardi, and Defabiani, *Ville Sabaude*, 18. For the connection between the Regio Parco and the city, which—in parallel to the situation at the castle of Mirafiori—inaugurated the radial-centric system of the "crown" of the Savoy villas, see Comoli Mandracci, *Torino*, 18–40 and 45–53; and Vera Comoli Mandracci, "La capitale per uno Stato: Torino e il Piemonte sabaudo," in *Centri e periferie del barocco: Corso internazionale di alta cultura*, eds. Gaetana Cantone and Marcello Fagiolo, 233–53 (Rome: Istituto Poligrafico e Zecca dello Stato, 1992).

29 Robert de Salnove, *La vénerie royale* (Paris: Favre, Chez Antoine de Sommaville, 1655). It should be remembered that Robert de Salnove took part in the Savoy hunts at the court of Duke Vittorio Amedeo.

30 Amedeo di Castellamonte, *Venaria reale, palazzo di piacere, et di caccia: Ideato dall'Altezza reale di Carlo Emanvel II, duca di Sauoia, Re di Cipro* (Turin: B. Zapatta, 1674), 3. At the Venaria Reale, the "Versailles" of Piedmont, the palace by Castellamonte was rebuilt in a French style after its destruction in 1693. (Michelangelo Garove even sent his preparatory drawings to Robert de Cotte, the architect of Louis XIV, to review.) Juvarra took over as architect of the church, stables, orangery, and new pavilion in 1716–28.

31 Facts about the Savoy residences should be compared with what we know about the displacements for hunting journeys of other Italian courts. See the *delizie* of the Este family in Ferrara, the residences of the Visconti and the Sforza in Milan, or the Medici villas in Florence. See notes 3 and 4.

32 ". . . quella Loggia in forma di Teatro, che si alza tanto, che la veduta resta nel seno di quella imprigionata." Castellamonte, *Venaria reale, palazzo di piacere, et di caccia*, 72.

33 "In lunghezza poi non si è voluto passar il doppio della larghezza, anzi per maggiormente proporzionarlo acciò confondendosi con la vastità dell'Aria, che lì và avanti fino alle montagne . . . " Ibid.

34 Roggero Bardelli, Vinardi, and Defabiani, *Ville Sabaude*, 65.

35 Ibid., 368–408.

36 Ibid., 61.

37 On the history of the castle of Rivoli, see ibid., 263–87; and Gianfranco Gritella, *Rivoli: Genesi di una residenza sabauda* (Modena: Panini, 1986), 38–39.

38 "Di un diramato sistema organizzativo del territorio, che si fa elemento centrifugo di appropriazione spaziale, in un esplicito invito alla caccia e alla fuga." Roggero Bardelli, Vinardi, and Defabiani, *Ville Sabaude*, 411.

39 "L'adeguamento del modello e del rito venatorio all'uso francese e delle altre Corti europee, richiedeva un territorio congruente per la coreografia e adatto a un disegno progettuale delle rotte di caccia esteso e variato." Ibid., 412.

40 Ibid, 254.

41 See Marcello Fagiolo, *Funzioni simboli valori della Reggia di Caserta* (Rome: Dell'Arco, 1963); Giancarlo Alisio, *Siti reali dei Borboni: Aspetti dell'architettura napoletana del Settecento* (Rome: Officina, 1976); G. L. Hersey, "Carlo di Borbone a Napoli e a Caserta," in *Storia dell'arte italiana*, 12:215–64 (Turin: G. Einaudi, 1983); Cesare de Seta, ed., *Luigi Vanvitelli e la sua cerchia* (Naples: Electa Napoli, 2000); and Marcello Fagiolo, "Los nuevos palacios reales entre Versalles y Caserta: Modelos borbónicos para una idea de palacio real-ciudad-parque," in *Real sitio de La Granja de San Ildefonso*,

retrato y escena del rey, eds. Delfín Rodríguez, Helena Pérez Gallardo, and Mercedes Simal López, 51–69 (Madrid: Patrimonio Nacional, 2000). During the reigns of Carlo di Borbone and his son Ferdinand IV, "enormous tracts of land came into possession of the royal patrimony, such as the island of Procida, Astroni, Agnano, Licola, Calvi, Capriati, the lake of Patria, Cardito and Carditello, Persano, Venafro, Torre Guevara, the spinning works (*fusaro*) of Maddaloni, the woods of Omodei at Caiazzo, S. Arcangelo di Caserta, the hill of Quisisana near Castellammare, and numerous other places. To them was reserved, together with the royal palaces of Capodimonte, Portici and Caserta, a special branch of the Bourbon administration called 'royal sites.'" ("entrarono a far parte del patrimonio reale un'enorme quantità di territori come l'isola di Procida, gli Astroni, Agnano, Licola, Calvi, Capriati, il lago di Patria, Cardito e Carditello, Persano, Venafro, Torre Guevara, il fusaro di Maddaloni, la selva Omodei di Caiazzo, S. Arcangelo di Caserta, il colle di Quisisana presso Castellammare e altre numerose località, a cui, insieme con i palazzi di Capodimonte, Portici e Caserta, fu riservato un ramo speciale dell'amministrazione borbonica con la denominazione di 'Siti Reali'") Alisio, *Siti reali dei Borboni*, 27.

42 Michelangelo Schipa, *Il regno di Napoli al tempo di Carlo di Borbone*, vol. 1, bk. 3 (Milan: Roma, 1923), 329.

43 Alisio, *Siti reali dei Borboni*, 66–106. In a letter to his brother Urbano on 20 December 1757, Luigi Vanvitelli wrote: "The forest of Persano is ten miles long; there are roads completed and graveled, which seem smooth rides, to go to the beats to wait for the game, hence this is a truly royal hunting ground." ("Il bosco di Persano è lungo 10 miglia; vi sono le strade fatte e sbrecciate, che paiono giochi lisci, per andare alle poste, onde è vera caccia reale.") In that same day, the king personally killed "19 wild boar, 5 wild goats and a fox" ("19 cignali, 5 caprii e una volpe"); all included, some fifty-six animals were killed, including "a large female deer with antlers" ("una gran cerva cornuta"). Ibid., 75.

44 Minister Bernardo Tanucci wrote: "In the middle of the forest is this Royal House built by the king; in plan it is like that of a monastery of friars. Each one of us has his own cell. It is a good residence, and certainly it is the most comfortable of all the houses of the king." ("In mezzo al bosco è questa Reale Casa edificata dal Re di pianta a guisa d'un Convento di Frati. Ognuno di noi ha la sua cella. È buona abitazione, e certamente la più comoda di tutte le case del re.") Enrica Viviani della Robbi, *Bernardo Tanucci ed il suo più importante carteggio*, vol. 2 (Florence: G. C. Sansoni, 1942), 39.

45 Alisio, *Siti reali dei Borboni*, 46–65.

46 Marcello Fagiolo and Maria Luisa Madonna, "Sicilia: La ristrutturazione del territorio; Una realpolitik feudale," in *San Leucio: Archeologia, storia, progetto*, 205–9 (Milan: Il Formichiere, 1977). See also Margherita de Simone, *Ville palermitane del XVII e XVIII secolo* (Genoa: Vitali e Ghianda, 1968); Margherita de Simone, *Ville palermitane: Dal XVI al XVIII secolo* (Palermo: SIAI Edizione d'Arte Nuovo Sud, 1974); Eliana Mauro, *Le ville a Palermo* (Palermo: U. La Rosa, 1992); and Rosario Scaduto, "Il trionfo del principe: L'arco della Santissima Trinità a villa Palagonia in Bagheria," in *Storia e restauro di architetture siciliane*, eds. Salvatore Boscarino and Maria Giuffrè, 71–80 (Rome: Bonsignori, 1996).

47 Like Bagheria, the town of Santa Flavia developed from a villa. The eighteenth-century borough may be considered a sort of mirror-image inversion of the Villa Filangieri (begun in 1666); the rectangular perimeters of both the villa and borough intersect each other with a crossing axis (that leads to the Villa Valdina and the castle of Solanto on one side and to the Villa Torremuzza on the other side), and they continue on the axial road leading to Porticello.

48 Karl Lohmeyer, *Palagonisches Barock: Das Haus der Laune des "Prinzen von Palagonia"* (Berlin: Maximilian-Gesellschaft, 1942); K. Brassai, "La Villa Palagonia: Une curiosité du baroque sicilien," *Gazette des beaux-arts* (1962): 351–64; Scaduto, "Il trionfo del principe"; Giuseppe la Monica, *Sicilia misterica: Fondazioni e restauri di monumenti tra Rinascimento e Barocco* (Palermo: S. F. Flaccovio, 1982); Natale Tedesco, *L'immago espressa, Villa Palagonia: Tra norma ed eccezione* (Siracusa: Ediprint, 1986); Marcello Fagiolo and Maria Adriana Giusti, "La stella e la rosa: Analisi della Villa Buonvisi-Santini a Camigliano," in *Il giardino delle muse: Arti e artifici nel barocco europeo*, eds. Maria Adriana Giusti and Alessandro Tagliolini, 199–254 (Florence: Edifir, 1995); E. H. Neil, "Architects and Architecture in Seventeenth- and Eighteenth-Century Palermo: New Documents," *Annali di architettura* 7 (1995): 159–76; and Lionello Puppi, "Il principe e i mostri," in *Studi in onore di Renato Cevese*, eds. Guido Beltramini, Adriano Ghisetti Giavarina, and Paola Marini, 385–99 (Vicenza: Centro Internazionale di Studi di Architettura Andrea Palladio, 2000).

49 The geometry of the main staircase inserted into the concavity of the facade is similar to the geometry of the grand staircase (built around 1690 and demolished in the nineteenth century) with concave-convex curves shown in a sketch by Fischer von Erlach for the Casino Althan near Vienna.

50 Dante Alighieri, *The Divine Comedy*, trans. Charles S. Singleton (Princeton, N.J.: Princeton University Press, 1973), 61.

51 Particularly evocative is a study by Claudia Lazzaro, "Italy is a Garden: The Idea of Italy and the Italian Garden Tradition," in *Villas and Gardens in Early Modern Italy and France*, eds. Mirka Beneš and Dianne Harris, 29–60 (Cambridge: Cambridge University Press, 2001), in which she analyzes in parallel the tradition of the "Italian" garden and the idea of "Italy." The essay, which was based on sources from antiquity to the twentieth century, also engages Dante's metaphor.

52 Castellamonte, *Venaria reale, palazzo di piacere, et di caccia*, 10.

53 See Andreina Griseri, "Urbanistica, cartografia e antico regime nel Piemonte sabaudo," *Storia della città* 12–13 (1979): 19–38; and Roggero Bardelli, Vinardi, and Defabiani, *Ville Sabaude*, 38–39.

54 On the geometric design of the hunting forests, with intersecting avenues and étoiles, see most recently Jérôme Buridant, "La forêt et la chasse au XVIe siècle," in *Chasses princières dans l'Europe de la Renaissance: Actes du colloque de Chambord, 1er et 2 octobre 2004*, eds. Claude d'Anthenaise and Monique Chatenet, 159–74 (Arles: Actes Sud, 2007). With respect to the system of avenues made more tangible with Louis XIV, a few archetypal examples can be cited, including the 1521 "Carrefour des Routtes" in the forest of Compiègne, the late sixteenth-century intersecting roads in the forest of Chantilly, and the ca. 1600 "Route ronde" (circular ring-road) of Fontainebleau.

55 Nicolás García Tapia, *Ingenieria y arquitectura en el Renacimiento español* (Valladolid: Secretariado de Publicaciones, Universidad de Valladolid, 1990); Catherine Wilkinson-Zerner, *Juan de Herrera, Architect to Philip II of Spain* (New Haven: Yale University Press, 1993), 146–51; Carmen Añon, José Luis Sancho, and José Martínez Millán, eds., *Jardín y naturaleza en el reinado de Felipe II* (Madrid: Sociedad Estatal Conme. Centenarios Felipe II–Carlos V, 1998); Ana Luengo Añon and Coro Millares, "El Real Sitio de Aranjuez," in *Jardín y naturaleza en el reinado de Felipe II*, 461–95; and José Luis Sancho, "Plano del Real Sitio de Aranjuez al final del reinado de Felipe II," in *Jardín y naturaleza en el reinado de Felipe II*, 497–503.

56 On cartographic experimentation in the age of Philip II, see García Tapia, *Ingenieria y arquitectura en el Renacimiento español*; and M. I. Vicente Maroto and Mariano Esteban Piñeiro, *Aspectos de la ciencia aplicada en la España del siglo de oro* (Salamanca: Junta de Castilla y León, Consejereia de Cultura y Bienestar Social, 1991).

57 Marcello Fagiolo, "La Roma di Sisto V: Le matrici del policentrismo," *Psicon* 8–9 (1976): 25–40.

58 Marcello Fagiolo, "L'universo della luce nell'idea di architettura del Vittone," in *Bernardo Vittone e la disputa fra classicismo e barocco nel Settecento: Atti del Convegno internazionale promosso dall'Accademia delle scienze di Torino nella ricorrenza del secondo centenario della morte di B. Vittone, 21–24 settembre 1970*, 2:117–74 (Turin: Accademia delle Scienze, 1972).

59 Marcello Fagiolo, "Il piano di L'Enfant per Washington," *Gran bazaar* (October–November 1988): 30–34; Fagiolo, "Washington: O simbolismo maçónico da nova capital dos Estados Unidos," in *Lisboa iluminista e o seu tempo*, 239–66 (Lisbon: Universidade Autónoma de Lisboa, 1997); and Marcello Fagiolo and Vincenzo Cazzato, eds., *Architettura e massoneria: L'esoterismo della costruzione* (Rome: Gangemi, 2007).

CHAPTER 4

Residences of the Emergent Classes in Two Areas of Southern Italy

VINCENZO CAZZATO

SOUTHERN ITALY (THE *MEZZOGIORNO*)—WITH the Sicilian exceptions of Piana dei Colli near Palermo and the Bagheria area—presents two main clusters of villas in the form of systems. They were consolidated during the eighteenth century and show many points in common, albeit with certain differences. On the one hand are the residences of the Neapolitan area, where the court aristocracy, following the construction of the royal palace at Portici by Carlo di Borbone, formed a veritable "city of villas" between Mount Vesuvius and the sea. This cluster extends along the "Golden Mile" as it was called, above the stretch of the royal highway of the Calabrias that runs between Naples and Torre del Greco, now called the Via Nazionale. On the other hand are the residences of the Salento region in Puglia, which took shape in some of the most fertile portions of the territory in less stately forms and at the initiative of members of the emerging classes (fig. 4.1). This network was reshaped between the nineteenth and the twentieth centuries in the period of eclecticism.

Both systems are distributed across large territories and are characterized by a long, gradual, and coherent stratification of groups of villas, documented from the sixteenth to the eighteenth centuries. In their disposition, a perfect harmony is established between art, architecture, and landscape; beauty, healthfulness, and fertility are its main attributes. For example, the first monograph dedicated to the royal villa of Portici, by Nicola Nocerino, praised the salubriousness of the site: "at the edge of the perfumed sea, gracefully placed in a slightly dominant location three miles from Naples, above the delightful slopes of Mount Vesuvius, crossed by a good mile of the Royal road (Strada Regia) straight, smooth, comfortable and spacious." As noted in ancient times by Galen, Procopius, and Strabo, the site is healthy because it lies "between the sea and Mont Vesuvius, the former with its salts mostly evaporated on the waves of the sea, the latter with its fire and sulfur," where "the climate is always and in every hour perfect all the year long. So you can come and live here in winter and in summer, in autumn and in spring time." The beauty of the site is undeniable, and "to the purity and healthiness of the air you should add the delight and the beauty of the sight of a calm and pleasant sea, and that of the near and bright hills of the neighboring town of Naples and of all the homes, villas and mounts that crown our crater."[1]

FIGURE 4.1. The kingdom of Naples.

Reprinted from Willem Janszoon Blaeu and Joan Blaeu, *Novus Atlas: Das ist Abbildung und Beschreibung von allen Ländern des Erdreichs* (Amsterdam: Wm. Blaeu, 1635).

Both systems of villas combined the function of agricultural production with *otium*.[2] An eighteenth-century Neapolitan chronicler affirmed that noble sites should signify their status and that villas should coexist harmoniously with the rustic residences of the farmer and with agricultural buildings "following the idea described by Columella."[3] Both the Bourbon residences and the Vesuvian villas adopted this concept, following the principles of classical treatises, but modified it in accordance with enlightened theories of agriculture and new agricultural techniques. In the Salento region, the spread of the country casino expressed the attitude of the emerging bourgeoisie that agriculture was not only the centerpiece of the kingdom's economy but also the basis for transforming the countryside into a healthy retreat where one could pursue pleasures. Unlike the Vesuvian villas, which were expressions of the aristocratic and ruling classes of a country devoted to a sovereign, the Salento residences issued from the economic power of noble families, landowners, merchants, and new professionals.

Vesuvian Villas

In 1959, the volume *Ville vesuviane del Settecento* was published with contributions by Roberto Pane and other scholars. "Few places in the world," wrote Pane, "can boast of such a favorable climate as that chosen by the Neapolitan aristocracy in the eighteenth century for their summer residence, between the slopes of Vesuvius and the sea. The alignment of the avenues, in axis with the villas, seems to have been spontaneously suggested by the gentle slope of the land down to the beaches; and likewise also the arrangement of the trees, so that, above the green slopes, one could glimpse on one side Mount Vesuvius, and on the other an uninterrupted clear blue line on the horizon."[4] Already in this excerpt, one sees the emphasis placed on the landscape value of these residences; this value was based on their spectacular views toward both the sea and the volcano (fig. 4.2).

Twenty-one years separated the *Ville vesuviane del Settecento* and the careful survey of these villas by Cesare de Seta, Leonardo di Mauro, and Maria Perone. De Seta wrote that "the system of villas that have been built in the course of many centuries in the shadow of what Giacomo Leopardi termed the *sterminator Vesevo* is an example, neither unique nor rare, of historical, social, economic and productive continuity."[5] The uniqueness of this

FIGURE 4.2. Saverio Xavier della Gatta, *Naples, vue du port de Portici* and *Vue du Palais Royal de Portici, avec le Vésuve en éruption*, 1784, engravings.

system, compared with other famous residential and productive clusters, lies in the nature of its patrons—mainly members of the aristocratic and ruling classes that were linked to the sovereign—and in its wholly unusual concentration—about one hundred and thirty villas in an extremely limited expanse of territory.[6]

This set of conditions, for which de Seta correctly uses the term "system," stretched over a time span which, starting in the period of the viceroyalty—but stemming from a more ancient tradition—reached its peak around the middle of the eighteenth century. In fact, the second half of the sixteenth century saw, on the one hand, the building of new urban residences by the feudatories, and, on the other hand, the conquest of the Vesuvian area by the viceroy, nobles, and members of the upper hierarchies of the state through the construction of sumptuous houses in the vicinity of the areas chosen for the summer residences of the court (i.e., in the plain to the east of the city overlooking Posillipo and the Riviera di Chiaia). But only in the first half of the eighteenth century—thanks to a positive economic situation brought about by the increase in prices of agricultural products, the growth of the population, and a succession of years of abundance (interrupted from 1759 to 1764 by five years of epidemics and famine)—did conditions foster the building of residences and villas on the Vesuvian slopes. During the same years, the policies of Carlo di Borbone opened the way for the creation of the "royal sites" ("siti reali"), public works, and productive commercial structures (fig. 4.3).[7]

Mount Vesuvius was the absolute protagonist of the region,[8] and not just in terms of landscape. "It is quite clear," wrote de Seta, "that the diversity and distribution of the settlements, their development or their crisis, the fortune of one center or area

FIGURE 4.3. Giovanni Carafa, Duke of Noja, detail of the *Mappa topografica della città di Napoli e de' suoi contorni* (Naples, 1775).

compared with another, depend in the long term on the structure that is geographically and topographically dominant. But in this case the structure is not a class, or an economic or political system, or all three of these put together, but a volcano, namely the Vesuvius."[9] Near the volcano, a terrifying instrument of destruction, was the sea and a lava terrain that was rich in vineyards and orchards. "These are essential elements for understanding the established relationship between nature and architecture," wrote de Seta. "The unsettling charm of these villas is entirely in the skill with which the relationship between *artifice* and *nature* is achieved in them . . ."[10] This relationship between the villas, the countryside, and Vesuvius is also—it might be added—that between hell and paradise, earth, water, air, and fire: that is, the hell and fire threatened by the active Vesuvius and the paradise of the villa landscapes, consisting of the earth of the fertile Vesuvian slopes and the balmy air and clear waters of the seaside.

According to Gerard Labrot, the nobility and the aristocracy vied with each other in seeking a direct, less rapacious relationship with nature. What makes these villas one of the great expressions of the Enlightenment is the breadth of cultural knowledge utilized by patrons and artists and the degree to which they synthesized architecture and nature in the landscape.[11]

The concentration of residences on the coastal side, where connections with the city, both by sea and by land, were more convenient, coincided with the decision of Carlo di Borbone to erect a royal palace at Portici in 1738 (figs. 4.4 and 4.5).[12] But there were, indeed, some villas completed before the royal palace, including the Villa d'Elboeuf and Villa Meola at Portici in 1711 and 1724, respectively; the Villa Pignatelli di Monteleone at Barra after 1728; the Villa Caravita at Portici in 1730; and the Villa San Gennariello at Torre del Greco around 1730. Together with the mild climate and the natural beauty of the site, it was the presence of the court as well as the granting of tax exemptions and other incentives to the entire "royal site" that fostered, above all from 1740 to 1770, the increase in the number of *casini di delizia* (villa palaces of delight).[13] In the *Istoria generale del reame di Napoli* (1750), Placido Troyli observed that the residence at Portici was surrounded by "a hundred other villas of princes, gentlemen,

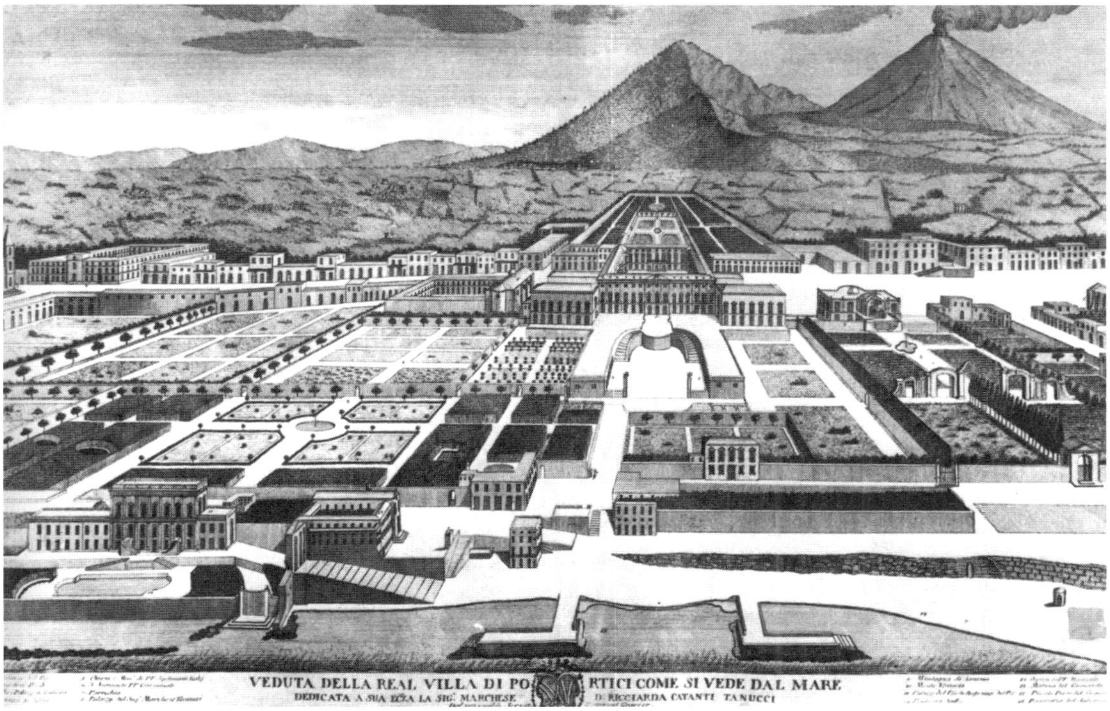

FIGURE 4.4. Giovanni Gravier, view of the royal palace of Portici, n.d., engraving.

FIGURE 4.5. Louis Chays, view of the royal palace of Portici, ca. 1770, engraving.

ministers, merchants, lawyers and other persons of good taste, which have been built here heedless of the expense, and with proper architecture."[14]

Preexisting structures were enlarged, restructured, or rebuilt *ex novo* by some of the best architects, painters, and decorators following the tastes and requirements of a cultured class that moved to the site to live in leisure, to follow the sovereign, and to enjoy a climate and a tranquility that a city like Naples—with three hundred thousand inhabitants in the mid-eighteenth century—was no longer able to guarantee. The site was also well situated for exercising control over the surrounding countryside, which was particularly fertile.[15] The lands, when not cultivated, were wooded, and hunting and fishing constituted one of the underlying reasons for the establishment of the royal palace of Portici and other residences.[16]

Among the architects who should be mentioned are Domenico Antonio Vaccaro with the Villa Maltese, Ferdinando Sanfelice with the Villa d'Elboeuf and the courtyard of the Villa Pignatelli di Monteleone, Luigi Vanvitelli with the Villa Campolieto at Ercolano (after 1762) and the Villa de Gregorio at Barra (1761), Ferdinando Fuga with the Villa Favorita at Ercolano (until 1768) and the Villa Pignatelli di Monteleone (until 1766), and further, Mario Gioffredo, Michelangelo Giustiniani, Giovan Battista Nauclerio, Giuseppe Astarita, and Pompeo Schiantarelli.

The splitting up of many vast and much older properties in the area and the intensive exploitation of the resulting smaller parcels reduced their productive character, as much of the previously cultivated land was covered with pleasure gardens and ornamental plantings. Goethe, who was in Naples in 1787 (when a large number of the villas built with the intention of creating a small court around Portici were already in existence), described in his *Italienische Reise* (*Viaggio in Italia*) the Neapolitan landscape as one of "verdant hills, sweet pastures, fertile lands and pleasure gardens."[17]

The highway from Naples to Portici carried out the function performed by the *navigli* (canals) in Lombardy or the river Brenta in the Veneto.[18] "The mildness of the climate," stated Giuseppe Maria Galanti, "the beauty of the situation and the sojourn of the court have made Portici the center of the vacations of Neapolitans. In October, particularly on feast days, the road from Naples to Portici presents a continuous passage of carriages and persons on foot. All the luxury of Naples is transported here during that month."[19]

The proliferation of villas is evident on a map made by the Duke of Noja that shows the Vesuvian area in 1775—nearly four decades after construction on the royal palace commenced.[20] See, for example, the area of Portici in figure 4.3. De Seta, di Mauro, and Perone described how "the villas do not appear scattered over the territory, but [are] spaced out and distributed in the agricultural area, according to an endless succession along the main highway and its main branches, becoming gradually denser as they approach the Royal palace, which acts in the same way as a pole of attraction in a magnetic field."[21] As Canon Carlo Celano wrote: "Here start the dwellings, which without any interruption reach as far as Portici and are called by three names: San Giovanni a Teduccio, Pietrabianca and Portici, which together resemble a magnificent and extremely beautiful city."[22] These words echo those of Annibale Caro, who, when writing to his friend Torquato Conti in 1563, hoped for the establishment of "a borough of villas from Poli to Rome."[23]

The road is, therefore, the backbone of this system. The royal residence of Portici itself is pierced by the "Strada delle Calabrie," its courtyard acting as a palatine piazza (fig. 4.6). The villas directly overlook the road, with their grounds or the surrounding countryside at their backs. There are some cases in which the main building, like the backdrop to a

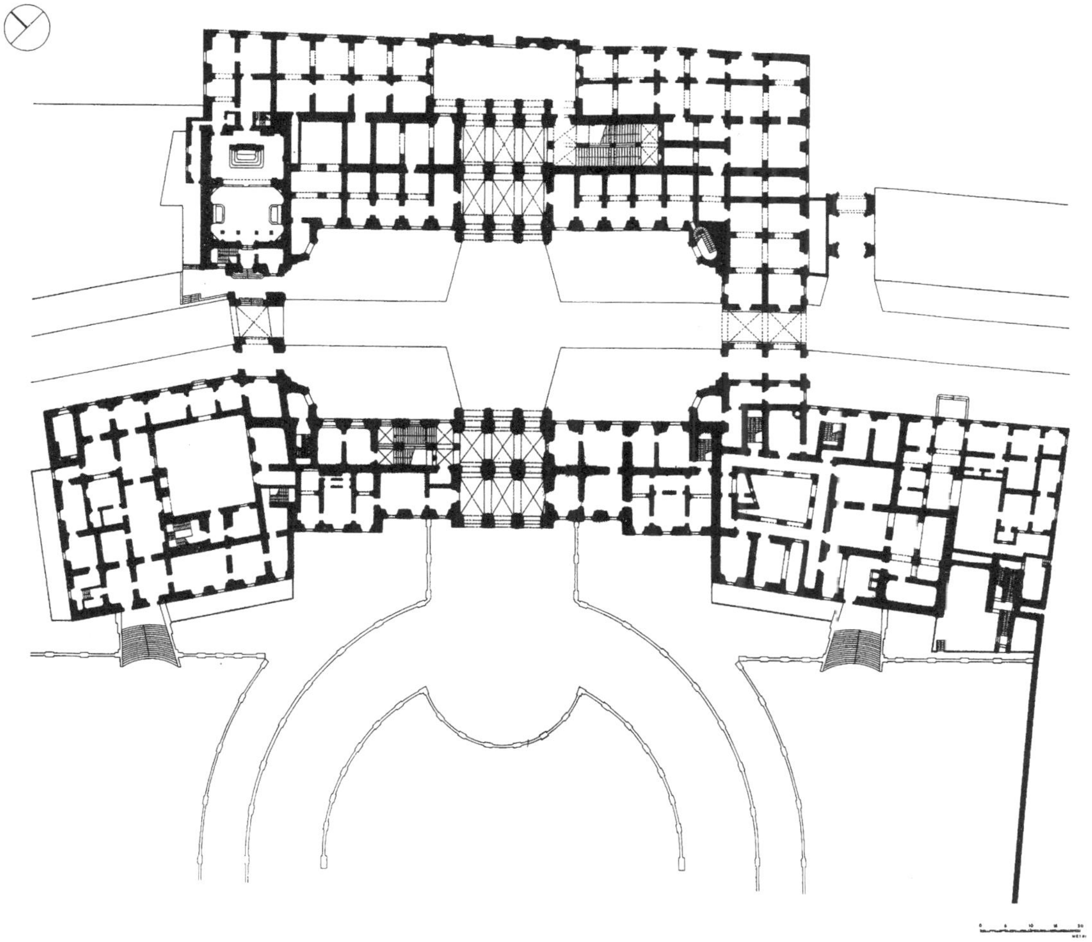

FIGURE 4.6.
Plan of the ground floor of the royal palace of Portici.

Private collection.

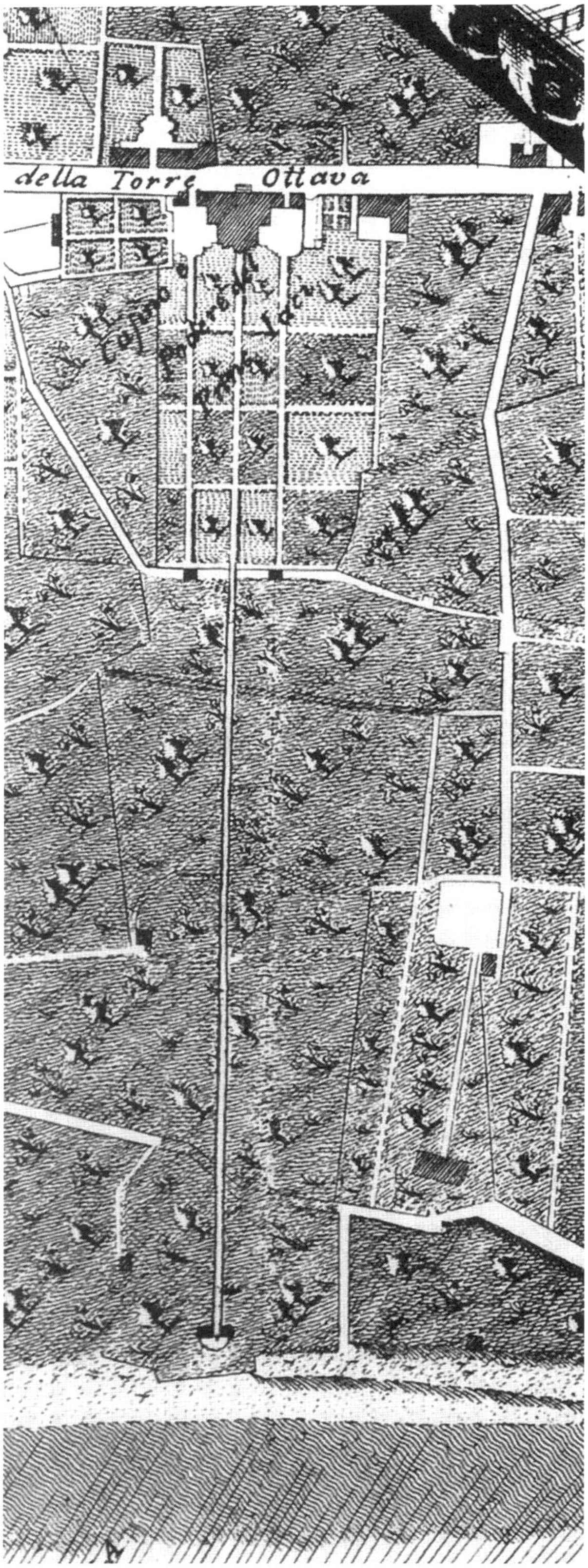

perspective, is simply announced by a portal—for example, in the Villa Prota at Torre del Greco, the drive starts from the monumental portal, which faces the road and consists of an arch flanked by two openwork balconies decorated with balustrades (an arrangement that is recalled in the loggia with a hanging arch in the foreground opening to a panorama of Vesuvius), and passes through the main building to continue toward the sea.[24]

De Seta proposed an exhaustive and convincing classification of the Vesuvian villas. Villas were classified by their location (i.e., in the vicinity of Mount Vesuvius or the sea) and their function (i.e., agricultural or recreational). (Already in Roman times there was a distinction between rustic villas in the foothills and maritime villas along the coast.)[25] The first group includes villas in which a productive function prevailed—for example, villa-farms, in which owners resided during certain periods of the year to manage the farm. Often isolated, these villas were situated on the slopes of the volcano. The various parts of the villa were distributed around a large courtyard in direct communication with the vineyards and orchards: the owner's premises were more refined and occupied multiple floors, while service wings and dependencies were less distinguished architecturally and were confined to the lower floors. The chapel was usually located alongside the main entrance to the villa or beside the portal giving access to the drive, and was used by the entire neighborhood. Typical examples of villas in the center of flourishing, extensive properties are the Villa Bifulco at Terzigno (with millstone, presses, and equipment for distilling wine, as well as a spacious panoramic terrace at the rear overlooking the slopes of Mount Vesuvius), Villa Figliola at San Sebastiano al Vesuvio, Villa Tufarelli di Sotto at San Giorgio a Cremano, and Villa Rota at Cercola.

The second group includes villas that served as places of pleasure, either exclusively or in addition

FIGURE 4.7.
Giovanni Carafa, Duke of Noja, Villa Favorita at Ercolano, detail of the *Mappa topografica della città di Napoli e de' suoi contorni* (Naples, 1775).

to their productive functions. Because they resulted from the merger of the villa-farm with the city mansion, they combined the features of both structures. These villas are situated in the vicinity of the coastal area and form an unbroken chain along the "Golden Mile." Only in rare cases are they located away from the road. De Seta makes a further distinction among these villas according to whether they are situated above or below the royal highway (fig. 4.7): "In the first case the facade overlooking the road faces the sea while the rear of the building looks beyond the garden toward the hill slopes; in the second case, the garden instead overlooks the sea and, therefore, the internal (private) facade of the building faces the sea while the public facade looks toward Vesuvius."[26] Two etchings of the Villa Favorita at Ercolano made by Francesco Sicuro in 1775 are significant in this respect, as they present the villa as viewed from the road and from the sea (figs. 4.8 and 4.9).

The *salones* (main halls) on the *primi piani* of these recreational villas permit views toward the sea and Mount Vesuvius. Typically stretching through the bodies of the buildings, the halls can be of different configurations. In the Villa Favorita and the Villa Pignatelli di Montecalvo, they are oval shaped; in the Villa del Cardinale at Torre del Greco, rectangular; and in the Villa Campolieto, as designed by Gioffredo and Vanvitelli, the alignment runs through the building from the Serlian balcony facing onto the road to the longitudinal salone, to a dome-vaulted hall that is brightly illuminated from above, and finally to the terrace overlooking the colonnade of the "rotunda."[27]

The relationship of the villa building's central axis with the garden or with the park—which in some cases (the Villa de Gregorio at Barra and the Villa Campolieto) is located at the side so as not to interrupt the relationship with the countryside—is often common to the great royal palace and the less courtly noble residence; in short, the motif of the axis, which at Caserta runs through the royal palace and seemingly extends to infinity, occurs also in the Vesuvian villas.[28]

Because it was also an architectural design, the garden was the natural continuation of the buildings of the Vesuvian villa. As Attanasio wrote: "The splendid, compact little courtyards of the villas help little to understand the spaces behind, and give no indication of the importance of the construction of the gardens; but when the portals are opened the effect is astonishing."[29] The garden architecture consists of hemicycles, rotundas, exedras, arcades, and coffee pavilions; the layout is regular with rectangular planting beds surrounded by hedges, thickets of holm-oaks, kiosks, and basins at the crossings of the avenues.

In the eighteenth-century Vesuvian villas, a close relationship was established between the form of the building and its immediate context. The construction criteria of the villa buildings were also applied to the design of parterres, avenues, and gardens, which mediated between Italian and French models. These outdoor elements were laid out in the same manner as the residential buildings, as may be evinced from the alignments, the disposition of the avenues, the markings of the flower beds, and the positions of the fountains and other decorative elements.

Radial structures were not lacking, as evidenced by the villa built by Giacomo d'Aquino of the Caramanico family in 1755 at San Giorgio a Cremano, which contained the largest park after that of the royal palace at Portici. Analogies are seen between the radial pattern at San Giorgio a Cremano and that of the hermitage in the upper park of the royal palace at Portici. The resemblance is not confined to their internal arrangements, for the symmetrical axis in Villa d'Aquino can be ideally extended as far as Portici, connecting the center of the two "suns."[30] One scholar considers that certain gardens are "veritable cultural and scientific manifestos, the sum of knowledge and expertise, in which spirituality and reason, magic and science, merge in a harmonious synthesis."[31]

It was noted already in the eighteenth century that the three traditional garden typologies of the region—flower gardens, fruit gardens (with grapes and citrus, in particular), and ornamental gardens—blended into an organic composition in Neapolitan residences: "—And finally the crowning delight—" wrote Nocerino in 1787, "is the view of so many gardens, avenues, parterres, espaliers, made with majestic design, and skill, all well provided with all sorts of citrus and other fruits, botanical herbs and the rarest and loveliest of flowers."[32]

FIGURE 4.8. Francesco Sicuro, view of the Villa Favorita at Ercolano from the road, 1777, engraving.

FIGURE 4.9. Francesco Sicuro, view of the Villa Favorita at Ercolano from the sea, 1777, engraving.

Terraces, open galleries, and balconies—as in the examples of the Villa Pignatelli di Monteleone and the Villa Signorini at Ercolano—had the function of making the surrounding spaces more readable from a higher level. As Filippo Barbera wrote: "The construction of viewpoints in the articulation of the designs of the villas did not have as its aim just taking generic advantage of the natural landscape (Vesuvius and the gulf), but the actual enjoyment of the rich geometries of the gardens annexed to the villas."[33]

The compositional axis of the villa commenced at the portal and—by means of a complex sequence of spaces constituted by the hall, the vestibule, and a loggia on the primo piano opening onto the landscape—crossed the courtyard, which is a spectacular prelude to the garden from which it is separated by an exedra that acts as a filter. This axis then continued either toward the sea (as at the Villa Favorita at Ercolano, the Villa Menna at Portici, the Villa Campolieto at Ercolano, and the Villa Prota at Torre del Greco) or in the direction of Mount Vesuvius (as at the Villa Ruggiero at Ercolano, the Villa de la Ville at Ercolano, the Villa del Cardinale at Torre del Greco, and the Villa Bifulco at Terzigno) (fig. 4.10).[34] Often the cultivated land was situated on the other side of the road and the axial alignment commenced at a portal in the center of an exedra (as at the Villa Meola at Portici, Villa del Cardinale at Torre del Greco, and Villa Pignatelli di Monteleone at Barra).

The hall, one of the elements that contributes most to an architecture of vision and permeable use, takes on complex forms. Although the main axis of the ellipse is perpendicular to the alignment of the architectural layout in the Villa Cerbone at San Giorgio a Cremano, it coincides with it in the Villa Pignatelli di Montecalvo at San Giorgio a Cremano. In the Villa Menna at Portici, the main hall is a sequence of three sectors differentiated by the decoration of the vaults, and in the Villa Ruggiero at Ercolano the central space has a lobate layout. In the Villa del Cardinale at Torre del Greco, one passes from a small hall to a vestibule whose size coincides with that of the courtyard, which is visible through the big arches of the double arcade. This arrangement enables the visitor, shortly after crossing the hall, to have a full view of the articulated, rich exedra in the background, which provides access to the garden.

In the Villa Campolieto at Ercolano (figs. 4.11–4.13), a deep entrance hall leads into a luminous vestibule; its luminosity is due to its proximity to the entrance that opens toward the sea and to the presence of a secondary cross alignment that, opening to the right onto the garden, provides light for the stairway on the left, whose position perpendicular to the main alignment recalls that of Caserta. After the entrance hall comes a portico with three functions: delimiting the courtyard, providing a covered walk, and supporting a terrace-belvedere with access from the *piano nobile*.

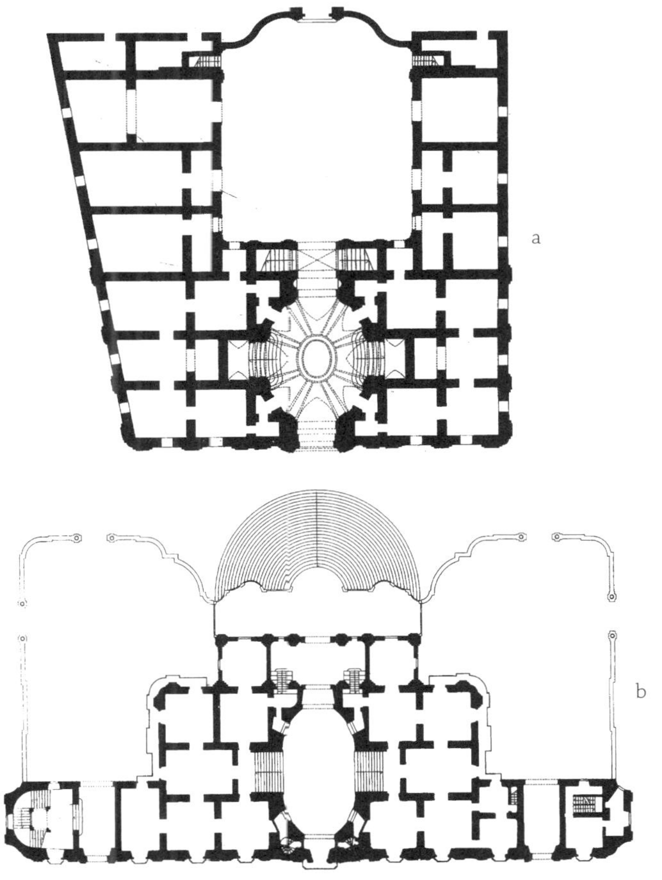

FIGURE 4.10.
Ground-floor plans of (a) the Villa Pignatelli di Montecalvo at San Giorgio a Cremano and (b) the Villa Favorita at Ercolano. Note the sequence of spaces along the central axis of each plan.

Reproduced by permission from Cesare de Seta, Leonardo di Mauro, and Maria Perone, *Ville vesuviane* (Milan: Rusconi, 1980), 63 and 169.

The staircases are, therefore, positioned in such a way as not to interrupt the alignment of the composition and the view; they take on a great scenographic value, whether constituted by a single block arranged laterally with respect to the axis of symmetry (with access from the entrance hall, from the vestibule, or directly from the courtyard) or by two symmetrical flights with respect to the longitudinal axis of the layout.[35]

FIGURE 4.11.
Exterior view of the Villa Campolieto at Ercolano.
Photograph by Vita Basile.

FIGURE 4.12.
Portico of the Villa Campolieto at Ercolano.
Photograph by Vita Basile.

FIGURE 4.13.
Staircase gallery of the Villa Campolieto at Ercolano.
Photograph by Vita Basile.

FIGURE 4.14.
Main elevation of the Villa Prota at Torre del Greco.

Reproduced by permission from Cesare de Seta, Leonardo di Mauro, and Maria Perone, *Ville vesuviane* (Milan: Rusconi, 1980), 348.

In the Villa Pignatelli di Montecalvo, the open stairway, which commences at the sides of the large arch leading into the courtyard from the hall, flanks the internal facade with its symmetrical flights and then turns to the side wings at right angles. The twin flights of stairs in the Villa Signorini at Ercolano are in a singular position—as in many Neapolitan palaces, they act as a backdrop to the courtyard. With their double central archway, whose back side also serves as the inner edge of the second courtyard, the stairs frame the opening to the garden and hence the sea. In the Villa Meola at Portici, the inner side of the courtyard contains two symmetrical stairways that act as a filter with respect to the park.

The three large arches in the Villa Bisignano at Barra, which frame a long avenue toward the countryside and Mount Vesuvius, also act as filters between the courtyard and the garden—as do the sinuous exedra of the Villa Pignatelli di Montecalvo at San Giorgio a Cremano, the openwork exedra that defines the limits of the courtyard in the Villa del Cardinale at Torre del Greco, the triumphal arch with three barrel vaults that separates the internal courtyard and the rear garden in the Villa Letizia at Barra, and the three archways (two arcuate and one architraved) that open toward the sea in the Villa Renna (Consiglio) at Ercolano.

These examples suggest the themes of permeability, transparency, and tracery. These themes are also recurrent motifs in the fastigia of the Vesuvian villas. In addition to the large opening with the hanging arch at the Villa Prota (fig. 4.14), we may think of the fastigium with the statue of the Blessed Virgin in the Villa Salvatore at Torre del Greco or the fastigium in the Villa San Gennariello at Torre del Greco, which is mixtilinear with two round eyes and contains a niche with a bust of San Gennaro looking toward Mount Vesuvius.

Because of past ravages and more recent degradations, many villas have lost their original features. As a result, the relationship between their parts and the whole have been obscured, and—above all—one no longer perceives how individual villas once belonged to a system. But already in 1829 Giuseppe Maria Galanti wrote: "Around a devastating volcano, a prodigious population clothes, through its industriousness, with a lush vegetation places once charred and devastated, opulence erects palaces and delights, there where the danger of losing them seems imminent, and a happy indifference becomes more productive and effective than a wise foresight."[36]

Residences in the Salento

In the Salento in the south of Puglia, the typology of the villa—known in its various forms as villa, casino, and casina[37]—led in the same years to the redesign of vast areas of the rural landscape through the formation of nuclei of suburban residences concentrated in specific parts of the territory, thereby giving rise to veritable systems.[38] The following section will analyze these different residential typologies; it is worthwhile to stress that in the Salento, as in the Neapolitan area, there were diversified typologies, ranging from the *masseria* (farm), of ancient origin and tradition, to the villa.

The Salentine masseria, a basic center for agricultural production and storage, was generally characterized by a turret-shaped building that served as the living quarters of the farmer, but it was also a lookout point and a defensive structure intended to protect inhabitants against the seaborne Saracen incursions (fig. 4.15). In the sixteenth century, the need for defense led to the creation of a system of coastal towers and fortified masserias in the Salento; this was a moment of profound transformation in the rural environment (fig. 4.16). But in spite of the presence of fortification elements, these complexes already displayed certain architectural features typical of villas. Furthermore, the custom of living in villas, although impacted by defense requirements, manifested itself clearly in the course of the sixteenth century. Consider, for example, the residences of a number of humanists around Lecce, from the villa of Scipione Ammirato to the villas of Fulgenzio and Giovanni Camillo della Monica.

The masseria would characterize the region without interruption until the mid-eighteenth century. Throughout the seventeenth and early eighteenth centuries, in fact, the landscape, marked by an economy based mainly on animal husbandry, did not evolve in any significant way due to demographic crises, labor shortages, famines, droughts, plagues, and price fluctuations. All economic and political interests were focused on the city, and it was not by chance that the explosion of the so-called Barocco Leccese was typically an urban phenomenon.

It was not until the second half of the eighteenth century, when the Turkish threat was over

FIGURE 4.15. Masseria di San Biagio at Salve Lecce. Photograph by the author.

and brigandage had run its course, that casinos were built *ex novo* in the countryside and that the old structures of fortified masserias were enlarged and adapted to new functions. Many masserias assumed the dignity of villas as they were converted from fortified masserias to masseria-casinos or masseria-villas (i.e., places intended as holiday retreats or seasonal residences for noble landowning families, traders, and professional men). Among the many masserias transformed from defensive structures into magnificent residences—with the presence of those typical villa features, such as balconies and open galleries—are the Masseria Brusca in Nardò (fig. 4.17), the Masseria Torre Pinta in Galatina, and the Masseria Lo Spagnulo in Ostuni. On the higher part of the Cupa, the Villa Mellone incorporated "courtyards, houses and sheds" of an earlier farm complex called "Curti grandi," and near its sheep pens were courtyards and enclosed gardens marked by avenues leading to a belvedere and a coffee pavilion.[39] The Villa Cerulli Bozzicorso and the Casino de Virgilis are also organized on the remains of a masseria.[40] And during the nineteenth century, it was not uncommon to find scenographic facades of villas masking earlier structures consisting of farm complexes.

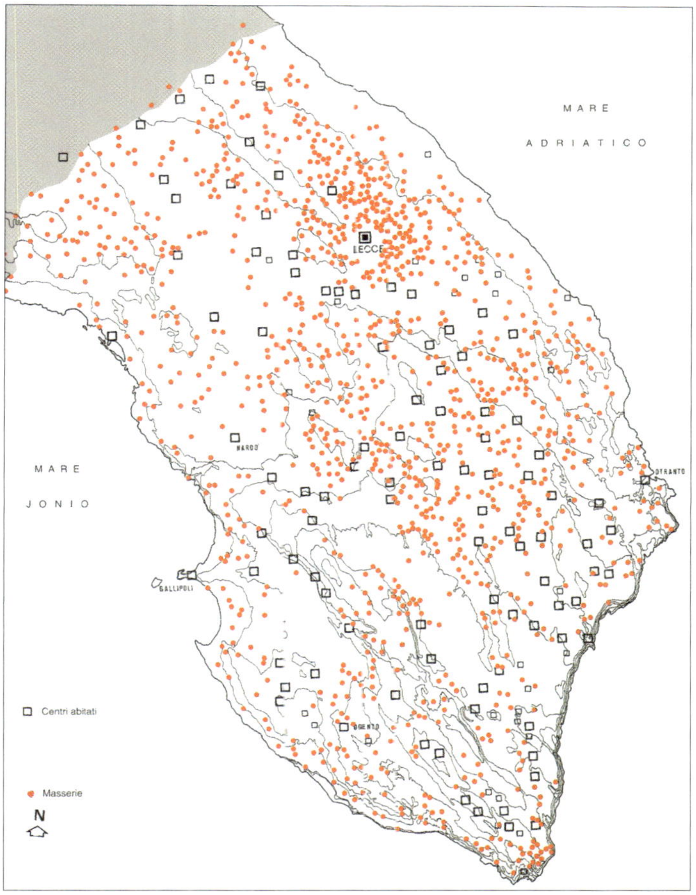

FIGURE 4.16. Distribution of masserias (in red) in relation to population centers in the province of Lecce.

Reproduced by permission from Antonio Costantini, *Le masserie del Salento: Dalla masseria fortificata alla masseria-villa* (Galatina: Mario Congedo, 1994).

The rural casino bore witness to a process of agrarian renewal that produced changes in the form and structure of rural buildings. This process marked the passage from a cereal-growing, pastoral economy to an economy based essentially on tree crops (e.g., olives, grapes, and almonds) and expressed the new relationship that was gradually established between landlords and peasant farmers in the second half of the eighteenth and the early part of the nineteenth century. The crisis in olive production and the expansion of vineyards were to have a considerable impact on the typology of the casino complex. The presence of a vineyard, which was more complex to run than an olive grove, required the construction of a permanent dwelling for the peasant farmer and the proprietor.

The casino was the architectural expression of a particular type of reconciliatory relationship between owners, who resided primarily in urban areas, and the peasant farmers who lived in the country. The two-story building combined the worker's house (along with the millstone, store, wine vault, and rooms for processing tobacco) on the ground floor and the owner's house (his temporary residence) on the upper floor without any explicit separation of the two social classes (fig. 4.18). Many casinos were referred to as villas, even when they were the result of radical transformations or extensions of more modest rural dwellings.

The process of agrarian renewal was particularly evident near a number of important urban centers and in places where the land was more fertile (an analogous situation can be found in Naples).[41] This was where wealthy families built elegant country houses, which, in the eighteenth century, simultaneously bore witness to the dissemination of the Baroque taste in rural areas and marked the decline of this style. The most significant examples of these villa clusters are found around Lecce (in the area known as the Cupa), near Nardò (in the locality of Cenate), in the Presicce area,[42] and in the Gallipoli hinterland.

FIGURE 4.17.
Masseria Brusca in Nardò.
Photograph by Michele Onorato.

FIGURE 4.18.
Villa Spirito at Sannicola. Note the continuity of treatment between the upper and lower floors.
Photograph by Michele Onorato.

The deep Cupa depression is an area of ancient population; its cultural patrimony includes prehistoric menhirs, the remains of two important Messapic cities (Rudiae and Cavallino), traces of the Roman centuriation, medieval street patterns, masseria-type settlements, and Baroque rural dwellings. Fertile land, abundant water, pure air, busy thoroughfares, and the proximity of the regional capital of Terra d'Otranto have all had an appreciable influence on the building of so many residences by owners intent on transferring urban qualities to a rural setting.[43] The Cupa was the "Tivoli of the inhabitants of Lecce"—the profiles of the domes and bell towers of numerous inhabited centers surround this valley, while the fruit orchards "of light green color" are "interspersed between villas and farmhouses which stand out brightly in that ocean of greenery." In the orchards—as we read in a nineteenth-century text—"Flora and Pomona, Bacchus and Minerva display oriental luxury" (fig. 4.19).[44]

There were also reasons for constructing the summer-autumn residences in the area around

Nardò known as the Cenate (fig. 4.20). Among them were the healthy air, the nearby sea, the vegetation, and the "great plain with a hundred shades of green" in which were scattered vineyards and orchards with their fig, pear, peach, and apricot trees.[45] The etymology of the area's name is uncertain, and perhaps derives from a type of grape (*acenata* or *cenata*) or the obligation of the *cenaticum*, the meal that the local populations had to guarantee for the Roman troops when they were stationed there. (The area was, in fact, crossed by the Via Sallentina, the continuation of the Via Appia.)[46]

Villas were also concentrated in the hinterland of Gallipoli, the most dynamic center in the Salento region throughout the course of the eighteenth century. Its port was, in fact, the main outlet for the oil produced in the province. Because of the impossibility of expanding the urban center beyond its fortification walls and because the presence of a vast feudal estate reserved for civic use prevented the urban inhabitants from having immediate access to the countryside, the nobility and the wealthy bourgeoisie were forced to build an appreciable number of small residences around the centers of the hinterland.[47] One of these centers, Alezio (known as Villa Picciotti until 1873), has been described as "a lovely jewel set in a ring of emeralds"[48] and as a "wonderful water lily amidst the green that crowns it on all sides" (fig. 4.21).[49] If the Cupa was the "Tivoli of the inhabitants of Lecce," then this was "the Schönbrunn of the inhabitants of Gallipoli" with its "white houses alternating with the greenery of its orchards, and its hundred villas, which are like voluptuous Naiads in that verdant ocean."[50] As Bartolomeo Ravenna wrote in 1836: "The people of Gallipoli more than all others in the Province have been and are more attached to and passionate about spending the best months of the year in enjoying the country air, and they stand out for the magnificence of their spacious casinos" (fig. 4.22).[51]

The system of villas and casinos—as some of these residences were called—was linked not only to the introduction of complex crop practices, but also to a new interest in the pleasures of rural living, which involved many families of the landed nobility and the bourgeoisie in the mid-eighteenth century. A number of inscriptions offer an interpretative key to their understanding of villeggiatura: "Here one

FIGURE 4.19.
Villa Cerulli Bozzicorso at Lecce.
Photograph by Michele Onorato.

FIGURE 4.20.
Villa Vescovile at Cenate, near Nardò.
Photograph by Michele Onorato.

FIGURE 4.21.
Villa Prandico at Alezio.
Photograph by Michele Onorato.

FIGURE 4.22.
Villa Pasca-Raeli at Sannicola.
Photograph by Michele Onorato.

FIGURE 4.23. Villa Ravenna at Sannicola.

Photograph by Michele Onorato.

lives honestly; here Pallas offers her gifts; here you will find peace, tranquility, fruits and health; 1770." At the entrance to the Casino Mimmo, built in the latter half of the eighteenth century by the Tufo family, is the inscription "Open to the good / closed to the bad," while above the arch of the entry portal to the Casino Lazzarello, probably built in 1725 by Ferdinando Sanfelice, it is possible to read: "Fui vil capanna e rustica pendice / or d'alte moli adorna e d'opre colte / Fatta son del piacer valle felice . . ." ("I was a humble hut and a rustic slope / Now adorned with tall structures and refined works / I became a happy valley of pleasure."[52])

The spread of the phenomenon of country villas and casinos was aided also by the views of agriculturalists such as Giovanni Presta, philosophers and poets such as Tommaso Nicolò d'Aquino, and illustrious economists such as Giuseppe Palmieri.[53] As he celebrated the pleasures of country living, encouraged agricultural investment and modernization, and generally revived the myth of the country nobleman, Palmieri also insisted on the continuous presence of the owner to supervise agricultural production—a concept taken up again a few decades later by Vincenzo Corrado in "Sul ritiro in campagna: Dialogo fra un Dottor Partenopeo ed un Filosofo Salentino."[54] Palmieri himself lived periodically in "his grand villa de'Rocci" near Gallipoli, "where he used to linger and where his greatest pleasure was that of roaming about his spacious garden, and enjoying those choice, abundant fruits, of seeing the olives being harvested on his lands: and at times, imitating the philosophers of yore, picking them with his own hands."[55]

The typological features of the gardens of the Salentine villas merit close examination and careful description. Portals and fences (figs. 4.23) announce and introduce the extraurban residence; their triumphal arches, which can be compared to town gates, help to illustrate their patrons' prestige. There are also significant portals at the garden entrances that are near to the residences.[56]

The residences have simple symmetrical facades—particularly in the area of Presicce—a simplicity that is dictated by function but is also the result of a careful study of volume and form. Their front doors, in the center, lead to entrance halls that run through the houses to the gardener's quarters (which included storerooms and sheds) and the enclosed gardens (fig. 4.24). The piani nobili often have alcove balconies, which sheltered the owner from the sun and enabled him to supervise the activity of the peasant farmers. Often the balconies run the entire length of the residence and become an external access corridor, but they occasionally remain broad terraces.

FIGURE 4.24. Front elevations of four casinos at Presicce. Note the central entryways and balconies on the primi piani.

Survey drawings by Patrizia Bovinelli and Luigi Nicolardi; reproduced by permission from Vincenzo Cazzato, ed., *Paesaggi e sistemi di ville nel Salento* (Galatina: Mario Congedo, 2006).

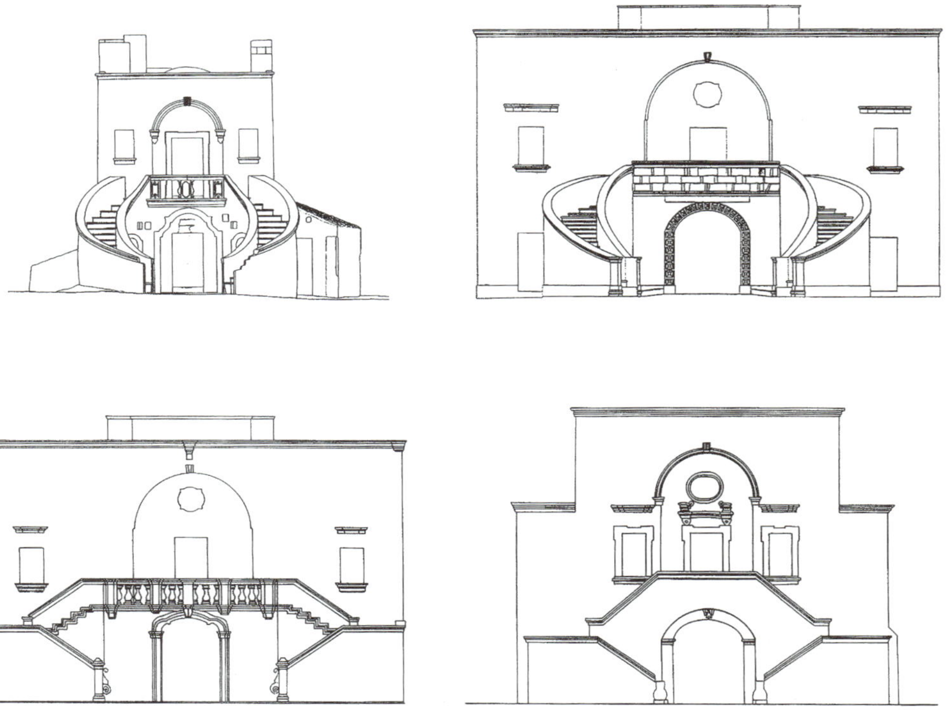

FIGURE 4.25. Casino degli Angeli at Presicce.

Photograph by Michele Onorato.

In some residences, the scenographic element that most ennobled the main prospect was the pincer-shaped external stairway, whose twin ramps ran *a tenaglia* (pincer-shaped), or parallel to the facade, in clear reference to Neapolitan architecture of the first half of the eighteenth century. In small casinos, these stairways are out of scale to the building and its facade (fig. 4.25).[57]

Most residences have a salone in their central core (fig. 4.26) with one or more windows opening onto the balconies overlooking the enclosed garden and onto the semicircular-shaped *piazzale* in front, where the chapel is also located. (Such chapels are also present in the Vesuvian villas; they served as the place where the owner's family, the peasants, and the gardener's family crossed paths, as well as a sign of the increased religiosity of the latter half of the eighteenth century.) The formal repertory of these residences draws extensively on urban architecture with their elaborate fastigia, polylobate windows, and elegant moldings.

Articulated in the garden are the scenographic perspectives of the avenues, which are covered by pergolas and flanked by columns or pilasters and

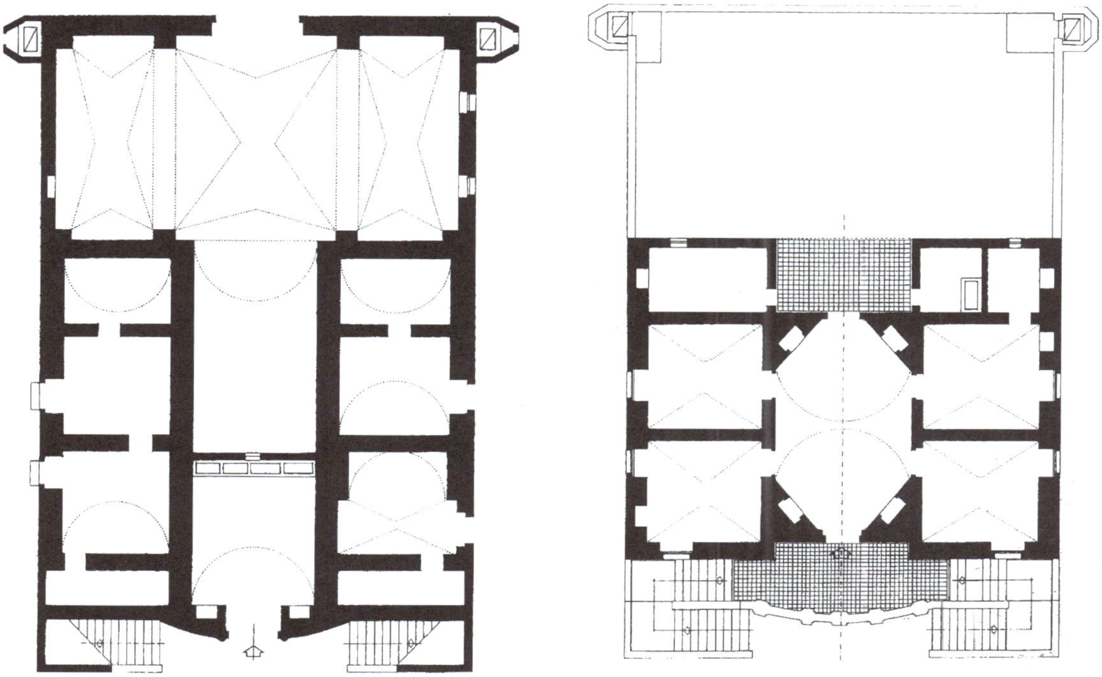

FIGURE 4.26. Plans of the ground floor and primo piano of the Casino Ceddhe at Presicce. Note the salone and balconies along the main axis.

Reproduced by permission from Antonio Costantini, *Le masserie del Salento: Dalla masseria fortificata alla masseria-villa* (Galatina: Mario Congedo, 1994).

which often end with an aedicule located in an alcove (fig. 4.27). Elegant stone seats are arranged along the avenues, or adjacent to the residence, flanking a portal, or terminating a view. Elaborate wells and cisterns (figs. 4.28 and 4.29) provide boldly innovative solutions to the problem of supplying water in a semi-arid climate. Ranging from canopy type to those with pergolas supported by columns, they are veritable hydraulic machines, with complex systems of stone ducts and channels leading off from them. The decorations on these wells frequently emphasize not only their functional character but also their strongly symbolic value.[58]

Salentine gardens—like their counterparts in the Neapolitan region—are generally productive.[59] But there are exceptions: the Garden of Statues in the Masseria Brusca at Nardò is divided into four parts by two perpendicular lines, at the crossing of which are twelve statues.[60] Their arrangement into groups (i.e., three statues in each quarter circle) follows a logic, whereby statues of the continents are flanked by one female and one male bust: *America* by *Pomona* and *Vertumnus*; *Africa* by *Diana* and *Sylvanus*; *Asia* by *Ceres* and *Bacchus*; and *Europe* by

FIGURE 4.27. Pergola, Villa d'Ambrosio at Cenate, near Nardò.

Photograph by Michele Onorato.

FIGURE 4.28. Well, Villa d'Ambrosio at Cenate, near Nardò.

Photograph by Michele Onorato.

Flora and *Faunus* (*Pan*). The male busts in the quarters on the left (*Vertumnus* and *Sylvanus*) are draped, while those in the quarters on the right (*Bacchus* and *Pan*) are naked or partly draped. The logic is reversed with the continents: *America* and *Africa*, on the left, are nude (or partly draped), while *Asia* and *Europe*, on the right, are wearing very elegant clothes (fig. 4.30).

While the busts represent divinities often found in gardens, the four continents are more unusual, as other quaternary groups (such as the elements or the seasons) are usually preferred. Certain divinities seem, however, to substitute for them in mimetic form. The seasons, for example, are evoked by flowers (and by *Flora* herself, who is often mistaken for Spring), by the ears of wheat forming a wreath crown for *Ceres* (Summer), by the grapes borne by *Bacchus* in his hand (Autumn), and by the old man in the guise of *Pan* (Winter). Agricultural themes are combined with pastoral ones: the figures of *Flora, Ceres, Pomona, Bacchus*, and *Vertumnus* are linked to agriculture, while those of *Sylvanus, Pan*, and *Diana* are connected with mainly pastoral themes. Also evident is an effort to portray nature in its various manifestations, which partially coincide with the four sculptural groupings: flower gardens (*Flora*), fruit gardens (*Pomona*), vegetable gardens and farmland (*Vertumnus, Ceres*, and *Bacchus*), and woods and groves (*Pan, Sylvanus*, and *Diana*).

In the light of what is now known of the history and typology of Salentine villa systems, we may, in part, rectify what Cesare de Seta has written about the Vesuvian area:

> This region has profoundly different cultural features from the countryside of the Mezzogiorno: where, . . . the *latifundium* (large landed estate) system is dominant, the landowner uses archaic farming methods, and sometimes gives the land over to a basely parasitic use. The profound crisis of the southern countryside is also caused by the fact that the owner has often

> moved into the city . . . When instead the landlord remains on the farm—and this occurs with the long stays in the nearby Vesuvian villas—the management of the land is very different: favored, moreover, by the absolutely exceptional fertility compared with the bare stretches of the large estates in Puglia, with the steep Calabrian hills, with the parched, meager plains of the South.[61]

This statement may, in fact, be valid in general, but it is not an absolute truth. The situation encountered in the Neapolitan countryside is not unique but occurred, even if in a situation of crisis for southern Italian agriculture, in other peripheral areas of the Mezzogiorno. As we have seen, in the Salento, the typology of the villa led in those same years to the redesign of vast areas of the rural landscape.

We are dealing with the recurrence of a phenomenon that had already appeared during the sixteenth century, as in the Neapolitan region, where the Vesuvian area began to prosper during the viceroyalty of Don Pedro di Toledo. It was precisely at that time that sumptuous residences were built and

FIGURE 4.29. Wells, Villa Spirito at Sannicola.

Photograph by Michele Onorato.

FIGURE 4.30. Garden of Statues in the Masseria Brusca at Nardò.

Photograph by Michele Onorato.

an impressive agrarian transformation took hold with the birth of the masseria and the reclamation of territory through improved cultivation. It was also in this period that many Vesuvian towns became free communities or municipalities and enjoyed tax exemption if they were located within twelve miles of Naples.

A variety of situations were present in eighteenth-century Salento in analogous fashion to what took place in the vicinity of Naples, where many villas were the result of the enlargement and the restructuring of older buildings.

The systems of villas in the Salento in the eighteenth century had more than a few elements in common with those in the Vesuvian area. For example, both systems had similar productive functions and shared the same formal arrangements—the axial perspectives, the circulation sequences, the pincer-shaped or twin-ramped external stairways, the porticos, and the double-facing salons—but of more limited and less stately dimensions in the Salento. But, as we have emphasized, the phenomenon in the Salento was an expression of local economic and social conditions, which were different from those that gave rise to the Vesuvian villas, that were manifestations of the aristocratic and ruling classes of an entire state associated with the figure of the sovereign.

Finally, in both areas, the nineteenth and twentieth centuries generated a new, important system of eclectic villas, which superimposed itself on the preceding one. This new configuration was a testimony to a bourgeois society that wished to imitate the eighteenth-century aristocracy in their construction of pleasure residences, inventing thereby the modern fashion of the out-of-town holiday.[62]

Conclusion

The methodological approach to these two areas of the Italian Mezzogiorno intentionally has not been of a monographic type dealing with single villas or groups of villas, nor has it intended to privilege specific aspects of architectural idioms and syntaxes. Rather it has aimed to analyze the villa as a signifying structure that reveals deep-seated and varied social and economic changes. From this standpoint, I have emphasized several points: first, systems of villas and gardens were brought about by economic, social, and political phenomena; second, the relations between the villa residence and its context consisted not only of connections with the garden but also with the broader landscape; and third, villa systems in minor geopolitical contexts or in geographical areas hitherto deemed less interesting by historians (such as the Salento) should be identified, because they can play a defining role in the creation of a new methodology for analyzing Italian villa and garden culture, and Italian villa systems in particular.

The interpretation of landscape as a "system" should also be extended to other typologies of properties. In the case of the Salento, for instance, the structure of the territory was constituted by an infinite history of polycentric systems connecting the sea, the city, and the countryside—from the sacral network of menhirs and dolmens to the orthogonal network of the Roman centuriation, and, in more recent times, from the system of coastal towers (together forming a defense network and a method of communication) to the masserias.

Such an approach could be particularly significant in territories not yet completely ruined by ongoing urbanization (such as the Salento) and in areas where the number of historical residential buildings has been reduced through systematic demolition (such as the Vesuvian countryside). In both cases, the identification of systems, or of their fragments, can provide opportunities for reflecting on their future protection, restoration, and improvement. Past failures in understanding the system of villas in the Neapolitan area has resulted in far-reaching transformations—for example, the installation of railroads and the expansion of urban areas in the twentieth century caused the severing of the relationship between the elements of the system (i.e., Vesuvius, the villas, the parks, the gardens, and the sea). Villas frequently have been separated from their gardens, most of which are then used as market gardens or divided into plots for intensive building. Now decontextualized, few of their original elements can presently be identified. Only the more permanent features—such as boundary walls, gates and portals, scenic backdrops, belvederes, segments of paths and avenues, and fragments of green spaces—remain to give a partial sense of the villa systems that they once constituted.

Notes

1 Nicola Nocerino, *La real villa di Portici* (Naples: Presso I fratelli Raimondi, 1787), 46–53.

2 "If we must find a single English word for *otium* it would be seclusion, or serenity, or relaxation, but the ancients thought of it rather as an opportunity to engage, often intensely, in worthwhile physical and mental pursuits." James S. Ackerman, *The Villa: Form and Ideology of Country Houses* (Princeton N.J.: Princeton University Press, 1990), 37.

3 Donato Perillo, *Ragguaglio delle ville, e luoghi prescelti per uso delle caccie, pesche, e simili diporti da regnanti, ed altr'insigni personaggi* (Naples: Niccolò Naso, 1737), 5.

4 Roberto Pane, "Le ville e la strada costiera," in *Ville vesuviane del Settecento*, eds. Roberto Pane et al., 1–18 (Naples: Edizioni Scientifiche Italiane, 1959). In the same volume, see also Arnaldo Venditti, "La costa vesuviana da Napoli a Torre del Greco e la mappa del Duca di Noja," 19–51; Giancarlo Alisio, "Le ville di Portici," 127–91; Lucio Santoro "Il palazzo reale di Portici," 193–235; and Paolo Di Monda, "Da Resina a Torre Annunziata," 237–325.

5 Cesare de Seta, Leonardo di Mauro, and Maria Perone, *Ville vesuviane* (Milan: Rusconi, 1980), 11.

6 Among other studies on Vesuvian villas, see Pietro Lezzi, *Le ville vesuviane* (Salerno: Arti Grafiche Boccia, 1977); Vittorio Gleijese, *Ville e palazzi vesuviani* (Naples: Società Editrice Napoletana, 1980); Pietro Lezzi and Paolo Romanello, *Le ville vesuviane* (Naples: Ente per le Ville Vesuviane, 1981); and Maria Perone, "Le ville vesuviane," in *Napoli*, ed. Cesare de Seta, 182–94 (Rome: Laterza, 1981). On the permanence of this character during the nineteenth and twentieth centuries, see Gaetano Amodio, *Ville vesuviane tra Ottocento e Novecento* (Naples: Edizioni Scientifiche Italiane, 2002).

7 Michelangelo Schipa, *Il regno di Napoli al tempo di Carlo di Borbone*, 2nd ed., 2 vols. (Milan: Roma, 1923); and Giovanni Aliberti, "Economia e società da Carlo III ai Napoleonidi, 1734–1806," *Storia di Napoli* 8 (1971): 77–164.

8 Giuseppe Imbò, *Il Vesuvio e la sua storia: caratteristiche, attività e danni* (Naples: Edizioni Scientifiche Italiane, 1984). See also the exhibition catalogue *All'ombra del Vesuvio: Napoli nella veduta europea dal Quattrocento all'Ottocento* (Naples: Electa, 1990).

9 De Seta, di Mauro, and Perone, *Ville vesuviane*, 16–18.

10 Ibid., 19.

11 Gerard Labrot, *Baroni in città: Residenze e comportamenti dell'aristocrazia napoletana, 1530–1734* (Naples: Società Editrice Napoletana, 1979); and Gerard Labrot, *Palazzi napoletani: Storie di nobili e cortigiani, 1520–1750* (Naples: Electa, 1993).

12 Nocerino, *La real villa di Portici*; Carlo Celano, *Notizie del bello dell'antico e del curioso della città di Napoli* (Naples: S. Palermo, 1792); Vincenzo Jori, *Portici e la sua storia* (Naples: Tipografia dei Comuni, 1882); N. del Pezzo, "Siti Reali: Il Palazzo Reale di Portici," *Napoli nobilissima* 5 (1896): 161–67 and 183–88; Giancarlo Alisio, "Una rilettura su inediti del Palazzo Reale di Portici," *L'Architettura* 20 (1974): 262–67; and Giancarlo Alisio, *Siti reali dei Borboni: Aspetti dell'architettura napoletana del Settecento* (Rome: Officina, 1976). See also Maria Luisa Margiotta, ed., *Il Real Sito di Portici* (Naples: Paparo, 2008), and in particular the essays by Maria Luisa Margiotta ("Il Sito Reale e il suo parco," 11–68) and Filippo Barbera ("I progetti della Reggia di Portici: Da Medrano a Canevari, da Vanvitelli a Fuga," 69–103).

13 On eighteenth-century architecture in Naples, see Roberto Pane, *Architettura dell'età barocca in Napoli* (Naples: Editrice Politecnica, 1939); Renato de Fusco, "L'architettura della seconda metà del Settecento a Napoli," *Storia di Napoli* 8 (1971): 410–12; Anthony Blunt, *Neapolitan Baroque and Rococo Architecture* (London: A. Zwemmer, 1975); Giuseppe Fiengo, *Documenti per la storia dell'architettura e dell'urbanistica napoletana del Settecento* (Naples: Editoriale Scientifica, 1977); *Civiltà del Settecento a Napoli, 1734–1799*, 2 vols. (Florence: Centro-Di, 1980), especially the essays by Anthony Blunt ("Caratteri dell'architettura napoletana dal tardobarocco al classicismo," 1:60–71), Giancarlo Alisio ("I Siti Reali," 1:72–85), and Mario de Cunzo ("Le ville vesuviane," 1:86–105); Cesare de Seta, ed., *Arti e civiltà del Settecento a Napoli* (Rome: Laterza, 1982); Gaetana Cantone, ed., *Barocco napoletano* (Rome: Istituto Poligrafico e Zecca dello Stato, Libreria dello Stato, 1992); and Giuseppe Fiengo, ed., *Architettura napoletana del Settecento* (Naples: Franco Di Mauro, 1993).

14 Placido Troyli, *Istoria generale del reame di Napoli: ovvero, Stato antico e moderno delle regioni e luoghi che 'l reame de Napoli compongono, una colle loro prime popolazioni, costumi, leggi, polizia, uomini illustri e monarchi* (Naples, 1747–54), vol. 4, part I.

15 Celeste Fidora Attanasio, *Ville vesuviane e siti reali* (Naples: Edizioni Scientifiche Italiane, 1998), 36–37. See also Celeste Fidora and Sergio Attanasio, *Ville e delizie vesuviane del '700: Passeggiata da Napoli a Torre del Greco* (Naples: Grimaldi, 2004).

16 Alisio, "Le ville di Portici," 127–91.

17 Johann Wolfgang von Goethe, *Viaggio in Italia*, trans. Aldo Oberdorfer (Florence: Vallecchi, 1955), 248.

18 Fidora Attanasio, *Ville vesuviane e siti reali*, 47.

19 Giuseppe Maria Galanti, *Napoli e contorni*, ed. Luigi Galanti (Naples: Borel e Comp, 1829), 319.

20 Venditti, "La costa vesuviana da Napoli a Torre del Greco e la mappa del Duca di Noja," 19–51; and Mario Bevilacqua, "Tra Napoli, Roma e l'Europa: Alcune lettere di Giovanni Carafa duca di Noja," *Napoli nobilissima* 34 (1995): 99–116.

21 De Seta, di Mauro, and Perone, *Ville vesuviane*, 24–25.

22 Celano, *Notizie del bello dell'antico e del curioso della città di Napoli*, 7.

23 "un Borgo di ville da Poli a Roma." Annibal Caro, *Delle lettere familiari del commendatore Annibal Caro* (Padua: Giuseppe Comino, 1742), 2:350.

24 Mario de Cunzo, "Le ville vesuviane," in *Civiltà del Settecento a Napoli, 1734–1799* (Florence: Centro-Di, 1980), 1:86–89.

25 De Seta, di Mauro, and Perone, *Ville vesuviane*, 25–29.

26 Ibid., 27.

27 On Vanvitelli and Gioffredo, see Jörg Garms, *Disegni di Luigi Vanvitelli nelle collezioni pubbliche di Napoli e di Caserta* (Naples: AGEA, 1973); Arnaldo Venditti, *L'opera napoletana di Luigi Vanvitelli* (Naples: Edizioni Scientifiche Italiane, 1974), 98–167; Giuseppe Fiengo, *Vanvitelli e Gioffredo nella villa Campolieto di Ercolano* (Naples: Arte Tipografica, 1974); and Giuseppe Fiengo, *Gioffredo e Vanvitelli nei palazzi dei Casacalenda* (Naples: Editoriale Scientifica, 1976), 3–57; Ciro Robotti, "L'opera di Gioffredo e Vanvitelli per il giardino di Villa Campolieto," *Storia dell'arte* 35 (1979): 49–58; Cesare de Seta, ed., *Luigi Vanvitelli e la sua cerchia* (Naples: Electa Napoli, 2000); Benedetto Gravagnuolo, ed., *Mario Gioffredo* (Naples: Guida, 2002); and Alfonso Gambardella, ed., *Luigi Vanvitelli, 1700–2000* (San Nicola la Strada: Edizioni Saccone, 2005).

28 De Cunzo, "Le ville vesuviane," 86–89.

29 Fidora Attanasio, *Ville vesuviane e siti reali*, 59–60.

30 Filippo Barbera, "Dalle ville nobiliari esoteriche al Palazzo Reale di Portici: Il simbolismo del sole e della luna nella Santa Coppa," in *Architettura e massoneria: L'esoterismo della costruzione*, ed. Marcello Fagiolo, 238–43 (Rome: Gangemi, 2006); and Filippo Barbera, *Cultura e scienza nei giardini delle ville vesuviane* (Portici: Effegi, 2007), 183–84.

31 Barbera, *Cultura e scienza nei giardini delle ville vesuviane*, 183–84.

32 Nocerino, *La real villa di Portici*, 46–53.

33 Barbera, *Cultura e scienza nei giardini delle ville vesuviane*, 183–84.

34 De Cunzo, "Le ville vesuviane," 86–89.

35 On the role of staircases in Neapolitan architecture, see Pane, *Architettura dell'età barocca in Napoli*, 182–95; Michele Capobianco, "Scale settecentesche a Napoli," *L'Architettura* 84 (1962): 406; Alfonso Gambardella, *Note su Ferdinando Sanfelice architetto napoletano* (Naples: Istituto Editoriale del Mezzogiorno, 1970), 57–80; Alfonso Gambardella, *Ferdinando Sanfelice architetto* (Naples: Arti Grafiche Licenziato, 1974); Blunt, *Neapolitan Baroque and Rococo Architecture*, 128–58; De Seta, di Mauro, and Perone, *Ville vesuviane*; Alastair Ward, *The Architecture of Ferdinando Sanfelice* (London: Garland, 1988); and Alfonso Gambardella, ed., *Ferdinando Sanfelice: Napoli e l'Europa* (Naples: Edizioni Scientifiche Italiane, 2004).

36 Galanti, *Napoli e contorni*, 318. On problems of deterioration and conservation of Vesuvian villas, see Paolo Romanello, "Problematica della conservazione integrata delle ville vesuviane," *Naples nobilissima* 26 (1987): 153; Urbano Cardarelli, Paolo Romanello, and Arnaldo Venditti, *Ville vesuviane: Progetto per un patrimonio settecentesco di urbanistica e di architettura* (Naples: Electa Napoli, 1988); Francesco La Regina, *Restauro, conservazione e valorizzazione delle ville vesuviane* (Naples: CUEN, 2004); and Emanuele Romeo, "Frammenti e memoria dei luoghi: Permanenze del sistema delle ville vesuviane," in *Giardini, contesto, paesaggio: Sistemi di giardini e architetture vegetali nel paesaggio*, eds. Laura Sabrina Pelissetti and Lionella Scazzosi, 619–30 (Florence: L. S. Olschki, 2005).

37 Antonio Costantini, *Guida alle ville del Salento: Del piacere di vivere in campagna: La villa, il giardino, la casina, il casino* (Galatina: Congedo Editore, 1992), 12–41. Of great importance, by the same author, is *Le masserie del Salento: Dalla masseria fortificata alla masseria-villa* (Galatina: Mario Congedo, 1994), 283–370.

38 See Vincenzo Cazzato, ed., *Paesaggi e sistemi di ville nel Salento* (Galatina: Mario Congedo, 2006), in particular "Sistemi di ville e di giardini nel Salento dal Barocco al Novecento," 34–45. See also Vincenzo Cazzato, "Puglia giardino del Sud," in *Parchi e giardini storici, parchi letterari: Conoscenza, tutela e valorizzazione; Atti del III Convegno (Primo Internazionale) "Paesaggi e giardini del Mediterraneo,"* (Pompeii: Ministero per i Beni Culturali e Ambientali, Comitato Nazionale per lo Studio e la Conservazione dei Giardini Storici, Soprintendenza Archeologica di Pompei, 1993), 2:81–94, especially the pages (88–90) devoted to systems of villas and gardens.

39 Antonio Costantini, "Ville, casini e casine nell'area della 'Cupa'," in *Paesaggi e sistemi di ville nel Salento*, ed. Vincenzo Cazzato (Galatina: Mario Congedo, 2006), 157.

40 Costantini, *Le masserie del Salento*.

41 Maria Antonietta Visceglia, *Territorio, feudo e potere locale: Terra d'Otranto tra Medioevo ed età moderna* (Naples: Guida, 1988).

42 Patrizia Bovinelli and Luigi Nicolardi, "I casini nel territorio di Presicce: Storia e proposte di restauro conservativo," in *Paesaggi e sistemi di ville nel Salento*, ed. Vincenzo Cazzato, 234–49 (Galatina: Mario Congedo, 2006).

43 Antonio Costantini, *Architettura e paesaggio rurale nell'area della Cupa* (Galatina: Salentina, 1997); and Costantini, "Ville, casini e casine nell'area della 'Cupa'."

44 Cosimo de Giorgi, *La provincia di Lecce: Bozzetti di viaggio*, 2 vols. (Lecce: Spacciante Editore, 1882–88), 1:42 and 226–27.

45 Ibid., 1:242.

46 Mario Mennonna, *Guida di Nardò: Arte, storia, centro antico* (Galatina: Congedo Editore, 2001), 103–22.

47 Antonio Costantini and Michele Paone, *Guida di Gallipoli: La città, il territorio, l'ambiente* (Galatina: Congedo

Editore, 1992), 116–26. See also Elio Pindinelli, "Ville e casini dell'entroterra gallipolino," in *Paesaggi e sistemi di ville nel Salento*, ed. Vincenzo Cazzato, 210–21 (Galatina: Mario Congedo, 2006).

48 De Giorgi, *La provincia di Lecce*, 1:60.

49 Ibid., 2:237.

50 Ibid., 1:51.

51 Bartolomeo Ravenna, *Memorie istoriche della città di Gallipoli* (Naples: R. Miranda, 1836), 85.

52 Vincenzo Cazzato and Andrea Mantovano, *Paradisi dell'eclettismo: Ville e villeggiature nel Salento* (Cavallino di Lecce: Capone, 1992), 242. See also Mario Cazzato, "Matino: Immagine di una comunità nel XVIII secolo," in *Matino: Natura ed arte; Una comunità meridionale nel '700*, ed. Giuseppe Schivano (Galatina: Congedo Editore, 1992).

53 Aldo Vallone, ed., *Illuministi e riformatori salentini: Giuseppe Palmieri, astore, milizia e altri minori* (Lecce: Milella, 1984), 100.

54 Vincenzo Corrado, "Sul ritiro in campagna: Dialogo fra un Dottor Partenopeo ed un Filosofo Salentino," in *Scuola di generale agricoltura, e pastorizia adattata alle varie Province del Regno di Napoli ed insieme il trattato delle api e dei filugelli*, ed. Vincenzo Corrado, 146–56 (Naples: Presso Vincenzo Orsino, 1804). On Vincenzo Corrado, see Vincenzo Cazzato and Andrea Mantovano, "La 'Fisiologia degli agrumi' e il giardino tardo barocco in Terra d'Otranto," in *Il giardino delle Esperidi: Gli agrumi nella storia, nella letteratura e nell'arte*, eds. Alessandro Tagliolini and Margherita Azzi Visentini, 245–68 (Florence: Edifir, 1996).

55 Francesco Saverio Salfi, "Sul Marchese Giuseppe Palmieri," nineteenth century, ms. XX, 57, folio F, recto and verso, Biblioteca Nazionale, Naples.

56 Vincenzo Cazzato and Andrea Mantovano, "Giardini di mura e giardini murati nel Salento," in *Il giardino e le mura: Ai confini tra natura e storia*, eds. Cristina Acidini Luchinat, Giorgio Galletti, and Maria Adriana Giusti, 235–50 (Florence: Edifir, 1997). See also Simonetta Politano, "Portali e recinti di ville nelle campagne salentine," in *Paesaggi e sistemi di ville nel Salento*, ed. Vincenzo Cazzato, 262–73 (Galatina: Mario Congedo, 2006).

57 Costantini, *Le masserie del Salento*, 309 and 363.

58 On the wells of Salento, see Vincenzo Cazzato, "Il Salento, le acque e il pozzo del chiostro," in *Il tempio di Tancredi: Il monastero dei Santi Niccolò e Cataldo in Lecce*, eds. Bruno Pellegrino and Benedetto Vetere 133–44 (Milan: Silvana, 1996); Patrizia Congedo, "Censimento di pozzi e cisterne del territorio neretino," in *Paesaggi e sistemi di ville nel Salento*, ed. Vincenzo Cazzato, 286–93 (Galatina: Mario Congedo, 2006); and Ugo Gelli, "Portali, pozzi, cisterne: Esperienze di rilievo architettonico," in *Paesaggi e sistemi di ville nel Salento*, ed. Vincenzo Cazzato 274–85 (Galatina: Mario Congedo, 2006).

59 Cazzato and Mantovano, "La 'Fisiologia degli agrumi' e il giardino tardo barocco in Terra d'Otranto," 246–68. See also Vincenzo Cazzato and Andrea Mantovano, "Giardino ed economia agraria negli scritti di Francesco Milizia e della 'scuola' pugliese,' in *Francesco Milizia e la cultura del Settecento*, eds. Mariella Basile and Grazia Distaso, 211–28 (Galatina: Congedo Editore, 2002).

60 Vincenzo Cazzato, "Il giardino di Statue della Masseria Brusca a Nardò, teatro del mondo e degli dei," in *Interventi sulla 'Questione Meridionale',"* ed. Francesco Abbate, 335–40 (Rome: Donzelli, 2005).

61 De Seta, di Mauro, and Perone, *Ville vesuviane*, 20–21.

62 Cazzato and Mantovano, *Paradisi dell'eclettismo*; and Andrea Mantovano, "Il bazaar degli stili: Ville e giardini nella Puglia di fine Ottocento," in *Ville e giardini fra Ottocento e Novecento: Studi e proposte*, ed. Alberta Campitelli (Rome: Edizioni Joyce, 1996), 121.

PART III

Agents of Landscape Transformation: From Microstoria to Policies of Stewardship

CHAPTER 5

From the Italian Countryside to the Italianate Landscape: Peasants as Gardeners and Foreign Observers in Italy, 1500–1850

MAURO AMBROSOLI

The Notion of the Italian Landscape: A Changing Paradigm Through the Centuries

THIS PAPER AIMS TO DISCUSS THE CONTRIBUtion of peasants as gardeners to the organization of the Italian landscape. The accounts of foreign travelers in Italy since the sixteenth century provide a continuous stream of commentary on the Italian landscape that suggests how this peasant-made landscape was being represented in new ways in the European context. The deep social changes of the countryside, which were brought about by the economic and political conditions of early modern Italy, initiated the invention of the Italianate landscape, a new stereotype that quickly superseded an older stereotype, that of the "fruitfulness" of the Italian peninsula.

In the context of the present volume, this discussion will take into consideration the development of garden history as a discipline predicated on the legacy of several centuries of gardening the landscape, understood as a social practice.[1] In his most recent edited volumes, Michel Conan suggested new approaches to the interpretation of garden history. He availed himself of the contributions of social scientists who have debated such topics as the definition of space and the creation of boundaries by means of cultivation and gardening practices. Conan's fruitful appeal for "New Challenges for Garden Studies" certainly deserves to be taken up.[2] Therefore, for the general purpose of this paper, I suggest that it is more useful to define a "garden" as any space determined by its social use and under intensive cultivation practices. Given this new definition of a garden, I believe that we will be able to comprehend a larger number of variables related to gardens and garden history, such as land ownership, weather, the perception of the seasons, and even the availability of plants according to soils, regional floras, and market conditions.[3]

The concept of the "Italian" or, more precisely, the "Italianate" landscape must be considered in association with the perspective of particular social groups who developed it in modern times. It was foreigners more often than Italians who championed the idea of the Italian landscape. Therefore, this story cannot be told without the help of these participant observers. But although we certainly cannot dispense with the Anglo-American perspective, we also cannot do without the Italian tradition of studying farming for a deeper comprehension of the regional systems of Italian agriculture. Recent historical research has made it possible to go beyond the limits of separate analysis and to bring together these two perspectives. New academic disciplines have been created in this way by treating subjects and sources synthetically; such is the case of garden history, which branched out from the history of architecture in the same way that a garden stems out from a house. Thus, it will be extremely useful to examine the writings of Leon Battista Alberti, the fifteenth-century humanist and architect, who devised his theory of the villa to connect family history and the history of family buildings (*famiglia* and *proprietà*).[4] The unity of buildings, gardens, and territories is reinforced by a cultural and economic approach, and today one cannot look at a given landscape without thinking of the surrounding region in cost-benefit terms. Both the aesthetic values and the socio-economic costs of creating a landscape have to be taken into consideration in any historical approach to the problems relating to gardens. The cost of every garden element can be determined, but the choices surrounding these elements are not purely economic, and only cultural analysis provides the tools needed to understand the garden as a composition and its place in the landscape or the surrounding territory.

Although there have been several important contributions to this line of research, what appears to be missing is a comprehensive social history of Italian gardens.[5] Therefore, it is important to discuss three interlocking (but somewhat neglected) issues: the relationship between masters and laborers in the construction of a landscape that extended well beyond the garden into the surrounding countryside, the physical activities by which the landscape was constructed, and the process by which the landscape became an object of imitation and representation.[6] Furthermore, I wish to consider those gardening practices that organized local and regional landscapes beyond the walls and borders of private gardens. A number of well-known historical, literary, and artistic sources (such as travel books and paintings) will provide eyewitness accounts of a landscape torn between evolution and stability. Finally, I will closely compare several Italian regional landscapes and foreigners' perceptions of Italy in order to cast light on the role of selected intellectuals who observed and appreciated the inhabitants' gardening techniques, which were widely shared and which made the improvement of vast areas possible.

The Fruitfulness of Italy in Early Modern Centuries: An Aging Stereotype?

The stereotype of the fruitful Italian peninsula, first formulated by Varro but endorsed by Pliny the Elder, Strabo, and Virgil, was a persistent one.[7] With Renaissance writers (such as Flavio Biondo and Leandro Alberti) it became a literary commonplace that was undermined only at times by unexpected events, such as the agricultural crises of the 1580s and 1620s. Leandro Alberti's *Descrittione di tutta Italia* fixed the description of the peninsula for subsequent centuries; the peninsula, according to this volume, was centered on cities, their history, and their dominion over the countryside (*contado*) (fig. 5.1).[8] The book was read and appreciated by the Italians and foreigners who traveled throughout the peninsula, and, in their travel accounts, we find a selection of themes and situations that caught their attention. Very accurate descriptions provide us with the perception of a landscape torn between the consolidation of extensive grain cultivation and the radical changes that brought more intensive cropping systems. Examples of these sudden changes are to be found in the descriptions of lands around Bologna: "for five miles around Bologna all the lands are dressed with lovely grape-vines and productive trees, among others olive trees . . . and are adorned with sumptuous buildings."[9] More "beautiful fields" (*belli campi*)—rich with wheat, barley, broad beans, flax, and hemp—are found as far as the Padusa marshes, and "one sees the manicured rows of trees on which are strung the vines, which hang down on all sides"[10] and more fruit trees, especially orange trees, growing in the private gardens of the townsfolk. The classes who lived in the countryside, gentry and peasants alike, improved their estates in this manner when general conditions allowed.

Michel de Montaigne visited Italy at length in 1580 and 1581. He took the waters wherever it was recommended, recorded the cost of living in the major cities, and described the landscape with an unprecedented attention.[11] He was possibly the first

FIGURE 5.1.

Italy, sixteenth to eighteenth century.

Reprinted from J. G. Bartholomew, *A Literary and Historical Atlas of Europe* (London: J. M. Dent & Sons, and New York: E. P. Dutton, 1910), 38–39.

traveler to comment on the landscaping practices of Italian peasant gardeners, which served as the culmination of a gradually unfolding geographical narrative that extended from France to central Italy. In Alsace, he first described the vineyard as a particular feature in the landscape. Even though the German territories extended as far as Bozen (Bolzano) and Trent (Trento), one already began to hear Italian spoken there; but it was only at Rovereto that the diet changed and the citrus, orange, and olive trees appeared as a feature in the landscape.[12] It was at Monselice, heading toward Padua, that "on either side of us there were very fertile plains that have, according to the custom of the country, amid their wheat fields many trees arranged in rows, from which hang their vines."[13] The same combination of wheat fields, fruit trees, and vine cultivation caused him great astonishment and enthusiasm at Narni and Spoleto, and again along the road from Pistoia to Lucca.[14] During his stay at La Villa (Bagni di Lucca), he noted "the mountains that shelter the said valley, all well cultivated and green all the way to the summit, full of chestnut and olive trees, and elsewhere of vines, which they plant around the mountains, girding the mountains with terraces. The edge of the terrace toward the outside, a little raised, is vine; the hollow of the terrace is wheat."[15] "One cannot praise too highly both for beauty and for utility this way of cultivating the mountains right up to the summit": as a matter of fact, the plain and the territory around Lucca were densely populated. This did not prevent him from noting the poverty of the inhabitants, giving the impression that they did not take their own share out of the rich crops they grew.[16] Montaigne was always drawn toward the combination of meadows, wheat, fruit trees, and vines growing in festoons; he

FIGURE 5.2. Conegliano (Treviso), from Anton von Zach, *Kriegskarte of the Duchy of Venice (1798–1805)*, sheet XIII-12. Note the predominance of arable fields bordered by trees, which are interspersed with vines.

Photograph courtesy of the Österreichisches Staatsarchiv, Vienna.

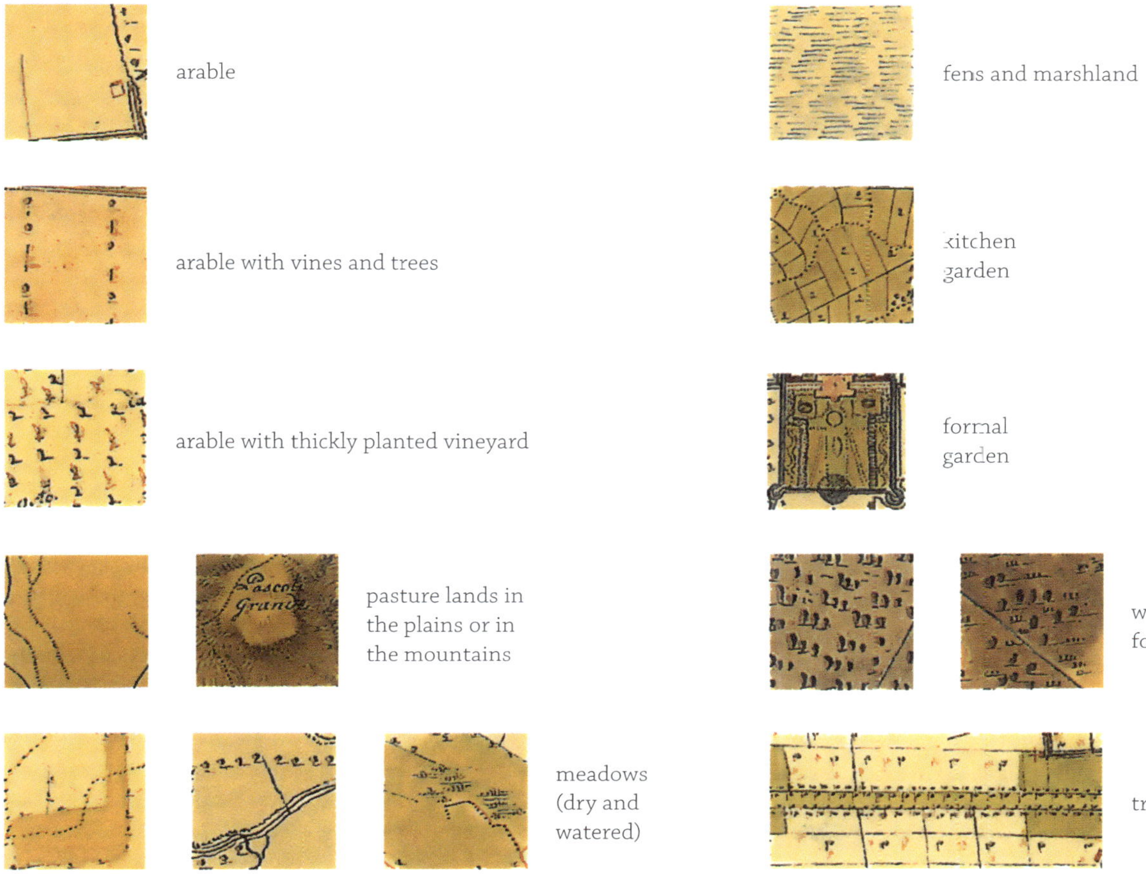

noticed this combination at Florence and Altopascio, as well as along the road linking Novara, Vercelli, and San Germano Vercellese.

Montaigne's journal remained unpublished for a long time,[17] but his impressions were shared by other travelers. Fynes Moryson's journals from the 1590s became reference texts for other foreigners who traveled along the same roads. Traveling from Vienna, he entered Italy at Pontebba Veneta and journeyed through the Friuli countryside, noting "wilde ground and stony fields of corne, and neere our journey's end . . . many Orchardes and Vineyards, to *Konian* [Conegliano]" (figs. 5.2 and 5.3).[18] He went along "through fruitful hils of corne, and by pleasant Vineyards, to *Treuigi* [Treviso], a City little in circuit, but fortified, and built of bricke."[19] He noted that it was only between Chioggia and Ferrara that "we passed a pleasant plain and fields of corne[20] divided by furrowes, in which furrowes elms were planted, and upon them Vines grew up to the tops. Such is the manuring of Lombardy, or the loward part of Italy toward the west, where the Vines growing high, yeeld not so rich wines, as in other parts of Italy upon mountaines and hills, upon the sides whereof the Vines suported with short stakes, and growing not high, yeeld much richer wines"[21] (figs. 5.4 and 5.5). Moryson realized that this peculiar form of cultivation was a system of "manuring" the soil: leaves replaced straw in the stables or were even fed to draft animals. He noted that this system of cultivation extended to Bologna and Imola, but that, in Ravenna, the land was better suited for rich crops of wheat and pasture. After moving south through Pesaro, Ancona, and Loreto, he reached "the city of

FIGURE 5.3. Symbols used to describe vegetation and farmland in Anton von Zach, *Kriegskarte of the Duchy of Venice* (1798–1805).

FIGURE 5.4. Ink silhouette showing vine and tree cultivation in the Villa Serego-Alighieri at Gargagnago (Verona), ca. 1700. Note the vines growing in festoons between the trees.

Photograph by Giuseppe Franco Viviani; reprinted from *La villa nel Veronese*, ed. Giuseppe Franco Viviani (Verona: Banca mutua poplare di Verona, 1975), 274, fig. 177.

FIGURE 5.5. Traditional cultivation pattern of olives and vines on terraces, Avesa (Verona).

Photograph by the author.

Spoleto, through a fertile plaine, but stony, yelding together in the same field, vines, corne, Almond and Olive trees."[22]

In central Italy, he (like Montaigne) noticed the *alberate* (vines growing in festoons from mature trees, as in the Po Valley). From Spoleto southward, the landscape was always very meticulously described; as he neared the city of Narni, for example, he took careful note of the wheat, vines, and olive trees.[23] At Castel Otricoli, he went through wooded mountains and valleys with olive trees and wheat grown together; he then came upon the Tiber, the cities of Rome and Marino, mountains "planted with vines and having a sweet prospect into the same plaine," and the numerous villas at Frascati and Tivoli. Particularly noteworthy was the Villa d'Este at Tivoli, with its wonderful gardens, fountains, statues, grottoes, groves, fishponds, aviaries, and nightingales flying freely in the groves. The Villa Mondragone (Frascati) of Cardinal Borghese was at the center of a large agricultural estate with woods, orchards, and vineyards.[24]

Moryson contended with a very dangerous journey to Naples, but—as he traveled through Sermoneta and Piperno—he passed through more hills covered with olive trees on the right side of the road, and rich wheat plains, orange groves, and citrus orchards on the left side of the road. He found a very similar landscape as he continued on to Terracina, Fondi, and Formia; he was full of admiration for the many "orchards of lemons."[25] Between Capua and Naples (in the so-called Terra di Lavoro), he came across more wheat as well as citrus and olive trees: "All this way from Capua to Naples, is a fruitfull plaine of corne and vines growing high upon Elme trees, according to the tillage of Lombardy, one and the same field yielding corne and wine and wood to burne."[26] (figs. 5.6–5.9)

FIGURE 5.6. Older fruit orchard on decaying stone terraces, Montecchio di Negrar (Verona).

Photograph by the author.

Montaigne and Moryson visited Italy in the 1580s and 1590s, at the end of the long decades of stability that led up to the so-called *Pax Hispanica*. There were major crises during and after the wars of 1500–30, and these were followed by an economic recovery that finally changed the late medieval situation. In the sixteenth century, the countryside was farmed by a smaller number of peasant families—either as owner-occupiers or as customary tenants on feudal or church lands—than one century earlier.[27] But the economic crisis of the late fifteenth and early sixteenth centuries, the Italian Wars of 1494–1559, the increased tax collection, and the price revolution forced many Italian peasant families to borrow money on their wheat crops from city merchants and local moneylenders. Because the loans would never be paid back, a large number of families lost their farms within ten or fifteen years after going into debt. The more fortunate families were allowed to remain on their former properties as tenants, while many others experienced further economic decline as they had no choice but to move around the countryside with annual tenancies.[28] City merchants and lawyers became landowners in the countryside, and they rearranged their estates on the villa model (a system that would last well into the second half of the nineteenth century).

Villa: Siti e contesti, a collection of seminar papers on the villa in the northern province of Treviso, has very recently made a major contribution to studies on the origins of the villa and its relationship with the rural landscape before and after the massive acquisition of lands by the Venetian nobility during the mid-sixteenth century. Private and fiscal sources, as well as historical maps, indicate that there was only one villa in the district of Treviso in 1470–1500.

FIGURE 5.7.
Giandomenico Tiepolo, *Peasants at Rest*, 1757, fresco in the Foresteria, Villa Valmarana ai Nani, Vicenza. Note the line of mulberry trees.

FIGURE 5.8.
Vines interspersed with mulberry trees, Ajello (Friuli).
Photograph by the author.

By 1518, there were eight villas; in 1542, there were eighty-three villas, as well as two hundred and fifty large farmhouses with villa characteristics (*ville-fattorie*) and four hundred and seventy estates.[29]

The agricultural and horticultural activities that spread through the Po Valley developed from forms of cultivation already practiced in other areas of Italy. A new wave of privately owned irrigation canals followed those built by free associations of peasants as early as the twelfth century,[30] and land drainage projects were undertaken with the financial support of wealthy landlords or local and regional governments. (For example, the Barbaro family was prominent in the reclamation of the marshes around Padua.) After the 1540s, new farms and estates sprang up in the countryside, population growth pushed cultivation to the newly reclaimed fens and up the hillsides, and—although the plague hit the major cities—immigration from the countryside helped to replenish the urban workforce. Because the flat country in the Po Valley had various kinds of limitations and wheat yields were low, arable fields were generally reserved for cereal production rather than grazing. As a result, tree-lined arable fields (*piantate*) were increasingly used in the landscape to solve the problem of the limited fodder supply for plow oxen. The great number of free-running rivers, streams, marshes, and fens allowed landowners to develop pastures into a system of outfields. Peasant families provided the workforce to perform multiple tasks on these intensive farms (*poderi*) with a ready return in terms of foodstuffs. And although the wheat crops were sometimes lower than the European average, the tree-lined arable fields allowed landowners to double and treble their crops on the best lands (figs. 5.10 and 5.11).

However, this growing prosperity began to be reversed by a series of wet summers, and in 1588

FIGURE 5.9.
Arable field with row of mulberry trees, Ajello (Friuli).
Photograph by the author.

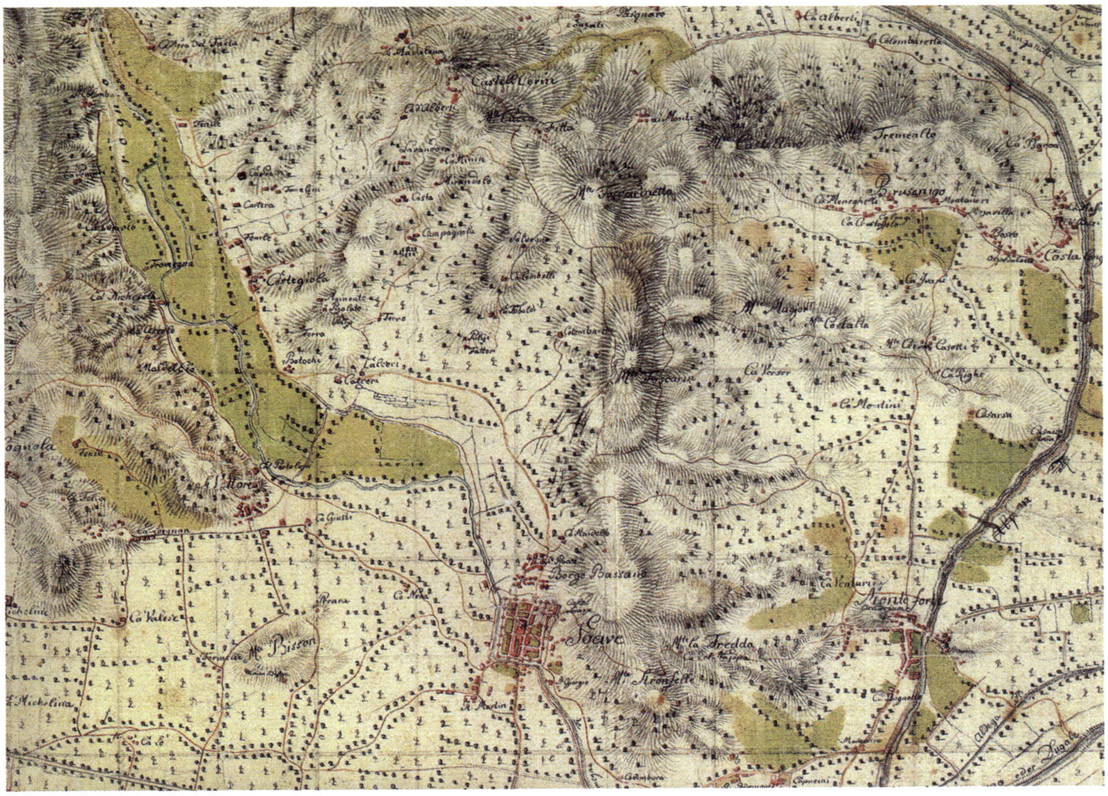

FIGURE 5.10.
Hills at Soave (Verona), from Anton von Zach, *Kriegskarte of the Duchy of Venice (1798–1805)*, sheet VIII-16. Note the extent of tree-lined arable fields.
Photograph courtesy of the Österreichisches Staatsarchiv, Vienna.

FIGURE 5.11. Plain and fens at Soave (Verona), from Anton von Zach, *Kriegskarte of the Duchy of Venice (1798–1805)*, sheet VIII-16.

Photograph courtesy of the Österreichisches Staatsarchiv, Vienna.

and 1589, poor wheat crops brought back famine after many decades of abundance. Major cities, such as Venice and Florence, used their well-established trade connections with Flanders and England to import grain from Antwerp and London. French merchants also increased their grain exports to Italy and from that date northern ships became a regular presence in Italian harbors. Northerners learned through this turn of affairs that they could go directly to the Mediterranean to buy the goods they wanted without the commercial mediation of Italian merchants back home.

Politics and Agriculture: The Italian Countryside and English Travelers during the Civil Wars

The number of Englishmen traveling in Italy increased after 1603, when the death of Queen Elizabeth I freed England from the papal interdict and enabled the country to renew diplomatic ties with the Italian states. Sir Henry Wotton was appointed ambassador to Venice. In his letters to King James I and other writings, Wotton freely discussed international politics, religion, and architecture. He is credited with introducing fennel—which he discovered in the Venetian orchards—to England.[31] As a result not only of this discovery but of Wotton's general laudation of the Venetian countryside, a considerable number of Englishmen, young and more mature, traveled regularly to Padua, which was then a center of advanced learning because of its private academies and its university.

Among these English visitors was John Evelyn, who traveled to Italy to escape the worst of the civil war (1642–51) between King Charles I and Parliament. During his trip, Evelyn kept a diary that included descriptions of the Italian countryside. We know from the editor of his papers, Esmond de Beer, that, when composing his diary, Evelyn occasionally consulted Fynes Moryson but more often a lesser-known travel writer, John Raymond, who was in Italy in 1646–47. The diaries of John Raymond and John Evelyn often praised the same circumstances and can be read together. Besides describing the fascinating marvels of the Roman villas of his time, Raymond commented extensively on Italian agriculture, noting especially the reasons for its productivity: "wee should have had such an esteem of this Cisalpine clod; the fertility of which I attribute not to the Soyle, but Site. The Earth yeldes five Harvests successively; First in June, that of Silke; in July of diverse fruits; in August that of Corne, which afterwards sow with Milio, Rice, Turkie Wheate, or the like graine, and within two moneths have another croppe. In September that of their wines. In October that of Oyle."[32]

Evelyn likewise included detailed observations of Italian agriculture in his diary. After a visit to the Villa Aldobrandini at Frascati, Evelyn noted that all the walls were "covered with Citron trees." As he traveled from Capua to Naples, he commented that

> what is extremely divertissant, is the incomparable fertility of the fields and grounds about it, which are planted about with fruit trees . . . but what much adds to the pleasures of these rusticities, is that the Vines climbing to the summit of the trees reach in festoon and fruitages from one tree to another, planted at exact

distances, which shewing like a greene Chayne about a field is pleasanter than any painting can describe it.[33]

After traveling from Rome to Siena, Leghorn, Lucca, Florence, Pietramala, Bologna, Ferrara, Padua, and Venice, he returned to Padua and matriculated at its university on 30 July 1645.[34] Finally leaving Padua and some of the important friends of his group in March or April 1646, Evelyn passed through Vicenza, Verona, Brescia, and Milan, and visited some of the most important Italian gardens, including those at the Villa Valmarana ai Nani at Vicenza (with its *cedrario*) and the Villa Giusti at Verona (with its cypresses).[35] Passing through Marignano, ten miles from Milan, he "went on with exceeding pleasure: for it is certainely the Paradise of all Lumbardy . . . the Fields to a vast extent planted with fruit about the inclosures and vines to every Tree . . . watered with frequent Streames . . . likewise much Corne and Olives in abundance"[36] (figs. 5.12 and 5.13).

Raymond exhibited similar enthusiasm when he passed through the countryside around Bologna and Ferrara, then crossed the Po River to reach Adria, Chioggia, Pellestrina, and Venice, and finally traveled to Padua along the river Brenta ("on both sides is a garden-like country and a multitude of villas or countryhouses, with gardens of orange trees and other greens after the Italian way").[37] Having gone through Vicenza (and the garden of the Villa Valmarana ai Nani with its "citron and Orange trees, together with the labyrinth") and passed over the hills around Lake Garda (with their "great store of olive, citron and orange trees"),[38] he approached Milan from Lodi "all which way the countrey is more Gardenlike then in any part of Lombardy . . . on both sides [of the highways] runne channels of water, on both sides trees planted and in the fields there is Corne, Wine, Fruits and Meadows altogether, till the very gates of Milan." Traveling across Lombardy,[39] Raymond stressed two major themes

FIGURE 5.12.
Avesa (Verona), from Anton von Zach, *Kriegskarte of the Duchy of Venice (1798–1805)*, sheet VII-15. Note the extent of vineyards and orchards on the hillsides.
Photograph courtesy of the Österreichisches Staatsarchiv, Vienna.

FIGURE 5.13.
Vineyards and olive trees, Avesa (Verona).
Photograph by the author.

in his assessment of the Italian landscape. The first was the continuity between the villa gardens and the surrounding countryside, which gave the effect of a "garden-like country." The second theme—which he was the first traveler to articulate—was that even though Italy was recognizably one country, there was a great difference between the landscape of Lombardy and that of the Italian peninsula beyond the Apennines. This proved to be a lasting concept in the perception of the Italian landscape, and it influenced the arrangement of English gardens dating from the latter part of the seventeenth century.

Garden Tools and the Making of the Peasant Countryside

The Italian countryside saw significant transformations during the 1540s, as the landed class began imposing rigid contracts on its tenants in the name of estate improvement. Tenants who wished to remain on an estate were compelled to accept the new conditions—even if they had dwelled on the property for generations. The general sharecropping contract (*mezzadria*) chiefly provided food for household consumption, not for the market, and therefore tenants found it more bearable to comply with the rigid clauses—such as planting and tending trees and maintaining soil drainage systems—than to seek more uncertain forms of livelihood. During crises, periods of depopulation, and wet winters, pasture and dairy farming became an option, together with planting trees (such as ash, alder, maple, and walnut, and especially willow, poplar, and mulberry) on the banks of rivers and canals to consolidate wetlands. Raymond and Evelyn visited Italy some fifteen years after the 1629–30 plague (which swept away one-third of the population between the Alps and Florence) and observed a cultivation system that combined infields of intensively farmed tree- and vine-lined arable fields with vast areas of frequently flooded outfields, consisting of pastures, meadows, and woods, where cattle and horses were kept in

FIGURE 5.14. Hamilton Maxwell, *Cadore—La Venegia di Paneveggio*, 1880s, watercolor. Private collection.

FIGURE 5.15. Women hoeing in the Veneto countryside, ca. 1984.

Photograph courtesy of Gianni Berengo Gardin.

folds, reeds were cut for fodder, and eels and fish were caught. To the learned foreign traveler, the Po Valley brought to mind Virgil's *Bucolics* and *Georgics*, as it combined areas of intensive cultivation with vast areas of pastures, woods, and marshlands.

It was a gardener's tool—the spade—that proved most useful for working the fields in a precise way. Various types of spades were advocated by the school of agriculture in Bologna through the mid-nineteenth century, and were used with great personal effort by tenants and sharecroppers, who had to complete by hand the work (i.e., turning and breaking the clods) of the plow.[40] Their labor was considered necessary for the cultivation of hemp (the most valuable cash crop), which required heavy manure, and then for the cultivation of the wheat crop that followed. While they were providing this intensive manual labor for agriculture, other farmers were growing extensive fruit-tree gardens around Ravenna for export for the benefit of the table of the Roman Curia.

Soil erosion was a major problem in many of the cultivated areas of Italy. And because of a combination of war, bad weather, and growing timber demand from city dwellers, the mountain landscapes were soon devastated as well. The Alps of the Veneto, in particular, showed signs of erosion and poor management (fig. 5.14). Even worse was the situation on the right bank of the Po River; the rivers coming from the Apennines brought so much mud that it left a fine deposit over the floodplain. However, these destructive events could also be managed to produce positive effects: since the thirteenth century, many lands had been improved through controlled floods, and from the 1650s on, this technique was put to work when possible in the provinces of Parma, Modena, and Ferrara. By contrast, landowners and *mezzadri* (sharecroppers) around Bologna went to great efforts to prevent the flooding of their piantate, or tree-lined arable fields used for hemp and wheat cultivation. The spade and the hoe were the primary tools used in these relentless operations. (See figure 5.15, a fine recent illustration of a team of women hoeing that is similar to those described by Carlo Poni in *Gli aratri e l'economia agraria*.) The same problems of soil erosion, silting, and flooding developed in Tuscany, and the responses by landowners over the centuries have produced its characteristic landscape. The landscape that was so beloved by the Anglo-American elite at the turn of the twentieth century, for example, owed its beauty to the diligence of Cosimo Ridolfi and his agronomy school at Meleto, which carried out extensive agricultural projects during the mid-nineteenth century that continued the traditional practices of sharecroppers.[41] Thus, the garden-like vistas of Tuscany were achieved only by the labor of the mezzadri through terrace construction, tree planting, water drainage, and erosion control.

FIGURE 5.16.
Vineyard grown as a pergola, Avesa (Verona).
Photograph by the author.

FIGURE 5.17.
Stone walls and terraces, Negrar (Verona).
Photograph by the author.

I would suggest that this struggle against environmental deterioration did not lead to the obsolescence of the main elements by which peasants for centuries had altered the landscape: the pergola, the terrace, and the drainage and irrigation structures. This system of simple technologies had been adopted whenever rural communities improved and defended their lands with earthworks and water control. I have previously pointed out that when the upper classes took the lead in land improvement in the sixteenth century, they employed these same techniques to embellish their formal and their landscaped gardens, such as when they adapted irrigation systems to create fountains (figs. 5.16 and 5.17).

The Invention of a New Stereotype: Painting the Landscape under the Roman Sky

By the mid-seventeenth century, two Italian landscapes began to compete within the European imagination: the real landscape dispersed in scores of local versions and the landscape idealized in paintings. Flemish, Dutch, and French painters contributed notably to the creation of what was later understood as the Italianate (or *italianisant*) landscape from the beginning of the seventeenth century. Rome (and later Naples) became the center of their activities because of the opportunities afforded by its low horizon and the particular light that came with it. Painters developed pastoral themes according to the literary fashions of the mid-seventeenth century, and used the semicultivated landscape of the Roman Campagna to please the Arcadian tastes of their wealthy patrons.

The works of the antiquarian Sir Richard Symonds (1617–92?) exemplify the complex relationship between mid-seventeenth-century politics, travel, the lure of classical antiquities, and landscape observation. His unpublished journals reveal that the two main aims of his travels in Italy were cultivating his antiquarian interests and learning to paint landscapes.[42] Having fought in the civil war on the side of King Charles I, Symonds left England for France in 1647 and, again, on 1 January 1649. He would stay abroad until the end of 1651. His interest in landscape painting made him very aware of the details in the countryside. For example, his attention to soil, plows, orchards, fruit trees, farmers' dwellings, and country seats was already manifest along the road from Calais to Paris. By the time he traversed the remainder of his French route into Italy, his fascination with vineyards and grafted trees had become equally apparent.[43] Symonds entered Italy through Savoy, and his description of the Mont Cenis crossing as "the most scarifull passage" is one of the earliest European accounts in which mountains are perceived as landscape. While traveling to Turin, he noted that the vineyards were "very different from those of France. For a row of maples growes into the corne sides upon ye vynes tree and hang. Here ye plowed land was deep ridged like our in England. Here grow a kind of beane not yet ripe and a tall stalked wheat which they call *formento turquesco.*"[44]

Notes taken during his trip from Rome to Naples in April 1651 and during his journey homeward show that he followed the same route as Raymond and Evelyn and even faced the same dangers of robbery. (Symonds had already been assaulted and robbed on the outskirts of Turin.) His journal entries also reveal a fascination with color in the landscape—olive trees and blue-hued rocks are singled out for special emphasis. His notes are filled with descriptions of children and *banditi,* and they include many comments about the government and customs of the Papal States and Naples.

Symonds's long residence in Italy indicates that English interests in the Italian peninsula were shifting. Having initially focused on the Po Valley and its garden-like agriculture—as well as on Venice and the University of Padua as possible partners for trade and cultural exchange—the English increasingly turned their attention to the kingdom of Naples and the port of Leghorn (Livorno). Studies have shown that, after the 1650s, English interests in the Mediterranean had to rapidly adjust to the demands of the domestic sector; semifinished agricultural products, such as oil and wrought silk, became the new priorities of the international markets until the 1730s.[45] After two population crises (in 1630 and 1657) and the industrial crisis that followed, Italy had to lower her expectations of becoming an active cultural partner to the growing elite that was developing new manners, tastes, and formalities in and around the emerging core of Europe (i.e., Paris, Amsterdam, and London). The Italian landscape, as an object of representation, had to reflect these new expectations, and artists added classical themes to their paintings to enhance their salability. The Italian countryside of those decades was literally dressed in Arcadian garb and offered as a pastoral stage set populated with shepherds, nymphs, gods, and goddesses: a theatrical representation of what was, in fact, a widespread ecological crisis.

Peasant Intensive Cultivation in Lombardy: A Model for Hartlib's Agricultural Projects and Evelyn's Plans for Forestry

The largely man-made landscape of the Po Valley became a focal point for an important circle of English social reformers and political activists during the years of the civil war and the commonwealth. Samuel Hartlib (1600–62), a Polish citizen born in the English merchant community of Elbing, Prussia, was a refugee from the Thirty Years War. He actively promoted political and social reforms in London, and his papers offer a profound understanding of the effects of agricultural practices on the landscape garden.[46] Hartlib's advocacy of a greener England as a solution to the economic problems that began in the 1620s and lasted throughout the civil war was taken seriously by a number of landowners, who showed a marked interest in planting trees, installing green hedges, growing soft fruits, planting flowers, and cultivating foreign seeds between the 1660s and the 1680s. Hartlib exchanged letters with several correspondents, including Robert Child, who received a degree in medicine in Padua in 1638, and showed a very good acquaintance with the European regions he visited in his discussions of the finer points of plowing, marl, chalk, soil "fermentation" (i.e., fertilization), and fruit cultivation.

The general theme of "the setting out of land" was crucial to the investigations and experiments of the Hartlib circle, a loose group of his contacts and associates. In England, Ireland, and America, many kinds of land awaited cultivation and needed to be managed in a new way. A new order was required, whether they were wastes or commons, outfields or pastures tilled for the first time. In response, Hartlib developed a wide-ranging project—based on his observations of the Po Valley—that employed plantations of fruit trees in commons and wastes, which, he felt, the commonwealth should enclose so that it might distribute the fruits produced to the poor, to whom they rightfully belonged.

Beginning with the decades of the English Restoration, a vexing question was whether the Italian landscape seen by foreign visitors belonged to the present or was a residual element of Italy's classical heritage.[47] It was a political as well as an academic question, and it required that participants in the debate choose political sides. Thus, when Hartlib sent John Evelyn a copy of his *Legacy of Husbandry* (1655), the gesture was not only intended to recognize the value of Evelyn's personal experience but also to bridge political differences with a partisan of the king.[48] By highlighting their common desire to harness the benefits of science and technology for the public interest, Hartlib sought to defuse the political question. The strategy proved successful—the gift was well received, and Evelyn produced an accurate manuscript index in his copy of the *Legacy of Husbandry*.[49] The *Legacy of Husbandry* contained important communications by Richard Child and John Beale on Italian agriculture.[50] Many years later, in a long letter dated 20 November 1669, Beale suggested to Evelyn that someone reprint Hartlib's book without "the cavils and Impertinences annexed . . . and to expurge some Antemonarchical Lines" because it was "full of Excellent and very useful Philosophy." He went on to ask "But why don't our universities reprint Cato, Varro, Columella et Palladius . . ."[51]

Beale's letters to Evelyn reveal two important preoccupations of the time: classical agriculture and English politics. Twenty years later, a small circle of Englishmen, including Evelyn, Beale, the illustrious physician William Harvey, and one of Harvey's nephews (who had all been to Italy during the same decades), were busily exchanging information and horticultural seeds. Beale revised some chapters of Evelyn's *Pomona* (1664); these few notes from their correspondence give us the sense of an ongoing relationship between classical learning and the new scientific movement.[52] In seeking to create an improved agricultural system in England, these men looked to Italian gardens and orchards because they considered them to have the potential to provide a useful seed bank of novel crop varieties, serving as they had for centuries as a center for the diffusion of new plants from warmer climates. The model for their vision was the intensive horticultural system they had observed between Venice and Milan, the most highly urbanized region in early seventeenth-century Europe. Evelyn and his followers were clearly thinking of a sustainable horticultural system that would employ the numerous laboring poor found in every English village. Their plan would have been advantageous to the landed classes, as it would have reduced the poor rates they paid in their parishes.

Evelyn had less success as a social reformer than as a designer of gardens for the elite. Italian and English patrons had many new sources of plants and gardening practices. Commercial nurseries became active in the 1680s, and their printed catalogues documented the variety of trees, fruit trees, shrubs, flowers, bulbs, and seeds on the market.[53] Also in Italy, new books contained illustrations of garden trees and flowers in the style of still-life representations created by seventeenth- and early eighteenth-century Dutch and Flemish painters.[54] Italian landowners capitalized on the available peasant technologies to create gardens that featured well-known elements of the working landscape formed by peasant labor, including terraces, pergolas, and drainage or irrigation systems (figs. 5.16 and 5.17). English landowners recreated Italianate cultivated landscapes with the help of specialized workers.

The Italian Countryside in the Eighteenth Century: "Semivirgilian Husbandry" in the Time of "High Farming"

In the decades of Augustan England (1689–1750), it was already apparent that Italian landscapes had, in one way or another, influenced the creation of landscape gardens in England. For the curious mid-seventeenth-century traveler in Italy, the classical authors of the *Rei rusticae* still provided the syntax for understanding the state of the landscape. Yet during the decades of the battle between the ancients and the moderns, a new grammar was being written on the basis of empirical observation. When Louis XIV's gardener, Jean de La Quintinie, printed the results of his work in 1692, 1695, and 1697, he boasted of the superiority of garden cultivation and practical experience at the Jardin des Plantes in Paris and the gardens of Versailles, which were well on their way to becoming world centers of botanical and horticultural diffusion. His book was translated and published in London in 1693 and in Bassano (Venice) in 1697.[55] In the same decades, the representation of the Italian landscape as a kind of wilderness was slowly (but steadily) replacing the stereotype of the fruitful Italian peninsula. In the battle between the ancients and the moderns, antiquarian interest in the peninsula remained high because classical authorities could be cited for each landscape type, providing weapons to both sides.

Virgil was seriously read by many, since he provided the most accessible key to understanding the Italian landscape. John Dryden's poetic license in his translation of Virgil's *Georgics* did not go unnoticed by agriculturists and scholars. In 1725, William Benson published an alternative version—it was less elegant but more accurate from an agricultural and horticultural point of view.[56] However, in this context, we should speak not of the battle of books but of the battle of weeds. Jethro Tull devised the horse hoe—for which he is justly famous—after reading about the Latin term *sarritio*, which means hoeing to prepare land for the cultivation of Lucerne-Alfalfa, as described by Columella. The debate on Virgilian husbandry engaged many agriculturists up to the 1760s. The expression "Virgilian husbandry" continued to be used by writers of the Augustan age because it evoked a system and a landscape known to the numerous Englishmen who traveled between Venice and Rome and who saw the beneficial effects of cross-plowing and applying horticultural methods to arable fields.[57] But one major question remained: Could a Virgilian landscape and Virgilian farming practices still be found anywhere in Italy (figs. 5.18 and 5.19)?

FIGURE 5.18.
Vittorio Amedeo Cignaroli, *Landscape with Peasants*, 1773, detail of a painting in the Sala degli Scudieri, Palazzina di Caccia di Stupinigi, Turin. Scene showing semivirgilian husbandry in Piedmont, foregrounding the technique of cross-plowing.

Photograph courtesy of the Fondazione Ordine Mauriziano.

FIGURE 5.19.
Cross-plowed fields showing the remains of semivirgilian husbandry, Basiliano (Udine).

Photograph by the author.

Dr. John Symonds (1730–1807) traveled extensively in Italy between 1765 and 1770. He visited Corsica, having heard James Boswell speak of Pascal Paoli's rebellion, and regularly ventured off the established routes of the Grand Tour, reaching Friuli and Istria in the east and Calabria and Sicily in the south. Symonds took extensive notes during his journeys, listing books to buy and to read and frequently abandoning classical antiquities for the study of present-day agriculture and political economy. In 1770, he went back to his hometown, Bury St. Edmunds, Suffolk, and was elected to the chair of modern history at Cambridge University in 1771. He strongly believed in the division of legislative and executive powers and their mutual checks and balances. In 1778, he supported the repeal of the Navigation Act in favor of the American colonies.[58] When Arthur Young (1741–1820), a writer on agricultural economy, moved to Bradfield Hall in 1779, he became a neighbor to Symonds; it was the beginning of a long-lasting friendship.[59] Symonds contributed some lengthy letters on Italian farming to Young's well-known journal, *Annals of Agriculture*. He dealt with subjects such as fodder, water, soil, climate, landscape, government, legislation, and ideas that were manifest in the Corn Laws, which were import tariffs later introduced in England in 1815 to protect domestic grain prices from foreign competition. He examined the stereotype of the fruitfulness of Italian agriculture so praised by Varro and Pliny, and this investigation became the major purpose of his travels.

Our vast bibliography on eighteenth-century Italy offers a confirmation, rather than a contradiction, of his assessment of agricultural conditions on the Italian peninsula. Symonds realized that the question of Virgilian husbandry was obsolete in the Italian context of the 1760s—the weight of political and religious institutions mattered more. Because he published his articles during an era of "high farming"—which emphasized high inputs and high yields—and heavy propaganda that favored large farms and capital-rich tenants, his memoirs remain an example of fairness toward Italian peasants, the tenacious sharecroppers who kept the countryside in order by fighting against water, weather, meager soils, and short-sighted public administration. In his eyes, a beautiful landscape meant good farming, and the best examples were to be found in Piedmont

FIGURE 5.20.
Giuseppe Pietro Bagetti, *Mowing the Hay in Piedmont*, late eighteenth century, watercolor.

Palazzo Reale, Turin. Photograph courtesy of the Direzione Regionale per i Beni Culturali e Paesaggistici del Piemonte, Soprintendenza per i Beni Architettonici e Paesaggistici per le province di Torino, Cuneo, Asti, Biella, Vercelli (Ministero per i Beni e le Attività Culturali).

FIGURE 5.21.
Red Spanish sainfoin in the pastures of the Monti Sibillini, May 2007.

Private collection.

(fig. 5.20), Lombardy, and Tuscany. Landscapes in the Veneto, Ferrara, and Bologna, on the other hand, had not been maintained with the necessary improvements, which in this context meant irrigated meadows and rice fields. His emphasis on good farming did not prevent him from admiring other landscapes, such as the blooming whitethorn enclosures of the Marches or the uncultivated pastures in Calabria ablaze with red Spanish sainfoin (*Hedysarum coronarium*) (which are still seen today in the Monti Sibillini [fig. 5.21]).

English political interests at this time, however, lay elsewhere—primarily in timber, oil, wrought silk, and the vast market for English manufactures.[60] For example, in 1795, the Royal Navy made the use of lemons against scurvy compulsory. Partly in response to this measure, additional citrus trees began to be cultivated throughout southern Italy in the beginning of the nineteenth century.[61]

The Transformed Landscape: From Pastoral Ideals to Political Propaganda

Italy's new position among European nations at the end of the Napoleonic era reinforced the view of an Italian landscape that was either classical or without definite configuration and that needed only the addition of human figures to give it a spatial or temporal setting. Travel writers did their best to share

FIGURE 5.22. Junius Hardwicke, *The Gulf of Policastro in Calabria*, 1894, watercolor. Private collection.

the feelings, events, and landscapes they had enjoyed in their journeys with those who did not have the means to go abroad. For example, the works of Edward Lear present a rare opportunity to comment on an ingenious and beautifully written journal with original landscape illustrations. After traveling to other parts of the Italian peninsula, Lear finally visited Calabria in 1847. To him, landscape meant not only "the fertile gardens, the wondrous coast scenes or the purple gorges of the heart of Calabrian mountains" but also the "numerous odoriferous silk factories, and many detached cheerful-looking houses, with lofty *pergolate*" at the Villa Musitano.[62] He continued: "Poussinesque landscape . . . None of your dense carpet-forests—your monotonies of verdure, but made up of separate combinations of pictorial effect . . . Claude and Salvatore Rosa at every step!"[63]; "gardens and fields . . . cottages surrounded by gourds . . . Bruzzano, placed as if arranged by G. Poussin for a picture."[64] After leaving Calabria, he described his entry into Melfi: "The picturesque buildings of the city . . . the valley below with its stream and great walnut trees; the numerous fountains . . . and the perfectly Poussinesque castle . . . commanding the whole scene . . . vine terraces . . . the pergolate, and (we) ate grapes in the vineyard."[65] A fashion for southern Italy developed as a result of such travel descriptions and lesser artists began making sketches of the region (fig. 5.22).

The increase in international trade during the nineteenth century led to more demand for timber, and tree cultivation in Italy rose in response. England, France, and Austria competed to acquire control over Italian agricultural and timber production, which was important for their industrial development. Oil was used in the textile industry and for lighting. In the 1840s and 1850s, half of the walnut timber used on English ships came from Italy. When olive oil and wine prices fell after 1815, evictions followed, trees were felled to pay off family debts, vines were heavily pruned to produce firewood, and peasants earned a meager living off the remaining arable land. According to the season, peasants left the tree orchards along the coasts to work in the outfields of the upper parts of Calabria and Puglia.[66] Deforestation and depopulation initiated the slow process of soil erosion—a process that altered the appearance of the landscape in the nineteenth century and that continues today when heavy rains wash away soil, crops, and houses.

The general view of Italian landscape that I have illustrated in these pages may seem rather in line with the historical tradition established by Emilio Sereni and Cesare de Seta; furthermore, this paper benefits from the long bibliography on the subject established in the last decades.[67] Sereni aimed to create a general picture of the Italian agrarian landscape; he used paintings to illustrate his arguments and produced a lasting piece of historical scholarship. However, he attributed a strong realism to paintings that somewhat overstates their documentary value; these attributions were challenged in 1978 by Giovanni Romano, who pointed out that landscape painting owed much more to formal academic conventions than to painting en plein air.[68] In light of more recent historical research, I prefer to direct my attention to the fact that the contribution of peasant gardening to the Italian landscape must be evaluated according to the changing position of Italy within the European context. Because of the declines in Italy's economy and in her political role in European affairs after the 1650s, the semicultivated landscapes of the Roman Campagna and the southern regions acquired priority in the eyes of foreign visitors.

Finally, to sum up my argument, I wish to remind my readers that the final representation of the Italian rural landscape—a cultural stereotype that served well both Arcadia and Neoclassicism—was developed by the combined actions of Italian peasants and their exacting landlords, foreign travelers, and landscape painters (both foreign and Italian). Among the foreigners, the English, whose interest in the countryside was well known, had most closely observed the results of the work and toil of the Italian peasants; their accounts reached many readers in other parts of Europe. Until 1650, the garden-like agriculture of the Po Valley drew the attention of foreigners in spite of the political rebellion, social unrest, religious dissent, and war throughout Europe. Following in the footsteps of Samuel Hartlib, John Evelyn projected a new type of English garden that developed national forestation for timber, orchards, nurseries, and pleasure. From the subsequent decades until the eighteenth century, English travelers shifted their attention according to changes in their commercial situation, while the interests of painters followed more closely the tastes of their patrons. Whig supremacy in England dictated new political alliances and new tastes at home and on the Italian peninsula, and the semicultivated countryside between Rome and Naples became a dominant trope in Europe. The Italian countryside, both as a real set of social and material relationships and as a representation, in paintings, was transformed into a highly politicized landscape by the time of the French Revolution and the Napoleonic era. Although the landlord-peasant relationship was no different from what it was elsewhere in Europe, by the time the Italian countryside became the object of visual representation, it was transformed in accordance with the taste of the political elite. The common people, laborers, journeymen, and shepherds—men and women alike—were removed from the picture and substituted with mythological figures. What emerged from this process can be considered a piece of political propaganda that served the English Whigs revolutionary Jacobins, and French Imperial notables—an idealized classical landscape defended by the conservative elite against the dangers of industrialization and mechanization as well as against a vigorous rural society still capable of resisting enclosures and evictions.

Acknowledgments

I exchanged views and thoughts with Michel Conan to develop this essay in a perspective useful for the present colloquium. I also wish to thank Dr. Joan Thirsk for her comments on an earlier version of this paper and Mr. Gianni Berengo Gardin for permission to reproduce one of his photos (fig. 5.15). The comments and the patience of my wife, Vanessa Maher, have also improved the final version of this paper. However, I am solely responsible for the views expressed in this essay. In the following notes, I refer only to major and recent works, which lead to more bibliographical information as the reader requires.

Notes

1 David R. Coffin, "The Study of the History of the Italian Garden until the First Dumbarton Oaks Colloquium," in *Perspectives on Garden Histories*, ed. Michel Conan, 27–36 (Washington, D.C.: Dumbarton Oaks Research Library and Collection, 1999).

2 Michel Conan, ed., *Sacred Gardens and Landscapes: Ritual and Agency* (Washington, D.C.: Dumbarton Oaks Research Library and Collection, 2007), 3.

3 A similar approach is suggested in Claudia Lazzaro, "Italy is a Garden: The Idea of Italy and the Italian Garden Tradition," in *Villas and Gardens in Early Modern Italy and France*, eds. Mirka Beneš and Dianne Harris, 29–60 (Cambridge: Cambridge University Press, 2001); Tracy L. Ehrlich, *Landscape and Identity in Early Modern Rome: Villa Culture at Frascati in the Borghese Era* (Cambridge: Cambridge University Press, 2002); and Conan, introduction to *Sacred Gardens and Landscapes*, 3–14.

4 Leon Battista Alberti, *Opere volgari*, ed. Cecil Grayson, 3 vols. (Bari: G. Laterza, 1960–73).

5 It might help to look at Everett—and Williamson—as models for a social history of gardens. Nigel Everett, *The Tory View of Landscape* (New Haven: Yale University Press, 1994); and Tom Williamson, *Polite Landscapes: Gardens and Society in Eighteenth-Century England* (Baltimore: Johns Hopkins University Press, 1995). Recent important contributions on Italian gardens include Mirka Beneš and Dianne Harris, eds., *Villas and Gardens in Early Modern Italy and France* (Cambridge: Cambridge University Press, 2001); Christopher J. Pastore, "Expanding Antiquity: Andrea Navagero and Villa Culture in the Cinquecento Veneto" (PhD diss., University of Pennsylvania, 2003); and Amanda Lillie, *Florentine Villas in the Fifteenth Century: An Architectural and Social History* (Cambridge: Cambridge University Press, 2005).

6 See the recent works by Giuliana Baldan Zenoni-Politeo and Antonella Pietrogrande, *Il giardino e la memoria del mondo* (Florence: L. S. Olschki, 2002); Michel Conan, *Essais de poétique des jardins* (Florence: L. S. Olschki, 2004); Franco Panzini, "Paesaggio versus giardino: La campagna come parco," in *Progettare la natura: Architettura del paesaggio e dei giardini dalle origini all'epoca contemporanea* (Bologna: Zanichelli, 2005), 217–51; and Hervé Brunon and Monique Bresson, "Ripensare i limiti del giardino," in *Per un giardino della terra*, ed. Antonella Pietrogrande, 9–30 (Florence: L. S. Olschki, 2006). See also an up-to-date bibliography in Marie Luise Schroeter Gothein, *Storia dell'arte dei giardini*, 2 vols. (Florence: L. S. Olschki, 2006).

7 Varro *Agricultura* 1.2, 3–8; Pliny *Naturalis Historia* 3.39–40; Strabo *Geographia* 6.4, 1–2; and Virgil *Georgicon* 2.136–76. For the best account of the problem, see Gaetano Forni and Arnaldo Marcone, eds., *Storia dell'agricoltura italiana*, vol. 1, bk. 2, *L'età antica: Italia romana* (Florence: Polistampa, 2002).

8 Leandro Alberti, *Descrittione di tutta Italia* (Venice: Ludovico degli Avanzi, 1568); and Massimo Donattini, ed., *L'Italia dell'inquisitore: Storia e geografia dell'Italia del Cinquecento nella 'Descrittione' di Leandro Alberti* (Bologna: Bononia University Press, 2007).

9 "per cinque miglia insino a Bologna tutti vestiti di belle vigne et di alberi fruttiferi, et tra gli altri di Olivi . . . et ornati di sontuosi edifici." Alberti, *Descrittione di tutta Italia*, 324v.

10 "si veggono gli artificiosi ordini di alberi sopra i quali sono le viti, che da ogni lato pendono." Ibid., 328v–329.

11 Montaigne's secretary actually wrote the journal for part of the journey. Commentators generally resolve the question of authorship by saying that he wrote at the instruction of his master, but some ambiguity remains in that we perceive the Italian landscape through the eyes of the secretary. Michel de Montaigne, *The Complete Works: Essays, Travel Journal, Letters*, trans. Donald M. Frame (London: Everyman's Library, 2003). The latest scholarly contribution on travels, travelers, and traveling in modern Italy is Attilio Brilli, *Il viaggio in Italia: Storia di una grande tradizione culturale* (Bologna: Il Mulino, 2006).

12 Montaigne, *Complete Works*, 1112–13.

13 Ibid., 1126.

14 Ibid., 1181 and 1183–85. For an analysis of the Umbria region, see Rita Chiacchella, *Regionalismo e fedeltà locali: L'Umbria tra Cinque e Settecento* (Florence: Nerbini, 2004).

15 Montaigne, *Complete Works*, 1201.

16 Ibid., 999. Marino Berengo, "Il pacifico et populare stato," in *Nobili e mercanti nella Lucca del Cinquecento* (Turin: G. Einaudi, 1965), 11–82.

17 Michel de Montaigne, *Journal du voyage de Michel de Montaigne en Italie, par la Suisse & l'Allemagne, en 1580 & 1581* (Rome and Paris: Chez Le Jay, 1774).

18 Fynes Moryson, *An Itinerary Written by Fynes Moryson Gent: First in the Latin Tongue, and Then Translated by Him into English; Containing his Ten Yeeres Travell Through the Twelve Dominions of Germany, Bohmerland, Sweitzerland, Netherland, Denmark, Poland, Italy, Turky, France, England, Scotland, and Ireland* (London: John Beale, 1617), 69.

19 Ibid.

20 The word "corn" retains its original meaning of wheat when it is quoted in sixteenth- and seventeenth-century English texts. Elsewhere, I have eliminated confusion using either "wheat" or "maize" as appropriate.

21 Moryson, *An Itinerary Written by Fynes Moryson Gent*, 90.

22 Ibid., 101.

23 Ibid., 102.

24 In 1630, more vineyards, chestnut, nut, and mulberry trees had been planted both for decorative and economic purposes. Ehrlich, *Landscape and Identity in Early Modern Rome*, 197–216.

25 On the history of citrus cultivation in Italy, see Alberta Cazzani, ed., *Giardini d'agrumi: Limoni, cedri e aranci nel paesaggio agrario italiano* (Brescia: Grafo, 1999).

26 Moryson, *An Itinerary Written by Fynes Moryson Gent*, 103–9.

27 Lillie, *Florentine Villas in the Fifteenth Century*, 24–38, describes the early formation of the landed estates around Florence.

28 Gigi Corazzol, *Fitti e livelli a grano: Un aspetto del credito rurale nel Veneto del '500* (Milan: Franco Angeli, 1979).

29 Renzo Derosas, ed., *Villa: Siti e contesti* (Treviso: Fondazione Benetton Studi Ricerche, 2006) provides a foundation for further research based on newly collected data.

30 Franco Cazzola, "Lo sviluppo storico delle bonifiche idrauliche," in *Un Po di terra: Guida all'ambiente della bassa pianura padana e alla sua storia*, eds. Carlo Ferrari and Lucio Gambi (Reggio Emilia: Diabasis, 2000); Derosas, *Villa*; Salvatore Ciriacono, *Building on Water: Venice, Holland, and the Construction of the European Landscape in Early Modern Times* (New York: Berghahn Books, 2007).

31 Henry Wotton, *Letters and Dispatches from Sir Henry Wotton to James the First and his Ministers, in Westminster in the Years MDCXVII–XX* (London: Printed by W. Nicol, 1850); and Henry Wotton, *The Elements of Architecture, Collected by Henry Wotton, Knight, from the Best Authors and Examples* (London: Longmans, Green, 1903). *Elements of Architecture* was written after Wotton's return from Venice in 1623 and published in London in 1624. For the Englishmen traveling in seventeenth-century Europe, see John Walter Stoye, *English Travellers Abroad 1604–1667: Their Influence in English Society and Politics*, rev. ed. (New Haven: Yale University Press, 1989); and Mayling Stubbs, "John Beale, Philosophical Gardener of Herefordshire Part I. Prelude to the Royal Society (1608–1663)," *Annals of Science* 39, no. 5 (September 1982): 470. For information on Venetian orchards, see Davide Busato, *Metamorfosi di un litorale: Origine e sviluppo dell'isola di Sant'Erasmo nella Laguna di Venezia* (Venice: Marsilio, 2006), 144ff; Mauro Ambrosoli, "Conservation and Diffusion of Species Diversity in Northern Italy: Peasant Gardens of the Renaissance and After," in *Botanical Progress, Horticultural Innovation, and Cultural Change*, eds. Michel Conan and W. John Kress (Washington, D.C.: Dumbarton Oaks Research Library and Collection, 2007), 188–89; and Joan Thirsk, *Food in Early Modern England: Phases, Fads, Fashions 1500–1760* (London and New York: Hambledon Continuum, 2006), 69. The 1630 plague epidemic was brought to Chioggia by some market gardeners sailing back from Venice. See Alessandro Rosina, Mirto Etoni, and Francesco Bilari, "La popolazione di Chioggia nel Seicento," in *La popolazione italiana nel Seicento: Relazioni presentate al convegno di Firenze, 28–30 novembre 1996* (Bologna: CLUEB, 1999), 611.

32 John Raymond, introduction to *An Itinerary Contayning a Voyage, Made through Italy, in the yeare 1646, and 1647* (London: Printed for Humphrey Moseley, 1648).

33 John Evelyn, *The Diary of John Evelyn*, ed. Esmond de Beer, vol. 2, *Kalendarium, 1620–1649* (Oxford: Clarendon Press, 1955), 324–25.

34 Ibid., 464–66.

35 Ibid., 478–79, 481, 483–84, and 487.

36 The term "paradise" is here used to evoke the concept of an enclosed garden. Ibid., 491. Esmond de Beer thought that the presence of olives and olive trees was "an original addition and probably incorrect" (491n1) on the part of Evelyn. On the contrary, this passage reveals Evelyn's attention to the existing tree varieties. Olive trees were a common feature on the sunny sides of the hills in the Po Valley in late medieval and early modern times. For the history of olive trees and the olive-oil trade, see Andrea Brugnoli and Gian Maria Varanini, eds., *Olivi ed olio nel medioevo italiano* (Bologna: CLUEB, 2005).

37 Raymond, *An Itinerary Contayning a Voyage*, 185–86.

38 Ibid., 234–35; and Cazzani, *Giardini d'agrumi*, 21–39.

39 Raymond followed Leandro Alberti in using the word "Lombardy" to designate the area in the Po Valley where the Longobards settled; this area bordered "Romania" (today Romagna) and began roughly at Ravenna.

40 Carlo Poni, *Gli aratri e l'economia agraria nel bolognese dal XVII al XIX secolo* (Bologna: Zanichelli, 1963); and Carlo Poni, *Fossi e cavedagne benedicon le campagne* (Bologna: Il Mulino, 1982).

41 Lucia Bonelli Conenna, Attilio Brilli, and Giuseppe Cantelli, *Il paesaggio toscano: Storia e rappresentazione* (Milan: Silvana, 2004); and Giuliana Biagioli, *Il modello del proprietario imprenditore nella Toscana dell'Ottocento—Bettino Ricasoli: Il patrimonio, le fattorie* (Florence: L. S. Olschki, 2000).

42 Symonds's study of landscape painting technique is discussed in Mary Beal, *A Study of Richard Symonds: His Italian Notebooks and their Relevance to Seventeenth-Century Painting Techniques* (New York: Garland, 1984). See also Henry V. S. Ogden and Margaret S. Ogden, *English Taste in Landscape in the Seventeenth Century* (Ann Arbor: University of Michigan Press, 1955), 68–71.

43 Egerton manuscript 1635, 62; Harley manuscript 943, 31–31v, 36, 76, and 98. British Library, London.

44 Harley manuscript 943, 85v. British Library, London.

45 Patrick Chorley, *Oil, Silk, and Enlightenment: Economic Problems in XVIIIth-Century Naples* (Naples: Istituto Italiano per Gli Studi Storici, 1965); Stefano Villani, "I consoli della nazione inglese a Livorno tra il 1665 e il 1673: Joseph Kent, Thomas Clutterbuck e Ephraim Skinner," *Nuovi studi livornesi* 11 (2004): 11–34; and Gigliola Pagano de Divitiis, *English Merchants in Seventeenth-Century Italy* (Cambridge: Cambridge University Press, 1997).

46 Charles Webster, *The Great Instauration: Science, Medicine, and Reform, 1626–1660* (London: Duckworth, 1975); and Mauro Ambrosoli, "The Political Context for the Agricultural Activities of the Hartlib Circle," in *Samuel Hartlib: An*

International Correspondence, ed. Scott Mandelbrote, 180–96 (Oxford: Oxford University Press, forthcoming).

47 Recent important studies have approached this question from the point of view of the achievements of Evelyn in England especially in terms of formal gardens. See Therese O'Malley and Joachim Wolschke-Bulmahn, eds., *John Evelyn's "Elysium Britannicum" and European Gardening* (Washington D.C.: Dumbarton Oaks Research Library and Collection, 1998); and John Evelyn, *Elysium Britannicum; or, The Royal Gardens*, ed. John E. Ingram (Philadelphia: University of Pennsylvania Press, 2001). I wish to focus on the Italian side of the story.

48 Samuel Hartlib, *Samuel Hartlib, his Legacy of Husbandry* (London, 1655).

49 Giles Mandelbrote, "John Evelyn and his Books," in *John Evelyn and his Milieu*, eds. Francis Harris and Michael Hunter (London: The British Library, 2003), 76–77 and 87.

50 Stubbs, "John Beale, Philosophical Gardener of Herefordshire"; and Peter H. Goodchild, "John Evelyn, John Beale and Blackberry Hill," *Garden History* 19 (1991): 105–37.

51 Add manuscript 78312, 113v. British Library, London.

52 John Evelyn, *Pomona; or, An Appendix Concerning Fruit-Trees, in Relation to Cider, the Making and Several Ways of Ordering It* (London: J. Martyn and J. Allestry, 1664).

53 See Webster, *The Great Instauration*; John Kingston Galpine, *The Georgian Garden: An Eighteenth-Century Nurseryman's Catalogue*, ed. John Harvey (Stanbridge, Wimborne, Dorset: Dovecote Press, 1983); and Ambrosoli, "The Political Context for the Agricultural Activities of the Hartlib Circle."

54 Paolo Boccone, *Museo di piante rare della Sicilia, Malta, Corsica, Italia, Piemonte, e Germania dedicato ad alcuni nobili patritii veneti protettori della botanica e delle buone lettere* (1697; repr., with introduction and notes by Francesco M. Raimondo, Christiane Garnero Morena, and Pietro Mazzola, Palermo: Ed. Grifo, 1996); and Paolo Bartolomeo Clarici, *Istoria e coltura delle piante: Che sono pe'l fiore più ragguardevoli, e più distinte per ornare un giardino in tutto il tempo dell'anno con un copioso trattato degli agrumi* (Venice: Andrea Poletti, 1726).

55 Jean de La Quintinie, *Instruction pour les jardins fruitiers et potagers, avec un traité des orangers, suivy de quelques reflexions sur l'agriculture*, 2nd ed., 2 vols. (Amsterdam: H. Desbordes, 1692). Translated by John Evelyn as *The Compleat Gard'ner; or Directions for Cultivating and Right Ordering of Fruit-Gardens and Kitchen-Gardens* (London, 1693). Subsequently published as *Le parfait jardinier, ou, Instruction pour les jardins fruitiers et potagers: Avec un traité des oranges, suivi de réflexions sur l'agriculture*, rev. ed. (Paris: C. Barbin, 1695) and *Trattato del taglio de gl' alberi fruttiferi* (Bassano, 1697). The recent restoration of the gardens at Versailles reveals this forgotten function of the *potager du roi* as a center for fruit and vegetable production through scientific horticulture.

56 Virgil, *Virgil's Husbandry, or an Essay on the Georgics*, trans. William Benson (London: William and John Innys, 1724); Virgil, *The Georgics*, trans. John Dryden (Ashington, Northumberland: Mid-Northumberland Arts Group, 1981); and Joseph Farrell, *Vergil's Georgics and the Traditions of Ancient Epic: The Art of Allusion in Literary History* (New York: Oxford University Press, 1991). See also John Henderson, *The Roman Book of Gardening* (London: Routledge, 2004) for the latest extremely intelligent account of the garden-like character of Virgilian agriculture.

57 Ambrosoli, "Conservation and Diffusion of Species Diversity in Northern Italy," 342, 345–48, 351, and 355–56; see also John Ingamells, *A Dictionary of British and Irish Travellers in Italy, 1701–1800* (New Haven: Yale University Press, 1997), 921–22.

58 John Symonds, *Remarks upon an Essay, Intituled, The History of the Colonization of the Free States of Antiquity, Applied to the Present Contest between Great Britain and her American Colonies* (London: Printed by J. Nichols, and sold by T. Payne, 1778).

59 Mauro Ambrosoli, *John Symonds: Agricoltura e politica in Corsica e in Italia (1765–1770)* (Turin: Fondazione Luigi Einaudi, 1974), 9–36. For further information, see also François de La Rochefoucauld, *A Frenchman's Year in Suffolk: French Impressions of Suffolk Life in 1784*, ed. and trans. Norman Scarfe (Woodbridge, Suffolk: Boydell Press, 1988).

60 Chorley, *Oil, Silk, and Enlightenment*; and John Robertson, *The Case for the Enlightenment: Scotland and Naples, 1680–1760* (Cambridge: Cambridge University Press, 2005).

61 Salvatore Lupo, *Il giardino degli aranci: Il mondo degli agrumi nella storia del Mezzogiorno* (Venice: Marsilio, 1990).

62 Peter Quennell, ed., *Edward Lear in Southern Italy: Journals of a Landscape Painter in Southern Calabria and the Kingdom of Naples* (London: W. Kimber, 1964), 11 and 35.

63 Ibid., 60–61 and 64.

64 Ibid., 66.

65 Ibid., 183.

66 Biagio Salvemini, *L'innovazione precaria: Spazi, mercati e società nel Mezzogiorno tra Sette e Ottocento* (Rome: Meridiana, 1995), 22, 36, and 44.

67 Emilio Sereni, *Storia del paesaggio agrario italiano* (Bari: Laterza, 1961); and Cesare de Seta, *Il paesaggio*, vol. 5 of *Storia d'Italia: Annali* (Turin: G. Einaudi, 1982). See also the rich bibliography in Fondazione Lelio e Lisli Basso-ISSOCO, *L'ambiente nella storia d'Italia: Studi e immagini* (Venice: Cataloghi Marsilio, 1989).

68 Giovanni Romano, *Studi sul paesaggio* (Turin: G. Einaudi, 1978).

CHAPTER 6

Gardens and Landscapes as "Open-Ended Works" between Continuity and Transformation: Notes on the Role of Historical Studies

LIONELLA SCAZZOSI

Historical Gardens: A History of Preservation Theories

OUR CURRENT CONCEPTION OF THE GARDEN AS a continuously changing artifact developed rather recently, as a result of a theoretical debate among specialists across the world and in Italy from the 1970s to the late 1990s. The international debate commenced with the creation of a special committee for historical gardens by the International Federation of Landscape Architects (IFLA) in 1967 and with the organization of the first "Colloque International sur la Conservation et la Restauration des Jardins Historiques" by the International Council on Monuments and Sites (ICOMOS) in Fontainebleau in 1971. Both organizations stated the importance of preserving historical gardens and set up a joint committee—the International Committee on Historic Gardens and Sites ICOMOS-IFLA—dedicated to them in Florence in 1981.

Before that, there had been a roughly thirty-year period (beginning in the 1940s) that was characterized by an evident lack of interest in historical gardens in Italy and abroad. Yet, still earlier, many national laws aimed at protecting historical and cultural heritage had already explicitly addressed gardens. For example, Italian "gardens and parks," "villas," and "natural beauties" were protected by Laws n. 1089 and n. 1497 of 1939 and partially by earlier laws and regulations.[1] The Venice Preservation Charter (*Carta del Restauro di Venezia*) of 1964—which continues to be the main international reference document for the protection of heritage sites—already recommended protection for "single architectural works" and the "urban or landscape environment," but it failed to refer explicitly to gardens.[2] The *Carta del Restauro* of 1972—which is still a milestone for Italian professionals specializing in the protection of heritage sites—made a leap forward as it explicitly stated that "gardens and parks" are part of the heritage to be protected, and even referred to the laws of 1939 still in force.[3] But it failed to include detailed operational instructions like those given for the other categories, such as architectural heritage, historical centers, paintings, sculptures, and archaeological heritage, and made no mention of landscape or "natural beauty," which was the term used by Law n. 1497 of 1939. These omissions betray the presence of a real intellectual problem. By the 1970s, in Italy and abroad, gardens came to be seen almost as a new kind of historical heritage, just as had happened in previous decades with historical centers, industrial archaeology, rural buildings, and diffused or so-called minor historical heritage.

The broad debate on the conservation and restoration of gardens that took place in Italy in the 1980s and 1990s included experts from many different disciplines and backgrounds.[4] For many of these naturalists, botanists, historians, architects, landscape architects, and agronomists, the problems associated with one of the garden's basic components—its rapidly changing vegetal material—are specific to gardens and have nothing to do with other historical artifacts. This fact discourages their reliance on the theoretical frameworks of other preservation disciplines. As a result, the field of garden preservation developed independently from the other preservation disciplines at multiple levels (theoretical, methodological, and operational), leading to interesting innovations as well as to contradictions, simplifications, gaps, and awkwardness. At the same time, the key figures in other disciplines used gardens to test how the theoretical, methodological, and operational models conceived for the preservation of works of architecture, painting, and sculpture could be broadened to cover other cultural artifacts. They hoped to establish a unified methodology that could be applied to the entire historical heritage. Their effort revisited (in abbreviated form) the more than one hundred years of debate on other kinds of historical heritage, dwelled on principles already explored and explained, developed new suggestions for a specific theory of gardens, and, finally, deepened and rethought existing theories and methodologies in ways that turned out to be relevant for other kinds of historical heritage.[5]

The main difficulty has been understanding what it really means to act on the fast-changing vegetal matter of gardens; a key principle, still essential to the restoration of historical heritage, holds that what is restored is not the work of art (and the historical document that it constitutes) but rather the material out of which it is made.[6] Because gardens are continuously changed by nature and man, they undermine the theoretical oppositions—work of art vs. document vs. monument, original vs. copy, authentic vs. fake, single vs. collective—followed in the restoration disciplines that are still considered to be the major conceptual and operational references at an international level. Italy has developed its own original point of view, which is different from the international approach codified by ICOMOS-IFLA.[7]

Enriched by input from other countries, the theoretical and methodological debate in Italy eventually helped to clarify the roles of the various preservation specializations, to bring mutual understanding to and integration between the different disciplinary viewpoints, and to consider the restoration of historical gardens as a specialized branch within the broader discipline of historic preservation. This debate enabled the informal training of professionals who operate with the awareness, rigor, competence, and knowledge that we would expect from anyone dealing with historical heritage.

The difference between the international and Italian viewpoints is clearly expressed in the documents produced during the animated discussions aimed at drawing up a specific charter for the preservation of historical gardens. There were two versions of the charter: an official text signed by ICOMOS-IFLA and an Italian text.[8] Although both versions referred to the general restoration principles stated in the Venice Preservation Charter, they reached different, and indeed incompatible, conclusions as to the criteria that should guide any intervention on the material structure of a garden. In particular, they disagreed as to whether the reconstruction of a past work was acceptable.[9] At that time, the core disagreement between ICOMOS-IFLA and Italy was due to a different idea of the meanings and roles of gardens in the contemporary world. ICOMOS-IFLA, in contrast with Italy, considered the form of a garden to be superior to its material, its symbolic meaning to be more important than its role as a material document (a repository of trees, paths, etc.), and the repair and rebuilding of its formal structure to be preferable to the ongoing diffused preservation of the accumulated material traces of the past. Italy remained faithful to its long theoretical and operational tradition of restoration—a tradition that kept its status as the unquestioned international standard.

The concept of "open-ended works" provided a framework for these theoretical debates, and reminded scholars and experts that any garden, landscape, building, and urban settlement (a) is the result of man's work and is a totally artificial artifact (even if it is mostly made out of vegetal materials); (b) is arranged as an architecture, whose vegetal walls and rooms, views and framed vistas, symmetries, and visual highlights have precise functions and meanings (like any other type of architecture); (c) requires continuous and diffused human action in order to keep the artificial character that uncontrolled nature would otherwise gradually—but sometimes quickly—cancel; and (d) should be seen as a collective work that results from both unique and recurrent interventions, as well as great signatures and routine work, by the designers, owners, gardeners, and users who intervened on it over time.[10] Change should be seen as a given of a site; it in no way undermines its historical specificity. A site, and even its remains, is largely made up of the traces left on it by time—that is, by nature's and man's work. Thus, each single trace matters as historical evidence and, as such, deserves to be passed on in its own appropriate way, whether material or immaterial. The concept of true or fake is not applicable, as any vegetal architecture or landscape is always and can only be authentic. What we see today is only the latest version, which bears readable traces of the past and records the present in its shaped materials.

Any present action, including the abandonment, destruction, or reconstruction of a past asset, is always a contemporary project; it leaves traces of the present and it never completely reproduces the past. Transformation is inevitable, unstoppable, and irreversible, but its outcomes must be controlled and guided in ways that are aware and respectful of historical characteristics and alert to new values added by man or nature over time. In other words, any present action must resist nostalgia for the past. It must respect past heritage, and strive to pass it on and make it visible in the present. But, at the same time, it must recognize the needs and innovative potential of present uses, formal compositions of places, and meanings through appropriate solutions. Reconstruction—or rebuilding a past asset—is not feasible, as it is impossible to reverse time and gain a full knowledge of the past to be reconstructed. Not only does reconstruction make arbitrary choices regarding the past, but it destroys a site's value as a layered material record of its history. Indeed, even restoration is impossible, if by this we mean the removal of accretions or alterations in order to return a garden or landscape to an earlier state. Any attempt to freeze a garden in its most recent state is equally impossible and displays a reductive understanding of so-called conservation methods.

Enlarging the Vision: Gardens, Contexts, Landscapes

The new approach to the field that subsequently emerged in Italy and Europe during the 1980s and 1990s, and was codified in the European Landscape Convention (Florence, 2000) promoted by the Council of Europe, has affected the reading of gardens.[11] This evolution began with the opening of the historical disciplines to material culture and to the "total history" of places and populations; this opening was rooted in cultural movements of the early twentieth century in the fields of history, geography, visual arts, literature, and theater. It led to the creation of new categories of cultural heritage—such as historical centers, industrial archaeology, rural buildings, and diffused heritage—after World War II. Moreover, it enlarged the concept of historical gardens by identifying new types and paying attention to so-called minor types, which are numerous and, therefore, extremely relevant in the building of territories. Gardens of recent historical periods (including middle-class gardens of the late nineteenth and early twentieth centuries), gardens by important contemporary landscape designers, and the early-twentieth-century restorations of historic gardens became newly valued as historical documents.

The Venice Preservation Charter of 1964 had already defined monuments as "not only great works of art but also more modest works of the past which have acquired cultural significance with the passing of time" (Article 1). Against this background, the expression, and concept of, vegetal architecture was meant not only for gardens and villa parks (which were the main focuses until then), but also for other architectures built with vegetal and mineral materials—including urban and rural tree-lined roads; tree-planted squares; public parks; public landscapes; lakesides; embankments; botanic gardens; zoological parks and gardens; gardens for schools, city halls, and rail stations; parks for spas; paths; memorial gardens dedicated to great personalities, historical events, and war heroes; battlefields; plantings in garden cities; and archaeological sites—as long as they were based on a single recognizable architectural project, even if they changed over time or were anonymous.[12] The term "vegetal architecture" was used for the first time in *Criteri per la tutela, la conservazione e l'uso delle architetture vegetali* (Principles for the Protection, Conservation, and Use of Works of Vegetal Architecture) (1987), a document published by the regional administration of Lombardy.[13] The conceptual basis for this broad view was partially present in some nineteenth-century treatises and art manuals on gardens and in the *Carta dei giardini storici* (Italian Charter of Historic Gardens) (1981). With the European Landscape Convention, an entire territory became an object of preservation and a site of identity and transformation for the populations (local and foreign) who helped create it, lived in it, and modified it through their daily activities: a historical heritage, where the degree to which the past persists and the means by which it is evident vary from place to place.

Two profound implications follow from these observations. The first has to do with how we read a site. The broadened definition of landscape requires a new way of looking, which is focused not on individual gardens and works of vegetal architecture divorced from their surroundings, but on the physical, functional, visual, symbolic, productive, and economic relationships that bound (and still bind) works of vegetal architecture to their surroundings. It is not just a question of analyzing the physical context of gardens and other vegetal architectures, or the relationships that they establish with the elements of their immediate, intermediate, and distant environments, since indeed the term "context" keeps the focus on a privileged item or site—the garden.[14] It is also a question of recognizing systems, where each constitutive element has a specific and joint function in the network of relationships linking it to the others and that actually are the system itself. Therefore, the landscape system becomes important too. This term recalls the concept of an ensemble, which is used internationally, especially for the census of architectural heritage.

The second implication is that we can use gardens to develop and test theories also applicable to landscapes in their outstanding and ordinary parts. After all, both gardens and landscapes are continuously changing artifacts. Many international experts are aware of the thematic closeness between gardens and landscapes. The ICOMOS-IFLA committee operated under a more encompassing name—the International Committee on Historic Gardens and Sites ICOMOS-IFLA—between 1982 and 1998. In 1998, it became the International Committee on Historic Gardens and Cultural Landscapes ICOMOS-IFLA; since 2005, it has been called the Committee on Cultural Landscapes ICOMOS-IFLA, but it has continued to deal with both gardens and landscapes.

Italy has recently begun to produce a number of theoretical documents dealing specifically with issues of landscape conservation and restoration.[15] Because of the convergence of garden and landscape issues, this interest in operational criteria has recently expanded within the field of garden history. Its importance as a specific topic is underscored by the reciprocal relationship between how we frame the historical study of a site and how we preserve and conserve that site.

In our current historical period, there is a growing awareness that the deep, epochal transformations occurring throughout many territories of the world are detrimental to the quality of those places. The specific character of a site is undermined by homogenization. And new designs and constructions all too often deal with the material specificity and meaning of a place through inappropriate strategies, such as juxtapositions, overlaps, indifference, incoherence, decontextualization, and contrast; or by various forms of mimeticism, including stylistic motifs taken from cultures that are alien to the place and simplistic imitations of local traditions. As we become aware of this bleak picture, we reach a growing consensus that innovations should integrate coherently with what already exists, thereby respecting our contemporary needs as well as the specific character of existing features and their role in cultural identity formation (which is one of the most essential needs of today). Scientific, technical, and cultural groups and communities are becoming aware of the negative transformations of landscape, and voices of protest are growing stronger and more numerous, even though they lack unanimity in defining what would constitute a good transformation. A careful and precise knowledge of a site is now generally seen as a point of departure for any transformation (whether conservation, addition, or remediation) that aims to deal with existing conditions with respect and dialogue rather than with exploitation and destruction.[16] An emerging issue is that of setting limits to the transformations of landscape through cultural initiatives as well as rules and policies. These limits should be formulated to ensure that any transformation attains a formal and functional quality in dialogue with what already exists. Another emerging issue is that of improving the quality of places that are generally regarded as deficient, such as areas with low-density sprawl, large linear conurbations, and peri-urban areas. Such places sometimes even host famous historical sites (for example, villas and gardens in many metropolitan areas, in regions like Milan, the Brianza, the Veneto, or along the Riviera del Brenta), as so many fragmentary elements lost in different rationalizations of territorial configuration. But these historical sites may become essential points of departure for a process of landscape requalification whose first move would be to invest them with new meanings and functions, chosen to enhance those already fixed in the collective memory.

The issues of limits and landscape requalification intersect with ongoing debates on the quality of innovation: the addition of new elements and new architecture, in its broader meaning, including, therefore, not only new and complex works (such as buildings, public parks, and infrastructure) but also numerous and diffuse interventions that change, add to, or transform the historical and nonhistorical buildings, vegetal arrangements and gardens, etc., that already exist.[17] These debates upend the customary concept of design, which is mainly (and sometimes even exclusively) focused on the functional and formal assets of new works, regardless of the effects on the specific character of the places where they will be built.[18]

All these considerations represent an expansion of the theoretical and operational horizons in the fields of historic preservation, architectural design, and territorial planning as well as underscore the essential contribution of historical knowledge—understood as knowledge of places, of the populations who built and lived in them, and of the meanings attributed to them.

Historical Studies of Gardens and Landscapes

Italian studies on the history of gardens have developed within this dynamic framework. They reflect various conceptions of the role of history writing, and they indirectly influence both the policies for the protection of historical heritage and the criteria and methods used in the tangible treatment of sites. They are also conditioned by questions arising from theoretical, methodological, and operational developments and choices related to conservation, restoration, and preservation. Let us remember that these studies are carried out not only by historians but also by experts from other disciplines (e.g., geography, botany, architecture, and restoration) for whom historical knowledge is an essential aspect of any protection policy or intervention to conserve the specific material aspects of gardens. Historical studies have been, and still are, necessary for a comprehensive understanding of the heritage of sites within a given territory, with regard not only to the most famous and celebrated gardens but also to minor ones and to other vegetal architectures.

In Italy, most historical studies of gardens—whether focused on the broad picture or on specialized topics—have followed long-established historiographical traditions.[19] They explore topics ranging from the effects of cultural, artistic, social, economic, and political factors on the design of gardens; to authors, patrons, and builders; to styles and symbolic meanings; to botany; to modern designers who are now considered part of history;[20] to unbuilt works; and to a broad range of vegetal architectures, such as public parks and cemeteries. These studies tend to use traditional sources of historical research, such as archives. To these forms of research we should add the archaeology of gardens, which has employed both direct tools (such as excavations) and indirect tools (such as aerial photographs and studies of surface remains) and has focused mainly on ancient gardens, in line with a deeply rooted Italian tradition of archaeological studies.[21]

Until recently, gardens and vegetal architectures were treated, both in Italy and abroad, as architectural works, and little attention was paid to the physical, functional, formal, and symbolic aspects of the contexts in which they were—and often are—embedded. Although they were rich in historical, cultural, and artistic meanings, they were seen as isolated entities, which were analyzed individually and not as constituent elements of the territory of which they were, and still are, a part. Since the second half of the eighteenth century, garden design has been seen as a branch of architecture charged with arranging external spaces, green rooms, and furnishings according to distinct social functions and meanings; this approach has remained basically unchanged, as evidenced by the numerous essays and treatises on the "art of gardens" that were published in the eighteenth and nineteenth centuries and by the sections devoted to gardens in the architecture manuals of the early twentieth century. This way of studying gardens is, indeed, very similar to that found in the fields of architectural history and criticism, of which garden studies forms a subfield. In addition, its methods belong to a strand of art history that focuses mainly on works and authors. Garden studies in Italy have little to say about the transformations of the territory as a whole, particularly outside of the cities. And even if historical studies of cities systematically cover most of the Italian territory, they tend to focus on the city as an artifact surrounded by its physical context (i.e., its rural and natural setting).

Historical monographs, guidebooks, technical manuals, and specialized journals of the past few decades have shown quite clearly the persistence of this historiographical approach, even if one considers nothing more than their illustrations and titles. Only in recent years can one detect a growing interest for the territories that were closely linked with gardens. Illustrations show a progressive shift from a focus on the isolated villa building—at a time when gardens were rarely considered cultural heritage—to an emphasis on the ensemble "villa with garden," and to the more recent, but still rare, contextualization of the villa-garden complex in its agricultural territory, whose management was one of the reasons, if not the main reason, for the settlement of villas in Italy before the second half of the nineteenth century. These historiographical developments are also evident in cases where scholars have shown that the original reason for constructing a villa was the management of a vast agricultural estate—notable examples include the Palladian villas and, more generally, the villas in the Veneto.[22] As Rudolf Borchardt observed in *Città italiane*, the villa residence with its adjoining garden was part—or better, the least important part—of a larger piece of real estate. Historically, the villa formed an organic whole with its surrounding landscape, dominating and shaping it and yet sharing its fate through the course of generations.[23]

Interactions between Historical Studies and Protection and Conservation Activities

Even though history typically posits itself as an autonomous discipline, its orientations have greatly determined, and still determine, the operational decisions for the protection of garden heritage, historical vegetal architectures, and landscape. Conversely, the orientations of the theoretical debate and the practices developed for the physical protection and conservation of historical heritage have also affected, and still affect, the choices made in historical studies, thus showing the close interaction that exists between these fields.

In particular, because historical studies in recent decades have focused primarily on gardens that critics regard as outstanding rather than minor, there has been a corresponding tendency, both in Italy and abroad, to list and protect only the most renowned and celebrated sites, and to ignore the existence of other sites within a given territory. The fact that historical studies traditionally have been interested in the garden as an architectural work and have favored certain historical periods and forms (such as formal gardens) over others has led to decisions to protect only parts of a complex—even when the gardens were thoroughly integrated with the surrounding landscape and territory.[24]

Moreover, it generally takes time for public opinions, administrators, and technicians from other disciplines to absorb and adopt the cultural innovations that come from specialized fields, such as historical research and historic preservation. This is particularly evident when examining the instruments for territorial planning and management (even the most recent ones) at the local and provincial level. These instruments typically consider gardens to be self-contained entities and fail to understand their connections to territories, in particular the essential relationship between the garden and its historical and contemporary contexts. An example of this failure is seen in the scholarship on areas where villa systems and related large properties are especially numerous, such as Piedmont, Lombardy, the Veneto, Tuscany, Latium, Sicily, and the Vesuvian area. On the other hand, the disciplines of conservation and territorial planning contributed to the solution of this problem by implementing forms of census—namely the collection and dissemination of historical data—to record the larger field of all vegetal architectures, making no distinction between major and minor ones. The aim of the census was indeed comprehensive: to know and protect the historical heritage that was physically present on a whole territory so that this heritage could be valued as an ecological, urbanistic, and economic resource and not only as a cultural one. Historians have participated in such censes by providing specialized analysis, classification of knowledge, historical and critical understanding, and interpretation.

Other studies linked with the operational aspect investigate more generally the transformations of territory and landscape. For example, they are currently integrating this broader conception of landscape heritage into the administrative structures charged with planning and managing the territory at the regional, provincial, and municipal levels. These studies are generally carried out by territorial designers and planners. Their aim is twofold: on the one hand, to understand territorial transformations and events and to arrange them chronologically on a timeline; and on the other hand, to identify the extant physical traces of the past and to locate them on a current map. Such studies require that results be presented in standardized formats in order to save time and reduce costs. They often rely on historical maps that cover large territorial areas[25] and make full use of extant historical studies, with the primary aim of representing transformations through maps rather than providing critical analysis. Their output is, thus, totally different from that of historians, yet it may be extremely useful for historians and worthy of their attention. Obviously this does not mean that the discipline of history should become the operational tool of territorial management, but there should be a broader interaction among the various disciplinary fields and a more systematic contribution to the knowledge of sites.

Stimuli from the operational landscape disciplines have recently encouraged historians to shift their attention from gardens to landscape systems, of which villas are a part. As we have seen, the historical Italian villa is an effective example of a landscape system: it is the core of a number of complex elements and relations adding up to an organic landscape unit, a web of utilitarian and recreational aims that was apparent both formally and functionally. Villas that include formal gardens and park landscapes are especially apt examples, as their merely decorative elements are not restricted to a well-defined area separate from the agricultural areas, but are extended either partially or completely to the agricultural areas. In some cases, these elements are so extensive that they create vast landscapes, encompassing the owner's house, pleasure gardens, pavilions, and woodlands as well as utilitarian elements, such as kitchen gardens, orchards, greenhouses, nurseries, farmlands, and connecting lanes.[26]

The research of villa systems is extremely relevant to landscape preservation decisions and yet administrators do not sufficiently avail themselves of this information. The failure to do so results in a lack of protection for sensitive sites and is often the reason why such sites are allowed to be destroyed or fragmented. Gaining a deeper insight into the villa systems may be methodologically useful to better understand other landscape systems that are qualified by different vegetal architectures, such as the pleasure gardens and kitchen gardens of rural settlements with their related systems for agricultural production and livestock breeding (fields, woods, pastures, trails, thickets and solitary trees, and equipment), as well as garden cities.

Conservation

The interaction between the theoretical orientations of history and the criteria of historic preservation is also visible in the actual practices for the protection and use/reuse of historical artifacts. The measures taken to conserve and/or restore artifacts reflect the many theoretical, methodological, and operational positions that experts in the protection disciplines have been debating for centuries. There are two camps in this debate: those who respect all traces of the transformations caused by man and nature over time as well as the authenticity of a site's materials and forms; and those who want to replace and remake the parts that aged, disappeared, or were never even built. With regard to historical gardens, the two operational approaches recall the deep reasons for the aforementioned discrepancy between the ICOMOS-IFLA protocol and the Italian document of 1981.

The respect for the age-value of historical heritage—which is defined as a clear perception of the passage of time through its traces, or the persistence of the historical physical substance —is often linked to the willingness to respect and preserve the specific cultural characteristics of a site and, through them, the identity of a population. The reconstruction of sites *ex novo*, whether partially or completely, sometimes reflects a wish to enhance their status by building exceptional iconic monuments or by building places rich with symbolic meaning for their populations. The decision to reconstruct these sites is supported by affirming their historical and artistic values, and the writings of historians are often invoked to corroborate these affirmations.

In Italy, the grand state-owned gardens (including Boboli, Caserta, Strà, the Villa d'Este at Tivoli, and Racconigi) have been seen by their administrators and the general public as monument-documents or open-air museums of their own history. This general consensus led to a focus on the preservation of accumulated historical character in its entirety. These gardens have been managed, presented, enhanced, and even defended on this basis despite the many problems associated with sites that are mainly used for tourist and cultural purposes and despite the disagreement among experts on particular theoretical and operational issues.[27] Overall, the traditional Italian approach to the restoration of historical heritage was followed at these state-owned gardens; the restorers were respectful of the traces of time and did not favor some historical periods over others. Their main focus was the site, with its current specific character and material elements. This perspective was codified in the "Italian Charter of Historic Gardens" (1981), which states that the material history of gardens is analogous to that of works of architecture: a garden that has been passed down to us is an architecture ("architectural resource"), "a whole built with different materials," and "a material artifact" (Article 1). It reflects the various ways in which the relationship between man and nature has been expressed over time, as well as the (many) civilizations that constructed it or were connected with it. As such, each site "represents a limited, fragile, not reproducible *unicum*" and has "its own development process, its own history [. . .] reflecting those societies and cultures that conceived, built, and used it or that were connected with it in any way" (Article 1). As a consequence, "whatever operation intended either to give priority to a single phase in the historical process over any of the others or to pursue it anew, to the detriment of the subsequent steps, would cause a reduction in resources and would result in a restrictive and anti-historical attitude" (Article 2). In these cases, historical studies, which are usually carried out by those in charge of the protection and conservation of a site and which are facilitated by easy access to archives, tend to focus on the following: creating an ideal—but not material—reconstruction of any knowable asset of the site for each period; understanding how and why each asset was created (this can be useful in solving problems of degradation that may have remote causes); and identifying, dating, and attributing all extant features. The frameworks used in historical studies and conservation are closely linked. However, restorers are still considering how they can realize concrete additions and alterations that clearly read as contemporary interventions while simultaneously respecting the historical character of a site. Some of the interventions realized in these state-owned gardens, such as the Villa Pisani at Strà, have been quite significant for how they connected with principles, experiences, and tastes of contemporary Italian and foreign landscape designers. In both their formal and material qualities, these works have been recognized as contemporary and appropriate.

Reconstruction

It has been rare in Italy for entire sites to be reconstructed *ex novo* from their foundations, and experts have tended to focus on the problems and contradictions inherent in this approach. The recent reconstruction of the large seventeenth- and eighteenth-century gardens of the Royal Palace of Venaria Reale, outside of Turin, which had been entirely destroyed due to historical choices and events, represents one of Italy's most exceptional and problematic interventions. (The building has also seen heavy-handed reconstruction and completion of some parts.) The existing historical research, which is rather substantial and long established, has carefully analyzed all of the transformations that the site has undergone, but its main focus has been on the construction, massive transformation, subsequent abandonment, and partial destruction of the town, royal palace, gardens, and farmland during the seventeenth and eighteenth centuries. Indeed, Venaria Reale is an important piece of our overall understanding of the dwellings of the House of Savoy. The curatorial decisions made since public acquisition—which until now have scarcely been documented in print—have relied on these empirical data to provide a critical judgment of historical events, to privilege one phase of the site's development as the moment of its maximum use and splendor, and to re-present it to visitors.[28] Archaeological tools, such as photo-interpretations of excavations, were used to reconstitute the site's formal characteristics and to dig up the few remains of that historical period. The new gardens of Venaria Reale reconstruct the perspectives, proportions, sizes, and elements—even the vegetal ones—of the eighteenth-century arrangement in the French style and mix them with traces from the seventeenth-century arrangement in the Italian style; they also introduce some new elements, such as the fishpond, that had been planned but were never built. The introduction of contemporary elements and materials (for example, furniture) does not make it evident that this is, in fact, a contemporary garden or an interpretation of the past as seen through the lens of the present. This reconstruction has been quite effective in generating mass appeal and tourism,[29] but it has been questionable, at the very least, in not promoting an awareness of the irreversibility of historical dynamics. Such an awareness is useful in dealing with gardens—and, even more broadly, it is useful in encouraging people to be more responsible when facing contemporary territorial and landscape choices.[30]

The rebuilt garden at Venaria Reale has been read mainly as an "architectural and vegetal composition," whose constituents "are defined by their formal qualities" rather than their material ones. It has been read as a testimony to a culture, style, and age, as well as to "the originality of a creative artist" ("Italian Charter of Historic Gardens," Articles 1 and 5). The primary goal of the restoration was to convey this reading to future generations; it was not to pay attention to historical dynamics. The restoration makes clear that contemporary landscape culture—and, more generally, architectural culture—does not quite know how to carry out interventions that are respectful of past histories and yet simultaneously legible as contemporary works.

Quite a different approach to restoration was adopted at the Roman gardens in Pompeii, where historical and archaeological knowledge was wisely and appropriately used and where research outcomes were actually displayed. New vegetal elements were added to the remains of the site—for instance, a living plane tree was placed in the palaestra near the mold of a Roman plane tree's roots; some garden forms and elements, such as trellises, were rebuilt; and some reconstructions of Roman gardens, dating back to the early twentieth century and already historicized, were enhanced. At Pompeii, historical evidence and didactic effectiveness have always been the primary concerns of restorers, as indicated by the use of boards, signs, and brochures that convey technical information regarding the site's past and its restoration.[31]

A New Meaning for Fragments and Remains of Gardens and Landscapes

Today, the field of historical garden preservation and conservation faces problems that are much more evident, widespread, and even newer than those of some decades ago, and the need for a contribution from historians is deeply felt. The concept of open-ended works was meant, and still is meant, to be useful in describing gardens and landscapes. Years after its introduction, it is becoming clear that this concept was intended primarily to cover sites that have remained recognizable as historical heritage and, to a lesser extent, sites that have undergone such deep transformations as to be regarded as fragments or remains (which were much less common then than today).

We can regard as decontextualized fragments those sites that underwent such massive and diffused destructions and/or replacements—including the rebuilding of whole parts, the introduction of large functional buildings and parking lots, and the overlay of infrastructures across a site—such that only a few elements have survived. These elements are scattered across a context responding to a totally different logic, yet their spatial, visual, functional, and symbolic relationships are still apparent to those who know how to read them. This is particularly true in low-density metropolitan areas.

Sites turn into remains when their composition is oversimplified—either through the removal or nonreplacement of its elements (such as underbrush, bushes, hedges, and flower beds), or through the addition of new elements inconsistent with its historical design or its botanical character. Sites become remains because of their poor maintenance, incoherent understandings of their character, and unclear plans for their appropriate use.[32] But sites also become remains when they are subjected to exaggerated maintenance (such as renovations and additions using new materials) that is not required by functional and formal lacunae or by the material state of degradation.[33] In these cases, the site looks well groomed, yet its historical architectural qualities—its design and material—are altered; its age-value disappears, and it becomes almost impossible to determine whether the site is of ancient or recent origin.[34] But neither is the site replaced by a contemporary project of quality.

In some cases—such as in minor villa gardens that are owned by local authorities—the parts that retain a strong historical character might coexist with parts that are affected by a gross oversimplification of their formal composition, a destructive introduction of equipment, an inappropriate selection of uses, and a fragmentation resulting from maintenance methods or use. This coexistence is often due to management and upkeep problems, poorly trained staff, and insensitive users, rather than to a conscious intent to distort a site.

The concept of open-ended works should not be used to justify interventions that will inevitably upend and destroy a site's historical character. Because such interventions stem from an attitude unsympathetic to the traces of time and are only interested in displaying contemporaneity, they shun any deep relationship with the character of a site based on knowledge and respect. Nor should the concept of open-ended works be used as the theoretical justification for valuing historical gardens primarily as places of change, rather than as places charged with acknowledging and transmitting cultural heritage.[35] Such an attitude usually leads to a series of piecemeal solutions, such as substitutions, additions, and innovations, that dominate and draw attention to themselves rather than integrate with the existing features.

In all such cases, an important problem arises: How can quality be added through innovations that respect preexisting features? Adding quality requires that both conservation and innovation become integral parts of the project, resulting in the mutual enrichment of the old and the new. Contemporary designers should find here a great opportunity to display their own abilities, as many realized works have already demonstrated. Historical studies have a crucial role to play here, as more extensive and in-depth studies on modern and contemporary landscape designers and, more generally, on architects[36] would be useful in illuminating the exact nature of the relationship between preexisting features and new additions. These case studies would focus on designed interventions from the past and recent times and analyze their authors' motivations and formal solutions. The knowledge gained from these analyses would provide a stronger critical and historical support to those designers who accept the challenges of attaching new meanings to the fragments of complex landscape systems, tackling the remains that recent times have produced, carrying out additions that maintain the strong historical character of a site, and restoring quality to sites that have lost it.

In this context, research on the history of garden restoration in Italy offers an essential, yet underdeveloped, chance for critical rethinking. Such research is useful in the historical and operational fields at many levels. First, it helps in dating historical remains correctly and focuses attention on the transformations carried out at sites in past and recent restoration interventions. Second, it underscores the relative and variable character of history's critical judgments over time; this is a well-known issue that is never sufficiently emphasized. Third, it calls attention to the value of gardens as documents inherited from the past and to the importance of preserving all traces of historical events (even the most recent ones). Gardens are real and living archives. Fourth, it brings a proper philological and critical approach to the study of all periods in the history of garden art, especially those periods defined by a tendency to imitate past models—a process that inevitably reinterprets those models in the service of a new style. In this regard, an important contribution was made by Vincenzo Cazzato in *La memoria, il tempo, la storia nel giardino italiano fra '800 e '900* (1999). The publication considered formal gardens in Italy in the late nineteenth and early twentieth centuries, when leading designers and critics wished to establish, celebrate, and reproduce the "Italian-style garden" as an unmatched artistic standard. This study involved many Italian scholars and experts and led to a reassessment of the character of Italian formal gardens from the fifteenth, sixteenth, and seventeenth centuries.[37]

Conferring Meanings and Values to Sites

Starting in the twentieth century, the open and responsible participation by many communities in the reception and transformation of artifacts has been increasingly evident in many fields of theory and practice. In the case of gardens and landscapes, this tendency can be seen today in the public's active participation in the selection and management of sites. This experiment in participation was extended to the planning and management of landscapes and territories in several European countries in the late 1990s and especially after 2000—the year in which the European Landscape Convention became ready for signature in Florence.

The convention had several aims that are pertinent to these considerations, but one, in particular, should be underscored. The convention sought to improve the quality of places, whether they were regarded as outstanding, ordinary, or degraded landscapes.[38] The convention made it clear that the public's perception of a site was an indispensable foundation for any proposed alteration, and it emphasized that it was both necessary and desirable that any choice about a transformation be shared by experts, politicians, officials, and the public. Preserving landscape quality entails safeguarding the specific characteristics of a site, since a site is fundamental to the identity of the population that created it and that shares responsibility for its transformation.[39] Thus, the minimum requirement for any acceptable transformation is the consent of the community, which transmits previous interpretations through tradition and continues to incorporate new ideas, whether explicitly or not. Hence the need to circulate information and to sensitize the public to the conclusions reached by scholars and technicians in their own specialized domains. It is, indeed, well known that the dissemination of historical studies promotes a deeper collective sensitivity for individual historical entities and affects the policies aimed at protecting them.

The process through which specialists and members of the general public assign meanings and value judgments to sites is quite complex but little understood, and research on the topic has been limited. It concerns the various relationships between the new and the preexisting in light of the different meanings and values that cultural and social groups have assigned to the material and immaterial heritage of the past. These relations were brilliantly analyzed by Alois Riegl at the beginning of the twentieth century. Riegl highlighted both the distinctions and overlaps within these categories, including historical value, antiquity value, novelty value, value as memory or commemoration, topical value, artistic value, art historical value, and use or functional value.[40] His contribution was a milestone, and is still very useful for understanding the diversity of current attitudes toward cultural heritage, including the goals, opportunities, and implications of consensus as well as the reasons that misunderstandings and conflict have arisen over historical heritage as a whole—not only with regard to monuments, to which Riegl refers, but with all that has come down to us from the past. In others words, broadened public participation has lent support to the view that the whole territory or landscape is a palimpsest marked by the traces of human and natural activity. Historical studies, as well as others done from geographical philosophical, and sociological perspectives, have attempted—most recently with regard to landscape—to reconstruct the processes by which social representation is inscribed within sites and persists over time.[41] Exploring this issue would prove extremely useful in light of the operational trends that have recently emerged in European landscape policies, which are essential not only in protecting garden heritage and related landscape systems, but also in implementing transformations that use remains and fragments to realize a new landscape quality.

To conclude, we could say that conferring the value of open-ended works on gardens and landscapes is still useful, although we should by now be well aware of the limits and, simultaneously, of the potential benefits of such open-endedness. In the latter, we should not see a lack of specific character, or of those characteristics that make a work unique, incomparable, and unrepeatable and that make it a document-monument and a resource even if it is degraded or left in remains and fragments. Any inherited work has, in its present shape, its own recognizability and individuality; its inevitable transformation (which may result merely from the passage of seasons) requires guidance within certain limits if we do not want it to be instrumentalized or destroyed. The challenge for historians and conservation experts in their conceptual, methodological, and operational work is to define appropriate—and not just compatible—solutions that are capable of addressing both the open-endedness and the limits of the work we have inherited. From this point of view, gardens and landscapes are not so different one from another, and are not so different from a historical town or building.[42] Two new areas of research—on the relationship of a work and its physical context, both past and present, and on the relational system or landscape system of which the work is one element—increasingly bring together landscapes and gardens in their methodological, cognitive, and operational aspects.

Notes

Translation revised by Francesco Passanti.

1 Legge 1 giugno 1939, n. 1089 "Tutela delle cose d'interesse artistico e storico"; Legge 29 giugno 1939, n. 1497 "Protezione delle bellezze naturali"; Legge 12 giugno 1902 n. 185, on the conservation of monuments and objects of antiquity and art; and Legge 13 giugno 1912 n. 262 for the preservation of monuments, towns, and parks.

2 The Venice Preservation Charter (or International Charter for the Conservation and Restoration of Monuments and Sites) was drawn up at the Second International Congress of Architects and Technicians of Historic Monuments in Venice, 25–31 May 1964.

3 Ministero della Pubblica Istruzione, *Carta del Restauro 1972*, circular no. 117, 6 April 1972. The Ministero della Pubblica Istruzione was in charge of historic heritage preservation in 1972.

4 The Italian bibliography on this issue is vast. See Luigi Zangheri, "Il restauro dei giardini storici in Italia dal 1980," in *Bibliografia del giardino e del paesaggio italiano, 1980–2005*, eds. Lucia Tongiorgi Tomasi and Luigi Zangheri, 135–59 (Florence: L. S. Olschki, 2008). The earliest reference is still Vincenzo Cazzato, ed., *Tutela dei giardini storici: Bilanci e prospettive* (Rome: Ministero per i Beni Culturali e Ambientali, Ufficio Studi, 1989), pts. 3 and 4, which collect all prior contributions and major publications by selected Italian researchers on the protection of historic heritage. An investigation of the creation of concepts and theories for the conservation and restoration of gardens in past centuries is found in Maria Adriana Giusti, *Restauro dei giardini: Teorie e storia* (Florence: Alinea, 2004).

5 Cazzato, *Tutela dei giardini storici*, pt. 4; Lionella Scazzosi, *Il giardino opera aperta: La conservazione delle architetture vegetali* (Florence: Alinea, 1993), 26–83; Giovanni Carbonara, *Trattato di restauro architettonico*, vol. 3 (Torino: UTET, 1996); and acts of the numerous congresses that took place in Italy in the 1980s and 1990s. See Lucia Tongiorgi Tomasi and Luigi Zangheri, eds., *Bibliografia del*

giardino e del paesaggio italiano, 1980–2005 (Florence: L. S. Olschki, 2008).

6 The term "restoration" indicates here the disciplines concerned with passing on the traces of the past to future generations, with their theoretical, methodological, and operational views (restoration, conservation, and reconstruction). Cesare Brandi, *Teoria del restauro* (1963; reprint, Torino: G. Einaudi, 1977), 7. The text forms the basis of the *Carta del Restauro 1972*. See also the law for the protection of historic and landscape heritage in Italy: *Codice dei beni culturali e del paesaggio*, Decreto Legislativo 42 and subsequent modifications, Article 29.

7 See the recent Italian contribution to terminological and conceptual clarity in *Codice dei beni culturali e del paesaggio, ai sensi dell'articolo 10 della legge 6 luglio 2002, n. 137*, Decreto Legislativo 42, 22 January 2004.

8 For the English and Italian versions of the "Italian Charter of Historic Gardens" ("Carta italiana dei giardini storici"), see Laura Sabrina Pelissetti and Lionella Scazzosi, eds., *Giardini, contesto, paesaggio: Sistemi di giardini e architetture vegetali nel paesaggio* (Florence: L. S. Olschki, 2005), 1:419–21. The publication also includes the English and Italian versions of the ICOMOS-IFLA charter.

9 However, these two versions had many common views on the coherence of uses, on enhancement, didactics, necessity of a census, etc.

10 Scazzosi, *Il giardino opera aperta*.

11 *European Landscape Convention*, European Treaty Series no. 176, 20 October 2000. Most European countries have adhered to the treaty—thirty have ratified it and six have signed it out of a total of forty-seven countries. http://conventions.coe.int/Treaty/en/Treaties/World/176.doc

12 Maurizio Boriani and Lionella Scazzosi, eds., *Natura e architettura: La conservazione del patrimonio paesistico* (Milano: Clup, 1987).

13 Regione Lombardia, *Criteri per la tutela, la conservazione e l'uso delle architetture vegetali* (Milan: Regione Lombardia, 1987).

14 The congress "Giardini, Contesto, Paesaggio" was organized by the Centro di Documentazione Storica di Cinisello Balsamo and the Politecnico di Milano to examine the relationship between the garden and its context. See Pelissetti and Scazzosi, *Giardini, contesto, paesaggio*. During the last decade, both institutions have helped to organize national and international biennial meetings on the issue of gardens and landscape.

15 See Lionella Scazzosi, "Il paesaggio opera aperta: Conservare/trasformare," in *La cultura del paesaggio in Europa tra storia, arte e natura: Manuale di teoria e pratica*, eds. Pierre Donadieu, Hansjörg Küster, and Raffaele Milani, 72–97 (Florence: L. S. Olschki, 2008). See also several pertinent speeches delivered during the congresses of the Associazione per il Restauro del Paesaggio, Ambiente e Territorio (ARSPAT) and published in their proceedings by Alinea Editrice (Florence).

16 This concept was emphasized by the European Landscape Convention in its *Guidelines for the Implementation of the European Landscape Convention*, Recommendation CM/Rec(2008)3, 6 February 2008 and in its specialized workshops (whose acts are published as individual monographs by the Council of Europe).

17 On this issue, Italy has organized several meetings, promoted by the Ministero per i Beni e le Attività Culturali through the Direzione Generale per l'Architettura e l'Arte Contemporanee (DARC), and many initiatives—even within the legal field—have been set up by the regional governments (in the Emilia-Romagna region, for example).

18 This concept has been used and codified in the *Relazione paesaggistica*, an administrative instrument at the national scale, for the control of the landscape quality of proposed designs (DPCM [Decreto del Presidente del Consiglio dei Ministri], 12 December 2005), as an enforcement of the *Codice per i Beni Culturali e del Paesaggio*, Article 146, Paragraph 2. Ministero per i Beni e le Attività Culturali, *La relazione paesaggistica: Finalità e contenuti* (Rome: Gangemi, 2006).

19 Margherita Zalum, "La storia del giardino italiano: Lineamenti ed evoluzione di una giovane disciplina," in *Bibliografia del giardino e del paesaggio italiano, 1980–2005*, eds. Lucia Tongiorgi Tomasi and Luigi Zangheri, 1–14 (Florence: L. S. Olschki, 2008).

20 The major reference is still the bibliography of historical studies on Italian gardens from 1980 to 2005 edited by Tongiorgi Tomasi and Zangheri. See also Vincenzo Cazzato, *Atlante del giardino italiano, 1750–1940: Dizionario biografico di architetti, giardinieri, botanici, committenti, letterati e altri protagonisti*, 2 vols. (Rome: Istituto Poligrafico e Zecca dello Stato, Libreria dello Stato, 2009).

21 Note, in particular, the archaeological studies of gardens in ancient Rome and Pompeii. Pompeii hosted a national congress organized by the Ministero per i Beni Culturali e Ambientali on 4–6 June 1993; the congress featured a presentation of scale models of Roman gardens based on archaeological studies. See *Parchi e giardini storici, parchi letterari: Conoscenza, tutela e valorizzazione; Atti del III Convegno (primo internazionale) "paesaggi e giardini del Mediterraneo" Pompei, 4–5–6 giugno 1993*, 3 vols. (Pompeii: Ministero per i Beni Culturali e Ambientali, Comitato Nazionale per lo Studio e la Conservazione dei Giardini Storici, Soprintendenza Archeologica di Pompei, 1993).

22 James S. Ackerman, *Palladio's Villas* (Locust Valley, N.Y.: Published for the Institute of Fine Arts, New York University, by J. J. Augustin, 1967); Lionello Puppi, "The Villa Garden of the Veneto from the Fifteenth to the Eighteenth Century," in *The Italian Garden*, ed. David R. Coffin, 81–114 (Washington, D.C.: Dumbarton Oaks Research Library and Collection, 1972); and Denis Cosgrove, *The Palladian*

Landscape: Geographical Change and its Cultural Representation in Sixteenth-Century Italy (Leicester: Leicester University Press, 1993).

23 Rudolf Borchardt, *Città italiane* (Milan: Adelphi, 1989), 34 and 36.

24 Quite significant is the case of the Villa Lante at Bagnaia. The formal garden, which historians have celebrated since the early twentieth century, is protected by law, while the park, which was an integral component of the landscape system, is not. The park was the starting point of a symbolic itinerary that expressed the centuries-long relationship between humans and nature; the itinerary ended in the formal garden, which represented man's control over nature. The neglect of the park has resulted in several problems: the destruction of some vegetal components and furnishings (such as statues and fountains) that were meant to convey those relationships; the inconsistent transformations and simplifications of the layout in order to open some areas as a public park; and the didactic lacunae due to the fact that the formal garden was given preferential treatment during visits and the overall meaning of the whole complex was not addressed.

25 See the maps of the Istituto Geografico Militare, which were drawn up in the late nineteenth century, as well as the land registers with maps, which were drawn up by most Italian states during the late eighteenth century.

26 Some interesting studies have focused directly on the role of the villa, and specifically the villa-farmhouse, in restructuring the territory in the regions of the Veneto and Friuli. These studies have provided an anthology of historical texts written by owners, agronomists, literati, architects, and technicians. Francesca Venuto, ed., *Agricoltura e villa nelle campagne friulane: Possidenti, operatori e sperimentazioni colturali dall'età veneta all'annessione al Regno d'Italia* (Turin: U. Allemandi, 2004).

27 For a recent examination of the conservation of state-owned gardens, see Vincenzo Cazzato and Marina Fresa, eds., *I nostri giardini: Tutela, conservazione, valorizzazione, gestione* (Rome: Gangemi, 2005).

28 Mirella Macera, "Il restauro dei giardini della Venaria Reale," in *Oltre il giardino: Le architetture vegetali e il paesaggio*, eds. Gabriella Guerci, Laura Pelissetti, and Lionella Scazzosi, 201–5 (Florence: L. S. Olschki, 2003); and Andrea Scaringella, *Il progetto "La Venaria Reale": Cronache, protagonisti e retroscena di una storia irripetibile* (Turin: Ananke, 2007).

29 See http://www.lavenaria.it for the past and present restoration work on the buildings and gardens at Venaria Reale.

30 The intervention was made on the basis of a winning design for a competition. Other competitors drew upon current historical knowledge and highlighted the remains (e.g., trails, visual and spatial connections, etc.) of the seventeenth- and eighteenth-century gardens, using them as markers within a project whose formal traits were entirely contemporary.

31 See the numerous studies on the ancient history and restoration of the gardens of Pompeii, especially those carried out for the national congress at Pompeii, such as *Parchi e giardini storici: Conoscenza, tutela e valorizzazione*, ed. Vincenzo Cazzato (Roma: Leonardo-DeLuca, 1991).

32 In Italy this happens mainly with historic gardens that have been made public and that, being quite small, are scarcely known and celebrated. They are generally regarded as having come down to us without having retained any notable historic character. They are often open to the public.

33 For example, when paving, flower-bed edging, and furniture are renovated, they are sometimes replaced by elements made from different materials and often of a different design. The renovated elements may appear attractive because they are new and undamaged, but they no longer possess the material and formal characteristics that made them unique and rich archives of garden history. Another example is the introduction of contemporary species of flowers and shrubs in modern arrangements whose forms and colors are incongruent with the site's specific character. Other examples include meadows that are mowed or weeded too frequently. The resulting grassy areas, which are more typical of groomed golf courses, are monotonous and lack the historical layering of the diverse plant communities they replace.

34 These well-groomed sites are typically characterized by a few grand old trees, which are isolated and almost separated from what is around them, on homogeneous well-watered meadows with clear signs of machine mowing, new well-cut hedges, modern-style flower beds with big, brightly colored flowers, and shrubs scattered here and there without a clear pattern. Innovation here is not respectful of the preexisting elements. There is a strong analogy with the effects that the total renovation of plasterwork, colors, fixtures, and decorative elements has on historic buildings.

35 Géza Hajós pointed out this danger when he enumerated what he believed to be the major threats facing historic gardens today. Géza Hajós, "Three Dangers to the Theory and Practice of Historic Garden Preservation," in *Giardini storici: A 25 anni dalle Carte di Firenze; Esperienze e prospettive*, eds. Laura Sabrina Pelissetti and Lionella Scazzosi, 1:207–26 (Florence: L. S. Olschki, 2009). The issue of the garden as a place of transformation is also examined in Erik A. de Jong, Erika Schmidt, and Brigitt Sigel, eds., *Der Garten—Ein Ort des Wandels: Perspektiven für die Denkmalpflege* (Zurich: Vdf. Hochschulverlag AG an der ETH Zürich, 2006).

36 Studies of this kind on architects and landscape designers are scarce. In Italy, it would be interesting, for example, to further analyze the work of Pietro Porcinai, an internationally renowned master of landscape design.

37 For many years, these gardens were erroneously believed to have contained no flowers, in part because interpretive and design trends in the early twentieth century precluded recognizing them as elements of the formal garden.

38 "'Landscape' means an area, as perceived by people, whose character is the result of the action and interaction of natural and/or human factors" (Article 1 of the European Landscape Convention—Definitions). "Subject to the provisions contained in Article 15, this convention applies to the entire territory of the Parties and covers natural, rural, urban and peri-urban areas. It includes land, inland water and marine areas. It concerns landscapes that might be considered outstanding as well as everyday or degraded landscapes" (Article 2 of the European Landscape Convention—Scope). The landscape policies are articulated in different actions: protection, innovation, and management (Article 1), but landscape action may also be a combination of these actions on a single territory, on a single part, or on its elements. *Guidelines for the Implementation of the European Landscape Convention*, Recommendation CM/Rec(2008)3, 6 February 2008.

39 "The issue of sustainable development, long-present in international documents, is enriched by the complete and global cultural dimension, which means referring to the whole territory: adding to it also, the social perception that populations have of their place of life and the awareness of their historic and cultural diversities and specificities, that are important as regards the respect and the preservation of their own *identity*, and individual and social enrichment." Ibid.

40 This is the account of the presentation of one of the first bills of law for the preservation of monuments in Austria. Alois Riegl, *Moderne Denkmalkultus: Sein Wesen und seine Entstehung* (1903; repr. as "Il moderno culto dei monumenti, la sua essenza, il suo sviluppo," in *Scritti sulla tutela e il restauro*, ed. Giuseppe La Monica and trans. Maria Annunziata Lima and Laura Bica, 27–82 [Palermo: La Palma, 1982]).

41 Various studies by geographers (Eugenio Turri and Francesco Fariello) and philosophers (Massimo Venturi Ferriolo, Paolo d'Angelo, and Raffaele Milani) are available in Italy.

42 There is a wide debate on the problems of transformations within UNESCO sites (such as towns and single monuments) with regard to the interventions of contemporary architecture.

PART IV

Ways of Seeing the Landscape: Reconstructing Horizons of Perception and the Imaginary

CHAPTER 7

The Imaginary of Generative Nature in Italian Mannerist Gardens

ANTONELLA PIETROGRANDE

Qual è, dimmi, il tuo più riposto kēpos,
l'orto in cui divini
brillano in rari scintillii, rare ombricole
i tuoi *semplici*
che nessuno ha mai
immaginato abbastanza . . .
—Andrea Zanzotto, *Kēpos*[1]

The "Renaissance of Ancient Paganism"

CRITICAL HYPOTHESES ABOUT THE RELATIONSHIP between the female element and the garden have developed in new and stimulating ways in recent decades. Several scholars have interpreted the garden as the site of a mythology that originated in the ancient world of Mediterranean cultures and survived uninterrupted through history, bequeathing to our epoch a complex of images referring to the maternal qualities of the earth and its creative spontaneity, an inexhaustible source of fertility and life.

Relying on a number of essays that offer an in-depth analysis of the main currents of Renaissance and Mannerist intellectual life, I hope to show that the Mediterranean mythic imagination appeared in sixteenth-century Italian gardens, which were shaped by the antiquarian tastes of the epoch, by a new conception of space, and by an idea of nature that was significantly different from that of the Middle Ages. The first part of this essay will focus on the growing interest of the Renaissance world in the Great Mother, while the second part will survey a number of the early twentieth-century studies in the history of religion (which have influenced the critical approaches of the last twenty years on which my thesis relies) and will stress some of the discontinuities between these recent theoretical approaches and earlier ones. The third part will show how a renewed focus on the Great Mother and "creative nature" represents an original contribution of the most recent scholarship that is capable of offering a different interpretation of Italian Mannerist gardens.

My analysis simultaneously presents two theses based in different theoretical approaches—to my mind, they are not opposed but complementary. The first thesis accounts for the presence in sixteenth-century Italian gardens of the ancient Mediterranean mythical undercurrent of pre-Olympian female deities, who are characterized by their knowledge and use of plants and their status as mistresses of the animal world. This set of deities is still seen within a theoretical perspective that interprets the garden as a system of signs. The second thesis, more radical and innovative, does not question but surpasses the method of iconological analysis of past studies; it invites us to consider the garden as a horizon of perception and understanding characterized by a mythic and emotional substratum and as a privileged site in which it is possible to reestablish the relationships between nature and history that have shaped the landscape. This is a fresh theoretical vision that could generate new fields of inquiry and a transformation of the main issues concerning the history of the garden.

I begin with the historical studies of Jacob Burckhardt, Aby Warburg, André Chastel, Michel Foucault, Eugenio Garin, and Carlo Ossola, which allow us to penetrate the close intellectual network and exchanges between the history of culture and the gardens of the Renaissance and Mannerist eras. My goal is to bring to light the cultural underworld that inspired artists to create, for their clients and the inner circles who gathered around them, gardens that were symbols of ancient civilization.

In his study of the relationship between Renaissance culture and classical antiquity, the philosopher Paul Oskar Kristeller pointed out that classical studies occupied a central place during the Renaissance, as had never happened in the prior history of Western Europe.[2] In his book *Futuro del "classico"* (2004), the art historian Salvatore Settis talked about a cyclical return or a renaissance of the "classic" as "not only an essential, but also a unique distinctive trait" of European cultural history. This preoccupation with classicism became a norm only during the Renaissance. Italian artists found a large repository of new expressive models and formulas in ancient ruins, especially those of Rome. Their desire to appropriate the visual lexicon of antiquity generated a growing interest in sculptures, marbles, and excavation materials that gave birth to antiquarian collecting.[3]

In the section "Le dimore degli dei e la rinascita dell'antico nel giardino umanistico-rinascimentale" of his essay "Picta poësis: Ricerche sulla poesia e il giardino dalle origini al Seicento" (1982), Gianni Venturi showed that Vaucluse, Francesco Petrarca's *locus amoenus* par excellence, marked the beginning of a mythic-rhetorical elaboration—which continued throughout the whole poetic humanistic tradition—of an ideal landscape codified by classical antiquity, whose most illustrious representatives are Theocritus and Virgil: "The garden loses its religious and edenic traits in order to become the residence of gods, a mythological place, a replica and a double of the *saturnia regna* that renew the celebration of the power of *antiquitas* over the present."[4]

Humanists, inspired by the ancient *auctores*, carried out a profound reflection on the mysterious forces of nature and on its incessant creative *vis*. In the sixteenth century, erudition fostered a return to the ancient sense of nature, which was inhabited by godly presences that manifested themselves in plants, animals, and water. In this respect—to quote the title of the famous collection of essays by Warburg—we can talk about the "renaissance of ancient paganism" through the reappearance of gods and especially goddesses, nymphs, and naiads, although this impulse is more precisely a Neoplatonic paganism, which had characterized the Italian Renaissance since Marsilio Ficino (1433–99).[5]

Eugenio Battisti investigated the dark side of the Renaissance, in a sharply provocative way, in *L'antirinascimento* (1989). For example, he regarded witchcraft as a tribute, no matter how distorted, to women, discussing it as something that concerned women almost exclusively. In his estimation, we are able to enter the core of the Neoplatonic theme of magic through sixteenth-century paintings of sorceresses, such as *Circe* (Galleria Borghese, Rome) and *Alcina* (National Gallery of Art, Washington, D.C.) by the Ferrarese painter Dosso Dossi (ca. 1486–1542). According to Battisti, Dossi painted the two sorceresses as demigoddesses, or queens of the universe, transforming them into symbols of love, a love beyond passion, which brought peace to the earth and to all beings. Battisti explained this special feature of sixteenth-century painting by saying that "the Renaissance feels in an exceptional way, even more than the too mystical Gothic, the feminine side, which regenerates in an orderly way, and moreover faithfully preserves society and the world. Almost all the ancient goddesses, such as Venus, Diana, and Cybele, are now immersed in the wider, more lyrical, and Arcadian natural context, almost as a promise of a regained earthly paradise."[6]

Providing a personal interpretation of the sixteenth-century conception of nature, Michel Foucault asserted that during that era erudition and magic were placed on the same level. Consequently, esoteric practices of magic and the body of knowledge rediscovered from antiquity were viewed with equal appreciation.[7] Building on these observations, one can add that, in sixteenth-century culture, the role of the feminine element was particularly strong, especially thanks to its connections to the figure of the sorceress, an expert in the secrets of nature and in the healing properties of the "simples," or the miraculous herbs, that were the sources of its power. We find evidence of this link in the painting and literature of the Renaissance, in which there is a clear connection between the Mediterranean Great Mother, an expert in the *pharmaka* (cures and poisons) and in an all-feminine pharmacopoeia drawn from nature, and the sorceresses-enchantresses of literature, the mistresses of splendid gardens. In the sixth canto of *Orlando furioso*, the poet Ludovico Ariosto outlined the enchanting powers of Alcina and her garden paradise, where, thanks to magic, it was always springtime. Similarly, in the famous octaves of the sixteenth canto of *La Gerusalemme liberata*, Torquato Tasso described Armida's magic arts as connected to her mazelike garden and as capable of diverting the hero Rinaldo from the enterprise of conquering Jerusalem.

In his volume *Le voile d'Isis: Essai sur l'histoire de l'idée de nature* (2004), Pierre Hadot retraced the history of the idea of nature from ancient times to the modern age. Following the tracks of Isis, a personification of nature who is identified with Artemis of Ephesus in iconography and literature, Hadot demonstrated the strong persistence of representations and images first conceived in ancient Greece. Yet he pointed out that the allegory of the Great Mother reappeared in painting and sculpture precisely at the beginning of the sixteenth century. As Hadot wrote, in the sixteenth century "nature is represented . . . according to the ancient model of Artemis of Ephesus, that is to say in the form of a female figure with a veiled and crowned head, with many breasts, and with the lower part of her body wrapped in a sheath dress on which various animals are visible. Numerous ancient statues bear testimony to this traditional representation of Artemis of Ephesus" (fig. 7.1).[8] To support this statement, the author reminded us that Raphael painted two Artemis figures representing nature on the arms of the throne on which Philosophy was seated in his 1508 fresco in the Room of the Signature in the Vatican Palace. The same model, as he pointed out, reappeared in Niccolò Tribolo's 1529 statue *Nature* (Château de Fontainebleau), where there are several animals attached to the goddess's breasts.[9] Commenting on this sculpture in

FIGURE 7.1. Statue of Artemis of Ephesus, Roman copy of a Hellenistic original of the second century BC., Capitoline Museum, Rome.

her article "Niccolò Tribolo e la Grotta degli Animali a Castello," Isabella Lapi Ballerini wrote that "the tangle of creatures" in the grotto at the Medici villa at Castello recalls "that animistic vitality of nature that Tribolo had already expressed in the *Allegory* of Fontainebleau."[10]

Hadot also signaled that "in the sixteenth century, in the iconography handbook *Le immagini degli dei* (1556), Vincenzo Cartari quotes . . . Macrobius in order to demonstrate that the ancients liked to represent Nature with the traits of Isis-Artemis. He stresses the fact that a statue of the same kind had been found in Rome, adding that he himself had seen a similar image on a medal of the emperor Hadrian."[11] In his analysis, Hadot mentioned that mythology handbooks with allegorical interpretations of pagan myths and deities, as well as books of emblems and collections of symbolic drawings, began to circulate in the Renaissance. For example, Artemis of Ephesus appeared in the *Emblemata* (1564) by Johannes Sambucus.[12]

At this point, in order to maintain a correct critical distance from scholarly interpretations of the sixteenth century, it must be pointed out that some contemporary archaeologists do not regard the protuberances on the torso of Artemis of Ephesus as breasts, but rather as the testicles of the bulls that were sacrificed on the altars of her temples. According to yet another theory, the testicles belonged to priests-eunuchs, who offered them to their goddess after being castrated as an extreme sacrifice in her honor. In all three hypotheses, there is a crucial reference to the idea of fertility, which seems to have particularly captured the imagination of the Renaissance artists who represented the Great Mother.

The Mediterranean School and the Great Mother

Artemis (who was often identified with the Anatolian goddess Cybele) can be traced back to a single Great Mother of Mediterranean origin; she is the mistress of the *kepos*, the secret garden where miraculous plants grow, often hidden in the middle of a forest or an island that serves to protect the sacred enclosure. The first function of the kepos, which generates life, is to grow pharmaka, which bring fertility, health, and eternal youth. Artemis, the prototype of the goddess-sorceress, keeps the *Artemisia*—that is, the *mater herbarum* that heals all the illnesses of women and children—in her garden.[13]

According to Massimo Venturi Ferriolo's research, the archetypal idea of the garden originated in the kepos. Venturi Ferriolo considered the earthly paradise of Eden—regarded by Christian tradition as a model of perfect nature to which man aspired to return—to be only one of the symbolic images associated with the garden. In his volume *Nel grembo della vita: Le origini dell'idea di giardino* (1989), he framed the question of the female presence in the garden in a philosophical and aesthetic context and reconsidered the interpretation of the garden as a symbol of Eden by Rosario Assunto, who maintained that in the well-known description in Genesis (2:8–9) it is possible to find everything people have always looked for in the garden.[14]

In order to broaden and refine the theory that regards the Genesis description as the reference point for the interpretation of the idea of the garden, Venturi Ferriolo followed, on the one hand, the groundbreaking work of Uberto Pestalozza, the first Italian professor of the history of religions and close colleague of the most prominent European scholars of the time (including Mircea Eliade),[15] and, on the other hand, the more recent research of the Belgian philosopher André Motte, who explored the role played by gardens and vegetation in Greek religion and thought in *Prairies et jardins de la Grèce antique: De la religion à la philosophie* (1973).

Pestalozza began his historical and religious research by focusing on the interpretation of pre–Indo-European Mediterranean religion, which arose in the neolithic period and had agricultural and matriarchal characteristics revolving around the cult of the Great Mother. Following the Homeric usage, he referred to the Great Mother as Potnia, and recognized her as the powerful mistress of the human, animal, and vegetal worlds and as a symbol of the "garden-woman." He was interested in the religious cultures and traditions of the ancient Near East, in which female deities—who manifested themselves in the rebirth of the earth, in the wombs of wild animals and women, and in the mountain caves and spring waters—were simultaneously goddesses, sorceresses, and women, endowed with the feminine power to give life and nourishment. Through a comparative and diachronic method, Pestalozza evoked the matriarchal era of the ancient Mediterranean world, which had already been investigated in the nineteenth century by the Swiss anthropologist Johann Jakob Bachofen and would later be corroborated by the Lithuanian archaeologist Marija Gimbutas.[16] Pestalozza was the founder of the so-called Milanese Mediterranean school, whose members included his disciples Mario Untersteiner and Momolina Marconi. In one of her essays, Marconi compared the archaeological finds in Hera's sanctuary at the mouth of the Sele River in Campania—a place of pilgrimage where women asked the goddess to protect them in childbirth and their children—with similar artifacts from other Mediterranean locations. The site contained a great many fictile votive offerings, including doves, pomegranates, apples, figs, almonds, and lilies, all of which referred to the sexual sphere. Marconi stressed the similarities between the Hera adored on the Sele River and Lêtô, the Aegean-Anatolian goddess—studied by Pestalozza[17]—who, like Hera, enjoyed being in the woods and in moist plains near water.[18]

The archaeologist Giovanni Patroni and the linguists Benvenuto Terracini, Vittorio Bertoldi, Piero Meriggi, and Vittore Pisani also belonged to the Milanese Mediterranean school.[19] In his *Commenti mediterranei all'Odissea di Omero* (1950), Patroni explained that the pre-Hellenic Potnia was the product of a series of elaborations, in which human reason and fantasy acted together. The world, that is to say Nature, was conceived as a female—as a mother and nourisher.[20] In this archaeologist's opinion, Homer was infused with a Mediterranean religious sensibility, as evidenced by Calypso, who lived on the island of Ogygia, a natural, violet-scented garden rich in spring waters that was as beautiful as a paradise, and Circe, who lived on the wooded island of Aeaea in a mysterious garden full of herbs (all of whose secret and prodigious properties she knew and used).[21] Both goddesses bore traces of the pre-Hellenic Potnia, upon whom the Minoan-Mediterranean theology was founded. The presence of the Great Mother was not erased by the arrival of Indo-European peoples in Greece, as the dominated peoples maintained strong religious beliefs; it was instead absorbed by the Achaean-Minoan religious reforms, although Zeus's accession to Olympus decreed the supremacy of the patrilineal system.

In this context, André Motte organized his research around two themes religion and philosophy. He demonstrated the existence of a pre-Hellenic religious legacy, with matriarchal and chthonian (of the underworld) features, in classical Greek religion, and the continuity between religious and philosophical thought in Greece. The author analyzed religious practices (with their worship rites and mythic expressions) and then compared them with philosophical literature. What emerged was a poetic and religious sentiment of nature that was peculiar to Greece, where humankind felt closely tied to its natural surroundings. Greeks were accustomed to communicating religiously with nature—for them, the perception of natural beauty spontaneously bordered on the sense of the divine. Motte examined the great goddesses of the Greek pantheon—Artemis, Hera, Demeter, Persephone, and Aphrodite—and pointed out that they bore many traces of Potnia's sovereignty over the vegetal, animal, and human worlds. Minor deities—such as the nymphs who governed childbirth, the muses who helped the memories of poets return to their origins, the charities who were Aphrodite's companions and the goddesses of grace and serene life, and the hours who were the symbols of beautiful spring days and the virtues generated by the earth—prolonged and multiplied the image of the Great Mother.[22]

Potnia's vital potency, which was identified with that of fecund nature, manifested itself in fertile places through a broad range of epiphanies. For this reason, Motte focused his studies of literary and philosophical works on the crucial images of the moist prairie (made luxuriant by the presence of water) and of the garden, which were found especially in the writings of Homer.[23] These images present microcosms that reveal a divine capacity to generate and nourish life, as well as archetypes that recurred in several cultures in the Mediterranean area. Focusing on the strong sentiment of the Great Mother, the eternal feminine in *De rerum natura*, and the important role of Venus in the poetry of Lucretius, Motte quoted Pestalozza, according to whom Lucretius "brings to life again, one thousand years after the victory achieved by patriarchal gods, the figure at the same time one and multiple, of the pre-Greek Potnia,"[24] which proves that Mediterranean religiousness also permeated the Roman world.[25]

Motte regarded the ancient feasts and rituals that were celebrated in gardens as sacred gestures meant to revive primordial divine actions. In the essay "Jardins et métaphysiques de l'eau," Michel Conan shared with Motte the idea that the urban feasts in classical Greece perpetuated the imaginary substratum of the Great Mother cults that had not ceased to animate the countryside. These feasts were "representations of the world [that] seem to us completely alien, irrational, and implausible. And yet a portion of the imaginary they shelter is preserved for us in the familiar images of grottoes, nymphs and fountains in the gardens."[26]

To account for the persistence of ancient religious themes in the modern age, Motte focused on Francesco Colonna's *Hypnerotomachia Poliphili*, published in Venice by Aldo Manuzio in 1499. The *Hypnerotomachia Poliphili*, one of the most well-known works of humanism, was infused with classical culture and characterized by an elaborate symbolism. Because it was the home of Venus—the woman par excellence and the goddess of love—and possessed a lush vegetation and a circular geometry referring to the cosmic symbolism of the center (or the point where the earth and sky meet), the garden of Cythera, where Poliphilus ultimately arrived, was regarded by Motte as the most perfect image of the love union (fig. 7.2).[27]

Neoplatonic Florentine culture in the fifteenth century also regarded the garden as the house of

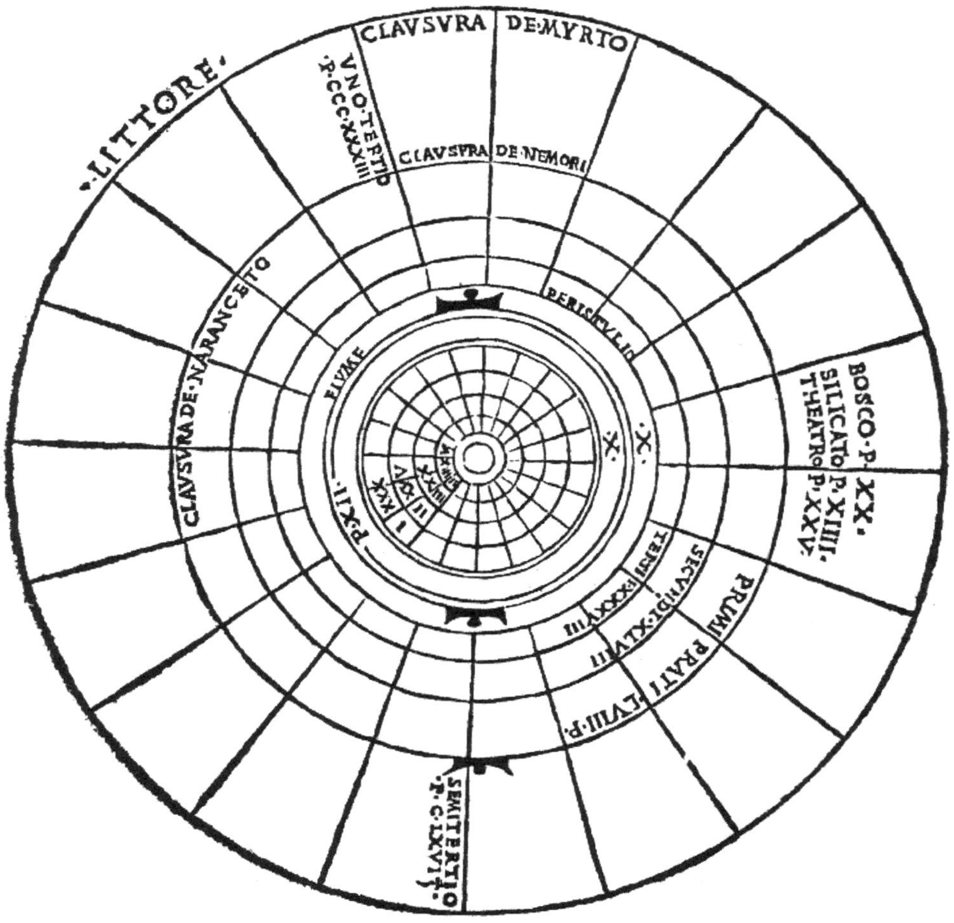

FIGURE 7.2.
The island of Cythera, from Francesco Colonna, *Hypnerotomachia Poliphili* (Venice: Aldus Manutius, 1499).

Venus and as the temple of poetry. The goddess of love—who, in the allegories of Ficino's circle, was associated with water, flowers, and springtime—was at the center of the *descriptio* in the literary gardens of this epoch, in which she preserved her ancient Mediterranean origin. For instance, in the *Stanze* by Angelo Poliziano (1454–94), the residence of Venus was situated in an island garden in Cyprus, upon a green and remote hill, surrounded by an idyllic natural landscape.[28] But the kepos of the goddess had lost its officinal properties; its meadows, in which medicinal herbs no longer grew, were instead characterized by a chromatic progression (from white to blue, yellow, and red) that only involved a mythological enumeration of flowers. Poliziano's Venus no longer grew the pharmaka, but she was still the mistress of plants and beasts—she thus preserved her Potnia-like attributes. In her eternal garden, animals fought for love as if jousting, and even the meekest ones followed the call of Eros without fear of being assaulted.

The Imaginary of Creative Nature

Unlike Pestalozza and the Milanese Mediterranean school, who researched the history of myths but did not investigate the garden culture of the Italian Renaissance, and unlike Motte, who cited the *Hypnerotomachia Poliphili*, Venturi Ferriolo gave a fresh interpretation of the Villa d'Este at Tivoli in his volume *Etiche del paesaggio: Il progetto del mondo umano* (2002). Coming on the heels of the (by now) historical reading of David R. Coffin, he argued that the villa was the result of an intellectual alliance between a cultured client, Cardinal Ippolito II d'Este, and an antiquarian architect, Pirro Ligorio.[29]

Starting from an iconological perspective, which considered myths as signs to be deciphered, Coffin identified in the gardens of the Villa d'Este the theme of the moral choice made by Hercules between vice (represented by the Grotto of Venus) and virtue (associated with the Grotto of Diana). Marcello Fagiolo, on the other hand, stressed that the Grotto of Venus, given its position and its significance, was not to be identified with lust, but rather with the Venus of generation.[30]

According to Coffin, the client (a second Hercules) and the privileged visitors to the gardens were faced with an ethical dilemma. In his article "Métaphore paysagère et métamorphose du temps" (2003), which took Coffin's study as a point of departure, Michel Conan introduced instead an analytical method based on the concept of space, through which we normally order our impressions of the visible world. It was an attempt to understand stylistic differences as responses to psychological needs. He observed that this conception of the garden, which was centered on the relationship between vice and virtue, generated, in the structure of the site, a new spatial device, that is to say, a T-shaped crossroads that had a strong visual pull toward the left (the northeast). The device oriented the choice of numerous visitors and engaged them as actors in the representation of a mythic story that they knew very well—that of Hercules, who opted for virtue and chastity and thus achieved immortality. By exploring the garden and trying to make sense of his discovery, the visitor would understand that Cardinal d'Este had to be compared with Hercules.[31]

Venturi Ferriolo did not refer to Coffin's interpretation; instead, he built on the studies by Maria Luisa Madonna and Marcello Fagiolo that opened the way to the perception of the various revelations of the Great Mother in the garden of the Villa d'Este. He identified in the spatial disposition of the site the ambiguity typical of the Renaissance; this ambiguity reversed the spiritual canons of the landscape: the original monastery, a place of inner peace, which was situated on a hill and detached from worldly matters and from nature itself (which was seen negatively), was transformed by Cardinal d'Este into a villa, "a terrace overlooking the world where the relationship garden-landscape and the idea of nature become important."[32] He interpreted the uphill walk to the palace, from the bottom upward through the entire garden,[33] as a "way towards the discovery of the landscape, in search of the revelation of nature."[34] According to Venturi Ferriolo, the structure of this admirable garden landscape—by virtue of its relation with the site (i.e., Tivoli and the valley overlooking Rome) and the capacity of art "to lend eloquence to matter"[35]—kept alive "the reading of the world that precedes philosophy,"[36] that is, the lost world of mythology and the memory of nature living in ancient cosmologies.

In the Villa d'Este, over which Ovid's *Metamorphoses* cast their long shadow, "we find the home of the Great Goddess, recognizable in its multiform individuality, Nature, alternately in the form of Artemis/Diana, Aphrodite/Venus, Mater Matuta/Sibyl Albunea, and the *nympha loci*, the sleeper in her lair: the Tiburtine landscape. Ovid's verses refer to a tradition of nature that comes from afar, from the ancient Mediterranean world, and which Lucas Cranach the Elder had painted only a few decades before, drawing on Dürer and Giorgione, with the following engraving: *Fontis nympha sacri somnum / ne rumpe quiesco* (I, Nymph of the sacred spring, disturb not my sleep, I am resting)."[37]

The various manifestations of the nature goddess that can be perceived in the landscape have been deciphered and transferred to the garden, thereby reconciling the past and its cultural memory. Thanks to the antiquarian knowledge of Pirro Ligorio and the learned milieu of the cardinal's court, the garden of the Villa d'Este became a horizon of perception and comprehension of the surrounding landscape. A series of fountains staged the Tiburtine territory and its ancient myths, beginning with those of the Sibyl Albunea and the various manifestations of the Great Mother. According to Ligorio's symbolic program, the Sibyl Albunea was the reincarnation of the Greek goddess Ino/Leucothea, who in Rome was called Mater Matuta (mother of waters and nature).[38] Given her capacity to predict the future, the Sibyl Albunea, to whom a wood and fountain in the forest where she gave responses were consecrated, was venerated as the Tiburtine Sibyl and a temple was dedicated to her in Tivoli.[39]

The real *genius loci* of Tivoli, the Sibyl Albunea in the garden of the Villa d'Este, was placed at the center of the Fountain of Tivoli, or Oval Fountain, which symbolizes the local waters and the Tiburtine mountains.[40] From here, through an underground maze of dark caverns, the visitor could penetrate the hidden secrets of nature. The figure of the Sibyl Albunea—who, as Mater Matuta, was associated with nutrition—was related to that of Artemis of Ephesus and the multibreasted Potnia of animals

FIGURE 7.3. Fountain of the Organ at the Villa d'Este at Tivoli.

and plants, whose sculpture was originally located in a dominant position above the Fountain of the Deluge, also known as the Fountain of the Organ, which included a waterfall that symbolized nature's vital potency (figs. 7.3 and 7.4).[41]

The Sibyl Albunea was also associated with the meaning of nourishment and with the soul of the world, which Ligorio attributed to water, an essential feature of this garden.[42] The elements of fertilization and nourishment, which were associated with the maternal component of water, were strictly related to the figure of Venus as generative nature, who created the elements to which, as has been seen, a grotto in the garden was dedicated.

According to Venturi Ferriolo, the Sleeping Venus or *nympha loci*, which was situated in the court of the Villa d'Este at the end of the upward path, was a figure of crucial importance in the reading of the site, as her position on the villa's main axis confirmed. The theme of the "sleeping woman" that reemerged in the Villa d'Este was very ancient; its tradition went back to the prehistoric sanctuaries of the Great Mother on the archipelago of Malta, where, among the votive gifts offered to this goddess of fertility, were two terracotta figures of sleeping women. Diodoro Siculo, Pausania, and Strabo also referred to the "sleeping woman," as healing sleep was a characteristic of the temples of Aesculapius (god of medicine), whose patients slept in the sacred enclosure.[43]

Venturi Ferriolo stressed that the sleep and quietness that characterized the Sleeping Venus were the "metaphor[s] of a culture represented by the Tiburtine landscape, the symbol of the ancient world with its images that are not to be revealed outside, to the profane. Silence is commanded: the veil is not to be lifted."[44] The Tiburtine landscape concealed its goddess: "the image of Diana [Artemis] of Ephesus, located in the background of the landscape, can also be seen in the hall of the sages and philosophers of the palace, which not only suggests a continuity between inner and outer space, but also prompts the viewer to seek outside the solution to her mysteries."[45]

Through his new theoretical approach toward the sixteenth-century garden of the Villa d'Este, which reflected the Tiburtine landscape as the place of Potnia's epiphany, Venturi Ferriolo demonstrated the originality of the "renaissance of ancient paganism" in Italian Renaissance culture. Thanks to the new imagination of the epoch, artists penetrated nature and restored the presence of the goddess in that landscape.[46] This was a new interpretation of the site, and could be considered to be the result of two of Venturi Ferriolo's converging interests. On the one hand, he explored in depth the origins of the idea of the garden, going beyond Eden, which had been the principal focus of previous studies, and emphasizing Nature and the Great Mother, who were closely connected to the processes of knowledge, intelligence, and creativity, and from whom Western philosophical culture had progressively distanced itself since the end of the pagan world. On the other hand, Venturi Ferriolo devoted his twenty-year research career to the concept of landscape; he

FIGURE 7.4. Fountain of Artemis of Ephesus at the Villa d'Este at Tivoli.

Photograph by Yair Haklai. Wikimedia Commons; GNU Free Documentation License.

focused on landscape as a nature altered by humans throughout the course of history, as a creation that expressed the main features and worldview of a people, and as a reality in which past and present coexisted, dwelling on ancient landscapes and their relationships with the sacred and on the connections between landscape and myth. Some of these concepts developed the arguments of Rosario Assunto, with whom Venturi Ferriolo had an intense and fruitful dialogue, but from whom, as we have seen, he sometimes dissociated himself.[47]

Reviving the custom of classical philosophers and authors, the early humanists (both clients and artists) turned the garden, which was decorated with ancient statues, into a privileged place for study and scholarly conversation. The Mannerist garden widened this sculptural layout, and exhibited mythological figurations that—using the language of allegory and drawing inspiration especially from Ovid's *Metamorphoses*—told the story of the birth and evolution of the landscape mainly in a feminine key. There one found the entire repertoire that was part and parcel of the symbolical narration of the most important Italian gardens of the time, such as the Villa Lante at Bagnaia (fig. 7.5), the Villa d'Este at Tivoli, the villas at Castello, Boboli, and Pratolino in Florence, and the Sacred Wood at Bomarzo in Viterbo.

In order to host the different phases of the mythological narrative conveyed by statuary, the space of the Mannerist garden obfuscated the clarity of the geometric and perspectival norms of the early Renaissance—symbols of the harmony of the cosmic order—to become a scenic form or a place of spectacle designed to excite wonder. Its path unraveled through a variety of episodes bearing witness to the different places and times that the visitor was expected to decipher by means of an experience that was not only physical and mental but also emotional.

The return to the sacredness of nature as the Great Mother and to the symbolization of its forces may also be found in the reinvention of some

FIGURE 7.5. Fountain of Pegasus and the Muses at the Villa Lante at Bagnaia.

Photograph by Tom Toft. Wikimedia Commons; GNU Free Documentation License.

FIGURE 7.6.
Medici villa at Poggio a Caiano, Florence.

Photograph by Niccolò Rigacci. Wikimedia Commons; GNU Free Documentation License.

Renaissance forms, which are constantly mediated by classical models. An example of a reinvented form is the grotto. Current scholarly interest in sixteenth-century grottoes and nymphaeums is attested by an international conference on the subject held in Florence and Lucca in 1998; the conference proceedings were published in *Artifici d'acque e giardini: La cultura delle grotte e dei ninfei in Italia e in Europa* (1999) and *Atlante delle grotte e dei ninfei in Italia*, vol. 2, *Italia settentrionale, Umbria e Marche* (2002).[48]

The frieze in the entrance hall of the Medici villa at Poggio a Caiano—a prototype of the humanistic aristocratic residence commissioned by Lorenzo de'Medici and used as dwelling of the *otium philosophicum* of the Neoplatonic Academy—shows a dark rock with a cave. At the center of the cave is a goddess-mother, a symbol of life-giving nature. Ernst Robert Curtius has pointed out that—through the Roman poet Claudius Claudianus, whose late antique theological conception still revolved around the Great Mother—Potnia spread her roots from the ancient Mediterranean world into the medieval consciousness and into the Florentine Neoplatonic culture of the Renaissance (fig. 7.6).[49]

The cavern—or the creative cave connected to the intimate depths of the earth—was the residence and the primitive temple of the Great Mother, understood as Nature in the full sense of cosmic power: there she hid the secrets of matter and expressed her infinite generative capacity. Cybele bore the designation of "empress of the cavern" in her very name.[50] An archetype of the maternal womb that was circumfused with sacred terror, the grotto was the center of initiation rituals and myths in Greco-Roman mystery cults. By recovering the grotto, which was identified with nature itself, humanistic Renaissance culture may also have performed its *regressus ad uterum*, in Eliade's sense of the word, as an initiatory journey through a microcosm that contains the primeval secrets of matter.[51]

The widespread presence of grottoes in Mannerist gardens indicates the supersession of the conception of nature as a stable system subjected to a single rational law that had been elaborated in the early Renaissance. Darker, more unstable aspects of the Mannerist period were studied in a highly provocative way by Eugenio Battisti in *L'antirinascimento*, a work to which I have already referred, and in essays more specifically dedicated to this topic that are now collected in his *Iconologia ed ecologia del giardino e del paesaggio* (2004). Thanks to its capacity to plunge into the heart itself of geological life, the grotto can be considered the emblem of one of the most frequent themes of Mannerist aesthetics: the interpenetration of art and nature. Artists imitate and emulate the organic world as if competing with it. The volcanic tuff walls of the cave give the visitor the impression of being underneath the earth's crust. Inside these caverns—as is the case with the last room of the Grotta Grande at the Boboli Gardens, created by Bernardo Buontalenti, which was regarded by Fagiolo as "the symbolic form of the artificial universe of the garden"[52]—it is possible to find the cosmic Venus, the primeval source par excellence, created by Giambologna; or, as is the case with Pratolino, it is possible to find hydraulic automata whose voices amplify the sacral effect of these dark places; or, as is the case with Castello, it is possible to find the bestiary of animals of the original creation. Therefore, it is possible to say that sixteenth-century artists—through a dynamic and creative relationship with the ancient world, rather than by means of a mere archaeological recovery—retrieved the signs of a lost world and engaged in an original interpretation of the myth of the Great Mother.

Luigi Zangheri explored the imaginary world of creative nature—the truly distinctive feature of the Mannerist garden—in *Pratolino, il giardino delle meraviglie* (1979). What emerged from his study was that the Grand Duke of Tuscany, Francesco I de'Medici, and his artists penetrated the secrets of nature by means of art, science, and technology, thus creating a fantastic world that emulated life through the mechanical wonders of hydraulic automata, grottoes, water gushing from rocks, and water jets that, in their variety, imitated meteorological phenomena.

In *Spazio e allegoria nel giardino manierista: Problemi di estetica* (1991), Fausto Testa interpreted the idea of nature, as expressed by Mannerist culture in the second half of the sixteenth century, as an "infinite germinal womb . . . the uncontested realm of metamorphosis."[53] He attributed this idea to a Neoplatonic doctrine that identified the cosmos with a large animal, which was the image of nature as a living whole in perpetual movement. The garden became an intricate labyrinth of messages and paths that no longer coincided with the image of Eden. Exploring the genetic aspect of the grotto as the "germinal repository of the earth,"[54] Testa defined it as the "fecund womb of metamorphic nature."[55]

Testa's work was referred to by Hervé Brunon in "Les mouvements de l'âme: Émotion et poétique du jardin maniériste"; in this essay, by examining the sequence of conflicting emotions that were typical of the path of the Mannerist garden, Brunon attributed to nature, as it was perceived by artists and clients of the epoch, the defining features of the Great Mother. He asserted that the Mannerist garden comprised the entire imaginary of nature—in other words, all that was good, dreadful, mysterious, and beautiful.[56]

Recent research on the figure of the Great Mother and on an array of great and small goddesses, initiators, and protectors of life has identified within Renaissance culture an original reinterpretation of these Mediterranean archetypes. The feminine element, which was connected to the creative power of the earth and to the magical arts, can be found in the sixteenth century in various artistic forms, from painting to poetry and from sculpture to gardens. Renaissance artists rediscovered the forms, imagination, and knowledge of the ancients, and they renewed and inserted them in the context of their epoch.

It is well known that the diffusion of the idea of creative nature—the outcome of the sixteenth-century "renaissance" of the ancient world—represented one of the major breaks between the medieval world and the modern age. In this respect, it is appropriate to insist on the originality of the studies that have been discussed. Unlike previous accounts of Renaissance history, which were mainly centered on the metaphorical use of the ancient world, these critical works recognized the originality of the Renaissance in representing ancient myths in an innovative way. This originality was due to the ability of sixteenth-century architects and clients to create gardens that were capable of restoring the presence of the deity and the sacred sense of nature.

I believe that the critical approaches discussed here may open the way to future theoretical interpretations not only applicable to sixteenth-century Italian gardens, but also to other historical gardens, thus bringing about an expansion of the issues that have been central to the field so far. For example, the iconological method of Coffin and his followers, which posited the garden as a system of signs to be intellectually deciphered against the background of universal nature, is not questioned, but rather surpassed by the new approaches, which embrace a conception of the garden as a horizon of perception and comprehension. As I have shown, the garden is considered to be a site of a reading of the world, and as a source of enlightenment capable of disclosing, beyond rationality, the imaginary of the landscape and its mythic and emotional substratum. The garden does not reveal precise meanings, but rather invites the production of meaning; it establishes a contact between visitors and nature by suggesting to them the *texture poétique*—that is, the complex of cultural, social, and mental contents that underlies its creation.[57]

But the perceptual horizon of gardens depends on their context, which obviously changes according to historical periods and the subjects involved. This new theoretical perspective might open up new directions of research: on the one hand, toward the horizon of perception, the mythical complex and memory of the world preserved in gardens and landscapes, and the relationships established between the creators of gardens and the genius loci; and, on the other hand, toward the transformations in the significance of the garden and its ornaments, in the patterns of behavior practiced there, and in the emotions and imaginations it has been able to generate.

Acknowledgments

An early and partial version of this essay, with the title "Il mito della Grande Madre e il giardino italiano del Cinquecento," was presented at the international conference *Giardini storici: A 25 anni dalle Carte di Firenze; Esperienze e prospettive* (Cinisello Balsamo, Milan, 9–11 November 2006), whose proceedings were published under the same title in Florence in 2009. This text is partially the result of the conversations I had with Michel Conan while writing it. I thank him very much for the variety of stimuli and interpretive suggestions he offered me.

Notes

Translated from the Italian by Anna de Biasio.

1 Patrick Barron, ed. and trans., *The Selected Poetry and Prose of Andrea Zanzotto* (Chicago: University of Chicago Press, 2006), 346.

2 Paul Oskar Kristeller, *La tradizione classica nel pensiero del Rinascimento* (1955; reprint, Florence: La Nuova Italia, 1987).

3 "una caratteristica non solo essenziale, ma unica." Salvatore Settis, *Futuro del "classico"* (Turin: G. Einaudi, 2004), 55–58 and 112.

4 "Il giardino perde la sua caratteristica religiosa ed edenica per divenire residenza di dei, luogo mitologico, replica e doppio dei *saturnia regna* che ritornano a celebrare il potere dell'*antiquitas* sul presente." Gianni Venturi, "Picta poësis: Ricerche sulla poesia e il giardino dalle origini al Seicento," in *Storia d'Italia: Annali*, eds. Ruggiero Romeno and Corrado Vivanti, vol. 5, *Il paesaggio*, ed. Cesare de Seta (Turin: G. Einaudi, 1982), 684–85.

5 Aby Warburg, *La rinascità del paganesimo antico* (1932; reprint, trans. Emma Cantimori, Florence: La Nuova Italia, 1996).

6 "Il rinascimento sente in modo eccezionale, più ancora che il troppo mistico gotico, il lato femminile, ordinatamente rigeneratore, e per altro fidatamente conservativo della società e del mondo. Quasi tutte le antiche dee,

Venere, Diana, Cibele, sono ora immerse nel più ampio, più lirico ed arcadico contesto naturale, quasi come promessa di un paradiso terrestre riconquistato." Eugenio Battisti, *L'antirinascimento* (1962; reprint, 2 vols., Milan: Garzanti, 1989), 1:160.

7 Michel Foucault, *Le parole e le cose: Un archeologia delle scienze umane* (1966; reprint, trans. Emilio Panaitescu, Milan: Rizzoli: 1978), 31–59.

8 "la Natura viene rappresentata in . . . conformità al modello antico dell'Artemide di Efeso, cioè nella forma di una figura femminile col capo velato e incoronato, con tanti seni e con la parte inferiore del corpo avvolta da una guaina stretta sulla quale si possono vedere rappresentati diversi animali. Parecchie statue antiche recano testimonianza di questa rappresentazione tradizionale dell'Artemide di Efeso." Pierre Hadot, *Il velo di Iside: Storia dell'idea di natura*, trans. Davide Tarizzo (Turin: G. Einaudi, 2006), 226.

9 Ibid.

10 "L'aggroppo di esseri viventi della sublime vasca coi pesci [della grotta di Castello richiama] quella vitalità animistica della natura che il Tribolo aveva già espressa nella *Allegoria* di Fontainebleau." Isabella Lapi Ballerini, "Niccolò Tribolo e la Grotta degli Animali a Castello," in *Artifici d'acque e giardini: La cultura delle grotte e dei ninfei in Italia e in Europa*, eds. Isabella Lapi Ballerini and Litta Maria Medri (Florence: Centro Di, 1999), 278. When describing the statue *Nature* of Fontainebleau in the section of *Le vite de' più eccellenti pittori scultori ed architettori* devoted to Tribolo, Giorgio Vasari wrote that the artist was approached in Florence by Giovanbattista della Palla, who was in charge of commissioning sculptures and paintings to be sent to King Francis I in France. Giorgio Vasari, *Le opere di Giorgio Vasari*, ed. Gaetano Milanesi, 9 vols. (1878–85; reprint, Florence: Sansoni, 1981).

11 "Nel Cinquecento, Vincenzo Cartari, nel manuale di iconografia *Le immagini degli dei* (1556), cita . . . Macrobio per provare che gli antichi amavano rappresentarsi la Natura coi tratti di Iside-Artemide. Egli precisa inoltre che è stata trovata a Roma una statua di quel genere e aggiunge di aver visto con i propri occhi una raffigurazione analoga su una medaglia dell'imperatore Adriano." Hadot, *Il velo di Iside*, 227.

12 Ibid., 229–30.

13 Massimo Venturi Ferriolo, "Mater herbarum: Il giardino dei semplici dall'antico mondo mediterraneo alla Scuola Medica Salernitana," in *Mater herbarum: Fonti e tradizione del giardino dei semplici della Scuola Medica Salernitana*, ed. Massimo Venturi Ferriolo, 13–27 (Milan: Guerini, 1995).

14 Rosario Assunto, "Fuga dal giardino e ritrovamento del giardino (con alcune varianti intorno ai consigli del serpente)," in *Il giardino: Idea natura realtà*, eds. Alessandro Tagliolini and Massimo Venturi Ferriolo (Milan: Guerini, 1987), 17; and Rosario Assunto, *Ontologia e teleologia del giardino* (Milan: Guerini, 1994), 143.

15 See the following sources by Uberto Pestalozza: *Pagine di religione mediterranea*, 2 vols. (Milan: G. Principato, 1942–45); *Nuovi saggi di religione mediterranea* (Florence: G. C. Sansoni, 1964); *Eterno femminino mediterraneo* (1954; reprint, Vicenza: Neri Pozza, 1996); and *I miti della donna-giardino: Da Iside alla Sulamita*, ed. Pier Angelo Carozzi (Milan: Edizioni Medusa, 2001).

16 Marija Gimbutas, *The Language of the Goddess: Unearthing the Hidden Symbols of Western Civilization* (San Francisco: Harper and Row, 1989); and Marija Gimbutas, "La 'Venere mostruosa' della preistoria: Creatrice divina," in *I nomi della Dea: Il femminile nella divinità*, eds. Joseph Campbell, Riane Esler, Marija Gimbutas, and Charles Musès, 28–44 (Rome: Astrolabio Ubaldini, 1992).

17 Uberto Pestalozza, "Lêtô phytia e le Ekdisya," *Memorie del Reale Istituto Lombardo di Scienze e Lettere: Classe di lettere, scienze morali e storiche* 24 (1938): 273–93.

18 Momolina Marconi, "Il santuario di Hera alla foce del Sele," *Rendiconti (Reale Istituto Lombardo di Scienze e Lettere: Classe di lettere e scienze morali e storiche)* 72 (1938–39): 441–58. Lêtô was worshipped in Crete as the mistress of plants, in Delos in the form of a palm tree, and in the woody and marshy area of Ortygia in the form of olive and oak trees.

19 Pier Angelo Carozzi, introduction to *I miti della donna-giardino: Da Iside alla Sulamita*, by Uberto Pestalozza, ed. Pier Angelo Carozzi (Milan: Edizioni Medusa, 2001), 12.

20 Giovanni Patroni, *Commenti mediterranei all'Odissea di Omero* (Milan: C. Marzorati, 1950), 109–208.

21 Homer *Odyssey* 5.55–75, 10.177ff.

22 André Motte, *Prairies et jardins de la Grèce antique: De la religion à la philosophie* (Brussels: Palais des Académies, 1973), 77–152.

23 Ibid., 5–25.

24 "Il fait revivre, mille ans après la victoire remportée par les dieux patriarcaux, la figure tout à la fois une et diverse de la Potnia pré-grecque." Ibid., 364.

25 Antonella Pietrogrande, "Echi mediterranei nei giardini italiani" and "La presenza di Roma antica nei giardini all'italiana," in *Attraverso giardini: Lezioni di storia, arte, botanica*, ed. Giuliana Baldan Zenoni Politeo, 123–38 and 139–54 (Milan: Guerini, 1995).

26 "Représentations du monde [qui] nous semblent totalement étrangères, irrationnelles, peu vraisemblables. Et pourtant une part de l'imaginaire qu'elles recèlent nous est conservée par des images familières de grottes, de nymphées et de fontaines dans les jardins." Conan's essay points out the essence of female water deities in the ancient Mediterranean metaphysics. Michel Conan, *Essais de poétique des jardins* (Florence: L. S. Olschki, 2004), 3–4.

27 Motte, *Prairies et jardins de la Grèce antique*, 200–201; and Marcello Fagiolo, "La rinascita della villa e del teatro nell'età dell'umanesimo," in *Lo specchio del paradiso:*

Giardino e teatro dall'antico al Novecento, eds. Marcello Fagiolo, Maria Adriana Giusti, and Vincenzo Cazzato (Cinisello Balsamo [Milan]: Silvana, 1997), 25–27. Fagiolo interprets the central high ground of Cythera island, described in the *Hypnerotomachia Poliphili*, as the synthesis of the feminine and generative elements of earth and water.

28 Angelo Poliziano, *Stanze cominciate per la giostra del Magnifico Giuliano de Medici* (1475–79; reprint, ed. Vincenzo Pernicone, Turin: Loescher-Chiantore, 1954), 1:68ff.

29 Massimo Venturi Ferriolo, *Etiche del paesaggio: Il progetto del mondo umano* (Rome: Editori Riuniti, 2002), 116–26; and David R. Coffin, *The Villa d'Este at Tivoli* (Princeton, N.J.: Princeton University Press, 1960).

30 Marcello Fagiolo, "Il significato dell'acqua e la dialettica del giardino: Pirro Ligorio e la 'Filosofia' della villa cinquecentesca," in *Il giardino storico italiano: Problemi di indagine, fonti letterarie e storiche; Atti del convegno di studi, Siena–San Quirico d'Orcia, 6–8 ottobre 1978*, ed. Giovanna Ragionieri, 198–210 (Florence: L. S. Olschki, 1981); and Isabella Barisi, Marcello Fagiolo, and Maria Luisa Madonna, *Villa d'Este* (Rome: De Luca, 2003).

31 Conan, *Essais de poétique des jardins*, 271–302.

32 "terrazza sul mondo dove risultano rilevanti il rapporto giardino-paesaggio e l'idea di natura." Venturi Ferriolo, *Etiche del paesaggio*, 117.

33 Today the paths lead in two directions. The upward path, which is the most logical and initiation-like, shows from the bottom all the visible elements, passes through the garden, and leads up to the palace. The downward path leads from the fountain of the Sleeping Venus or the *nympha loci* (the point of arrival of the upward path) in the courtyard-cloister of the palace to near the fountain of the Tiburtine Sibyl. Maria Luisa Madonna, "Il genius loci di Villa d'Este: Miti e misteri nel sistema di Pirro Ligorio," in *Natura e artificio: L'ordine rustico, le fontane, gli automi nella cultura del manierismo europeo*, ed. Marcello Fagiolo, 190–226 (Rome: Officina, 1981).

34 "cammino verso la scoperta del paesaggio, alla ricerca del disvelamento della natura." Venturi Ferriolo, *Etiche del paesaggio*, 118.

35 "fa parlare le cose." Ibid., 119.

36 "la lettura del mondo che precede la filosofia." Ibid., 116–17.

37 "Troviamo la dimora della Grande Dea, identificabile nella sua multiforme individualità, la Natura, nelle vesti ora di Artemis/Diana, Aphrodites/Venus, Mater Matuta/Sibilla Albunea, Nimpha loci, la dormiente nella sua tana: il paesaggio tiburtino. I versi di Ovidio rinviano alla tradizione della natura che viene da lontano, dall'antico mondo mediterraneo e che Lucas Cranach il vecchio ha dipinto pochi decenni prima riprendendo Dürer e Giorgione, con la seguente incisione: *Fontis nympha sacri somnum / ne rumpe quiesco* (Ninfa della sacra fonte / non turbare il sonno)." Ibid., 119.

38 "In the central grotto [of the Fountain of Tivoli] is seated the local Tiburtine Sibyl Albunea with her right hand resting on the back of a nude boy, probably Melicertes, who stands beside her. He was the son of Ino, who was transformed into Leucothea, and she, in turn, is often assimilated with the Sibyl Albunea." Coffin, *Villa d'Este at Tivoli*, 31. "The rectangular panel on the northeast [wall of the second Tiburtine room] depicts Ino, transformed into Mater Matuta or Albunea, the Tiburtine Sibyl . . . The Romans also knew Leucothea as Mater Matuta or Albunea, the Tiburtine Sibyl." Ibid., 63–64.

39 Maria Luisa Madonna, "Pirro Ligorio e Villa d'Este: La scena di Roma e il mistero della Sibilla," in *Il giardino storico italiano: Problemi di indagine, fonti letterarie e storiche; Atti del Convegno di Studi, Siena–San Quirico d'Orcia, 6–8 ottobre 1978*, ed. Giovanna Ragionieri (Florence: L. S. Olschki, 1981), 185.

40 Marcello Fagiolo, "Grotte, ninfei, teatri delle acque: I modelli romani," in *Atlante delle grotte e dei ninfei in Italia: Italia settentrionale, Umbria e Marche*, eds. Vincenzo Cazzato, Marcello Fagiolo, and Maria Adriana Giusti (Milan: Electa, 2002), 26.

41 Artemis of Ephesus was also situated at the center of the lobby of the sixteenth-century Casino of Pius IV in the Vatican Gardens. Fagiolo and Madonna connected the nymphaeum of the casino—regarded as the muses' temple due to the presence of fountains, river deities, and sea creatures—to the Fountain of the Organ at the Villa d'Este, which originally housed the goddess's statue. Marcello Fagiolo and Maria Luisa Madonna, "La Casina di Pio IV in Vaticano: Pirro Ligorio e l'architettura come geroglifico," *Storia dell'arte* 15–16 (1972): 237–81.

42 Madonna, "Pirro Ligorio e Villa d'Este," 191.

43 Franz Baumer, *La grande madre: Scenari da un mondo mitico*, trans. Giuseppina Quattrocchi (Genova: ECIG, 1995), 75–79.

44 "metafora di una cultura costituita dal paesaggio tiburtino, simbolo del mondo antico con le sue immagini non rivelabili all'esterno, ai profani. Si richiede silenzio: non si può sollevare il velo.' Venturi Ferriolo, *Etiche del paesaggio*, 122.

45 Ibid., 124–25.

46 In referencing the recitation of lyric poetry in the gardens of ancient Greece, Calame maintained that the ability to evoke the presence of the deity had a "performative character." I have also discussed the garden's ability to evoke the presence of the deity and to grasp the memory of a distant past and its myths in the landscape, in order to give a new interpretation of the seventeenth-century gardens at the Villa Barbarigo (Padua), whose sovereign deity is Diana. Called forth from the most remote forests of the ancient inhabitants of the Veneto, through an uninterrupted chain of references, the Great Mother Reitia, the goddess of the mountains and of savage nature, reappeared in

this garden, spread out among the woods in the Euganei hills. Claude Calame, "Gardens of Love and Meadows of the Beyond: Ritual Encounters with the Gods and Poetical Performances in Ancient Greece," in *Sacred Gardens and Landscapes: Ritual and Agency*, ed. Michel Conan, 43–56 (Washington, D.C.: Dumbarton Oaks Research Library and Collection, 2007); and Antonella Pietrogrande, *I giardini di Reitia: Storia e tipologie dei giardini del Parco dei Colli Euganei* (Este: Grafica Atesina, 1998), 31–50.

47 Rosario Assunto, *Il paesaggio e l'estetica* (Naples: Giannini, 1973).

48 Patrizia Castelli, "L'antro delle Ninfe," in *Artifici d'acque e giardini: La cultura delle grotte e dei ninfei in Italia e in Europa*, eds. Isabella Lapi Ballerini and Litta Maria Medri, 153–63 (Florence: Centro Di, 1999); and Antonella Pietrogrande, "'Una spelonca di dolci acque amena': Grotte e ninfeo tra Umanesimo e Manierismo," in *Artifici d'acque e giardini: La cultura delle grotte e dei ninfei in Italia e in Europa*, 180–85.

49 Ernst Robert Curtius, *Letteratura europea e medio evo latino* (1948; reprint, ed. Roberto Antonelli and trans. Anna Luzzato and Mercurio Candela, Florence: La Nuova Italia, 1992), 123–25; André Chastel, *Arte e umanesimo a Firenze al tempo di Lorenzo il Magnifico* (Turin: G. Einaudi, 1964), 225–30 and 447; and Margherita Azzi Visentini, *La villa in Italia: Quattrocento e Cinquecento* (Milan: Electa, 1995), 59–71.

50 Pestalozza, *Eterno femminino mediterraneo*, 28–29.

51 Mircea Eliade, *La nascita mistica: Riti e simboli d'iniziazione* (Brescia: Morcelliana, 1974), 88–91.

52 "forma simbolica dell'universo artificiale del giardino." Fagiolo, "Grotte, ninfei, teatri delle acque," 17.

53 "infinito grembo germinale . . . regno incontestato della metamorfosi." Fausto Testa, *Spazio e allegoria nel giardino manierista: Problemi di estetica* (Florence: Nuova Italia, 1991), 22.

54 "ricettacolo germinale della terra." Ibid., 46.

55 "grembo fecondo di una natura metamorfica." Ibid., 47.

56 Hervé Brunon, "Les mouvements de l'âme: Émotion et poétique du jardin maniériste," in *Felipe II: El rey íntimo; Jardín y naturaleza en el siglo XVI*, ed. Carmen Añón Feliú, 103–36 (Madrid: Sociedad Estatal para la Conmemoración de los Centenarios de Felipe II y Carlos V, 1998).

57 Conan, *Essais de poétique des jardins*, x–xi.

CHAPTER 8

Toward an Archaeology of the Gaze: The Perception and Function of Garden Views in Italian Renaissance Villas

DENIS RIBOUILLAULT

THE CRITICAL ANALYSIS OF GARDEN VIEWS IS a relatively recent concern among garden historians. Although garden views have been included in the scholarship since the late nineteenth and early twentieth centuries, they are rarely put under critical scrutiny. Rather, images of gardens functioned in these publications essentially as illustrations or documents that provide a visual stimulus to help readers understand the topography of the landscape and imagine the atmosphere and beauty of the gardens. These images, which are generally considered faithful representations of a particular state of the garden, have been employed to provide information about the garden's topography and history.[1] In this, historians have followed the discourse associated with topographical images during the Renaissance, a genre that was predominantly linked with the idea of truthfulness and objectivity.[2] A topographical view of a city or garden was almost always presented by its authors as being derived from direct observation, "from a true relationship with the world seen, not from a written account, nor from a purely conventional model, nor even from an abstract idea." For example, Georg Braun, in his preface to the *Civitates orbis terrarum* (1572–1618), stated that "the painters really went through the towns they drew and assumed the real world as their starting point."[3] His statement was obviously not true, as most images were constructed through the use of previous models, a variety of textual and visual information, and, most importantly, a good dose of artistic imagination.[4]

Since the 1990s, historians have suggested other ways in which images could be used to gain a better understanding of gardens, and several publications have been entirely dedicated to the tradition of garden representation.[5] For example, during the 1989 Dumbarton Oaks symposium, Linda Cabe Halpern noted that garden views are "useful not only for the topographical information they can convey, but also for communicating the assumptions and expectations of previous centuries concerning gardens . . . They tell us what mattered to the villa owners, and in many respects they are most interesting in their contradiction to physical reality."[6] The methodology adopted by Halpern has since been employed by a number of scholars, such as Hervé Brunon, Claudia Lazzaro, Mirka Beneš, John Dixon Hunt, and Dianne Harris.[7] What all of these authors stress is the necessity of considering the very status of garden images and the way they are constructed and of readdressing the question of their original function and their reception by coeval audiences.[8] As a result, images of gardens, which were previously considered to be "documents," are now starting to be examined as "monuments"—this follows an emblematic epistemological shift suggested some decades ago by Erwin Panofsky for the visual arts, Michel Foucault for the history of human sciences, and Jacques Le Goff and the *Annales* school for the discipline of history.[9] Foucault wrote: "The document, then, is no longer for history an inert material through which it tries to reconstitute what men have done or said, the events of which only the trace remains; history is now trying to define within the documentary material itself unities, totalities, series, relations." Where before, history was essentially preoccupied with authenticating and dating "sources," it must now explore the condition of their genesis and the transmission of their traces to unravel their apparent meaning or to interrogate their silence. In its relation to documents, history "aspires to the condition of archaeology, to the intrinsic description of the monument."[10]

Focusing on fresco paintings in Italian villas, this paper suggests new ways of using images for the history and archaeology of gardens, and raises new questions about the relationship between vision, representation, motion, and memory in Renaissance villa culture. Three important issues are addressed in order to offer new theoretical perspectives for garden historians. First, I explore the function of garden views as projects or *disegni*, and address the vexed question of synchronism between the creation of the garden and the production of its printed or painted model. I then analyze the theoretical significance of garden images in the Renaissance. Finally, I suggest a reconsideration of the visual environment of such images, so that their reception is analyzed not only in terms of vision

FIGURE 8.1. Girolamo Muziano, projected design of the gardens at the Villa d'Este, 1565–68, fresco in the main salone of the Villa d'Este, Tivoli.

Photograph by the author.

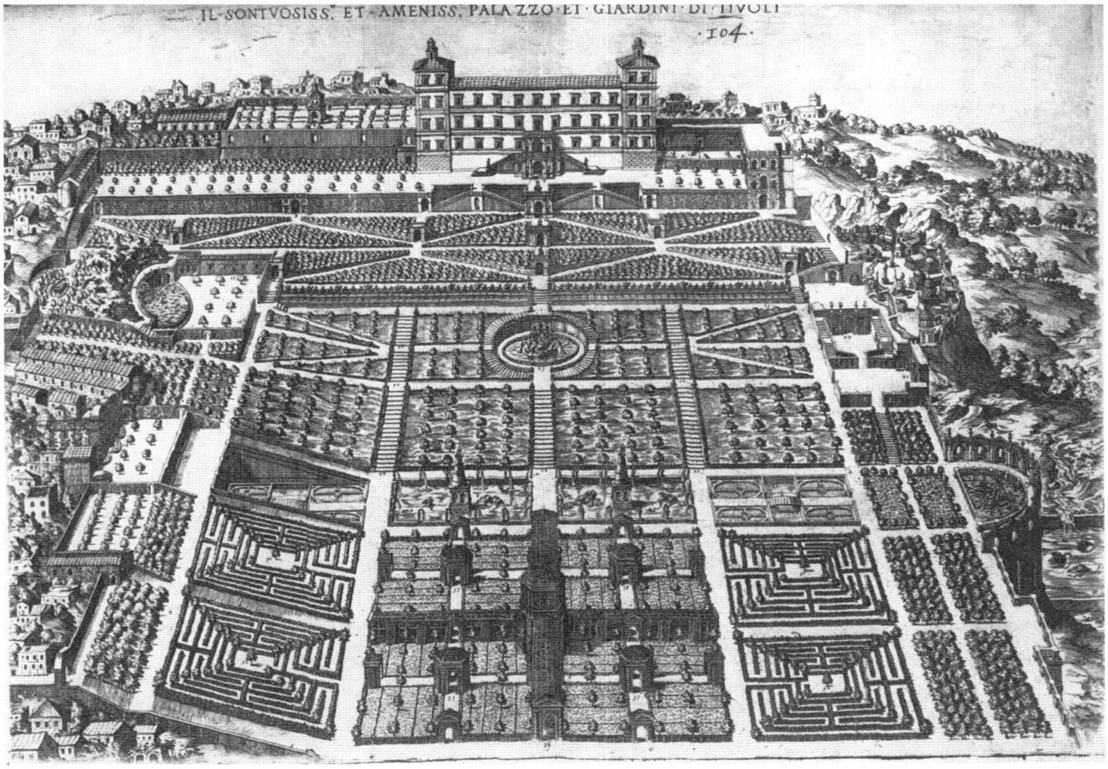

FIGURE 8.2.
Étienne Dupérac, projected design for the Villa d'Este at Tivoli, 1573, engraving.
Published as *Ritratto nel quale si rappresenta il vero sito dell'horti et fontane che con ingeniosissimi adornamenti e meraviglie si vedono nella villa in Tivoli fatta dalla Fe. Me. D. Hippolito da Este Card. di Ferrara* by Ambrosius Brambilla (Rome: Claude Duchet, 1581).

but also in terms of movement through the villa. For this method of contextualized analysis, I have coined the term "archaeology of the gaze," thereby implying that a certain vision of space is encoded, both at a conscious and an unconscious level, in historical images and their particular constructs. This term underscores the fundamental relationships established in the *Gesamtkunstwerk* that is the Italian Renaissance villa between the garden, its wider landscape, and the villa's painted decoration; between inside and outside space; and between past and present. The main focus of this paper will be not so much the images themselves but their role in the construction of a specific horizon of perception and understanding of space.

Garden Views as Projects

Although we have already noted that topographical images were generally associated with the idea of truthfulness and objectivity, the earliest commentaries on garden images during the Renaissance were anything but naive. For example, after admiring in 1576 the view of the Villa d'Este at Tivoli painted by Girolamo Muziano in the main *salone*, Nicolas Audebert reported that it showed the villa "not as it is, but as it would be if it were completed" (fig. 8.1).[11] Commenting on an engraving made of the same villa and its gardens by Étienne Dupérac in 1573, the French traveler demonstrated his awareness of the deformation of the perspective in the portrayal of the villa: "But one must remark that the length [of the garden] must be taken from the Palace to the Garden's gate leading to the street, that is twice its width: whereas in the portrait it seems the opposite; this comes from the fact that perspective represents all things in foreshortening" (fig. 8.2).[12]

Audebert's testimony tells us two important things. First, the gardens were not finished in 1576; the fresco in the salone was known to be a *disegno* and not a representation of reality. Audebert used the old French word *desseing*, meaning both a drawing and a project. Second, people such as Audebert were well aware of the difficulties of creating a representation that truly reproduces one's perceptions when present in a garden. Audebert's critical attitude toward the artificiality of topographical views was still alive in the seventeenth century; it is well known that the "art of prospect," while praised for its capacity to simulate the truth, was held in deep suspicion by many who regarded it as a "pernicious fantasy" that created "deceptive visions."[13]

Thus, from the point of view of their function, garden images were understood not as truthful depictions of sites but as projects and designs—that is, as material expressions of the ideas of architects. Desseing or disegno, in this instance, not only signified drawing and project, but was understood theoretically and conceptually as the result of a creative genius, the graphic translation of an idea, and the key of all imaginative process. It was this "idea" that was celebrated in engravings and frescoes of gardens during the Renaissance, and whose prestige, in turn, glorified the patrons that made possible its actual materialization.

One interesting example of this paradigm is the fresco of the Villa Lante at Bagnaia, which was based on the original *bozzetto grafico* (or disegno) for the villa that was possibly provided by Vignola himself (fig. 8.3).[14] A comparison of the fresco and the inventory of the villa taken in 1588 after the death of Cardinal Gianfrancesco Gambara shows that nearly all of the elements indicated on this fresco were eventually realized (with the exception of the second palazzina, which was completed by Cardinal Alessandro Peretti di Montalto).[15] We can, therefore, hypothesize that the inclusion of the disegno in the loggia of the Palazzina Gambara between 1574 and

FIGURE 8.3. Fresco in the loggia of the Palazzina Gambara at the Villa Lante, Bagnaia, ca. 1574. The fresco shows the projected design of the villa gardens.

Photgraph courtesy of the Bridgeman Art Library.

FIGURE 8.4. Jacopo Zucchi, project for the gardens of the Villa Medici, 1576, fresco in the garden pavilion of the Villa Medici, Rome.

Photograph courtesy of the Fototeca Nazionale, Istituto Centrale per il Catalogo e la Documentazione (ICCD).

1578 must have acted as a guarantee that the gardens would be finished in accordance with their original plan. Nonetheless, for more than ten years, the gardens certainly did not look like the fresco. In fact, we could say that the garden imitated the fresco rather than the opposite.[16] The same holds true for the fresco of the Villa d'Este at Tivoli (fig. 8.1).

The importance of this potential or apparent synchronism between the building of gardens and their representations also explains the function of the famous garden views at the Villa Medici in Rome (fig. 8.4). Created in 1576 by Jacopo Zucchi, these three frescoes—which were located in a small casino at the back of the villa garden—possessed an important legal dimension and should not be seen as mere illustrations.[17]

The rental contract drawn by Cardinal Ferdinando de'Medici and his advisors assured him the use of the villa, but left to the leaseholders, the Crescenzi and the Garzoni families, a certain number of rights over the land and what was built on it. In case the leaseholders would want to reclaim their possessions, the terms of the contract stated that they would have to pay for any addition to the land that was dedicated to its pure embellishment ("melioramenta voluntaria et ad delectationem") but not for additions that were seen as economically and financially productive ("melioramenta utilia et necessaria").[18] It is likely that, in order to prevent eventual contestations, Ferdinando de'Medici asked Jacopo Zucchi to represent with precision his plans for transforming and embellishing the gardens. The first two views thus show the villa as it would look with the cardinal's projected improvements and as it appeared in its original state as the Vigna Crescenzi. By showing that he had adorned his garden without increasing its productivity, and by recording the "before and after" states of the gardens, Ferdinando de'Medici might have intended to dissuade any descendants of the Crescenzi or Garzoni families from claiming what he himself had built, given that it would not be financially advantageous for them to do so. The third garden view is related to a major building project for a magnificent fountain and ramp in front of the villa on a piece of land belonging to the Garzoni family. Since the fountain and ramp would have embellished the entire city and would have provided the villa with a grand new focus, Pope Gregory XIII approved the project in 1576 (the same year that the views were painted), stating that it would be "in the interest of Garzoni [who was Quirino Garzoni's son] and his descendants, and for the great ornament of the city."[19] Again, the views worked as true legal arguments.

The situation must have been slightly different at the Villa Lante (fig. 8.3). I have already suggested that the representation of the villa in the Palazzina Gambara might have acted as a guarantee that the gardens would be completed in accordance with the original project. This supports an attribution of the initial conception of the gardens to the architect Vignola. In the late sixteenth century, only Pirro Ligorio, who also served as architect of Saint Peter's Basilica after the death of Michelangelo, was as celebrated in Rome as Vignola. Ligorio's splendid realizations for Pope Pius IV were, in fact, praised in a similar fashion in four views depicted on the vault of the stairway in the Casino of Pius IV at the Vatican Gardens. These views represent the pope's gardens in Rome: the Casino of Pius IV, the Nicchione del Belvedere, the vigna on the Quirinale, and the palazzina on the Via Flaminia.[20] At the Villa Lante in Bagnaia, the role of Tommaso Ghinucci in the conception and elaboration of the gardens has been recently reevaluated, but was the Sienese architect and engineer so renowned that his project would at so early a stage be celebrated in a painting?[21] It is likely that the fresco decoration had been motivated by Cardinal Gambara's desire to stress the originality and prestigious authorship of his villa's disegno as much as that of the villa itself. At the time the frescoes were completed, the villa was far from being finished; its future completion would be further compromised by the recriminations addressed to Cardinal Gambara by Cardinal Carlo Borromeo in 1580.[22] This hypothesis of the villa's authorship is reinforced by the recent discovery of a disguised portrait of Vignola in the loggia frescoes at the Villa Lante; the portrait is found in one of the *telamoni* framing the garden views, and is exactly in front of the views of two of Vignola's buildings for Cardinal Alessandro Farnese, the Palazzo Farnese and the Barco at Caprarola.[23] The connections established between the different villas represented in the loggia were meant to stress what the Villa Lante owed to the other famous residences, as the written verses accompanying each fresco also suggest.[24]

The importance given to a disegno during the Renaissance is demonstrated by the many drawings and prints that remain for projects that were never realized. For example, for his engraving of Michelangelo's project for Saint Peter's Basilica in Rome, Étienne Dupérac used the architect's wooden model as well as his drawings for the design of the facade, which when combined produced a complete image of the church as it would appear in reality.[25] Dupérac's engraving for the Villa Giulia was also based on drawings of early projects.[26] Finally, we should mention the Frenchman's most celebrated image of Roman gardens, that of the Villa d'Este at Tivoli (fig. 8.2). As noted by Elizabeth Eustis, this image was—at least for many viewers—more real than the garden itself and recalled the relation between disegni and unrealized projects: "Dupérac's view was reissued time and again by the original publisher and his heirs, and copied and imitated by other printmakers for eighty years or more. His idealized design, more perfectly geometric and more complete than the garden, was copied by subsequent printmakers, rather than corrected by reference to the actual garden. The print remained constant as a model of garden design even more widely influential than the garden itself."[27]

Vision and Memory

As a category of images, Renaissance garden views (like other topographical images) belonged to the epideictic category of *descriptio*, as they derived both from ancient geography and rhetoric and, as such, played an important mnemonic and didactic function in the villa and its garden. During the Renaissance, topographical images helped visitors to better remember the places they visited. Likewise, sixteenth-century garden views were often meant to accompany an *ekphrasis*, or literary description, of a site even though most authors acknowledged that visual images were more effective than literary descriptions. For example, Nicolas Audebert wrote at the end of his description of the Villa d'Este: "For better intelligence and demonstration of what [has been described] above, I have made a small portrait [of the villa], in order to represent what can only be made understandable through painting."[28] A preference for garden views is also evident in a famous letter by Bartolomeo Ammannati to Marco Mantova Benavides that described the Villa Giulia in Rome and in the description of the Villa Aldobrandini at Frascati attributed to Giovanni Battista Agucchi.[29] Moreover, the famous engraving of the Villa d'Este by Etienne Dupérac was originally commissioned to accompany a written description of the villa, the so-called Parisian manuscript, which was sent to both Catherine de'Medici of France and Maximilian II of Austria (fig. 8.2).[30]

As elements of *epideixis* (the rhetoric of praise and blame), descriptio and ekphrasis were not limited to literal description, but were meant to convince and to make objects appear as truthful as possible, a practice that Latin rhetoricians have called *evidentia, illustratio,* or *demonstratio.* In this context, garden views belonged to a genre that was celebratory and ideological.[31]

From a more practical point of view, the views of the garden and its surrounding territory enabled visitors to replicate a technique employed by travelers to fix in their memory the character and configuration of the places they had visited. During a trip to Rome, for example, Montesquieu wrote of his habit of seeking out such landscape panoramas: "When I arrive in a city, I always climb up the highest bell tower, to see the whole before seeing the parts; and, upon leaving I do the same to gather my ideas."[32]

The mnemonic and didactic function of garden views corresponded fully to the role given to images by the new directives of the Council of Trent, and it comes as no surprise that most Renaissance garden images were produced for cardinals of the church. In his 1582 description of topographical views and geographical maps, Cardinal Gabriele Paleotti recalled that places can be better remembered when they have been seen represented in painting.[33] Previously, in the *De Cardinalatu* (1510), Paolo Cortesi had stressed the suitability of such images for the decoration of a cardinal's palace and for the edification of the visitor:

> The summer rooms should be decorated in almost the same way. The more subtle a mathematical concept (*subtilior mathematica ratio*) a painting displays, the more learned (*litteratior*) the picture will appear. For instance there could be a painting something like a hydraulic or cthesibian machine the which [representation] permits more subtle reasoning [by the viewer]. The same thing should be said about systems of drawing water, hoisting, laying siege or channeling streams of water such as we contrived at San Gimignano to build the lake on the Cortesi family estate . . . And likewise there is no less delight to the learned in a painted picture of the world (*pinax*) or the depiction (*descriptio*) of its parts . . . And the same holds true for paintings done from life (*zo[o]graphiae describendae ratio*) . . .[34]

The resemblance between Cortesi's description of a cardinal's ideal *triclinium* and well-known rooms with garden and landscape views, such as the salone at the Villa d'Este at Tivoli (which is itself described as a triclinium), the *stanzino* of Ferdinando de' Medici at the Villa Medici in Rome, and the loggia of the Villa Lante at Bagnaia, is particularly striking and can shed new light on how garden views were understood by their contemporaries.[35] For Cortesi, garden views (as descriptio) were seen as edifying images that appealed directly to the intellect. In *De Cardinalatu,* he doubtless evoked the decoration of his own villa; the representation of the hydraulic works carried out in his garden at San Gimignano might have been an example he had right before his eyes. Similarly, many of the water features represented in contemporary views of gardens at Tivoli, Bagnaia, and elsewhere were examples of the fountains, water channeling systems, and wonder-inducing hydraulic machines recommended by Cortesi as suitable subjects for triclinium decoration.[36] The Fountain of the Organ and the Fountain of the Owl at Tivoli were possibly inspired by Vitruvius's description of a water organ invented by the Roman engineer Ctesibius (which Cortesi clearly evoked in his text), and the Avenue of the Hundred Fountains in the gardens of the Villa d'Este was nothing but a construction to channel streams (fig. 8.5).[37] The expression "subtilior mathematica ratio" can also be read to imply the use of trompe l'oeil representations and self-reflective visual techniques (such as *jeux de miroirs* and *mises en abîme*), which, as we will see, abound in the decoration of such villas. Finally, birds and animals were often depicted next to painted views of gardens ("zo[o]graphiae describendae ratio").

This combination of pictorial themes is especially apparent in the decoration of sixteenth-century villas, such as the Villa d'Este at Tivoli and the Villa Madama in Rome. The Villa Madama contains some of the pictorial themes mentioned by Cortesi, including a *mappamondo,* representations of exotic beasts, and scenes from Philostratus.[38] And in addition to the views of the villa and its gardens in the small stanzino of Ferdinando

FIGURE 8.5. View of the Avenue of the Hundred Fountains with the Fountain of Tivoli, detail of a fresco in the salone of the Villa d'Este, Tivoli.

Photograph by the author.

de'Medici at the Villa Medici in Rome, there are depictions of many species of fish as well as illustrations of Aesop's fables among the grotesques; the adjacent room is painted to look like an extraordinary bird cage with the rarest species known at the time, including birds and plants only found in America.[39] Garden views, thus, belonged to a category of images evoking wonder that were especially praised by Renaissance collectors.[40]

Perhaps the image of a peacock in front of the main view of the villa in the salone at the Villa d'Este alluded to the mnemonic function of the garden views and to the primacy of sight in the understanding of the world (fig. 8.1). In his *Dialogues* (19–20), the Greek rhetorician Lucian of Samosata claimed that no one could listen to the song of a nightingale while admiring a silent peacock, for "the pleasure of the eyes seems invincible . . . because words are winged and fly as soon as they depart from our lips, whilst the beauty of visible things is always present and capture the spectator whether he wants it or not."[41] This kind of learned riddle was considered appropriate in a cardinal's villa during the Renaissance. Paolo Cortesi concluded his discussion by recommending "the depiction of riddles (*aenigmata*) and fables (*apologi*). Their interpretation sharpens the intelligence and [inspection of] their learned representations fosters the cultivation of the mind."[42] Many riddles existed in the highly complex, antiquarian program of the Villa d'Este's decorations. They stimulated the intellect and the philological knowledge of the highly learned guests of the cardinal, leading the courtier Ercole Cato to describe this assembly as "an Academy, a cenacle, a theatre of the world."[43]

Garden views were, therefore, intended to stimulate both the imagination and the intellect. This model of perception was rooted in ancient Greek sources, a point that Cortesi emphasized: "For [by the sight of these paintings] either the appetite of the soul is aroused or the capacity for motion—the which consists, according to Aristotle, in the combination of imagination (*imaginatio*) and the intellectual understanding of things (*intelligentia*)—may be prompted by the striking lifelike imitation, in the painting, of the thing represented."[44]

Finally, it should be remarked that, in light of Cortesi's humanist background, the parallel between his understanding of the function of garden views and the ancient art of memory is striking. As Quintilian, Cicero, and the anonymous author of the *Ad Herrenium* explained, the *loci* (or mnemonic sites; here the painted views) should be placed within a short distance of each other. They should be well and carefully lit, and should be as realistic as possible. The images (i.e., ideas, concepts, or texts) associated with each *locus* are then perceived through the motion of the viewer within the mnemonic landscape: a walk through a public building or a city, a long journey through the country, or a series of paintings. The process of moving, seeing, and knowing described for the ancient *ars memoriae* closely corresponds with the way in which topographical cycles and gardens were plastically and spatially organized and perceived during the Renaissance.[45]

FIGURE 8.6.
Giusto Utens, *Castello*, 1599. Museo Firenze Com'era, Florence.

Photograph courtesy of the Ministero per i Beni e le Attività Culturali.

A Look at Giusto Utens's Views of Medicean Villas

Spatial context and motion is, thus, of crucial importance for the understanding of garden views during the Renaissance. A case in point is garden historians' use of Giusto Utens's famous lunettes for the Medici villa at Artimino.[46] Painted between 1598 and 1602, this pictorial cycle—which shows the villas and gardens associated with the Medici family—provides invaluable evidence for reconstructing the original planting of the gardens.[47] Yet the use of these lunettes as historical evidence is fraught with problems. The first problem is with chronology: the views represent the gardens as they seem to have appeared around 1600, but they have often been employed to document the state of gardens made considerably earlier, in the fifteenth or early sixteenth century.[48] The second problem is with accuracy: in addition to manipulating the perspective in the garden views, many aspects of the depicted gardens have been simply invented or corrected.[49] For example, in his view of the Medici villa at Castello, Utens modified the central axis of the garden to correspond with the main axis of the villa—an adjustment that Étienne Dupérac also made in his 1573 engraving of the Villa d'Este (figs. 8.2 and 8.6).[50]

In order better to understand the raison d'être and the historical meaning of Utens's lunettes, we should attempt to place them in the context in which they were meant to be seen (i.e., in one of the two main reception rooms of the villa at Artimino).[51] Where these views truly depart from reality is not so much in the "corrections" that have already been highlighted, but in the singular absence of light, atmospheric, and distance effects. No clouds are apparent or winds suggested, and the time of day remains indeterminate. The limited palette (which is reduced to only three colors), the meticulousness of the line work, and the geometrical precision used to depict even the most natural elements in the gardens imbue the lunettes with the timeless dimension of a map. The human figures must be understood, like the other elements of the landscape, as generic symbols rather than factual illustrations. They have been inserted into the lunettes to describe the activities (hunting, games and leisure, and agriculture) associated with each villa.

The emphasis on generic elements denotes a desire to unify all of the lunettes at the villa at Artimino. As Claude Lévi-Strauss noted in his discussion of the reduced-scale model, reduction and simplification imply that "the knowledge of the whole precedes that of the parts."[52] In other words, the views at Artimino exist as a series before they exist as individualized representations of particular villas. The great diversity of architectural and topiary typologies that the paintings present—the villas were built between 1451 and 1595—is subordinated, when seen in situ, to the stylistic unity, the uniformity of line and color, and the repetition of the formatted elements of the landscape and the architecture. The images become the metaphor of a grand duchy of Tuscany conceived as a centralized political and administrative system, of which the villas are the active agents on the territory.[53] In short, Utens's lunettes, by simultaneously offering a detailed and overall view of the landscape of the Medici villas, form an ideologically ordered inventory.[54]

The absence of the villa at Artimino in the lunette cycle can be explained by the fact that the villa had become, for Ferdinando de'Medici, the center of the territory and the point from which the network of villas was organized. The centripetal disposition of the views transformed the room into a microcosm of the entire territory, so that the spectator looking and moving within the room was both virtually and in reality at the center of Ferdinando de'Medici's domain. The villa at Artimino, which was located at one of the higher points in Tuscany, indeed afforded magnificent panoramic views of the surrounding countryside. Furthermore, the sequential disposition of the views around the room, producing "a kind of diorama in the filmic succession of the images," suggested to the visitor a mental journey around the territory and recalled the ceaseless traveling of Ferdinando de'Medici and his court from one villa to another.[55] The unity and uniformity achieved in the cycle reflected not only the unifying presence of the prince, but also his fundamental ideological project for the Medici villas. Villas, old and new, were built or refurbished with careful attention paid to the relationship between the architecture and the landscape.[56] Beyond serving as informal country retreats, these villas also urbanized the countryside by laying a grid of orderly and unifying structures over the landscape for political, military, and economic purposes. James Saslow described the action of looking over the land from the villas as "laying bare the surrounding territory to a gaze of visual and social surveillance."[57] Thus, Utens's series documents through an appropriation of space—both macroscopic (the territory) and microscopic (the topography of each place)—the organizational system, visual domination, and aesthetic appreciation of the landscape that the architecture of the villa itself—"eine prominente Synthese" of former Medicean villas' architectural styles and typologies[58]—was constructing and projecting. Painted landscape and real landscape were the recipients and the metaphors of the gaze of Ferdinando de'Medici, whose presence was materialized by a bust set above the principal loggia, dominating the stupendous panorama.[59]

Toward an Archaeology of the Gaze

The need to consider garden images in relation to space and movement thus calls for a reconsideration of our methodological tools. In his book *Representing Place: Landscape Painting and Maps*, the philosopher Edward Casey suggested an approach that would be "concerned less with how representation works . . . or with its cultural content or historical position or political purport . . . than with how the representation of landscape places affects us, the viewers—affects us not socially or politically as such but experientially . . . it is not just a matter of 'eye and mind' (as Merleau-Ponty put it) but of the eye—and hand and foot and back and neck, each of these in actual as well as virtual forms of realization."[60]

Some historians dealing with prints or easel paintings have already considered this important aspect of bodily motion in their analysis of garden imagery. Dianne Harris noted that the physical experience of the viewer was central to the understanding of Marc'Antonio dal Re's printed views of Lombard villas: "The theatrical quality of the panoramas in the 1726 edition . . . is enhanced by the drama of unfolding the prints for viewing. Turning the large pages requires extended arm motions and even stepping back and forth or sideways to unfold pages."[61] These observations are even more important for historians dealing with fresco paintings, which are bound to the architecture and, like architecture, need to be apprehended spatially.

The following discussion will stress the importance of this phenomenological reception of garden views and will unravel the significance of their location in Renaissance villas. I will demonstrate that garden views need not be considered separate from the garden, but (like statues, fountains, and belvederes) should be considered part of the garden itself. Furthermore, I will argue that representations of gardens were necessary to impress upon visitors a particular visual knowledge of these garden spaces. I will, therefore, regard the garden views as symptoms of a "way of seeing" a garden, as images that enable us to put into practice an "archaeology of the gaze." I use the first expression in the sense given to it by Erwin Panofsky, John Berger, and Denis Cosgrove, who wrote that "landscape first emerged as a term, an idea, or better still, *a way of seeing* the external world, in the fifteenth and early sixteenth centuries."[62] The second expression derives from the hypothesis that the conventions by which historical images were constructed convey a certain vision of space that is by definition different from ours, and that an understanding of these images varies over time depending on the historical system of cultural references to which the viewing subject belongs.[63] In his book *Geography of the Gaze: Urban and Rural Vision in Early Modern Europe*, Renzo Dubbini argued that "the process of constructing images—whether of natural or artificial environments—interests us as a vision of the world related to the specificity of place; . . . they are attempts to analyze the structure of the historical space of existence and represent its true aspects."[64] Looking at garden views, therefore, not only in the Italian Renaissance but in all times and periods, offers a way of understanding how gardens were meant to be experienced and perceived.[65]

Space and Place at the Villa d'Este at Tivoli

The vision of and movements in gardens and villas were closely related during the Renaissance.[66] What a visitor learned inside the villa determined his understanding of the garden, and vice versa. Most descriptions of Renaissance gardens started or ended with a discussion of the pictorial or sculptural decoration in the villa, which was either the first or the last stage of the journey through the site. This is particularly clear with respect to the Villa d'Este at Tivoli built for Cardinal Ippolito II d'Este between 1550 and 1572.[67]

The garden at Tivoli was built around two main axes. The first axis was, as David Coffin has shown, that of Hercules. It leads from the villa's main entrance at the lower level of the garden to the two main reception rooms: the salone (or Room of the Fountain) and the Room of Hercules. The presence of different statues of Hercules along the main axis stands as a metaphor of Hercules's journey and many deeds. The Fountain of the Dragon, for example, symbolizes one of the deeds of Hercules stealing the golden apples from the Garden of the Hesperides, an appropriate image for the Villa d'Este garden. The other statues that were placed along the main axis are (from bottom to top): Hercules and the Hydra of Lerna, Hercules resting on the spoils of his labors, and Hercules adored as a god for his attainment of immortality.

The second axis conveys a geographical theme and employs water features to make a symbolic connection between Tivoli and Rome. Located in the northeastern section of the garden, the monumental Fountain of Tivoli recalls the water that flows from the mountains to the northeast of Tivoli to form the Aniene River. In the southwestern section of the garden, in the direction of Rome, the Fountain of Rome (the so-called *Rometta*) is shaped like a model of the ancient city, with the Tiber River, Tiberine Island, and the gates and main temples of Rome. Linking these two fountains is the Avenue of the Hundred Fountains, which represents the Aniene River as it runs through the Tiburtine territory and terminates in the Tiber River. The little boats at the top of the fountain identify the channel as a river and evoke the navigability of the ancient Aniene River according to Pliny the Elder and Strabo. Like several other Renaissance gardens in Italy, such as the gardens at Castello or Pratolino, the garden at the Villa d'Este acted as a geographical model; it provided a monumental translation with fountains and sculptures of the entire region of Tivoli and its water system.[68] When moving through the garden, visitors were transported through wide spaces and times, and were asked to take part, as on a theater stage, in a narrative in which they implicitly became actors: "Their own motion through the garden, whatever their intentions during their visit, paralleled Hercules's ancient choice between virtue and vice, which anticipated the cardinal's."[69]

The territorial and mythical symbolism of the gardens—what Michel Conan has called a "landscape metaphor"—was also translated in the main room of the villa, the so-called salone (fig. 8.7).[70] Its walls were painted between 1565 and 1568 by Girolamo Muziano and his workshop; they feature a fictive colonnade opening onto landscapes and vistas, among them views of the main fountains of the garden, which gives the impression that the entire room was an open loggia dominating the surrounding landscape.

The axis of Hercules ends inside the villa in the central ceiling panels of the salone and the adjacent Room of Hercules. Hercules is welcomed to the feast of the gods in the salone, and to the council of the gods in the Room of Hercules. The visitor's journey through the gardens to the interior of the villa is, therefore, a reenactment of Hercules's journey—of his choice between virtue and vice at the crossroads, and eventually of his apotheosis and accession to immortality. In the fresco of Hercules at the Feast of the Gods, the hero is strategically placed in the composition as if, coming from the real space of the garden, he had just entered the pictorial space of the Olympian triclinium (fig. 8.8). His head is turned in a calculated movement toward the door leading to the gardens, in direct relation to the line of sight of a visitor entering the room and looking up toward the fresco.

Let us now look at the Tivoli-Rome axis. On the northeastern wall of the salone, the fontanina, like the Fountain of Tivoli in the garden, evokes the local topography by showing the Temple of the Sibyl overlooking the famous cascade on the Aniene River

FIGURE 8.7. Salone in the Villa d'Este, Tivoli.

Photograph by the author.

FIGURE 8.8. Federico Zuccaro, *Hercules at the Feast of the Gods*, 1565–68, fresco in the salone of the Villa d'Este, Tivoli.

Photograph by the author.

(fig. 8.9). The location of this rustic fountain in the room echoes that of the real temple and cascade at the northeastern end of Tivoli. On the opposite wall, the large view of the Villa d'Este was painted from the north looking to the southwest, precisely in the direction of Rome (fig. 8.1). So, just as it does in the garden, the Aniene River flows metaphorically from one end of the room, passes through the rustic fountain on the northeastern wall, and reappears at the other end of the room in the fresco of the Villa d'Este. Evidence for this reading can be found in the shape of the fountain basin itself—it is a barge that stands on two big fish symbolizing the Aniene River, which figuratively floods the salone (fig. 8.9). It directly refers to the barges of the same shape that ornament the upper channel of the Avenue of the Hundred Fountains in the gardens. The salone should, therefore, be seen as a painted transposition to the walls of the room of the garden's topographical layout, its geographical orientation, and its iconographic program.

The position of the different views of the garden's fountains on the salone walls and the perspective adopted by the artists to depict them provide further clues for understanding the specific nature of the decoration. For example, the Fountain of Tivoli is represented in the eastern corner of the salone, just as the real fountain stands in the eastern corner of the garden. On the opposite wall, in the northern corner of the salone, the painter depicted the Fountain of the Organ, which stands in the northern section of the garden. Muziano also represented the two major bridges on the Aniene River (i.e., the Ponte Lucano and the Ponte Cornuto), as well as the ancient villas of Tibur that Pirro Ligorio studied in *Libro delle antiche ville tiburtine* before working as the architect of the Villa d'Este. The villa of Manlio Vopisco, the villa of Horace, the Temple of the Sibyl (which Ligorio associated with the Villa Gelliana), and the villa of Augustus were all represented on the walls of the salone according to their geographical location in the territory.[71]

FIGURE 8.9. Fontanina in the salone of the Villa d'Este, Tivoli.

Photograph by the author.

The topography of two different places has, therefore, been translated into the space of the room by a process of homothetic imitation, i.e., an enlargement or diminution of scale that preserves the basic layout. The territory, with its ancient villas, and the garden—which is itself a geographical model of the territory—are harmoniously united by the fact that all their spaces (both real and virtual) share the same geographical orientation. A complex play of placement and displacement situates the spectator in both a real and virtual realm, and profoundly "intensifies" his apprehension and comprehension of the locus, Tivoli, as an ancient and actual place.[72] This extremely elaborate spatial disposition corresponded to a conscious desire during the Renaissance not only to represent geographical space but to reproduce a "feeling" of its presence. As Edward Casey noted, landscape is what Jean-Paul Sartre has called a "detotalized totality," something that while being apprehended as a whole cannot be reduced to the sum of its parts. Landscape is, therefore, always partially "invisible" or limited to its literal visibility. It surrounds the spectator and cannot be visually grasped in its totality.[73]

When considered in this light, it is not surprising that most Renaissance artists chose to paint landscape scenes that were panoramic in nature, piecing together "fragments" of a setting in order to create a condensed representation that simulated the totalizing experience of being in the landscape.[74] Thus, at both Tivoli and Artimino, circumambulation is the bodily counterpart to the circumambience of the perceived landscape. Renaissance artists would ultimately respond to this perceptual limitation by translating geographical knowledge not only to the two-dimensional surface of a painting or print but to the three-dimensional spaces, such as geographical rooms, geographical gardens, and (later) georamas, that Jean-Marc Besse has called "les espaces de l'imagination géographique."[75]

Aside from the salone of the Villa d'Este at Tivoli, the most exemplary and famous of these realizations can be found in the Gallery of Maps in the Vatican. The architectonic space of the gallery, which was painted around 1580 for Pope Gregory XIII, is a metaphor for the Italian peninsula. The maps—which are positioned on each wall according to their geographical location (either toward the Adriatic Sea or the Mediterranean)—are themselves a metaphor for the all-powerful gaze of the pope.[76] Walking through the gallery, the visitor is transported across vast geographic spaces; the historical vignettes inserted into the maps and the religious episodes depicted on the vault, moreover, allow him to travel through time and to witness the most salient episodes of early Christian history. The Ptolemaic notion that "Geography is the eye of History" found in the gallery its most complete illustration during the Renaissance.[77]

In the salone of the Villa d'Este (as in the Gallery of Maps), the notions of place and time have been transformed by art, as if the ancient history of the place were continuously reenacting itself within the actuality of the present. In addition to the views of the garden and the landscape with its ancient villas, the paintings of the salone show the four seasons, the four elements, and the gods of the Roman pantheon. It is as if the implicit passage between the real and the theoretical panorama implied not only the passage from a *sujet regardant* to a *sujet connaissant*, but also the passage from an instantaneous and objective vision to a historical, symbolic, or mythological knowledge of the landscape and its significant sites.

Moving and Looking in the Villa and the Garden

The conflation of space and time in topographical views is especially clear if one examines in its context a view of the Fountain of Tivoli under construction in the first Tiburtine room at the Villa d'Este at Tivoli. The view was described in a recent guide book as "a kind a photograph of the fountain under construction" (fig. 8.10).[78] The two Tiburtine rooms, located logically to the east of the salone in the direction of Tivoli, are dedicated to the mythological foundation and ancient history of the city. The view only reveals its full significance when the viewer is confronted with the historical episodes represented in the room. At the center of the vault, the battle of the brothers Tiburtus and Catillus against the Latins after their disembarkation in Italy is accompanied by two scenes evoking the building of the ancient town of Tibur and two scenes pertaining to its foundation (fig. 8.11).[79] The view of the fountain under construction immediately echoes the two frescoes of the ancient city shown as a building site, and therefore equates the construction of the garden and the Fountain of Tivoli with the refoundation and rebirth of the ancient city. The explicit visual and metonymical parallel between the images and their subjects within the space of the room gives to the apparently objective and "innocent" view of the garden's fountain a precise meaning and a strong historical dimension.

Furthermore, the view of the fountain under construction was strategically placed close to the

FIGURE 8.10.
View of the Fountain of Tivoli, ca. 1569, fresco in the first Tiburtine room of the Villa d'Este, Tivoli. The real fountain is visible from the adjacent window.
Photograph by the author.

FIGURE 8.11.
The construction of Tibur, ca. 1569, fresco in the first Tiburtine room of the Villa d'Este, Tivoli.
Photograph by the author.

only window in the room, from which the real fountain in the garden is visible. By placing the painted image in this location, the artist appropriated the actual view onto the fountain to the historical order of the narrative that is at work in the frescoes. The play between inside and outside blurs the distinctions between vision and representation and between representation and historical imagination. The understanding of this complex intensification of the notion of place is only possible through movement, specifically the movement of the gaze across the walls, through the window, and into the garden.

That this system of visual echoes was not accidental is proven by the repetition of similar visual and intellectual games in earlier, contemporary, and probably later villas. As early as the fourteenth century, such plays between painted representations and actual landscapes were common. At the Torre dell'Aquila at Trento in northern Italy, where one of the earliest calendar cycles was painted around 1400, a painter represented the Castello del Buonconsiglio as it could be seen in reality through the window of the tower.[80] Another such visual game is present in the Sala delle Prospettive painted by Baldassare Peruzzi around 1516 at the Villa Farnesina in Rome. It has already been noted by other scholars that the painted scenes—presented as views through the columns of fictive loggias at either end of the hall—corresponded to the actual surroundings of the villa: a representation of the city on the eastern side of the hall, and a representation of the then-rural landscape of Trastevere on the western side.[81] What is generally unnoticed is the presence of a view of the Villa Farnesina between the fictive columns. It shows the Porta Settimiana, with a glimpse of the villa beyond, outside of the city gate from a position to the southwest of the villa, on the Via Settimiana (fig. 8.12). Interestingly, the painter chose to place this fresco in the southwestern side of the room, next

FIGURE 8.12.
View of the Porta Settimiana and the Villa Farnesina between the fictive columns, ca. 1516, fresco in the Sala delle Prospettive of the Villa Farnesina, Rome. The Porta Settimiana would have been visible through the window to the right of the fresco.

Photographs by the author.

FIGURE 8.13. View of the summer garden under construction, ca. 1562–65, fresco in the Room of the Farnese Deeds of the Palazzo Farnese, Caprarola. The painting reproduces the view from the window.

Photograph by the author.

to a window from which the original viewpoint was visible. Although the Accademia dei Lincei currently obstructs the view of the gate, no building was there in the early sixteenth century. Thus, the spectator was afforded a reflective gaze: the view from the window was literally mirrored, or rather mise en abîme, in the painted view. Only a slight movement of the head or eyes was necessary in order to see both views.

In the Room of the Farnese Deeds at the Palazzo Farnese at Caprarola, only the attentive visitor can spot the view painted in a *tondo* in the embrasure of one of the windows (fig. 8.13). It represents the summer garden under construction, as it would have appeared through the window. The view is the earliest representation of the garden, probably showing it as it looked around 1561.[82] The view is located immediately to the left of the window, as if to indicate where the visitor should direct his gaze.

One final and remarkable image takes us back to the Villa d'Este at Tivoli. In a small room situated next to the main room of the *primo piano*, a view was painted above a window that represented exactly the portion of landscape that could be seen through it (fig. 8.14). The Monti Corniculani are clearly recognizable, as they frame the famous Mount Soratte in the distance, with the sanctuary of Santa Maria di Quintiliolo also visible. More than four centuries later, the landscape has barely changed. To the view that he had before his eyes, the painter added only a hunter and two pilgrims walking toward the sanctuary.[83]

This example illustrates particularly well the concept of landscape as a representation and as a way of seeing in the Renaissance. The view from the window is the object of a double representation: first, a given portion of the landscape is framed by the architecture itself; and second, the mirrored image of the landscape is carefully placed above the window so that a slight shift of the gaze, this time vertically rather than laterally, enables the viewer

FIGURE 8.14. View of the Monti Corniculani, Mount Soratte, and Santa Maria di Quintiliolo, fresco in the Villa d'Este, Tivoli. The painted landscape mirrors the view from the window (at right).

Photographs by the author.

to compare the views and verify their similarities. The operation requires the transformation of land into landscape and of landscape into art.[84] But the apprehension of the two landscapes as identical depends on the position of the spectator in front of the window. Compared to our previous examples, this landscape is highly unremarkable. In order to perceive the similarity between the painted landscape and the view from the window, the visitor must pause at a very precise spot. He must detach himself from the architectural space of the room and enter the pictorial space of the view. From this position, he can perceive the continuity between the main axis of the garden and the topography of the surrounding landscape, as the axis of Hercules points directly toward Mount Soratte. If the spectator were to move, the two landscapes would no longer appear identical, since their sameness is fully established only when the spectator is facing the window. Thus, the image simultaneously affirms and questions the possibility of the landscape's existence outside of its Albertian frame—an existence imposed by man's vision. The image helps to create a mental image of the villa's space and landscape that is governed by a system of orthogonal axes, simultaneously visual and symbolic.

That the landscapes around the villa and the garden itself, as "representations," are conceived as paintings, is not a new development for garden historians. In the words of Augustin Berque, a garden gives the natural world in which it appears "a new dimension characteristic of a painting."[85] Reading the way the Villa d'Este was described by contemporary visitors makes this statement abundantly clear. Nicolas Audebert conceived his itinerary of the garden in terms of an alternation of movements and pauses for "viewing," understood as both an act of seeing and understanding. Like the position of the visitor in the small room described above, his movement in the garden was controlled by set "views." His steps and gazes were channeled through the allées, which led to objects that merited his consideration and demanded his static attention: a statue, a fountain, a belvedere, or a window that was the architectonic equivalent of the painted view. The allées, which were framed by parallel rows of trees, hedges, or architecture, served as both paths for walking and as perspectival lines (fig. 8.15).[86]

At Tivoli and Caprarola, many allées lead to large framed openings or belvederes that offer beautiful panoramas of the Roman countryside. The views onto the landscape are fully associated with paintings, recalling Pliny the Younger's remark on the painterly quality of the landscape seen from his Tuscan villa (fig. 8.16).[87] Evidence of the particularly strong conflation of painted and real views in Renaissance gardens is found in the many

FIGURE 8.15.
An allée leading to a framed view in the garden of the Palazzo Farnese, Caprarola.
Photograph by the author.

celebratory descriptions of the views from villas by Renaissance writers, as well as by small mistakes made by garden historians themselves.[88] For example, in her recent discussion on Italian Renaissance gardens, Malgorzata Szafranska commented on the views described by Vasari from the belvedere of the gardens at Castello as "a wide, painted panorama."[89] But in his "Life of Tribolo," Vasari was, in fact, describing the real view from the loggia, which would have included the ducal villas of Poggio a Caiano, Florence, Prato, and Siena. The confusion possibly lies in the fact that if the first three sites were indeed visible from the loggia, then a view of Siena would be impossible. For Claudia Lazzaro, this could only mean that Vasari, like Utens in his paintings, idealized his description of the view: "The view from the loggia, we realize, is not just a literal one; and the villa not just a grand palace with a beautiful garden, but a sign of the duke's rule over his dominion of Tuscany."[90]

This organization of space was also applied a century later in the gardens of Versailles, which were composed as a "constellation of specially arranged views."[91] Louis XIV himself devised different itineraries for visits to the gardens. These itineraries (*La manière de montrer les jardins de Versailles*) are punctuated by comments that encourage the visitor to stop, pause, and consider the views. The principal view, which was shown to the visitor on three occasions during his visit, was of the main axis of the garden. Like the axis of Hercules in the gardens at Tivoli, this grand allée was not intended for circulation, but instead played a fundamental role in the visual and iconographical composition of the garden. While sixteenth-century allées could end at a window or door that opened onto the surrounding countryside, seventeenth-century allées sometimes ended with painted views, or "perspectives," that extended the natural perspective created by the allées. In general, these views were mural paintings, usually landscapes, but, as this type of garden

FIGURE 8.16.
Sunset framed by one of the garden windows at the Villa d'Este, Tivoli.
Photograph by the author.

FIGURE 8.17. View of a project for the upper gardens at the Palazzo Farnese, 1586, fresco in the loggia of the palazzina at the Villa Farnese, Caprarola.
Photograph by the author.

decoration became increasing popular, the murals began to be supplanted by canvases stretched on the wall, "so that these beautiful prospects could be removed from the injurious effects of weather whenever one wished."[92]

The tradition of combining real and painted views in the garden may derive from the ancient Roman concept of *topiaria opera*—the art of representing place—that applied equally to gardens, painted landscapes, and theater sets, and whose primary aim was to create pictorial effects.[93] If the Italian Renaissance garden can be understood as a juxtaposition of views (*varietates topiorum*), like the *ars topiaria* of ancient Roman art, then the relationship between vision and representation, between the garden and its painted image, can provide a fruitful ground for research.[94]

For example, in an unpublished mid-sixteenth-century treatise on agriculture, Girolamo Fiorenzuola recommended that small allées radiating out from the wide principal allée terminate in painted or sculpted depictions on the walls enclosing the garden.[95] And already at the beginning of the sixteenth century, Baldassare Peruzzi had painted a fresco with the vision of Saint Bernard of Clairvaux set in a landscape scene on the wall of the garden of Sant' Andrea al Quirinale. This tradition of painting landscape frescoes on garden walls continued in the seventeenth century in the Jesuit garden of San Vitale.[96] Giovanni Battista Armenini, writing at the end of the sixteenth century in his *De' veri precetti della pittura* (1586), summed up the subjects appropriate for outdoor decoration as "games of shepherds, of nymphs . . . fauns, satyrs, wood sprites, centaurs, sea monsters, along with other aquatic and wild things"—all subjects related to landscape.[97] The garden and frescoed views were, thus, bound together in a unique vision of the landscape as a sacred or pastoral site.

Painted garden views were carefully placed in the palazzina of the upper gardens behind the Palazzo Farnese at Caprarola to highlight the main axis of the garden and to control the gaze of the viewer along the main sight lines. Only one of these views has been identified. It shows the project or state of the garden as it was conceived by Giacomo del Duca around 1584 (fig. 8.17).[98] The view is situated above a door in the lower loggia of the palazzina, on the southern side, from which one had a commanding view of the entire garden as it sloped down in a sequence

FIGURE 8.18.
View of a project for the upper gardens showing the uppermost terrace behind the palazzina, 1586, loggia of the palazzina at the Palazzo Farnese, Caprarola.

Photograph by the author.

of terraces and fountains. Above the opposite door, thus mirroring the first view, is another view of the garden, which shows the palazzina's hillside facade (*a monte*) as it was originally projected, plus the open landscape and hill above the palazzina (fig. 8.18). The one-story elevation of the building is clearly recognizable, including the three arcades of the loggia and the belvedere. These features, as well as the pergolas on the upper terrace, are visible in both views. The group of houses on the right, which are gathered around what looks like a medieval tower, likely includes the caretaker's house and the Porta di San Rocco (also known as the Porta del Giglio), whose presence and function as an entrance gate to the park are documented.[99] Just as he might have had at Tivoli, the visitor, after reaching the loggia from the garden, could have a complete image of his own ascent and a view of the site as it would appear once it was completed (fig. 8.19). The site—which was only progressively and sequentially revealed to the viewer during this climb—now became entirely visible in both its present and future aspects.

Renaissance villas that included depictions of their gardens and landscapes gave access to a superior sort of knowledge—a knowledge of the villa

FIGURE 8.19.
View from the loggia of the palazzina at the Palazzo Farnese, Caprarola.

Photograph by the author.

as a whole, not only of its garden, fountains, and surrounding territory, but also of its past history, its subsequent glory and immortality, and its deeper philosophical meaning. The painted decoration of a villa thus becomes, like the garden, a visual and symbolic synthesis of the place or locus; it provides the viewer with a mnemonic tool to situate himself both physically and virtually within the actual and represented space. In this "theater of memory," the eye and gaze of the visitor—a "window of the soul" according to Leonardo da Vinci—are the only media by which the story told in the garden can once again come alive.[100]

Conclusion and Perspectives

What new perspectives can this approach offer to the study of Italian gardens? Although the traditional use of garden views as documents will remain crucial for reconstructing historical gardens, historians need to exercise caution. Renaissance topographical images had the power to make spaces that were often invented or profoundly manipulated appear to be truthful representations or striking lifelike imitations of nature. But if these images are understood as rhetorical constructions—as propagandistic, didactic, and mnemonic tools—then they can yield a wealth of information on how the spaces and landscapes of a villa were perceived and understood.

The history of Italian gardens and landscapes will continue to benefit from the social and political approach in the wake of the seminal studies done by Reinhard Bentmann and Michael Müller and later by James Ackerman.[101] Today, this approach, together with the development of regional studies of gardens, is the most important avenue of research. Another approach, inspired by a phenomenology of perception, considers how space itself was constructed and experienced.[102] While garden historians have started to address these important questions—for example, in the Dumbarton Oaks symposium "Landscape Design and Experience of Motion" organized by Michel Conan—I have shown that a similar direction could be taken based on an analysis of images. Jean-Marc Besse, Denis Cosgrove, and Renzo Dubbini have attempted to do this in recent years by developing a new epistemology of historical geography.[103] The methodology used by historians of Roman art is also essential and can provide the historian of the Renaissance with new tools to understand landscape representations. Pierre Grimal, Wilhelmina Jashemski, Bettina Bergmann, and Jás Elsner examine painted decorations to understand the architectural and garden spaces in a way that historians of the Renaissance do not.[104] This is puzzling if we consider that most Renaissance villas were based on an understanding of the principles found in ancient writings by Pliny, Vitruvius, and others. The Sala delle Prospettive at the Villa Farnesina and the salone at the Villa d'Este, for example, are, in essence, reconstructions of ancient Roman dining rooms.[105]

I have used the word "symptoms" to designate views of gardens. This clearly indicates a shift from the study of the garden as a material object to the study of the garden as a social and political space, and as a space of experience. To engage in such an approach is to literally create new "immaterial objects" of study, such as a view from a window or a visual axis—that is, objects that are created by man but do not belong to the category of fine arts. Marcello Fagiolo's recent essay, which deals with the construction of urban-scale visual axes through the topographical arrangement of villas and palaces in Rome (the so-called axes of historical memory), demonstrated the importance of this historically informed perception of space in the economy of the Renaissance villa.[106] In this paper, I have shown how, in some villas of Renaissance Italy, vision and representation were purposefully blurred—rather than confounded—in order to create a third level of perception and understanding that was liberated from the constraints of time and space. I would like to call this phenomenon a "third nature" of perception and historical imagination, or what Michel Conan has termed intersubjectivity: "Motion through a landscape metaphor engages visitors into a hermeneutical activity that reactivates the meaning of a cultural tradition at the same time that it enables them to bring new meaning to their lives. In that respect, intersubjectivity, as mediated by the experience of motion through a landscape metaphor, contributes to the development of the individual and the cultural community to which the individual belongs."[107]

Finally, from a theoretical point of view, the approach developed in this paper calls into question the notion of pure landscape, which is still advocated by art historians dealing with sixteenth- and seventeenth-century landscape painting and *vedute*. Several authors have noted that views of landscapes and gardens in sixteenth-century Italian villas were among "the first representations of pure landscape."[108] Yet the notion of pure landscape in the historiography of art history is, as W. J. T. Mitchell has shown, comparable to "a kind of quest-romance in which pure landscape is the grail to be obtained."[109] At most, it can be justified in purely formal terms. Thus, instead of talking about a rise of pure landscape, I suggest we talk about a process by which landscape becomes autonomous as a cultural, rather than a natural, discourse. Autonomy is marked within the image by the replacement of figures by a memorial immanence of the landscape, which does not unfold a narrative as a linear sequence, but contains, *en puissance*, its memory: this is, in short, the translation of the subjective vision of the artist or the patron onto the landscape that surrounds him, which, in turn, suggests to the viewer a specific horizon of perception and comprehension of the place. Pure landscape cannot exist without pure vision, which exists, precisely, only in theory.

Notes

1 See Alessandro Tagliolini, *Storia del giardino italiano: Gli artisti, l'invenzione, le forme, dall'antichità al XIX secolo* (Florence: La Casa Usher, 1988); and David R. Coffin, *Gardens and Gardening in Papal Rome* (Princeton, N.J.: Princeton University Press, 1991).

2 Dianne Harris notes that "past works of art actually work at prefiguring the shape of their subsequent histories," and that "representational practices encoded in works of art continue to be encoded in their commentaries." See Dianne Harris, "Landscape and Representation: The Printed View and Marc'Antonio dal Re's *Ville di Delizie*," in *Villas and Gardens in Early Modern Italy and France*, eds. Mirka Beneš and Dianne Harris (Cambridge: Cambridge University Press, 2001), 179.

3 On the question of "truthfulness" in topographical representation during the Renaissance, see Lucia Nuti, "The Perspective Plan in the Sixteenth Century: The Invention of a Representational Language," *The Art Bulletin* 76 (1994): 107 (for the quotations).

4 Claudia Swan, "*Ad vivum, naer het leven*, From the Life: Defining a Mode of Representation," *Word and Image* 11 (1995): 353–72.

5 Marcello Fagiolo and Maria Adriana Giusti, eds., *Lo specchio del paradiso: L'immagine del giardino dall'antico al Novecento* (Cinisello Balsamo [Milan]: Silvana, 1996).

6 Linda Cabe Halpern, "The Use of Paintings in Garden History," in *Garden History: Issues, Approaches, Methods*, ed. John Dixon Hunt (Washington, D.C.: Dumbarton Oaks Research Library and Collection, 1992), 183–84.

7 John Harris, *The Artist and the Country House: A History of Country House and Garden View Painting in Britain, 1540–1870* (London: Sotheby Parke-Bernet, 1979); Françoise Boudon, "Images de jardins au XVIème siècle: Les plus excellents bastiments de France," in *Histoire des jardins de la Renaissance à nos jours*, eds. Monique Mosser and Georges Teyssot (Paris: Flammarion, 1991); Maurizio Gargano, "Villas, jardins et fontaines de Rome: Les gravures de Giovanni Battista Falda," in *Histoire des jardins: De la Renaissance à nos jours*, eds. Monique Mosser and Georges Teyssot, 162–64 (Paris: Flammarion, 1991); Cristina Acidini Luchinat, "Alle origini del 'ritratto di giardino'," in *Giardini regali: Fascino e immagini del verde nelle grandi dinastie; Dai Medici agli Asburgo*, ed. Monica Amari, 159–64 (Milan: Electa, 1998); Monique Mosser, "Hortésie cartographique: De l'écriture classique des parcs à la française à la calligraphie poétique des jardins anglo-chinois," in *Le paysage des cartes: Genèse d'une codification; Actes de la 3e journée d'études du Musée des Plans-Reliefs, Paris, Hôtel des Invalides, 19 novembre 1998*, ed. Catherine Bousquet-Bressolier, 99–119 (Paris: Le Musée, 1999); Hervé Brunon, "De l'image à l'imaginaire: Notes sur la figuration du jardin

sous le règne de Louis XIV," *XVIIe siècle* 209 (2000): 671–86; Roy C. Strong, *The Artist and the Garden* (New Haven: Yale University Press, 2000); Harris, "Landscape and Representation"; Claudia Lazzaro, "Italy is a Garden: The Idea of Italy and the Italian Garden Tradition," in *Villas and Gardens in Early Modern Italy and France*, eds. Mirka Beneš and Dianne Harris (Cambridge: Cambridge University Press, 2001), 56–60; Elizabeth S. Eustis, "The Garden Print as Propaganda, 1573–1683," in *European Pleasure Gardens: Rare Books and Prints of Historic Landscape Design from the Elizabeth K. Reilley Collection*, ed. Elizabeth S. Eustis, 41–51 (Bronx, N.Y.: New York Botanical Garden, 2003); Claudia Lazzaro, "Representing the Social and Cultural Experience of Italian Gardens in Prints," in *The Changing Garden: Four Centuries of European and American Art*, ed. Betsy G. Fryberger, 29–39 (Berkeley, Calif.: Iris and B. Gerald Cantor Center for Visual Arts at Stanford University, 2003); and Dianne Harris, *The Nature of Authority: Villa Culture, Landscape, and Representation in Eighteenth-Century Lombardy* (University Park: Pennsylvania State University Press, 2003). For a philosophical and theoretical consideration of the garden and its representation, see also Massimo Venturi Ferriolo, "L'art dei giardini tra pittura e realtà," in *Il giardino dipinto nella pittura lombarda dal Seicento all'Ottocento*, ed. Paolo Biscottini, 13–16 (Milan: Skira, 1995); and John Dixon Hunt, *Greater Perfections: The Practice of Garden Theory* (Philadelphia: University of Pennsylvania Press, 2000), 143–79.

8 According to Mirka Beneš, they should be considered "not only as documents of landscapes and gardens or as models for the picturelike construction of landscape designs, but with a structural focus, taking into account all the relevant categories of reference, or the framework of meanings in which a society addressed its concerns with landscape." Mirka Beneš, "Recent Developments and Perspectives in the Historiography of Italian Gardens," in *Perspectives on Garden Histories*, ed. Michel Conan (Washington, D.C.: Dumbarton Oaks Research Library and Collection, 1999), 61–62. See also Mirka Beneš, "Italian and French Gardens: A Century of Historical Study (1900–2000)," in *Villas and Gardens in Early Modern Italy and France*, eds. Mirka Beneš and Dianne Harris, 1–16 (Cambridge: Cambridge University Press, 2001).

9 Erwin Panofsky, *Meaning in the Visual Arts* (1957; translated by Bernard and Marthe Teyssèdre as *L'oeuvre d'art et ses significations: Essais sur les "arts visuels,"* Paris: Gallimard, 1969), 35–38; Michel Foucault, *The Archaeology of Knowledge* (London: Tavistock Publications, 1972), 6–8; Jacques Le Goff, "Documento/monumento," in *Enciclopedia* (Turin: G. Einaudi, 1977–), 5:38–48; and Jacques Le Goff, *Storia e memoria* (Turin: G. Einaudi, 1982), 443–55. For examples of this methodology applied to the analysis of garden images and landscape historiography, see Brunon, "De l'image à l'imaginaire"; and Hervé Brunon, "Documents ou monuments? Les textes littéraires dans la panoplie méthodologique des histoires du paysage," in *Le paysage dans la littérature italienne: De Dante à nos jours*, ed. Giuseppe Sangirardi, 17–28 (Dijon: Éditions Universitaires de Dijon, 2006).

10 Foucault, *Archaeology of Knowledge*, 6–8.

11 "Contre la gallerie est une grande Sale ornée de belles peintures, & entre aultres a un bout d'icelle est le pourtraict et desseing du Palais, Jardin, et Fontaines de Tyvoly, non comme il est, mais comme il seroit estant achevé . . ." Ronald Lightbown, "Nicolas Audebert and the Villa d'Este," *Journal of the Warburg and Courtauld Institutes* 27 (1964): 171.

12 "Mais il fault remarquer que la longueur se doibt prendre depuis le palais jusques a la porte du Jardin respondante en la rue, qui est deux foys plus que la largeur: combien que par le pourtraict il semble au contraire; ce qui provient de la perspective qui représente les choses toutes raccourcyes quand elles nous sont directement opposées, et fort eslognées de nostre veue . . ." Ibid., 190; and Claudia Lazzaro, *The Italian Renaissance Garden: From the Conventions of Planting, Design, and Ornament to the Grand Gardens of Sixteenth-Century Central Italy* (New Haven: Yale University Press, 1990), 219.

13 James Turner, "Landscape and the 'Art Prospective' in England, 1584–1660," *Journal of the Warburg and Courtauld Institutes* 42 (1979): 290–93.

14 Claudia Lazzaro, "The Villa Lante at Bagnaia" (PhD diss., Princeton University, 1974), 1:37–40; and David R. Coffin, "Some Aspects of the Villa Lante at Bagnaia," in *Arte in Europa: Scritti di storia dell'arte in onore di Edoardo Arslan*, 569–75 (Milan: Tipografia Artipo, 1966).

15 The inventory is published in Sabine Frommel, ed., *Villa Lante a Bagnaia* (Milan: Electa, 2005), 360–62.

16 For the date of the fresco, see Andrea Alessi, "La decorazione pittorica della Palazzina Gambara a Bagnaia," *Biblioteca e società* 21, no. 1–2 (2002): 22–24. Marcello Fagiolo suggested a later date of 1580, after the visit of Carlo Borromeo, in *Vignola: L'architettura dei principi* (Rome: Gangemi, 2007), 211. For a summary of the chronology of the works in the garden, see Christoph Luitpold Frommel, "Villa Lante e Tommaso Ghinucci," in *Villa Lante a Bagnaia*, ed. Sabine Frommel (Milan: Electa, 2005), 92–93.

17 See Suzanne B. Butters, "Ferdinand et le jardin du Pincio," in *La Villa Médicis*, ed. André Chastel, vol. 2, *Études*, eds. Glenn M. Andres et al. (Rome: Académie de France à Rome, École Française de Rome, 1991), 1:50–52 and 2:363–64; and David R. Coffin, "The Self-Image of the Roman Villa during the Renaissance," *Architectura: Zeitschrift für Geschichte der Baukunst* 28 (1998): 201. On the decoration of the stanzino, see also Eric Darragon, "Le studiolo du Cardinal Ferdinand à la Villa Médicis," *Revue de l'art* 19 (1973): 63–77; and Philippe Morel, "Le Parnasse astrologique: Les décors peints pour le cardinal Ferdinand de Médicis," in *La Villa Médicis*, eds. André Chastel and Philippe Morel, vol. 3, *Le Parnasse astrologique*, by Philippe

Morel, 45–88 (Rome: Académie de France à Rome, École Française de Rome, 1991).

18 Suzanne B. Butters, "Ferdinand et le jardin du Pincio," 364.

19 Ibid., 363.

20 Graham Smith, *The Casino of Pius IV* (Princeton, N.J.: Princeton University Press, 1977), 87 and 98–99; and Denis Ribouillault, "Paysage et pouvoir: Les décors topographiques à Rome et dans le Latium au XVIe siècle," 3 vols. (Doctoral thesis, Université Paris I Panthéon-Sorbonne, 2006), 248–50.

21 During the symposium on the Villa Lante at Bagnaia held at Viterbo in April 2004, architectural historians reopened the debate concerning the authorship of the villa. Historians such as Christoph Frommel, Fabiano Tiziano Fagliari Zeni Bucchichio, and Richard Tuttle discarded the name of Vignola in favor of Tommaso Ghinucci, who indeed appears to have been the main actor on the building site. Other historians, such as Bruno Adorni and Marcello Fagiolo (following Claudia Lazzaro and David Coffin's pioneering suggestions), continue to defend the idea that Vignola was at the origin of the design, although no documentation exists that shows his involvement in the actual construction process. See the respective articles in Frommel, *Villa Lante a Bagnaia*. A nineteenth-century source seems to confirm the hypothesis that Ghinucci had been working after ideas first suggested by Vignola: "Il prelodato Gambara nel 1568 col disegno del celeberrimo Vignola, eseguito sotto l'assistenza del valente fiorentino Francesco Chisiucci [Ghinucci], nobilitò e perfezionò vieppiù sempre la Villa già incominciata e formata dai suoi antecessori . . ." Mattia Natilj, *Cenno storico e compendiosa descrizione della Villa di Bagnaia com' era avanti al 1820* (Rome: Sinimberg, 1864), 7.

22 After the visit of Cardinal Carlo Borromeo in 1580, it seems that no other fountains or buildings were built. On Borromeo's visit, see Alexander Koller, "Giovan Francesco Gambara (1533–1587): Profilo di un cardinale," in *Villa Lante a Bagnaia*, ed. Sabine Frommel (Milan: Electa, 2005), 28–29.

23 Andrea Alessi, "La palazzina Gambara: Gli architetti e i pittori," in *Villa Lante a Bagnaia*, ed. Sabine Frommel (Milan: Electa, 2005), 110–12. The presence of disguised portraits of artists and architects is common in Renaissance villas. For example, Vignola is represented several times in the frescoes of the Palazzo Farnese at Caprarola. Marcello Fagiolo has recently discovered that the four caryatids in the main courtyard of the Villa Giulia in Rome were portraits of the four famous architects of the villa: Michelangelo, Vignola, Giorgio Vasari, and Bartolomeo Ammannati. Fagiolo, *Vignola*, 90–91.

24 Coffin, "Some Aspects of the Villa Lante at Bagnaia," 572–73. The verses were added later. See also Alessi, "La palazzina Gambara," 114.

25 Lazzaro, "Villa Lante at Bagnaia," 47.

26 John Coolidge, "The Villa Giulia: A Study of Central Italian Architecture in the Mid-Sixteenth Century," *The Art Bulletin* 25 (1943): 224–25.

27 Eustis, "The Garden Print as Propaganda," 43.

28 "En fin, pour plus facile intelligence & demonstration de tout ce que dessus, Jay bien voulu en faire un petit pourtraict pour representer ce qui ne se peult aultrement comprendre que par la peinture." Lightbown, "Nicolas Audebert and the Villa d'Este," 190.

29 "E perchè Vostra Eccellenza la veggia prima con l'imaginativa che co'l senso, cercaro a parte per parte farglila vedere, ma non cosi bene e per ordine con la penna, come farei co'l disegno. Bench'io spero fra pochi giorni mandarle ancho questo . . ." Bartolomeo Ammannati to Marco Benavides, 2 May 1555. MS 374, vol. II, fol. 91–96, Biblioteca Oliveriana, Pesaro See Tilman Falk, "Studien zur Topographie und Geschichte der Villa Giulia in Rom," *Römisches Jahrbuch für Kunstgeschichte* 13 (1971): 171. "Mi ha Vostra Altezza comandato piu volte, che io Le mandi un dissegno della mia villa di Frascati, che Belvedere si chiama, et per obedirla già ho dato commissione che il dissegno si faccia, et si può dire egli essere sotto il torchio delle stampe. Ma perché vorrei più presto al desiderio dell'Altezza Vostra haver satisfatto, ho pensato mentre maestra mano, et con intagli et con colori, et in prospettiva, et in profilo procura di far venire la mia villa in mano di Lei, di farla comparire anco io descritta nel suo cospetto, acciò Vostra Altezza congiongendo la fatica dell'intaglio e del penello con quella della penna, meglio si rappresenti le cose di essa à parte à parte nell'imaginativa, et estimandole ne possi far più certo giuditio et io goda di saper quello che vi è bono et quello che vi è di errore, con l'intendere ciò che da Lei verrà approvato, et riprovato, percioche sol quello mi sarà caro, che dalla finezza del Suo giuditio per ben fatto approverassi." Cesare d'Onofrio, *La Villa Aldobrandini a Frascati* (Rome: Staderini, 1963), 82. On the function of garden views in eighteenth-century Rome, see also David R. Marshall, "'Farò la villeggiatura sopra la tela': Cardinal Patrizi and Adriaen Manglard's 'Vedute' of the Villa Patrizi," *The Burlington Magazine* 144, no. 1193 (2002): 497–501.

30 David R. Coffin, *The Villa d'Este at Tivoli* (Princeton, N.J.: Princeton University Press, 1960), 141.

31 On descriptio and ekphrasis, see the fundamental study of Ernst Robert Curtius, *European Literature and the Latin Middle Ages* (1948; reprint, trans. Willard R. Trask, Princeton, N.J.: Bollingen Series, 1953), 68–71, 157–58, and 183–202. See also Denis Ribouillault, "Le salone de la villa d'Este à Tivoli: Un théâtre des jardins et du territoire," *Studiolo: Revue d'histoire de l'art de l'Académie de France à Rome* 3 (2005): 84–85; and Jean-Marc Besse, *Face au monde: Atlas, jardins, géoramas* (Paris: Desclée de Brouwer, 2003), 107.

32 Charles de Secondat Montesquieu, *Voyages* (Paris: Arléa, 2003), 183. Other examples are in Lucia Nuti, "I 'teatri' di città e l'Italia del secolo XVII," in *Cartographiques: Actes du colloque de l'Académie de France à Rome, 19–20 mai*

1995, ed. Marie-Ange Brayer (Paris: Réunion des Musées Nationaux, 1996), 118–21; and Thomas Frangenberg, "Chorographies of Florence: The Use of City Views and City Plans in the Sixteenth Century," *Imago Mundi* 46 (1994): 41–64.

33 "le quali vedendosi espresse in pittura e potendosi con questo mezzo conservar meglio nella memoria." Gabriele Paleotti, *Discorso intorno alle imagine sacre e profane* (1582; reprinted in *Trattati d'arte del Cinquecento, fra manierismo e Controriforma*, ed. Paola Barocchi, Bari: G. Laterza, 1960–62), 2:354–56.

34 I have followed the translation published in John F. D'Amico and Kathleen Weil-Garris, "The Renaissance Cardinal's Ideal Palace: A Chapter from Paolo Cortesi's *De Cardinalatu*," *Memoirs of the American Academy in Rome* 35 (1980): 94–97.

35 The salone of the Villa d'Este at Tivoli is called "triclinium" in Uberto (Uberti Folietae) Foglietta, *Tyburtinum Hippolyti Estii* (1569), vol. 1 of *Antiche descrizioni della Villa d'Este a Tivoli*, trans. Franco Sciaretta (Tivoli: Tiburis Artistica, 2003), 7.

36 See, for example, Audebert, who speaks about "un Jardin incomparable pour les rares exellences qui y sont, & les fontaines artificielles, qui non seulement sont tres ingenieuses, mais aussy admirables, et peult estre incroyables a plusieurs qui ne les auront veues . . ." Lightbown, "Nicolas Audebert and the Villa d'Este," 169–70. See also the descriptions of the fountains of the Villa Lante at Bagnaia by Fabio Arditio in 1578 and Michel de Montaigne in 1581 in Frommel, *Villa Lante a Bagnaia*, 347–48.

37 Vitruvius *Ten Books* 9.8, 10.8. See also Isabella Barisi, Marcello Fagiolo, and Maria Luisa Madonna, *Villa d'Este* (Rome: De Luca, 2003), 104–9.

38 D'Amico and Weil-Garris, "The Renaissance Cardinal's Ideal Palace," 118n123.

39 Morel, "Le Parnasse astrologique," 45–88.

40 Acidini Luchinat, "Alle origini del 'ritratto di giardino'," 160. On gardens as museums and collections of rarities, see John Dixon Hunt, "Curiosities to Adorn Cabinets and Gardens," in *The Origins of Museums: The Cabinet of Curiosities in Sixteenth- and Seventeenth-Century Europe*, eds. Oliver Impey and Arthur MacGregor, 193–203 (Oxford: Clarendon Press, and New York: Oxford University Press, 1985); and Elisabeth Blair MacDougall, "A Paradise of Plants: Exotica, Rarities, and Botanical Fantasies," in *The Age of the Marvelous*, ed. Joy Kenseth, 145–57 (Hanover, N.H.: Hood Museum of Art, Dartmouth College, 1991).

41 This was first suggested by Patrizia Cavazzini when discussing the decoration by Agostino Tassi of the Palazzo Lancellotti in Rome in *Palazzo Lancellotti ai Coronari: Cantiere d'Agostino Tassi* (Rome: Istituto Poligrafico e Zecca dello Stato, Libreria dello Stato, 1998), 59. The relationship between the peacock and the sense of sight is made very clear in many Flemish paintings, where peacocks are usually depicted against landscape views. See, for example, Jan Brueghel the Elder, *The Sense of Sight*, 1617 (Museo del Prado, Madrid).

42 D'Amico and Weil-Garris, "The Renaissance Cardinal's Ideal Palace," 96–97. On the depiction of riddles and fables, and for examples of how these recommendations were followed in sixteenth-century Roman palaces, see 117–19.

43 "Un accademia, un cenacolo, un teatro del mondo." Ercole Cato, *Oratione fatta dal cavaliere Hercole Cato nelle essequie dell'illustriss. & reverendiss. sig. D. Hippolito d'Este card. di Ferrara, celebrate nella città di Tivoli* (Ferrara: Per Vittorio Baldini, stampator ducale, 1587). The highly intellectual program of the Villa d'Este is illustrated in the decidedly esoteric approaches of some art historians. See David Dernie, *The Villa d'Este at Tivoli* (London: Academy Editions, 1996); and Gérard Desnoyers, *La Villa d'Este à Tivoli, ou, Le songe d'Hippolyte: Un rêve d'immortalité héliaque* (Paris: Myrobolan, 2002).

44 D'Amico and Weil-Garris, "The Renaissance Cardinal's Ideal Palace," 90–91.

45 Quintilian *Institutio oratoria* 11.2.17–22; and *Ad Herrenium* 3.22. See Francis A. Yates, *L'art de la mémoire*, trans. Daniel Arasse (Paris: Gallimard, 1975), 14–15 and 19–22. See also Isabelle Rieusset-Lemarié, "Des palais de mémoire aux paysages virtuels: Le rôle du parcours dans les paysages urbains imaginaires," in *Les enjeux du paysage*, ed. Michel Collot (Brussels: Ousia, 1997), 250–55. Recent historians have stressed the importance of the ancient art of memory for the understanding of topographical images. See especially Giorgio Mangani, "Da icone a emblemi: Cartografia morale delle città (secoli XIV–XVI)," in *Tra oriente e occidente: Città e iconografia dal XV al XIX secolo*, ed. Cesare de Seta, 10–21 (Naples: Electa Napoli, 2004); and Giorgio Mangani, *Cartografia morale: Geografia, persuasione, identità* (Modena: Franco Cosimo Panini, 2006). This was also suggested by Elisabeth Blair MacDougall, "*Ars Hortulorum*: Sixteenth-Century Garden Iconography and Literary Theory in Italy," in *Fountains, Statues, and Flowers: Studies in Italian Gardens of the Sixteenth and Seventeenth Centuries*, ed. Elisabeth Blair MacDougall (Washington, D.C.: Dumbarton Oaks Research Library and Collection, 1992), 124–25; and André Chastel, "Les jardins et les fleurs," *Revue de l'art* 51 (1981): 43.

46 On Utens's views, see Daniela Mignani, *Le ville medicee di Giusto Utens* (Florence: Arnaud, 1982).

47 Lazzaro, *Italian Renaissance Garden*, 5–6.

48 See Raffaella Fabiani Giannetto, "'Grafting the Edelweiss on Cactus Plants': The 1931 Italian Garden Exhibition and Its Legacy," this volume.

49 "The villas are shown frontally . . . and from an elevated viewpoint, which means that two modes of construction coexist in each painting and that they use two theoretical, simultaneous, and intersecting planes of observation, one giving a frontal view of the buildings' facades from

ground level, and the other an aerial view of the entire landscape." Renzo Dubbini, *Geography of the Gaze: Urban and Rural Vision in Early Modern Europe* (Chicago: University of Chicago Press, 2002), 36. See also the analysis of Utens's views in Acidini Luchinat, "Alle origini del 'ritratto di giardino'," 161–62.

50 This was noted in Lazzaro, *Italian Renaissance Garden*, 219.

51 The lunettes must also be understood in relation to the wider decorative scheme at the Medici villa at Artimino. Two other cycles of paintings existed inside the villa: the first depicted the women of the Medici family, and the second depicted battle scenes in seventeen lunettes (the same number of paintings used in the *salone delle ville*). Ferdinando de'Medici, following most aristocratic courts in Europe at the time, used these cycles to build the image of his dynasty on the ideological triad of territorial domination, genealogy, and conquest. On the decoration of the villa of Artimino, see Enrica Cassarino, *La villa medicea di Artimino* (Florence: Becocci-Scala, 1990); Nadia Bastogi, "La villa Ferdinanda di Artimino," in *Fasto di corte: La decorazione murale nelle residenze dei Medici e dei Lorena*, vol. 1, *Da Ferdinando I alle Reggenti, 1587–1628*, ed. Mina Gregori, 45–65 (Florence: Edifir, 2005); and Nadia Bastogi, "Magnificenza, decoro morale e celebrazione dinastica nei cicli di affreschi per il Granduca Ferdinando I: Il caso della villa di Artimino," *Fontes* 7, no. 13–16 (2004–5 [2007]): 53–82; and Suzanne Butters, "Land, Women, and War: Constructing Ferdinando I de'Medici's Artimino," forthcoming.

52 Claude Lévi-Strauss, *The Savage Mind* (Chicago: University of Chicago Press, 1962), 63.

53 On the Medici villa system as an ideological instrument of territorial control, see Vittorio Franchetti Pardo, *I Medici nel contado fiorentino: Ville e possedimenti agricoli tra Quattrocento e Cinquecento* (Florence: Clusf, 1978), 42–57.

54 "Utens's 'manner' was highly influential but it operated within a strongly ideological iconographic program having little to do with any objective desire to survey the lands he was depicting." Dubbini, *Geography of the Gaze*, 38. See also James M. Saslow, who wrote that Utens's series "functioned not simply as visual records, but more profoundly as a collective document of ownership and control, a catalogue of holdings that asserts possession of the individual pieces while establishing their common identity as parts of a coherent whole" in *The Medici Wedding of 1589: Florentine Festival as Theatrum Mundi* (New Haven: Yale University Press, 1996), 133–38.

55 On Ferdinando de'Medici's travel between his different villas, see Mignani, *Le ville medicee di Giusto Utens*, 15–17; and Maria Adriana Giusti, "La veduta documento e le serie 'catastali'," in *Lo specchio del paradiso: L'immagine del giardino dall'antico al Novecento*, eds. Marcello Fagiolo and Maria Adriana Giusti (Cinisello Balsamo [Milan]: Silvana, 1996), 51.

56 Franchetti Pardo, *I Medici nel contado fiorentino*, 54; and Matthias Quast, "Die Medici-Villen als Spiegel frühabsolutistischer Herrschaft. Beobachtungen zur Instrumentalisierung der Villenarchitektur unter Grossherzog Ferdinand I. (1587–1609)," in *Gedenkschrift für Richard Harprath*, eds. Wolfgang Liebenwein and Anchise Tempestini, 375–85 (Munich: Deutscher Kunstverlag, 1998).

57 Saslow, *Medici Wedding of 1589*, 134 and 138.

58 Quast, "Die Medici-Villen als Spiegel frühabsolutistischer Herrschaft. Beobachtungen zur Instrumentalisierung der Villenarchitektur unter Grossherzog Ferdinand I. (1587–1609)," 379.

59 On the architecture of the villa of Artimino by Bernardo Buontalenti and the relationship between architecture and landscape, see Matthias Quast, "La villa di Artimino del Buontalenti: Rilettura tipologico-stilistica," in *Kunst des Cinquecento in der Toskana*, ed. Monika Cämmerer, 365–71 (Munich: F. Bruckmann, 1992). On the Medicean villas at the time of Ferdinando de'Medici as instruments of the absolutist power of the Grand Duke, see Quast, "Die Medici-Villen als Spiegel frühabsolutistischer Herrschaft. Beobachtungen zur Instrumentalisierung der Villenarchitektur unter Grossherzog Ferdinand I. (1587–1609)"; and Franchetti Pardo, *I Medici nel contado fiorentino*, 54–56.

60 Edward S. Casey, *Representing Place: Landscape Painting and Maps* (Minneapolis: University of Minnesota Press, 2002), xvi. The same methodological direction has been suggested by W. J. T. Mitchell, preface to *Landscape and Power*, ed. W. J. T. Mitchell, 2nd ed. (Chicago and London: University of Chicago Press, 2002), vii–xii; and by the French epistemologist and geographer Jean-Marc Besse, "Représenter la ville ou la simuler? Réflexions autour d'une vue d'Amsterdam au XVIe siècle," *Ligeia: Dossiers sur l'art* 19–20 (1996–97): 55.

61 Harris, "Landscape and Representation," 182.

62 John Berger, *Ways of Seeing* (London: British Broadcasting Corporation, and New York: Penguin Books, 1972); and Denis Cosgrove, "Prospect, Perspective and the Evolution of the Landscape Idea," *Transactions of the Institute of British Geographers*, n.s., 10 (1985): 46.

63 The expression "archaeology of the gaze" should not be understood as a direct derivation from the archaeological method used by Michel Foucault in *The Archaeology of Knowledge*, since Foucault's approach is essentially philosophical and its aim is quite different from mine. However, it is tempting to have his epistemological method coincide to some extent with my attempt to contextualize images of place within a convincing horizon of cultural perception, both at a conscious and unconscious level. As I have already explained, his discussion of the "document," which history now transforms into "monument," is highly relevant for my purpose. See Foucault, *Archaeology of Knowledge*, 6–8.

64 Dubbini, *Geography of the Gaze*, 8–10. It is worth signaling here the pioneering work of Bruno Toscano, who,

in an article on Perugino's representation of the Umbrian landscape, called for the development of such an archaeology of the gaze: "Il tema coinvolge anche lo studio delle attitudini e delle abitudini visive (per esempio: degli olandesi rispetto agli italiani), e non solo degli artisti; si tratta di uno dei più interessanti canali di ricerca della storia dell'arte del nostro secolo preoccupata di approfondire i concetti di naturalismo, imitazione, descrizione, da Gombrich a Baxandall alla Alpers ai nostri Romano e Castelnuovo. Quanto all'argomento affrontato in queste pagine, l'obbiettivo, che richiede strumenti di analisi più sottili di quelli per solito usati, sarebbe di accostarsi il più possibile al modo di vedere il paesaggio che possiamo ritenere peculiare del Perugino e dei suoi contemporanei: guardare cioè, in un certo senso con il loro occhio." Bruno Toscano, "Una nota su paesaggio dipinto e paesaggio reale (rileggendo la prima annata di Paragone)," *Paragone* 42 (1991): 33–34n28. I have found that the expression "archaeology of the gaze" has been used twice so far: in a very different context from ours by Regina Stefaniak ("Correggios's Camera di San Paolo: An Archaeology of the Gaze," *Art History* 16, no. 2 [1993]: 203–38), who considers different types of gazes, the "phallic gaze," the "burning eye, the piercing eye, the biting eye, the grasping eye," and by Massimo Quaini ("Per una archeologia dello sguardo topografico," *Casabella* 575–76 [1991]: 13–17), an important Italian geographer and historian of cartography.

65 This approach reflects a recent reorientation of the field by some garden historians. John Dixon Hunt, in particular, has stressed the necessity of developing a history of reception and consumption of gardens in "Approaches (New and Old) to Garden History," in *Perspectives on Garden Histories*, ed. Michel Conan (Washington, D.C.: Dumbarton Oaks Research Library and Collection, 1999), 89; and *The Afterlife of Gardens* (Philadelphia: University of Pennsylvania Press, 2004).

66 A number of historians have recently readdressed the question of motion in gardens. See Michel Conan, "Landscape Metaphors and Metamorphosis of Time," in *Landscape Design and the Experience of Motion*, ed. Michel Conan, 287–317 (Washington, D.C.: Dumbarton Oaks Research Library and Collection, 2003); and Malgorzata Szafranska, "Place, Time and Movement: A New Look at Renaissance Gardens," *Studies in the History of Gardens and Designed Landscapes* 26, no. 3 (2006): 194–208.

67 On circulation in Renaissance gardens, see David R. Coffin, "The 'Lex Hortorum' and Access to Gardens of Latium during the Renaissance," *Journal of Garden History* 2 (1982): 201–32.

68 Coffin, *Villa d'Este at Tivoli*, 78–92.

69 Conan, "Landscape Metaphors and Metamorphosis of Time," 293.

70 Ibid. The landscape decoration of the salone of the Villa d'Este has been thoroughly analyzed in Ribouillault, "Le salone de la villa d'Este à Tivoli," and "Le ville dipinte del cardinale Ippolito d'Este a Tivoli: L'architettura di fronte all'antico, la tradizione ferrarese, e un nuovo documento su Belriguardo," in *Delizie estensi e architetture di villa nel rinascimento italiano ed europeo*, eds. Francesco Ceccarelli and Marco Folin, 341–71 (Florence: L. S. Olschki, 2009).

71 See Pirro Ligorio, *Libro dell'antica città di Tivoli e di alcune famose ville*, ed. Alessandra Ten (Rome: De Luca, 2005). On Ligorio's studies of ancient villas, see Antonella Ranaldi, *Pirro Ligorio e l'interpretazione delle ville antiche* (Rome: Quasar, 2001), 132–33. For the identification of the views, see Ribouillault, "Le salone de la villa d'Este à Tivoli."

72 On the perception and the complex layering of space at the Villa d'Este, see also Besse, *Face au monde*, 162.

73 Casey, *Representing Place*, 6.

74 Ibid., 7.

75 Besse, *Face au monde*, 9.

76 Rolando Ferri, "Una 'passeggiata per l'Italia': L'anonima Ambulatio gregoriana," in *La galleria delle carte geografiche in Vaticano/The Gallery of Maps in the Vatican*, eds. Lucio Gambi and Antonio Pinelli, 73–82 (Modena: F. C. Panini, 1994); Besse, *Face au monde*; and Francesca Fiorani, *The Marvel of Maps: Art, Cartography and Politics in Renaissance Italy* (New Haven: Yale University Press, 2005), 171–232, especially p. 174.

77 Abraham Ortelius, *Theatrum Orbis Terrarum* (Antwerp, 1581), preface.

78 Isabella Barisi, *Guide de la Villa d'Este* (Rome: De Luca, 2004), 40.

79 On the iconographical program of the room, see Coffin, *Villa d'Este at Tivoli*, 60–63.

80 Enrico Castelnuovo, *Il ciclo dei Mesi di Torre Aquila a Trento* (Trento: Museo Provinciale d'Arte, 1987), 41.

81 Coffin, "The Self-Image of the Roman Villa during the Renaissance," 184–85.

82 The fresco was first published in Luciano Passin, *Caprarola: Il paese e la sua storia* (Rome: Manfredi, 2002), 106. It is dated around 1561 in Rosalba Canton, "I giardini della Villa Farnese di Caprarola: Loro evoluzione, fortuna critica e prospettive di recupero," in *Vignola e i Farnese*, eds. Christoph Luitpold Frommel, Maurizio Ricci, and Richard J. Tuttle (Milan: Electa, 2003), 124. See also Luciano Passini, "Le vedute di paesaggi nel Palazzo Farnese di Caprarola," *Biblioteca e società* 26, no. 1–2 (2007): 36–42.

83 For the significance of this view and its theoretical implications for the understanding of the concept of landscape in the Renaissance, see Denis Ribouillault, "Landscape *all'antica* and Topographical Anachronism in Roman Fresco Painting of the Sixteenth Century," *Journal of the Warburg and Courtauld Institutes* 71 (2008): 211–37.

84 On this fundamental question of the passage from land to landscape, see the useful analysis in Malcolm Andrews, *Landscape and Western Art* (Oxford: Oxford University Press, 1999), 2–3. For a discussion of the idea

of "representation" in garden art, see Hunt, *Greater Perfections*, 76–115.

85 Augustin Berque, "La demeure des choses: Jardin, écoumène, espace virtuel," in *Le jardin planétaire*, eds. Claude Eveno and Gilles Clément, 155–63 (Châteauvallon: Aube, 1997); and Venturi Ferriolo, "L'art dei giardini tra pittura e realtà," 13.

86 Carl Lamb affirmed that the system of points of view (whereby various artistic elements become visible unexpectedly from a close perspective) was developed for the first time at a large scale at the Villa d'Este. *Die Villa d'Este in Tivoli* (Munich: Prestel, 1966), 43. See also Isabella Barisi, "Il disegno del giardino e l'architettura vegetale," in *Villa d'Este*, eds. Isabella Barisi, Marcello Fagiolo, and Maria Luisa Madonna (Rome: De Luca, 2003), 64–65.

87 Pliny the Younger *Epistulae* 5.6.7–13.

88 On descriptions of the panorama from the Villa d'Este, see Lazzaro, "The Sixteenth-Century Central Italian Villa and the Cultural Landscape," in *Architecture, jardin, paysage: L'environnement du château et de la villa au XVe et XVIe siècles*, ed. Jean Guillaume (Paris: Picard, 1999), 34–35.

89 Szafranska, "Place, Time and Movement," 196.

90 See Lazzaro, "The Sixteenth-Century Central Italian Villa and the Cultural Landscape," 32. Another more straightforward solution to this riddle would be to read "Sina" and not "Siena" in Giorgio Vasari, *Le opere di Giorgio Vasari*, ed. Gaetano Milanesi, 9 vols. (Florence: G. C. Sansoni, 1878–85), 6:76.

91 Malgorzata Szafranska, "Comment le roi visitait ses jardins: Louis XIV au sujet de Versailles," *Biuletyn historii sztuki* 59, nos. 1–2 (1997): 115.

92 André Mollet, *Le jardin de plaisir* (Stockholm: Chez Henry Kayser, 1651), chap. 9. See Szafranska, "Comment le roi visitait ses jardins," 117. On vision and movement in the gardens at Versailles, see also Hervé Brunon, "Les promenades du roi," in *Le jardin, notre double; Sagesse et déraison*, ed. Hervé Brunon, 157–82 (Paris: Éditions Autrement, 1999); and Chandra Mukerji, "The Political Mobilization of Nature in Seventeenth-Century French Formal Gardens," *Theory and Society* 23–25 (1994): 670–71.

93 See Pierre Grimal, *Les jardins romains*, 3rd ed. (Paris: Fayard, 1984), 88–98.

94 Vitruvius *De architectura* 7.5.2. On the ancient ars topiaria and Renaissance landscape painting, see Ribouillault, "Landscape *all'antica* and Topographical Anachronism in Roman Fresco Painting of the Sixteenth Century," 225–26.

95 See Alessandro Tagliolini, "Girolamo Fiorenzuola ed il giardino nelle fonti della metà del '500," in *Il giardino storico italiano: Problemi di indagine, fonti letterarie e storiche; Atti del convegno di studi, Siena–San Quirico d'Orcia, 6–8 ottobre 1978*, ed. Giovanna Ragionieri (Florence: L. S. Olschki, 1981), 300–301, quoted in Coffin, *Gardens and Gardening in Papal Rome*, 80, with other seventeenth-century examples.

96 On S. Silvestro al Quirinale, see Cynthia Stollhans, "Fra Mariano, Peruzzi and Polidoro da Caravaggio: A New Look at Religious Landscapes in Renaissance Rome," *Sixteenth Century Journal* 23 (1992): 513. On the garden of San Vitale, see Arnold A. Witte, *The Artful Hermitage: The Palazzetto Farnese as a Counter-Reformation Diaeta* (Rome: "L'Erma" di Bretschneider, 2008), 107; and Louis Richeome, *La peinture spirituelle ou l'art d'aimer en toutes ses œuvres* (Lyon: P. Rigaud, 1611), 666–71.

97 Giovanni Battista Armenini, *De veri precetti della pittura* (Ravenna: Francesco Tebaldini, 1587), bk. 3, chap. 13, quoted in Elisabeth Blair MacDougall, "Imitation and Invention: Language and Decoration in Roman Renaissance Gardens," in *Fountains, Statues, and Flowers: Studies in Italian Gardens of the Sixteenth and Seventeenth Centuries*, ed. Elisabeth Blair MacDougall (Washington, D.C.: Dumbarton Oaks Research Library and Collection, 1992), 125.

98 On the upper gardens at Caprarola, see Lazzaro, *Italian Renaissance Garden*, 100–108. The view is discussed in Sandro Benedetti, *Giacomo del Duca e l'architettura del Cinquecento* (Rome: Officina, 1973), 256–57.

99 See Passini, "Le vedute di paesaggi nel Palazzo Farnese di Caprarola," for the documents; and Ribouillault, "Paysage et pouvoir," 422–26.

100 Leonardo stressed the priority of sight over the other senses in the memorization of objects and situations. Leonardo da Vinci, *The Literary Works of Leonardo da Vinci*, ed. Jean Paul Richter, 2 vols. (1883; reprint, London: Phaidon, 1970), 1:62.

101 Reinhard Bentmann and Michael Müller, *Die Villa als Herrschafts-architektur: Versuch einer kunst- und sozialgeschichtlichen Analyse* (1970; translated by Tim Spence and David Craven as *The Villa as Hegemonic Architecture*, Atlantic Highlands, N.J.: Humanities Press, 1992); and James S. Ackerman, *The Villa: Form and Ideology of Country Houses* (Princeton, N.J.: Princeton University Press, 1990). On the historiography of landscape and gardens in Italy, see Beneš, "Recent Developments and Perspectives in the Historiography of Italian Gardens"; Brunon, "Documents ou monuments?"; and the contributions in this volume.

102 Hunt, "Approaches (New and Old) to Garden History," and *The Afterlife of Gardens*.

103 Cosgrove, "Prospect, Perspective and the Evolution of the Landscape Idea"; Denis Cosgrove, *The Palladian Landscape: Geographical Change and its Cultural Representations in Sixteenth-Century Italy* (Leicester: Leicester University Press, 1993); Dubbini, *Geography of the Gaze*; Conan, "Landscape Metaphors and Metamorphosis of Time"; and Besse, *Face au monde*.

104 Grimal, *Les jardins romains*; Wilhelmina Mary Feemster Jashemski, *The Gardens of Pompeii, Herculaneum and the Villas Destroyed by Vesuvius*, 2 vols. (New Rochelle,

N.Y.: A. D. Caratzas, 1979–93); Bettina Bergmann, "Painted Perspectives of a Villa Visit," in *Roman Art in the Private Sphere: New Perspectives on the Architecture and Decor of the Domus, Villa, and Insula*, ed. Elaine K. Gazda, 49–70 (Ann Arbor: University of Michigan Press, 1991); Bettina Bergmann, "Exploring the Grove: Pastoral Space on Roman Walls," in *The Pastoral Landscape*, ed. John Dixon Hunt, 21–46 (Washington, D.C., National Gallery of Art, 1992); Jaś Elsner, "The Viewer in the Roman Landscape," *Apollo* 60 (1999): 13–17; and Bettina Bergmann, "Playing with Boundaries: Painted Architecture in Roman Interiors," in *The Built Surface*, vol. 1, *Architecture and the Visual Arts from Antiquity to the Enlightenment*, ed. Christy Anderson, 15–46 (Burlington, Vt.: Ashgate, 2002).

105 See Manfred Luchterhandt, "Im Reich der Venus: Zu Peruzzis 'Sala delle Prospettive' in der Farnesina," *Römisches Jahrbuch der Bibliotheca Hertziana* 31 (1996): 230–39; and Ribouillault, "Le salone de la villa d'Este à Tivoli,“ 66–68.

106 Marcello Fagiolo, "Da Villa Madama a Villa Giulia e al Gianicolo: Gli assi della memoria storica," in *Roma: Il verde e la città; Giardini e spazi verdi nella costruzione della forma urbana*, eds. Roberto Cassetti and Marcello Fagiolo, 2:31–47 (Rome: Gangemi, 2002). See also Margherita Azzi Visentini, "Alle origini dell'architettura del paesaggio: Considerazioni in margine al rapporto tra gli edifici, i giardini e il sito nelle ville laziali del Cinquecento," in *Villa Lante a Bagnaia*, ed. Sabine Frommel, 190–205 (Milan: Electa, 2005).

107 Conan, "Landscape Metaphors and Metamorphosis of Time," 308.

108 "Le prime rappresentazioni di paesaggi puri . . ." Claudia Cieri Via, "Alle origine della pittura di paesaggio," *Semestrale di studi e ricerche di geografia* 2 (1993): 54. We may note the use of the expression in a recent discussion of landscape painting in early modern Rome in Patrizia Cavazzini, "Towards the Pure Landscape," in *The Genius of Rome, 1592–1623*, ed. Beverly Louise Brown, 208–47 (London: Royal Academy of Arts, and New York: Harry N. Abrams, 2001).

109 W. J. T. Mitchell, "Nature for Sale: Gombrich and the Rise of Landscape," in *The Consumption of Culture, 1600–1800: Image, Object, Text*, eds. Ann Bermingham and John Brewer (London: Routledge, 1995), 104. On the notion of "pure landscape" and the "invention" or "rise" of landscape, see also Serge Briffaud, "De 'l'invention' du paysage: Pour une lecture critique des discours contemporains sur l'émergence d'une sensibilité paysagère en Europe," *Compar(a)ison: An International Journal of Comparative Literature* 2 (1998): 35–55.

Contributors

Mauro Ambrosoli

Mauro Ambrosoli is professor of modern history at the Università di Udine; he taught at the Università di Torino from 1976 to 1994. His research focuses on agricultural development in early modern Europe. Inspired by the "green revolution" of the 1970s, he began with studies of early agricultural books, seed exchanges, and the connections between botany and agriculture. Following several years of research in Italy, France, and England, Ambrosoli received a visiting fellowship at Magdalen College, Oxford (1987–88), where he delivered the Waynflete Lectures on the subject of fodder grasses in European agriculture from 1350 to 1850. These lectures were published in 1992 as *Scienziati, contadini e proprietari: Botanica e agricoltura nell'Europa occidentale 1350–1850*; this book was translated into English as *The Wild and the Sown: Botany and Agriculture in Western Europe, 1350–1850* in 1997. In addition to studying horticultural innovations in early modern Europe, Ambrosoli also works on the history of textiles and institutions. His most recent research is on the role of the garden as a seed bed of development.

Mirka Beneš

Mirka Beneš is associate professor of landscape architecture in the School of Architecture at the University of Texas at Austin. She first trained as a painter, and then received her B.A. from Princeton University and her PhD in the history of art from Yale University. From 1988 to 2005, she taught the history of landscape architecture at the Graduate School of Design of Harvard University. Her teaching interests range from Mediterranean antiquity to Islamic gardens, and from Baroque Rome to contemporary landscape architecture. Her scholarship and publications focus on the city of Rome and its countryside in the early modern period (1500–1700), in particular the design of its villas, gardens, and parks, which are studied in the contexts of their social-geographical structures, agrarian landscapes, Rome's artistic and architectural culture, and its urban and suburban development. She is coeditor, with Dianne Harris, of *Villas and Gardens in Early Modern Italy and France* (2001). She also publishes on the seventeenth-century landscape painter Claude Lorrain, on modernism in landscape architecture, and on issues of historiography and methodology. Beneš has been a fellow of Dumbarton Oaks, and twice a fellow of the American Academy in Rome.

Vincenzo Cazzato

Vincenzo Cazzato is professor of the history of modern architecture and garden art at the Università di Lecce. From 1981 to 2001, he was the coordinating senior architect in the research office of the Ministero per i Beni e le Attività Culturali. Since 1989, he has coordinated the Centro di Studi sul Barocco di Lecce, and has served as a research lecturer at the Centro di Studi sulla Cultura e l'Immagine di Roma. He has participated in the compilation of a thematic atlas of Baroque noble residences, villas, and gardens in central and southern Italy. He has been the scientific coordinator of the Comitato Nazionale per lo Studio e la Conservazione dei Giardini Storici since its establishment in 1982. As scientific head of the *Quaderni* series, he has directed the series *Architettura e città* and *Studi e documenti*, as well as the series *Natura e artificio* with Marcello Fagiolo. Winner of the Grinzane Cavour-Giardini Botanici Hanbury Award in 1999 with *La memoria, il tempo, la storia nel giardino italiano fra '800 e '900* and in 2005 with *Ville e giardini italiani: I disegni di architetti e paesaggisti dell'American Academy in Rome*, he has just coordinated and published a national project with more than one thousand biographies of landscape architects and gardeners, *Atlante del giardino italiano, 1750–1940* (2009).

Raffaella Fabiani Giannetto

Raffaella Fabiani Giannetto is assistant professor of landscape architecture at the University of Pennsylvania. Before that, she taught in the landscape architecture programs at the University of Maryland and Ohio State University. She has lectured at the Studienkurs des Kunsthistorischen Institut in Florence, the Sixth International Conference for Word and Image Studies in Hamburg, the New School University in New York, the University of Pennsylvania, and Dumbarton Oaks. She trained as an architect at the University of Palermo before earning a PhD in architecture and a MLA in landscape architecture from the University of Pennsylvania. After receiving her doctorate, she held a postdoctoral fellowship in Garden and Landscape Studies at Dumbarton Oaks, where she worked toward the completion of her book *Medici Gardens: From Making to Design* (2008).

Marcello Fagiolo

Marcello Fagiolo is professor of architectural history at the Università di Roma "La Sapienza." He received his *laurea* degree in art history at the Università di Roma in 1963. He created, directed, or co-directed the journals of architectural history *Psicon* (Florence, 1974–77), *QUASAR* (Florence, 1989–93), and *Palladio* (1988–); and he is the director of various publication series, including the *Atlante del Barocco in Italia* (planned with thirty regional and ten thematic volumes) and series on architecture and gardens with the publishers Officina Editrice (Rome), Gangemi (Rome), and Electa Napoli (Naples). Since 1980, he has been the head of the Corsi Internazionali di Alta Cultura dell'Accademia dei Lincei. He created and currently directs the Centro di Studi sulla Cultura e l'Immagine di Roma, as well as the Centri di Studi sul Barocco of Siracusa, Lecce, and Foligno. He is vice president of the Istituto Zorzi per le Arti dello Spettacolo (Florence). Among his leadership responsibilities in the organization of scholarly initiatives in Italy, he has served as a consultant to the Ministero per i Beni Culturali, the scientific secretary of the Comitato Nazionale per Bernini and the Comitato Nazionale per Raffaello, the coordinator of the Comitato Nazionale per Sisto V, and the president of the Comitato Nazionale per Pirro Ligorio and of the Comitato Nazionale per Roma e la nascita del Barocco. He is also the president of the Comitato Nazionale per lo Studio e la Conservazione dei Parchi e dei Giardini Storici and the secretary for the *Edizione nazionale delle opere di Pirro Ligorio* (planned in forty volumes).

Michael G. Lee

Michael G. Lee is a postdoctoral associate in Garden and Landscape Studies at Dumbarton Oaks. His research focuses on ideological constructions of nature at the intersection of philosophy, literature, and landscape design. He is the author of *The German "Mittelweg": Garden Theory and Philosophy in the Time of Kant* (2007), which examines the structural affinities between German Enlightenment garden design and topographical metaphors in Kantian philosophy. His most recent projects include a study of bureaucratic vision and landscape planning in nineteenth-century Prussia and an analysis of landscape and gender in Weimar modernism. He has lectured at Humboldt Universität zu Berlin, the Stiftung Fürst-Pückler-Park Bad Muskau, and the National Gallery of Art in Washington, D.C. Trained as a landscape architect and historian, Lee received a BSLA from Texas A&M University and a MLA and PhD in landscape architecture from Harvard University. He has taught at the Harvard Graduate School of Design, the Rhode Island School of Design, and Connecticut College.

Antonella Pietrogrande

Antonella Pietrogrande is coordinator of curriculum for the "Gruppo Giardino Storico dell'Università di Padova," for which she plans and organizes an annual interdisciplinary course on garden and landscape culture in the Dipartimento di Biologia-Orto Botanico. She took her first degree in literary studies from the Università di Padova, and a second degree in drama, arts, and music from the Università di Bologna. Since the early 1990s, she has published widely on garden and landscape history, in particular on the Veneto region, with much of her research focusing on the relationships among gardens, theater, and literature. She has participated in numerous conferences both in Italy and abroad, and has taught courses in architectural history at the Politecnico di Milano with Margherita Azzi Visentini. Some of her most recent work will appear in the Veneto section of the *Atlante del Barocco in Italia*, directed by Marcello Fagiolo and supported by the Accademia dei Lincei of Rome.

Denis Ribouillault

Denis Ribouillault is a pensionnaire at the Académie de France à Rome. Prior to his residency in Rome, he was a Florence J. Gould Fellow at the Villa i Tatti in Florence (2008–9) and a lecturer in early modern art at the Courtauld Institute of Art in London (2006–8). Before these appointments, he taught sixteenth- and seventeenth-century Italian art at the Université Paris I Panthéon-Sorbonne, where he received a PhD in 2006 with a dissertation on topographical landscape cycles in sixteenth-century Rome and Latium. Ribouillault's research addresses the function and meaning of landscape painting in Renaissance and early modern Italy. He has published several articles on the villas of Rome and the Roman countryside (including those at Tivoli and Bagnaia) and has completed a book on landscape fresco decoration in sixteenth-century Rome, *Paysage et pouvoir: Les décors topographiques à Rome et dans le Latium au XVIe siècle*. He has benefited from the support of several institutions during the course of his research, including the Dutch Institute for Art History in Florence, the École Francaise de Rome, the Académie de France à Rome, Dumbarton Oaks, and the Warburg Institute in London.

Lionella Scazzosi

Lionella Scazzosi is an architect who holds a PhD in historic preservation. She is currently associate professor at the Politecnico di Milano in the areas of architectural restoration and the preservation and management of historical gardens and landscapes. Since 1998, she has been a consultant to the Ministero per i Beni e le Attività Culturali on Italian landscape policies and conservation rules. She has also served as the permanent Italian representative at the Council of Europe since 2002, as an expert at the Council of Europe for the application of the European Landscape Convention since 2005, and as a member of the ICOMOS-IFLA International Committee on Historic Gardens and Cultural Landscapes since 2006. She is the scientific director of the Centro per la Ricerca e Documentazione Internazionale per il Paesaggio (PaRID) at the Politecnico di Milano, and also serves as a scientific director for several national and international research projects focused on garden and landscape preservation. Her field work includes the restoration of the Botanical Garden of Brera-Milan and the Renaissance gardens of the Vertemate Franchi Palace in Piuro.

Bibliography

Abulafia, David, ed. *The Mediterranean in History*. Los Angeles: J. Paul Getty Museum, 2003.

Accati, Elena et al. *Il restauro del giardino storico: Metodologie per la conoscenza e strumenti operativi per gli interventi di conservazione*. Vernasca (Piacenza): Flortecnica, 2002.

Acidini Luchinat, Cristina. "I giardini dei Medici: Origini, sviluppi, trasformazioni; L'architettura, il verde, le statue, le fontane." In *Giardini medicei: Giardini di palazzo e di villa nella Firenze del Quattrocento*, edited by Cristina Acidini Luchinat, 46–59. Milan: F. Motta, 1996.

———. "Il modello del giardino fiorentino del Quattrocento nella mostra del 1931." In *Giardini medicei: Giardini di palazzo e di villa nella Firenze del Quattrocento*, edited by Cristina Acidini Luchinat, 138–45. Milan: F. Motta, 1996.

———. "Alle origini del 'ritratto di giardino'." In *Giardini regali: Fascino e immagini del verde nelle grandi dinastie; Dai Medici agli Asburgo*, edited by Monica Amari, 159–64. Milan: Electa, 1998.

Acidini Luchinat, Cristina, ed. *Giardini medicei: Giardini di palazzo e di villa nella Firenze del Quattrocento*. Milan: F. Motta, 1996.

Ackerman, James S. *The Cortile del Belvedere*. Vatican City: Biblioteca Apostolica Vaticana, 1954.

———. "Art History and the Problems of Criticism." In *The Visual Arts Today*, edited by Gyorgy Kepes, 257–67. Middletown, Conn.: Wesleyan University Press, 1960.

———. *Palladio's Villas*. Locust Valley, N.Y.: Published for the Institute of Fine Arts, New York University, by J. J. Augustin, 1967.

———. Review of *The Villa in the Life of Renaissance Rome*, by David R. Coffin. *Journal of the Society of Architectural Historians* 39 (1980): 242–43.

———. *The Villa: Form and Ideology of Country Houses*. Princeton, N.J.: Princeton University Press, 1990.

———. "Style." Chap. 1 in *Distance Points: Essays in Theory and Renaissance Art and Architecture*. Cambridge, Mass.: MIT Press, 1991.

———. *Interviews with Art Historians, 1991–2002*. Malibu, Calif.: Getty Research Institute, 1994.

———. "Richard Krautheimer, 6 July 1897–1 November 1994." *Proceedings of the American Philosophical Society* 148, no. 2 (June 2004): 229–34.

Ady, Mrs. Julia Mary Cartwright. *Italian Gardens of the Renaissance, and Other Studies*. London: Smith, Elder, 1914.

Ago, Renata. "Gli storici italiani e le fortune dell'antropologia: Il dibattito sulla storia sociale in Italia." In *Orientamenti marxisti e studi antropologici italiani: Problemi e dibattiti*, edited by Renata Ago et al., 223–29. Milan: F. Angeli, 1980.

———. *Carriere e clientele nella Roma barocca*. Rome: Laterza, 1990.

———. *Economia barocca: Mercato e istituzioni nella Roma del Seicento*. Rome: Donzelli, 1998.

———. *Il gusto delle cose: Una storia degli oggetti nella Roma del Seicento*. Rome: Donzelli, 2006.

Alberti, Leandro. *Descrittione di tutta Italia*. Venice: Ludovico degli Avanzi, 1568.

Alberti, Leon Battista. *Opere volgari*. Edited by Cecil Grayson. 3 vols. Bari: G. Laterza, 1960–73.

Alessi, Andrea. "La decorazione pittorica della Palazzina Gambara a Bagnaia." *Biblioteca e società* 21, no. 1–2 (2002): 21–30.

———. "La palazzina Gambara: Gli architetti e i pittori." In *Villa Lante a Bagnaia*, edited by Sabine Frommel, 110–21. Milan: Electa, 2005.

Aliberti, Giovanni. "Economia e società da Carlo III ai Napoleonidi, 1734–1806." *Storia di Napoli* 8 (1971): 77–164.

Alisio, Giancarlo. "Le ville di Portici." In *Ville vesuviane del Settecento*, edited by Roberto Pane et al., 127–91. Naples: Edizioni Scientifiche Italiane, 1959.

———. "Una rilettura su inediti del Palazzo Reale di Portici." *L'Architettura* 20 (1974): 262–67.

———. *Siti reali dei Borboni: Aspetti dell'architettura napoletana del Settecento.* Rome: Officina, 1976.

All'ombra del Vesuvio: Napoli nella veduta europea dal Quattrocento all'Ottocento. Naples: Electa, 1990.

Alpers, Svetlana. "Is Art History?" *Daedalus* 106, no. 3 (Summer 1977): 1–13.

Alpers, Svetlana, ed. "Art or Society: Must We Choose?" Special issue, *Representations* 12 (Fall 1985).

Ambrosoli, Mauro. *John Symonds: Agricoltura e politica in Corsica e in Italia (1765–1770).* Turin: Fondazione Luigi Einaudi, 1974.

———. *Scienzati, contadini e proprietari: Botanica e agricoltura nell'Europa occidentale, 1350–1850.* Turin: G. Einaudi, 1992.

———. *The Wild and the Sown: Botany and Agriculture in Western Europe, 1350–1850.* Cambridge: Cambridge University Press, 1997.

———. "Agronomi e società tra Italia ed Europa: Realizzazioni e contraddizioni da Pier de'Crescenzi a Filippo Re." *Atti del Convegno Internazionale Bologna, 31 maggio–1 giugno 2007.* Special issue, *Schede umanistiche* 21, no. 1–2 (2007).

———. "Conservation and Diffusion of Species Diversity in Northern Italy: Peasant Gardens of the Renaissance and After." In *Botanical Progress, Horticultural Innovation, and Cultural Change,* edited by Michel Conan and W. John Kress, 177–98. Washington, D.C.: Dumbarton Oaks Research Library and Collection, 2007.

———. "The Political Context for the Agricultural Activities of the Hartlib Circle." In *Samuel Hartlib: An International Correspondence,* edited by Scott Mandelbrote, 180–96. Oxford: Oxford University Press, forthcoming.

Amodio, Gaetano. *Ville vesuviane tra Ottocento e Novecento.* Naples: Edizioni Scientifiche Italiane, 2002.

Andrews, Malcolm. *Landscape and Western Art.* Oxford: Oxford University Press, 1999.

Añon, Carmen, José Luis Sancho, and José Martínez Millán, eds. *Jardín y naturaleza en el reinado de Felipe II.* Madrid: Sociedad Estatal Conme. Centenarios Felipe II–Carlos V, 1998.

Anthenaise, Claude d', and Monique Chatenet, eds. *Chasses princières dans l'Europe de la Renaissance: Actes du colloque de Chambord, 1er et 2 octobre 2004.* Arles: Actes Sud, 2007.

Assunto, Rosario. "Fuga dal giardino e ritrovamento del giardino (con alcune varianti intorno ai consigli del serpente)." In *Il giardino: Idea natura realtà,* edited by Alessandro Tagliolini and Massimo Venturi Ferriolo, 17–44. Milan: Guerini, 1987.

———. *Ontologia e teleologia del giardino.* Milan: Guerini, 1994.

———. *Il paesaggio e l'estetica.* 2 vols. 1973. Reprint, Palermo: Novecento, 1994.

———. *Retour au jardin: Essais pour une philosophie de la nature, 1976–1987.* Besançon: Les Éditions de l'Imprimeur, 2003.

Aymard, Maurice. "Les *Annales* et l'Italie." *Mélanges de l'École Française de Rome: Moyen âge* 93, no. 1 (1981): 401–17.

Azzi Visentini, Margherita. *La villa in Italia: Quattrocento e Cinquecento.* Milan: Electa, 1995.

———. "Storia dei giardini: Osservazioni in margine al recente sviluppo di questa disciplina in Italia." In *Storia e storie di giardini: Fortune e storia del giardino italiano e verbanese nel mondo; Atti del Convegno, Verbania, sabato 31 agosto 2002,* edited by Leonardo Parachini and Carlo Alessandro Pisoni, 45–86. Verbania: Alberti Libraio, Comune di Verbania, Magazzeno Storico Verbanese, 2003.

———. "Islands of Delight: Shifting Perceptions of the Borromean Islands." In *Baroque Garden Cultures: Emulation, Sublimation, Subversion,* edited by Michel Conan, 245–89. Washington, D.C.: Dumbarton Oaks Research Library and Collection, 2005.

———. "Alle origini dell'architettura del paesaggio: Considerazioni in margine al rapporto tra gli edifici, i giardini e il sito nelle ville laziali del Cinquecento." In *Villa Lante a Bagnaia,* edited by Sabine Frommel, 190–205. Milan: Electa, 2005.

———. "Riflessioni intorno alla fortuna critica del giardino storico italiano negli Stati Uniti negli ultimi trentacinque anni." In *Giardini storici: A 25 anni dalle Carte di Firenze; Esperienze e prospettive,* edited by Laura Sabrina Pelissetti and Lionella Scazzosi, 1:31–46. Florence: L. S. Olschki, 2009.

Azzi Visentini, Margherita, ed. *L'arte dei giardini: Scritti teorici e pratici dal XIV al XIX secolo.* 2 vols. Milan: Il Polifilo, 1999.

Bagatti Valsecchi, Pier Fausto, and Andreas Kipar, eds. *Il giardino paesaggistico tra Settecento e Ottocento in Italia e in Germania: Villa Vigoni e l'opera di Giuseppe Balzaretto.* Milan: Guerini, 1996.

Baglione, Giovanni. *Le vite de' pittori, scultori et architetti dal pontificato di Gregorio XIII sino à tutto quello d'Urbano Ottavo.* Rome: M. Manelfi, 1649.

Baldan Zenoni-Politeo, Giuliana, and Antonella Pietrogrande. *Il giardino e la memoria del mondo.* Florence: L. S. Olschki, 2002.

Barbanera, Marcello. *L'archeologia degli italiani: Storia, metodi e orientamenti dell'archeologia classica in Italia.* Rome: Editori Riuniti, 1998.

Barbera, Filippo. "Dalle ville nobiliari esoteriche al Palazzo Reale di Portici: Il simbolismo del sole e della luna nella Santa Coppa." In *Architettura e massoneria: L'esoterismo della costruzione*, edited by Marcello Fagiolo, 238–43. Rome: Gangemi, 2006.

———. *Cultura e scienza nei giardini delle ville vesuviane.* Portici: Effegi, 2007.

———. "I progetti della Reggia di Portici: Da Medrano a Canevari, da Vanvitelli a Fuga." In *Il Real Sito di Portici*, edited by Maria Luisa Margiotta, 69–103. Naples: Paparo, 2008.

Barisi, Isabella. "Il disegno del giardino e l'architettura vegetale." In *Villa d'Este*, edited by Isabella Barisi, Marcello Fagiolo, and Maria Luisa Madonna, 55–81. Rome: De Luca, 2003.

Barisi, Isabella, Marcello Fagiolo, and Maria Luisa Madonna. *Villa d'Este.* Rome: De Luca, 2003.

Barrell, John. *The Dark Side of the Landscape: The Rural Poor in English Painting, 1730–1840.* Cambridge: Cambridge University Press, 1980.

Bastogi, Nadia. "La villa Ferdinanda di Artimino." In *Fasto di corte: La decorazione murale nelle residenze dei Medici e dei Lorena.* Vol. I, *Da Ferdinando I alle Reggenti, 1587–1628*, edited by Mina Gregori, 45–65. Florence: Edifir, 2005.

———. "Magnificenza, decoro morale e celebrazione dinastica nei cicli di affreschi per il Granduca Ferdinando I: Il caso della villa di Artimino." *Fontes* 7, no. 13–16 (2004–5 [2007]): 53–82.

Battisti, Eugenio. "*Natura Artificiosa* to *Natura Artificialis.*" In *The Italian Garden*, edited by David R. Coffin, 1–36. Washington, D.C.: Dumbarton Oaks Research Library and Collection, 1972.

———. "The Role of Semiology in the Visual Arts." In *A Semiotic Landscape: Proceedings of the First Congress of the International Association for Semiotic Studies*, edited by Seymour Chatman, Umberto Eco, and Jean-Marie Klinkenberg, 744–48. The Hague: Mouton, 1979.

———. *L'antirinascimento.* 1962. Reprint, 2 vols. Milan: Garzanti, 1989.

———. *Iconologia ed ecologia del giardino e del paesaggio.* Edited by Giuseppa Saccaro Del Buffa. Florence: L. S. Olschki, 2004.

Baumer, Franz. *La grande madre: Scenari da un mondo mitico.* Translated by Giuseppina Quattrocchi. Genoa: ECIG, 1995.

Baxandall, Michael. *Giotto and the Orators: Humanist Observers of Painting in Italy and the Discovery of Pictorial Composition, 1350–1450.* Oxford: Clarendon Press, 1971.

———. *Painting and Experience in Fifteenth-Century Italy: A Primer in the Social History of Pictorial Style.* Oxford: Oxford University Press, 1972.

Beal, Mary. *A Study of Richard Symonds: His Italian Notebooks and their Relevance to Seventeenth-Century Painting Techniques.* New York: Garland, 1984.

Bédarida, François, ed. *L'histoire et le métier d'historien en France 1945–1995.* Paris: Éditions de la Maison des Sciences de l'Homme, 1995.

Belli Barsali, Isa. *Ville di Roma.* 1970. Reprint, Milan: Rusconi, 1983.

Belli Barsali, Isa, and Maria Grazia Branchetti. *Ville della campagna romana.* Milan: SISAR, 1975.

Benedetti, Sandro. *Giacomo del Duca e l'architettura del Cinquecento.* Rome: Officina, 1973.

Beneš, Mirka. "Villa Pamphilj (1630–1670): Family, Land, and Gardens in Papal Rome." PhD diss., Yale University, 1989.

———. "Landowning and the Villa in the Social Geography of the Roman Territory: The Location and Landscapes of the Villa Pamphilj, 1645–70." In *Form, Modernism, and History: Essays in Honor of Eduard F. Sekler*, edited by Alexander von Hoffmann, 187–209. Cambridge, Mass.: Harvard University Graduate School of Design, 1996.

———. "The Social Significance of Transforming the Landscape of the Villa Borghese, 1606–1630: Territory, Trees, and Agriculture in the Design of the First Roman Baroque Park." In *Gardens in the Time of the Great Muslim Empires: Theory and Design*, edited by Attilio Petruccioli, 1–31. Leiden: Brill, 1997.

———. "Recent Developments and Perspectives in the Historiography of Italian Gardens." In *Perspectives on Garden Histories*, edited by Michel Conan, 37–76. Washington, D.C.: Dumbarton Oaks Research Library and Collection, 1999.

———. "Italian and French Gardens: A Century of Historical Study (1900–2000)." In *Villas and Gardens in Early Modern Italy and France*, edited by Mirka Beneš and Dianne Harris, 1–16. Cambridge: Cambridge University Press, 2001.

———. "Pastoralism in the Roman Baroque Villa and in Claude Lorrain: Myths and Realities of the Roman Campagna." In *Villas and Gardens in Early Modern Italy and France*, edited by Mirka Beneš and Dianne Harris, 88–113. Cambridge: Cambridge University Press, 2001.

———. "A Tribute to Two Historians of Landscape Architecture: David R. Coffin and Elisabeth B. MacDougall." *Journal of the Society of Architectural Historians* 63, no. 2 (June 2004): 248–54.

———. "Claude Lorrain's Pendant Landscapes of 1646–50 for Camillo Pamphilj, Nephew of Pope Innocent X: Classicism, Architecture, and Gardens as Contexts for the Artist's Roman Patronage." *Storia dell'arte* 112 (2005): 37–90.

Beneš, Mirka, and Dianne Harris, eds. *Villas and Gardens in Early Modern Italy and France.* Cambridge: Cambridge University Press, 2001.

Benocci, Carla. *La villa della famiglia Doria Pamphilj a Roma.* Milan: Electa, 1988.

———. *Villa Doria Pamphilj*. Rome: Editalia, 1996.

———. *Villa Il Vascello*. Rome: Erasmo, 2003.

Benocci, Carla, ed. *I giardini Chigi tra Siena e Roma: Dal Cinquecento agli inizi dell'Ottocento*. Siena: Protagon, Fondazione Monte dei Paschi di Siena, 2005.

Benocci, Carla, and F. Catalli. *Villa Doria Pamphilj*. Rome: Comune di Roma, 2005.

Bentmann, Reinhard, and Michael Müller. *Die Villa als Herrschafts-architektur: Versuch einer kunst- und sozial-geschichtlichen Analyse*. Frankfurt: Suhrkamp, 1970.

———. *The Villa as Hegemonic Architecture*. Translated by Tim Spence and David Craven. Atlantic Highlands, N.J.: Humanities Press, 1992.

Berengo, Marino. *Nobili e mercanti nella Lucca del Cinquecento*. Turin: G. Einaudi, 1965.

Berger, John. *Ways of Seeing*. London: British Broadcasting Corporation, and New York: Penguin Books, 1972.

Bergmann, Bettina. "Painted Perspectives of a Villa Visit." In *Roman Art in the Private Sphere: New Perspectives on the Architecture and Decor of the Domus, Villa, and Insula*, edited by Elaine K. Gazda, 49–70. Ann Arbor: University of Michigan Press, 1991.

———. "Exploring the Grove: Pastoral Space on Roman Walls." In *The Pastoral Landscape*, edited by John Dixon Hunt, 21–46. Studies in the History of Art 36. Washington, D.C.: National Gallery of Art, 1992.

———. "Playing with Boundaries: Painted Architecture in Roman Interiors." In *The Built Surface*. Vol. 1, *Architecture and the Visual Arts from Antiquity to the Enlightenment*, edited by Christy Anderson, 15–46. Burlington, Vt.: Ashgate, 2002.

Berque, Augustin. "La demeure des choses: Jardin, écoumène, espace virtuel." In *Le jardin planétaire*, edited by Claude Eveno and Gilles Clément, 155–63. Châteauvallon: Aube, 1997.

Besse, Jean-Marc. "Représenter la ville ou la simuler? Réflexions autour d'une vue d'Amsterdam au XVIe siècle." *Ligeia: Dossiers sur l'art* 19–20 (1996–97): 43–55.

———. *Face au monde: Atlas, jardins, géoramas*. Paris: Desclée de Brouwer, 2003.

Bevilacqua, Mario. "Tra Napoli, Roma e l'Europa: Alcune lettere di Giovanni Carafa duca di Noja." *Napoli nobilissima* 34 (1995): 99–116.

Bevilacqua, Mario, and Maria Luisa Madonna, eds. *Stato pontificio e granducato di Toscana*. Vol. 2 of *Il sistema delle residenze nobiliari*, edited by Marcello Fagiolo. Rome: De Luca, 2003.

Bhatt, Ritu. "The Significance of the Aesthetic in Postmodern Architectural Theory." *Journal of Architectural Education* 53 (May 2000): 229–38.

Biagioli, Giuliana. *Il modello del proprietario imprenditore nella Toscana dell'Ottocento—Bettino Ricasoli: Il patrimonio, le fattorie*. Florence: L. S. Olschki, 2000.

Bloom, Harold. *The Anxiety of Influence: A Theory of Poetry*. Oxford: Oxford University Press, 1973.

Blunt, Anthony. *Neapolitan Baroque and Rococo Architecture*. London: A. Zwemmer, 1975.

Boccone, Paolo. *Museo di piante rare della Sicilia, Malta, Corsica, Italia, Piemonte, e Germania dedicato ad alcuni nobili patritii veneti protettori della botanica e delle buone lettere*. Venice: Zuccato, 1697. Reprint, with introduction and notes by Francesco M. Raimondo, Christiane Garnero Morena, and Pietro Mazzola. Palermo: Ed. Grifo, 1996.

Bonadonna Russo, Maria Teresa. "Renato Lefevre." *Archivio della Società Romana di Storia Patria* 127 (2004): 293–99.

Bonelli Conenna, Lucia, Attilio Brilli, and Giuseppe Cantelli. *Il paesaggio toscano: Storia e rappresentazione*. Milan: Silvana, 2004.

Borchardt, Rudolf. *Città italiane*. Milan: Adelphi, 1989.

Borea, Evelina. "La scomparsa di Paola della Pergola: La signora della Galleria Borghese." *Il giornale dell'arte* 11, no. 108 (1993): 3.

Boriani, Maurizio, and Lionella Scazzosi, eds. *Natura e architettura: La conservazione del patrimonio paesistico*. Milan: Clup, 1987.

Bosio, Gherardo. "Invito alla visita delle Ville Medicee a proposito della mostra fiorentina del giardino." *Domus* 39 (March 1931): 56–58.

Botero, Giovanni. *The Reason of State*, and *The Greatness of Cities*. New Haven: Yale University Press, 1956.

Boudon, Françoise. "Images de jardins au XVIème siècle: Les plus excellents bastiments de France." In *Histoire des jardins de la Renaissance à nos jours*, edited by Monique Mosser and Georges Teyssot, 96–98. Paris: Flammarion, 1991.

Bourdieu, Pierre. "Champs intellectuel et projet créateur." 1966. Reprinted in *Anthologie des sociologues français contemporains*, edited by Jean Duvignaud. Paris: Presses Universitaires de France, 1970.

———. "Champs du pouvoir, champs intellectuel et habitus de classe." *Scolies* 1 (1971): 7–26.

———. "The Genesis of the Concepts of *Habitus* and of *Field*." *Sociocriticism* 2 (December 1985): 11–25.

Bousquet-Bressolier, Catherine, ed. *Le paysage des cartes: Genèse d'une codification; Actes de la 3e journée d'études du Musée des Plans-Reliefs, Paris, Hôtel des Invalides, 19 novembre 1998*. Paris: Le Musée, 1999.

Bovinelli, Patrizia, and Luigi Nicolardi. "I casini nel territorio di Presicce: Storia e proposte di restauro conservativo." In *Paesaggi e sistemi di ville nel Salento*, edited by Vincenzo Cazzato, 234–49. Galatina: Mario Congedo, 2006.

Brandi, Cesare. *Teoria del restauro.* 1963. Reprint, Turin: G. Einaudi, 1977.

Branduini, Paola, and Franco Sangiorgi. "L'accesso a Milano dal Parco Agricolo Sud: Riconoscibilità e qualificazione del paesaggio rurale." In *Oltre il giardino: Le architetture vegetali e il paesaggio,* edited by Gabriella Guerci, Laura Sabrina Pelissetti, and Lionella Scazzosi, 87–101. Florence: L. S. Olschki, 2003.

Brassai, K. "La Villa Palagonia: Une curiosité du baroque sicilien." *Gazette des beaux-arts* (1962): 351–64.

Braudel, Fernand. *La Méditerranée et le monde méditerranéen à l'epoque de Philippe II.* 1949. Reprint, Paris: A. Colin, 1966.

———. *The Mediterranean and the Mediterranean World in the Age of Philip II.* Translated by Sián Reynolds. 2 vols. New York: Harper and Row, 1972.

Brayer, Marie-Ange, ed. *Cartographiques: Actes du colloque de l'Académie de France à Rome, 19–20 mai 1995.* Paris: Réunion des Musées Nationaux, 1996.

Bredekamp, Horst. *Vicino Orsini und der Heilige Wald von Bomarzo: Ein Fürst als Künstler und Anarchist.* 2 vols. Worms: Werner, 1985.

———. *Vicino Orsini e il bosco sacro di Bomarzo: Un principe artista ed anarchico.* Translated by Franco Pignatti. Rome: Edizioni dell'Elefante, 1989.

Briffaud, Serge. "De l''invention' du paysage: Pour une lecture critique des discours contemporains sur l'émergence d'une sensibilité paysagère en Europe." *Compar(a) ison: An International Journal of Comparative Literature* 2 (1998): 35–55.

Brilli, Attilio. *Il viaggio in Italia: Storia di una grande tradizione culturale.* Bologna: Il Mulino, 2006.

Brinckmann, Albert E. *Baukunst des 17. und 18. Jahrhunderts in den romanischen Ländern.* Berlin-Neubabelsberg: Athenaion, 1919.

———. *Plastik und Raum als Grundformen künstlerischer Gestaltung.* Munich: R. Piper, 1922.

———. *Platz und Monument als künstlerisches Formproblem.* Berlin: E. Wasmuth, 1923.

Brothers, Cammy. "The Renaissance Reception of the Alhambra: The Letters of Andrea Navagero and the Palace of Charles V." *Muqarnas* 11 (1994): 79–102.

Brown, Horatio. "Inglesi e scozzesi all'Università di Padova dall'anno 1618 sino al 1765." In *Monografie storiche sullo studio di Padova,* 137–213. Venice: Ferrari, 1922.

Brown, Jonathan, and John H. Elliott. *A Palace for a King: The Buen Retiro and the Court of Philip IV.* New Haven: Yale University Press, 1980.

Browne, Thomas. *Hydriotaphia, Urne-Buriall; or, A Discourse of the Sepulchrall Urnes Lately Found in Norfolk; Together with The Garden of Cyrus, or the Quincunciall, Lozenge, or Net-work Plantations of the Ancients, Artificially, Mystically Considered; With Sundry Observations.* London: Printed for Hen. Brome, 1658.

———. *The Works of Sir Thomas Browne.* Edited by Geoffrey Keynes. 6 vols. London: Faber and Gwyer, 1928.

Brugnoli, Andrea, and Gian Maria Varanini, eds. *Olivi e olio nel medioevo italiano.* Bologna: CLUEB, 2005.

Brunon, Hervé. "Les mouvements de l'âme: Émotions et poétique du jardin maniériste." In *Felipe II: El rey íntimo; Jardín y naturaleza en el siglo XVI,* edited by Carmen Añón Feliú, 103–36. Madrid: Sociedad Estatal para la Conmemoración de los Centenarios de Felipe II y Carlos V, 1998.

———. "Les promenades du roi." In *Le jardin, notre double; Sagesse et déraison,* edited by Hervé Brunon, 157–82. Paris: Éditions Autrement, 1999.

———. "De l'image à l'imaginaire: Notes sur la figuration du jardin sous le règne de Louis XIV." *XVIIe siècle* 209 (2000): 671–86.

———. "Pratolino: Art des jardins et imaginaire de la nature dans l'Italie de la seconde moitié du XVIe siècle." Doctoral thesis, Université Paris 1 Panthéon-Sorbonne, 2001.

———. "Dalle 'fiere non rapaci' ai 'fruttiferi e pomati arbori': Villa Lante a Bagnaia e l'evoluzione del barco nel Rinascimento." In *Villa Lante a Bagnaia,* edited by Sabine Frommel, 31–43. Milan: Electa, 2005.

———. "Documents ou monuments? Les textes littéraires dans la panoplie méthodologique des histoires du paysage." In *Le paysage dans la littérature italienne: De Dante à nos jours,* edited by Giuseppe Sangirardi, 17–28. Dijon: Éditions Universitaires de Dijon, 2006.

———. "L'essor artistique et la fabrique culturelle du paysage à la Renaissance." *Studiolo: Revue d'histoire de l'art de l'Académie de France à Rome* 4 (2006): 261–90.

———. "La chasse et l'organisation du paysage dans la Toscane des Médicis." In *Chasses princières dans l'Europe de la Renaissance: Actes du colloque de Chambord, 1er et 2 octobre 2004,* edited by Claude d'Anthenaise and Monique Chatenet, 219–46. Arles: Actes Sud, 2007.

———. "Articuler pratiques et représentations paysagères en histoire de l'art: Recherches récentes sur l'Italie à la Renaissance." In *Paysage et environnement: De la reconstitution du passé aux modèles prospectifs,* edited by Didier Galop, 461–69. Besançon: Presses Universitaires de Franche-Comté, 2008.

———. "Questions et méthodes de l'histoire des jardins en France." In *Giardini storici: A 25 anni dalle Carte di Firenze; Esperienze e prospettive,* edited by Laura Sabrina Pelissetti and Lionella Scazzosi, 1:11–21. Florence: L. S. Olschki, 2009.

Brunon, Hervé, and Monique Mosser. "Ripensare i limiti del giardino." In *Per un giardino della terra,* edited by Antonella Pietrogrande, 9–30. Florence: L. S. Olschki, 2006.

Bruschi, Arnaldo. *Bramante architetto.* Bari: Laterza, 1969.

Büchel, Daniel, and Volker Reinhardt, eds. *Die Kreise der Nepoten: Neue Forschungen zu alten und neuen Eliten Roms in der frühen Neuzeit.* Bern: P. Lang, 2001.

Burckhardt, Jacob. *Der Cicerone: Eine Anleitung zum Genuss der Kunstwerke Italiens.* Basel: Schweighauser'sche Verlagsbuchhandlung, 1855.

———. *The Civilisation of the Period of the Renaissance in Italy.* Translated by S. G. C. Middlemore. London: C. Kegan Paul, 1878.

———. *The Cicerone: An Art Guide to Painting in Italy for the Use of Travelers and Students.* Translated by Mrs. A. H. Clough. New York: Scribner, 1908.

Burguière, André. *L'école des annales: Une histoire intellectuelle.* Paris: O. Jacob, 2006.

Buridant, Jérôme. "La forêt et la chasse au XVIe siècle." In *Chasses princières dans l'Europe de la Renaissance: Actes du colloque de Chambord, 1er et 2 octobre 2004,* edited by Claude d'Anthenaise and Monique Chatenet, 159–74. Arles: Actes Sud, 2007.

Burke, Peter. *The Historical Anthropology of Early Modern Italy: Essays on Perception and Communication.* Cambridge: Cambridge University Press, 1987.

———. *The French Historical Revolution: The Annales School, 1929–89.* Stanford: Stanford University Press, 1990.

Burns, Howard, and Paul Davies. "Mediterranean dialogues: Palladio and Sinan." In *Palladio,* edited by Guido Beltramini and Howard Burns, 236–43. London: Royal Academy of Arts, 2008.

Busato, Davide. *Metamorfosi di un litorale: Origine e sviluppo dell'isola di Sant'Erasmo nella Laguna di Venezia.* Venice: Marsilio, 2006.

Butters, Suzanne B. "Ferdinand et le jardin du Pincio." In *La Villa Médicis,* edited by André Chastel. Vol. 2, *Études,* edited by Glenn M. Andres et al., 350–411. Rome: Académie de France à Rome, École Française de Rome, 1991.

———. "Pressed Labor and Pratolino: Social Imagery and Social Reality at a Medici Garden." In *Villas and Gardens in Early Modern Italy and France,* edited by Mirka Beneš and Dianne Harris, 61–87. Cambridge: Cambridge University Press, 2001.

Calame, Claude. "Gardens of Love and Meadows of the Beyond: Ritual Encounters with the Gods and Poetical Performances in Ancient Greece." In *Sacred Gardens and Landscapes: Ritual and Agency,* edited by Michel Conan, 43–56. Washington, D.C.: Dumbarton Oaks Research Library and Collection, 2007.

Campitelli, Alberta. *Villa Borghese: Da giardino del principe a parco dei romani.* Rome: Istituto Poligrafico e Zecca dello Stato, Libreria dello Stato, 2003.

Campitelli, Alberta, ed. *Villa Borghese: I principi, le arti, la città dal Settecento all'Ottocento.* Milan: Skira, 2003.

———. *Verdi delizie: Le ville, i giardini, i parchi storici del Comune di Roma.* Rome: De Luca, 2005.

———. *Villa Borghese: Storia e gestione.* Milan: Skira Editore, 2005.

Canestrini, Francesco, Francesca Furia, and Maria Rosaria Iacono, eds. *Il governo dei giardini e dei parchi storici: Restauro, manutenzione, gestione.* Naples: Edizioni Scientifiche Italiane, 2001.

Cantone, Gaetana, ed. *Barocco napoletano.* Rome: Istituto Poligrafico e Zecca dello Stato, Libreria dello Stato, 1992.

Cantone, Rosalba. "I giardini della Villa Farnese di Caprarola: Loro evoluzione, fortuna critica e prospettive di recupero." In *Vignola e i Farnese,* edited by Christoph Luitpold Frommel, Maurizio Ricci, and Richard J. Tuttle, 118–43. Milan: Electa, 2003.

Capobianco, Michele. "Scale settecentesche a Napoli." *L'Architettura* 84 (1962): 401–17; 86 (1962): 549–60; 88 (1963): 695–706.

Capodiferro, Alessandra, and Cornelia Lauf, eds. *Georgina Masson (1912–1980): Selections from the Photographic Archive.* Milan: Charta, 2003.

Carbonara, Giovanni, ed. *Trattato di restauro architettonico.* 4 vols. Turin: UTET, 1996.

Carboneri, Nino. *Ascanio Vitozzi: Un architetto tra Manierismo e Barocco.* Rome: Officina Edizioni, 1966.

Cardarelli, Urbano, Paolo Romanello, and Arnaldo Venditti. *Ville vesuviane: Progetto per un patrimonio settecentesco di urbanistica e di architettura.* Naples: Electa Napoli, 1988.

Caro, Annibal. *Delle lettere familiari del commendatore Annibal Caro.* 2 vols. Padua: Giuseppe Comino, 1742.

———. *Lettere familiari.* Edited by Aulo Greco. 3 vols. Florence: Le Monnier, 1957–61.

Carozzi, Pier Angelo. Introduction to *I miti della donna-giardino. Da Iside alla Sulamita,* by Uberto Pestalozza, edited by Pier Angelo Carozzi, 5–12. Milan: Edizioni Medusa, 2001.

"Carta dei giardini storici (1981, Firenze)." In *Giardini, contesto, paesaggio: Sistemi di giardini e architetture vegetali nel paesaggio,* edited by Laura Sabrina Pelissetti and Lionella Scazzosi, 1:419–21. Florence: L. S. Olschki, 2005.

Casey, Edward S. *Representing Place: Landscape Painting and Maps.* Minneapolis: University of Minnesota Press, 2002.

Caskey, Jill. *Art and Patronage in the Medieval Mediterranean: Merchant Culture in the Region of Amalfi.* Cambridge: Cambridge University Press, 2004.

Cassarino, Enrica. *La villa medicea di Artimino.* Florence: Becocci-Scala, 1990.

Castellamonte, Amedeo di. *Venaria reale, palazzo di piacere, et di caccia: Ideato dall'Altezza reale di Carlo Emanuel II, duca di Sauoia, Re di Cipro.* Turin: B. Zapatta, 1674.

Castelli, Patrizia. "L'antro delle Ninfe." In *Artifici d'acque e giardini: La cultura delle grotte e dei ninfei in Italia e in Europa*, edited by Isabella Lapi Ballerini and Litta Maria Medri, 153–63. Florence: Centro Di, 1999.

Castelnuovo, Enrico. "Per una storia sociale dell'arte." *Paragone* 27, no. 313 (March 1976): 3–30; 27, no. 314 (January 1977): 3–34.

———. *Il ciclo dei Mesi di Torre Aquila a Trento*. Trento: Museo Provinciale d'Arte, 1987.

Cato, Ercole. *Oratione fatta dal cavaliere Hercole Cato nelle essequie dell'illustriss. & reverendiss. sig. D. Hippolito d'Este card. di Ferrara, celebrate nella città di Tivoli*. Ferrara: Per Vittorio Baldini, stampator ducale, 1587.

Cavazzini, Patrizia. *Palazzo Lancellotti ai Coronari: Cantiere d'Agostino Tassi*. Rome: Istituto Poligrafico e Zecca dello Stato, Libreria dello Stato, 1998.

———. "Towards the Pure Landscape." In *The Genius of Rome, 1592–1623*, edited by Beverly Louise Brown, 208–47. London: Royal Academy of Arts, and New York: Harry N. Abrams, 2001.

Cazzani, Alberta, ed. *Giardini d'agrumi: Limoni, cedri e aranci nel paesaggio agrario italiano*. Brescia: Grafo, 1999.

Cazzato, Mario. "Matino: Immagine di una comunità nel XVIII secolo." In *Matino: Natura ed arte; Una comunità meridionale nel '700*, edited by Giuseppe Schivano. Galatina: Congedo Editore, 1992.

Cazzato, Vincenzo. "I giardini del desiderio: La Mostra del Giardino Italiano (Firenze 1931)." In *Il giardino romantico*, edited by Alessandro Vezzosi, 80–91. Florence: Alinea, 1986.

———. "Firenze 1931: La consacrazione del 'primato italiano' nell'arte dei giardini." In *Il giardino: Idea natura realtà*, edited by Alessandro Tagliolini and Massimo Venturi Ferriolo, 77–108. Milan: Guerini, 1987.

———. "Puglia giardino del Sud." In *Parchi e giardini storici, parchi letterari: Conoscenza, tutela e valorizzazione; Atti del III Convegno (Primo Internazionale) "Paesaggi e giardini del Mediterraneo,"* 2:81–94. Pompei: Ministero per i Beni Culturali e Ambientali, Comitato Nazionale per lo Studio e la Conservazione dei Giardini Storici, Soprintendenza Archeologica di Pompei, 1993.

———. "Il Salento, le acque e il pozzo del chiostro." In *Il tempio di Tancredi: Il monastero dei Santi Niccolò e Cataldo in Lecce*, edited by Bruno Pellegrino and Benedetto Vetere, 133–44. Milan: Silvana, 1996.

———. *Ville e giardini italiani: I disegni di architetti e paesaggisti dell'American Academy in Rome*. Rome: Istituto Poligrafico e Zecca dello Stato, Libreria dello Stato, 2004.

———. "Il giardino di Statue della Masseria Brusca a Nardò, teatro del mondo e degli dei." In *Interventi sulla 'Questione Meridionale',"* edited by Francesco Abbate, 335–40. Rome: Donzelli, 2005.

———. "Sistemi di ville e di giardini nel Salento dal Barocco al Novecento." In *Paesaggi e sistemi di ville nel Salento*, edited by Vincenzo Cazzato, 34–45. Galatina: Mario Congedo, 2006.

Cazzato, Vincenzo, ed. *Tutela dei giardini storici: Bilanci e prospettive*. Rome: Ministero per i Beni Culturali e Ambientali, Ufficio Studi, 1989.

———. *Parchi e giardini storici: Conoscenza, tutela e valorizzazione*. Roma: Leonardo-DeLuca, 1991.

———. *La memoria, il tempo, la storia nel giardino italiano fra '800 e '900*. Rome: Istituto Poligrafico e Zecca dello Stato, 1999.

———. *Paesaggi e sistemi di ville nel Salento*. Galatina: Mario Congedo, 2006.

———. *Atlante del giardino italiano, 1750–1940: Dizionario biografico di architetti, giardinieri, botanici, committenti, letterati e altri protagonisti*. 2 vols. Rome Istituto Poligrafico e Zecca dello Stato, Libreria dello Stato, 2009.

Cazzato, Vincenzo, Marcello Fagiolo, and Maria Adriana Giusti. *Teatri di verzura: La scena del giardino dal barocco al Novecento*. Florence: Edifir, 1993.

Cazzato, Vincenzo, Marcello Fagiolo, and Maria Adriana Giusti, eds. *Atlante delle grotte e dei ninfei in Italia*. Vol. 1, *Toscana, Lazio, Italia meridionale e isole*. Milan: Electa, 2001.

———. *Atlante delle grotte e dei ninfei in Italia*. Vol. 2, *Italia settentrionale, Umbria e Marche*. Milan Electa, 2002.

Cazzato, Vincenzo, and Marina Fresa, eds. *I nostri giardini: Tutela, conservazione, valorizzazione gestione*. Rome: Gangemi, 2005.

Cazzato, Vincenzo, and Andrea Mantovano. *Paradisi dell'eclettismo: Ville e villeggiature nel Salento*. Cavallino di Lecce: Capone, 1992.

———. "La 'Fisiologia degli agrumi' e il giardino tardo Barocco in Terra d'Otranto." In *Il giardino delle Esperidi: Gli agrumi nella storia, nella letteratura e nell'arte*, edited by Alessandro Tagliolini and Margherita Azzi Visentini, 245–68. Florence: Edifir, 1995.

———. "Giardini di mura e giardini murati nel Salento." In *Il giardino e le mura: Ai confini tra natura e storia*, edited by Cristina Acidini Luchinat, Giorgio Galletti, and Maria Adriana Giusti, 235–50. Florence: Edifir, 1997.

———. "Giardino ed economia agraria negli scritti di Francesco Milizia e della 'scuola' pugliese." In *Francesco Milizia e la cultura del Settecento*, edited by Mariella Basile and Grazia Distaso, 211–28. Galatina: Congedo Editore, 2002.

Cazzola, Franco. "Lo sviluppo storico delle bonifiche idrauliche." In *Un po di terra: Guida all'ambiente della bassa pianura padana e alla sua storia*, edited by Carlo Ferrari and Lucio Gambi, 487–515. Reggio Emilia: Diabasis, 2000.

Ceccarelli, Francesco, and Marco Folin, eds. *Delizie estensi: Architetture di ville nel Rinascimento italiano ed europeo.* Florence: L. S. Olschki, 2009.

Celano, Carlo. *Notizie del bello dell'antico e del curioso della città di Napoli.* Naples: S. Palermo, 1792.

Charlton, D. G. *New Images of the Natural in France: A Study in European Cultural History, 1750–1800.* Cambridge: Cambridge University Press, 1984.

Chastel, André. *Arte e umanesimo a Firenze al tempo di Lorenzo il Magnifico.* Turin: G. Einaudi, 1964.

———. "Les jardins et les fleurs." *Revue de l'art* 51 (1981): 42–50.

Chastel, André, ed. *La Villa Médicis.* 3 vols. Rome: Académie de France à Rome, École Française de Rome, 1989–91.

Chatenet, Monique, ed. *Maisons des champs dans l'Europe de la Renaissance: Actes des premières Rencontres d'architecture européenne, Château de Maisons 10–13 juin 2003.* Paris: Picard, 2006.

Chiacchella, Rita. *Regionalismo e fedeltà locali: L'Umbria tra Cinque e Settecento.* Florence: Nerbini, 2004.

Chiarelli, Renzo. *I Tiepolo a Villa Valmarana.* Florence: Sadea/Sansoni, 1965.

Chorley, Patrick. *Oil, Silk, and Enlightenment: Economic Problems in XVIIIth-Century Naples.* Naples: Istituto Italiano per gli Studi Storici, 1965.

Christian, Kathleen W. "Landscapes of Ruin and the Imagination in the Antiquarian Gardens of Renaissance Rome." In *Gardens and Imagination: Cultural History and Agency,* edited by Michel Conan, 117–37. Washington, D.C.: Dumbarton Oaks Research Library and Collection, 2008.

Ciacci, Margherita. "Non tutti i giardini di delizie sono uguali." In *I giardini delle regine: Il mito di Firenze nell'ambiente preraffaellita e nella cultura americana fra Ottocento e Novecento,* edited by Margherita Ciacci and Grazia Gobbi Sica, 12–39. Florence: Sillabe, 2004.

Ciarallo, Annamaria. *Flora pompeiana antica: Guida all'orto botanico.* Naples: Electa Napoli, 2007.

Cieri Via, Claudia. "Alle origini della pittura di paesaggio." *Semestrale di studi e ricerche di geografia* 2 (1993): 39–58.

Ciriacono, Salvatore. *Building on Water: Venice, Holland, and the Construction of the European Landscape in Early Modern Times.* New York: Berghahn Books, 2007.

Civiltà del Settecento a Napoli, 1734–1799. 2 vols. Florence: Centro-Di, 1980.

Clarici, Paolo Bartolomeo. *Istoria e coltura delle piante: Che sono pe'l fiore più ragguardevoli, e più distinte per ornare un giardino in tutto il tempo dell'anno con un copioso trattato degli agrumi.* Venice: Andrea Poletti, 1726.

Clark, Stuart, ed. *The Annales School.* 4 vols. London and New York: Routledge, 1999.

Coffin, David R. *The Villa d'Este at Tivoli.* Princeton, N.J.: Princeton University Press, 1960.

———. "Some Aspects of the Villa Lante at Bagnaia." In *Arte in Europa: Scritti di storia dell'arte in onore di Edoardo Arslan,* 569–75. Milan: Tipografia Artipo, 1966.

———. *The Villa in the Life of Renaissance Rome.* Princeton, N.J.: Princeton University Press, 1979.

———. "The 'Lex Hortorum' and Access to Gardens of Latium during the Renaissance." *Journal of Garden History* 2 (1982): 201–32.

———. *Gardens and Gardening in Papal Rome.* Princeton, N.J.: Princeton University Press, 1991.

———. "The Self-Image of the Roman Villa during the Renaissance." *Architectura: Zeitschrift für Geschichte der Baukunst* 28 (1998): 181–203.

———. "The Study of the History of the Italian Garden until the First Dumbarton Oaks Colloquium." In *Perspectives on Garden Histories,* edited by Michel Conan, 27–36. Washington, D.C.: Dumbarton Oaks Research Library and Collection, 1999.

Coffin, David R., ed. *The Italian Garden.* Washington, D.C.: Dumbarton Oaks Research Library and Collection, 1972.

Comba, Rinaldo, and Stefano A. Benedetto, eds. *Torino, le sue montagne, le sue campagne: Rapporti, metamorfosi, tradizioni produttive, identità (1350–1840).* Turin: Archivio Storico della Città di Torino, 2002.

Comoli Mandracci, Vera. *Torino.* Rome: Laterza, 1983.

———. "La capitale per uno Stato: Torino e il Piemonte sabaudo." In *Centri e periferie del barocco: Corso internazionale di alta cultura,* edited by Gaetana Cantone and Marcello Fagiolo, 233–53. Roma: Istituto Poligrafico e Zecca dello Stato, 1992.

Compte rendu du premier colloque international sur la conservation et la restauration des jardins historiques, Fontainebleau, France, 13–18 septembre 1971. Paris: Conseil International des Monuments et des Sites, 1973.

Conan, Michel. Introduction to *Perspectives on Garden Histories,* edited by Michel Conan, 1–16. Washington, D.C.: Dumbarton Oaks Research Library and Collection, 1999.

———. "Landscape Metaphors and Metamorphosis of Time." In *Landscape Design and the Experience of Motion,* edited by Michel Conan, 287–317. Washington, D.C.: Dumbarton Oaks Research Library and Collection, 2003. Translated as "Métaphore paysagère et métamorphose du temps," in *Essais de poétique des jardins,* 271–302 (Florence: L. S. Olschki, 2004).

———. *Essais de poétique des jardins.* Florence: L. S. Olschki, 2004.

———. "Jardins et métaphysiques de l'eau." In *Essais de poétique des jardins,* 3–14. Florence: L. S. Olschki, 2004.

Originally published as "Ogrody i Metafyzika Wod," in *Ogród, forma, symbol, marzenie,* edited by Malgorzata Szafrańska, 213–21 (Warsaw: Zamek Królewski w Warszawie, 1998).

———. "New Horizons of Baroque Garden Cultures." In *Baroque Garden Cultures: Emulation, Sublimation, Subversion,* edited by Michel Conan, 1–36. Washington, D.C.: Dumbarton Oaks Research Library and Collection, 2005.

———. "Introduction: The Cultural Agency of Gardens and Landscapes." In *Sacred Gardens and Landscapes: Ritual and Agency,* edited by Michel Conan, 3–14. Washington, D.C.: Dumbarton Oaks Research Library and Collection, 2007.

———. "Introduction: In Defiance of the Institutional Art World." In *Contemporary Garden Aesthetics, Creations and Interpretations,* edited by Michel Conan, 3–15. Washington, D.C.: Dumbarton Oaks Research Library and Collection, 2007.

———. "The Significance of Bodily Engagement with Nature." In *Performance and Appropriation: Profane Rituals in Gardens and Landscapes,* edited by Michel Conan, 3–16. Washington, D.C.: Dumbarton Oaks Research Library and Collection, 2007.

———. "Methods and Perspectives for the Study of Gardens and their Reception." In *Gardens and Imagination: Cultural History and Agency,* edited by Michel Conan, 3–17. Washington, D.C.: Dumbarton Oaks Research Library and Collection, 2008.

Conan, Michel, ed. *Perspectives on Garden Histories.* Washington, D.C.: Dumbarton Oaks Research Library and Collection, 1999.

———. *Baroque Garden Cultures: Emulation, Sublimation, Subversion.* Washington, D.C.: Dumbarton Oaks Research Library and Collection, 2005.

———. *Sacred Gardens and Landscapes: Ritual and Agency.* Washington, D.C.: Dumbarton Oaks Research Library and Collection, 2007.

Conan, Michel, José Tito Rojo, and Luigi Zangheri, eds. *Histories of Garden Conservation: Case-Studies and Critical Debates.* Florence: L. S. Olschki, 2005.

Conan, Michel, and Chen Wangheng. "City Gardens, Intercommunication and Culture." In *Gardens, City Life, and Culture: A World Tour,* edited by Michel Conan and Chen Wangheng, 3–13. Washington, D.C.: Dumbarton Oaks Research Library and Collection, 2008.

Congedo, Patrizia. "Censimento di pozzi e cisterne del territorio neretino." In *Paesaggi e sistemi di ville nel Salento,* edited by Vincenzo Cazzato, 286–93. Galatina: Mario Congedo, 2006.

Connors, Joseph. "The Casa dei Filippini in Rome." PhD diss., Harvard University, 1978.

———. *Borromini and the Roman Oratory: Style and Society.* New York: Architectural History Foundation, 1980.

———. "Alliance and Enmity in Roman Baroque Urbanism." *Römisches Jahrbuch für Kunstgeschichte* 25 (1989): 207–94.

———. "Ars Tornandi: Baroque Architecture and the Lathe." *Journal of the Warburg and Courtauld Institutes* 53 (1990): 217–36.

———. "Virtuoso Architecture in Cassiano's Rome." In *Cassiano Dal Pozzo's Paper Museum,* edited by Ian Jenkins et al., 2:23–40. Milan: Olivetti, 1992.

———. "Comment interpréter un édifice? Le cas de Saint-Yves-de-la-Sapience." In *Méthodes en histoire de l'architecture,* edited by Sabine Frommel, 97–108. Paris: Monum, 2002.

Coolidge, John. "The Villa Giulia: A Study of Central Italian Architecture in the Mid-Sixteenth Century." *The Art Bulletin* 25 (1943): 177–225.

Corazzol, Gigi. *Fitti e livelli a grano: Un aspetto del credito rurale nel Veneto del '500.* Milan: Franco Angeli, 1979.

Corrado, Vincenzo, ed. *Scuola di generale agricoltura e pastorizia adattata alle varie Province del Regno di Napoli ed insieme il trattato delle api e dei filugelli.* 2 vols. Naples: Presso Vincenzo Orsino, 1804.

Cosgrove, Denis. *Social Formation and Symbolic Landscape.* London: Croom Helm, 1984.

———. "Prospect, Perspective and the Evolution of the Landscape Idea." *Transactions of the Institute of British Geographers,* n.s., 10 (1985): 45–62.

———. *The Palladian Landscape: Geographical Change and Its Cultural Representations in Sixteenth-Century Italy.* Leicester: Leicester University Press, 1993.

Cosgrove, Denis, and Stephen Daniels, eds. *The Iconography of Landscape: Essays on the Symbolic Representation, Design, and Use of Past Environments.* Cambridge: Cambridge University Press, 1988.

Costantini, Antonio. *Guida alle ville del Salento: Del piacere di vivere in campagna: La villa, il giardino, la casina, il casino.* Galatina: Congedo Editore, 1992.

———. *Le masserie del Salento: Dalla masseria fortificata alla masseria-villa.* Galatina: Mario Congedo, 1994.

———. "Ville, casini e 'casine' nell'area della Cupa." In *Paesaggi e sistemi di ville nel Salento,* edited by Vincenzo Cazzato, 138–69. Galatina: Mario Congedo, 2006.

Costantini, Antonio, ed. *Architettura e paesaggio rurale nell'area della Cupa.* Galatina: Salentina, 1997.

Costantini, Antonio, and Michele Paone. *Guida di Gallipoli: La città, il territorio, l'ambiente.* Galatina: Congedo Editore, 1992.

Coste, Jean. "I casali della Campagna di Roma all'inizio del Seicento." *Archivio della Società Romana di Storia Patria* 92 (1969): 41–115.

———. "La topographie médiévale de la campagne romaine et l'histoire socio-économique: Pistes de recherche." *Mélanges de École Française de Rome: Moyen âge, temps modernes* 88, no. 2 (1976): 621–75.

———. "Description et délimitation de l'espace rural dans la campagne romaine." In *Sources of Social History: Private Acts of the Late Middle Ages*, edited by Paolo Brezzi and Egmont Lee, 185–200. Toronto: Pontifical Institute of Mediaeval Studies, 1984.

Council of Europe. *European Landscape Convention.* European Treaty Series no. 176, 20 October 2000.

———. *Guidelines for the Implementation of the European Landscape Convention.* Recommendation CM/Rec(2008)3, 6 February 2008.

Court, Benoît de. *Hortorum libri triginta.* Lugduni (Lyon): Joannes Tornaesius, 1560.

Croce, Benedetto. *La Spagna nella vita italiana durante la Rinascenza.* Bari: G. Laterza & Figli, 1917.

———. *Storia dell'età barocca in Italia: Pensiero, poesia e letteratura, vita morale.* Edited by Giuseppe Galasso. Milan: Adelphi Edizioni, 1993.

Culatti, Marcella. *Villa Montalto Negroni: Fortuna iconografica di un luogo perduto di Roma.* Venice: Istituto Veneto di Scienze, Lettere ed Arti, 2009.

Curtius, Ernst Robert. *European Literature and the Latin Middle Ages.* 1948. Reprint, translated by Willard R. Trask. Princeton, N.J.: Bollingen Series, 1953.

———. *Letteratura europea e medio evo latino.* 1948. Reprint, edited by Roberto Antonelli, and translated by Anna Luzzato and Mercurio Candela. Florence: La Nuova Italia, 1992.

Cusset, François. *French theory: Foucault, Derrida, Deleuze & Cie et les mutations de la vie intellectuelle aux États-Unis.* Paris: Découverte, 2003. Translated by Jeff Fort, Josephine Berganza, and Marlon Jones as *French Theory: How Foucault, Derrida, Deleuze & Co. Transformed Intellectual Life in the United States* (Minneapolis: University of Minnesota Press, 2008).

Dacos, Nicole. *Roma quanta fuit, ou, L'invention du paysage des ruines.* Paris: Somogy, and Brussels: Musée de la Maison d'Erasme, 2004.

Dami, Luigi. "L'arte italiana dei giardini." *Rivista mensile del Touring Club Italiano* (August 1914): 553–59.

———. *Il giardino italiano.* Milan: Bestetti and Tumminelli, 1924. Translated by L. Scopoli as *The Italian Garden* (New York: Brentano's, 1925).

D'Amico, John F., and Kathleen Weil-Garris. "The Renaissance Cardinal's Ideal Palace: A Chapter from Paolo Cortesi's *De Cardinalatu.*" *Memoirs of the American Academy in Rome* 35 (1980): 45–123.

Dandelet, Thomas James. *Spanish Rome, 1500–1700.* New Haven: Yale University Press, 2001.

Daniels, Stephen. "Marxism, Culture, and the Duplicity of Landscape." In *New Models in Geography*, edited by Richard Peet and Nigel Thrift, 196–220. London and Boston: Unwin-Hyman, 1989.

———. *Humphry Repton: Landscape Gardening and the Geography of Georgian England.* New Haven: Yale University Press, 1999.

Darnton, Robert. "Two Paths through the Social History of Ideas." In *The Darnton Debate: Books and Revolution in the Eighteenth Century*, edited by Haydn T. Mason, 251–96. Oxford: Voltaire Foundation, 1998.

———. "'What Is the History of Books?' Revisited." *Modern Intellectual History* 4, no. 3 (November 2007): 495–508.

Darragon, Eric. "Le studiolo du Cardinal Ferdinand à la Villa Médicis." *Revue de l'art* 19 (1973): 63–77.

De Cunzo, Mario. "Le ville vesuviane." In *Civiltà del Settecento a Napoli, 1734–1799*, 1:86–89. Florence: Centro-Di, 1980.

De Fusco, Renato. "L'architettura della seconda metà del Settecento a Napoli." *Storia di Napoli* 8 (1971): 369–449.

De Giorgi, Cosimo. *La provincia di Lecce: Bozzetti di viaggio.* 2 vols. Lecce: Spacciante, 1882–88.

Deinhard, Hanna. "Reflections on Art History and Sociology of Art." *Art Journal* 35, no. 1 (Fall 1975): 29–32.

Della Pergola, Paola. *Villa Borghese.* Rome: Istituto Poligrafico dello Stato, Libreria dello Stato, 1962.

Del Pezzo, Nicola. "Siti Reali: Il Palazzo Reale di Portici." *Napoli nobilissima* 5 (1896): 161–67 and 183–88.

Del Re, Antonio. *Dell'antichità tiburtine: Capitolo V.* Rome: Appresso Giacomo Mascardi, 1611.

Delumeau, Jean. *Vie économique et sociale de Rome dans la seconde moitié du XVIe siècle.* 2 vols. Paris: E. de Boccard, 1957–59.

Dernie, David. *The Villa d'Este at Tivoli.* London: Academy Editions, 1996.

Derosas, Renzo, ed. *Villa: Siti e contesti.* Treviso: Fondazione Benetton Studi Ricerche, 2006.

De Sanctio, Gabriello. *Stato della popolazione del Regno delle due Sicilie messo a confronto tra gli anni 1823 e 1843.* Naples, 1844.

Deseine, François-Jacques. *Rome moderne, première ville de l'Europe, avec toutes ses magnificences et ses delices.* Leiden: P. Vander Aa, 1713.

De Seta, Cesare, ed. *Arti e civiltà del Settecento a Napoli.* Rome: Laterza, 1982.

———. *Il paesaggio.* Vol. 5 of *Storia d'Italia: Annali.* Turin: G. Einaudi, 1982.

———. *Luigi Vanvitelli e la sua cerchia.* Naples: Electa Napoli, 2000.

De Seta, Cesare, Leonardo di Mauro, and Maria Perone. *Ville vesuviane.* Milan: Rusconi, 1980.

De Simone, Margherita. *Ville palermitane del XVII e XVIII secolo.* Genoa: Vitali e Ghianda, 1968.

———. *Ville palermitane: Dal XVI al XVIII secolo.* Palermo: SIAI Edizione d'Arte Nuovo Sud, 1974.

Desnoyers, Gérard. *La Villa d'Este à Tivoli, ou, Le songe d'Hippolyte: Un rêve d'immortalité héliaque.* Paris: Myrobolan, 2002.

Dezzi Bardeschi, Marco. "La carta dei giardini storici otto anni dopo." In *Tutela dei giardini storici: Bilanci e prospettive,* edited by Vincenzo Cazzato, 195–205. Rome: Ministero per i Beni Culturali e Ambientali, Ufficio Studi, 1989.

Di Gaddo, Beata. *Villa Borghese: Il giardino e le architetture.* Rome: Officina Edizioni, 1985.

Di Monda, Paolo. "Da Resina a Torre Annunziata." In *Ville vesuviane del Settecento,* edited by Roberto Pane et al., 237–325. Naples: Edizioni Scientifiche Italiane, 1959.

Dolcetta, Bruno, ed. *Paesaggio veneto.* Milan: A. Pizzi, 1984.

Donadieu, Pierre, Hansjörg Küster, and Raffaele Milani, eds. *La cultura del paesaggio in Europa tra storia, arte e natura: Manuale di teoria e pratica.* Florence: L. S. Olschki, 2008.

Donattini, Massimo, ed. *L'Italia dell'inquisitore: Storia e geografia dell'Italia del Cinquecento nella 'Descrittione' di Leandro Alberti.* Bologna: Bononia University Press, 2007.

D'Onofrio, Cesare. *Le fontane di Roma: Con documenti e disegni inediti.* Rome: Staderini, 1957.

———. *La Villa Aldobrandini a Frascati.* Rome: Staderini, 1963.

———. *Roma nel Seicento.* Florence: Vallecchi, 1969.

———. *Il Tevere e Roma.* Rome: U. Bozzi, 1970.

Dubbini, Renzo. *Geography of the Gaze: Urban and Rural Vision in Early Modern Europe.* Chicago: University of Chicago Press, 2002.

Duvignaud, Jean. *Anthologie des sociologues français contemporains.* Paris: Presses Universitaires de France, 1970.

Eagleton, Terry. "Base and Superstructure in Raymond Williams." In *Raymond Williams: Critical Perspectives,* edited by Terry Eagleton, 165–75. Boston: Northeastern University Press, 1989.

Eagleton, Terry, ed. *Raymond Williams: Critical Perspectives.* Boston: Northeastern University Press, 1989.

Eco, Umberto. *Opera aperta: Forme e indeterminazione nelle poetiche contemporanee.* Milan: Bompiani, 1962.

———. *I limiti dell'interpretazione.* Milan: Bompiani, 1990.

Ehrlich, Tracy L. *Landscape and Identity in Early Modern Rome: Villa Culture at Frascati in the Borghese Era.* Cambridge: Cambridge University Press, 2002.

———. "Pastoral Landscape and Social Politics in Baroque Rome." In *Baroque Garden Cultures: Emulation, Sublimation, Subversion,* edited by Michel Conan, 131–81. Washington, D.C.: Dumbarton Oaks Research Library and Collection, 2005.

Eisler, Colin. "*Kunstgeschichte* American Style: A Study in Migration." In *The Intellectual Migration: Europe and America 1930–1960,* edited by Donald Fleming and Bernard Bailyn, 544–629. Cambridge, Mass.: Belknap Press of Harvard University Press, 1969.

Eliade, Mircea. *La nascita mistica: Riti e simboli d'iniziazione.* Brescia: Morcelliana, 1974.

Elsner, Jaś. "The Viewer in the Roman Landscape." *Apollo* 60 (1999): 13–17.

Empathy, Form, and Space: Problems in German Aesthetics, 1873–1893. Santa Monica, Calif.: The Getty Center for the History of Art and the Humanities, 1994.

Ermini Pani, Letizia. "Il contributo della Società Romana di Storia Patria allo studio della topografia di Roma e del Lazio nel medioevo." *Archivio della Società Romana di Storia Patria* 130 (2007 [2008]): 123–37.

Espace français: Vision et aménagement, XVIe–XIXe siècle. Paris: Archives Nationales, 1987.

Esposito, Daniela. "Vigneti e orti entro le mura: Utilizzo del suolo e strutture insediative." In *Roma: Le trasformazioni urbane nel Quattrocento,* edited by Giorgio Simoncini, 2:205–28. Florence: L. S. Olschki, 2004.

Etlin, Richard A. *Modernism in Italian Architecture, 1890–1940.* Cambridge, Mass.: MIT Press, 1991.

Eustis, Elizabeth S. "The Garden Print as Propaganda, 1573–1683." In *European Pleasure Gardens: Rare Books and Prints of Historic Landscape Design from the Elizabeth K. Reilley Collection,* edited by Elizabeth S. Eustis, 41–51. Bronx, N.Y.: New York Botanical Garden, 2003.

Evelyn, John. *Pomona; or, An Appendix Concerning Fruit-Trees, in Relation to Cider, the Making and Several Ways of Ordering It.* London: J. Martyn and J. Allestry, 1664.

———. *The Diary of John Evelyn,* edited by Esmond de Beer, vol. 2, *Kalendarium, 1620–1649.* Oxford: Clarendon Press, 1955.

———. *Elysium Britannicum; or, The Royal Gardens.* Edited by John E. Ingram. Philadelphia: University of Pennsylvania Press, 2001.

Everett, Nigel. *The Tory View of Landscape.* New Haven: Yale University Press, 1994.

Fabiani Giannetto, Raffaella. *Medici Gardens: From Making to Design.* Philadelphia: University of Pennsylvania Press, 2008.

Fagiolo, Marcello. *Funzioni simboli valori della Reggia di Caserta.* Rome: Dell'Arco, 1963.

———. "Villa Aldobrandina Tusculana." *Quaderni dell'Istituto di Storia dell'Architettura* 62–66 (1964): 61–92.

———. "L'universo della luce nell'idea di architettura del Vittone." In *Bernardo Vittone e la disputa fra classicismo e barocco nel Settecento: Atti del Convegno internazionale *promosso dall'Accademia delle scienze di Torino nella ricorrenza del secondo centenario della morte di B. Vittone, 21–24 settembre 1970*, 2: 117–74. Turin: Accademia delle Scienze, 1972.

———. "La Roma di Sisto V: Le matrici del policentrismo." *Psicon* 8–9 (1976): 25–40.

———. "Il significato dell'acqua e la dialettica del giardino: Pirro Ligorio e la 'Filosofia' della villa cinquecentesca." In *Il giardino storico italiano: Problemi di indagine, fonti letterarie e storiche; Atti del convegno di studi, Siena–San Quirico d'Orcia, 6–8 ottobre 1978*, edited by Giovanna Ragionieri, 198–210. Florence: L. S. Olschki, 1981.

———. Introduction to *Tracce di memoria: Arte e cultura a Genzano di Roma*, by Mariano Apa. Genzano di Roma: Comune di Genzano, 1982.

———. "Le due anime nelle ville della Tuscia." In *Il giardino d'Europa: Pratolino come modello nella cultura europea*, edited by Alessandro Vezzosi, 68–81. Milan: Mazzotta, 1986.

———. Introduction to *Lazio delle delizie: Le dimore della nobiltà, teatro del lusso e dell'illusione*, edited by Marco Fabio Apolloni et al., 15–22. Milan: Franco Maria Ricci, 1988.

———. "Il piano di L'Enfant per Washington." *Gran bazaar* (October–November 1988): 30–34.

———. "Gli assi segreti delle ville nel sistema sacrale del *Latium vetus*." In *Atti del Convegno "Il giardino storico nel Lazio": Indirizzi per la conservazione e il restauro*, 16–26. Rome: Associazione Dimore Storiche Italiane, 1990.

———. "Ricordo di Eugenio Battisti: Il cavaliere dell' Antirinascimento." *Quaderni di storia dell'architettura e restauro* 3 (1990): 101–2.

———. *Roma delle delizie: I teatri dell'acqua, grotte, ninfei, fontane*. Milan: Franco Maria Ricci, 1990.

———. "Struttura e significato di Villa Lante a Bagnaia." In *Ville e parchi storici: Storia, conservazione e tutela*, edited by Alberta Campitelli, 219–30. Rome: Argos, 1994.

———. "La rinascita della villa e del teatro nell'età dell'umanesimo." In *Lo specchio del paradiso: Giardino e teatro dall'antico al Novecento*, edited by Marcello Fagiolo, Maria Adriana Giusti, and Vincenzo Cazzato, 22–41. Cinisello Balsamo (Milan): Silvana, 1997.

———. "Washington: O simbolismo maçónico da nova capital dos Estados Unidos." In *Lisboa iluminista e o seu tempo*, 239–66. Lisbon: Universidade Autónoma de Lisboa, 1997.

———. "Los nuevos palacios reales entre Versalles y Caserta: Modelos borbónicos para una idea de palacio real-ciudad-parque." In *Real sitio de La Granja de San Ildefonso, retrato y escena del rey*, edited by Delfín Rodríguez, Helena Pérez Gallardo, and Mercedes Simal López, 51–69. Madrid: Patrimonio Nacional, 2000.

———. "Da Villa Madama a Villa Giulia e al Gianicolo: Gli assi della memoria storica." In *Roma: Il verde e la città; Giardini e spazi verdi nella costruzione della forma urbana*, edited by Roberto Cassetti and Marcello Fagiolo, 2:31–47. Rome: Gangemi, 2002.

———. "Grotte, ninfei, teatri delle acque: I modelli romani." In *Atlante delle grotte e dei ninfei in Italia: Italia settentrionale, Umbria e Marche*, edited by Vincenzo Cazzato, Marcello Fagiolo, and Maria Adriana Giusti, 16–35. Milan: Electa, 2002.

———. "Sistemi di ville in Italia: Roma e il Lazio, il Piemonte Sabaudo, i Siti Reali borbonici, le ville di Bagheria." In *Paesaggi e sistemi di ville nel Salento*, edited by Vincenzo Cazzato, 14–33. Galatina: Mario Congedo, 2006.

———. *Vignola: L'architettura dei principi*. Rome: Gangemi, 2007.

———. "Battisti, il giardino delle idee." In *Eugenio Battisti: Storia, critica, progetto nella continuità della ricerca*, edited by Antonio Piva and Pierfranco Galliani, 33–39. Rome: Gangemi, 2009.

Fagiolo, Marcello, ed. *La città effimera e l'universo artificiale del giardino*. Rome: Officina, 1980.

———. *Natura e artificio: L'ordine rustico, le fontane, gli automi nella cultura del Manierismo europeo*. Rome: Officina, 1981.

———. *Il sistema delle residenze nobiliari*. Vol. 1, *Italia settentrionale*. Atlante tematico del barocco in Italia. Rome: De Luca, 2009.

Fagiolo, Marcello, and Vincenzo Cazzato, eds. *Architettura e massoneria: L'esoterismo della costruzione*. Rome: Gangemi, 2007.

Fagiolo, Marcello, and Maria Adriana Giusti. "La stella e la rosa: Analisi della Villa Buonvisi-Santini a Camigliano." In *Il giardino delle muse: Arti e artifici nel barocco europeo*, edited by Maria Adriana Giusti and Alessandro Tagliolini, 199–254. Florence: Edifir, 1995.

Fagiolo, Marcello, and Maria Adriana Giusti, eds. *Lo specchio del paradiso: L'immagine del giardino dall'antico al Novecento*. Cinisello Balsamo (Milan): Silvana, 1996.

Fagiolo, Marcello, Maria Adriana Giusti, and Vincenzo Cazzato, eds. *Lo specchio del paradiso: Giardino e teatro dall'antico al Novecento*. Cinisello Balsamo (Milan): Silvana, 1997.

Fagiolo, Marcello, and Maria Luisa Madonna. "La Casina di Pio IV in Vaticano: Pirro Ligorio e l'architettura come geroglifico." *Storia dell'arte* 15–16 (1972): 237–81.

———. "Sicilia: La ristrutturazione del territorio; Una realpolitik feudale." In *San Leucio: Archeologia, storia, progetto*, 205–9. Milan: Il Formichiere, 1977.

Fagliari Zeni Buchicchio, Fabiano Tiziano. "Tommaso Ghinucci." In *Dizionario biografico degli italiani* 53:781–83. Rome: Istituto della Enciclopedia Italiana, 1999.

Falk, Tilman. "Studien zur Topographie und Geschichte der Villa Giulia in Rom." *Römisches Jahrbuch für Kunstgeschichte* 13 (1971): 102–78.

Farhat, Georges, ed. *André Le Nôtre, fragments d'un paysage culturel: Institutions, arts, sciences & techniques.* Sceaux: Musée de l'Île-de-France, Domaine de Sceaux, 2006.

Fariello, Francesco. *Arte dei giardini.* Rome: Edizioni dell'Ateneo, 1956.

———. *Architettura dei giardini.* Rome: Edizioni dell'Ateneo, 1967.

Farneti, Fauzia. "La legislazione medicea sulle bandite, la caccia e la pesca." In *La legislazione medicea sull'ambiente,* edited by Giovanni Cascio Pratilli and Luigi Zangheri, 95–117. Florence: L. S. Olschki, 1988.

Farrell, Joseph. *Vergil's Georgics and the Traditions of Ancient Epic: The Art of Allusion in Literary History.* New York: Oxford University Press, 1991.

Ferrara, Fernando. "Raymond Williams and the Italian Left." In *Raymond Williams: Critical Perspectives,* edited by Terry Eagleton, 95–107. Boston: Northeastern University Press, 1989.

Ferri, Rolando. "Una 'passeggiata per l'Italia': L'anonima Ambulatio gregoriana." In *La galleria delle carte geografiche in Vaticano/The Gallery of Maps in the Vatican,* edited by Lucio Gambi and Antonio Pinelli, 73–82. Modena: F. C. Panini, 1994.

Fidora Attanasio, Celeste. *Ville vesuviane e siti reali.* Naples: Edizioni Scientifiche Italiane, 1998.

Fidora, Celeste, and Sergio Attanasio. *Ville e delizie vesuviane del '700: Passeggiata da Napoli a Torre del Greco.* Naples: Grimaldi, 2004.

Fiengo, Giuseppe. *Vanvitelli e Gioffredo nella villa Campolieto di Ercolano.* Naples: Arte Tipografica, 1974.

———. *Gioffredo e Vanvitelli nei palazzi dei Casacalenda.* Naples: Editoriale Scientifica, 1976.

———. *Documenti per la storia dell'architettura e dell'urbanistica napoletana del Settecento.* Naples: Editoriale Scientifica, 1977.

Fiengo, Giuseppe, ed. *Architettura napoletana del Settecento.* Naples: Franco Di Mauro, 1993.

Fiorani, Camillo. *Giardini d'Italia: Arte, carattere e storia del giardino italiano.* Rome: Edizioni Mediterranee, 1960.

Fiorani, Francesca. *The Marvel of Maps: Art, Cartography and Politics in Renaissance Italy.* New Haven: Yale University Press, 2005.

"The Florence Charter 1982–Charter for Historic Gardens and Landscapes (1981, Firenze, ICOMOS-IFLA)." In *Giardini, contesto, paesaggio: Sistemi di giardini e architetture vegetali nel paesaggio,* edited by Laura Sabrina Pelissetti and Lionella Scazzosi, 1:423–26. Florence: L. S. Olschki, 2005.

Foglietta, Uberto (Uberti Folietae). *Tyburtinum Hippolyti Estii.* 1569. Vol. 1 of *Antiche descrizioni della Villa d'Este a Tivoli,* translated by Franco Sciaretta. Tivoli: Tiburis Artistica, 2003.

Folin, Marco. "Borso a Schifanoia: Il Salone dei Mesi come *speculum principis.*" In *Il Palazzo Schifanoia a Ferrara,* edited by Salvatore Settis and Walter Cupperi, 9–38. Modena: F. C. Panini, 2007.

Fondazione Lelio e Lisli Basso-ISSOCO. *L'ambiente nella storia d'Italia: Studi e immagini.* Venice: Cataloghi Marsilio, 1989.

Forni, Gaetano, and Arnaldo Marcone, eds. *Storia dell'agricoltura italiana.* Vol. 1, bk 2, *L'età antica: Italia romana.* Florence: Polistampa, 2002.

Forster, Kurt W. "Metaphors of Rule: Political Ideology and History in the Portraits of Cosimo I de' Medici." *Mitteilungen des Kunsthistorischen Institutes in Florenz* 15, no. 1 (1971): 65–104.

———. "Back to the Farm: Vernacular Architecture and the Development of the Renaissance Villa." *Architectura* 1 (1974): 1–12.

Foucault, Michel. *Le parole e le cose: Un archeologia delle scienze umane.* 1966. Reprint, translated by Emilio Panaitescu. Milan: Rizzoli, 1978.

———. *The Archaeology of Knowledge.* London: Tavistock Publications, 1972.

Franchetti Pardo, Vittorio. "Le ville medicee nel contado fiorentino (sec. XV–XVI): Ideologia di un investimento patrimoniale." *Storia della città* 6 (1978): 42–57.

Franchetti Pardo, Vittorio, and Giovanna Casali. *I Medici nel contado fiorentino: Ville e possedimenti agricoli tra Quattrocento e Cinquecento.* Florence: Cooperativa Editrice Universitaria, 1978.

Franck, Carlludwig. *Die Barockvillen in Frascati, ihre Gestaltung aus den landschaftlichen Gegebenheiten.* Munich: Deutscher Kunstverlag, 1956.

———. *The Villas of Frascati, 1550–1750.* New York: Transatlantic Arts, 1966.

Frangenberg, Thomas. "Chorographies of Florence: The Use of City Views and City Plans in the Sixteenth Century." *Imago Mundi* 46 (1994): 41–64.

Freedberg, David, and Jan de Vries, eds. *Art in History/History in Art: Studies in Seventeenth-Century Dutch Culture.* Santa Monica, Calif.: The Getty Center for the History of Art and the Humanities, 1991.

Frommel, Christoph Luitpold. *Die Farnesina und Peruzzis Architektonisches Frühwerk.* Berlin: De Gruyter, 1961.

———. *Der römische Palastbau der Hochrenaissance.* 3 vols. Tübingen: E. Wasmuth, 1973.

———. "Papal Policy: The Planning of Rome during the Renaissance." *Journal of Interdisciplinary History* 17, no. 1 (1986): 39–65. Reprinted in *Art and History: Images and Their Meanings*, edited by Robert I. Rotberg and Theodore K. Rabb, 39–65. Cambridge: Cambridge University Press, 1988.

———. "Villa Lante e Tommaso Ghinucci." In *Villa Lante a Bagnaia*, edited by Sabine Frommel, 79–93. Milan: Electa, 2005.

Frommel, Sabine, ed. *Villa Lante a Bagnaia*. Milan: Electa, 2005.

———. *Bomarzo: Il sacro bosco*. Milan: Electa Architettura, 2009.

Fusaro, Maria. *Uva passa: Una guerra commerciale tra Venezia e l'Inghilterra (1540–1640)*. Venice: Il Cardo, 1996.

Galanti, Giuseppe Maria. *Napoli e contorni*. Edited by Luigi Galanti. Naples: Borel e Comp, 1829.

Galpine, John Kingston. *The Georgian Garden: An Eighteenth-Century Nurseryman's Catalogue*. Edited by John Harvey. Stanbridge, Wimborne, Dorset: Dovecote Press, 1983.

Gambardella, Alfonso. *Note su Ferdinando Sanfelice architetto napoletano*. Naples: Istituto Editoriale del Mezzogiorno, 1970.

———. *Ferdinando Sanfelice architetto*. Naples: Arti Grafiche Licenziato, 1974.

Gambardella, Alfonso, ed. *Ferdinando Sanfelice: Napoli e l'Europa*. Naples: Edizioni Scientifiche Italiane, 2004.

———. *Luigi Vanvitelli, 1700–2000*. San Nicola la Strada (Caserta): Edizioni Saccone, 2005.

Gantner, Joseph. "Erinnerungen an Heinrich Wölfflin und Benedetto Croce." *Jahrbuch für Aesthetik und allgemeine Kunstwissenschaft* 3 (1955–57): 129–52.

García Tapia, Nicolás. *Ingenieria y arquitectura en el Renacimiento español*. Valladolid: Secretariado de Publicaciones, Universidad de Valladolid, 1990.

Gargano, Maurizio. "Villas, jardins et fontaines de Rome: Les gravures de Giovanni Battista Falda." In *Histoire des jardins: De la Renaissance à nos jours*, edited by Monique Mosser and Georges Teyssot, 162–64. Paris: Flammarion, 1991.

Garms, Jörg. *Disegni di Luigi Vanvitelli nelle collezioni pubbliche di Napoli e di Caserta*. Naples: AGEA, 1973.

Geertz, Clifford. *The Interpretation of Cultures*. New York: Basic Books, 1973.

———. *A Life of Learning: Charles Homer Haskins Lecture for 1999*. New York: American Council of Learned Societies, 1999.

Gelli, Ugo. "Portali, pozzi, cisterne: Esperienze di rilievo architettonico." In *Paesaggi e sistemi di ville nel Salento*, edited by Vincenzo Cazzato, 274–85. Galatina: Mario Congedo, 2006.

Gimbutas, Marija. *The Language of the Goddess: Unearthing the Hidden Symbols of Western Civilization*. San Francisco: Harper and Row, 1989.

———. "La 'Venere mostruosa' della preistoria: Creatrice divina." In *I nomi della Dea: Il femminile nella divinità*, edited by Joseph Campbell, Riane Esler, Marija Gimbutas, and Charles Musès, 28–44. Rome: Astrolabio Ubaldini, 1992.

Ginzburg, Carlo. "A proposito della raccolta dei saggi storici di Marc Bloch." *Studi medievali*, 3rd ser., 6, no. 1 (1965): 335–53.

———. *I benandanti: Ricerche sulla stregoneria e sui culti agrari tra Cinquecento e Seicento*. Turin: G. Einaudi, 1966.

Giusti, Maria Adriana. "La veduta documento e le serie 'catastali'." In *Lo specchio del paradiso: L'immagine del giardino dall'antico al Novecento*, edited by Marcello Fagiolo and Maria Adriana Giusti, 44–57. Cinisello Balsamo (Milan): Silvana, 1996.

———. *Restauro dei giardini: Teorie e storia*. Florence: Alinea, 2004.

Gleijeses, Vittorio. *Ville e palazzi vesuviani*. Naples: Società Editrice Napoletana, 1980.

Goethe, Johann Wolfgang von. *Viaggio in Italia*. Translated by Aldo Oberdorfer. Florence: Vallecchi, 1955.

Golombek, Lisa. "From Timur to Tivoli: Reflections on *Il Giardino all'Italiana*." In *Frontiers of Islamic Art and Architecture: Essays in Celebration of Oleg Grabar's Eightieth Birthday*, edited by Gülru Necipoglu and Julia Bailey, 243–54. Special issue, *Muqarnas* 25 (2008).

Goodchild, Peter H. "John Evelyn, John Beale and Blackberry Hill." *Garden History* 19 (1991): 105–37.

Gothein, Marie Luise Schroeter. *Storia dell'arte dei giardini*. 2 vols. Florence: L. S. Olschki, 2006.

Gouesbier, Yvan. *La maison de sable: Histoire et politique en Italie, de Benedetto Croce à Renzo de Felice*. Rome: École Française de Rome, 2007.

Gradi, Adriano. "Il paesaggio agrario-forestale toscano nel XV secolo e sue trasformazioni." In *L'arte al potere: Universi simbolici e reali nelle terre di Firenze al tempo di Lorenzo il Magnifico*, edited by Domenico A. Conci, Vittorio Dini, and Francesco Magnelli. Bologna: Editrice Compositori, 1992.

Gravagnuolo, Benedetto, ed. *Mario Gioffredo*. Naples: Guida, 2002.

Grieco, Allen J., Michael Rocke, and Fiorella Gioffredi Superbi, eds. *The Italian Renaissance in the Twentieth Century: Acts of an International Conference, Florence, Villa I Tatti, June 9–11, 1999*. Florence: L. S. Olschki, 2002.

Grimal, Pierre. *Les jardins romains*. 3rd ed. Paris: Fayard, 1984.

Griseri, Andreina. "Urbanistica, cartografia e antico regime nel Piemonte sabaudo." *Storia della città* 12–13 (1979): 19–38.

Gritella, Gianfranco. *Rivoli: Genesi di una residenza sabauda.* Modena: Panini, 1986.

———. *Stupinigi: Dal progetto di Juvarra alle premesse neoclassiche.* Modena: Panini, 1987.

———. *Juvarra: L'architettura.* Modena: Panini, 1992.

Guerci, Gabriella, Laura Sabrina Pelissetti, and Lionella Scazzosi, eds. *Oltre il giardino: Le architetture vegetali e il paesaggio.* Florence: L. S. Olschki, 2003.

Guerrieri Borsoi, Maria Barbara. *Villa Belpoggio a Frascati: Storia della villa dei Vestri, Cesi, Borromeo, Visconti, Pallavicini, Sciarra dal XVI al XX secolo.* Rome: Gangemi, 1997.

———. *Villa Sora a Frascati.* Rome: Gangemi, 2000.

———. "I Contugi e Francesco da Volterra: Il palazzo romano all'Aracoeli e la villa tuscolana." *Palladio* 40 (2007): 103–16.

———. *Villa Rufina Falconieri: La rinascita di Frascati e la più antica dimora tuscolana.* Rome: Gangemi, 2008.

Guillaume, Jean, ed. *Architecture, jardin, paysage: L'environnement du château et de la villa aux XVe et XVIe siècles.* Paris: Picard, 1999.

Günther, Hubertus. "Urbanistica del Rinascimento a Roma." In *D'une ville à l'autre: Structures matérielles et organisations de l'espace dans les villes européennes, XIIIe–XVIe siècles,* edited by Jean-Claude Maire Vigueur, 382–406. Rome: École Française de Rome, 1989.

Hadot, Pierre. *Le voile d'Isis: Essai sur l'histoire de l'idée de nature.* Paris: Gallimard, 2004. Translated by Davide Tarizzo as *Il velo di Iside: Storia dell'idea di natura* (Turin: G. Einaudi, 2006).

Hajós, Geza. "Three Dangers to the Theory and Practice of Historic Garden Preservation in the Last Twenty-Five Years (in German-Speaking Countries)." In *Giardini storici: A 25 anni dalle Carte di Firenze; Esperienze e prospettive,* edited by Laura Sabrina Pelissetti and Lionella Scazzosi, 1:207–26. Florence: L. S. Olschki, 2009.

Halpern, Linda Cabe. "The Use of Paintings in Garden History." In *Garden History: Issues, Approaches, Methods,* edited by John Dixon Hunt, 183–202. Washington, D.C.: Dumbarton Oaks Research Library and Collection, 1992.

Harris, Dianne. "The Post-Modernization of Landscape: A Critical Historiography." *Journal of the Society of Architectural Historians* 58, no. 3 (September 1999): 434–43.

———. "Landscape and Representation: The Printed View and Marc'Antonio dal Re's *Ville di Delizie.*" In *Villas and Gardens in Early Modern Italy and France,* edited by Mirka Beneš and Dianne Harris, 178–206. Cambridge: Cambridge University Press, 2001.

———. *The Nature of Authority: Villa Culture, Landscape, and Representation in Eighteenth-Century Lombardy.* University Park: Pennsylvania State University Press, 2003.

Harris, Dianne, and D. Fairchild Ruggles, eds. *Sites Unseen: Landscape and Vision.* Pittsburgh, Pa.: University of Pittsburgh Press, 2007.

Harris, Francis, and Michael Hunter, eds. *John Evelyn and His Milieu.* London: British Library, 2003.

Harris, John. *The Artist and the Country House: A History of Country House and Garden View Painting in Britain, 1540–1870.* London: Sotheby Parke-Bernet, 1979.

Hartlib, Samuel. *Samuel Hartlib, His Legacy of Husbandry.* London, 1655.

Harvey, David. Afterword to *The Production of Space,* by Henri Lefebvre, 425–34. Translated by Donald Nicholson-Smith. Oxford and Cambridge, Mass.: Blackwell, 1991.

Harwood, Edward, Tom Williamson, Michael Leslie, and John Dixon Hunt. "Whither Garden History?" *Studies in the History of Gardens and Designed Landscapes* 27, no. 2 (April–June 2007): 91–112.

Haskell, Francis. *Patrons and Painters: A Study in the Relations between Italian Art and Society in the Age of the Baroque.* London: Chatto and Windus, 1963.

Heikamp, Detlef. "I viaggi di Federico Zuccaro." Pts. 1 and 2. *Paragone* 9, no. 105 (1958): 40–63; 9, no. 107 (1958): 41–58.

Heilmann, Christoph H. "Die Entstehungsgeschichte der Villa Borghese in Rom." *Münchner Jahrbuch für Kunstgeschichte* 15 (1973): 97–158.

Henderson, John. *The Roman Book of Gardening.* London and New York: Routledge, 2004.

Hersey, G. L. "Carlo di Borbone a Napoli e a Caserta." In *Storia dell'arte italiana,* vol. 12, 215–64. Turin: G. Einaudi, 1983.

Hibbard, Howard. "Palazzo Borghese Studies, 1. The Garden and its Fountains." *The Burlington Magazine* 100, no. 663 (June 1958): 204–12, 215.

———. "Scipione Borghese's Garden Palace on the Quirinal." *Journal of the Society of Architectural Historians* 23, no. 4 (December 1964): 163–92.

———. *Carlo Maderno and Roman Architecture, 1580–1630.* London: Zwemmer, 1971.

Hobsbawm, Eric, and Terence Ranger, eds. *The Invention of Tradition.* Cambridge: Cambridge University Press, 1983.

Hoskins, William George. *The Making of the English Landscape.* Harmondsworth, England: Penguin, 1955.

Hunt, John Dixon. "Curiosities to Adorn Cabinets and Gardens." In *The Origins of Museums: The Cabinet of Curiosities in Sixteenth- and Seventeenth-Century Europe,* edited by Oliver Impey and Arthur MacGregor, 193–203. Oxford: Clarendon Press, and New York: Oxford University Press, 1985.

———. *Garden and Grove: The Italian Renaissance Garden in the English Imagination, 1600–1750*. Princeton, N.J.: Princeton University Press, 1986.

———. "The Garden as Cultural Object." In *Denatured Visions: Landscape and Culture in the Twentieth Century*, edited by Stuart Wrede and William Howard Adams, 19–32. New York: Museum of Modern Art, 1991.

———. "Approaches (New and Old) to Garden History." In *Perspectives on Garden Histories*, edited by Michel Conan, 77–90. Washington, D.C.: Dumbarton Oaks Research Library and Collection, 1999.

———. *Greater Perfections: The Practice of Garden Theory*. Philadelphia: University of Pennsylvania Press, 2000.

———. *The Picturesque Garden in Europe*. London: Thames and Hudson, 2002.

———. *The Afterlife of Gardens*. Philadelphia: University of Pennsylvania Press, 2004.

Hunt, John Dixon, ed. *Garden History: Issues, Approaches, Methods*. Washington, D.C.: Dumbarton Oaks Research Library and Collection, 1992.

———. *The Italian Garden: Art, Design, and Culture*. Cambridge: Cambridge University Press, 1996.

Hunt, John Dixon, and Joachim Wolschke-Bulmahn, eds. *The Vernacular Garden*. Washington, D.C.: Dumbarton Oaks Research Library and Collection, 1993.

Imbò, Giuseppe. *Il Vesuvio e la sua storia: caratteristiche, attività e danni*. Naples: Edizioni Scientifiche Italiane, 1984.

Ingamells, John. *A Dictionary of British and Irish Travellers in Italy, 1701–1800*. New Haven: Yale University Press, 1997.

Italy, Ministero della Pubblica Istruzione. *Carta del Restauro 1972*. Circular no. 117, 6 April 1972.

Italy, Ministero per i Beni e le Attività Culturali. *La relazione paesaggistica: Finalità e contenuti*. Rome: Gangemi, 2006.

Italy, Presidente della Repubblica. *Codice dei beni culturali e del paesaggio, ai sensi dell'articolo 10 della legge 6 luglio 2002, n. 137*. Decreto Legislativo 42, 22 January 2004.

Jacques, David. *Georgian Gardens: The Reign of Nature*. London: B. T. Batsford, 1983.

Jardins et sites historiques. Madrid: Doce Calles, 1993.

Jashemski, Wilhelmina Mary Feemster. *The Gardens of Pompeii: Herculaneum and the Villas Destroyed by Vesuvius*. 2 vols. New Rochelle, N.Y.: A. D. Caratzas, 1979–93.

Jauss, Hans Robert. *Literaturgeschichte als Provokation*. Frankfurt: Suhrkamp, 1970. Translated by Claude Maillard as *Pour une esthétique de la réception* (Paris: Gallimard, 1978) and by Timothy Bahti as *Toward an Aesthetic of Reception* (Minneapolis: University of Minnesota Press, 1982).

Jong, Erik A. de, Erika Schmidt, and Brigitt Sigel, eds. *Der Garten—Ein Ort des Wandels: Perspektiven für die Denkmalpflege*. Zurich: Vdf. Hochschulverlag AG an der ETH Zürich, 2006.

Jori, Vincenzo. *Portici e la sua storia*. Naples: Tipografia dei Comuni, 1882.

Kemp, Wolfgang. *Der Anteil des Betrachters: Rezeptionsästhetische Studien zur Malerei des 19. Jahrhunderts*. Munich: Mäander, 1983.

Koller, Alexander. "Giovan Francesco Gambara (1533–1587): Profilo di un cardinale." In *Villa Lante a Bagnaia*, edited by Sabine Frommel, 23–29. Milan: Electa, 2005.

Krautheimer, Richard. "Introduction to an 'Iconography of Medieval Architecture.'" *Journal of the Courtauld and Warburg Institutes* 5 (1942): 1–33. Reprinted in *Studies in Early Christian, Medieval, and Renaissance Arts*. New York: New York University Press, 1969.

Krautheimer, Richard, ed. *Redefinitions of Style*. Special issue, *College Art Journal* 17, no. 2 (Winter 1958).

Kristeller, Paul O. *La tradizione classica nel pensiero del Rinascimento*. 1955. Reprint, Florence: La Nuova Italia, 1987.

Kultermann, Udo. *Geschichte der Kunstgeschichte: Der Weg einer Wissenschaft*. Munich: Prestel Verlag, 1990. Translated as *Storia della storia dell'arte* (Vicenza: Neri Pozza, 1997).

Labrot, Gerard. *Baroni in città: Residenze e comportamenti dell'aristocrazia napoletana, 1530–1734*. Naples: Società Editrice Napoletana, 1979.

———. *Palazzi napoletani: Storie di nobili e cortigiani, 1520–1750*. Naples: Electa, 1993.

Lamb, Carl. *Die Villa d'Este in Tivoli*. Munich: Prestel, 1966.

La Monica, Giuseppe. *Sicilia misterica: Fondazioni e restauri di monumenti tra Rinascimento e Barocco*. Palermo: S. F. Flaccovio, 1982.

Langdale, Allan. "Aspects of the Critical Reception and Intellectual History of Baxandall's Concept of the Period Eye." In *About Michael Baxandall*, edited by Adrian Rifkin, 17–35. Oxford and Malden, Mass.: Blackwell, 1999.

Lanman, Susan Warren. "Meaning and Change in the Walled Kitchen Gardens of Nineteenth-Century Britain." In *Performance and Appropriation: Profane Rituals in Gardens and Landscapes*, edited by Michel Conan, 79–92. Washington, D.C.: Dumbarton Oaks Research Library and Collection, 2007.

Lapi Ballerini, Isabella. "Niccolò Tribolo e la Grotta degli Animali a Castello." In *Artifici d'acque e giardini: La cultura delle grotte e dei ninfei in Italia e in Europa*, edited by Isabella Lapi Ballerini and Litta Maria Medri, 268–83. Florence: Centro Di, 1999.

La Quintinie, Jean de. *Instruction pour les jardins fruitiers et potagers, avec un traité des orangers, suivy de quelques reflexions sur l'agriculture*. 2nd ed. 2 vols. Amsterdam: H. Desbordes, 1692.

———. *The Compleat Gard'ner; or, Directions for Cultivating and Right Ordering of Fruit-Gardens, and Kitchen-Gardens. Now Compendiously Abridg'd, and Made of More Use, with Improvements, by George London and Henry Wise*. London, 1704.

La Regina, Francesco. *Restauro, conservazione e valorizzazione delle ville vesuviane*. Naples: CUEN, 2004.

La Rochefoucauld, François, duc de. *A Frenchman's Year in Suffolk: French Impressions of Suffolk Life in 1784*. Edited and translated by Norman Scarfe. Woodbridge, Suffolk: Boydell Press, 1988.

Lasansky, D. Medina. *The Renaissance Perfected: Architecture, Spectacle, and Tourism in Fascist Italy*. University Park: Pennsylvania State University Press, 2004.

Lazzaro, Claudia. "The Villa Lante at Bagnaia." PhD diss., Princeton University, 1974.

———. "The Villa Lante at Bagnaia: An Allegory of Art and Nature." *The Art Bulletin* 40, no. 4 (December 1977): 553–60.

———. *The Italian Renaissance Garden: From the Conventions of Planting, Design, and Ornament to the Grand Gardens of Sixteenth-Century Central Italy*. New Haven: Yale University Press, 1990.

———. "The Sixteenth-Century Central Italian Villa and the Cultural Landscape." In *Architecture, jardin, paysage: L'environnement du château et de la villa aux XVe et XVIe siècles*, edited by Jean Guillaume, 29–44. Paris: Picard, 1999.

———. "Italy is a Garden: The Idea of Italy and the Italian Garden Tradition." In *Villas and Gardens in Early Modern Italy and France*, edited by Mirka Beneš and Dianne Harris, 29–60. Cambridge: Cambridge University Press, 2001.

———. "Representing the Social and Cultural Experience of Italian Gardens in Prints." In *The Changing Garden: Four Centuries of European and American Art*, edited by Betsy G. Fryberger, 29–39. Berkeley, Calif.: Iris and B. Gerald Cantor Center for Visual Arts at Stanford University, 2003.

———. "Politicizing a National Garden Tradition: The Italianness of the Italian Garden." In *Donatello among the Blackshirts: History and Modernity in the Visual Culture of Fascist Italy*, edited by Claudia Lazzaro and Roger J. Crum, 157–69. Ithaca, N.Y.: Cornell University Press, 2005.

Leach, Andrew. *Manfredo Tafuri: Choosing History*. Ghent, Belgium: A&S Books, 2007.

Lee, Vernon. "Old Italian Gardens." In *In Praise of Old Gardens*. Portland, Maine: Thomas B. Mosher, 1912.

Lefebvre, Henri. *The Production of Space*. Translated by Donald Nicholson-Smith. Oxford and Cambridge, Mass.: Blackwell, 1991.

Lefevre, Renato. "Il patrimonio cinquecentesco dei Medici nel Lazio e in Abruzzo." *Archivio della Società Romana di Storia Patria* 98 (1975): 95–133.

Le Goff, Jacques. "Documento / monumento." In *Enciclopedia* 5:38–48. Turin: G. Einaudi, 1977–.

———. "Les *Annales* et l'histoire de l'Italie médiévale." *Mélanges de l'École Française de Rome: Moyen âge* 93, no. 1 (1981): 349–60.

———. *Storia e memoria*. Turin: G. Einaudi, 1982.

Le Goff, Jacques, Roger Chartier, and Jacques Revel, eds. *La Nouvelle Histoire*. Paris: Retz, 1978.

Lensi Orlandi Cardini, Giulio Cesare. *Le ville di Firenze*. 2 vols. Florence: Vallecchi, 1954.

Leonardo, da Vinci. *The Literary Works of Leonardo da Vinci*. Edited by Jean Paul Richter. 2 vols. 1883. Reprint, London: Phaidon, 1970.

Levine, Neil. "Introduction" and "Vincent Scully: A Biographical Sketch." In *Modern Architecture and Other Essays*, edited by Vincent Scully, 8–11 and 12–33. Princeton, N.J.: Princeton University Press, 2003.

Lévi-Strauss, Claude. *The Savage Mind*. Chicago: University of Chicago Press, 1962.

Lezzi, Pietro. *Le ville vesuviane*. Salerno: Arti Grafiche Boccia, 1977.

Lezzi, Pietro, and Paolo Romenello. *Le ville vesuviane*. Naples: Ente per le Ville Vesuviane, 1981.

Lightbown, Ronald. "Nicolas Audebert and the Villa d'Este." *Journal of the Warburg and Courtauld Institutes* 27 (1964): 164–91.

Ligorio, Pirro. *Libro dell'antica città di Tivoli e di alcune famose ville*. Edited by Alessandra Ten. Rome: De Luca, 2005.

Lillie, Amanda. *Florentine Villas in the Fifteenth Century: An Architectural and Social History*. Cambridge: Cambridge University Press, 2005.

Lingohr, Michael. "The Palace and Villa as Spaces of Patrician Self-Definition." In *Renaissance Florence: A Social History*, edited by Roger J. Crum and John T. Paoletti, 240–72. New York: Cambridge University Press, 2006.

Lohmeyer, Karl. *Palagonischer Barock: Das Haus der Laune des "Prinzen von Palagonia."* Berlin: Maximilian-Gesellschaft, 1942.

Luchterhandt, Manfred. "Im Reich der Venus: Zu Peruzzis 'Sala delle Prospettive' in der Farnesina." *Römisches Jahrbuch der Bibliotheca Hertziana* 31 (1996): 207–43.

Luciani, Domenico. "Ritrovare e reinventare i 'giardini italiani': L'aporia del restauro." In *Storia e storie di giardini: Fortune e storia del giardino italiano e verbanese nel mondo;*

Atti del Convegno, Verbania, sabato 31 agosto 2002, edited by Leonardo Parachini and Carlo Alessandro Pisoni, 35–43. Verbania: Alberti Libraio, Comune di Verbania, Magazzeno Storico Verbanese, 2003.

Luengo Añon, Ana, and Coro Millares. "El Real Sitio de Aranjuez." In *Jardín y naturaleza en el reinado de Felipe II*, edited by Carmen Añon, José Luis Sancho, and José Martínez Millán, 461–95. Madrid: Sociedad Estatal Conme. Centenarios Felipe II–Carlos V, 1998.

Lupo, Salvatore. *Il giardino degli aranci: Il mondo degli agrumi nella storia del Mezzogiorno*. Venice: Marsilio, 1990.

MacDougall, Elisabeth Blair. "The Villa Mattei and the Development of the Roman Garden Style." PhD diss., Harvard University, 1970.

———. "*Ars Hortulorum*: Sixteenth-Century Garden Iconography and Literary Theory in Italy." In *The Italian Garden*, edited by David R. Coffin, 37–59. Washington, D.C.: Dumbarton Oaks Research Library and Collection, 1972. Reprinted in *Fountains, Statues, and Flowers: Studies in Italian Gardens of the Sixteenth and Seventeenth Centuries*, edited by Elisabeth Blair MacDougall, 89–111. Washington, D.C.: Dumbarton Oaks Research Library and Collection, 1994.

———. "A Paradise of Plants: Exotica, Rarities, and Botanical Fantasies." In *The Age of the Marvelous*, edited by Joy Kenseth, 145–57. Hanover, N.H.: Hood Museum of Art, Dartmouth College, 1991.

———. "Imitation and Invention: Language and Decoration in Roman Renaissance Gardens." In *Fountains, Statues, and Flowers: Studies in Italian Gardens of the Sixteenth and Seventeenth Centuries*, edited by Elisabeth Blair MacDougall, 113–26. Washington, D.C.: Dumbarton Oaks Research Library and Collection, 1994.

MacDougall, Elisabeth Blair, ed. *Fons Sapientiae: Renaissance Garden Fountains*. Washington, D.C.: Dumbarton Oaks Research Library and Collection, 1978.

———. *Fountains, Statues, and Flowers: Studies in Italian Gardens of the Sixteenth and Seventeenth Centuries*. Washington, D.C.: Dumbarton Oaks Research Library and Collection, 1994.

MacDougall, Elisabeth Blair, and Richard Ettinghausen, eds. *The Islamic Garden*. Washington, D.C.: Dumbarton Oaks Research Library and Collection, 1976.

Macera, Mirella. "Il restauro dei giardini della Venaria Reale." In *Oltre il giardino: Le architetture vegetali e il paesaggio*, edited by Gabriella Guerci, Laura Pelissetti, and Lionella Scazzosi, 201–5. Florence: L. S. Olschki, 2003.

Madonna, Maria Luisa. "Il genius loci di Villa d'Este: Miti e misteri nel sistema di Pirro Ligorio." In *Natura e artificio: L'ordine rustico, le fontane, gli automi nella cultura del manierismo europeo*, edited by Marcello Fagiolo, 190–226. Rome: Officina, 1981.

———. "Pirro Ligorio e Villa d'Este: La scena di Roma e il mistero della Sibilla." In *Il giardino storico italiano: Problemi di indagine, fonti letterarie e storiche; Atti del Convegno di Studi, Siena–San Quirico d'Orcia, 6–8 ottobre 1978*, edited by Giovanna Ragionieri, 173–96. Florence: L. S. Olschki, 1981.

Maire-Vigueur, Jean-Claude. "Les grands domaines de la Campagne Romaine dans la seconde moitié du XIVe siècle." Thèse d'état, Université Paris I Sorbonne, 1974.

Mandelbrote, Giles. "John Evelyn and His Books." In *John Evelyn and His Milieu*, edited by Francis Harris and Michael Hunter, 71–94. London: The British Library, 2003.

Mangani, Giorgio. "Da icone a emblemi: Cartografia morale delle città (secoli XIV–XVI)." In *Tra oriente e occidente: Città e iconografia dal XV al XIX secolo*, edited by Cesare de Seta, 10–21. Naples: Electa Napoli, 2004.

———. *Cartografia morale: Geografia, persuasione, identità*. Modena: Franco Cosimo Panini, 2006.

Magnani, Lauro. "The Rise and Fall of Gardens in the Republic of Genoa, 1528–1850." In *Bourgeois and Aristocratic Cultural Encounters in Garden Art, 1550–1850*, edited by Michel Conan, 43–76. Washington, D.C.: Dumbarton Oaks Research Library and Collection, 2002.

Mantovano, Andrea. "Il bazaar degli stili: Ville e giardini nella Puglia di fine Ottocento." In *Ville e giardini fra Ottocento e Novecento: Studi e proposte*, edited by Alberta Campitelli, 121–25. Rome: Edizioni Joyce, 1996.

Marconi, Momolina. "Il santuario di Hera alla foce del Sele." *Rendiconti (Reale Istituto Lombardo di Scienze e Lettere: Classe di lettere e scienze morali e storiche)* 72 (1938–39): 441–58.

Margiotta, Maria Luisa. "Il Sito Reale e il suo parco." In *Il Real Sito di Portici*, edited by Maria Luisa Margiotta, 11–68. Naples: Paparo, 2008.

Margiotta, Maria Luisa, ed. *Il Real Sito di Portici*. Naples: Paparo, 2008.

Mariage, Thierry. *L'univers de Le Nostre*. Brussels: P. Mardaga, 1990. Translated by Graham Larkin as *The World of André Le Nôtre* (Philadelphia: University of Pennsylvania Press, 1999).

Marin, Louis. *Le portrait du roi*. Paris: Les Éditions du Minuit, 1981. Translated by Martha M. Houle as *Portrait of the King* (Minneapolis: University of Minnesota Press, 1988).

Marshall, David R. "'Farò la villeggiatura sopra la tela': Cardinal Patrizi and Adriaen Manglard's 'Vedute' of the Villa Patrizi." *The Burlington Magazine* 144, no. 1193 (2002): 497–501.

Masson, Georgina. *Italian Gardens*. New York: Harry N. Abrams, 1961.

Matteini, Milena. *Pietro Porcinai, architetto del giardino e del paesaggio*. Milan: Electa, 1991.

Mauro, Eliana. *Le ville a Palermo*. Palermo: U. La Rosa, 1992.

Mennonna, Mario. *Guida di Nardò: Arte, storia, centro antico*. Galatina: Congedo Editore, 2001.

Merleau-Ponty, Maurice. *Phénoménologie de la perception*. Paris: Gallimard, 1945.

Michels, Karen. *Transplantierte Kunstwissenschaft: Deutschsprachige Kunstgeschichte in amerikanischen Exil*. Berlin: Akademie, 1999.

Mignani, Daniela. *Le ville medicee di Giusto Utens*. Florence: Arnaud, 1982.

Millon, Henry A. *A Life of Learning: Charles Homer Haskins Lecture for 2002*. New York: American Council of Learned Societies, 2002.

Mitchell, W. J. T. "Nature for Sale: Gombrich and the Rise of Landscape." In *The Consumption of Culture, 1600–1800: Image, Object, Text*, edited by Ann Bermingham and John Brewer, 103–18. London: Routledge, 1995.

———. Preface to *Landscape and Power*, edited by W. J. T. Mitchell, vii–xii. 2nd ed. Chicago and London: University of Chicago Press, 2002.

Mollet, André. *Le jardin de plaisir*. Stockholm: Chez Henry Kayser, 1651.

Montaigne, Michel de. *Journal du voyage de Michel de Montaigne en Italie, par la Suisse & l'Allemagne, en 1580 & 1581*. Rome and Paris: Chez Le Jay, 1774.

———. *The Complete Works: Essays, Travel Journal, Letters*. Translated by Donald M. Frame. Stanford: Stanford University Press, 1958.

Montesquieu, Charles de Secondat. *Voyages*. Paris: Arléa, 2003.

Moos, Stanislaus von. *Turm und Bollwerk: Beiträge zu einer politischen Ikonographie der italienischen Renaissancearchitektur*. Zurich: Atlantis, 1974.

Morel, Philippe. "Le Parnasse astrologique: Les décors peints pour le cardinal Ferdinand de Médicis." In *La Villa Médicis*, edited by André Chastel and Philippe Morel. Vol. 3, *Le Parnasse astrologique*, by Philippe Morel, 45–88. Rome: Académie de France à Rome, Ecole Française de Rome, 1991.

Moryson, Fynes. *An Itinerary Written by Fynes Moryson Gent: First in the Latin Tongue, and Then Translated by Him into English; Containing his Ten Yeeres Travell Through the Twelve Dominions of Germany, Bohmerland, Sweitzerland, Netherland, Denmark, Poland, Italy, Turky, France, England, Scotland, and Ireland*. London: John Beale, 1617.

Mosser, Monique. "Hortésie cartographique: De l'écriture classique des parcs à la française à la calligraphie poétique des jardins anglo-chinois." In *Le paysage des cartes: Genèse d'une codification; Actes de la 3e journée d'études du Musée des Plans-Reliefs, Paris, Hôtel des Invalides, 19 novembre 1998*, edited by Catherine Bousquet-Bressolier, 99–119. Paris: Le Musée, 1999.

Mostra del Giardino Italiano: Catalogo. 2nd ed. Florence: Palazzo Vecchio, 1931.

Motte, André. *Prairies et jardins de la Grèce antique: De la religion à la philosophie*. Brussels: Palais des Académies, 1973.

Movimento Italiano per l'Architettura Razionale (MIAR). "L'architettura razionale italiana 1931." *La casa bella* 40 (April 1931): 69–82.

Mukerji, Chandra. "The Political Mobilization of Nature in Seventeenth-Century French Formal Gardens." *Theory and Society* 23–25 (1994): 651–77.

———. *Territorial Ambitions and the Gardens of Versailles*. Cambridge: Cambridge University Press, 1997.

Muraro, Michelangelo. "Civiltà delle ville venete." In *Arte in Europa: Scritti di storia dell'arte in onore di Edoardo Arslan*, 533–43. Milan: Tipografia Artipo, 1966.

———. "Feudo e ville venete." *Bollettino del Centro Internazionale di Studi di Architettura 'Andrea Palladio'* 20 (1978): 203–23.

Natilj, Mattia. *Cenno storico e compendiosa descrizione della Villa di Bagnaia com'era avanti al 1820*. Rome: Sinimberg, 1864.

Necipoglu, Gülru. "The Suburban Landscape of Sixteenth-Century Istanbul as a Mirror of Classical Ottoman Garden Culture." In *Gardens in the Time of the Great Muslim Empires: Theory and Design*, edited by Attilio Petruccioli, 32–71. Leiden and New York: Brill, 1997.

Neil, Erik H. "Architects and Architecture in Seventeenth- and Eighteenth-Century Palermo: New Documents." *Annali di architettura* 7 (1995): 159–76.

Neubauer, Erika. "The Garden Architecture of Cecil Pinsent, 1884–1964." *Journal of Garden History* 3, no. 1 (1983): 35–48.

Nichols, Rose Standish. *Italian Pleasure Gardens*. New York: Dodd, Mead, 1931.

Nocerino, Nicola. *La real villa di Portici*. Naples: Presso I Fratelli Raimondi, 1787.

Norberg-Schulz, Christian. *Genius loci: Paesaggio, ambiente, architettura*. Milan: Electa, 1979.

Nussdorfer, Laurie. "City Politics in Baroque Rome, 1623–1644." PhD diss., Princeton University, 1985.

———. *Civic Politics in the Rome of Urban VIII*. Princeton, N.J.: Princeton University Press. 1992.

———. "The Politics of Space in Early Modern Rome." *The Memoirs of the American Academy in Rome* 42 (1997): 161–86.

Nuti, Lucia. "The Perspective Plan in the Sixteenth Century: The Invention of a Representational Language." *The Art Bulletin* 76 (1994): 105–28.

———. "I 'teatri' di città e l'Italia del secolo XVII." In *Cartographiques: Actes du colloque de l'Académie de France à Rome, 19–20 mai 1995*, edited by Marie-Ange Brayer, 105–23. Paris: Réunion des Musées Nationaux, 1996.

Ogden, Henry V. S., and Margaret S. Ogden. *English Taste in Landscape in the Seventeenth Century*. Ann Arbor: University of Michigan Press, 1955.

Ojetti, Ugo, ed. *I palazzi e le ville che non sono più del re*. Milan: Fratelli Treves, 1921.

O'Malley, Therese, and Joachim Wolschke-Bulmahn, eds. *John Evelyn's "Elysium Britannicum" and European Gardening*. Washington, D.C.: Dumbarton Oaks Research Library and Collection, 1998.

Ortelius, Abraham. *Theatrum Orbis Terrarum*. Antwerp, 1581.

Pagano, Giuseppe. "I 'materiali' nella nuova architettura." *La casa bella* 41 (May 1931): 10–14.

Pagano de Divitiis, Gigliola. *English Merchants in Seventeenth-Century Italy*. Cambridge: Cambridge University Press, 1997.

Paleotti, Gabriele. *Discorso intorno alle imagine sacre e profane*. Bologna, 1582. Reprinted in *Trattati d'arte del Cinquecento, fra manierismo e Controriforma*, edited by Paola Barocchi, 117–509. Bari: G. Laterza, 1960–62.

Pane, Roberto. *Architettura dell'età barocca in Napoli*. Naples: Editrice Politecnica, 1939.

———. "Le ville e la strada costiera." In *Ville vesuviane del Settecento*, edited by Roberto Pane et al., 1–18. Naples: Edizioni Scientifiche Italiane, 1959.

———. "Civiltà del Settecento a Napoli." *Napoli nobilissima*, 3rd ser., 19 (1980): 83–98.

Panofsky, Erwin. "Three Decades of Art History in the United States: Impressions of a Transplanted European." In *Meaning in the Visual Arts*, 321–46. Garden City, N.Y.: Doubleday, 1955.

———. *Meaning in the Visual Arts*. Garden City, N.Y.: Doubleday, 1955. Translated by Bernard and Marthe Teyssèdre as *L'oeuvre d'art et ses significations: Essais sur les "arts visuels"* (Paris: Gallimard, 1969).

———. *Perspective as Symbolic Form*. 1924–25. Reprint, translated by Christopher S. Wood. New York: Zone Books, 1991.

Panzini, Franco. *Progettare la natura: Architettura del paesaggio e dei giardini dalle origini all'epoca contemporanea*. Bologna: Zanichelli, 2005.

Parchi e giardini storici: Conoscenza, tutela e valorizzazione. Rome: Leonardo-De Luca, 1991.

Parchi e giardini storici, parchi letterari: Conoscenza, tutela e valorizzazione; Atti del III Convegno (primo internazionale) "paesaggi e giardini del Mediterraneo" Pompei, 4–5–6 giugno 1993. 3 vols. Pompeii: Ministero per i Beni Culturali e Ambientali, Comitato Nazionale per lo Studio e la Conservazione dei Giardini Storici, Soprintendenza Archeologica di Pompei, 1993.

Pareyson, Luigi. *Estetica: Teoria della formatività*. Milan: Bompiani, 1988.

Passini, Luciano. *Caprarola: Il paese e la sua storia*. Rome: Manfredi, 2002.

———. "Le vedute di paesaggi nel Palazzo Farnese di Caprarola." *Biblioteca e società* 26, no. 1–2 (2007): 36–42.

Pastore, Christopher J. "Expanding Antiquity: Andrea Navagero and Villa Culture in the Cinquecento Veneto." PhD diss., University of Pennsylvania, 2003.

Patroni, Giovanni. *Commenti mediterranei all'Odissea di Omero*. Milan: C. Marzorati, 1950.

Pechère, René. "Memorandum sur la naissance et les origines de l'IFLA et du Comité International des Jardins et des Sites Historiques ICOMOS-IFLA." In *Jardins et sites historiques*, 259–61. Madrid: Doce Calles, 1993.

Pelissetti, Laura Sabrina, and Lionella Scazzosi, eds. *Giardini, contesto, paesaggio: Sistemi di giardini e architetture vegetali nel paesaggio*. 2 vols. Florence: L. S. Olschki, 2005.

———. *Giardini storici: A 25 anni dalle Carte di Firenze; Esperienze e prospettive*. 2 vols. Florence: L. S. Olschki, 2009.

Perillo, Donato. *Ragguaglio delle ville, e luoghi prescelti per uso delle caccie, pesche, e simili diporti da regnanti, ed altr'insigni personaggi*. Naples: Niccolò Naso, 1737.

Perone, Maria. "Le ville vesuviane." In *Napoli*, edited by Cesare de Seta, 182–94. Rome: Laterza, 1981.

Pestalozza, Uberto. "Lêtô phytia e le Ekdisya." *Memorie del Reale Istituto Lombardo di Scienze e Lettere: Classe di lettere, scienze morali e storiche* 24 (1938): 273–93.

———. *Pagine di religione mediterranea*. 2 vols. Milan: G. Principato, 1942–45.

———. *Eterno femminino mediterraneo*. 1954. Reprint, Vicenza: Neri Pozza, 1996.

———. *Nuovi saggi di religione mediterranea*. Florence: G. C. Sansoni, 1964.

———. *I miti della donna-giardino: Da Iside alla Sulamita*. Edited by Pier Angelo Carozzi. Milan: Edizioni Medusa, 2001.

Pietrogrande, Antonella. "Echi mediterranei nei giardini italiani." In *Attraverso giardini: Lezioni di storia, arte, botanica*, edited by Giuliana Baldan Zenoni Politeo, 123–38. Milan: Guerini, 1995.

———. "La presenza di Roma antica nei giardini all'italiana." In *Attraverso giardini: Lezioni di storia, arte, botanica*, edited by Giuliana Baldan Zenoni Politeo, 139–54. Milan: Guerini, 1995.

———. *I giardini di Reitia: Storia e tipologie dei giardini del Parco dei Colli Euganei.* Este: Grafica Atesina, 1998.

———. "'Una spelonca di dolci acque amena': Grotte e ninfeo tra Umanesimo e Manierismo." In *Artifici d'acque e giardini: La cultura delle grotte e dei ninfei in Italia e in Europa*, edited by Isabella Lapi Ballerini and Litta Maria Medri, 180–85. Florence: Centro Di, 1999.

Pietrogrande, Antonella, ed. *Per un giardino della terra.* Florence: L. S. Olschki, 2006.

Pietrosanti, Susanna. *Le cacce dei Medici.* Florence: Vallecchi, 1992.

Pindemonte, Ippolito. *Su i giardini inglesi e sul merito in cio dell'Italia.* Verona: Dalla Tipografia Mainardi, 1817.

Pindinelli, Elio. "Ville e casini dell'entroterra gallipolino." In *Paesaggi e sistemi di ville nel Salento*, edited by Vincenzo Cazzato, 210–21. Galatina: Mario Congedo, 2006.

Piva, Antonio, and Pierfranco Galliani, eds. *Eugenio Battisti: Storia, critica, progetto nella continuità della ricerca.* Rome: Gangemi, 2009.

Platt, Charles A. *Italian Gardens.* New York: Harper and Brothers, 1894.

Pliny, the Elder. *Natural History.* 10 vols. Cambridge, Mass.: Harvard University Press, 1961–67.

Politano, Simonetta. "Portali e recinti di ville nelle campagne salentine." In *Paesaggi e sistemi di ville nel Salento*, edited by Vincenzo Cazzato, 262–73. Galatina: Mario Congedo, 2006.

Poliziano, Angelo. *Stanze cominciate per la giostra del Magnifico Giuliano de Medici.* 1475–79. Reprint, edited by Vincenzo Pernicone. Turin: Loescher-Chiantore, 1954.

Poni, Carlo. *Gli aratri e l'economia agraria nel bolognese dal XVII al XIX secolo.* Bologna: Zanichelli, 1963.

———. *Fossi e cavedagne benedicon le campagne.* Bologna: Il Mulino, 1982.

Pozzana, Mariachiara. "Il giardino del Trebbio." In *Giardini medicei: Giardini di palazzo e di villa nella Firenze del Quattrocento*, edited by Cristina Acidini Luchinat, 148–52. Florence: F. Editore, 1996.

Pozzana, Mariachiara, ed. *I giardini del XX secolo: L'opera di Pietro Porcinai.* Florence: Alinea, 1998.

Puppi, Lionello. "The Villa Garden of the Veneto from the Fifteenth to the Eighteenth Century." In *The Italian Garden*, edited by David R. Coffin, 81–114. Washington, D.C.: Dumbarton Oaks Research Library and Collection, 1972.

———. "L'ambiente, il paesaggio e il territorio." In *Materiali e problemi: Ricerche spaziali e tecnologiche*, pt. 1, vol. 4 of *Storia dell'arte italiana*, edited by Giovanni Previtali, 44–99. Turin: G. Einaudi, 1980.

———. "Il principe e i mostri." In *Studi in onore di Renato Cevese*, edited by Guido Beltramini, Adriano Ghisetti Giavarina, and Paola Marini, 385–99. Vicenza: Centro Internazionale di Studi di Architettura Andrea Palladio, 2000.

Quaini, Massimo. "Per una archeologia dello sguardo topografico." *Casabella* 575–76 (1991): 13–17.

Quast, Matthias. *Die Villa Montalto in Rom: Entstehung und Gestalt im Cinquecento.* Munich: Tuduv, 1991.

———. "La villa di Artimino del Buontalenti: Rilettura tipologico-stilistica." In *Kunst des Cinquecento in der Toskana*, edited by Monika Cämmerer, 365–71. Munich: F. Bruckmann, 1992.

———. "Die Medici-Villen als Spiegel frühabsolutistischer Herrschaft. Beobachtungen zur Instrumentalisierung der Villenarchitektur unter Grossherzog Ferdinand I. (1587–1609)." In *Gedenkschrift für Richard Harprath*, edited by Wolfgang Liebenwein and Anchise Tempestini, 375–85. Munich: Deutscher Kunstverlag, 1998.

Quazza, Guido. *La decadenza italiana nella storia europea: Saggi sul Sei-Settecento.* Turin: G. Einaudi, 1971.

Quennell, Peter, ed. *Edward Lear in Southern Italy: Journals of a Landscape Painter in Southern Calabria and the Kingdom of Naples.* London: W. Kimber, 1964.

Ragionieri, Giovanna, ed. *Il giardino storico italiano: Problemi di indagine, fonti letterarie e storiche.* Florence: L. S. Olschki, 1981.

Ranaldi, Antonella. *Pirro Ligorio e l'interpretazione delle ville antiche.* Rome: Quasar, 2001.

Ravenna, Bartolomeo. *Memorie istoriche della città di Gallipoli.* Naples: R. Miranda, 1836.

Raymond, John. *An Itinerary Contayning a Voyage, Made through Italy, in the yeare 1646, and 1647.* London: Printed for Humphrey Moseley, 1648.

Regione Lombardia. *Criteri per la tutela, la conservazione e l'uso delle architetture vegetali.* Milan: Regione Lombardia, 1987.

Reinhard, Wolfgang. "Papa Pius: Prolegomena zu einer Sozialgeschichte des Papsttums." In *Von Konstanz nach Trient: Beiträge zur Geschichte der Kirche von den Reformkonzilien bis zum Tridentinum; Festgabe für August Franzen*, edited by Remigius Bäumer, 261–99. Munich: F. Schöningh, 1972.

———. "Ämterlaufbahn und Familienstatus. Der Aufstieg des Hauses Borghese 1537–1621." *Quellen und Forschungen aus Italienischen Archiven und Bibliotheken* 53 (1974): 328–427.

———. *Papstfinanz und Nepotismus unter Paul V (1605–1621): Studien und Quellen zur Struktur und zu quantitativen Aspekten des päpstlichen Herrschaftsystems.* 2 vols. Stuttgart: A. Hiersemann, 1974.

———. "Nepotismus. Der Funktionswandel einer papstgeschichtlichen Konstanten." *Zeitschrift für Kirchengeschichte* 86 (1975): 145–85.

———. "Herkunft und Karriere der Päpste, 1417–1963: Beiträge zu einer historischen Soziologie der römischen Kurie." *Mededelingen van het Nederlands Instituut te Rome* 38 (1976): 87–108.

———. *Freunde und Kreaturen: 'Verflechtung' als Konzept zur Erforschung historischer Führungsgruppen; Römische Oligarchie um 1600.* Munich: Ernst Vögel, 1979.

Reinhardt, Volker. *Kardinal Scipione Borghese (1605–1633): Vermögen, Finanzen und sozialer Aufstieg eines Papstnepoten.* Tübingen: M. Niemeyer, 1984.

Relazioni del X Congresso Internazionale di Scienze Storiche. Vol. 4, *Storia moderna.* Florence: G. C. Sansoni, 1955.

Ribouillault, Denis. "Le salone de la villa d'Este à Tivoli: Un théâtre des jardins et du territoire." *Studiolo: Revue d'histoire de l'art de l'Académie de France à Rome* 3 (2005): 65–94.

———. "Paysage et pouvoir: Les décors topographiques à Rome et dans le Latium au XVIe siècle." 3 vols. Doctoral thesis, Université Paris I Panthéon-Sorbonne, 2006.

———. "Landscape *all'antica* and Topographical Anachronism in Roman Fresco Painting of the Sixteenth Century." *Journal of the Warburg and Courtauld Institutes* 71 (2008): 211–37.

———. "*Paesaggio dipinto, paesaggio reale*: Notes sur une fenêtre de la Villa d'Este à Tivoli." In *Delizie in villa: Il giardino rinascimentale e i suoi committenti*, edited by Gianni Venturi and Francesco Ceccarelli, 269–87. Florence: L. S. Olschki, 2008.

———. "Le ville dipinte del cardinale Ippolito d'Este a Tivoli: L'architettura di fronte all'antico, la tradizione ferrarese, e un nuovo documento su Belriguardo." In *Delizie estensi: Architetture di villa nel rinascimento italiano ed europeo*, edited by Francesco Ceccarelli and Marco Folin, 341–71. Florence: L. S. Olschki, 2009.

Richeome, Louis. *La peinture spirituelle ou l'art d'aimer en toutes ses œuvres.* Lyon: P. Rigaud, 1611.

Riegl, Alois. *Moderne Denkmalkultus: Sein Wesen und seine Entstehung.* 1903. Reprinted in *Scritti sulla tutela e il restauro*, edited by Giuseppe La Monica, and translated by Maria Annunziata Lima and Laura Bica. Palermo: La Palma, 1982.

Rieusset-Lemarié, Isabelle. "Des palais de mémoire aux paysages virtuels: Le rôle du parcours dans les paysages urbains imaginaires." In *Les enjeux du paysage*, edited by Michel Collot, 249–65. Brussels: Ousia, 1997.

Robertson, John. *The Case for the Enlightenment: Scotland and Naples, 1680–1760.* Cambridge: Cambridge University Press, 2005.

Robotti, Ciro. "L'opera di Gioffredo e Vanvitelli per il giardino di Villa Campolieto." *Storia dell'arte* 35 (1979): 49–58.

Roccia, Rosanna, ed. *Theatrum sabaudiae.* Turin: Archivio Storico della Città di Torino, 2000. Originally published as *Theatrum statuum regia celsitudinis sabaudia ducis* (Amsterdam: Apud Haeredes Ioannis Blaev, 1682).

Roggero Bardelli, Costanza, Maria Grazia Vinardi, and Vittorio Defabiani. *Ville Sabaude.* Milan: Rusconi, 1990.

Romanello, Paolo. "Problematica della conservazione integrata delle ville vesuviane." *Naples nobilissima* 26 (1987): 153.

Romanello, Paolo, and Cinzia Parrotta, eds. *Le ville vesuviane.* Naples: Provincia di Napoli, 1991.

Romano, Giovanni. *Studi sul paesaggio.* Turin: G. Einaudi, 1978.

Romeo, Emanuele. "Frammenti e memoria dei luoghi: Permanenze del sistema delle ville vesuviane." In *Giardini, contesto, paesaggio: Sistemi di giardini e architetture vegetali nel paesaggio*, edited by Laura Sabrina Pelissetti and Lionella Scazzosi, 619–30. Florence: L. S. Olschki, 2005.

Romitti, Ines, ed. *Alessandro Tagliolini paesaggista, scultore e storico del giardino.* Florence: Alinea Editrice, 2001.

Rosa, Salvatore. *Lettere.* Edited by Gian Giotto Borrelli. Bologna: Il Mulino, 2003.

Rosina, Alessandro, Mirto Etoni, and Francesco Bilari. "La popolazione di Chioggia nel Seicento." In *La popolazione italiana nel Seicento: Relazioni presentate al convegno di Firenze, 28–30 novembre 1996*, 607–42. Bologna: CLUEB, 1999.

Rotberg, Robert I., and Theodore K. Rabb, eds. *Art and History: Images and Their Meanings.* Cambridge: Cambridge University Press, 1988. Originally published in *Journal of Interdisciplinary History* 17, no. 1 (1986).

Ruggles, D. Fairchild. *Gardens, Landscape, and Vision in the Palaces of Islamic Spain.* University Park: Pennsylvania State University Press, 2000.

Rupprecht, Bernhard. "Villa: Zur Geschichte eines Ideals." In *Wandlungen des Paradiesischen und Utopischen: Studien zum Bild eines Ideals*, edited by Hermann Bauer, 210–50. Berlin: De Gruyter, 1966.

———. "L'iconologia nella villa veneta." *Bollettino del Centro Internazionale di Studi di Architettura 'Andrea Palladio'* 10 (1968): 229–240.

Salerno, Luigi, Luigi Spezzaferro, and Manfredo Tafuri. *Via Giulia: Una utopia urbanistica del 500.* Rome: A. Staderini, 1973.

Salnove, Robert de. *La venerie royale.* Paris: Favre, Chez Antoine de Sommaville, 1655.

Saltini, Antonio, and Maria Sframeli. *L'agricoltura e il paesaggio italiano nella pittura dal Trecento all' Ottocento.* Florence: Octavo, 1995.

Salvemini, Biagio. *L'innovazione precaria: Spazi, mercati e società nel Mezzogiorno tra Sette e Ottocento.* Rome: Meridiana, 1995.

Sancho, José Luis, "Plano del Real Sitio de Aranjuez al final del reinado de Felipe II." In *Jardín y naturaleza en el reinado de Felipe II*, edited by Carmen Añon, José Luis Sancho, and José Martínez Millán, 497–503. Madrid: Sociedad Estatal Conme. Centenarios Felipe II–Carlos V, 1998.

Sansa, Renato. *L'oro verde: I boschi nello stato pontificio tra XVIII e XIX secolo.* Bologna: CLUEB, 2003.

Santoro, Lucio. "Il palazzo reale di Portici." In *Ville vesuviane del Settecento*, edited by Roberto Pane et al., 193–235. Naples: Edizioni Scientifiche Italiane, 1959.

Saslow, James M. *The Medici Wedding of 1589: Florentine Festival as Theatrum Mundi.* New Haven: Yale University Press, 1996.

Scaduto, Rosario. "Il trionfo del principe: L'arco della Santissima Trinità a villa Palagonia in Bagheria." In *Storia e restauro di architetture siciliane*, edited by Salvatore Boscarino and Maria Giuffrè, 71–80. Rome: Bonsignori, 1996.

Scaringella, Andrea. *Il progetto "La Venaria Reale": Cronache, protagonisti e retroscena di una storia irripetibile.* Turin: Ananke, 2007.

Scazzosi, Lionella. *Il giardino opera aperta: La conservazione delle architetture vegetali.* Florence: Alinea, 1993.

———. "Giardini, contesto, paesaggio." In *Giardini, contesto, paesaggio: Sistemi di giardini e architetture vegetali nel paesaggio*, edited by Laura Sabrina Pelissetti and Lionella Scazzosi, 1:3–15. Florence: L. S. Olschki, 2005.

———. "Il paesaggio opera aperta: Conservare/trasformare." In *La cultura del paesaggio in Europa tra storia, arte e natura: Manuale di teoria e pratica*, edited by Pierre Donadieu, Hansjörg Küster, and Raffaele Milani, 72–97. Florence: L. S. Olschki, 2008.

———. "Giardini e paesaggi 'opera aperta': I limiti delle trasformazioni." In *Giardini storici: A 25 anni dalle Carte di Firenze; Esperienze e prospettive*, edited by Laura Sabrina Pelissetti and Lionella Scazzosi, 1:131–57. Florence: L. S. Olschki, 2009.

Scazzosi, Lionella, ed. *Leggere il paesaggio: Confronti internazionali/Reading the Landscape: International Comparisons.* Rome: Gangemi, 2002.

Schiavo, Armando. *Villa Doria Pamphilj.* Milan: Alfieri and Lacroix, 1942.

———. *Villa Ludovisi e Palazzo Margherita.* Rome: Editrice Roma Amor, on behalf of the Banca Nazionale del Lavoro, 1981.

Schipa, Michelangelo. *Il regno di Napoli al tempo di Carlo di Borbone.* 2nd ed. 2 vols. Milan: Roma, 1923.

Schneider, Uwe, and Gert Gröning, eds. *Stolo: Bibliographische Findmittel zur Gartenkultur.* Vol. 1, *Italien.* Worms: Wernersche Verlagsgesellschaft, 2009.

Schwager, Klaus. "Kardinal Pietro Aldobrandinis Villa di Belvedere in Frascati." *Römisches Jahrbuch für Kunstgeschichte* 9–10 (1961–62) 291–382.

Scott, Geoffrey. *The Architecture of Humanism: A Study in the History of Taste.* 1914. Reprint, New York: W. W. Norton, 1999.

Scotti, Aurora. *Ascanio Vitozzi: Ingegnere ducale a Torino.* Florence: La Nuova Italia, 1969.

Scully, Vincent J. *The Earth, the Temple and the Gods: Greek Sacred Architecture.* New Haven: Yale University Press, 1962.

———. *Architecture: The Natural and the Manmade.* New York: St. Martin's Press, 1991.

———. *Modern Architecture and Other Essays.* Princeton, N.J.: Princeton University Press, 2003.

Sella, Domenico. *Crisis and Continuity: The Economy of Spanish Lombardy in the Seventeenth Century.* Cambridge, Mass.: Harvard University Press, 1979.

Sereni, Emilio. *Storia del paesaggio agrario italiano.* Bari: Laterza, 1961. Translated by R. Burr Litchfield as *History of the Italian Agricultural Landscape* (Princeton, N.J.: Princeton University Press, 1997).

Sette, Maria Piera, ed. *Gustavo Giovannoni: Riflessioni agli albori del XXI secolo.* Rome: Bonsignori, 2005.

Settis, Salvatore. *Futuro del "classico."* Turin: G. Einaudi, 2004.

Shearman, John. "A Functional Interpretation of Villa Madama." *Römisches Jahrbuch für Kunstgeschichte* 20 (1983): 313–27.

Silk, Mark. "The Hot History Department: Princeton's Influential Faculty." *New York Times Magazine*, 19 April 1987.

Simoncini, Giorgio. "Gustavo Giovannoni, Vincenzo Fasolo e la concezione integrale della storia dell'architettura." In *Principi e metodi della storia dell'architettura e l'eredità della "Scuola Romana,"* edited by Flavia Colonna and Stefania Costantini, 63–72. Rome: Centro Stampa Ateneo, 1994.

Sitwell, George. *On the Making of Gardens.* 1909. Reprint, with a foreword by John Dixon Hunt. Boston: David R. Godine, 2003.

Smith, Graham. *The Casino of Pius IV.* Princeton, N.J.: Princeton University Press, 1977.

Sohm, Philip L. *Pittoresco: Marco Boschini, His Critics, and Their Critique of Painterly Brushwork in Seventeenth- and Eighteenth-Century Italy.* Cambridge: Cambridge University Press, 1991.

Sombart, Werner. *Die römische Campagna*. Leipzig: Duncker & Humblot, 1888. Translated as *La campagna romana: Studio economico-sociale* (Turin: Loescher, 1891).

Sonnino, Eugenio, ed. *Popolazione e società a Roma dal Medioevo all'età contemporanea*. Rome: Il Calamo, 1998.

Stefaniak, Regina. "Correggios's Camera di San Paolo: An Archaeology of the Gaze." *Art History* 16, no. 2 (1993): 203–38.

Steinberg, Ronald M. "The Iconography of the Teatro dell'Acqua at the Villa Aldobrandini." *The Art Bulletin* 47 (1963): 453–63.

Stollhans, Cynthia. "Fra Mariano, Peruzzi and Polidoro da Caravaggio: A New Look at Religious Landscapes in Renaissance Rome." *Sixteenth-Century Journal* 23 (1992): 509–25.

Stoye, John Walter. *English Travellers Abroad 1604–1667: Their Influence in English Society and Politics*. Rev. ed. New Haven: Yale University Press, 1989.

Strabo. *The Geography of Strabo*. Translated by Horace Leonard Jones. Cambridge, Mass.: Harvard University Press, 1960–69.

Strong, Roy C. *Splendour at Court: Renaissance Spectacle and the Theatre of Power*. London: Weidenfield and Nicolson, 1973.

———. *Art and Power: Renaissance Festivals 1450–1650*. Woodbridge, Suffolk: Boydell, 1984.

———. *The Artist and the Garden*. New Haven: Yale University Press, 2000.

Stubbs, Mayling. "John Beale, Philosophical Gardener of Herefordshire. Part I. Prelude to the Royal Society (1608–1663)." *Annals of Science* 39, no. 5 (September 1982): 463–89.

Swan, Claudia. "*Ad vivum, naer het leven*, From the Life: Defining a Mode of Representation." *Word and Image* 11 (1995): 353–72.

Symonds, John. *Remarks upon an Essay, Intituled, The History of the Colonization of the Free States of Antiquity, Applied to the Present Contest between Great Britain and her American Colonies*. London: Printed by J. Nichols, and sold by T. Payne, 1778.

Szafranska, Malgorzata. "Comment le roi visitait ses jardins: Louis XIV au sujet de Versailles." *Biuletyn historii sztuki* 59, nos. 1–2 (1997): 112–22.

———. "Place, Time and Movement: A New Look at Renaissance Gardens." *Studies in the History of Gardens and Designed Landscapes* 26, no. 3 (2006): 194–208.

Tafuri, Manfredo. *Teorie e storia dell'architettura*. Bari: Laterza, 1968.

———. "Via Giulia: Storia di una struttura urbana." In *Via Giulia: Una utopia urbanistica del 500*, edited by Luigi Salerno, Luigi Spezzaferro, and Manfredo Tafuri, 65–152. Rome: A. Staderini, 1973.

———. *Materiali per il corso di storia dell'architettura II.a A. 1978/79 (Francesco Borromini)*. Venice: CLUVA Libreria Editrice and Istituto Universitario di Architettura di Venezia, Dipartimento di Analisi Critica e Storica, 1979.

———. "'Roma instaurata': Strategie urbane e politiche pontificie nella Roma del primo '500." In *Raffaello Architetto*, edited by Christoph Luitpold Frommel, Stefano Ray, and Manfredo Tafuri, 59–106. Milan: Electa, 1984.

———. *Ricerca del Rinascimento: Principi, città, architetti*. Turin: G. Einaudi, 1992.

———. "History as Project: An Interview with Manfredo Tafuri." By Luisa Passerini. *Architecture New York (ANY)* 25–26 (2000): 10–70.

Tagliolini, Alessandro. *I giardini di Roma: Folclore, poesia e storia della città attraverso l'evoluzione delle 'isole verdi,' la riscoperta di una rinascimentale bellezza in un'ideale sintesi tra natura e arte*. Rome: Newton Compton, 1980.

———. "Girolamo Fiorenzuola ed il giardino nelle fonti della metà del '500." In *Il giardino storico italiano: Problemi di indagine, fonti letterarie e storiche; Atti del convegno di studi, Siena–San Quirico d'Orcia, 6–8 ottobre 1978*, edited by Giovanna Ragionieri, 295–308. Florence: L. S. Olschki, 1981.

———. *Storia del giardino italiano: Gli artisti, l'invenzione, le forme, dall'antichità al XIX secolo*. Florence: La Casa Usher, 1988. Reprint, Rome: Ponte alle Grazie, 1994.

Tagliolini, Alessandro, ed. *Il giardino italiano dell'Ottocento nelle immagini, nella letteratura, nelle memorie*. Milan: Guerini, 1990.

Tagliolini, Alessandro, and Massimo Venturi Ferriolo, eds. *Il giardino: Idea natura realtà*. Milan: Guerini, 1987.

Tantillo Mignosi, Almamaria, ed. *Villa e paese: Dimore nobili del Tuscolo e di Marino*. Rome: De Luca, 1980.

Tarchiani, Nello. "La Mostra del Giardino Italiano in Palazzo Vecchio a Firenze." *Domus* 38 (1931): 15–17.

Tedesco, Natale. *L'immago espressa, Villa Palagonia: Tra norma ed eccezione*. Siracusa: Ediprint, 1986.

Testa, Fausto. *Spazio e allegoria nel giardino manierista: Problemi di estetica*. Florence: Nuova Italia, 1991.

Thirsk, Joan. *Food in Early Modern England: Phases, Fads, Fashions 1500–1760*. London and New York: Hambledon Continuum, 2006.

Tino, Pietro. *Campania felice? Territorio e agricolture prima della grande trasformazione*. Catanzaro: Meridiana Libri, 1997.

Tinti, Mario. "La Mostra del Giardino Italiano." *La casa bella* 41 (May 1931): 37–40 and 67.

Tongiorgi Tomasi, Lucia, and Luigi Zangheri, eds. *Bibliografia del giardino e del paesaggio italiano, 1980–2005*. Florence: L. S. Olschki, 2008.

Toscano, Bruno. "Una nota su paesaggio dipinto e paesaggio reale (rileggendo la prima annata di Paragone)." *Paragone* 42 (1991): 20–34.

Toubert, Pierre. *Les structures du Latium médiéval: Le Latium méridional et la Sabine du IXe siècle à la fin du XIIe siècle.* 2 vols. Paris: École Française de Rome, 1973.

Trezzani, Ludovica, ed. *La pittura di paesaggio in Italia: Con saggi d'introduzione dall'antichità al Rinascimento; Il Seicento.* Milan: Electa, 2004.

Troyli, Placido. *Istoria generale del reame di Napoli: ovvero, Stato antico e moderno delle regioni e luoghi che 'l reame de Napoli compongono, una colle loro prime popolazioni, costumi, leggi, polizia, uomini illustri e monarchi.* 5 vols. Naples, 1747–54.

Turner, James. "Landscape and the 'Art Prospective' in England, 1584–1660." *Journal of the Warburg and Courtauld Institutes* 42 (1979): 290–93.

Turner, Richard. *The Vision of Landscape in Renaissance Italy.* Princeton, N.J.: Princeton University Press, 1966.

Vallone, Aldo, ed. *Illuministi e riformatori salentini: Giuseppe Palmieri, Astore, Milizia e altri minori.* Lecce: Milella, 1984.

Varro, Marcus Terentius. *On Agriculture.* Translated by William Davis Hooper. Cambridge, Mass.: Harvard University Press, 1935.

Vasari, Giorgio. *Le opere di Giorgio Vasari.* Edited by Gaetano Milanesi. 9 vols. Florence: G. C. Sansoni, 1878–85. Reprint, Florence: Sansoni, 1981.

Venditti, Arnaldo. "La costa vesuviana da Napoli a Torre del Greco e la mappa del Duca di Noja." In *Ville vesuviane del Settecento,* edited by Roberto Pane et al., 19–51. Naples: Edizioni Scientifiche Italiane, 1959.

———. *L'opera napoletana di Luigi Vanvitelli.* Naples: Edizioni Scientifiche Italiane, 1974.

Venturi, Franco. "L'Italia fuori d'Italia." In *Storia d'Italia,* edited by Ruggiero Romano and Corrado Vivanti. Vol. 3, *Dal primo Settecento all'Unità,* 985–1481. Turin: G. Einaudi, 1973.

———. *Settecento riformatore.* Vol. 5, pt. 1, *L'Italia dei lumi, 1764–1790.* Turin: G. Einaudi, 1987.

Venturi, Gianni. "Picta poësis: Ricerche sulla poesia e il giardino dalle origini al Seicento." In *Storia d'Italia: Annali,* edited by Ruggiero Romano and Corrado Vivanti. Vol. 5, *Il Paesaggio,* edited by Cesare de Seta, 665–749. Turin: G. Einaudi, 1982.

Venturi, Gianni, and Francesco Ceccarelli, eds. *Delizie in villa: Il giardino rinascimentale e i suoi committenti.* Florence: L. S. Olschki, 2008.

Venturi Ferriolo, Massimo. *Nel grembo della vita: Le origini dell'idea di giardino.* Milan: Guerini, 1989.

———. "L'arte dei giardini tra pittura e realtà." In *Il giardino dipinto nella pittura lombarda del Seicento all'Ottocento,* edited by Paolo Biscottini, 13–16. Milan: Skira, 1995.

———. "Mater herbarum: Il giardino dei semplici dall'antico mondo mediterraneo alla Scuola Medica Salernitana." In *Mater herbarum: Fonti e tradizione del giardino dei semplici della Scuola Medica Salernitana,* edited by Massimo Venturi Ferriolo, 13–27. Milan: Guerini, 1995.

———. *Giardino e paesaggio dei romantici.* Milan: Guerini, 1998.

———. *Etiche del paesaggio: Il progetto del mondo umano.* Rome: Editori Riuniti, 2002.

Venuto, Francesca, ed. *Agricoltura e villa nelle campagne friulane: Possidenti, operatori e sperimentazioni colturali dall'età veneta all'annessione al Regno d'Italia.* Turin: U. Allemandi, 2004.

Vezzosi, Alessandro, ed. *Il giardino d'Europa: Pratolino come modello nella cultura europea.* Milan: Mazzotta, 1986.

———. *Il giardino romantico.* Florence: Alinea, 1986.

Vicente Maroto, M. I., and Mariano Esteban Piñeiro. *Aspectos de la ciencia aplicada en la España del siglo de oro.* Salamanca: Junta de Castilla y León, Consejereia de Cultura y Bienestar Social, 1991.

Vidler, Anthony. *The Writing of the Walls: Architectural Theory in the Late Enlightenment.* Princeton, N.J.: Princeton University Press, 1987.

Villani, Stefano. "I consoli della nazione inglese a Livorno tra il 1665 e il 1673: Joseph Kent, Thomas Clutterbuck e Ephraim Skinner." *Nuovi studi livornesi* 11 (2004): 11–34.

Virgil. *Virgil's Husbandry, or an Essay on the Georgics.* Translated by William Benson. London: William and John Innys, 1724.

———. *The Eclogues and Georgics of Virgil.* London: Everyman's Library, 1950.

———. *The Georgics.* Translated by John Dryden. Ashington, Northumberland: Mid-Northumberland Arts Group, 1981.

Visceglia, Maria Antonietta. *Territorio, feudo e potere locale: Terra d'Otranto tra Medioevo ed età moderna.* Naples: Guida, 1988.

Visceglia, Maria Antonietta, and Gianvittorio Signorotto, eds. *La corte di Roma tra Cinque e Seicento: Teatro della politica europea.* Rome: Bulzoni, 1998. Translated as *Court and Politics in Papal Rome: Sixteenth and Seventeenth Centuries* (Cambridge: Cambridge University Press, 2002).

Viviani, Giuseppe Franco, ed. *La villa nel veronese.* Verona: Banca Mutua Popolare di Verona, 1975.

Viviani della Robbia, Enrica. *Bernardo Tanucci ed il suo più importante carteggio.* Florence: G. C. Sansoni, 1942.

Wacquant, Loïc J. D. "Sociology as Socioanalysis: Tales of Homo Academicus." *Sociological Forum* 5, no. 4 (1990): 677–89.

Warburg, Aby. *La rinascità del paganesimo antico.* 1932. Reprint, translated by Emma Cantimori. Florence: La Nuova Italia, 1996.

Ward, Alastair. *The Architecture of Ferdinando Sanfelice.* London: Garland, 1988.

Warnke, Martin. *Bau und Überbau: Soziologie der mittelalterlichen Architektur nach den Schriftquellen.* Frankfurt: Syndikat, 1976.

———. *Politische Architektur in Europa vom Mittelalter bis heute: Repräsentation und Gemeinschaft.* Cologne: DuMont, 1984.

———. *Politische Landschaft: Zur Kunstgeschichte der Natur.* Munich: C. Hamer, 1992. Translated as *Political Landscape: The Art History of Nature* (London: Reaktion, 1994).

Weber, Max. *Die römische Agrargeschichte in ihrer Bedeutung für das Staats- und Privatrecht.* Stuttgart: F. Enke, 1891. Translated by S. Franchi as *Storia agraria romana dal punto di vista del diritto pubblico e privato* (Milan: Il Sagiatore, 1967).

Webster, Charles. *The Great Instauration: Science, Medicine, and Reform, 1626–1660.* London: Duckworth, 1975.

Wescoat, James L., Jr., and Joachim Wolschke-Bulmahn, eds. *Mughal Gardens: Sources, Places, Representations, and Prospects.* Washington, D.C.: Dumbarton Oaks Research Library and Collection, 1996.

Wharton, Edith. *Italian Villas and Their Gardens.* 1904. Reprint, with introductory notes by Arthur Ross, Henry Hope Reed, and Thomas S. Hayes. New York: Da Capo Press, 1988.

Wilkinson-Zerner, Catherine. *Juan de Herrera, Architect to Philip II of Spain.* New Haven: Yale University Press, 1993. Translated by Isabel Bal Sinde as *Juan de Herrera, arquitecto de Felipe II* (Madrid: Ediciones Akal, 1996).

Williams, Raymond. "Base and Superstructure in Marxist Cultural Theory." *New Left Review* (November–December 1973): 3–16.

———. *The Country and the City.* London: Chatto and Windus, 1973.

———. *Marxism and Literature.* Oxford: Oxford University Press, 1977.

———. "Plaisantes perspectives: Invention du paysage et abolition du paysan." *Actes de la recherche en sciences sociales* 17–18 (November 1977): 29–36.

———. *Keywords: A Vocabulary of Culture and Society.* 1976. Reprint, New York: Oxford University Press, 1983.

Williamson, Tom. *Polite Landscapes: Gardens and Society in Eighteenth-Century England.* Baltimore: Johns Hopkins University Press, 1995.

Witte, Arnold A. *The Artful Hermitage: The Palazzetto Farnese as a Counter-Reformation Diaeta.* Rome: "L'Erma" di Bretschneider, 2008.

Wölfflin, Heinrich. *Renaissance und Barock: Eine Untersuchung über Wesen und Entstehung des Barockstils in Italien.* Munich: T. Ackermann, 1888. Translated by Kathrin Simon as *Renaissance and Baroque* (Ithaca, N.Y.: Cornell University Press, 1966).

Wollheim, Richard. *Painting as an Art.* Princeton, N.J.: Princeton University Press, 1987.

Wolschke-Bulmahn, Joachim, with contributions by Angeliki E. Laiou and Michel Conan. *Twenty-Five Years of Studies in Landscape Architecture at Dumbarton Oaks: From Italian Gardens to Theme Parks.* Washington, D.C.: Dumbarton Oaks Research Library and Collection, 1996.

Wotton, Henry. *Letters and Dispatches from Sir Henry Wotton to James the First and his Ministers, in the Years MDCXVII–XX.* London: Printed by W. Nicol, 1850.

———. *The Elements of Architecture, Collected by Henry Wotton, Knight, from the Best Authors and Examples.* London: Longmans, Greene, 1903.

Yates, Francis A. *L'art de la mémoire.* Translated by Daniel Arasse. Paris: Gallimard, 1975.

Zach, Anton von. *Kriegskarte, 1798–1805: Il ducato di Venezia nella carta di Anton von Zach = Herzogtum Venedig auf der Karte Antons von Zach.* 2 vols. Treviso: Fondazione Benetton Studi Ricerche, 2005.

Zalum, Margherita. "La storia del giardino italiano: Lineamenti ed evoluzione di una giovane disciplina." In *Bibliografia del giardino e del paesaggio italiano, 1980–2005*, edited by Lucia Tongiorgi Tomasi and Luigi Zangheri, 1–14. Florence: L. S. Olschki, 2008.

Zangheri, Luigi. *Pratolino, il giardino delle meraviglie.* 1979. Reprint, Florence: Gonnelli, 1987.

———. "Il restauro dei giardini storici in Italia dal 1980." In *Bibliografia del giardino e del paesaggio italiano, 1980–2005*, edited by Lucia Tongiorgi Tomasi and Luigi Zangheri, 135–59. Florence: L. S. Olschki, 2008.

Zangheri, Luigi, Brunella Lorenzi, and Nausikaa M. Rahmati. *Il giardino islamico.* Florence: L. S. Olschki, 2006.

Index

Note: Illustrations are indicated by page numbers in *italic* type.

Dumbarton Oaks Colloquium on the History of Landscape Architecture

PUBLISHED BY DUMBARTON OAKS RESEARCH LIBRARY AND COLLECTION, WASHINGTON, D.C.

The Dumbarton Oaks Colloquium on the History of Landscape Architecture series volumes are based on papers presented at scholarly meetings sponsored by the Garden and Landscape Studies program at Dumbarton Oaks. These meetings provide a forum for the presentation of advanced research on garden history and landscape architecture; they support a deepened understanding of landscape as a field of knowledge and as a practice carried out by landscape architects, landscape artists, and gardeners.

Further information on Garden and Landscape Studies publications can be found at www.doaks.org/publications.

1 *The Italian Garden*, edited by David R. Coffin

2 *The Picturesque Garden and Its Influence Outside the British Isles*, edited by Nikolaus Pevsner

3 *The French Formal Garden*, edited by Elisabeth B. MacDougall and F. Hamilton Hazlehurst

4 *The Islamic Garden*, edited by Elisabeth B. MacDougall and Richard Ettinghausen

5 *Fons sapientiae: Renaissance Garden Fountains*, edited by Elisabeth B. MacDougall

6 *John Claudius Loudon and the Early Nineteenth Century in Great Britain*, edited by Elisabeth B. MacDougall

7 *Ancient Roman Gardens*, edited by Elisabeth B. MacDougall and Wilhelmina F. Jashemski

8 *Beatrix Jones Farrand (1872–1959): Fifty Years of American Landscape Architecture*, edited by Diane Kostial McGuire and Lois Fern

9 *Medieval Gardens*, edited by Elisabeth B. MacDougall

10 *Ancient Roman Villa Gardens*, edited by Elisabeth B. MacDougall

11 *Prophet with Honor: The Career of Andrew Jackson Downing, 1815–1852*, edited by George B. Tatum and Elisabeth B. MacDougall

12 *The Dutch Garden in the Seventeenth Century*, edited by John Dixon Hunt

13 *Garden History: Issues, Approaches, Methods*, edited by John Dixon Hunt

14 *The Vernacular Garden*, edited by John Dixon Hunt and Joachim Wolschke-Bulmahn

15 *Regional Garden Design in the United States*, edited by Therese O'Malley and Marc Treib

16 *Mughal Gardens: Sources, Places, Representations, and Prospects*, edited by James L. Wescoat, Jr., and Joachim Wolschke-Bulmahn

17 *John Evelyn's "Elysium Britannicum" and European Gardening*, edited by Therese O'Malley and Joachim Wolschke-Bulmahn

18 *Nature and Ideology: Natural Garden Design in the Twentieth Century*, edited by Joachim Wolschke-Bulmahn

19 *Places of Commemoration: Search for Identity and Landscape Design*, edited by Joachim Wolschke-Bulmahn

20 *Theme Park Landscapes: Antecedents and Variations*, edited by Terence Young and Robert Riley

21 *Perspectives on Garden Histories*, edited by Michel Conan

22 *Environmentalism in Landscape Architecture*, edited by Michel Conan

23 *Bourgeois and Aristocratic Cultural Encounters in Garden Art, 1550–1850*, edited by Michel Conan

24 *Landscape Design and the Experience of Motion*, edited by Michel Conan

25 *Baroque Garden Cultures: Emulation, Sublimation, Subversion*, edited by Michel Conan

26 *Sacred Gardens and Landscapes: Ritual and Agency*, edited by Michel Conan

27 *Performance and Appropriation: Profane Rituals in Gardens and Landscapes*, edited by Michel Conan

28 *Botanical Progress, Horticultural Innovation, and Cultural Change*, edited by Michel Conan and W. John Kress

29 *Contemporary Garden Aesthetics, Creations and Interpretations*, edited by Michel Conan

30 *Gardens and Imagination: Cultural History and Agency*, edited by Michel Conan

31 *Middle East Garden Traditions: Unity and Diversity; Questions, Methods, and Resources in a Multicultural Perspective*, edited by Michel Conan

32 *Clio in the Italian Garden: Twenty-First-Century Studies in Historical Methods and Theoretical Perspectives*, edited by Mirka Beneš and Michael G. Lee